The 1857 Jihad

The 1857 Jihad

Authored by

Prof. Sheshrao B. More

Translated by

Bhalchandrarao C. Patwardhan

Manas Publications

New Delhi-110002 (INDIA)

MANAS PUBLICATIONS
(Publishers, Distributors, Importers & Exporters)
4402/5-A, Ansari Road (Opp. HDFC Bank)
Darya Ganj, New Delhi - 110 002 (India)
Phones: Off.: 011-23260783, 23265523,
Res.: 011-23842660
E-mail: manaspublications@gmail.com
manaspub6@gmail.com
www.manaspublications.in

2017

ISBN: 978-81-7049-337-2
Rs. 795/-

Designed at
Manas Publications

Printed in India at
R.K. Print Services, Delhi
and published by Mrs Suman Lata for
Manas Publications, 4402/5-A,
Ansari Road (Opp HDFC Bank),
Darya Ganj, New Delhi - 110002 (INDIA)

Contents

2

Prologue 7

1. A Century before the Jihad – I 13
2. A Century before the Jihad – II 49
3. 1857 : Pre-Uprising—Conditions and Causes 81
4. 1857 : The Course of Events 111
5. Promoters, Leaders and Beneficiaries of the Uprising – I (i.e. Jihadi Core of the Uprising) 174
6. Promoters, Leaders and Beneficiaries of the Uprising – II (i.e. Jihadi Core of the Uprising) 253
7. Promoters, Leaders and Beneficiaries of the Uprising – III (i.e. Jihadi Core of the Uprising) 318
8. Jihadi Proclamations during the Uprising 360
9. Hindu-Muslim Struggle during the Uprising 417

Epilogue 440

Appendix I : List of Reference Books 447

Appendix II : The Nature of the Uprising–Conclusions of Eminent Scholars. 455

Appendix III : The So-called 'Constitution' Drafted by Revolutionaries of 1857 474

Index 489

Method of Citing References:

References from other books are indicated by two numbers in brackets separated by a hyphen. The first number refers to the serial number of the book in the 'List of Reference Books' in Appendix I and the second number refers to the page number in that book. Where only a single number (or numbers separated by commas) is given; it refers to the page number in the book previously cited (i.e. *ibid* or *op.cit.*).

Abbreviations : n. = footnote; q. = quoted.

Prologue

Dr. Babasaheb Bhim Rao Ambedkar wrote in 1940 that the 1857 Uprising was a *Jihad* for converting India into a 'Dar-ul Islam'; it was a rekindling of the *Jihad* that had been initiated a few decades before the 1857 Uprising by Sayyid Ahmad. (2-295) We had read this statement some years ago but had not paid serious attention to it. Enthralled as we were by Savarkar's Marathi opus, '*1857 Che Swatantrya Samar*', we tended to be skeptical, even indignant, about every opinion adverse to it. Anybody viewing the 1857 Uprising as a 'sepoy mutiny' seemed to us pro-British and opposed to India's political independence. Indeed, we had avoided reading N. R. Phatak's well researched Marathi book, *1857 Chi Shipai Gardi* (or, Sepoy Mutiny of 1857) merely on account of its title. In fact, till about four years ago, we had not read any book discussing the 1857 Uprising other than Savarkar's. We held the firm belief that the Uprising could not have been anything but a war for India's independence because it was fought against the British, especially when Nanasahib, Tatya Tope and Rani Laxmibai had participated in it and unprecedented Hindu-Muslim unity had characterized it.

However, Taylor's *What Really Happened During the Mutiny (1857-59)*, published by the Oxford University Press (1999), made us restless. The book contained an exhaustive bibliography of resources on the 1857 Uprising that had been published till that time. The list comprised 901 items that included books, theses, essays and reports. Also provided was a separate list of 47 novels and plays. Taylor had devoted eighty-four pages to this bibliography. (132–237 to 310) We were overcome by a feeling of guilt when we realized that barring the singular exception of Savarkar's book, we had read absolutely nothing. We immediately resolved to undertake an in-depth study of the subject. The process of collecting reference books began. It was impossible to acquire and study every one of Taylor's references. Nevertheless, we managed to reach a figure of around 200.

We were forced by our study to change our previous views. We awoke to the realization that not Savarkar's, but Dr. Ambedkar's conclusions were both objective and accurate. We are placing that study and conclusion before our readers.

Dr. Ambedkar's analysis contains reference to a certain Sayyid Ahmad (Barelvi). We had no inkling of the precise identity of the man till after we had finished reading about 50 of our references. He was the first Indian leader to proclaim a *Jihad* against the British but was killed in 1831 during his *Jihad* against the Sikhs. His followers continued the *Jihad* against the British, which ultimately led to the 1857 Uprising. It is impossible to comprehend the nature of the 1857 Uprising without a thorough acquaintance of Sayyid Ahmad's thoughts and work. Dr. Ambedkar had undertaken that study. Contrastingly, Savarkar's opus does not even fleetingly mention Sayyid Ahmad. (Many do not even know that this Sayyid Ahmad is distinct from 'Sir Sayyid Ahmad Khan'.)

To follow the development of the Uprising, it is equally important to study the inspiration provided by Sayyid Ahmad's mentor, Shah Abdul Aziz and his father, Shah Waliullah (1702–1763). What is generally (but mistakenly) known as the 'Wahabi' movement has its roots in Shah Waliullah's activism, which may really be called the 'Waliullahi' movement. Shah Abdul Aziz had declared by his 1803 Fatwa, that India had become a 'Dar-ul Harb'. The 1857 Uprising has a historical genesis going back a hundred years to the Battle of Plassey in 1757. As a result, all those who ignored revolutionary activism of this interregnum of a century invariably erred in their assessment of the 1857 Uprising. We have discussed all those attempts in two chapters that follow this introduction.

Our use of the word 'Jihad' in the title should not alarm anyone. The word appears innumerable times in Savarkar's own tome. Frequent references affirm that it was directed against 'kafirs'. His descriptions of events contain a sumptuous fare of green flags and cries of 'Deen-Deen'. Bahadur Shah is acknowledged as 'Emperor of Free India', Maulana Ahmad Shah as the 'hero of heroes' and Nakkhi Khan as its 'head'. Praise and exaltation as revolutionaries is showered on Muslims all through the book, while any expression of the author's disdain is only reserved for some among the Hindus. Sikhs and Gurkhas are condemned as outright traitors, while the apathy of South India including Maharashtra and Rajputana is compared with the supreme inertia characteristic of 'dead weights'.

'Jihad' means a struggle in the cause of Islam. It is waged for five purposes: *protection* and *propagation* of Islam, and *institution, protection* and *expansion* of the Islamic State. *Jihad* being a sacred religious obligation, none at that time harboured any sentiment of apprehension, compunction or reservation in identifying the 1857 Uprising as such. On the contrary, Muslims took immense pride in calling it one. Indeed, what emerges from evidence is that the Uprising had been acknowledged as a *Jihad* (or Muslim revolt) in fatwas of the clergy, edicts and decrees of rulers, handbills and appeals of activists, oaths taken by holy warriors, parlance used by Muslim laity, reports of British officials and judgements of courts. The milieu was suffused with the sentiment of *Jihad*. Savarkar, too, had been sucked into the vortex of that emotion, which had pervaded contemporaneous records and literature. Therefore, in calling the event as a *Jihad* we are stating nothing new or adverse. We are merely placing before our readers what was already in existence a hundred and fifty years ago, attempting in the process to accord due justice to the true nature of the 1857 Uprising. While we entertain no doubt, we will earn the grateful endorsement of Muslims, we feel Hindus need to brace their minds against unsettling facts and ponder profoundly on a rethinking of their notions about 1857.

Lest we are accused of making bizarre or unfounded statements, we have furnished in the Appendix II a list of forty-three impeccable sources that corroborate our evaluation. We are certain those would suffice to urge our readers to introspection.

The Uprising involved three participants: the British, the Hindus and the Muslims. While all three, during the actual event and its immediate aftermath, concurred that it was a *Jihad,* each split into two, according to their view in later times.

One group of British opinion continued, as before to view it as a *Jihad.* But while conceding that it was an agitation by Muslims, the second shifted ground from historical to political considerations because they felt it was dangerous to themselves to continue regarding Muslims as rebels. They advocated the need for peaceful coexistence with Muslims in order to continue ruling over India. As a result, they initiated a policy of holding Hindus culpable for the 1857 Uprising along with Muslims. (That the 1857 Uprising was not a war of independence but a 'sepoy mutiny', is quite another position.)

Among Muslims, one group continued viewing it as a *Jihad.* But a second faction assumed a stance quite similar to that of their British counterparts. It was led by Sir Sayyid Ahmad Khan, who had served as a judge in the British administration during the Uprising. In order to safeguard Muslims from post-Uprising British ire and vendetta, he began vigorously promoting the idea that Muslims were not rebels but had always been – and were – loyal subjects. He even wrote a book, *The Loyal Mohomedans of India* for the purpose. His aim was to cause a reversal in British perceptions that 1857 was a Muslim rebellion and tried to propagate the view that remaining loyal British subjects was immensely more beneficial for Muslims than engaging in *Jihad* against them. In order to avert another Uprising, he had also tendered valuable advice to the British government of creating rifts between the two communities and instituting separate armies of Hindu and Muslim soldiers to be used against one another.

None had dared before Savarkar to call the 1857 Uprising a 'war of independence'. Thereafter, however, Hindu opinion split into two, not over the issue of whether it was a Muslim agitation or (*Jihad*), but whether it was a 'war of independence' or a 'sepoy mutiny'. Barring a few exceptions like Dr. Ambedkar, none viewed the Uprising from the former aspect. The Hindu had never even thought on those lines. Savarkar's novel and its inventive interpretation, that it was a cooperative struggle for independence, proved both inspiring and useful. It moved the likes of Subhash Chandra Bose and Bhagat Singh with patriotic fervour. The 'first' war of independence began to be discussed as motivation for winning the 'second'. Moreover, because Savarkar's work underscored the principle of Hindu-Muslim unity, an issue very dear to the Hindu heart, it became immensely popular among Hindus subscribing to all hues of opinion. Veritably, it became a standard commentary on the 1857 Uprising. On the other hand, even Ambedkar's followers paid no attention to what their own venerable leader-statesman had written about 1857, virtually consigning his findings to the dustbin. None felt the need of critically studying his claims and determining the veracity of his findings. It would almost seem that the entire nation had practically forgotten what Ambedkar wrote (assuming of course that it was aware of it in the first place!).

A nationwide celebration is planned in 2008 to mark the 150th anniversary of the 1857 Uprising, in which the government, all political parties, organizations and individual citizens will participate. The Indian government has appealed to neighbouring Pakistan and Bangla Desh that the three states and their people should jointly participate in the event. Quite naturally, the appeal evoked no response from those countries. We are not aware of the official reason for their silence, but it is very likely that their reaction might have been something in the nature of: "How is (Hindu) India connected with the first war of independence? That war, which was our first struggle for independence, had been fought by us. We had lost that first war and had to wait 90 years for attaining partial independence in the second war. The third war will, of course, not be fought against the British." The Government of Pakistan published the four-volume *A History of the Freedom Movement (Being the Story of Muslim Struggle for the Freedom of Hind-Pakistan, 1707-1947)* in 1957 to mark the centenary of the 1857 Uprising. (1707 is the year of Aurangzeb's death.) Thus both our neighbours concur with conclusions stated in our book.

A century and a half has elapsed, and the British have left. Is it not the high time that the 1857 Uprising be studied objectively?

* * *

Chapter 1

A Century before the Jihad – I

It is well-known that the 1857 Uprising was aimed at wresting political power from the British and reinstating the rule of the last Mughal Emperor, Bahadur Shah. The causes and nature of such a momentous event in Indian history may never be determined if the scope of research is limited to events that were but a few months or years old, like cartridges or annexation of States, for instance. A long history of events preceding them needs to be unravelled.

Rationale of Muslim Aggressions

Dr. Ambedkar wrote his *Pakistan* in 1940 to address questions like, 'should India be partitioned?' and 'can Hindus and Muslims coexist as a single nation?' He needed an overview of history from Muhammad bin Qasim's 711 C.E. invasion of India. He went on to study various subsequent invasions to determine their motivation, as well as objectives of the Islamic administrations that came to be established as a result. The exercise was dictated because Muslims still (1940) entertained the same rationale, purpose and aim that had actuated those invasions.

The same Muslim psyche was dominant during the 1857 Uprising, which necessitates an inquiry into history from

711 C.E. in order to appreciate its nature and causes. Dr. Ambedkar's analysis in this respect can serve as a guideline for 1857 as well.

Briefly narrating various Muslim invasions from 711 to 1761, Dr. Ambedkar states why they occurred: "These Muslim invasions were not undertaken merely out of lust for loot or conquest. There was another object behind them....There was no doubt that striking a blow at the idolatry and polytheism of Hindus and establishing Islam in India was also one of the aims of such expeditions (of Muhammad bin Qasim). In one of his dispatches to Hajjaj....(he) is quoted to have said: '....the infidels (have been) converted to Islam or destroyed. Instead of idol-temples, mosques and other places of worship have been created....' ....Muhammad Mahmood Ghazni also looked upon his numerous invasions of India as the waging of a holy war." (2-56)

He writes further: "Mahommad Ghori was actuated by the same holy zeal in his invasions of India. Hasan Nizami, the historian, describes his work in the following terms: 'He purged by his sword the land of Hind from the filth of infidelity and vice, and freed the whole of that country from the thorn of God-plurality and impurity of idol-worship, and by his royal vigour and intrepidity left not one temple standing.' Taimur has in his memoir explained what led him to invade India. He says: 'My object in the invasions of Hindustan is to lead a campaign against the infidels, to convert them to the true faith according to the command of (Prophet) Muhammad, to purify the land from the defilement of mischief and polytheism, and overthrow the temples and idols, whereby we shall be *Ghazis* and *Mujahids,* companions and soldiers of the faith before God.'" (56)

He also shows how not merely the invader, but even long established rulers followed the same tradition. As examples of this finding, he discusses the regimes of Qutubuddin Aibak, Alauddin Khilji, Sultan Firoz Shah and Emperor Shah Jahan. Stating that 'It was left to Aurangzeb to make a final attempt to overthrow idolatry', he shows how the unchanging pattern had continued (60).

Concession of 'Jiziya' to Hindus

He writes, "All this was not the result of mere caprice or moral perversion. On the other hand, what was done, was in accordance with the ruling ideas of Islam in the broadest aspects". Dr. Ambedkar then cites the example of the following reply to a question posed by Allauddin Khilji to his qazi (judge) about the status of Hindus according to Islamic Law: "They are called payers of tribute.....The due subordination of the Dhimmi is exhibited in this humble payment... The glorification of Islam is a duty.... God holds them in contempt, for He says, 'Keep them in subjection'. To keep the Hindus in abasement is especially a religious duty, because they are the most inveterate enemies of the Prophet, and because the Prophet has commanded us to slay them, plunder them, and make them captive.... (The) great doctor (Hanifah), to whose school we belong, has assented to the imposition of jizya on Hindus[1]; doctors of other (three) schools[2] (of Islam) allow no other alternative but 'Death or Islam '." (2–63; also, 138–40) Dr. Ambedkar further demonstrates that infighting between various invading races like the Turks, Afghans or Mughals notwithstanding, all of them were unanimous and united in destroying Hinduism and establishing Islam. (57)

In short, the aim of Muslim invasions was to establish and strengthen their rule in order to make India Islamic. This intention had never been concealed by them. They desired to convert all Hindus to Islam and rid them of ignorance. As they longed to rule the country and also because it was not possible to convert all Hindus at once, they treated them as a subjugated people, exacting the jiziya (poll tax) as a symbol of their subjugation and allowing them a concession from the alternatives of Islam or Death. They always viewed Hindus

---

1. According to Ayat 9:29 of the Quran, provision for levying jiziya is only available for 'people of the book' like Jews and Christians. It is not prescribed for polytheists. (For additional discussion, see 128–467; 129–320).

2. These are the Hanbali, Maliki and Shaafi Schools.

as a conquered nation and believed unremittingly that the right to rule had been exclusively bestowed upon them by Allah. They considered it irreligious to submit to the suzerainty of others or concede their right of governance. Moreover, they even regarded it as demeaning of Islam to agree willingly to coexist with others on equitable terms[3].

Principles of the Islamic State

Their religious beliefs regarding the Islamic state were crystal clear: Allah's Law was sovereign; it was explained in the Quran and *Hadis*; Muslims were bound to submit to that law; it was un-Islamic to obey man-made laws if they were at variance with Allah's law. Muslims could be loyal only to a state founded on Allah's Law[4]; it was Allah's command that in the absence of an Islamic state (*Dar-ul-Islam*), the territory was to be regarded as the Land of War (*Dar-ul-Harb*) and a migration (*hijrat*) was to be undertaken to an Islamic country. If that be not possible, religious diktats prescribed *Jihad* against the non-Islamic state. It became a religious duty of the global Muslim community to help brethren-in-faith for that purpose[5]. The Quran promises that this religion of Allah, which is the

---

3. Dr. Ambedkar writes in this regard: "For six hundred years, the Musalmans had been the masters of the Hindus. The British occupation brought them down to the level of the Hindus. From masters to fellow subjects was degradation enough, but a change from the status of fellow subjects to that of subjects of the Hindus (on the basis of the democratic principle) is really humiliation." (2-49) (It was to escape from this situation that they made a demand for partition.)

4. Dr. Ambedkar writes: "Among the tenets, one that calls for notice is the tenet of Islam which says that in a country which is not under Muslim rule wherever there is a conflict between Muslim law and the law of the land, the former must prevail over the latter and a Muslim will be justified in obeying the Muslim law and defying the law of the land." (2-49)

5. Dr. Ambedkar's comment: "It might also be mentioned that *Hijrat* is not the only way of escape to Muslims who find themselves in a *Dar-ul-Harb*. There is another injunction of Muslim Canon Law

(Contd.)

only true and final faith, shall prevail over all the others[6]. It is incumbent upon each Muslim to strive to his utmost to implement Allah's promise, aim and will. For the head of an Islamic state (Khalifa), in fact, this becomes a duty absolutely intrinsic to his office. It is his prime responsibility to propagate Islam throughout the world and bring the whole of the mankind under Islamic rule. Struggle for the fulfillment of Allah's work is called 'Jihad' in Islamic parlance. Taking up arms to do so is not just sanctioned but even commanded. Not accepting the one and only God, Allah, is tantamount to disobedience; it is a rebellion against Him; it is nothing short of war against Him. Worshipping other gods or regarding them as partners with Allah (*shirk*) is the greatest injustice and crime[7]. Islam commands a *Jihad* against all those who do not accept Allah and defy His commandments.

Familiarity with these Islamic principles and resulting Muslim sentiments, along with knowledge of the history of invasions since 711 C.E., is essential for an appreciation of reasons for Muslim invasions of India, the nature of the Islamic states that were sought to be established, and why and against whom a *Jihad* is fought.

Misguided Akbar and Sirhindi, the Defender of the Faith

It is not merely sufficient for the king to be Muslim; the state has to be administered according to Islamic principles. Under such conditions, it becomes necessary for the clergy to struggle for ushering in pure Islam and Islamic governance. Such a struggle had occurred during the reign of Emperor Akbar (1556-1605). He ruled by turning away from Islam. Not only was the jiziya on Hindus abolished, but they were even

---

called *Jihad* (crusade) by which it becomes incumbent on a Muslim ruler to extend the rule of Islam until the whole world shall have been brought under its sway..... Not only can they proclaim *Jihad* but they can call the aid of a foreign Muslim power to make *Jihad* a success, or if the foreign Muslim power intends to proclaim a *Jihad*, help that power in making its endeavour a success." (2-295, 6)

6. Quran: *9:33; 48:28; 61:9.*

7. Quran: *31:13.*

being treated with respect. Cow slaughter was banned. A new religion, *Din-e Ilahi,* was founded. Akbar began subscribing to the view that all religions were equal. Clearly, he had strayed from the path of true Islam. The great cleric, Shaikh Sayyid Ahmad Sirhindi (1562–1624), emerged at this critical juncture to protect Islam from Akbar.

Sirhindi is regarded as 'the Mujaddid (Renewer of Faith) of the Second Millennium.' He rose a thousand years after the Prophet. His great work consisted of ridding Islam of improper un-Islamic practices that had crept into it during the millennial interregnum. (30-265; 143-93) He was "one of the two greatest Muslim theologians produced on the subcontinent."[8] (52-57) His thoughts continue to influence Muslim clergy even in the 21st Century. (58) He is regarded as "a great decisive factor on the Indian scene" (63) and enjoys the prime position in the list of famous Muslim freedom fighters. (28-17) Maulana Azad eulogizes him as a hero of the Indian nationalists. (30-215) He also venerated Sirhindi as 'a radical reformer in the field of religion' who had dared to express dissent over un-Islamic practices of Akbar's time and to even raise a rebellion in opposition to the Emperor. (23-106) "The result of this peaceful revolution of the Shaikh was that Akbar's *Din-e-Ilahi,* an un-Islamic movement, received its death kriell forever and died out." (143-96)

Sirhindi held that "*Kufr* and Islam are opposed to each other. The progress of one is possible only at the expense of the other and coexistence between these two contradictory faiths is unthinkable. To honour the one amounts to insulting the other.... The honour of Islam lies in insulting *Kufr* and *Kafirs.* One who respects *Kafirs,* dishonours the Muslims.... The real purpose in levying Jiziya on them (the non-Muslims) is to humiliate them.... It is intended to hold them under contempt and to uphold the honour and might of Islam." (30-248, 9; 21-185; 33-66) Sirhindi believed in the Islamic

8. The second was Shah Waliullah, whose career is discussed later.

prescription that "the *Shara* was beneath the sword and its glory depended on the rulers." (30-234)

He had likewise taken strong exception to the inclusion of Hindus in the administrative hierarchy. (23-75) He preached that cows ought to be slaughtered to demonstrate the predominance of Islam. (73)

He considered participation in Hindu festivals like Diwali, or even giving them greetings, as *kufr*. "It is a folly of great magnitude to treat Rama and Rahim as one." (30-254; 121-186) In his view, Hindus ought only to be given the choice between Islam and death. (30-249)

Thus, the trend of his thoughts and the nature of pristine Islam become amply clear.

Aurangzeb — the 'Star' Pupil

Sirhindi made it known to Akbar that enforcing all these Islamic principles and practices was the duty of the Khalifa. He raised his voice against Akbar's successor, Jahangir, who had continued his father's policies. He appealed to the armed forces as well as all sections of society to disobey the Emperor's orders, and dispatched hundreds of his disciples all over the Mughal territory to preach these thoughts. He was arrested by Jahangir and imprisoned for treason. (28-28) However, realizing the immense influence Sirhindi enjoyed over the population, especially the military, Jahangir released him honourably. The Emperor acknowledged his teachings and appointed him as an advisor at the court. Those teachings were implemented. (29) He was entrusted with the work of imparting Islamic instruction to the army, which he did for five years. (143-97) Shah Jahan, who succeeded Jahangir, and his son Aurangzeb — the 'symbol of victory of orthodoxy' — became ardent followers of Sirhindi's teachings. (33-20) This was a reason for Aurangzeb's religious fanaticism, bigotry and anti-Hindu policies! (23-107; 52-63)

Sirhindi has gained a prominent place in history for neutralizing the peril created for Islam by Akbar, the 'culmination of the success of heterodoxy', rescuing its pristine form and saving the Islamic state. (33-20) Other redeemers in

India of later times drew inspiration from Sirhindi. He is regarded as the progenitor of the call and movement, 'go back to the Quran'.

Decline of the Mughal Empire

The Empire had reached its zenith in both geographical extent and Islamic excellence during Aurangzeb's reign. A region of Afghanistan had become a *suba* (administrative division). However, the decline began with Aurangzeb's death in 1707. The blazing meridian sun began setting. His successors lacked sense of purpose, and were profligate and incompetent; succession to the throne was a blood-soaked affair. Aurangzeb's eldest son, Bahadur Shah (1707-12), killed two of his brothers in battle. After his death, his son Jahandar Shah, in turn, liquidated three brothers. Within a year, his nephew had murdered him to wrest the throne (1713). This new Emperor was killed (1719) by two influential and scheming courtiers, the Sayyid brothers, who installed three incumbents on the throne, according to their whim and fancy within a span of just seven months. All of these 'Emperors' were thoroughly inept. It was around this time that the Amir of Persia, Nadir Shah, invaded India (1739) and further weakened the already rickety empire. He stayed in Delhi for 57 days and even kept the Emperor in confinement. Over twenty thousand were put to the sword in Delhi. He returned to Persia after seizing the prized Koh-i-Noor diamond, the Emperor's famed Peacock Throne, immense booty and possession of all territory beyond the Indus. (133-526) The prestige of the Mughal empire was lost. It became clear to the world that it now had no strength to survive.

This notwithstanding, rebellion and bloodthirsty intrigue for the throne continued unabated. No control remained over the vast territory of the empire and its regional Subedars (governors). Imperial orders began to be flouted with impunity. This had two principal effects.

First, Subedars of three large provinces began acting as independent rulers. While they exhibited loyalty and respect for the 'Emperor of the Muslims', it was merely notional and none obeyed his orders in any real sense. Soon, Hyderabad

(1724), Ayodhya (1723) and Bengal (1740) became autonomous. The process of fragmentation of the empire had begun. These provincial governors were proving to be more powerful than the central authority.

Maratha Challenge to Muslim Power

Secondly, three non-Muslim powers had emerged in India around this time — Marathas, Sikhs and the British. The Marathas were the strongest. In fact, Aurangzeb had breathed his last while campaigning against Maratha resistance. His death marked the beginning of the disintegration of the Mughal Empire on the one hand and the rise of Maratha power on the other. With an already firmly entrenched power base in the South, they turned their eyes northward and began expanding in all directions.

They began taking interest in Delhi politics from 1719. They even participated in the intrigues of succession. (33-527) Peshwa Bajirao I (1720–40), aimed to reestablish what was known as the Hindupad Padshashi (or rule by majority Hindus). (538) He had based his policy on the view that once the central Mughal Empire is dismantled, its branches will automatically fall off. Accordingly, he began conquering territories of North India. Maratha armies ranged all over those provinces. (134-71) He invaded Bengal several times and also conquered Orissa. (71) He reached the environs of Delhi in 1737 but did not force his way into the city out of the consideration his Hindu mindset evinced for the Emperor's feelings. (33-538)

The Marathas had become a force to reckon with in the Imperial Court at Delhi. They had a say in the appointment of the Vizirs. They had won control of Punjab in 1758, and of Attock, Peshawar and Multan later in the same year. (139-127) In short, all signs clearly indicated the disappearance of the Mughal Empire and the emergence and victory of the Maratha Empire. The prospect was sufficient to terrify the autonomous Nawabs of Bengal, Ayodhya, Hyderabad and Rohilkhand, as the overall power structure had become threatened by the Marathas.

Advent of Clerics as Saviours of the Empire

In Muslim societies, the clergy is more anxious than statesmen themselves about the health of the state. A cleric, Shah Waliullah (1703–62), emerged at this time to analyze the causes of the Muslim debacle and suggest remedial action.

Shah's historic fame, capability and the place he enjoys in collective Muslim consciousness are beyond description. He was the second great reformer of Islam in India after Shaikh Sirhindi. He had carried Sirhindi's work forward. (121-202; 25-7) There was little difference in their thinking. Sirhindi had to intervene to save Islam from Akbar during the ascendancy of Muslim power, while Shah redeemed Islam from the Hindus during its decline.

He was not only a religious scholar, but also an illustrious redeemer of the faith, accomplished philosopher, great thinker and seasoned politician. He was a socialist and an economist. (27-61; 28-48) There might scarcely be a single Muslim religious organization in India or Pakistan that has not come under the influence of Shah's thoughts. (33-539) It is not possible to comprehend the Muslim mind of the 18th and 19th Century without taking due note of Shah. (540) He is eulogized as, "The greatest Muslim scholar that Muslim South Asia produced, (who) has left a very deep impact on subsequent generations." (25-6) His thoughts have created a deep impression on the minds of later Muslim generations and history. (28-48; 25-6) Hundreds of clerics graduated from the Madarsa-i-Rahimiya, which was founded by Shah in Delhi, to take his work ahead.

The following observation by Prof. Safdar Mahmood and Javaid Jafar about 1857 is amply illustrative of Shah's influence: "The consciousness aroused by Shah Waliullah continued to inspire the reformers and freedom fighters. The great struggle to throw off the British yoke in 1857 was to a great extent the outcome of this movement."[9] (53-7)

---

9. This is not all they say. They write further that, "(His) movement, therefore, is the forerunner of the movement which led to the creation of Pakistan." (53-9)

Redeemer of the Faith, Shah Waliullah

When, at the age of 29, he was on a pilgrimage to Mecca, it is believed that the Prophet had appeared to him in a vision and given him his blessings for bringing Muslims together. (33-494, 518) He analyzed reasons for the decline of Muslim power after returning to India. He realized that pure, pristine Islam had all but disappeared from their midst and that it was because Muslims, particularly the rulers, had strayed from the original teachings of the Quran and the Prophet, that calamity had befallen them. The Quran was then available only in Arabic. Shah translated it into Persian so that laity may be able to read it. He followed this up by cries of 'Go back to the Quran' and 'Islam is in danger.' (26-3; 74-127)

Through many centuries of contact, some Hindu principles, traditions and practices had crept into the Islam practised by Indian Muslims. Indeed, they had even begun to believe that what they were practising was Islam. "He painted pictures of the lack of moral standards in the Muslim society and attributed this to their contact with the Hindus and the converts. In the company of the Hindus and the converts, the Muslims had forgotten....Islam.... Muslims had become Indians." (74-127) "(He) was suggesting that the less they shared with their non-Muslim neighbours, the better servants of God Indian Muslims would be." (43-30) He wanted to ban Hinduism. (54-226)

So he began preaching pure Islam. A campaign was launched against Hindu customs and traditions. (74-127) He was a firm believer that Muslim power depended on practising pure Islam and desired to revitalize Islam as a force. (126) He recognized that Muslims would never remain political masters unless they took support of pristine Islam. Aurangzeb's successors had neglected to do this, kept the teachings of Islam aside and lost all recollection of Sirhindi. Muslim society, generally, had strayed from pristine Islam. Shah traced the loss of political power to these causes.

Shah's Islam-Inspired Objective

Muslim society in general and the ruling class in particular had lost sight of the supremacy of Islam, its purpose and need for *Jihad* because they had forgotten Islamic principles. Prof. Jalbani, a biographer of Shah and commentator of his teachings, writes thus about his *Aims and Aspirations*: "What Shah Waliullah wanted to see it (sic) achieved, what were his aims and aspirations, and for what he was so anxious and impatient? All this is contained in the following verse of the Quran: "*'It is He Who has sent His Apostle with guidance and the religion of truth, to proclaim it over all religions even though the polytheists like it not.'* (9:33) Commenting on this verse, he argues that even though the fall of the empires of Chosroes and Caesar was equivalent to the complete prevalence of Islam as achieved during the reign of the first two Caliphs[10] (after the Prophet), it is not permissible for the Muslims that they should remain content with their present deplorable condition with the sweet memory of their glorious past. He says that the prevalence of Islam should continue uninterruptedly, and be of such a nature that the rest of the world should stand before it in submission. Islam should be perpetually predominant, magnificent, illustrious and splendidly clear." (26-159) "His sole anxiety, all the time had been to see the Muslims....powerful and strong.... Though the overthrow of the Roman and Persian Empires during the reign of the first two Caliphs, in a way, amounted to world domination, he wants to see the Muslim domination perpetual and continuous." (27-99)

Allah commands *Jihad* for fulfillment of all these things. "(He) believed that the decline (of Islam) could not be stopped until Muslims won victories on the battlefield." (52-87) Prof. Jalbani writes about Shah's thoughts on *Jihad*: "Besides what Shah Sahib feels so sorry about, and for which he so bitterly laments, is the apathy and negligence on the part of the Muslims towards *Jihad* which in fact is continuous and permanent. So long as the spirit of *Jihad* was alive among them, they were successful and victorious wherever they went, but no sooner it disappeared from them than they were

---

10. These two Khalifas were Abu Bakr (d.634) and Umar (d.644). They had conquered the entire Persian and half the Roman Empire in a matter of 10–12 years. (129-621)

subjugated and held in contempt everywhere. The verse of the Holy Quran : *'And fight on with them until there is no more tumult or oppression (i.e. persecution)*[11]*, and there prevail justice and faith in God altogether and everywhere....'* (8:39), clearly points out that the necessity of continuation of *Jihad* until the emergence of Islam as a dominant force." (26-161; also: 27-81)

Shah Waliullah's Quran-inspired stance was that Islam was the one and only and ultimate religion acceptable to Allah. All humanity must accept it. Anyone not doing so was acting against Allah's wish and is thus subject to punishment meted out by Him. Only acceptance of Islam will ensure global good. (26-137)

He desired a state ruled according to Islamic principles or the *Shariat* as it had been during the time of the first four rightly-guided Khalifas[12]. (33-535; 51-72) He longed to see Muslims of his time emulating especially the first two *Khalifas* and becoming a colossal force to subjugate the world. (27-99) It was the responsibility of the Khalifa to make Islam prevail over other religions. Likewise, it was also his duty to ensure that traditions and customs of other religions were not followed by Muslims[13]. (36-159) He felt that there ought to be only one universal Khilafat (Islamic state) for all Muslims. He also insisted that such Khilafat must remain with the Quraysh[14]. (21-106)

---

11. The essential meaning of 'persecution' is 'unbelief' (*kufr*). (128-418)

12. This period is called the 'golden age'. For details see: 129-627 to 34.

13. Dr. I. H. Qureshi writes: "Waliullah did not want the Muslims to become part of the general milieu of the subcontinent; he wanted them to keep alive their relations with the rest of the Muslim world...." (74-128q.) Dr. S. A. A. Rizvi says: "Though his ancestors had migrated to India in the 13th century, he considered himself as an alien." (51-72)

14. Prophet Muhammad belonged to the Quraysh tribe. He was the head of the first Islamic state. The first four Khalifas, too, were Quraysh. Moreover, the Prophet had himself ordained that the Khilafat must remain in Quraysh hands. (128-632; 129-41)

Exhortation to Rulers, Soldiers

Besides being a cleric, redeemer of the religion and a thinker, Shah was also a motivator and source of inspiration to people for undertaking actual action. He was a skillful preacher. He wrote hundreds of letters to administrators, nawabs, nobles, generals as well as laity explaining to them what constituted Islamic duty[15]. (26-42) Those letters clearly reveal the nature of the inspiration and teaching he imparted. He regarded the Emperor at Delhi as the 'King of Islam'. (21-106)

In the letters he addressed to administrators and rulers, he wrote: "I tell the rulers that this time, it is the will of God that you should draw out your swords from the scabbards, and should not insert them back until God makes a distinction between the Muslims and the infidels.... You continue your fight against the infidels and idolaters, until the religion of God prevails....and make such arrangement that everything is done according to the Law (*Shariah*)." (26-163)

To soldiers, he wrote: "I tell the soldiers : O soldiers, God has raised you for the Holy War, and for the purpose of making the truth prevail, and that you subdue the idolaters and root out their idolatry; but you have neglected all this, and are anxiously eager to increase your wealth.... Have fear of God....and follow the path of the *Shariah,* as prescribed." (164)

His Favourite Disciple — Najeeb Khan

The most urgent need before him was arresting the threat posed to Muslim power by Hindu forces. Military strength was needed for that purpose. He made an unsuccessful attempt to unite various Muslim nawabs and subedars. Ultimately, his hopes became concentrated on two Muslim leaders : Najeeb-ud-Daula (or Najeeb Khan) and the Amir of Afghanistan, Ahmad Shah Abdali. (21-208; 22-89)

Although Najeeb Khan was uneducated, he was tactful, well-versed in politics, capable, ambitious, courageous and

15. His letters have been published from Aligadh. (1950) (47-31)

skillful as a general. He hailed from Rohilla Afghan stock. Shah made him his favourite disciple and instilled in him faith in religion and commitment to cause. Najeeb wielded great influence over Rohillas who had become an independent state known as Rohilkhand. Najeeb, however, paid more attention to events in Delhi political circles. He was in correspondence with Ahmad Shah Abdali. He had mobilized a force of 40,000 to assist Abdali in his 1757 invasion when Abdali had captured Delhi without a fight. Emperor Alamgir had personally gone up to the Fatehpuri Masjid to welcome the invader and a joint darbar (court) was held on the following day in the imperial palace. Abdali had allowed the Emperor to continue as such in future, but reorganized the administration. Najeeb was appointed as Commander-in-Chief of the Mughal army and Abdali's representative in India. Abdali's name was included as Emperor in the *khutba* of Friday prayer at the Delhi mosque. (33-271)

However, no sooner Abdali had gone back, than the Marathas captured Delhi and drove Najeeb out of office, appointing a prime minister of their choice. Marathas now controlled Delhi. (113) Shah was observing all these events unfolding around him while he was in Delhi. He resolved to eliminate Hindu Maratha influence with the help of Abdali and Najeeb, and to make Muslim rule in Delhi strong, prosperous and sovereign.

He wrote to his favourite disciple, Najeeb: "The overthrow of both the Marathas and the Jats has been decided in the 'Court of Heaven.' Until and unless the Marathas, Jats and Sikhs are completely vanquished, no Muslim ruler can rule in peace and security." (26-152)

He groomed Najeeb to do what the Mughal Emperor ought actually to have done but had not. (33-529) Najeeb wrote several letters to Abdali, now convinced by the scheme of inviting him to India. (280)

Shah Invites Abdali to Invade India

Shah himself wrote to Abdali: "Amongst the non-Muslims there is a nation called Marathas.... Their activities have actually brought the whole of India under their influence.... Thus, by and by, the Marathas became very powerful and acquired sway over the major part of the world of Islam (i.e. South Asia).... The empire of Delhi became a child's play."

About the unenviable position of Muslims in India, he wrote: "In short, the plight of the Muslims is pitiable. All control of the government machinery is in the hands of the Hindus.... All wealth and prosperity is to be found in their houses while there is nothing for the Muslims but poverty and misery."

After praising Abdali, he concluded with the request: "At present there is no king more powerful and dignified than you. It is your duty to make for India, so as to break the power of Marathas and rescue the hapless Muslims held in the bondage by the nonbelievers.... We, the humble servants of God, seek the intercession of the Holy Prophet Muhammad, and in the name of Allah, ask Your Majesty to use your valour and gallantry to wage *Jihad* against the infidels of this area so that the beautiful reward is written in Your Majesty's record before Almighty Allah and your exalted name is included among those who do *Jihad* in the way of Allah." (25-98, 104; 26-152; 33-532; 22-91; 74-129)

Battle of Panipat (1761)

The Mughal Emperor, too, had sent Abdali an invitation for the same purpose. (33-280) This invitation from brothers-in-faith was accepted and Abdali marched into India at the close of 1759 with a large army. The entire strength of the Rohillas from Rohilkhand was deployed by Najeeb-ud-Daula behind the Afghan army. The Nawab of Ayodhya, Shuja-ud-Daula, too, joined forces[16]. Out of the total force of 60,000 ranged on Abdali's side, 30,000 was Indian Muslim. (543) All North Indian Muslim subedars and nobles united with Abdali[17], but no Hindu king, subedar or noble sided with the

16. The Marathas had sought cooperation from Shuja-ud-Daula. But Najeeb had met him and convinced him how "It was a conflict between Islam and infidelity." (33-287)

17. The Nawab of Bengal had been reduced to the status of a British stooge, and could not lend support.

Marathas. The Marathas were routed in the resulting battle at Panipat in January 1761. Barely 10,000 Maratha soldiers, out of a total force of 50,000, could escape because they fled. This was a devastating blow to Maratha power and its dream of founding the Hindupad Padshahi. (25-171; 33-295)

Shah Waliullah was elated by the Maratha defeat, but saddened because Abdali did not act according to his expectations. Abdali returned to Afghanistan after giving sanction to Shah Alam as Emperor of India[18], naming Najeeb as Commander-in-Chief, and appointing a vazir and other officials. (33-114) Shah had desired Abdali to set up the Muslim power at Delhi on a firm footing; that he back it up with permanent presence of his entire strength; or that he himself become Emperor[19]. Unfortunately, this did not happen and the dejected Shah died the following year. (140-8)

The Battle of Plassey (1757): The Emergence of British Power

A study of why the Battle of Panipat was engineered becomes indispensable for an understanding and appreciation of what Muslims, especially those in North India, wanted as a polity. The political ascendancy and power of Hindus of that time caused Muslims to regard them as their competitors and enemies. Shah Waliullah had tried to unite Muslims as a force in order to challenge the threat. However, after his death, the British emerged as a third force and became a new competitor

---

18. In a sense, he had become a vassal of Persia.

19. Mohiuddin Ahmad writes about Abdali's invasion: "Had Ahmad Shah Abdali....not left India like Nadir Shah, he might have extended his dominion from Afghanistan to Bengal. But his hasty return from India,....paved the way for gradual emergence of the British as the supreme power in India." (112-8) Likewise, Mohammad Ilyas Nadvi says: "The Almighty had mercy on Muslims and Ahmad Shah Abdali with an army of 90,000 soldiers....exterminated more than 2 lakh Marhatha soldiers to give the Muslims a sigh of relief, though short-lived.... Had he ruled Delhi for some years, the Mughal empire could have been saved from disintegration. Alas ! Nothing like that happened and the influence of the British, if not the Marathas, began to increase in the country." (41-7)

for them. From very early times, the East India Company had shrewdly begun spreading its tentacles of political power through conspiracies, agreements, conflicts and treaties. Bengal was their main centre. Four years before Panipat, in 1757, the British had defeated the Nawab of Bengal at Plassey and assumed control over the province. Their choice of the new Nawab, as desired by them, was only a stooge. The victory led to their emergence as a new challenge to Muslim power. The Hindu population of Bengal was opposed to the Nawab's rule, and secretly sympathetic to the British. (31-85; 34-335) It is for this reason that the Battle of Plassey of 1757 is viewed historically as a revolutionary event. However, as the consequences of the battle began to become apparent only after two or three years; Shah had not taken note of either the event or the British emergence[20].

Now the British as the Enemy!

The effects of the Battle of Plassey became evident after the Battle of Buxar, fought seven years later in 1764 mainly between the British and the Nawab of Ayodhya, in which battle the Nawab's army was put to rout. However, since Emperor Shah Alam and the recently deposed Nawab of Bengal had at that time sought asylum with the Nawab of Ayodhya and assisted him in the battle, Buxar is regarded as a joint defeat of all three. By a tripartite agreement executed thereafter (1765), the British acquired two districts in the Ayodhya province and, from the Emperor of Delhi, the divani rights to Bengal and Orissa provinces. Several restrictions were imposed on the Nawab of Ayodhya. By this agreement, the Ayodhya province came under British sway while the Mughal Emperor was forced to surrender to the British and give up possession of Bengal.

---

20. This battle was fought on 23rd June 1757. The situation in Delhi at the time was as follows: Abdali had arrived in Delhi on the Emperor's invitation in January 1757. He reorganized the administrative system. He remained in Delhi till April 1757. (33-274) Marathas acquired control over the Delhi administration soon after Abdali went back. Under such conditions, who could have bothered about what happened at Plassey?

The foundations of British power became more extensive with this agreement. The Muslim power now faced a real threat and that too from the British. It became amply clear by the end of the 18th Century that the British, and not the Marathas, were going to emerge as the supreme power in India. In 1803, in fact, they defeated the Marathas and seized Delhi after which the Mughal Emperor was reduced to the position of a pawn in their hands. The British had thus become 'Enemy no. 1' for the Muslims.

Fatwa: India Declared a 'Dar-ul-Harb'

Clerics trained and groomed by Shah Waliullah's inspiration and thoughts now stood up against the British. Shah's son, Shah Abdul Aziz (1746–1824), continued the struggle after his father's death. In the same year that the British became masters of Delhi (1803), he issued a *fatwa* (Muslim religious edict) against them. According to his edict, India was declared as a 'Dar-ul-Harb' (or enemy territory, vis-à-vis Islam). It is said about this declaration that it was "the most important and epoch-making *fatwa* in the history of Muslim South Asia." (25-172; 76-2)

That historic edict stated:

"According to the celebrated and trusted books (of Islamic jurisprudence), a territory of *Dar-ul-Islam* turns into *Dar-ul-Harb* if three conditions are met :

i. The enforcement of the orders of Ahl al-shirk (polytheists);
ii. Its annexation by the *Dar-ul-Harb;* and
iii. That no Muslim or *Dhimmi* (protected non-Muslim citizen of Islamic state) can live there enjoying the same peace and security as previously granted to him (by the Islamic state).

"A *Dar-ul-Harb* can also turn into *Dar-ul-Islam* with the enforcement of Islamic Laws there.

"*Dar-ul-Islam* has been defined in *al-kafi* as a state where the orders of a Muslim ruler are enforced (according to the laws of Islam) and that state is under his full and independent authority. By *Dar-ul-Harb* we mean a state where the laws of the *Shariah* are not enforced and that state is under the full and independent authority of infidels.

"In this country (i.e. India), the orders of the Muslim ruler are not enforced in reality. On the other hand, the orders of the Christian rulers are enforced without any hindrance. By the enforcement of the orders of *Kufr,* we mean that the infidels have sovereign control in matters such as state administration.... No Muslim or *dhimmi*[21] can enter this city....without their permission.... the supremacy of Christians extends from this city (Delhi) to Calcutta..

"As far as *Hadis* literature and the conduct of the Companions is concerned, the same principles can be deduced from them. We know that (the first Caliph) Abu Bakr[22] during his caliphate declared Yanbu to be *Dar-ul-Harb* on the grounds that its inhabitants had refused to pay *zakat,* although the *Jumuah, Idayn, adhan* and such other commandments of the *Shariah* were still operative there.... Even the Holy Prophet considered places like Fadak and Khaibar to be *Dar-ul-Harb* in spite of the fact that a good number of Muslims were living there...." (25–174; 118-391; 120-24; 76-3)

The entire Muslim society was stirred with this *fatwa.* It became the legal basis for *Jihad* in the years that followed. (15–50) The debate and discussion whether or not India was

---

21. 'Zimmis' (Dhimmis) are subjugated populations afforded protection by the Islamic state. Hindus were zimmis under Mughal rule. Here, the word has been used for Hindus, and intentionally, instead of 'Hindu'. What is implicit in the statement is that the 'zimmi' status of Hindus would remain unaltered even after the British had been driven out and Muslim rule had been reinstated.

22. Abu Bakr had fought (i.e. waged *Jihad*) against people in those areas. (More details: 129–61 to 83)

a *'Dar-ul-Harb'* continued not just till 1857 but also 1947[23]. The edict continued to be useful for whipping up an atmosphere of *Jihad* against the British[24]. Shah had extensively preached his thoughts in North India. Besides personally journeying far and wide, he had created a cadre of preachers and sent them in all directions for the purpose. Although the Shah, father and son duo, had not actually performed *Jihad,* they had succeeded in accomplishing the preliminary groundwork of forging Muslim public opinion and motivating them to action. Physical engagement in *Jihad* was left to his disciples and followers after his death (1824 C.E.). (See ch.3.)

Shah Abdul Aziz was succeeded in Delhi by his grandson, Shah Muhammad Ishaq (1782–1864). He found himself in a predicament when Sayyid Ahmad (Shaheed), Abdul Aziz's other favourite disciple who had undertaken the responsibility for the *Jihad,* was killed at Balakot in 1831. To ensure success of his aims, therefore, he drew up comprehensive plans and programmes as a part of which he travelled to Turkey via Mecca in 1841 to meet and seek help from the Khalifa of the global Muslim community. No information is available about the outcome of that meeting. He died in 1846 while he was still in Mecca. (74-134)

Tipu's Challenge to the British in the South

While Muslim Northern India was being churned with anti-British sentiment, a Muslim power emerged in the South

---

23. Many clerics including Maulana Azad had issued a *fatwa* in 1921 declaring that Muslims ought to migrate to Afghanistan as India had become a 'Dar-ul Harb'. (125-100; 2-295)

24. Writing about the nature of this edict, Prof.Faruqi states: "It amounted to a call to religiously conscientious Muslims to mobilize themselves, in the absence of any powerful Muslim warlord, under popular leadership and rise in defiance of the foreign power." (76-2)

Likewise, Prof. Nizami writes about its influence: "It was a political verdict couched in religious terminology. It became the focal point of Muslim Political thought in the decades that followed and, in fact, Muslim activity in the political sphere drew inspiration from this *fatwa* and centered round it." (120-3)

to challenge the British. The name of this religious hero was Tipu Sultan (1740–99). He was the son of Haider Ali, the capable general of the Hindu king of Mysore. In 1782, he inherited territory of 80,000 sq.miles and a military force of 88,000. (33-425; 41-9) He is credited as "the only Indian ruler during the 18th Century who saw clearly the danger to the independence of India from the British.... His life was continuous struggle against establishment of British rule; this was the central purpose of his life." (33-427) He is known to have led forces of a hundred thousand into battle. (28-73) He was ultimately martyred while fighting against the British. An inscription on a marble slab on his tomb in Mysore reads: "As Tipu Sultan vowed to wage a holy war, the Almighty conferred the rank of Martyrdom on him." (84)

What was his motivation to fight the British? What was going to be the nature of the state he wished to usher in after he had driven the British away? Answers to these questions are important and essential for understanding the 1857 Uprising.

Tipu had to contend with his neighbours, Marathas, British and his coreligionist Nizam. The fact that these four powers, subscribing to three different religious persuasions, were in constant conflict with one another, especially when the Nizam had allied himself with other non-Muslim powers on many occasions against Tipu, is likely to lead to the erroneous conclusion that religion *per se* had nothing to do with those struggles. Tipu's stand vis-à-vis the Nizam, which becomes very clear from a letter he (Tipu) wrote, needs to be understood in this connection.

Appeal to the Nizam for Islamic Brotherhood

Tipu's biographer Nadvi writes: "As Tipu was a great patriot, in a similar manner he was a staunch lover of Islam too. Therefore, it became a part of his mission to strive for the global unity and brotherhood among Muslims. This was the reason why he abstained from fighting against the Nizam of Hyderabad and Nawab of Karnataka till the very end. He sent his messengers very often to the Nizam to promote unity and harmony. In this connection, his letters are a sure evidence of his irresistible desire for Islamic brotherhood. In a letter to the Nizam in 1784, Tipu had reiterated his wish to help the Islamic sultanates always and his desire to sacrifice his life and property in the name of Islam." (41-128)

On one occasion Tipu wrote that, "the British deceptively don't allow us to come together. If both of us join hands, the Marathas would never dare to think of attacking us". (275) To achieve such unity, Tipu had even offered to return territory he had previously won from the Nizam. He had also suggested a marriage alliance between his and the Nizam's families to facilitate solidarity. However, the Nizam was not prepared to entertain Tipu's overtures." (275)

He had also written to a close connection in the Delhi court requesting him to urge the Nizam to cooperate with him for the enhancement of Islamic interests. (274)

Further, Tipu wrote to the Nizam's son-in-law and the subedar of Adhoni: "It is wrong that the Nizam had sided with the *Kafir* (Marathas)." (47-187)

An Appeal to the Mughal Emperor, too

Keeping the same Islamic aim in view, he wrote to Emperor Shah Alam: "This humble servant of Islam is presently involved in suppressing the rebellion of the Christians[25].... Having firm belief in the Almighty, this servant of Islam intends to fight against the anti-Islamic forces and wipe them out." (41-274)

To a top ranking official, Mohammed Beg, in the Mughal court, he wrote: "I am sure you must be aware how this friend of yours crushed the debauched Christians[25]. Presently, I am engaged in suppressing the revolt of Muslim rulers who united with the Christians[25] against Islam. In this connection, recently I distributed leaflets listing the duties towards Islam and the sayings of Prophet Muhammad throughout the country. A copy of the same is being attached along with for your perusal. It is essential to be united under one banner to protect and

25. It needs to be noted that instead of 'British' or 'English', the word 'Christian' was used intentionally.

preserve our religion and to challenge Christian onslaught with our full might so that Islam continues to prosper.... Our past glory can be retained if all the Muslims unite themselves." (41-275)

Liaison with Khalifa of Turkey

Finding it impossible to unite all Muslim powers in India, Tipu decided to seek military assistance from Salim, the Khalifa of Turkey, who was notionally the religious and political head of the Muslims all over the world. Other Muslim rulers legitimized their royalty by obtaining regalia of kingship from him. Tipu wanted that endorsement too.

He dispatched a large delegation, 900-strong, to Turkey in 1796. In a letter accompanying gifts of diamonds, jewellery, Rs.10 lacs in cash and four elephants, Tipu wrote to the Khalifa: "Our struggle is against the Christians in this country. We seek your help in this supreme effort." (41-276) He requested help to crush the enemy and perpetuate Islamic values. (134)

Expressing anxiety for Islam, not merely in India but all over the world, Tipu wrote further: "I, not only take it as a duty of the Indian citizens to resent and protest against the moves of the British, rather I feel this *Jihad* is mandatory on the part of the entire Islamic community world-wide. Moreover, our mission is to uphold the grandeur of Islam more than the protection of our country." (131)

A draft for a bipartite agreement was also sent with the delegation. It proposed letting of the port of Basra to Tipu on rental basis in return for any port of the Khalifa's choice in Tipu's territory, as this arrangement would facilitate trade and enhancement in maritime and naval power, to ultimately benefit Islam. Under one Article in the draft, Tipu also sought military help, expenses for which would be borne by Tipu; in return, Tipu would send his own troops *gratis* if the Khalifa felt the need for them[26].

---

26. Dr. I. H. Qureshi writes about this proposal: "If the Ottoman Empire had been strong and vigorous, it would have welcomed this opportunity of expanding its influence in South Asia. The decay of Mughal Empire could have added to its opportunities." (33-38)

The prevailing international situation precluded the *Khalifa* from accepting this proposal from his brother-in-faith. Nevertheless, he acceded to Tipu's request for sanctioning investiture of royalty. At the same time, Tipu was granted permission to include his name as Emperor in the *khutba* and also to strike coins in his name. The delegation returned to India bearing the investiture with it. (33-452; 93-137; 21-53) With those regal trappings, Tipu's status surpassed even that of the Emperor at Delhi from the religious viewpoint, as the latter called himself 'Emperor' without such investiture!

Appeal to Afghanistan for Help

Not disheartened by noncommittal response for military help from the 'Khalifa of Islam', Tipu sent a similar embassy to Zaman Shah, the Amir of Afghanistan (grandson of Ahmad Shah Abdali), in 1797. In the letter accompanying the delegation, he wrote: "The Almighty's blessings are invoked after every Friday prayer upon your Kingdom for its further expansion and consolidation. We have always been praying for the unity and mutual understanding amongst the Muslim rulers on the basis of religion. At present, we are in dire straits since the anti-Islamic forces are preparing for a war against us. Keeping these facts in view, we seek your help earnestly. Hope you will support our endeavours in this crusade." (41-176) He had asked for cavalry of 20,000. (88-39)

In his reply, Zaman Shah wrote: "Since anti-Islamic forces are on the threshold of wiping out an Islamic Sultanate, we extend our support to you. We are coming up to you along with a gigantic force so that the country may be cleansed of idolatry and innovations in religion." (41-177)

He mobilized a force of 33,000 and set off towards India for the succour of his coreligionists. This created a panic in the British camp. But Zaman Shah had to return from the Indian border because the British managed to engineer a diversionary attack on Afghanistan by the Shah of Iran. (33-489; 41-177)

Embassy to Iran, too

Thereafter, Tipu sent a delegation seeking help from Karim Khan, Shah of Iran. The Persian Empire used to be considered powerful at the time. The Shah acceded to just one of Tipu's requests: permission to reciprocal use of one port belonging to one another. In a letter of thanks to the Shah, Tipu wrote: "By the grace of Almighty as expected, you, too, are concerned about the unity and amity between the two. You ought to consider all my areas and territories yours, on the same pattern as I think." (41-178) However, owing to an emergent warlike situation in Iran, this pact could not be implemented[27].

Jihad against Nonbelievers

Tipu was thus unable to muster any tangible support from three of the world's powerful Muslim empires[28].

By a royal edict in 1786, Tipu had appealed to Muslim residents of British India to immigrate to his territory : "The Muslims should quit the country of nonbelievers and wait until the Sultan either converts those rascal nonbelievers to Islam or forces them to pay *Jiziya*[29].... Our aim is to wage *Jihad* against them." (41-276)

---

27. In later years, when a prince of the Persian royal family visited Mysore, Tipu accorded him a royal welcome. He also reiterated to the prince before he returned, "You, Amir of Afghanistan and myself together shall strive utmost to establish Islamic rule in India." (44-187)

28. Commenting on Tipu's initiative of engaging in correspondence with foreign powers, his biographer Nadvi writes: "The letters were also written with the aim of preservation of an Islamic Sultanate rather than for his individual gains or security of his Sultanate. Furthermore, he wrote that their cooperation would imply the resurgence of Islam in India, its prosperity and security." (41-276)

29. Tipu has stated here the Doctrine of Hijrat.

Tipu had published a book to inculcate the spirit of *Jihad* in Muslims. It was entitled *Fateh-al-Mujahideen* (Victory of Religious Soldiers) (94-95) Directives and sayings from the Quran and *Hadis* dealing with *Jihad* were included in it. Besides his own territories, copies of the book were also distributed in Hyderabad, Bengal and Delhi among other places. (41-276) The book explicated how *Jihad* against aggressive nonbelievers was true Islam. "(He) did fight to preserve the political power of Islam." (33-427)

Proponent of the Ideal Muslim State

Tipu called his army the 'Lashkar-e-Mujahideen' ('army of religious warriors'). To ward off the possibility of defections, he had ultimately begun recruiting what he thought were 'pure' Muslims in the army. (93-378) He named his Kingdom as, "'Saltanat-i-Khudadad' (God given state)." (93-378) The coin he struck in his name was called the 'imani' ('believer' or 'faithful'). On it were inscribed the words, '"Islam saw its glory with the victories of Hyder." (41-276). Tipu is also known as the 'sword of Islam' of the 18th Century. (94-212)

Tipu was a proponent of pristine Islam. (28-74) Shah Waliullah's teachings had influenced him to a great extent. "He had always aspired to keep his Muslim subjects free from all sorts of innovations in religion, un-Islamic rituals and nonsensical beliefs because living together with the Hindus for centuries altogether, the Muslims had borne an imprint of their culture and rituals." (41-277) He had issued ordinances to forbid non-Islamic practices. (278) Prohibition was imposed in his state because Islam disapproves of liquor. (38-74) Hundreds of cities, towns and places were renamed with Islamic names. (94-217) 70,000 Hindus in the Coorg province were made Muslims. (93-363; 94-96) "The Sultan intended to establish an exemplary Islamic society in his Sultanate." (41-279) In other words, Tipu was Shah Waliullah's ideal Khalifa. "He had always been concerned for the superiority of Islam in the world." (276)

Tipu was killed in 1799 in a battle with the British. The noted Urdu poet, Iqbal, said about him: "Tipu was the last arrow in our quiver in the great struggle between religion and irreligion (i.e. Islam and Kufr)." (47-192)

War of Independence, but for Who?

A study of Tipu's career is significant in connection with the 1857 uprising. First, he is revered as a freedom fighter because he opposed the British[30]. Can merely ousting the British be sufficient justification for the uprising to be regarded a war of independence? Even though replacement of British power by Muslim rule (like that of Tipu Sultan) may have meant independence for minority Muslims, what did it entail for majority Hindus? This same consideration applies to the 1857 uprising.

Secondly, Tipu needs to be studied in order to understand the nature and intensity of Indian Muslim sentiment when it became quite clear (after 1757 or 1765) that the British were certain to replace Muslim rule. The same feelings that actuated North India were apparent in the South. Both cleric and ruler alike were animated by the same sentiment. Both had agitated to perform *Jihad,* both regarded India as *Dar-ul-Harb.* Tipu made significant impact on all-India Muslim psyche, which increased after his death. Tipu's career had become a model of the true Islamic *Jihad* that an ideal Muslim ruler must perform.

For this reason, a scrutiny of the life of Tipu serves as a criterion to ascertain what sentiment inspired Indian Muslims before 1857, why they rose against the British and whether the uprising can be viewed as a war of independence.

---

30. In the Karnataka Government publication, *A History of Freedom Struggle in Karnataka,* Haider Ali and Tipu Sultan have been eulogized as freedom fighters and more than 200 pages devoted to their biographies. (47-181) Information about Tipu occupies 74 pages in Pakistan Government publication: *A History of the Freedom Movement.* (33–427 to 90)

Revolt by Vazir Ali of Ayodhya

Like Tipu in the South, the deposed Nawab of Ayodhya, Vazir Ali Khan (1781–1818) was also striving around the same time to secure military help from foreign Islamic powers for the purpose of overthrowing British rule. His attempts are known in history as 'Revolt / Conspiracy of Vazir Ali '. Prof. Sashi Bhushan Chaudhary believes it was a 'national revolt'. (80-76) Endowed with a sharp intellect and acumen for diplomacy, Vazir Ali who had ascended the throne with British consent at the age of 17, soon began acting in disregard of them. He was deposed as soon as the British thought that he was "unlikely to be obedient to the English; and finally as altogether adverse to the English likely to use his utmost endeavours to free himself from their yoke."[31] (33-226) This made him bitterly anti-British. He shifted residence to Benares under instructions from them. He was very popular among his subjects and had a large following. A large part of the army had become sympathetic to him. (117-19; 80-76)

Conspiracy by Indian Muslim Powers

While he was at Benares, Vazir Ali sent an embassy to Zaman Shah of Afghanistan along with a gift of Rs. 50,00,000 and sought military assistance. (117-15) At the same time, he established relations with the Nawabs of Murshidabad, in Bengal, and Dacca, who were fed up with British subjugation and had also already sent envoys to Zaman Shah[32]. (117-16;

---

31. Dr. Chaudhary's comment on his dismissal: "Real intentions of the British" was not to have "another" Tipu'....in the North" (80-74)

32. Dr. Chaudhary comments on this arrangement: "The papers found in possession of Vazir Ali, show that he was the main link in the chain of conspiracies started from Dacca and Murshidabad with Zaman Shah of Kabul as the centre of Muslim aspirations. Vazir Ali might have acted in concert with the Dacca and Murshidabad chiefs, and was waiting to receive an Afghan force. As Kaye writes, Zaman Shah of Kabul was stirring up the Muhammadan princes of India to continue in a religious war against the usurping *feringhee*." (80-75)

80-75; 32-21) In his letter to Zaman Shah, the Nawab of Dacca implored the Afghan to destroy British power in the region for Islam's sake. (80-74) This was not all. At the same time, Emperor Shah Alam's envoy had also reached Zaman Shah's court. (88-39) Vazir Ali had reached an understanding with Shah Alam. (39) On his part, Zaman Shah too was not idle and, according to historian John Kaye, was instigating Muslim rulers in India for *Jihad* against the British.(80-75q.) Tipu's envoy had also reached Kabul around the same time. Relations had also been established between Vazir Ali and Tipu. (88-316) Indeed, this was a comprehensive and concerted conspiracy hatched by Indian Muslim powers of the time to invite Zaman Shah to invade India. (88-63; 18-192; 67-26)

Zaman Shah Marches towards India

The British intelligence network soon got wind of the scheme and the administration became anxious about India's security. (88-26; 65-101) News began doing the rounds: 'Zaman Shah has crossed the river Jhelum and is on his way to Lahore' (January 1797); 'the British and Marathas are planning to jointly resist the invasion' (88-27). But Zaman Shah had to return owing to the home situation. News was again received (August 1797) that he had reached Kandahar on his way to India. (39) But once again he had to abandon the campaign for the same reason. It was learnt again in October 1797 that he had left with a force of 60,000. (90) He captured Lahore unopposed in November 1797. (92) He also won control of Amritsar and was expected to launch an attack on Delhi which the British were preparing to repel. (93) It became common knowledge that the Emperor, Shah Alam, was proceeding to Sirhind to meet Zaman Shah. (97) The Shah's invasion was going to be a signal to Indian Muslim rulers to rise up against the British simultaneously. (194)

Incapable of facing the threat militarily, the British used diplomatic and political stratagems to force Zaman Shah to abort his campaigns by either instigating his neighbours to make incursions into his territory or creating rebellions within his state, saving India from aggression in the process[33]. Although this invasion was a failure because it remained incomplete, it succeeded as an inspiration by rekindling in the Muslim psyche an intense ambition to perform *Jihad* for re-establishing their Islamic empire. Mere news about the prospective invasion was sufficient to electrify them. Note must be taken of this invasion to appreciate why Muslims had desired to end British rule and which regime they had aspired to usher in as its successor[34]. It must be remembered that

---

33. The Amir of Afghanistan had several times from 1761 to 1919 been invited by Indian Muslims to invade India. Dr. Ambedkar comments about the 1919 invitation: "Whether the invasion would have resulted in the emancipation of India or whether it would have resulted in its subjugation, it is not possible to say because the invasion failed to take effect." (2-295)

34. Here are some contemporary British reactions about the invasion:

i. The *Calcutta Review* wrote: "The hopes and aspirations of Muhammedans on the northern frontier of Hindustan rose up to a fever pitch. They envisioned the restoration of the lost dignity of the House of Timur." (88-312q.)

ii. The then governor general wrote (on 22.4.1799) to his superiors: "I am already in possession of sufficient evidence to prove that a conspiracy had been hatched for the purpose of not only restoring Vazir Ali to the throne of Oudh but also favouring the invasion of Zaman Shah, and of expelling the British from the provinces of Bengal, Bihar and Orissa.... persons concerned in this treason are almost exclusively Muhammedans, several of them of high rank." (88-194q.) "Mornington (the governor)....(and other officials) were far more concerned with the theory of a conspiracy for a serious Muslim uprising in India, led by persons of Royalty of bygone days." (302)

iii. Aniruddha Ray informs: "The English then, against the background of Zaman Shah's invasion, had been looking at the Muslim royalties with suspicion. The 'conspiracy' had proved to (them)....that 'no dependence can be placed on the gratitude or attachment of the highest of Mussalmans." (305)

simultaneous appeals for aggression had been made barely 60 years before the 1857 uprising by the Nawabs of Ayodhya, Dacca and Murshidabad, Tipu Sultan of Mysore, and the Emperor of Delhi, who had all been in close communication with one another.

The 'Farazi' Movement of Bengal

Just as Muslim rulers and administrators were striving to overthrow British rule elsewhere, the cleric Shariatullah (1781–1840) had initiated a Jihadi movement for the same purpose in Bengal. It began as a reaction against exploitation of Muslim peasants in Bengal. The exploiters were Hindus and the British. The actual injustice was being done by the Hindus, but the British rulers were aiding and abetting it by making laws that allowed it to occur.

The Emperor of Delhi had awarded the 'diwani' rights of Bengal by the 1765 treaty to the British who now controlled all affairs of that province. They used this authority to enact various new laws concerning lands and revenue that were primarily intended to benefit themselves, but effectively proved advantageous to Hindus and disadvantageous to Muslims. A majority of Bengal's zamindars (landholders) were Hindu and the peasants, Muslim. (77-146; 124-33) Rich Hindus and poor Muslims was the general norm. The new laws increased this disparity. Hindus emerged as collectors of revenue while Muslims became victims of their unjust ways and were reduced to landlessness. Hindus began buying Muslim lands. In this manner, with the loss of political power, Muslim society was faced with economic crisis[35].

Shariatullah mobilized and organized Muslim society into a mass movement against British rule. This agitation was similar to that of Shah Waliullah and Shah Abdul Aziz with this difference that economic issues were treated as distinct from others. Shariatullah is rated among noted Muslim freedom fighters. (28-85)

---

35. For more information about the unenviable condition of Muslims bereft of political power: see Chap. 4.

He went on the Hajj pilgrimage with his father at the age of 18 and stayed on in Mecca to pursue religious studies for 18 or 19 years (spending two years at the Al Azhar University in Egypt), returning to India in 1818.

On his return, he saw the pitiable condition of Muslims among the peasantry and working classes, and initiated the 'farazi' movement[36] to alleviate their suffering. It was directed against both, the Hindu zamindars as well as British rulers. Muslims joined the agitation in large numbers as economic issues were irksome to them and were sought to be addressed. (83-63) The Muslim peasant and worker classes became united and organized under Shariatullah's leadership. (120-81) The perpetrators of economic injustice were forced to regard the movement with due seriousness. (28-93) He was on one occasion arrested and forced to shift his residence. (83-65; 28-97)

However, this was nothing like an agitation of economically exploited classes conducted by communists. Having spent two decades in Mecca, which enabled him to observe pure Islam in action, Shariatullah was influenced by Wahabi[37] thought prevalent in Saudi Arabia. His agitation was not called anything like, say, "Peasants'-Workers' Agitation", but "Agitation for Implementing Allah's Commandments".[36] It was just coincidental that he had hit upon the economic angle in addition to the essentially religious motive to unite Muslims.

Like Shah Waliullah, Shariatullah was a proponent of 'pure' Islam. He assiduously maintained that original Islam was only what was conveyed through the Quran by Allah and preached through the *Hadis* by Muhammad, that Muslims ought to

---

36. 'Farazi' means 'Allah's commandments'. 'Farazi Movement' means 'an agitation for implementing Allah's commandments'.

37. The Arab cleric, Abdul Wahab (1703-92), was a proponent of pristine Islam as prescribed by the Quran and *Hadis*. He had also received royal patronage. His teachings became better known outside Arabia. For that reason, it became a practice thereafter to call anyone promoting pristine Islam as a 'wahabi'.

practice only that Islam and shun all non-Islamic practices that had later found their way into the religion. (120-79) Muslims had begun following many Hindu customs; they participated in Hindu religious observances. Shariatullah sought to prohibit all such practices. (28-94) It is for this reason that those following only original religious prescriptions or Allah's commandments, to the exclusion of all others, are known as 'farazis'. (33-546)

India: 'Dar-ul-Harb'

The second vital postulation by Shariatullah was that India under British rule had been rendered a '*Dar-ul-Harb*' (territory inimical to Islam). (33-547; 120-80) This was similar to the edict issued by Shah Abdul Aziz, except that Shariatullah banned the Friday public namaz and the annual Id rites in Bengal because their observance lacked scriptural sanction in a *Dar-ul-Harb*. (83-64) His principal objective was driving the British out and transforming the '*Dar-ul-Harb*' into a '*Dar-ul-Islam*'. For the time being, he only contemplated reestablishing Muslim rule in Bengal. (32-11; 67-34; 124-17)

Dadu Miyan: 80,000 followers

In real terms, it was his son who set the agitation into actual motion. Dadu Miyan became the leader of the movement after Shariatullah's death (1840). His resolve became more firm after he performed the Hajj pilgrimage of Mecca. (83-66) He was not merely a preacher and redeemer of religion, but also an effective and vigorous leader. The movement gained strength and inculcated a fighting spirit under his leadership. He brought eighty thousand followers into the agitation and made it a hub of power. They commenced a struggle against zamindars with all their might. The activists were armed with swords, shields and other weapons. (83-68) They would demonstrate their power by occasional shows of strength and create an atmosphere of terror. (69) They also engaged in many armed struggles against the zamindars. (74-163) As the latter were predominantly Hindus, the agitation assumed an anti-Hindu complexion. As rulers, the British sided with the

Hindus[38]. Dadu Miyan was charged with treason, murder and dacoity, and many criminal cases were filed against him. (83-76; 120-84) The farazis had emerged as a great predicament for the government. (83-75)

In accordance with his acceptance of the principle of Dar-ul-Harb, "Their ultimate objective is the expulsion of the present rulers of the land, and the restoration of Muhammedan power." (95) He declared that as the whole earth belonged to Allah, none had the hereditary right to either live off it or impose tax on mankind against 'Allah's sanction'. (120-84; 77-149; 33-548; 124-18) He thus declared that all taxes imposed by the British were illegitimate, antireligious and condemnable. (83-91) Support for this contention was drawn from the Prophet's following *Hadis*: It was 'illegal to pay rent especially to an infidel.' (92)

The agitation drew on for several years thereafter. Dadu Miyan and his followers had actively participated in the 1857 Uprising. (83-73 to 5) He was also arrested at that time. He died in 1862.

British Apprehension of Uprising

The challenge posed to British authorities by the agitation was clearly spelled out in a communication sent by the Police

---

38. Bengal Muslims were being consistently told that, "(In Bengal) the Muslims in particular were constantly taught to regard their European masters as *Kafirs*.... The followers of the Prophet were reminded that the hated oppressors were the enemies of Islam, who had not only usurped the sovereignty of the country, but were also exploiting the Muslim peasantry in collusion with the Hindu landlords, and therefore *Jihad* against them was the sacred duty of all true believers." (124-13)

39. Another movement for ushering in pristine Islam had begun in Bengal around the same time under the leadership of Titu Mir. It was opposed to both the British and Hindus. "(The sect) claimed the sovereign power as the hereditary right of Mohammedans." (77-154) "The movement led by Titu Mir was solely directed against the Hindus.... (The sect) looked upon the whole community of Hindus as their enemies." (83-104q.)

chief of Bengal to the secretary of the central administration: "The Muhammedan population in the Eastern Districts (of Bengal) are all what is called Farazis, that is Wahabis, strongly united together, very fanatic, under the control of particular leaders and inimical to our government and they need to be watched most carefully, for if there is any danger of an outbreak in these provinces, it is from the ultra fanaticism of this sect." (83-94)

The farazis had, as their aim, the uprooting of British rule and reestablishment of Muslim power with which motive alone they had participated in the *Jihad* of 1857.

Prof. Mujeeb Ashraf concludes in respect of all these movements: "Their final goal was to establish a purely Islamic State in India." (77-154)

* * *

Chapter 2

A Century before the Jihad – II

India's First Freedom Fighter: Sayyid Ahmad Shaheed

The most effective and accomplished person among Indian Muslims in the century before the 1857 Uprising was Sayyid Ahmad Barelvi (Shaheed)[1] (1786-1831). 'Sayyid Ahmad', to whom Dr. Ambedkar refers as the person whose uprising of a prior few decades was rekindled as the *Jihad* of 1857, was this Sayyid Ahmad[2]. He is regarded as 'the greatest reformer and Mujahid (holy warrior) of the early 19th Century.' (112-i) "He was the first popular, political leader (amongst the Muslims) in this subcontinent." (33-580; 25-189) Shaikh Sirhindi is regarded as the redeemer and Imam Mahdi[3] (Mujahid Alf Thani) of the 2nd (Hijri) Millennium while Sayyid Ahmad, that of the 13th (Hijri) Century. (75-184; 115-1; 15-60) He possessed

---

1. He is referred to as 'Shaheed' because he was martyred on the battlefield, and 'Barelvi' from the name of his birthplace (Bareilly).

2. It should be noted that 'Sir Sayyid Ahmad' (1817-98), British loyalist, was an entirely different person than this Sayyid Ahmad.

3. 'Mahdi' is a divine messenger who appears from age to age to resurrect the religion.

an extraordinary personality and it was claimed that he was born in the Prophet's lineage. It was believed that he could converse with Allah and the Prophet. (75-184) About his movement it is said that, "Of all the movements which the British rule in India called into existence the Wahabi Movement was the most remorselessly anti-British." (116-335) He is credited with the honour of being 'India's first freedom fighter'. (120-50)

Such was Sayyid Ahmad's extraordinary career and historic significance that Abul Hassan Ali Nadvi of India needed to write a thousand pages in two volumes to cover his biography, while Ghulam Rasool Meher of Pakistan, 1,921 pages in four volumes. He was a great organizer and able leader who actually implemented the teachings of Shah Waliullah and Shah Abdul Aziz amid the milieu already created by them[4]. It is held that the history of the Indian freedom movement would remain incomplete without the inclusion of the activism of Sayyid Ahmad Barelvi. (115-10) "His thought was greatly affected by the teachings of Shaikh Sirhindi and more directly by Shah Waliuallah." (120-43) "Their movement was a sequel to Shah Waliullah's efforts for the revival and reform of Islam." (33-508) "The *Jihad* movement was only another facet of Shah Waliullah's movement." (25-201) He is believed to have held that 'My way is the way of my grandfather (i.e.

---

4. His agitation is popularly known as the 'Wahabi' Movement. The term 'Wahabi' is used for the thoughts of Abdul Wahab, a religious teacher in Saudi Arabia. In actual fact, except for the commonality of insistence on 'pristine Islam', Sayyid Ahmad's thoughts and work are quite distinct. Many scholars have made it clear that it is incorrect to call his movement the 'Wahabi' agitation. He himself had called it the 'Tariqah-i-Muhammadiya' (Way of Muhammad). He was inspired not by Wahab, but the Shah father and son! His school of thought and agitation might correctly be called 'Waliullahi'. However, since many scholars and authors have called it the 'Wahabi' Movement and the word cannot be avoided while referring to their writings, we have been unable to completely eliminate its use.

Waliullah).' (52-89) "Thus on this fundamental issue Sayyid Ahmad Shaheed practically accepted the teachings of (Shaikh Sirhindi)." (33-573)

Disciple of Shah Abdul Aziz

Sayyid Ahmad was born in 1784 to the well-known Sayyid family in Rae Bareli in the Ayodhya province. *Jihad* had enchanted him since his very childhood. (112-28) He travelled to Delhi at the age of twenty with seven colleagues and met Shah Abdul Aziz. The Shah had only recently issued a religious decree declaring India a '*Dar-ul-Harb*'. Impressed by the young man's sharp intellectual abilities, the Shah kept him as his guest. Soon, he became a disciple. So pleased was the Shah with Sayyid Ahmad that he said, "My son, you have been blessed by God with the prophetic enlightenment." (37) It was believed that the Prophet had appeared to him several times during this period. (40) He returned to his home town after 3–4 years.

With his teacher's permission, he went to the Nawab of Tonk, Amir Khan, and took up employment in his army (1811), which gave him the opportunity to learn military skills. Tonk was an independent kingdom in Rajputana, and not under British control (*Dar-ul-Harb*). (112-50; 77-124) The Nawab was highly impressed by his personality and thoughts, and became his follower. Six years later, when the Nawab signed a treaty with the British and Tonk did not remain sovereign in the strict sense, Sayyid resigned from service and left for Delhi (1818). (112-59)

Selection as Successor for Jihad

He went to meet his preceptor in Delhi. According to a pious belief, the Shah had a vision about Sayyid's imminent arrival and the beginning of the great work of reestablishing Islam. (62) The Shah named Sayyid Ahmad as his successor for waging *Jihad* and began urging everyone to accept his tutelage and receive instruction from him. The reluctance of a certain learned Maulavi to do so was dispelled by the Shah, with the words, "Mulla, you would attain the stages under him in 12 days that would take 12 years under me." (112-62)

This extraordinary respect shown by the teacher for his disciple was sufficient for that Maulavi to become Sayyid's adherent. Members of the Shah's family also became his followers. Among them, Maulana Abdul Hai (Shah's son-in-law) and Maulana Shah Muhammad Ismail (Shah's nephew), later rose to fame as Sayyid's able lieutenants. Hundreds of Muslims from Delhi and environs began thronging to Sayyid to become his disciples.

Tours for Preaching Jihad

Soon thereafter, Sayyid Ahmad took permission from the Shah and embarked upon a tour of provinces outside Delhi with the purpose of preaching the philosophy of *Jihad*. The Shah had also sent him his own cloak. (This was in the nature of a blessing or benediction.) Accompanied by twenty disciples, Sayyid toured various districts[5] of North India. People, including Maulvis, rushed to become his followers at each of the places he visited. In Meerut, the throngs were so large that he had to stay in the town for fifteen days. (63) In Nanauta, it became impossible for Sayyid to induct everyone individually – his turban was unwound and spread out, and everyone touching it was declared inducted. He would give discourses at various places where huge crowds gathered to hear him. Even some Hindus became his disciples (after embracing Islam) under the influence of this charged atmosphere. Sayyid returned to his birth town in June 1819 after preaching *Jihad* intensively for seven months and inducting hundreds of thousands of followers. (66)

Thereafter, he undertook a similar tour of the Rae Bareli district. Then he went on to another tour towards Allahabad. Ordinarily, the distance between Rae Bareli and Allahabad could be covered in four days but Sayyid needed over a month for the journey owing to more inductions en route. (112-70) He then went to Benares. A senior official of the Hindu Raja

5. These included: Ghaziabad, Meerut, Muzaffarnagar, Deoband, Fular, Nanauta, Saharanpur, Thanabhavan, Moradabad, Rampur and Bareilly. (112-63; 32-23)

of Benares, Shaikh Ghulam Ali, became a follower. About 10,000 local Muslims were also inducted. Religious discourses were delivered on the way. His lieutenant, Maulana Hai, was a popular speaker who drew huge crowds. At Sultanpur, where he won followers in large numbers, the district governor Ghulam Hassan Khan and hundreds of soldiers from the Ayodhya region joined the movement. (70)

With 170 of his followers, Sayyid then went to the capital of Ayodhya, Lucknow, where he was even more successful than Allahabad or Benares. People queued up from dawn till late night every day to be inducted. Even Shi'ah Muslims, who were in majority in the capital, became his followers. Muslims in large numbers including those belonging to the ruling family, as well as several military officers, joined the movement. (71) All of them began viewing Sayyid as a messenger sent to them by Allah. (33-532) Preaching *Jihad* along the way, he returned to Rae Bareli by a different route.

Emphasis on Jihad in Discourses

In their discourses, Sayyid Ahmad and Maulana Hai would tell their listeners of the importance of pure Islam and *Jihad.* They would impress upon the minds of the audience that *Jihad* was the highest service to Allah. (112-74) They would at times appear armed with a sword or musket, which sent the crowds into raptures. Sayyid presented a musket to a disciple with the words, "Make up your mind to take part in *Jihad,* learn the use of arms for that purpose and try to build up your health. God willing, we shall fight the infidels." (112-74) Someone asked, "You carry arms, swords, shields and matchlocks. Are these not the ways of ignorant folk ?" (112-74) He retorted indignantly : "God allowed His prophets the use of these means in fighting the nonbelievers. Did not our own Prophet take up arms against the infidels to diffuse the light of Truth ? Had he not done so, we would not have been believers today." (112-75) Any invitation from weapon-wielding youth would please him immensely. He used to tell them, "Young men like you are needed by me. I do not want the weak and sickly sons of the *pirs.*" (112-75)

Thereafter he toured the towns and surrounding areas of Kanpur, Kura, Jehanabad and Fatehpur. Here, too, he won the following of thousands as at other places he had toured earlier. (82)

Hajj Pilgrimage: Veritable Jihad Tour

Sayyid Ahmad's tours for preaching pristine Islam and *Jihad* went on for two years and nine months. He had succeeded in alluring much of North India (and the whole of the then North-Westerly provinces) with the spirit of *Jihad*. At this juncture, Sayyid decided to perform the Hajj pilgrimage. He set out from Rae Bareli with 400 select followers several months in advance of the date of his actual embarkation from Calcutta for Mecca. He had deliberately chosen to sail from Calcutta so that the longer route might provide further opportunity to preach on the way. (25-194) For all practical purposes, it was a tour for preaching *Jihad*! He broke journey for 12 days in Allahabad and a month in Benares. During an eight-day stay in Patna, he inducted Nawab Qutb-ud-Din Khan, some noblemen and a large number of others. With halts for discourses and inductions at other places in Bihar like Bhagalpur, Murshidabad, Surajgadh and Rajmahal, he reached Calcutta in November 1821, three months after he had set out from Rae Bareli.

Calcutta was the British capital. In the entire period of his three-month halt there, he and members of his party undertook tours of the surrounding regions. People thronged from remote places like Sylhet, Chittagong, Dacca and Assam to hear him. Again, as individual induction became impossible, several turbans were tied to one another with Sayyid Ahmad holding one end so that everyone touching any portion of it was deemed inducted. This had become a daily practice[6]. (74-132; 112-86)

It was around this time that some of Tipu Sultan's sons, who were residing there, became Sayyid's followers. They

6. Moved by his compelling appeal, some 300 or 400 Hindus had also converted to Islam and accepted his teachings. (112-86)

said that Tipu's family had become disciples of Sayyid's uncles[7] who themselves subscribed to Sayyid's thoughts, a matter that Sayyid confirmed with his approbation. (25-190, 4; 112-86; 41-310)

Sayyid then set sail for Mecca from Calcutta with 750 followers. Many Hindus had also been present at the dock to bid him farewell. He reached Mecca in May 1822 and returned to India after a stay of 14 months. He reached his home in April 1824 after another preaching-packed journey from Calcutta to Rae Bareli. (112-98)

Headquarters for Jihad Programme: Peshawar

Sayyid had acquired millions of followers by this time. The whole of north India had been stirred up by his thoughts and preaching. He advocated in his preaching the same thoughts that were promoted by the Shah father and son. He was fully convinced by his mentor's declaration that India had become a '*Dar-ul-Harb*'. *Jihad* was needed to transform it into a '*Dar-ul-Islam*', which responsibility he had assumed. Now he began making plans and programmes to realize it.

Sayyid was faced with the question of selecting a place to be utilized as the centre for the *Jihad*; whether it ought to be located within or outside India. Two difficulties surfaced in selecting a place within India. First, would the launching of the *Jihad* from within India, that had become a '*Dar-ul-Harb*', be religiously correct and proper? According to the *shariat*, a Khalifa is necessary for conducting *Jihad*. In the absence of a truly independent Muslim state within India, there was obviously none who qualified as Khalifa. Second, was it feasible to immediately begin and sustain a successful *Jihad* against the British? For, before declaring *Jihad* it has to be first

7. Their names were Sayyid Abu Said and Sayyid Abul Laith. They had participated in Waliullah's movement. Haider Ali was a disciple of theirs, and they had maintained excellent relations with Tipu. (25-194)

considered whether it would succeed[8], which was not the case in prevailing conditions. (118)

'One Enemy at a Time'

It was decided, on the basis of these two considerations, to establish the principal centre outside the *'Dar-ul-Harb'*, at Peshawar, and initially commence a *Jihad* against the neighbouring infidel Sikh state. It was possible to obtain support of Pathan tribes in the region and neighbouring Muslim state of Afghanistan for the undertaking. (50) Moreover, migrating (*hijrat*) from *'Dar-ul-Harb'* to 'Dar-ul Islam' was a pious duty. (116-325; 32-25) Sayyid appealed to all those who were unable to perform *hijrat,* to carry out in India the work of motivating people with the message of *Jihad* and mobilizing funds for the struggle across the border[9]. (116-341) Patna was made the headquarters for the movement in India.

The aim of *Jihad* was to establish a state that will conduct itself according to Islamic law (like the 'golden age' during the rule of the first four 'rightly guided' Khalifas). Sayyid Ahmad desired to found just such a truly Islamic state in India. (116-130; 120-45) "This implied the launching of a consistent struggle against all non-Muslim rulers." (77-117) The anti-Sikh *Jihad* was just a step in the direction of the ultimate goal, inspired by the common principle of war, 'one enemy at a time'. (33-578; 77-127)

---

8. As a precedent for emulation, Sayyid Ahmad had before him the Prophet's example of how he had refrained from armed *Jihad* during his Mecca years when he lacked requisite following, but how he had led an army to subdue Mecca within eight years after establishing an Islamic state in Madina.

9. Prof. Nizami writes in connection with this plan: "Sayyid Ahmad was fully conscious that the lost political supremacy in India could be reestablished only by starting a struggle in the north and consolidating power in the northwest frontier which would be used as a base of operations for further expansion in the country." (120-32)

Jihad Tour Towards Peshawar

Sayyid Ahmad left for Peshawar in January 1826 along with 500 selected companions after making arrangements for propagation of his philosophy in India. (116-43; 112-43) A long route had deliberately been chosen so that he could preach *Jihad* in the western part of North India, which he had not previously visited. This was certain to cause the remaining parts of North India to become enthused with the cause. Some events that occurred on the way are noteworthy.

When Sayyid was in Gwalior, a message from Maharaja Daulatrao was brought by his son-in-law and chief minister, Hindurao, to the effect that the Maharaja could not come out to meet Sayyid as he was unwell and would Sayyid come to the palace? Sayyid went with his associates to see the Maharaja who accorded him a respectful welcome. The Maharaja requested guidance on meditation but Sayyid declined, stating that it was first necessary to believe in Allah (or become Muslim). However, on the Maharaja's persistence, Sayyid offered some instructions. While Sayyid was still in the Maharaja's presence, it was time for offering namaz, and he offered prayers collectively with all Muslims present[10].

The Maharaja requested Sayyid to spend a year in Gwalior, but as the latter was in a hurry to commence *Jihad* against infidels, so he declined the request. The Maharaja offered to provide arms and ammunition for the *Jihad*. Sayyid was given robes of honour and a state banquet. (154)

During his stay at Gwalior, Sayyid secured the release of a grandson of Ahmad Shah Abdali who was under detention of Maharaja. The man was given a state escort, and left for Hyderabad (Sind). (154)

The Jihadis were given a warm welcome when they reached Tonk. The Nawab, Amir Khan, was already a disciple.

---

10. Mohiuddin Ahmad writes that this was the first occasion when *azan* was given and *namaz* offered at the Gwalior palace. (112-154)

The Khan's son, many courtiers, army chiefs, soldiers and citizens became his disciples. (33-582)

Sayyid had to proceed through Sind where he was given a welcome by the Muslim chief at the capital, Hyderabad Sind, and was assured of his support for the *Jihad*. Many nobles, high ranking officials and citizens in large numbers received the benefit of induction from Sayyid. (112-157; 33-582) A certain influential Maulavi at Ranipur in the Sind province commanded veneration of thousands of disciples. He declared support for Sayyid's *Jihad* and directed his followers to participate in it. (ibid)

Sayyid then crossed the Indus and began making his way towards Afghanistan through Baluchistan. Stopping at places like Quetta, Kandahar and Ghazni, the Jihadi force reached Kabul in October 1826. Many in Quetta registered their names for the *Jihad* and thousands also in Kandahar. But they were instructed to await actual orders before acting. Sultan Muhammad Khan of Kabul treated Sayyid and his men to a royal reception, while the people welcomed him to the town thunderously. (112-161; 135-22)

The kingdom of Afghanistan was balkanized into small, quarrelsome, ineffectual groups. Some of them supported Sayyid Ahmad, some were opposed to him while others were neutral. Sayyid halted at Kabul for 45 days in an attempt to bring about unity among them, but failed. (112-162; 33-584) His position would have been very strong if he had succeeded.

From Kabul, Sayyid went to the final destination, Peshawar. The region was inhabited by an independence-loving, brave and warlike 'Yusufi' Pathan tribe. He planned to garner their support for launching the *Jihad*. News of his arrival spread like wildfire and the martial sentiment among the tribes became ever more pronounced.

Sayyid had reached Peshawar in November 1826 after a journey lasting ten months and covering 5,000 kms. He made Naushera the headquarters in December. This was a veritable *Jihad* tour! The passage of this fully armed Jihadi force through their territories stirred Muslims in the vicinity. Preaching *Jihad* and performing inductions at places on the way was a routine practice, and the Jihadi sentiment was all-pervasive. The British chose to ignore this *Jihad* tour because it was not directed against them, but the Sikhs. (120-11) The stimulating influence of this remarkable and unprecedented expedition on Muslims needs no reiteration[11]. What matters for a historical appreciation of the unrest and uprising of later times, is not its actual success but how it accomplished the great work of instilling Jihadic inspiration in North Indian Muslims.

'Why I Came Here'

Explaining his aim in undertaking the journey, he addressed nobles, tribal chieftains, Maulvis and laity in the following words: "I have been thinking of a place of peace in India where I should take the Muslims and organize *Jihad.* Although Hindustan is a sprawling country with an expanse of hundreds of miles, I could not find a suitable place to which I could migrate. Many friends advised me to start the hostilities within India and promised to provide me with men, money and the munitions of war required for the *Jihad,* but I did not agree to their suggestion. I wanted to rise in arms strictly in

---

11. Khushwant Singh writes about this expedition: "Early in 1827 the whole of the northwest frontier was in ferment. This time they were roused by one Syed Ahmad who had come all the way from India through Sindh to lead a *Jihad* against the Sikhs. Before coming to the Pathan country, Syed Ahmad (and his two Lieutenants)....had gone on an extensive tour of Hindustan and addressed mammoth gatherings of Indian Muslims, raised corps of volunteers and large sums of money. Among the patrons was the Mughal emperor and many Muslim rulers of Indian states, notably the Nawab of Tonk. The British Government made no attempt to check this crusade against a state with which it had signed a treaty of friendship. Thousands of volunteers were trained and armed in India and then permitted to cross over to Sindh.... Organizations which collected arms and money for the crusaders were allowed to function without let or hindrance in many big cities of India." (18-271)

accordance with the precepts and practice of the Holy Prophet.... Some of your brothers, who happened to be there, told me that if I were to migrate to their (i.e. your) country, hundreds of thousands of Muslims would join me, particularly, because Ranjit Singh was perpetrating great excesses in their (i.e. Muslims) land....burnt Mosques[12].... In the Panjab itself, I was told, the Sikhs did not allow Muslims to give call for prayers and turned the Mosques into stables.... Believing what your brothers told me to be correct, I considered it advisable to emigrate to your country to unite and call the Muslims to arms for launching a *Jihad* against the infidels in order to rescue our brothers from their clutches.'" (112-120; 120-103)

Elected as Khalifa of the Islamic State

Everyone accorded support to Sayyid's aims and objectives of launching *Jihad*. Now a Khalifa was needed to lead them and administer captured territories according to Islamic principles. Sayyid was unanimously elected 'Khalifa (the Commander of the Faithful)'[13] (11th January 1827). (25-199; 112-175) An Islamic state was established simultaneously and his name was included in the Friday *khutba*. His followers began referring to him as 'Sayyid Badshah.' (120-46; 112-175) A coin was also struck in his name which bore the inscription, "Ahmad the Just, Defender of the Faith : the glitter of whose scimitar spreads destruction among the infidels." (18-273; 114-171; 42-9) "He called himself as the messenger of Allah." (135-22)

Maharaja Ranjit Singh was fully aware of Sayyid's precise intentions. He dispatched a force of 7,000 under the command of his cousin, Sardar Budha Singh, to deal with the Jihadis. (112-169) When reports of the approaching army reached him, Sayyid prepared to give battle along with 1,500 holy warriors. The Sikh forces had camped at Akor, 25 kms from the Jihadi headquarters at Naushera.

---

12. Prof. Ram Gopal writes: "An excuse for *Jihad* was invented on the imaginary pretext that Sikhs were mistreating Muslims" (135-22)

13. The second Khalifa, Umar (d.644), had instituted this title for the head of the Islamic state. (129-157)

Sikhs Given Three Choices of Jihad

According to Islamic principles, an ultimatum was dispatched to the Sikh general before declaring *Jihad* against them. They were given three choices: Accept Islam and live as brothers of Muslims with equitable rights in an Islamic state, accept status as zimmis (protected vassals) and pay jiziya (tax), or allow the sword to decide[14]. (112-166; 25-199)

The Sikhs were also warned, in the event they chose the third alternative, to note that Sayyid enjoyed support of all the Pathans as well as Indian Muslims who considered death more pleasing than life. (112-167) A religious edict was then issued declaring the commencement of *Jihad* and summoning Muslims to participate: "The Sikh nation have long held sway in Lahore and other places. Their oppressions have exceeded all bounds. Thousands of Muhammadans have been unjustly killed.... Hazrat Sayyid Ahmad with his single object, the protection of the faith....going in the direction of Kabul and Peshawar, succeeded in rousing Muhammadans.... Praise be to God, some thousands of believers became ready at his call to tread the path of God's service.... The *Jihad* against the infidel Sikhs begins."[15] (120-11; 42-7)

First Overwhelming Triumph

Adopting guerilla tactics since their numbers were few, Sayyid launched a sudden and fierce attack one night. The Sikh army was terrified and in the battle that ensued, they lost 700 men while the rest turned tail and deserted to save their lives. On the other hand, the Jihadis lost just 82 men killed and 72 wounded. (112-117) The Sikhs were thoroughly

---

14. The same three choices used to be given every time during the rule of the four rightly guided khalifas who succeeded the Prophet, before giving battle to nonbelievers.

15. Copies of this edict of commencement of *Jihad* were simultaneously dispatched with messengers to all towns in North India in order to inspire Indian Muslims. (42-7)

defeated in their very first encounter on 21st February 1827 at Akor, and Sayyid had triumphed. This further enthused Pathan tribes in larger numbers to participate in future Jihads. (172) Sayyid's reputation and sway in the region increased.

The vanquished general Budha Singh wrote to Sayyid decrying his guerilla warfare, expressing doubts about the intentions of *Jihad* and challenging him to a battle on open ground. In his reply, Sayyid Badshah wrote: "It seems you have not understood the purpose of my campaign.... I desire nothing save to serve my Lord and Master and strive to make His chosen faith (i.e. Islam) dominant, as promised by Him[16].... I neither desire to make show of my bravery nor I want to carve out a kingdom for me. And you can test my sincerity. If any one amongst the nobles and chiefs of the Sikhs accepts Islam, I shall at once pledge my loyalty to him and try my best to extend his (Muslim) dominions." (178)

Letters to All : Reason for Jihad

Jihad was inevitable since the Sikh state was never going to become Islamic through appeals like these. Sayyid was fully aware that Maharaja Ranjit Singh was not likely to take this humiliating defeat lying down and that a fiercer battle would soon be fought. He wrote a total of 32 letters to Muslim rulers, clerics, tribal chieftains and laity to seek their participation in the *Jihad*. All the letters were generally similar in content, with only small variations to suit specifics, and are useful for understanding the intention of Sayyid's *Jihad* and his methods of preaching.

Each letter said: "The time for action has arrived.... Therefore, every true believer and sincere Muslim ought to betake himself for getting enlisted among the Mujahideen. Verily, God will accomplish the laudable task we have set before ourselves and cause the religion of Prophet Muhammad

16. This promise is given in the Quran. (*9:33; 61:9; 48:28*)

to gain ascendancy over all others[17]. Whoever shall sacrifice his life for this cause shall earn the eternal bliss and whoever shall be lagging behind today, remorse and grief shall be his lot on the Day of Judgement." (112-117)

He wrote to the Sultan of Bukhara: "When the non-Muslims begin to dominate Islamic cities, the Muslims in general and the great rulers in particular ought to continue encountering and killing the infidels so long as the Islamic cities are not retrieved from their possession. Otherwise they will be committing sin.... They will thus be deprived of the blessings of the proximity to God." (120-97)

In letters sent to the Sultans of Kabul and Ghazni, Sayyid wrote: "My motive behind accepting the leadership is nothing more than that of arraying forces for *Jihad*.... To my mind the value of the crown of Faridoon and the throne of Alexander is tantamount to a grain of barley. The kingdom of Kasra and Caesar are immaterial and insignificant to my eyes. I do, however, aspire to promulgate the orders of the Creator of the world, called the principles of Faith, among the entire humanity." (100) He wrote to Shah Sulaiman: "The underlying purpose for arraying the forces and leading encounters is nothing but to raise the words of Faith and resuscitate the acts of the Holy Prophet.... There is no other motive than this at all." (101) In another letter he wrote: "(In India) the Christians and infidels have come to dominate the major portion of the country. .... The customs of profanity and polytheism have taken an upper hand while the manners of the Faith are thrown into oblivion. Such a state of affairs has brought great sorrow to us,....the heart is blushing with shame and there is a passion for *Jihad* or religious crusade." (101)

---

17. The statement, "When India will be freed from aliens and enemies....the high ranks of the state and politics will be assigned to those who covet them," from a letter Sayyid wrote to Chief Minister Hindurao of Gwalior, is often cited to prove that Sayyid envisaged a joint administration by Hindus and Muslims for India. (120-50; 116-365) That statement and the thoughts expressed in the present letter make an interesting comparison.

To Prince Kamran, he wrote: "The country (Frontiers) after having been purged of the impurities of polytheism and the filth of dissonance, will be handed over to those who are deserving,....provided they are grateful to God for the boon and always ready to continue the holy war through fire and water.... Then I will set out with my followers for India with a view to purifying the country from polytheism and infidelity.... My real motive is to launch an attack over India and not to seek domicility in Khurasan (in Frontiers and Afghanistan)." (100)

Humiliating Defeat in Second Battle

Sayyid received heartening response to these appeals and several Muslim rulers declared their support for his initiative. (112-177) Everyone was prepared to recognize him as Khalifa. The assistance rendered by Yar Muhammad Khan, Sultan of Peshawar, and his brother, Sultan Muhammad Khan, proved very significant. With the contingent of 20,000 troops sent by Muhammad Khan, the total force assembled under Sayyid Badshah's banner was 100,000 strong. (33-587; 120-47; 11-182)

Maharaja Ranjit Singh deployed additional troops under Hari Singh to crush the Jihadis. Budha Singh now had a fighting force of 20,000. (112-182) They also had 8 cannons. The two armies met at Shaidu, which is not too far from Akor where the first big battle was fought. Sayyid was taken ill around this time and was unable to personally lead his army. Their overwhelming numbers ensured initial gains when the battle broke out and the Sikh army began retreat under the pressure. Their valorous general, Budha Singh, was killed. Victory for the Jihadis seemed certain and some associates even offered felicitations to the Khalifa in advance. (184)

It was at this juncture that Sultan Yar Muhammad Khan of Peshawar withdrew his force of 20,000 from the scene of battle. He had been ruling over Peshawar under the aegis of Maharaja Ranjit Singh and had never been too enthusiastic in his mind for the *Jihad*. However, Sayyid Ahmad's popularity and peer pressure from other Muslim rulers had brought him to the battlefield. The mood of the battle changed completely when Muhammad Khan's open withdrawal became apparent. At the same time, the Sikhs attacked with tremendous determination, while the Jihadis began a demoralized retreat in the belief that they had been defeated due to Muhammad Khan's withdrawal. Sikh soldiers fell furiously upon the Jihadis under cover of cannon fire and slaughtered 6,000 of them. A certain victory was turned into a total rout by Yar Muhammad Khan's treachery. (112-184; 33-588)

Conceding that the defeat was divine punishment for their mistakes, Sayyid supplicated himself for Allah's forgiveness and prayed that true guidance would dawn upon those who had committed treachery. (186) Ranjit Singh was overjoyed by the Shaidu victory (1827) because it had dispelled the Jihadi threat to the Sikh state. A great celebration took place in Lahore, with the whole city being illuminated and largesse distributed to the poor. (112-186; 33-589)

Relocation of Jihad Center (1827)

Sayyid Badshah was not disheartened by this debacle. When he recovered from his illness, he moved the *Jihad* center from Naushera to Panjatar in the Swat Valley and resumed intensive preaching among local Pathan tribes. His efforts evoked tremendous response with several tribal chieftains becoming his disciples. (112-189) Sayyid set himself to the Herculean task of uniting local tribes and inducing them to *Jihad*. They were fiercely independence-loving, eternally in conflict with one another and many un-Islamic practices had entered their way of life. He was only emulating the Prophet, who had likewise united the many different tribes in Arabia. His companions began to be referred to by local tribesfolk as 'muhajirs' (refugees) and themselves as 'ansars' (helpers)[18]. (190) Like the Prophet, who had transformed first Mecca into a '*Dar-ul-Islam*' with the help of the Madinaites and then the whole of Arabia, Sayyid Badshah too desired to first subdue Punjab and then the whole of India.

---

18. The Prophet's companions, who had performed *hijrat* and arrived in Madina, are called 'muhajirs', while the locals in Madina who afforded refuge to them are called 'ansars'.

Organization Work in India

Sharp reactions to the induction of thousands in the North-Western provinces and their resolve to perform *Jihad*, began to be felt in North India. Detailed information about the *Jihad* work was regularly conveyed through messengers to Indian counterparts. Maulvis began leading groups of young men aspiring for *Jihad* from North India. Twenty-one such groups had arrived at the time[19] and included Maulvis from places like Meerut, Roorkee, Kanpur, Delhi and Patna. (189, 199)

Although Sayyid was concentrating on the local *Jihad*, he was also attentive to strengthening and dissemination of the *Jihad* network in India[20]. To that end, he had made suitable arrangements before leaving India. Moreover, several preachers and organizers were dispatched from across the border with specific charge of various parts of India[21]. Special messengers were appointed to bring dispatches of letters and wealth from India. (200)

Implementation of the Shariat Law (1829)

The Islamic state became well established in two years (1827–29). The aim was to usher in a state similar to the one that had prevailed during the time of the first four Khalifas, along with total implementation of the *Shariat* law. (33-539) Sayyid believed it was time for doing so. Accordingly, he summoned an assembly of sultans, noblemen, tribal chieftains and Maulvis in his jurisdiction and declared the adoption of the *shariat* after discussions with them. This resulted in the imposition of many restrictions on the free, tribal lifestyles of

---

19. Each group had between 40 and 100 youths.

20. According to Mohiuddin: "(F)or the Sayyid, the *Jihad* in the Frontier and missionary activities in India were two aspects of the same endeavour, for reform and regeneration of Islam in the sub-continent." (112-201)

21. For instance, Mumbai Region: Maulana Muhammad Qasim of Panipat; Hyderabad Region: Maulana Vilayat Ali of Patna; Ayodhya Region: Maulana Sayyid Hasan; Bengal Province: Maulana Inayat Ali. (112-200)

Pathans. Perceived loss of their former freedom gave occasion to murmurs of dissatisfaction from some quarters. But Khalifa Sayyid made it clear that those who did not accept the divine Islamic law were free to leave the state. (112-209) His ultimate desire was the establishment of just such a state in India.

Peshawar Taken (1830)

He had to fight against Islamic rebels. He decided to punish Yar Muhammad Khan whose treachery had resulted in the debacle of the previous battle. Khan was defeated in a battle with Jihadi forces and later died of the severe wounds he had sustained. This event proved to be the forerunner of Muslim internecine conflict.

Khan's brother, Sultan Muhammad Khan, succeeded as chief of Peshawar. He had been Sayyid's disciple from the very beginning and had disapproved of his brother's secret opposition to Sayyid. Nevertheless, with his brother's death, he adopted an anti-Sayyid stance. (112-228; 116-55) Ultimately, Sayyid had to subdue him in a battle. A 3,500 Jihadi force defeated the Khan's force of 10,000 at Mayar and made a triumphant entry into Peshawar (1830). Citizens illuminated the town and distributed sweets to welcome the holy warriors. The victory produced a remarkable effect on Muslim psyche. "His reputation stood at its zenith" (33-596)

Proposals to One Another

Skirmishes were continuing simultaneously with the Sikhs. The Maharaja was reaching the end of his patience. With the aim of settling the issue, he sent an envoy with the offer of a *jagir* (fief) for Sayyid if he stopped agitating against the Sikh state and supplicated to Allah for the peace, happiness and prosperity of the Maharaja's kingdom. Rejecting the proposal Sayyid wrote back to the Maharaja that he had come to wage a holy war for the sake of God alone and that he could not give up his errand even if the latter gave him the whole of his Kingdom. But if the Maharaja were to accept the precepts of true faith, added the Sayyid in his reply, he would fight to extend his dominions. (112-237)

Seeing his overture for peace thus rejected, the Maharaja dispatched a large force under the command of Ventura to act more as a deterrent to the Jihadis. The army camped near the border of the Islamic state, and in response to the commander's initiative, Sayyid sent a Maulavi as his envoy to hold talks. The commander inquired how Sayyid hoped with his ill-equipped horde to subdue the powerful and rising power of the Sikhs. The Maulavi replied, "Such a phenomenon was not entirely without a precedent, for, all the Prophets of God had to contend with powerful tyrants although they had no force behind them except their weak and poor followers. Had not the Prophets come out successful against mighty empires?" (237) However, the two forces did not engage in battle at that time.

Treachery by the Subedar of Peshawar

In the meantime, Sultan Muhammad Khan of Peshawar approached Sayyid expressing remorse over past deeds and made an entreaty to be appointed Subedar of the region. Despite cautioning by several associates, Sayyid accepted his repentance, conceded the request and appointed him Subedar of Peshawar under the Islamic state. (116-56; 112-249)

But Sultan Muhammad Khan turned out to be treacherous. Within a short time of his appointment, he commenced spreading ill feeling against the Khalifa and inciting the Pathans, who were already unhappy about the application of the *Shariat* against them. The compulsory appropriation of 2.5% of individual earnings to the state as *zakat* (religious tax) was a sore point with the freedom loving tribes. Taking advantage of these circumstances and using his authority as Subedar, Sultan executed a well-planned conspiracy one night and eliminated all officials connected with revenue collection, besides innumerable holy warriors. (33-596; 112-259)

New Headquarters at Balakot

Sayyid Badshah was shocked by this news and lost all faith in the Pathan tribes in the area. Taking his remaining followers with him, he left the region and moved towards the Hazara region of Kashmir making Balakot the new center of his state (1830). (112-264; 33-597)

Preaching *Jihad* and inducting many followers from the area, he began preparations to fight the Sikhs once again. (112-264)

Sayyid Badshah Martyred (1831)

The Jihadi base in the area was a great threat to the Sikhs. A force of 8,000 was dispatched under Sher Singh's command to neutralize it. The Sikhs fell upon the Jihadis in the bitter battle that ensued, Sayyid Ahmad and his closest lieutenant Muhammad Ismail joined in the fray brandishing their weapons. However, they could not resist the well-equipped and trained Sikh army. Sayyid, Ismail and many senior associates were killed in battle along with about 600 Jihadis. The Sikhs lost 700 men. (112-283; 33-598) The battle was fought on 6th May 1831.

Maharaja Ranjit Singh was ecstatic at this unprecedented victory, and the messenger carrying the news that Sayyid had been killed, was awarded a pair of gold *kadas* (an ornament worn on the wrist), headgear and two shawls. All provincial governors were sent orders to celebrate the victory. Lahore and Amritsar towns were illuminated and triumphant cheers were heard everywhere. (112-286; 116-75) Chroniclers and historians make special mention of these celebrations to emphasize the great significance attached by Sikhs to the end of Sayyid's activism.

The motive for Sayyid's migration to the Pathan tribal region and the expectations he had from them remained unfulfilled. It was quite impossible for an arbitrarily patched up force of *Jihad*-inspired unprofessional holy warriors to defeat a strong, well-trained and equipped Sikh army. Moreover, Sayyid had failed in understanding the Pathan mindset. (33-599) Their traditional inter-tribe strife, free and willful nature, propensity to rebel under excessive control and, despite being Muslim, their lack of purely Islamic lifestyles and absence of a perception of Muslim brotherhood, were some of the reasons for his failure to unite all of them under his banner. They were not happy with the imposition of the *Shariat,* compulsory collection of *zakat* and other pristine Islamic prescriptions. They preferred life under their tribal chieftain than the ideal Islamic state. Sayyid's pure Islam became the greatest hindrance. (116-340) The tribal Pathans were unable to comprehend the lofty aims of Sayyid's movement and *Jihad.* Nevertheless, Sayyid accomplished unprecedented success during his lifetime in respect of the four million *Jihad* inspired disciples he had gained. Moreover, he had converted 40,000 Hindus to Islam. (25-204) "In this subcontinent he first used the technique of winning the support of the masses for his programme and created a political organization for its furtherance and execution." (33-580) He exemplified for Muslims the ideals and lustrous inspiration of martyrdom and *Jihad* in the cause of Allah's work.

The *first phase* of the movement ends at this point.

The Work Continues

Sayyid's removal from the scene did not spell the end of the movement. Dr. Tara Chand rightly says : "The fires of holy war once lighted were kept burning for half a century.... Before he left for the Frontier, Sayyid Ahmad had established a network of centers and agents to prepare the Indian Muslims for *Jihad....*" (32-27) Founded on doctrinal principles and ideals considered noble by Muslims, it had spread from Peshawar to Bengal. (27) "He was a tremendously popular figure among many Muslims. His popularity even increased after his death." (52-95) An aura of martyrdom and sacrifice had grown around his name. Seven hundred loyal warriors from the region regrouped after the defeat at Balakot and elected Sayyid's nephew, Shaikh Wali Muhammad, as the new Khalifa. (116-78; 112-288) He shifted the center of the state from Panjatar to Sitana on the banks of the Indus and began spreading the movement from there with the support of the local sultan, Sayyid Akbar Shah. (112-300)

At about the same time (April 1835), a certain Maulana Nasiruddin of Delhi, inspired by Sayyid's teachings, was leading 200 *Jihad* enthusiasts towards Sitana when they were stopped on the way in Sind. Realizing that the region was eminently suitable as a center for *Jihad,* they decided to stay there and not go further. Following the practice of Sayyid Badshah, Nasiruddin began correspondence with rulers and nobles in surrounding areas. (301) Over a hundred letters were simultaneously sent to prominent Muslims in North India, appealing for their help for the *Jihad.* (303) The holy warriors at Sitana, impressed by Nasir's ability, elected him as Khalifa. (306)

Dost Muhammad, Amir of Afghanistan, who had always supported Sayyid Badshah in the past, took notice of Nasir's increasing strength. Being engaged in a war with the British at the time, he requested help from Nasir who responded immediately by dispatching a contingent of a thousand holy warriors[22]. (116-86; 115-10; 112-306) Nasiruddin died in 1840 and was succeeded by Mir Ali as Khalifa.

This marks the end of the *second phase* of the Jihadi movement. (112-306)

Work of the Ali Brothers

The *third phase* of the movement upto 1857 is very important.

Two brothers hailing from the well-known Sadiqpur family of Patna, Maulana Vilayat Ali (1790–1852) and Maulana Inayat Ali (1794–1858), known as the 'Ali Brothers', command an extraordinary status by their contribution to the movement. Not just the two of them, but their entire family had accepted Sayyid Ahmad's tutelage when the latter was in India. (112-308; 116-31) He had visited their home in Patna on his return journey after the Hajj pilgrimage. The two, along with a third brother Tariq, had participated in Sayyid's *Jihad* beyond India's frontiers in one of which Tariq was killed.

---

22. Sir William Hunter's comment on this military assistance: "They sent a great force to help our enemies in the Kabul War, and a thousand of them remained steadfast against us to the death. In the fall of Ghazni alone, 300 obtained the joys of Martyrdom from the points of English bayonets." (42-13)

The brothers were skillful organizers and workers. Sayyid Badshah had sent them to India in 1828 with specific charge of organizing *Jihad* respectively in the Hyderabad and Bengal provinces. Although the *Jihad* was not faring too well beyond the border, the brothers were successful in establishing a widespread and strong organization on a firm footing within India for the approaching struggle[23].

Maulana Vilayat Ali did valuable work when he was the *Jihad* preacher of the Hyderabad region (1828–31), and one of his most significant accomplishments was the successful enlistment of the Nizam's brother, Nawab Mubarizuddaulah, as an ardent disciple and supporter of the cause. Converting rulers, influential courtiers, military leaders and soldiers along with common people to his ideology, was one of the chief policies of his movement. Support from such people was only going to strengthen his activism. (112-308; 116-125)

The Hyderabad Conspiracy (1839)

Nawab Mubarizuddaulah, under guidance of Maulana Vilayat Ali, finalized a scheme of an uprising against the British and established liaison with the nawabs of Kurnool and Bhopal for that purpose. Vilayat Ali had been successful in arranging for the propagation of his teachings among Indian soldiers in the British army at Hyderabad[24]. (ibid) The nawab had set up facilities for training activists, while soldiers were going to revolt and join them after the mutiny had broken out. This

---

23. Sir William Hunter writes: "We have seen how, time after time, when the cause appeared ruined, they again and again, raised the standard of Holy War from the dust. Indefatigable as missionaries, careless of themselves, blameless in their lives, supremely devoted to the overthrow of the English Infidels, admirably skillful in organizing a permanent system for supplying money and recruits, the Patna Khalifas stand forth as the types and exemplars of the Sect." (42-60)

24. His assistants would disguise themselves as fakirs (mendicants) and enter military camps. (116-126) Fakirs, as religious workers, were not prohibited from camps.

nawab, who was to become the vice-Khalifa of the Islamic state that would be established in Hyderabad, had even had two seals of office made. They bore the inscriptions: 'Protector of Established Religion, the Defender of Faith and Mussalmans' and 'Mubariz, the Naib of Martyred Syed Ahmad.' (116-126) This was a scheme to found the first Islamic state within the Indian territory on the principles laid down by Sayyid Ahmad.

However, the British got wind of this conspiracy early enough to take action, and suppressed it expeditiously. Although the Nizam had not supported the plan, he had ignored what was brewing. As a consequence of these events, which are known as the 'Hyderabad Conspiracy' (1839), many of Mubarizuddaulah's co-conspirators were arrested and he was sentenced to life imprisonment. (112-309; 116-128) Although local British authorities took a serious view[25] of the plot, the central administration had not[26]. (116-128)

Khalifa Vilayat Ali's Organizational Work

Vilayat Ali moved from Hyderabad to the headquarters at Patna after Sayyid Ahmad's death in 1831 and assumed all-

---

25. Reports by some of the local administrators are notable.

The Resident wrote: "Mubariz's intention was to move out, collect Wahabi adherents and slaughter the English to possess himself of the country and the government. His followers had gained admittance into the companies of various officers and soldiers in the guise of faqirs, etc. and were endeavoring to seduce the Sepoys to Wahabism and....to sedition." (116-126)"

Stonehouse, the magistrate, wrote to the secretary to the government: "that a considerable number of Muhammadans in different parts of India had embraced Wahabism, among whom are persons who, from rank and position, exercise considerable influence over their brethern.... That their ultimate object had been the overthrow of the British power in India and that with this view they had been endeavoring to make converts among the native army." (116-127)

26. Prof. Qeyamuddin comments upon this neglect: "It shows a lack of understanding of the wider political unrest against the British rule of which they were the symptoms." (116-128)

India leadership of the movement. He organized the work exceedingly well, dividing the country into provinces and sub-divisions with an independent leader given charge of each. The village mosque was the smallest unit. (112-309) The network began exhorting the public neither to have any dealings with the British nor approach their law courts. (116-105; 115-16) Facilities for dispensing justice according tc Islamic law were set up in every place. The chief of every mosque became the *qazi* (judge). (112-309) Various heads were assigned to different administrative departments, including a system for collecting the *zakat* that was necessary for the organization. For all intents and purposes, it had become an Islamic administration with the chief aim of readying Muslims for the *Jihad*. Intensive preaching of *Jihad* was begun and a permanent network was established for that purpose in every district[27]. (135-23)

The work of the movement, including transfer of manpower and, particularly, funds needed for the *Jihad* across the border, was done in secrecy. Encrypted messages were used to communicate with one another. (112-311) Two separate printing presses were set up to propagate Sayyid Ahmad's teachings throughout India. (314)

Islamic State in Hazara Region

While Maulana Vilayat Ali was engaged in organizational work in India, Maharaja Ranjit Singh had died in 1839 and struggle for the throne had broken out among his heirs resulting in anarchy. Subedars began disobeying their king. It was to take advantage of these circumstances that Zamin Shah, a supporter of the Jihadis in the Hazara region[28] and leader of

---

27. Sir William Hunter writes: "The Wahabis have a permanent machinery throughout the rural districts for spreading their faith.... The term Wahabi was a synonym for traitor. A Wahabi preacher had appeared in a lonely village, and forthwith several thousands Muhammedans gathered around him." (42-63,5)

28. Sayyid Ahmad was killed in the Battle of Balakot (1831) in this same region.

the Sayyids, invited Vilayat Ali to go there and complete Sayyid Ahmad's unfinished work. (317)

In response, Vilayat Ali dispatched 2,000 Jihadis under command of his brother, Inayat Ali. They reached Hazara in 1844 in phased out batches to escape attention of the government. Zamin Shah and his innumerable associates became Inayat Ali's followers and chose him as their Khalifa. The combined forces wrested Balakot from the Sikhs and, within a year, 22 other strongholds. By similar victories, the entire Hazara region soon passed under the control of the Jihadis. (112-319; 115-11)

Inayat Ali then founded (1845) an Islamic state in the region with its capital at Fatehgad, renamed 'Islamgarh', and governance began according to *Shariat* laws. (112-320)

The Indian Khalifa, Vilayat Ali, along with many associates, made a journey to Hazara from Patna to inspect the victorious Jihadi army and the new Islamic state (1846). After accepting a regal welcome from the army at the border, he proceeded to the capital where all the subjects took an oath of loyalty to him as the head of the whole Islamic state (October 1846). (112-320; 116-112)

Seven months before this event, on 16th March 1846, the British had entered into a treaty with the Sikhs (after the latter had been defeated in 1845), according to which some territories of the Sikh state including a large part of the Hazara province had been transferred to Gulab Singh of Kashmir against a tribute payable by him to the British. Consequently, a large combined force of British and Sikhs entered the Islamic state to take physical possession (1847).

The tribal subjects of the Islamic state were reluctant to give battle as defeating this force seemed impossible to them. Having no other recourse, the Khalifa made a compromise. The British dispatched the Ali brothers and their lieutenants to Patna and a security of Rs.10,000 each was taken from them as guarantee of peaceable conduct. All these people arrived in Patna towards the end of 1847. (116-124; 226-13)

After returning to Patna, they resumed their preaching and organizational work once again. In 1848, Amir Akbar Shah of Swat, who was a great patron of Jihadis in his area, invited Vilayat Ali to come to his region.

Vilayat Ali's Influence in Delhi (1850)

Vilayat Ali left for Swat towards the end of 1849 and halted at Delhi for two months where he gave several discourses on *Jihad* in the Jama Masjid and other masjids. Hearing of these sermons, Emperor Bahadur Shah reverentially invited him to his palace. He went there with 75 followers and delivered a sermon. The famous Urdu poet Momin, mentor of Empress Zeenat Mahal, Iman Ali, and many others became followers. The Emperor was so impressed that he ordered fifty plates of a variety of delicacies to be sent to Vilayat Ali the next day, along with an entreaty that he may spend some more time with him at the palace. But, apprehensive of drawing undue attention of the British, the offer was declined. Large crowds went up to the Yamuna River to see him off when he finally left Delhi. (115-12; 116-120) He had succeeded in creating a huge impact in Delhi by his teaching.

Vilayat Ali and his followers, and Inayat Ali, who had travelled by a different route, reached Swat by the beginning of 1851.

The British, Now, Instead of the Sikhs

The victorious British had in the meantime annexed Punjab in March 1849 after the war with the Sikhs. The Jihadis were therefore obliged to fight the British as infidels instead of the Sikhs who were henceforth going to be their enemy from Patna to Sitana. As the struggle was going to be difficult, Vilayat Ali postponed immediate hostilities and advocated the policy of strengthening the organization. Inayat Ali, however, insisted that the *Jihad* should be continued. (112-324; 116-122) He cherished the prospect of being able to emulate the Prophet, who had wrested Mecca and Arabia despite lack of military strength. (77-138) Vilayat Ali died in November 1852.

Khalifa Inayat Ali's Work (1852–58)

Inayat Ali, who was chosen as Khalifa, moved the headquarters of the state from Sitana to nearby Mangalthana in 1854. There were many skirmishes with the British forces during the period, and the Jihadis even managed to win the fort of Kotla on the banks of the Indus from them for a while. (34-150) The local magistrate recorded the following about Inayat's activities: "He laboured to organize his followers and inflame them with a hatred of the English kafirs. The crescentaders were drilled daily, sometimes twice a day and, on parade, were taught to recite hymns extolling the glories of *Jihad* and on Fridays....sermons extolling them to wait patiently until the time appointed for subjugation of the British India would arrive." (112-326; 116-183)

His work was progressing in stages. Governor General Dalhousie issued instructions to keep a close watch on the activities of the organization. The British needed to send 33,000 soldiers in 16 expeditions between 1850 and 1857 to suppress the unrest across the border. (41-15; 115-22; 67-37)

Inayat Ali had dismissed an 1856 British proposal of amnesty if he surrendered and returned to his native place. The 1857 Uprising that was sparked off soon thereafter presented his activism with a fresh opportunity. (112-327)

Attempts to Spread Mutinous Sentiment in British Army

These events mark the end of the *third phase* of Sayyid Ahmad's agitation, a notable aspect of which was the propagation of his thoughts within the rank and file of the British Indian army, which was one of its principal aims. This was achieved through a well-planned strategy by which an officer or soldier in an army camp would first be befriended and indoctrinated, and subsequent close association with him utilized to assemble and address specific groups of soldiers. Monetary allurement was also sometimes employed to influence soldiers to their way of thinking. The preacher would disguise himself as a fakir (mendicants were permitted by army rules to visit camps) to gain entry to the camp and preach rebellion to soldiers. Moreover, suitably indoctrinated youths were encouraged to seek recruits[29]. The *Shariat* injunction, of not having anything to do with government, did not apply in this case because the real aim of joining the army was not to serve the enemy but infuse treason among the soldiers and prepare them for the mutiny. This work was carried out in utmost secrecy.

Contribution of the Waliullahi Movement

Sayyid Ahmad and his well-organized movement[30] had stirred up the whole of India and Afghanistan by the declaration of *Jihad*. The Indian Muslim mind was captivated by the prospect of *Jihad*. Indian Muslims, particularly, felt that they were engaged in the transborder *Jihad* because holy warriors from every district in North India had gone to participate in it, every kind of help and support was being provided by them, and their hearts and ears were tuned in to the happenings there. This was a period when the whole of

---

29. Some comments by eminent authors about this:

i) Prof. Qeyamuddin Ahmad: "The Wahabis were the earliest to realize the crucial role of the Indian Units of the Army in the struggle against the English and they made conscious attempts to win them over, or to 'tamper their allegiance.". (116-338) He devotes 28 pages to the subject under the heading 'Infiltration by Wahabis into the Indian Army'.

ii) The Administration Report of the British Government states: "In 1852, a treasonable correspondence was seized by the Punjab authorities which disclosed an attempt on the part of the Hindustani 'fanatics' in the hills to tamper with the 4th Regiment of Native Infantry at Rawalpindi. The conspiracy was found to have originated at Patna." (115-16; 42-19; 34-370) A munshi of this platoon, Muhammad Wali, had a big hand in this. He was later convicted and punished. (115-18) Eleven other Waliullahi (Wahabi) ring leaders were also tried and punished. (120-37; 34-373)

iii) Says Sir William Hunter: "In 1853, several of our native soldiers were convicted of correspondence with the traitors." (42-15)

30. Sir William Hunter writes: "To trace the Wahabi warlike ramifications throughout India, would swell this little book to a great volume." (42-34)

North India was under the spell of *Jihad* with events across the border inspiring and enthusing people here. Preaching of *Jihad* from outside the country had been successful on a scale that was many times more than what might have been achieved from home. The success of this movement lay not in what it achieved across the border, but in how it was able to enthuse the Indian Muslim mind for the great *Jihad* that was to come.

Some comments by eminent authors about this:

1. Prof. M.Mujeeb: "The movement started by Sayyid Ahmad Shaheed was like a smouldering fire for a number of years and contributed to the outburst which unexpectedly took the form of the upheaval of 1857." (118-425)
2. Prof. Aziz Ahmad: "This hostility (started by Sayyid Ahmad) grew from 1840 to 1857 when it allied itself with the Indian Mutiny." (21-216)
3. Dr.Tara Chand says: "Syed Ahmad's movement failed, but it left a trail of far reaching consequences. It gave a strong impetus to separatist tendencies in Indian society.... The memory of Syed Ahmad's movement kept alive the desire for freedom among the Muslims. The Maulvis lent their powerful aid in all subsequent struggles against British rule, e.g. the Revolt of 1857." (32-30)
4. Prof. Jayanti Maitra observes: "Armed with a consistent anti-British ideology, and with the backing of a network of organizational centers spread all over Northern India, the Wahabi leaders exercised a moral influence on the Muslim intelligentsia throughout the country, and aroused the Muslim masses to free themselves from the political tyranny of the British..." (124-12)
5. Prof. Qeyamuddin Ahmad, an authority on the subject, comments: "When the great conflagration of 1857 took place the Wahabis had already been working for about three decades, but this fact has not been properly emphasized." (116-215)

6. Prof. Nizami writes about Sayyid Ahmad's movement: "His followers travelled to every nook and corner of the country and recruited people. The whole of the northern India, from the remotest corner of East Bengal to the Northern most hills of the Frontier, almost every town had a secret organization centered around the local mosque and guided by a band of noble spirits. For nearly half a century the energy of the people in northern India was utilized under his leadership to regain lost power." (120-47) "The Wahabi slogan of *Jihad* from the time of Shah Abdul Aziz had prepared the soil for the outbreak of the movement of 1857." (91)
7. Safdar Mahmood reports: "After the demise of Aurangzeb, the edifice of the Muslim empire raised by the Mughals had begun to crumble. Shah Waliullah foresaw the danger to the future of the Muslims. He himself started a movement amongst the Muslim masses which was to revive the spirit of Islam. It was the first mass movement in India. It rekindled the spirit of *Jihad,* aroused Muslim mass consciousness, and organized the Muslims to meet the challenge of the Sikhs, Jats and Marathas. The movement spread underground and one of its offshoots was the War of Independence, 1857." (113-1)

The Efforts of a Hundred Years

The outbreak of 1857 did not happen suddenly. Seeds of the Uprising were planted by Shah Waliullah, and the process had begun from the Battle of Plassey in 1757. Inviting Ahmad Shah Abdali or Zaman Shah of Afghanistan to invade India on the one hand, and actually migrating to those provinces to seek support from local Muslims for *Jihad* to liberate India on the other, were identical as far as aims and results were concerned. The propaganda, current in 1857, that British rule would be uprooted a hundred years after Plassey, was not mere prophetic inspiration. It was a manifestation of the emotional conviction that Muslims would be rewarded in 1857 for the incessant work they had put in for a century!

❋ ❋ ❋

Chapter 3

1857: Pre-Uprising Conditions and Causes

-1-

It is amply clear from the foregoing discussion that, for a century before 1857, Indian Muslims were making attempts to reestablish their lost empire with participation of erstwhile rulers, Nawabs, governors, nobles, Maulvis and even the common people. With the exception of Tipu Sultan, all these activists belonged to North India which they had been ruling for eight centuries. They had developed a psyche according to which they firmly believed that they had both the religious and legitimate right to rule.[1] The Rajputs had made attempts

1. Writing about the significance that North India held for Muslims, Francis Robinson writes: "The UP, with the city of Delhi on its Western border, was the traditional centre of Muslim rule and civilization in India. Here were cities redolent with the past glories of Muslim power : Jaunpur, capital of the Sharqi Kings; Fathepur Sikri, city of Akbar; Agra, city of Shah Jahan; Bareilly, centre of the

(Contd.)

to establish and sustain independent kingdoms, but had failed. Muslims had unceasingly sought to reduce the Sikh kingdom that had arisen in the Punjab during the decline of Mughal empire. Broadly speaking, in North India the Muslim has always seen himself as the ruler, while the Hindu has remained content with life as a vassal.

Mindset of North Indians

However, the situation in Southern India, where Hindu kingdoms had emerged in the teeth of Muslim opposition, was different. Southern Hindus had demonstrated many times that they could found independent kingdoms, the Marathas among them had even subdued remote territories like Attock and reduced the Mughal Emperor to a mere puppet. It was for the express purpose of salvaging their power that Muslims had invited Ahmad Shah Abdali to invade India. Northern Hindus had not supported the Marathas in the Battle of Panipat that resulted from Abdali's invasion. That the Marathas had looted their territories in the past, was hardly a plausible or only reason for this apathy. Muslim rulers had not looted them any the less, for spoils of war after battle and jiziya after political subjugation was a norm dictated by their religion. The reason, more accurately, was that the North Indian Hindu mindset preferred to remain content with vassal status rather than struggle for independence. This factor not only explains why Muslims of North India strove for a rejuvenation of their erstwhile empire but also why the 1857 Uprising remained largely confined to that half of the country.

Historians and commentators of the 1857 Uprising have generally ignored developments — discussed in the last two

---

Rohilla Kingdom; Faizabad and Lucknow, in turn the seats of the Kings of Oudh; and 'seven-cities' Delhi, witness of the glory and the destruction of Muslim empires.... Here the distinctive character of Indian Muslim civilization was formed." (12-11)

sections — during the preceding century.[2] Restricting their research only to a few years before the Uprising, these writers discuss the effect of the British conquest of Delhi – and the political dispossession that it spelled for Muslims – on the sociopolitical life in the country, along with the development of discontent against the British and how this contributed to the 1857 Mutiny. It is as clear as day that discontent felt by Indians against British rule led to the Uprising. However, it is imperative to ascertain which of the causes and reasons are fundamental, principal or decisive and which are secondary, topical or incidental. Let us briefly review the various factors proffered so far as reasons for the Uprising.

- 2-

Causes for the Uprising

The *first cause*: After the British conquest of Delhi, the status of the Emperor was gradually devalued and compromised, which had resulted in Muslim discontent. Second, only to their religion, the king (khalifa or badshah) was of immense significance to Muslims.[3] His role in religious matters is equally

---

2. Dr. Sashi Bhushan Chaudhary, an eminent historian who describes the 1857 Uprising as a 'war of independence', wrote a book *Civil Disturbances During the British Rule in India (1765 – 57)*, specially devoted to the study of pre-1857 anti-British agitations. However, just two pages each are devoted to Vazir Ali's revolt and the Farazi movement, and no mention at all is made of Sayyid Ahmad Shaheed's activism. Savarkar takes no cognizance of any movement prior to 1857. While Prof. Dutta mentions Vazir Ali's revolt and the Farazi movement along with some information about some Wahabi-related incidents in Patna in his book *Anti-British Plots and Movements before 1857* (Ref.No.117 in bibliography), he omits reference to any of the movements led by Sayyid Ahmad Shaheed. Prof. Mujumdar provides some information about Sayyid's movement, but does not link it to the subsequent 1857 Uprising. (67-26, 36)

3. Henry Mead writes: "In spite of the utter subjection in which the Padshah lived for well nigh a hundred years, the Mussalmans

(Contd.)

vital: the religion is practically 'orphaned' without him. The British first accorded the Emperor a nominal status. Proclaiming, *khulk khuda ka, mulk badshah ka, hukum company sarkar ka* (the earth is Allah's, the land is the Emperor's, the administration is the Company's, the British had arrogated to themselves all rights of kingship, retaining the Emperor only in name. Even jurisdiction over the city of Delhi that was at first given to the Emperor, was reduced to one over just the Red Fort. The annual custom of offering *nazrana* (fealty) by the British to him was discontinued from 1844. In the words of Prof. Nizami, "The Mughul Emperors became not only pensioners but prisoners in the hands of the East India Company." (120-3) They even began conferring sovereign status in their territories to former governors and noblemen. It was with this very intention that the British had recognized the Nawab of Ayodhya as 'king'.

Apprehensions about Nominal Emperor

Being fully aware of past attempts by Indian Muslims to resurrect the Mughal Empire, British authorities were opposed to continuation of even this notional status of the Emperor because they feared[4] that all Muslims might make him their

---

still continued to regard him as being the fountain of honour, the rightful monarch of Hindustan. The Mughal is the only person to whom the Mahomedans can look up as their natural head. The founders of the royal houses of the Deccan, Carnatic and Oudh, of Holkar and Scindhia, were the deputies and servants of his ancestors. His divine right to universal dominion still exists." (103-94)

4. i) Prof. Mujeeb Ashraf of the Jamia Millia says: "The Hindus had no reason to be hostile to British rule, whereas the Muslims had many historical, religious, cultural and psychological reasons. After the establishment of British rule in India, the various sections of the Muslim community endeavoured to realize, through their respective approaches, the same goal viz. regeneration and re-establishment of the Muslim power and prestige." (77-28) "To the Muslims, the Uprising (of 1857) was the logical culmination of their vigorous resistance to alien rule. It was based on definite ideals and objectives which converged towards a single purpose viz. to re-establish

(Contd.)

leader, rally around him and make yet another bid against them. Lord Dalhousie, Governor General during pre-1857 years (1856), stated: "The British Government has become indeed and in truth the paramount Sovereign in India. It is not expedient that there should be, even in name, a rival in the person of a sovereign whose ancestors once held the paramountcy we now possess." (78-12) The British viewed the Emperor as their potential enemy. (12) Even Lord Hardinge, Governor General (1848) before Dalhousie, had been insistent on doing away with this veil of pretense and making an open declaration of British sovereignty. He urged the need for declaring that, "the pretensions of British sovereignty should be unveiled." (69-8) "He did not want the notion of the paramountcy of the King of Delhi to prevail as it was

---

Muslim rule in India. As a matter of fact this movement was mainly organized by the Muslims; in fact all the sections of the Muslim community participated wholeheartedly except for a microscopic group of nobles and elite." (77-161)

ii) Dr. Srivastava says: "Muslims looked upon the British people as usurpers of their sovereignty over India." (90-40)

iii) K. M. Panikkar expresses: "The Muslims had been the ruling class in India in the Gangetic Valley for over 500 years. They found all of a sudden that their power had vanished for ever; that even the last remnants of their glory had disappeared with the annexation of Oudh." (122-22)

iv) Prof. Mallik of the Aligarh University observes: "The Mughal ghost continued to rekindle popular imagination for a century with nostalgia of the past greatness that was irrevocably gone until it was finally laid down and buried in 1858." (24-192)

v) G. S. Hodgson states: "By 1818, the British had become the paramount power in most of India, ruling directly in Bengal and Ganges plain where Islam was very strong. Within a few decades the British had also absorbed the lands of the Indus basin, almost solidly Muslim. In some cases, the advent of British rule meant a transfer from one sort of infidel rule (in part of the Punjab, that of the Sikhs) to another… . (I)t became evidently that British rule." (104-333) 'dangerous to uphold for the Mussalmans rallying point....'"[5] (8)

However, authorities in London perceived implementation of these suggestions more hazardous, because they feared an uprising resulting from adverse reaction of Muslims, loyal to the Emperor. "The British had a genuine fear that if they destroyed the whole Muslim empire militarily, the defeated Muslims would declare a holy war against them. They, therefore, adopted...(go slow) policy and put it into practice with great caution in India...letting the Muslim political power die a natural death." (77-6)

It was for this very reason that higher authorities had not sanctioned the Governor General's demand for moving the Emperor to some other habitation after evicting him from the Red Fort, on account of which frequent differences of opinion between British authorities in India and London had occurred. Which option was more hazardous: deposing the Emperor, or letting him remain for some time?[6] Allowing him to remain notional Emperor was fraught with the possibility of Muslims

---

5. Historian Sir John Kaye writes: "For fifty years the Master of the Delhi Palace had been, in estimation of the English, merely a pageant and a show. But the pageantry, the show, the name, had never ceased to be living influences in the minds of princes and people of India.... If the Empire of Delhi had passed into a tradition, the tradition was still an honoured one. It had sunk deeply into the memories of the people." (78-1) "Even in the depths of his misery and degradation, the King's name was a pillar of strength." "Lord Wellesley saw clearly that if the ancestral State of the Mughal were perpetuated — if he were left to reside in the palace of Shah Jahan, with all the accompaniments of his former grandeur around him, in the midst of a Muhammadan population still loyal to the House of Taimur — there might some day be an attempt to reconstruct the ruined monarchy in the person of one of Shah Alam's successors, which might cause us grievous annoyance." (5)

6. A British official of the time, Charles Metcalfe, wrote: "It was deemed a better policy to tolerate a double executive authority in the city, to retain the shadow of Mughal dynasty, lest the King's

(Contd.)

uniting under his leadership and rising against the British; deposing him might lead to Muslim ire, but it would lack both centralized leadership and unity of command. The first option was proved more hazardous by later history.

The British administration in India then adopted the policy of progressively limiting the Emperor's nuisance value.

Bahadur Shah was fairly old by that time. The British, in pursuance of a policy of protecting his heirs, disallowed the Emperor to nominate Prince Jawan Bakht, his son from favourite queen Zeenat Mahal, as his successor. Instead, proffering the just reason that Bahadur Shah had seven sons who were older than Jawan Bakht, they made a pact with the eldest heir and accorded him recognition as successor. One of the conditions of the pact was that the new Emperor, upon his coronation, would vacate the palace. (141-66) In effect, this policy, which was aimed at neutralizing both the authority of the Emperor as well as his propensity to create unrest, was adopted under the ever present fear of a Muslim uprising. The British had not felt the need for like consideration in respect of the Chhatrapati of Satara because the Chhatrapati as well as the Hindu population of that state were completely harmless for their interests, and posed no threat.

Annexation of Ayodhya

Thus, this first cause points to the possibility of the Uprising being a Muslim initiative.

---

deposition should alarm the whole Mahommedan race in India.... (I)t was rightly deemed impolitic to wound the(ir) feelings....by his removal from Delhi.... (But) not so much a fear of a revival of the Mahommedan power was entertained, as that the King might become the rallying-point of a confederacy of native states. From time to time the English newspapers pressed the necessity of removing the King. The English were living over a volcano ready to burst forth into a deadly violence at any moment, but they could not, or would not, apprehend their danger. Of warnings there (by officers) were plenty; but they made little impression (on the Government)." (121-14 to 9)

The British policy of annexing native states under various pretexts like the absence of an heir, a denial of sanction for adoption of a successor and misgovernance is mentioned as a *second cause*. (States that were not annexed, were made tributaries.) Naturally, these centers of erstwhile power assumed an anti-British stance and played an important role in the 1857 Uprising, for which reason the mutiny is also referred to as 'mutiny of the states'.

Ayodhya was the most important among such states. While it derived its name from the holy city of Ayodhya which was the capital in the Ramayana era, its headquarters was at Lucknow. Bad governance of the state was given as the excuse for annexing it in 1856 — an act considered as a significant contributing factor for the 1857 Uprising — and, indeed, the lion's share of that Uprising is attributable to this state. Even those who call the 1857 Uprising a 'sepoy mutiny' have labelled the events in Ayodhya as a 'war of independence'. (95-153; 141-413) There existed certain specific reasons for Ayodhya assuming such overriding importance.

The Importance of Ayodhya

Situated adjacent to the Himalayas and Nepal in the northeast, the state enjoyed vital significance as the virtual hub of India. (66-1) Watered by the Gomti and the Ganga, the fertile land had made the territory so prosperous that it was referred as "The Garden of India". (1) The population was given to martial traits, agriculture and military service being their primary occupations. Eighty-five percent of the British army in Bengal was drawn from Ayodhya. (106-18) The state was a veritable recruiting center for them. (130-10) The king's force of 60,000 was entirely locally enlisted. (90-24) There was no family that had not sent at least one youth for military service. (106-18) Ayodhya was thus known as 'the great nursery of sepoys'. (106-17; 79-218) The king released soldiers from his service when the state was annexed, while several platoons from the British army were disbanded for their role in the Uprising. As the annexation of Ayodhya had proved deleterious to every such soldier, they became messengers at large to spread the sentiment of discontent far and wide. (130-10)

Of greater substance than the above aspect was the fact that Ayodhya was a Muslim state. Sadat Khan, a Shi'ah emigrant from Iran, had established a principality in Ayodhya in 1720 under aegis of the Delhi Emperor. (54-40) Nadir Shah had invaded India in 1739 on the advice of Baharan Mulk, the then Nawab of Ayodhya, and had perpetrated heinous massacres in Delhi, after which the Nawab became the Indian representative of the Shah of Iran. (41) As the authority of the Emperor declined, the power of this Shi'ah Nawab progressively waxed with support from his Shi'ahite Iranian patron, resulting in an increase in the Shi'ah population of the region. (106-2) The incumbent Nawab also became the vazir (prime minister) in the Delhi court after 1748, held both titles simultaneously and was referred to as the 'Nawab-Vizir'. The arrangement continued in later periods, too. (46-7) Emperor Shah Alam, for some time, took asylum with the Nawab and both of them were jointly defeated by the British at Buxar (1764). Nawab Vazir Ali Khan established liaison with the Amir of Afghanistan in 1797 in order to free himself from the British. From 1819, the Nawab of Ayodhya was accorded British recognition as a sovereign ruler.[7] When the last Nawab, Wajid Ali Shah, ascended the throne in 1847 and was crowned by the British Resident, he assumed the usual titles : "The Father of Victory, The Supporter of Religion, The Grandeur of Alexander, The Just King, The King of the Age, The Sultan of the Universe, Muhammad Wajid Ali Shah the King of Avadh." (95-11) This gives an idea about the contemporaneous importance of Ayodhya and its ruler.

---

7. The British took exception to the incorporation of the titles, 'Padshah-e-Ghazi'/'Shah-e-Zaman' in the Nawab's new throne name. According to them, the use of the word 'ghazi' suggested that Muslims were rulers and the British government was *kafir*, whereas sanction was given for use of the title 'Shah-e-Zaman' under the condition of also using 'King of Ayodhya' in conjunction with it. (46-10)

Ayodhya had developed into an important center of Islamic learning. Lucknow ranked fourth among most populous Indian cities and 40% of the population of 600,000 was Muslim. (126-165; 46-4) In terms of population as well as its Islamic culture, signs of which were plainly visible everywhere, Lucknow surpassed even Delhi. It used to be compared with Oxford. (87-2) Mirza Ghalib had called it the "Baghdad of India". (17-149) Indian Muslims regarded it with immense gratification, second only to Delhi and both these places were the hubs of Islamic revival. After the British had recaptured Delhi in 1857, the leaders of the Uprising and sepoys there had left for Lucknow along with their men.

Another aspect about Ayodhya was that the British suddenly annexed the state in February 1856, under the pretext of maladministration, despite the fact that the Nawab was loyal to them. This plunged him in great sorrow and brought tears to his eyes. Placing his crown at the Resident's feet, he declared his resolve to seek redress for the injustice by visiting London. (95-149; 77-70) He went to Calcutta before proceeding to London along with a delegation of 1,000. The people of Lucknow were deeply moved by these events and the entire population turned up to bid him a sad farewell. (95-153) Public opinion was opposed to the annexation of the state, and the event became a topic of unhappy household discussion in Uttar Pradesh. (34-241) Muslims evinced sentiments of despair that even this — their important Islamic state — had been dissolved. The Nawab was forced to abandon his intention of going to England as he fell ill while he was in Calcutta and British authorities detained him there under their watchful eye. He died in 1887. This affair of annexation is regarded as an important cause of the 1857 Uprising.[8]

---

8. Some notable comments: Charles Metcalfe: "It may be accepted as a historical fact that the annexation of Oudh intensified the prevailing disaffection and hastened the Rebellion." (121-9)

Dr. Sashi Bhushan Chaudhary: "And when the news (of annexation of Oudh) leaked out in Feb. 1857.... 'all Oudh has been up in arms against' the British.... William Edwards, an able and

(Contd.)

Therefore, it is clear that this *second reason* also indicates that the Uprising was fostered by those anxious to reinstate the Nawab's Islamic rule.

Opposition to English Language and Education

The several adverse effects that British rule had on the educational, economic, social and psychological life of Indians is regarded as the *third cause* for the Uprising. Daring attempts were made to usher in radical transformation in every field through new laws and replacement of traditional systems. All historians take note of the nature of public dissatisfaction over these reforms and how it spread. Education being the basis of all these proposed transformations, we will review it as a third cause separately.

The official language used in the administration and education, which was Persian or Urdu during the Mughal era, was replaced (1837) by English. This adversely affected Muslims, who refused to accept it as the official *lingua franca* or receive instruction — more so Western education — through its medium. Contrastingly, Hindus welcomed it. "As they had learnt Persian and Urdu under the Muslims, so they were willing to learn English under the British." (73-543; also 42-169) The Hindu attitude to their new rulers and their systems was conciliatory, which the Muslims were loath to emulate.

Out of Perceptions of Superiority

Despite loss of political power, Muslims firmly believed that their religion, social system, language and culture were

---

discerning British officer of N.W. Provinces, noticed a feeling of irritation — a marked change in the demeanour of the Mahommedans since that time." (81-14)

Governor General Canning wrote to Commander-in-chief Campbell: "Every eye in India is upon Oudh, as it was upon Delhi : Oudh is not only the rallying place of the sepoys, the place to which they all look but it represents a dynasty; there is the King of Oudh 'seeking his own Oudh, and our dealings with it, have been in every native's mind for the last two years." (126-335)

superior to all others and were reluctant to make any compromises on that count. "They objected to the study of English because they feared English education would undermine their religion." (73-54) "The change of language served as a constant reminder to the Muslim of the fact that they were now among the subject races of mankind."[9] (77-22; 75-191) The head of the British Intelligence department had sent a report to the government that, "(They) have a strong prejudice against learning the language of the idolater Hindu, and that of the *Kafir* English." (124-27) In Prof. Mujeeb Ashraf's opinion, "The Muslims resented official interference in their religious and educational institutions more bitterly than the Hindus did, because religious beliefs in Islam had a revolutionary significance." (77-143) "The religious leaders of Delhi....regarded India under British rule as a *Dar-ul-Harb*.... They hated Western education, and they hated to see Muslims accepting service under the British. They aimed at establishing an Islamic State in India. For that purpose, they planned a final confrontation with the British; and they did fight the British in 1857-8." (77-118) "They determined to boycott the Western institutions which were rapidly taking root and flourishing everywhere. This prohibition...included the teaching of English and modern science. Using vehement language the reactionary *Maulvis* inveighed against the institutions of the infidels. The faithful were warned that the end of such education was sure and certain and that those who attended such schools, or permitted their sons to do so, would be accounted as apostates. Even life itself was

---

9. G. S. Hodgson wrote: "(W)hen the British decided to eliminate Persian in favour of English, it became evident that British rule — which for Hindus was mostly a change of masters — for Muslims meant a deposition from the position of ruling class which had presupposed the prestige and wealth that came with power." (104-333) Also, Prof. Safdar Mahmood writes: "On the other hand, the Hindus accepted the new order with an open heart because for them it meant only a change of Masters." (113-1)

threatened...."[10] (75-193) Maulvis commenced on a propaganda which "consisted of admonishing people and telling them to stick to Arabic education and abstain from learning English, and also appealing them to found *madrassas*.... Every village in Eastern Bengal had half a dozen *Mullahs,* and every *Mullah* had at least twenty pupils... ."[11] (124-15)

Pandit Nehru writes about the result of this antagonism, "But the Muslims generally had then retired into their shells far more than the Hindus, avoided English education, and lived in daydreams of a restoration of the old order...Hindus had gone far ahead in education and service." (101-345) Prof. M.T. Titus observed, "The result of this attitude...was that for many decades Muslims in India fell farther and farther behind their Hindu compatriots in the matter of education; for the latter were not at all slow to adapt themselves to changing circumstances and the requirements of the new Government." (75-193) As early as in 1817, the 'Hindu College' had been established in Calcutta to give Western education in English to Hindus. (124-71) A 'Muslim College', too, had been founded but did not provide English education. (77-285)

Curse and Boon

Boycotting western education and English, had a long term effect on the life of Muslims. Modern education and the English

---

10. Nevertheless, Shah Abdul Aziz, author of the *fatwa* declaring India as a '*Dar-ul-Harb*', had allowed Muslims to study sufficient English to engage in correspondence and comprehend cryptic words used by the enemy. (77-122)

11. Prof. Ram Gopal writes: "The earlier (upto 1857) decades had been decades of great upheaval in which a large number of Muslims, calling themselves Wahabis, raised a revolt against British rule. The result was deep-rooted hatred against English education and culture, and Muslim families in the front rank of society boycotted government educational institutions. Hindus had not done so, and were therefore ahead of the Muslims in modern educational attainments." (97-vii)

language had become a necessity in every department of the new administration and a virtual passport to government employment (124-172). Consequently, Muslims were precluded from seeking those jobs. (77-22) With disappearance of their special old titles and positions of employment resulting from loss of Muslim political power on the one hand, and bleak prospects of obtaining jobs under the new dispensation on the other, Muslims began receding in every sphere in contrast to Hindus who were making rapid progress. They were disturbed by the fact that Hindus, who had not only been their subjects for centuries but also 'hitherto the object of their contempt' were overtaking them. (77-286) "(I)t was largely the Hindus who took the training necessary for positions of responsibility, commercial or governmental, while the Muslims had the added pain of seeing their former subjects taking the lead over them." (104-334) "The end of the Mughul Empire had meant unemployment not only to those who were engaged in the armed forces or in the administration but also to the artists, the poets, the Muslim scholars." (34-242) Qazis and other Muslims, who had been rendered redundant under the new laws and systems of dispensing justice, made their way to Ayodhya to seek employment. However, after annexation of that state, their situation became insufferable. (243) According to orders issued by the government, only Hindus could apply for jobs; Muslims were not to be given employment. (125-42; 55-74; 34-342) They had become 'people without careers'. (124-72)

In short, "The government's firm determination to carry out a system of English education proved unfavourable to the Muslims and a great boon to the Hindus."[12] (73-54)

---

12. Conclusions by some noted scholars:

i. Prof. Faruqi: "The British domination in India posed a great danger to the hegemony of the Muslims in their country's life, they reacted strongly and bitterly. The Muslims, as the ruling class, had been dominant for centuries. Hence the changes in the old order were affecting them most." (76-8) "The Hindus, on the other hand,

(Contd.)

This situation continued right up to the 1857 uprising. Thereafter, Sir Sayyid Ahmad advised Muslims to declare loyalty to the British and opt for Western education. "(He) saw with his own eyes the descendants of Muhammad b. Tughluq cultivating in villages near Tughlaqubad and met a great grandson of....an eminent noble of Shah Jahan, who earned his livelihood by performing menial service to the people." (98-13) He expressed the apprehension that, "The speed with which decline has set in is so rapid that it seems imminent that within a few years the Muslims will not be found anywhere excepting serving in stables and kitchens or mowing the grass." (13)

---

welcomed the new change and adjusted themselves to the new situation. They took full advantage of the official encouragement to carve out a bright future for themselves." (13)

ii. Dr. Tara Chand: "The conquest of Bengal and many measures struck hard blows on the Muslims. New laws reduced the Muslim aristocracy to penury. Deep-rooted hatred of the alien government spread. The Muslims became jealous of the Hindus; their – opposition movement continued till the Mutiny (of 1857)." (73-x)

iii. Ashok Mehta: "They (Muslims) rejected English education and thereby steadily lost ground in professions and in the Government services. While the Hindus were absorbing Western ideas and adjusting themselves to the new circumstances, the Muslims remained aloof." (122-61)

iv. Harprasad Chattopadhyaya: "The spread of higher education through the medium of English, though much appreciated by the Hindus, did not find favour with the Muslims.... The 'Mollas' (i.e. Mullas) used to forbid it on religious grounds, but the aversion of the Muslims to it (English) closed to them every avenue of prosperity in public life. The eagerness of the Hindus for imbibing western culture, on the other hand, raised the social prestige and decidedly gave them a primacy over the followers of Islam in India. Though the Muslims were thus themselves responsible for (this), still they entertained ill feeling against Government. They meditated a revenge on the British Government on the eve of the Mutiny." (55-74)

Some historians are of the view that anticipating grave threats to their rule posed by Islam and the psyche that it fostered, the British had initiated remedial measures very early in their Indian advent. Prof. Mujeeb Ashraf of the Jamia Millia says: "With this began the final attempt to remove the great obstacle, viz. Islam, from the way of progress of Western civilization. Thus, right from 1765 onwards, the English carried out intelligently and imperceptibly their policy of removing the obstacle that was Islam and eliminating its impact on society in order to impose their own 'progressive' civilization." (77-24) In support of this contention, he cites Sir William Hunter: "India passed from a country of Islam into a country of the Enemy, by absolutely imperceptible gradations." (77-24q.; 42-131) He also cites Hafiz Malik : "Their strategy was to oust the Muslims from the professions and positions of economic and administrative control. This policy ultimately pauperized them." (77-22) While doing so, "The English started placing reliance on the goodwill and co-operation of the Hindus rather than the Muslims." (23)

Thus, this *third* reason — language and education — adversely affected only Muslims and caused them to rise in protest; every motivation for Hindus to do so on this count, was nonexistent.

Economic Consequences of British Rule

British economic policy is given as a *fourth cause* of the Uprising.

Economic policies and reforms introduced by the British also adversely affected the people, particularly the Muslims. Muslim monopoly over the muslin trade in Bengal came to an end with the establishment of weaving mills. (34-244) Other trades also progressively suffered similar setbacks. Ship-building, which was a Muslim monopoly, went into British hands. Generally, trade suffered immeasurably. Several traders in Bengal, reputed to be wealthier in terms of working capital than even the Bank of England, suffered depletion of trade on account of new British competitors and laws they framed to benefit themselves. The new rulers also took over monopolies enjoyed by some of the local traders, while the entire maritime trade went into British hands. (246)

New policies adopted by the British created discontent among zamindars and talukdars. The 'permanent land settlement' law gave rise to a new class of zamindars who remitted the determined revenue to the government treasury but enforced excess collection from the cultivators. Lands belonging to defaulters would be auctioned off by the government, to be bought over by big capitalists who enjoyed government protection. Innumerable cultivators had to lose their holdings in this manner. Talukdars, who held numerous villages, had to give up many of them as a result of this law. For instance, Rana Beni Madhav, had to give up 116 out of the 223 villages he held. (87-36) Talukdars in the Ayodhya province held 25,543 villages at the time of annexation; 11,903 had to be surrendered. (34-250) Seething discontent about the British was the result. There were some Hindus among those talukdars, too, and many of them participated in the Uprising. Cultivators and talukdars who owned villages united during the period of the Uprising, began evicting purchasers to take forcible repossession of their lands.

In pre-British times, revenue collection was entrusted to Muslim jagirdars. Under the new system, the jagirdar was eliminated and replaced by a Collector. This was a crushing blow to Muslims. (77-22) Prof. Mujeeb Ashraf asks a question in this respect: "Was it necessary to ruin the Muslims by taking their lands? Was it necessary to deprive them of their influence and wealth and impoverish them?" (22)

Many land grants had been given to Muslims under Mughal rule, but the holders possessed no documentary proof of their title. British authorities confiscated such lands, and many landholders lost their holdings as a result. Muslims were adversely affected by this policy. (22) It used to be said, "A hundred and seventy years ago, it was almost impossible for a well-born Musalman in Bengal to become poor; at present it is almost impossible for him to continue rich." (42-150)

Thus, although this *fourth* cause generated ire of both Hindus and Muslims against the British, it were the Muslims who were more unfavourably affected.

Social Reforms

Discontent occasioned by several laws enacted by the British government to introduce social reforms in Indian society, especially affecting the Hindu population, is stated as a *fifth cause* of the Uprising. Laws prohibiting the practice of *sati*, encouragement to widow remarriage, prohibition of child killings and several other social customs were viewed as interference with the established norms and infringement of religious liberty. Such laws were not enacted even under Mughal rule, and Hindus began regarding the British more anti-Hindu than the former. Caste consciousness had immense significance for the Hindu psyche. With the advent of the railroad, all castes of Hindus had to share the same compartment, which was perceived as an attack on their traditional caste distinction. It is said that this was one of the reasons for Hindu participation in the Uprising.

Missionary Activity

The general feeling that British rule had been established to enable missionaries to preach their religion to Hindus and Muslims, in order to convert the whole of India to Christianity, is given as a *sixth cause* of the Uprising. Some British officials openly preached and promoted Christianity. It is suggested that since both Hindus and Muslims dearly loved their respective faiths, they had jointly participated in the Uprising.

Some Topical Causes

Besides the causes discussed so far, there remain some others of a topical nature. The affair of cartridge case can be cited as one of them. Because the casing of a new type of cartridge was smeared with fat obtained from cows and pigs and it was necessary to bite off the casing before the rifle could be loaded, this meant a loss of caste for Hindus and injury to religious sensitivities of Muslims. It is said that the sepoys revolted against this requirement. It is also believed that besides this immediate reason, the sepoys also had grievances concerning their salary, uniform, housing and other issues. Their complaints fell on deaf ears and sepoys welcomed the prospect of a better deal after the successful outcome of the Mutiny.[13] (126-389)

The Fundamental Cause

While each one of the causes discussed here are true, primarily some of them are fundamental and vital, and others are secondary, topical or incidental. Soldiers and civilians alike, always have some grudge against the administration even under a democracy, but these scarcely lead to bloody revolution. Second, it must be determined how many of these causes affected Muslims and how many affected Hindus. It is amply clear that all these causes came into play only because the previous Muslim supremacy had been ended and replaced by British rule. Even Hindus who joined the Uprising had unequivocally accepted that Muslim rule would be established as a result of the successful outcome of the Mutiny. There was no possibility whatsoever of a Hindu state run by the majority population under a Hindu Emperor of India. In effect, the Uprising aimed to resuscitate the Muslim empire, the reason why Muslims engaged in it. The loss of political power had reduced them to the status of 'subjects' on a par with Hindus and, with all their special rights and privileges having disappeared, they developed perceptions that injustice was being done to them. They craved their lost position and status. This was the real and fundamental cause of the 1857 Uprising.

Contrastingly, the Uprising only meant a change of masters to the Hindus. Even if we concede that Hindus who had taken part in the Uprising had done so sincerely and thoughtfully, it still implies nothing more than their preference for their previous masters over the new one. During the several centuries of slavery under Muslim rule, it is quite natural that some Hindus had become so accustomed to their old masters

13. Saul David discusses grievances of the sepoys in a separate 15 page section, 'Professional Grievances.' (126-19 to 33)

that they were reluctant to immediately accept someone else in their place.

Therefore, the chief (perhaps, even singular) cause for the Uprising was political dispossession of Muslims, while all other reasons were merely subordinate to it.

Abnormal, Illogical, Astonishing

Historically, it was uncharacteristic of Hindus to rise up in an armed struggle on account of a certain injustice done to them by the British. What they had undergone during seven centuries of Islamic rule was many times more grievous than anything the British had done. Moreover, Muslim rulers openly and proudly proclaimed that it was their obligatory, scripturally ordained duty to establish a Muslim state and convert the whole of India to Islam. In actual fact, millions of conversions took place under their rule, so that almost the entire population of Muslims in later times was the progeny of such converts. On the contrary, the British Government had not declared their aim of converting India, and their hundred year rule had not yielded more than a hundred thousand converts. (3-288) Even these had mostly happened through preaching and appeals to the intellect or at the most by way of giving incentives or enticement; no evidence suggests that they had been done either by coercion or at the point of the sword. It is illogical to suggest that Hindus, who had already lost 20% of their number to Islam, could have become annoyed at the conversion of a handful of them to Christianity.[14] Thus, it is uncharacteristic of the Hindu, who

---

14. A Christian mission school was functional even in Bithoor, the principality of Nanasahib Peshwa who is considered as a leader of the 1857 Uprising. Likewise, the Bible was being taught in a school established by Jaynarayan Ghoshal in Benares, the epicenter of Hindu devotion. (108-31) This helps in estimating precisely how irked were Hindus at Christian evangelization.

Dr. Sen writes in connection with the effects of Christian evangelism on Hindus and Muslims: "The enlightened Hindu in his tolerant attitude might concede that ultimately all religions led

was content in being able to observe as much of his religion as he was permitted while loyally serving his Muslim masters, to rise up in arms for his faith against the British.

Although the numerical strength of Hindus in the Mughal army was higher than Muslims, they had never contemplated rising in revolt against their Islamic masters even for the sake of religion, country, caste, self-respect, happiness, prestige, honour of their women or human rights. It was only a few of the pre-Islamic kingdoms or Hindu powers established by some exceptional persons with prodigious foresight like Shivaji, who ever stood up against Islamic might. Moreover, it is a fact of history that Shivaji faced more opposition from Hindus than Muslims even to establish a Hindu power. It rarely, if ever at all happened that even a few out of the hundreds of thousands of Hindus serving Aurangzeb, cast off their 'loyalty' and joined hands with Shivaji. So, how were Hindu soldiers suddenly inspired by a desire and urge on account of religion to rise against the British only in 1857? It must be astonishing that those who had no desire to rise in order to establish their own independent state, were now up in arms to depose one master and replace him by another.

At Variance with Hindu Character

The contention that Hindus or Hindu soldiers were provoked by the various social reform laws enforced by the British, too, does not appeal to logic. It went against Hindu nature. The characteristic Hindu response to every such law that seemingly conflicted with religion and tradition, usually went through the following stages:

---

to God, but the Muslim who firmly believed that he has the only true faith could not logically make that concession." (141-9)

The Advocate General submitted before court in Bahadur Shah's trial: "Even the forcible conversion of the Hindus to Mahomedanism under former emperors of India seems to have been insufficient to rouse them (i.e. Hindus) to resistance." (107-385) His argument was that evangelism was not a reason for Hindus joining the Uprising.

1) express intellectual protest;
2) oppose it as nonviolently as possible;
3) ensure in practice that the law only remained on paper;
4) begin to follow it gradually after some time, and
5) after some more time, laud the Hindu authors of the law as social revolutionaries (continuing quietly with old practices even after that).

Armed conflict against any such law is abnormal of Hindu society. On the other hand, there always were some in that society who both acclaimed and promoted such law or reform from its very inception. No one killed them for their views. Rising in armed rebellion against the king, indigenous or alien, was at variance with basic Hindu nature. It is therefore unrealistic to suggest that such a society could have promoted the 1857 Uprising in an armed revolt against a law perceived to be antireligion, or against alien rule.

What was the Need for an Armed Uprising?

In the first place, reformers from Hindu society themselves had pressed for those 'antireligious' laws that are stated as a reason for Hindu participation in the 1857 Uprising. It was for such social activism that Raja Rammohan Roy, Keshuv Chandra Sen and Ishwarchandra Vidyasagar became famous in Bengal. Similar social reform movements were also active in Maharashtra. Armed struggle as a remedy was both illogical and implausible. Moreover, since these movements aimed at ultimate social good, the propriety of contemplating armed struggle against their introduction must also be examined. What percentage of the Hindu population actually came under the purview of laws like *sati* prohibition and widow remarriage? Widows were remarrying and the custom of *sati* was absent among a majority of Hindus from very ancient times. Note the irony of the whole issue. Would Hindus collaborate in an armed struggle against the British, who made laws to protect widows declining to perform *sati* and to rehabilitate them through remarriage, with those whose invasions and atrocities had in the first place forced widows of Hindu martyrs to adopt that custom in a bid to save what was left of their honour?

Further, what was the necessity of armed struggle when it was conveniently possible to disregard the law? A widow desirous of ending her life could easily have quietly committed suicide instead of performing *sati,* and no British authority would have been the wiser. The law did not force a widow to remarry — she could very well have continued to live as a widow. The law merely sought to give her protection in the event that she decided upon remarriage. We may take the example of the celebrated 21–22-year old widowed Rani Laxmibai who had assumed the veritable incarnation of the Goddess of War in the Uprising. Even conceding that the legal ban on *sati* had prevented her from ritualistically and openly performing that rite, society had not excised her for choosing not to do so. On the contrary, she was lauded. She had not remarried despite her young age and the protection afforded by law. When such means for not abiding by the law were so easily available, the need for an armed struggle becomes incomprehensible.

Another absurd reason for Hindu participation in the Uprising was the perceived apprehension of losing caste on account of British legislation and use of fat smeared cartridges. Loss of caste and subsequent ostracism was not an arbitrary event but needs to be decided by an assembly of elders (*jaat panchayat*). No record is available of the number of persons that were actually excluded from their castes during British rule. Likewise, there is no evidence of exclusion of a sepoy from his caste on account of the use of cartridges. Possibly, there was no Hindu who had been thus ostracized. The actual consequences of using the cartridges had yet to be seen, because the new rifles which were to be used had not been issued to the army. In reality, none had lost his caste; only a fear that it would be lost had been created. Even in the event of an infringement of caste rules, a provision for performing a penance (*prayashchitta*) to continue to live within the caste was already available in caste rules. So, where was the need to rise in armed rebellion? Moreover, the religion itself had made provision of creating a new caste if the offender could not return to his original fold. In fact, this is a reason for the existence and prolific growth of castes within Hindu society. So, it is fanciful to claim that Hindus took part in the Uprising out of their fear of losing caste.

By Instigation

It will thus be seen that all the fundamental, principal or decisive causes primarily and exclusively affected Muslims. Those relating to Hindus were merely topical or local in nature. Before plunging into the Uprising, Hindus had not seriously contemplated the nature of the government that was expected to replace British rule; they had spared no thought to ascertain which of the two would have been progressive and beneficial, or at least good for themselves. It would appear as if secondary issues, to them, had been more important than political freedom. A thorough inquiry reveals that a majority of Hindus taking part had actually been instigated by Muslims. Realizing that it was impossible to fight the British without Hindu support, Muslims tried to befriend them by emphasizing the alien origin and ethnicity of the British, and instilling the idea that they were hostile towards both religions. They had told Hindus how the latter could again become chiefs, talukdars and zamindars once the British had been driven out. Characteristically, the Hindu is overwhelmed by such friendly advances and was more than willing to let bygones be bygones. This is precisely what happened in 1857 and Muslims were able to take some Hindus with them.

- 4 –

The Uprising – Only in North India

With the exception of a few insignificant and sporadic incidents south of the Narmada River, which were immediately put down locally, the Uprising remained almost restricted to North India. None of them were of cognizable seriousness. In a pertinent comment, Mahamahopadhyay Datto Vaman Potdar says: "The game of 1857 was played out mainly in North India. Some smoke was visible in the South, but no flames were seen."

(111- Preface 11) Savarkar wrote how Madras or Bombay were 'dead weights hampering the national movement.' and how it would have been exhilarating if a secret organization had also taken root in the South as it had in the North. (1-73, 161, 203) Dr. Ishwari Prasad calls the uprising 'The Great Northern Revolt'. (145-3)

In actual fact, the Uprising had not consumed even the whole of North India. The North Western provinces[15], Ayodhya (with its capital at Lucknow) and Rohilkhand are the three areas, now mainly known as Uttar Pradesh, that are most often encountered while reading the history of the Uprising. "The North-Western Provinces destined to become the main theatre of the anti-British war." (84-3) "It was in the North-Western Provinces, Oudh and Rohilkhand that the revolt attained the greatest success." (141-411) Dominated by Muslims, this territory had for several centuries been the centre of Islamic culture and, before passing into British hands, was ruled mainly by Muslim Nawabs and chiefs. The region was located in the doab of the Ganga and Yamuna rivers and Muslim zamindars were the dominant class here. (78-195) Islam was a powerful force. (104-333) Under Islamic influence, the entire region had 'Muslimized sections'. (75-191)

---

15. The provinces were subdivided into districts as follows:

i. Meerut: Meerut, Muzaffarnagar, Saharanpur, Bulandshahar and Dehra Dun.

ii. Delhi: Delhi, Gurgaon, Hissar, Panipat and Rohtak.

iii. Agra: Agra, Mathura, Mainpuri, Etawah, Aligarh and Farrukhabad.

iv. Allahabad: Allahabad, Fatehpur, Kanpur, Banda and Hamirpur.

v. Benares: Mirzapur, Jaunpur, Gorakhpur, Ghazipur and Azamgarh.

vi. Some writers include Rohilkhand within this province. Rohilkhand: Bareilly, Shahjahanpur, Moradabad, Bijnor, Budaun, Pilibhit, Naini Tal and Rampur.

Four *other* groups of territory are noteworthy in connection with the North Indian uprising:

1) Bengal and Bihar
2) Punjab and border areas of Peshawar
3) Rajputana and Malwa (present-day Rajasthan and Madhya Pradesh)
4) Bundelkhand, particularly its Jhansi division.

We will review details of the uprising that occurred at all these places in the next section.

-5-

British India and the States

India was politically divided into two parts — British India and the Native States. The former was under complete control of the British who had appropriated it through treaties, plots, annexations and battles. The native states had been accorded vassal status through treaties that varied in content according to expediency. Armies were posted within each state at the latter's cost for its security. In addition, each ruler had his own military force. A British officer, called the 'Resident', was appointed to supervise the affairs of states, with powers to sanction successors to the ruler or annex the state for reasons like maladministration. Generally, three fourths of India was 'British' and the remaining under 'native states'.

India was divided into three parts for administration: Bengal, Bombay and Madras, with a governor general for each. Among the three, the governor general of Bengal was supreme, and had overriding control over the other two. Lord Canning was the incumbent during this period with his headquarters at Calcutta. Each province had its independent military organization, which was known by the respective name of the province. Some platoons in each army were entirely composed of British troops while others had native soldiers, known as 'sepoys'. Even though the native platoons had Indian soldiers, they were commanded by British officers.

The Military in India

The total strength of the British army at that time was 2,77,000 of which 2,32,000 (or 84%) was Indian and 45,000 (or 16%) British. Of this total force, the Bengal Army had 1,59,000 (1,35,000 Indian and 24,000 British) men.[16]

The Bengal Army, all stationed in North India from Peshawar to Calcutta, had taken predominant part in the Uprising. A force of 60,000 had been posted to the border region of Punjab-Peshawar as it was unsecured. Ten thousand of these were British. (19-103) 14,000 British soldiers had been thinly spread over the vast remaining areas that had risen in revolt. Four British platoons were stationed at Dum-Dum near Calcutta in the Bengal province. Some British platoons were at Danapur near Patna in Bihar, 344 miles away. A few more British platoons were at Lucknow, 356 miles to the west of Danapur. Effectively, over a distance of 700 miles, British troops were present only at one place in the middle. This is very significant vis-à-vis the Uprising. While there were some British platoons at Meerut, there was none in nearby Delhi. Thus, British presence was minimal in the areas in which the Uprising occurred.

How Many Soldiers Revolted?

The Bengal Army had 74 infantry, 22 cavalry and 23 artillery platoons. (111-271; 126-26) Fifty-four platoons of the infantry took part in the Mutiny, 17 were disarmed while 3 remained loyal. (126-19) Sixteen cavalry and 11 artillery platoons had joined the mutineers. About 1,00,000 sepoys had rebelled. (132-31) Other narratives state that 70,000 rebelled, 30,000 had been disbanded or disarmed and the remaining 40,000 had remained loyal. (141-408) According to yet another source, only 11 platoons had remained loyal. (70-390) In a nutshell, about 70 to 75% of the Bengal Army had rebelled.

---

16. In comparison, the Bombay and Madras Armies were much smaller with a combined strength of 1,18,000 (96,000 Indian and 22,000 British). (126-26)

Contrastingly, out of a total of 29 platoons in the Bombay Army, some sepoys from three platoons had revolted. There was no Uprising at all in the Madras Army. Out of 52 platoons, only the sepoys in one platoon (No.36, infantry) had declined to move to Bengal in August 1857. (126-19) As there was no revolt in this region, Bombay and Madras Army were sent north during the Uprising. In short, rebellion in South is not considered cognizable.

Cavalry in the Lead

An important aspect of the Bengal Army was that the infantry was mostly composed of Hindus, while Muslims were in majority and dominant in the cavalry and artillery. (126-396; 89-50) The risaldars (chief officers) of almost all the cavalry platoons were Muslims.[17] (106-18) Commissioner Lawrence clarified that the Bengal irregulars (i.e. cavalry) were mostly well-born Muslims. (126-30) Among the Muslims, those from Delhi (the Doab) region and Rohilkhand outnumbered the rest. The 18th cavalry platoon consisted of sepoys from the same region.[18] (25) Cavalry soldiers were also called 'Turkswar'. (85-1) In view of the fact that the cavalry was in the lead in the Uprising, this information is both important and enlightening.

The Ayodhya State Army

As discussed earlier, an important aspect of the Bengal Army was that 80 to 85% of the sepoys had been recruited from the Ayodhya state. It is necessary to understand the nature of the Ayodhya state army which the Nawab had

---

17. Roshan Taqvi cites a representative example of the 7th cavalry platoon. Out of a total strength of 586 sepoys, 474 were Muslims while the rest were from various Hindu castes. (106-18) Historian Kaye writes: "As ever, the cavalry were foremost in the work of mutiny — foremost in their greed of blood." (78-472)

18. Valbezen writes: "The regular and irregular cavalry of the Bengal army was almost exclusively composed of Mussalmans belonging to Rohilkhand and to the Doab of the Ganges." (70-12)

disbanded after annexation. It was composed of 16 cavalry, 56 infantry and eight artillery platoons and each had been given a separate name. Chiefs of all the cavalry and artillery platoons were Muslim — not a single one of them was Hindu. (106-16) Roshan Taqvi provides a list of the names of chiefs of only 20 infantry platoons of which 18 were Muslim and two were Hindu. (16) Although names of the chiefs of the remaining 36 platoons are not available, the situation could not have been too different. This is a pertinent fact because the same disbanded soldiers turned into agents for spreading discontent.

Complex Account

The 1857 Uprising was not a coherent or organized struggle under unified command. Despite the potent underlying inspiration and the common cause of ending the British rule, the Uprising actually was the sum total of various events that took place independently of one another at different places. For instance, it was nothing like the Battle of Panipat that was fought between two contending armies. In contrast, the 1857 Uprising occurred at various places in North India at different times between May 1857 and the end of that year. They did not begin simultaneously, nor were they subdued at the same time. Some of the incidents were related to one another from the beginning; some became relevant to one another after they had broken out; some were completely isolated. While everyone had notionally accepted the post-Uprising leadership of Bahadur Shah as Emperor, he was not controlling the mutiny.

British historians Kaye and Malleson had to write six large volumes to narrate this entire history. They needed to discuss, for each one of those hundreds of incidents that occurred over a period of two years and at hundreds of places, their leaders, their relationships, the sepoys who participated, their inspiration and aspirations, British officers, triumphs of the opposing parties, individual victories and defeats, incidents of vendetta and massacres, loss of life and financial setbacks. Most books dealing with the subject are replete with such accounts. Yet, even after reading all such books, one is unable to get a comprehensive, cohesive picture of the Uprising. All one is able to gather is that there was general anarchy and rebellion, perhaps a reason why N.R. Phatak called it 'The Sepoy Anarchy of 1857'.

After a certain amount of reading, one appears to be going through identical repetition in each description. Narrating a sequential account of the Uprising is a formidable task. If accounts specific to an uprising at a certain place are traced from beginning to end, their mutual relationship and consequences with those at other places cannot be grasped, whereas a serial presentation of all the uprisings in chronological sequence makes it impossible to understand any particular one of them. Thus a judicious use of both approaches remains the only method of narration.

In the following chapter, we will only attempt to trace the history of various events that together make up the 1857 Uprising, in as coherent a manner as possible.

***

Chapter 4

1857: The Course of Events

-1-

News spread in January 1857 in the Dum-Dum Musketry Depot near Calcutta, that the new issue of Enfield rifles used a projectile that was part of a self-contained paper cartridge incorporating both ball and powder charge. It required only the end to be bitten off and the cartridge then rammed down the muzzle of the weapon. To facilitate this process the cartridge was heavily greased with cow and pig fat. This information circulated in no time to other camps.

Mangal Pandey

The 34th and 19th Native Infantry Regiments at Barrackpur and Behrampur respectively, refused to accept the cartridges at paradés during the following month. Despite government assurance that they contained no substance of the description, as well as the concession of removing the casing manually, the sepoys remained adamant. Finally, a decision was taken in the following month to disband those regiments.

However, before that, on 29th March, Sepoy Mangal Pandey of the 34th N.I. at Barrackpur rebelled all alone and shot at his commanding officer. He was tried by court martial and sentenced to death by hanging. He is regarded 'the first freedom fighter' as the Uprising was initiated by his act. (142-10)

The regiments were disbanded

Around the same time, between January and April, 'chapatis' (wheat bread) were suddenly observed circulating in various army camps. British officers were unable to trace either their source or motive. Messages for the Uprising were being conveyed through their use as a medium of communication.

Meerut

Three British and three native regiments were stationed at the large army camp at Meerut, 55 kilometers from Delhi. Orders were issued, with the intention of testing their loyalty, to 90 sepoys of the 3rd cavalry to receive the new cartridges. Eighty-five of them refused to obey the Colonel's order, which insubordination was tantamount to revolt. All of them were tried by court martial, sentenced to 10 years rigorous imprisonment, and made to walk, in front of all the other sepoys, in chains to the prison two miles away. (130-43)

Incensed by this humiliating treatment of their associates, the entire cavalry rose up in rebellion the next day (10th May). Attacking the prison house in the evening, they freed all the internees (700–800) and succeeded in perssuading many from the infantry regiments to their side. The infantry, too, joined the rebels. Eighty-two British officers were killed and the General Barely escaped with his life. None from the British regiments stationed there offered any resistance. Sepoys and civilians went on a looting spree through the town, making the Bengali population their special targets. (57-95) The local police also joined hands with the rebels. (96) Thereafter, they left in batches for Delhi; the British did not even attempt to give chase.

Bahadur Shah Crowned Emperor

Thirty horsemen, who were in the lead, overcame all hurdles, rode to the Emperor's palace in the morning of the

11th May and implored him to assume leadership. The Emperor was astonished to see them there. (107-414) Although skeptical initially, he ultimately consented rather reluctantly. He was proclaimed as Emperor of India. Thereafter, the remaining 2,000 sepoys from Meerut also arrived in Delhi. (78-54) British officers were present in Delhi, but no British troops were in station. Regiments of native sepoys stationed in the town defected to the rebels. British officers and Christian civilians were slaughtered. (130-57)

The Emperor began ruling in Delhi. The eldest of his 13 sons, Mirza Mughal, became Commander-in-Chief. No trace of British authority had remained in Delhi.

Echoes of the Meerut uprising and establishment of Mughal rule in Delhi began resounding all over North India and rebellions occurred at various places. It is said that 31st May had been appointed as the date for a unified revolt (which was also the conclusion of Col. Wilson who later conducted an inquiry into the Uprising on behalf of the British government). Nevertheless, perhaps because the Meerut revolt was premature, insurgency at each of the other places occurred separately according to local convenience. Almost the entire North India was in the grasp of rebellion by 15th June. It was not possible for British authorities to immediately put down all those mutinies because they lacked sufficient number of their own soldiers. A large part of their troops was deployed in the Punjab, which could not be mobilized till peace had been established in that region.

Let us follow the situation in Punjab.

Punjab Province

The Brigadier at Mian Mir near Lahore, where 4 native regiments had been stationed, learnt from a Sikh soldier on 12th May that the sepoys had conspired to rise in rebellion, seize the Fort at Lahore, free 2,000 prisoners and kill the British officers. (132-49) He immediately decided to disarm the men and disband the regiments, which was accordingly done the next day under supervision of British soldiers. A very dangerous situation was thus averted by dispersing the 2,500 sepoys. (132-50; 141-328)

Three native regiments were stationed at Firozpur in the same division. The Brigadier decided to test the loyalty of his men a day after news of the Meerut uprising reached on the third day. However, before the Brigadier could do so, news of the capture of Delhi also reached them. Two Native Regiments immediately revolted, setting fire to the Church, 16 officers' bungalows, and the dispensary before riding away towards Delhi. The unrest was subdued with the help of British troops.

The 55th N.I. at Hotimardan in the same division hoisted the flag of rebellion on 20th May. The commanding Colonel who had trusted the sepoys was so shocked that he committed suicide. A hundred and twenty sepoys remained loyal, forty were executed by being blown to bits by cannon and the remainder fled. The 10th cavalry which was stationed at the place, refused to act against the rebels. It was disarmed and disbanded with the help of British troops. The fleeing sepoys were pursued, 150 were apprehended and 120 killed while the others managed to escape.

A large force of 10 regiments comprising 13,000 soldiers was deployed at Peshawar out of which 10 regiments of 10,000 were Indian and three of 3,000 were British. (126-137; 141-331) Sensing that the Indian troops were on the verge of rebellion, the commandant decided to disarm them on 22nd May. Accordingly, 3,000 infantry and 500 cavalry sepoys were disarmed after positioning artillery assisted troops in front of and behind them. Several sepoys of the 51st infantry, however, escaped under cover of darkness. But some of them were later caught and executed. (141-332; 132-54) The 64th N.I. had become most discontented and rebellious.

A movable column of 2,500 soldiers had been formed to deal with prospective rebellions at the various army camps. Along with British troops, it included Sikh and Gurkha soldiers who had remained loyal.

In response to news about uprisings at various places, it had been decided to disarm the three native regiments at Jalandhar. But on 7th June, they rebelled before that could be done and headed for Delhi after opening fire at the Colonel's bungalow and killing one person. British troopers went in pursuit but could not apprehend them.

As soon as the sepoys from Jalandhar reached Philaur and Ludhiana en route, sepoys stationed at those two places revolted (9th June), engaged in some looting, set prisoners free and although it was possible to take over control of the fort at Ludhiana, proceeded to Delhi without doing so. (141-330)

One native regiment at Kangra and two at Multan were disarmed on 15th May and 10th June respectively.

The native regiment at Rawalpindi was disarmed with the help of British troops on 7th July. (337) On the same day, the 14th N.I. at Jhelum stoutly refused to disarm and armed conflict broke out, lasting for a day. However, the rebels could not hold out and 150 out of 500 were killed. About 180 of them were caught while they were fleeing and later executed, while 120 were arrested by the Hindu King of Kashmir and delivered to the British. Only 50 succeeded in escaping. (132-95; 141-337)

The 9th cavalry and 46th N.I. at Sialkot rebelled on 9th July after learning of the resistance at Jhelum. No British regiment had been stationed there. Several Christians — men and women — were killed. Some rebels took refuge in Sikh king Tej Singh's fortress that was in the vicinity. Rebels looted the treasury and the camp, and escaped towards Delhi before British troops could arrive. However, the movable column under Nicolson's command went in pursuit and caught them as they were crossing the Ravi River. Five hundred were killed on the spot and many others were later hanged. Another 200 that had escaped were rounded up by the Maharaja of Kashmir and handed over to the British, and were either sentenced to death or transported for life. (132-97; 130-184)

The Infantry Regiment at Amritsar was disarmed on the same day, while the rebellions at Hissar, Hansi, Sirsa, Rohtak, Gurgaon and other places were put down.

All Native Regiments of the Bengal Army in the Punjab division, with stray exceptions, were disarmed and disbanded in this manner. (141-340) The British had commenced recruiting soldiers from among the Sikh population which had remained loyal to them. Chief Commissioner Lawrence had made a public statement on 1st June that fighting forces for subduing the rebellion were available to them in abundant numbers, and that they could recruit 50,000 sepoys within a month.[1] (335) The British trusted Sikh States like Patiala, Nabha, Kapurthala and Jind who were helping them in every possible manner. (126-134)

The Punjab region was thus rendered secure by the end of July. Now the British turned their attention to Delhi — acquiring control over Delhi again was a political necessity.[2] The loss of that city and environs had created a significant psychological effect. The feeling that Mughal rule had been reestablished with the occupation of Delhi and British power had ended, was providing new inspiration for uprisings everywhere. But with Punjab secured, it was going to be possible to send British forces towards Delhi.

Before reviewing British recapture of Delhi, let us see what was happening at other places in the interregnum.

Agra Province

The rebels had contemplated the capture of Delhi by control of Agra, 185 kms away. It was the headquarters of the North-Western Province and was commanded by an officer of the rank of lieutenant general. The capital had been shifted

---

1. Dr. Sen writes: "They raised the Sikh strength in the army almost to the point of saturation." (141-345)

2. So vital was reoccupation of Delhi regarded by the British, that the Commissioner of the Punjab Division had even suggested that the Peshawar province be ceded to the Amir of Afghanistan so the military forces deployed there could be withdrawn and sent to Delhi. The proposal was not adopted because other officials were opposed to it. (130-183)

from Delhi to Agra for some time during erstwhile Mughal rule. In 1857, Delhi was placed under the jurisdiction of Agra.

Some detachments of 9th N. I. were stationed 80 kms away at the district town of Aligarh in the Agra division, and also at Mainpuri and Etawah in the same district. No British troops were present at any of these places. Hearing that a Brahmin zamindar had been hanged at Aligarh on charges of sedition on 20th May, the sepoys there suddenly rebelled, looting the treasury, setting prisoners free and heading towards Delhi. However, no officers were molested. (130-68) Sepoys at Etawah, receiving news of the revolt at Aligarh, went on a similar rampage on 22nd May, looting the treasury, freeing prisoners from the gaol and making their way towards Delhi. (126-148) Magistrate Hume (one of the founders of the Indian National Congress of later times) had managed to escape disguised in female attire. The same action was repeated at Mainpuri, except that the rebels could not loot the treasury because of the help given to the British by Rao Bhavani Singh, brother of the local Hindu ruler. (132-54) The sepoys left for Delhi. All these three places were now under rule of the rebels.

Three important places in the division having fallen to the rebels, Agra was in imminent danger of an uprising. One British regiment had been stationed there, but the situation had been complicated by the soldiers of the Gwalior State. Agra adjoined Maharaja Jayajirao Shinde's Gwalior State, which had not been annexed. (The distance between the two towns is 105 kms.) Although the Maharaja was a British loyalist, and had been requested to provide military assistance after the Meerut revolt for the protection of Agra, he had clearly informed them that he could not trust his army in the situation. (130-73) This was true, for a detachment of 100 horsemen of the Gwalior army at Hathras had rebelled on 24th May and left for Delhi. (132-54)

Sepoys at Mathura in the Agra division rebelled on 30th May, looting the treasury, freeing prisoners, firing at officers' bungalows, killing one of them, and heading for Delhi. Rebel rule was established there towards the end of September. (81-82; 130-74)

Realizing that the two native regiments at Agra were likely to rebel, they were disarmed with the assistance of the British regiment on 31st May.

By a revolt in the Farrukhabad district, the local Nawab proclaimed his independence on 16th June. (132-78) On the third day, the 10th N. I. rebelled at nearby Fatehgarh. British officers and their families rushed to the fort. When defence became impossible, they fled towards Kanpur in three boats. Many of them were killed in the firing that ensued, while the others died after reaching Kanpur. The Fatehgarh fort, which also housed a gun foundry, was taken over by the rebels and the Nawab's dominion was established in the district. (141-232; 44-120)

Thus all six districts in the Agra division had been wrested from British control. By the end of June, the city of Agra had become isolated and completely insecure.

In this situation, rebel forces from Neemuch, Malwa and other places assembled in the early days of July at Fatehpur-Sikri to attempt to gain control over Agra, 37 kms away, and their numbers swelled to 4,000 infantry, 1,500 cavalry and 15 cannons. British officers began preparing for the defence of Agra with just 742 soldiers and 6 cannons. They faced defeat at Sasia (Shahganj), eight kms from Agra, on 5th July in a fierce battle which left 45 killed and 105 wounded. The rebels lost over 500 dead. The remaining British troops went into the fort, and the victorious rebels, instead of investing the fort, left towards Delhi where they were greeted with a grand salute as the 'victors of Agra.' (130-168) This is known as 'the Battle of Shahganj.'

For two or three days after the victory, locals went on a spree of killing Christians in which at least thirty lost their lives. Along with a sack of the town, empty houses of officers were torched. A proclamation of independence was immediately made in the name of the Emperor. British officers, troops and their people were confined to the fort, while the rebels ruled outside, this situation continued till October 1857. Since the fort was not under siege, British troops would occasionally emerge from the fort to take out a flag march. (141-325)

Meerut Division

Let us review events in the Meerut Division.

Although the Uprising had originally commenced from Meerut, none of the rebels had remained behind, and since British troops were present in large numbers, it remained peaceful and under their control.

Hearing of the Uprising in Meerut, the Magistrate of Muzaffarnagar, 40 kms away, panicked and declared a three-day closure of government offices. This decision aggravated the already tense situation and rumour became rife. A feeling developed that British administration had collapsed. (7-76) The local zamindars patched up small bands of militia and looted the treasury, set fire to officers' bungalows, destroying barracks and government offices. They enjoyed support of the tehsildar and kotwal. (80) The 4th cavalry rebelled on 21st June and killed the commander, Smith.

Shamli and Thanabhavan became main centers of the uprising in the district, where rebels set up their own administration. (17-143)

Saharanpur, a district adjacent to Muzaffarnagar on the north, rebelled in May itself. The local Gujars rose up with several incidents of looting of banks and moneylenders. It was more of an uprising against classes other than those in the administration. (7-94) The local kotwal had defected to the rebel cause. The only armed force at the time was the 85 sepoys posted there for protection of the treasury. The British had no trust in them. (97) Nevertheless, the British had not lost all control over the place. (141-411)

One detachment of the 9th N. I. was stationed at Bulandshahar in the Meerut Division. This rebelled on 22nd May, immediately after detachments of the same regiment stationed at Aligarh, Mainpuri and Etawah had revolted. The

British lost control of that district. (132-54) The Nawab of Malgadh in the same district established his rule. (7-51)

Rebels thus acquired control of most of the Meerut Division.

Allahabad Division

Let us see what happened in the Allahabad Division.

The rebellion in Kanpur is especially significant because Nanasahib Peshwa became its leader. Kanpur was an important district headquarters as well as a vital military station. It was located on the banks of the Ganga river, which facilitated river transport to places like Allahabad. It was also famous for its industry.

Nanasahib lived at Bithoor (Brahmavarta), 25 kilometers from Kanpur. He had inherited property at Bithoor as adopted son of Bajirao II Peshwa. However, the British administration had denied to him a pension of Rs. eight lacs that Bajirao II used to receive during his lifetime, claiming that pensions could not be inherited. Nanasahib engaged in protracted correspondence with the administration on this account and had even sent Azeemullah Khan to London in 1853 as his representative to plead his case. However, these efforts had proved fruitless and Nanasahib was aggrieved with the British. Yet, he had the friendliest and cordial relations with local British officials, especially the veteran Major General Wheeler and Collector Hillersdon who had great trust in him. (111-347; 108-9) With the sanction of British authorities, he had 500 sepoys and 3 cannons under his command.

The British began fearing that a rebellion might occur in Kanpur. Security of the treasury, ammunition store and British citizens was of vital importance. They approached Nanasahib for assistance, which he provided by marching to Kanpur on 22nd May with the 500 sepoys and 3 cannons. A temporary entrenchment was dug near the ammunition dump.[3] Women

3. It consisted of a four foot high wall around the site with a ditch of medium depth dug to surround it. This was referred to as the entrenchment. (111-349)

and children were moved there and a British guard was placed around it. The entrenchment held about 1,000 people of whom 400 were women and children. Four hundred able bodied men were given crash training in use of weapons. Nanasahib even stayed at the barracks in order to oversee the discharge of the responsibility he had accepted. (111-346)

The British had stationed four regiments — three infantry and one cavalry — at Kanpur. The 2nd cavalry rebelled at midnight on 4th June and opened fire with pistols on the sleeping British officers. The remaining regiments also joined them on the following day. Bungalows, stables and office buildings were torched after which the treasury was attacked and looted. Then they broke into the prison, released inmates and took control of the ammunition dump. In order to prevent the use of river transport, they also cut fastenings of boats to set them adrift. British officers were ensconced in their homes; none was harmed. The sepoys then prepared to leave for Delhi. (111-353; 90-56)

After they had gone some distance, however, they turned back, returned to Kanpur and pressed Nanasahib to assume leadership and go to Delhi with them. When he refused to do so, they coerced him to accept. (141-333; 108-71) But, instead of going to Delhi, they decided to remain in Kanpur to fight the local British. Nana's name was declared as their leader, his rule began and various administration officials were appointed. (126-191)

On the same day (6th June), Nanasahib wrote to Wheeler to warn him that rebels were contemplating an attack on the entrenchment. The General was shocked at the news. (126-192) Nanasahib had sent him advance intimation so that it should not appear as breach of trust.

Sepoys went on a rampage of looting in the town and commenced killing Christians. (194) Attacks were launched on the entrenchment and a siege was laid. The situation of the British trapped within it became precarious. Wheeler sought permission to leave the place and go away. The rebels were in ample numbers to break into the entrenchment and take everyone in their custody, but they did not do so.

There was no let up in the siege, and provisions of water and food were getting exhausted. About 250 besieged persons died for a variety of reasons during the 20 days. (111-361; 126-195) Finally, Wheeler gave in on 26th June and it was agreed by the terms of surrender that all of them would be allowed safe passage by river to Allahabad.

Arrangements were accordingly made the next day (27th June) to send all of them by boat to Allahabad. The party reached the Satichaura Ghat where thousands of locals had gathered to witness the exodus. Besides, armed sepoys were also present.

However, sepoys opened fire when the British refugees boarded their boats, and many were killed as a result. Wheeler, too, was killed. When Nanasahib learned what was going on, he issued orders to spare women and children. Consequently, about 125 women and children were saved, taken back to the town and kept in a place called the Bibighar. Only few Englishmen managed to escape, the rest fell prey to sepoy wrath. It is said that this was in reaction to the unspeakable persecution inflicted on the civilian population of the Allahabad region by the British commander, General James Neill. The incident is notorious in history as the 'Satichaura Ghat Massacre'.

Nanasahib was then enthroned at a grand coronation at Bithoor on 1st July. He immediat y issued his proclamation. The same was repeated at Kanp. :. (44-50)

It is necessary to mention an incident that occurred thereafter, recorded in the annals of history as condemnable. All the women and children kept within the Bibighar were brutally slaughtered on 15th July and the corpses were disposed off by being thrown into a well. This number was about 200.[4] (132-102; 111-416) Most historians concur that this act was not ordered by Nanasahib.

---

4. The number rose on account of women and children who were brought there from other places.

On the heels of the Kanpur rebellion, an infantry Regiment at Fatehpur, 80 kilometers away on the Allahabad-Kanpur Grand Trunk Road, rebelled on 9th June. The local Indian deputy magistrate joined the revolt and later proclaimed his rule in the district. All British officers were driven out except the judge, who was put to death. (130-70) With Kanpur and Fatehpur in control of rebels, the Calcutta-Peshawar highway was closed for the British. (71)

Some detachments of two Kanpur regiments were detailed to Hamirpur. Those detachments rebelled on 14th June, took possession of the treasury and dispatched it to Nanasahib in Kanpur. With the exception of one, all British were put to death. (44-432; 132-76) The rebel leader proclaimed his rule.

Some detachments of one Kanpur regiment were also stationed in Banda district. Like the Hamirpur detachments, these also rebelled on 14th June and looted the treasury. The British abandoned the place and the local Nawab proclaimed his rule.

Allahabad proper was the fifth district in the Allahabad province. It was a very important place for political, geographical and military reasons. It was situated at a strategic point, on the main Kanpur-Delhi route and on the confluence of the Ganga and Yamuna rivers. Communication of Calcutta and environs with western areas would have broken down if it went under control of rebels. It was also referred to in those days as 'the armed gate'[5] to Kanpur and Lucknow. (130-97)

The entire military force there was native sepoys. It had a strong fort that had been built by Akbar. Stationed there was a contingent of 400 Sikh and 80 N. I. sepoys. (141-150) The British had great faith in the native sepoys, and the 6th N. I. had even shown their willingness to go to Delhi and fight the rebellion there, for which the governor general had sent them a message expressing his gratitude. That message was read out to them on 6th June, but within just three hours they rebelled and killed their trusting Captain along with 21 other officers. (130-99; 126-

5. It was also known as 'the gateway to the Doab.' (126-234)

234) cavalry and artillery sepoys from other regiments joined them. A detachment of the N.I. in the fort was disarmed with the assistance of Sikh sepoys and driven out. British officers who had escaped death took refuge within the fort, which they succeeded in holding. (130-100; 126-235)

But violence was rampant in the cantonment and the town. As usual, the treasury was looted; 3,000 prisoners were freed; offices of the railway and government were destroyed and telegraph lines cut; houses belonging to Europeans were looted; Englishmen were killed wherever found. Citizens took part in the carnage; they had found a leader from among themselves. He proclaimed his rule on 7th June no sooner than British presence in the town (excluding the fort) was removed. (90-74, 101)

Thus, British control over Allahabad district had ended in June and rebel administration was established.

Benares Division

We turn to the Uprising in the Benares Division.

Sepoys at Benares rebelled on the same day (4th June) as those at Kanpur, 80 kilometers away. This was a place of pilgrimage for Hindus. Stationed there, were the native 37th N.I. and 13th cavalry, the Ludhiana Regiment consisting of Sikhs and a company of British soldiers and artillery. It was decided to disarm the infantry as it began showing signs of rebellion. They enjoyed sympathy of the cavalry. At the actual time of the disarming, a few soldiers refused to surrender their weapons and, instead, opened fire at British soldiers, killing ten of them, along with the Captain. British forces then opened fire at the sepoys, in the course of which a bullet, by mistake, hit one of the Sikh soldiers who were actually fighting on their side. This led to a misunderstanding and Sikhs opened fire on the British. Feeling that Sikhs had turned coat, the British retaliated by training their rifles on them. Several Sikhs lost their lives and many sepoys of the 37th N. I. managed to escape in the confusion that ensued. (130-122; 132-64) The rebellion was ultimately suppressed.

This incident caused the Sikh regiment to turn anti-British. But later, one of their leaders succeeded in dispelling the misunderstanding and close the issue.

Sikh soldiers stationed at Jaunpur (65 kilometers away), hearing of this incident in Benares, reacted sharply and rose in rebellion on the following day (5th June), killing several British officers, looting their homes and the treasury. (126-233; 44-429) British officials handed over administration of the district to local leaders and left. (6-23) These incidents were exceptions, occasioned by a mere misunderstanding, to the consistent pro-British stance of Sikhs.

Sepoys of the 17th N.I. at Azamgarh, 100 kilometers from Benares, rebelled on 3rd June and killed two officers. British rule ended and the rebels set up their administration. (132-62)

As an effect of events in Benares and Azamgarh, sepoys in Gorakhpur in the same Benares Division were itching to rebel. They attempted to break into the prison house on 7th June and also made determined efforts to gain access to the treasury the next day. A public proclamation declaring the end of the British regime and establishment of the Nawab's rule was made in the third week of June. Muhammad Hasan came forward on 20th July and declared himself ruler. (6-157) The British abandoned the district on 13th August. (6-294; 132-113)

Arrival of Fresh British Forces

In the meantime, the British administration was drawing up plans for containing the rebellion. Governor General Canning was engaged in this work ever since the Meerut uprising. One method of suppressing the revolt was disarming rebellious regiments. The second was deploying loyal detachments brought in from other places in India, while raising a fresh force from the trustworthy among the Indian population, was the third. All three methods were employed. Recruitment of loyal Sikhs was already under way in Punjab, and the task of mobilizing troops from other places had begun.

Accordingly, a British regiment from Rangoon had already arrived. The 900-strong Madras Fusiliers was brought in from

Madras. Two regiments that had been detailed towards Persia (their campaign there having ended) had reached. One Regiment came from Ceylon. A regiment ordered to go to China was kept back. Six or seven regiments were thus immediately available for suppressing the rebellion. Besides, a requisition was sent to England for additional forces to be sent to India. (108-124; 130-67)

Allahabad Back in British Hands

The British Commander, Neill, had reached Benares with a special force and had quelled the rebellion that had recently broken out there, accompanied by unspeakable atrocities committed on the local population. He moved to reach Allahabad on 11th June and entered the fort. The task of restoring order and breaking up the rebel administration in the city began the next day. This was accomplished by 16th June. The rebel subedar left Allahabad and escaped to Kanpur on 16th June. (130-124) That marked the end of the rebel rule lasting 8 or10 days, and reestablishment of British control over the town. (90-115) Then Neill unleashed a regime of untold atrocity, as vendetta in the town and deterrent in the surrounding areas.[6] (115, 6)

The Fatehpur Battle

Plans were then prepared to take Fatehpur and Kanpur. A force was sent in two stages under command of Major Renauld and General Havelock. Renauld left Allahabad on 30th June and Havelock on 7th July. Renauld had 820 soldiers, and Havelock 1,353. (130-125; 90-117) Renauld looted and destroyed all villages on his way. Havelock was in overall command and was regarded as a skilled and daring commander. Fatehpur was 130 kilometers from Allahabad and Kanpur, a further 80.

---

6. Historian Sir John Kaye, who may be expected to have a pro-British bias, says that Neill slaughtered at least 6,000 men, women and children. (90-116 q.) This should give an idea of the carnage.

When Nanasahib received the news of the advancing British force, he detailed his General, Jwala Prasad with 3,500 sepoys and 12 field guns, to scatter it beyond Fatehpur. Tatya Tope was also in the expeditionary force. The two forces met in a fierce battle near Fatehpur on 12th July. Jwala Prasad could make no headway and the result became apparent within the first ten minutes of the engagement. (44-52; 108-130) Nana's force suffered a great defeat. The victorious British looted Fatehpur to their heart's content. This is known as the Battle of Fatehpur.

Kanpur Back Under British Control

The British force then left for Kanpur. Two more battles were fought on the way, in both of which they prevailed. Nanasahib personally took the field with a force of 5,000 on 16th July, but was defeated and, on 17th July, the British seized control of Kanpur once again. Thus ended Nana's rule that had lasted just about a fortnight. (111-409) He went to Bithoor and thereafter to other places.

Havelock made Kanpur the special object of his vengeance. Citizens of Kanpur were slaughtered in numbers far exceeding that of English men, women and children massacred at the Satichaura Ghat and Bibighar. It is said that about 10,000 citizens were put to death. (34-323)

Ayodhya Province

Let us now take a look at the Uprising in the important Ayodhya Province.

Ayodhya was one of the two provinces where the Uprising had assumed the nature of a civil rebellion. (The other was Rohilkhand.) Lucknow, the most important city after Delhi, was capital of this province.

Three native infantry, one cavalry and one artillery regiment were in Lucknow in May 1857, along with one British regiment and one artillery. (130-91) Sir Henry Lawrence, an officer of great capability and tact, held the dual charge as Commissioner and Brigadier General. The atmosphere in Ayodhya had begun getting restive ever since the State was annexed. Members of the erstwhile ruling family, too, were involved in this.

Rebellion on 3rd May

The 7th cavalry rebelled on 3rd May, killing some of its officers. When an attempt was made on the same day to disarm it under cover of artillery, all except 120 sepoys managed to escape; the 120 were disarmed. (132-43; 89-92) Twenty of them were hanged on 14th May. (56-64) Civilian residents of the town made an attempt to rise against British authorities, also on the same day. It is said for this reason, that the 1857 Uprising truly began not on 10th May in Meerut, but on 3rd May in Lucknow. (106-60) It is pertinent to note that news of this 3rd May incident in Lucknow had reached Meerut on the 9th. Attempts to turn the populace against the British continued till the end of May. (67)

Observing that rebellions were occurring in many areas of North India and that Lucknow, too, had begun showing signs of following suit, Lawrence began making preparations to secure the region under his charge. It was necessary to ensure safety of British officers and persons, and protect the treasury and munition dumps. Two places in town were selected for this purpose. Munitions were moved to the Machhibhavan, while the treasury and personnel were sent to the Residency, which was a fortified palace where the Commissioner dwelt. Soldiers, assisted by artillery pieces, were posted at both places for their security. Besides, adults were given firearms after quickly training them in the use of weapons. All these arrangements were complete by 24th May. (130-92; 141-179)

Revolts had begun to erupt at other places in the Ayodhya Province. Lawrence had to deploy a detachment to suppress a rebellion that occurred on 27th May at Malihabad, 24 kilometers from Lucknow, while another force of 400 soldiers was sent on the same day across the northern boundary. However, these detachments themselves rebelled after reaching their destinations, killing all of their officers, except one. (130-92)

Regiments in Lucknow rebelled on the night of 30th May and the next day successively. Officers' houses came under gunfire; the Brigadier and some others were killed, while several were wounded. (130-92; 106-72) However, Lawrence suppressed this revolt with the help of British troops and the artillery. Three thousand and five hundred of the 4,000 native soldiers participated in the rebellion. Forty of them were arrested and hanged on the same day outside the Machhibhavan in full public view. The other rebels escaped towards Delhi. (132-57; 141-181)

Civilians in the town also rose in revolt on 31st May and attempted to join with rebel sepoys but could not, since the latter were already on their way to Delhi. This revolt was also broken up. Twenty-two conspirators were caught and executed, for their role in instigating sepoys to rebel, by tying them to muzzles of cannons and blasting them to pieces. (126-171)

Violence erupted thereafter at many places in the Ayodhya Province. All four regiments stationed at Sitapur, a divisional headquarter located 72 kilometers from Lucknow, rebelled on 3rd June. The colonel and six other officers were killed along with 24 Christian men and women. (130-93; 46-171)

News of the incident in Sitapur reached Malaun, 65 kilometers away, and a similar rebellion occurred there on 4th June. All the officers there fled to Lucknow. (132-63) Another revolt on the same day in the Mohammadi district, which adjoined Rohilkhand, resulted in the massacre of several Christian men and women. (132-93; 46-171) Many officers, men and women took refuge with the Hindu Raja of Mithauli who secretly hid them in the forests in his jurisdiction. (130-93)

Likewise, all four regiments at the district place of Faizabad rose in rebellion on 8th June. They looted the treasury but permitted British officers to leave the area instead of putting them to death. However, 16 of the 22 of them were later killed while they were on their way. (46-171) They then freed the condemned convict, M. Ahmad Shah, from incarceration and declared him their leader. (108-81; 141-183)

Similar rebellions took place the following day at Dariabad, Sikrora, Saloni and Sultanpur. Treasuries were looted at each place. (126-179) The cavalry at Sultanpur killed their Captain and a majority of other officers. (46-171) On the day after that, Gonda and Pershadipur saw similar revolts. (132-73) Immediately thereafter, revolts occurred also at Purwa, Bahraich and other places. (130-93) In this manner, revolts occurred at places all over the province. By 12th June, Lawrence came to the realization that there remained only one secure place in the entire Ayodhya province — the Lucknow Residency! (93)

Chinhat: British Defeat

He thus made slight modifications in the security arrangements in Lucknow by shifting his headquarters as well as all troops from Machhibhavan and the cantonment to the Residency, stocking it with food, supplies and munitions, and strengthening the fortification. Defending the Residency with the assistance of artillery now remained his main aim. He received intelligence on 14th June that rebels were contemplating an attack on Lucknow from all directions and this was likely to happen on 18th or 19th. (126-181; 106-87)

Lawrence believed that the fate of Lucknow hung by the outcome at Kanpur; that success in holding Kanpur would secure Lucknow. He received news on 28th June that rebels had taken Kanpur and their forces were assembling at Chinhat, eight miles from Lucknow. (130-95) Lawrence set out from the Residency to counter the rebel army. His force comprised less than 700 soldiers and 10 field guns. (89-183; 130-95) Included in his contingent were some Ayodhya horsemen and cannoneers believed to be loyal to the British. By 30th June, the rebel force had grown to 5,500 infantry and 800 cavalry sepoys — a total force of 6,300 and 12 guns. (106-95; 89-190) M. Ahmad Shah, who had been freed from the Faizabad prison 22 days ago, was leading them. The British were thoroughly defeated in the battle that ensued (30th June). The Ayodhya soldiers who had accompanied the British force defected at a critical juncture. (132-85) The British lost 293 soldiers killed. (81-128) Rebels lost just 11 with M.Ahmad Shah suffering some wounds. This is known as the Battle of Chinhat.

Lucknow passed under rebel control and the Maulvi set up his headquarters at a suitable place in town.

The Residency and Machhibhavan were invested on 1st July, thus severing British communication between them. A system was devised by the British to communicate through exchange of signals from suitable elevated areas within the two places. When it became impossible to hold the Machhibhavan any longer, the British troops stationed there, ignited the ammunition dump one night and escaped to the Residency in the darkness. (106-103) All the 3,000 British personnel were now caught inside the Residency — 1,720 of them were regular soldiers while the rest were civilians. Lawrence was killed by a bullet on 4th July.

Enthronement of the Nawab's Son

Most of Lucknow's population had become rebellious. Birjis Qadar, 11-year old son of deposed Nawab Wajid Ali Shah then imprisoned in Calcutta, was enthroned as ruler on 5th July. Being a minor, the administration was entrusted to his mother as Regent, and appointment of ministers and officials was made. The whole of the Ayodhya Province, except the Residency, was now ruled by rebels.

Frequent attacks, big and small, were continuing on the besieged Residency. One particularly fierce attack, led by the Maulvi, was notable. It filled the defenders with great fear. The southeastern wall of the Residency collapsed under artillery fire and some rebel sepoys even entered the precincts through the breach. However, their supply of ammunition became exhausted and they were forced to return to their base. (112) Another attack on 20th July, also led by the Maulvi, was so severe that the British felt their end had come and prayers for deliverance began to be said. (119) Fourteen of them were killed and twelve wounded. (132-103) However, the British defenders did not lose hope but continued the barrage of cannon fire determinedly. The Maulvi's troops suffered heavy damage. In the attack of 10th August, in fact, the Maulvi lost over 450 dead. (126-311) This saga of attacks and bipartite loss continued till the British gained final victory over Lucknow.

Attempts to Relieve the Residency

British authorities feared that the same fate as that of their Kanpur compatriots would befall personnel besieged in the Residency unless efforts were made to free them. Havelock undertook the task after he had established control over Kanpur. Lucknow was 66 kilometers away. He took 1,500 soldiers with him and crossed the Ganga River on 20th July. They were offered stiff opposition all along the way not just by the Nawab's forces but also by the civilian population. Two hard battles had to be fought at Unnao and Bashratganj. Although they emerged victorious in both and managed to inflict heavy losses on the rebels (500 dead), they too had to suffer many a casualties. The British lost 88 men, while 112 suffered wounds. (106-126; 130-139) Seeing that they could not hope to achieve success in their task with so few men, the expeditionary force decided to cancel the mission and return to Kanpur. Accordingly, they turned back on 31st July. It is said that a force of 100,000 had assembled under command of the Nawab at Lucknow. (141-208, 219)

Havelock made adequate preparations and set out for Lucknow once again on 5th August. Another battle was won at Bashratganj after slaying 200 rebels. However, he was forced once again to abandon the mission on 13th August for the same reason as before. (44-65; 130-141)

Attacks on the Residency were continuing. It is astonishing that rebels did not make a concerted assault to force their way in and take control although that was well within their capability. Havelock set out from Kanpur for the third time on 19th September with more reinforcements to make an attempt to lift the siege of the Residency in Lucknow. He had help this time of the Commander-in-Chief, Outram, who had just arrived in Kanpur four days earlier (15th September). While Outram was the supreme Commander in principle, Havelock had been given full authority to direct the operation. He now had a total of 3,200 soldiers with him. (126-310)

They crossed the Ganga, neutralized all resistance on the way, established control over Unnao and Bashratganj, and advanced a further 25 kilometers to encamp at Banni. Lucknow was 25 kilometers away. Rebels had stationed the 1st Cavalry and 4th N. I. at Alambagh, 6 kilometers from Lucknow, to block the advance of any force from the direction of Kanpur. A plan was drawn up on 23rd September to take Alambagh and then force a way into the Residency. Then, after intense conflict, the British were able to enter the Residency on the third day (25th September). They suffered a casualty of 600 dead. (132-131) 'The idol of the British Army', the valiant but cruel Neill, was killed in this battle. (141-217)

The Residency had not been liberated by this campaign, only the defenders had been reinforced by additional troops. The siege continued. (106-159) A much larger number of soldiers was required for raising the siege. Havelock managed to hold control of the strategic Alambagh, which remained so till Lucknow was finally captured by the British. (132-130)

Rohilkhand Province

We now turn to Rohilkhand.

Contiguous to the Meerut Province and stretching in the north up to the Himalayan foothills, Rohilkhand was the most rebellious province in the 1857 Uprising. It was here that rebel administration had lasted the longest. Like Ayodhya, the civil population of this province participated in the Uprising. The region was the 'nursery of warlike races'. (141-346) It had acquired its name from the fact that Rohilas had ruled over it for a long period. Their regime had ended with the British conquest in 1801 and the local population was eager to overthrow the latter.

Bareilly was the capital (population at the time — 120,000) of the province and stationed there was an entire brigade, comprising one cavalry, one artillery and two infantry regiments. All these regiments revolted one after another on 31st May under the leadership of a rebellious Subedar Bakht Khan. The British brigadier was put to death. (7-193) Sepoys looted and robbed Christians and Bengali Baboos. (141-350)

Three thousand prisoners were set free. (7-177) All British personnel were driven away. On the same day, Khan Bahadur Khan became Nawab and began his rule in the name of the Emperor of Delhi. (132-59) Bakht Khan became 'Brigadier General'. A royal decree was issued, declaring death to anyone who gave refuge to any Christian. (141-349)

Sepoys in the district place of Shahjahanpur rebelled on the same day, attacked Christians who had gone to church for prayers. Many were killed. (7-197) Twenty-six of them, who had fled towards Mohammadi, were also later caught and killed. Two persons were then jointly installed as rulers. (296) Rebel rule began.

Preparations for rebellion had begun in Moradabad ever since the news of Meerut rebellion had reached. Although sepoys were in readiness to rebel on 31st May, they actually did so the following day. However, they did not kill their officers, who went away towards Meerut and Naini Tal. (234) Sepoys took charge of the treasury. Subordinate British officers, however, were killed. (132-61) On 3rd June, British rule was completely repudiated and rebel administration commenced.[7] (7-241)

Sepoys in the fourth district, Badaun, rebelled on 1st June. The treasury was looted, prisoners freed and the town as well as district plundered. Officers' houses were torched. (7-211) British control over the district ended. Khan Bahadur Khan commenced his rule. (132-61)

Events in the Bijnor district merit special attention. Signs of a revolt had become apparent during May. There was no cantonment in the place. The prison was broken into on 20th May. (7-249) The officers of the British administration, seeing the entire region up in rebellion, decided to hand over charge to the local population and leave the place. Accordingly, they approached the Chaudhary with the proposal, which he turned

---

7. Details of how rebellion occurred at 17 important places in the district and how rebel administrations were established, may be found at 7-243 to 5.

down. They then handed over authority to Mahmud Khan, Nawab of Najibabad in the same district, and left the place. (269) The Nawab declared his rule and began administration. (331)

Rebels from Bareilly arrived in Pilibhit district the day after (1st June) they rebelled in the former place. On getting this news and seeing the developing explosive situation, the local Tahsildar and Kotwal decided to leave. A huge crowd had gathered between the Tahsil and Kotwali. (229) The two officials asked the people to assume administration. They then left in safety. (230) New appointments were made by the Nawab of Bareilly. (327)

Nawab Muhammad Yusuf Ali Khan of Rampur, however, remained loyal to the British. He was undaunted by the rebellious milieu all around his principality. (271) He continued assisting the British.

Thus, almost the entire Rohilkhand region had passed under control and administration of rebels.[8] (7-219)

Rajputana Province

Eighteen states and principalities, large and small, constituted the Rajputana (Rajasthan) province. Sixteen of these remained loyal to the British.[9] (130-177) Sepoys in the remaining two states (Bharatpur and Kota) rebelled but they were not backed by the rulers. Rebels did not get the opportunity to raise their heads because of local Rajputs. (158-319) It is said that : "If the Rajput princes had responded to the call of religion, British authority would have vanished from the desert area stretching from Delhi to Gujarat." (141-

---

8. Savarkar writes: "In this manner, the whole province of Rohilkhand rose in a day! In Bareilly, Shahjahanpur, Moradabad, Badaun, and other district towns, the military, the police and the citizens issued proclamations and deported the British power in the space of a few hours !" (1-176)

9. That is why Savarkar writes that Rajputana was lying like 'dead weights hampering the national movement.' (1-203)

307) The region was known for its warlike Hindu patriots and valiant royalty. "The Rajputs in general, remained 'a rock of strength' to the British power during the critical days." (81-235) Malleson refers to the region as 'loyal Rajputana.' (130-178)

While the local Rajput princes and population sided with the British, sepoys in cantonments, which were mainly located at Ajmer, Nasirabad and Neemuch, joined the rebellion.

Ajmer was regarded as the key to Rajputana. It had a strong fort, and a munitions and weapons store. Security of these was a high priority for the British and two detachments of the 15th N.I. were stationed there for the purpose. No British soldiers were stationed there. The 15th N.I. had just arrived from Meerut. Their loyalty became suspect after the revolt. Immediately, therefore, replacement sepoys from other regiments were brought in and they were dispatched to reunite with their original Regiment in Nasirabad. (141-308) Ajmer was thus secured in May itself.

Nasirabad is 20 kilometers from Ajmer and 353 from Delhi. Two native infantry (15th and 30th) and one artillery regiment were stationed there. It was decided to bring in British troops from other places because those sepoys could not be trusted any more. When this information became known to sepoys, they rebelled on 28th May before the British troops had reached. Two officers were killed and two wounded, while others were forced to leave the cantonment. (141-308; 130-177) The sepoys then left for Delhi.[10]

Neemuch, 192 kilometers from Nasirabad and 371 from Delhi, had three regiments — two native infantry (15th and 30th) and one artillery. An oath of loyalty was extracted from

10. Savarkar writes: "(At Nasirabad) the revolutionaries took treasury, and their unanimously elected leader gave presents to the sepoys in the name of the Emperor of Delhi. The houses of the Englishmen were burnt. Then the army composed of thousands of Sepoys marched towards Delhi brandishing their arms to the tune of enthusiastic military airs!" (1-166)

them on 2nd June. British troops from other locations had in the meantime been called in. But when sepoys heard of the move, they rebelled on 4th June before those troops arrived. The treasury was sacked and officers houses torched. A sergeant's wife and three children were killed. British officers fled from the place. The rebels left for Delhi via Agra. (141-309; 130-177)

Later, rebels attacked and gained control over Neemuch for a short period, but they had come from outside Rajasthan.

The Maharaja of Kota was loyal to the British but his sepoys were not. They rebelled on 15th October 1857. There were four infantry regiments, 10 detachments of cavalry, 300 artillery and 1,500 armed policemen. The Maharaja had already informed British authorities that these sepoys could not be trusted. (132-137) The civil population was unaffected by the rebellion. (81-234)

Malwa Province

Known now as Madhya Pradesh, Malwa is adjacent to Rajputana east of the Chambal River and included the principal States of Gwalior, Indore, Dhar, Dewas, Bhopal and Jawra. They had not been annexed but were tributaries of the British.

Gwalior was the most powerful Indian State after Hyderabad. Twenty two-year old Jayajirao Shinde was on the throne at the time and had a standing force of 10,000 (Gwalior troops).[11] Macpherson was appointed as Resident to monitor administration of the State. Besides the Gwalior troops, there also was a British force of native soldiers. In addition to these, the Maharaja had a most trustworthy force called the 'Maratha Guards'. (141-288)

While the Maharaja was loyal to the British, the native British force was showing signs of rebellion. The Maharaja had alerted the Resident about this fact and indeed, a cavalry detachment at Hathras and a Regiment at Neemuch rebelled

---

11. Besides this number, Gwalior State had 7,500 trained soldiers, not in regular service but ready 'on call'.

on 24th May and 4th June respectively. The Maharaja's Diwan (Prime Minister) was insulted and threatened with his life on 26th May when he visited the cantonment. (5-128; 50-24) Sepoys had taken an oath on 27th May to assist one another. It was learnt on 28th May that they were preparing to leave for Delhi. (5-129) Several British women and children were taken into the palace on 29th May for their safety.

Actually, however, all regiments in Gwalior rebelled at once on 14th June. (183) Furious sepoys began butchering their officers and torching their houses. (86-102) Nineteen were put to death and 43 who had escaped alive were sent to Agra under military escort by the Maharaja. Resident Macpherson, too, left for Agra.

Rebel sepoys then went to the Maharaja and asked him to lead them in an attack first on Agra and then on Delhi. In case he declined to do so, they wanted him to provide them with Rs.12-15 lacs, equipments and conveyance to reach their destination. He was threatened that if he did not agree to do any of those things, they would rain cannon fire on the town and palace, plunder the inhabitants, loot the treasury, take control of the fort and imprison the Maharaja. (5-168; 39-129)

However, the Maharaja conceded none of their demands but, tactfully using every stratagem, managed to convince them with his assurance of joining them after the rainy season was over, and to stall them with sops of enhanced pay and other such allurements. The Resident had especially asked the Maharaja to do everything to keep the rebels pinned down in Gwalior and not allow them to proceed to Agra or Delhi. Accordingly, sepoys were paid three months' advance salary and rewards. If, despite all this, sepoys did make attempts to go to Agra, plans had been put in place to waylay and loot them en route, as well as to withdraw ferries across the Chambal River to prevent them from crossing over. (86-103) Five thousand fresh, trustworthy soldiers were also recruited thereafter. (36-194) In effect, the Maharaja succeeded in forcing rebel sepoys to remain in Gwalior till the fall of Delhi to the British (September 1857).

In the meantime, the situation in Gwalior became difficult once again when sepoys who had rebelled on 1st August at Indore and Mhow, came there with the intention of taking local rebels with them to Agra and Delhi. (86-134)

Indore was an important State in the southern part of Malwa, north of the Narmada River. Twenty one-year old Tukojirao Holkar was its ruler. The main British military base was situated 20 kilometers away at Mhow with one infantry regiment, a detachment of cavalry and British artillery. (132-174) Some troops were also stationed at Mahidpur and Indore. The former was headquarters of the united Malwa army, and Indore that of the Malwa-Bhil force.[12] Besides these troops, the Maharaja had a personal force of 10,150. (86-89)

British officers had come to the conclusion that the troops at Mhow could not be trusted on account of rebellions taking place everywhere. They had received information that cavalry soldiers were inciting the infantry to rebel. (141-312) They feared a rebellion at Mhow on 16th May itself. (86-121) For this reason, efforts were made to bring in troops from other places. Sepoys at Neemuch in Rajputana were in close contact with those at Mhow. Thus, British officers became unsettled when news of the 4th June revolt at Neemuch reached them. Sepoys at Mahidpur rebelled on 10th June, killing two British officers. This provided further encouragement to sepoys at Mhow. An entreaty for assistance had been sent by the British to the Maharaja, who had even detailed some troops in response. (122) The Maharaja himself had cautioned the British about the rebellious tendency of the army. (141-313) Moreover, he also had apprehensions that his own state army might rebel.

Preparations for rebellion were completed by the end of June and sepoys were merely awaiting a suitable opportunity. Finally, it was decided that they would revolt on 1st July, with the state army taking the lead. (86-124)

---

12. The total deployment at the three bases was as follows : Mhow: 1,679 (120 British officers); Mahidpur: 1,566; Indore: 560. (86-87, 8)

Accordingly, the state army at Indore rebelled on 1st July. The Residency was attacked. The detachment of Bhopal sepoys that had been brought in to curb possible rebellion, disobeyed their officers' commands and, instead of opposing rebels, actually went and joined up with them. (124) Their leaders later took principal roles in the uprising. Consequently, finding it impossible to counter rebels, the British quietly moved out from the scene on the same day. Twenty-eight Englishmen were killed in this incident. The Residency was evacuated and rebels plundered it. Houses were set on fire. (130)

The commander of the cavalry then went to the Palace and demanded more troops from the Maharaja. When his identity as rebel leader was discovered, the Maharaja had him arrested, only to release him later in view of the military power he enjoyed. The man then began conducting himself as 'Nawab Sadat Khan'. (131)

The Maharaja immediately informed the British administration that he had no hand in the rebellion and explained that he had no control left over his troops. As those circumstances were factual, it did not take the British long to be convinced. Thereafter, rebels were in control in Indore for three days.

As previously planned, sepoys in Mhow rose in rebellion on the same night, immediately after news of the Indore revolt was received. Local officers were killed. Then, the Mhow and Indore rebels left for Agra via Gwalior. They carried with them all that they had looted.

Rebel Forces Towards Agra

The Maharaja sent a force in pursuit to apprehend them, but there was a tacit understanding and sympathy between the two forces, and the pursuers returned without success. By several stages, the rebel force reached Gwalior on 1st August. They intended to take the Gwalior rebels with them. Prince Firoz Shah was encamped in the place with 1,000 soldiers. (111-475) The Maharaja of Gwalior just about managed to somehow prevent them from leaving Gwalior for Agra. The Indore and Mhow rebels halted for one month and moved out on 5th September for Agra via Dholpur. As the Raja of Dholpur refused to assist them, an armed conflict ensued in which 25 of the Raja's soldiers were killed and rebels took control of Dholpur. Firoz Shah was leading the rebels at the time. (141-314)

Thorough preparations were made to launch an assault on Agra. Five hundred ladders were made for scaling the Agra ramparts. The rebel force, led by Prince Firoz Shah, was 22 kilometers away from Agra on 10th October. (86-106) British forces had captured Delhi just twenty days ago and troops, sent from there for providing security to Agra, had arrived. The rebels would now have to engage this force.

Uprisings in these larger States in Malwa were bound to affect smaller States and principalities. Dhar, located 50 kilometers from Indore, was ruled by 13-year old Anandrao. Taking advantage of internecine strife among courtiers, sepoys rebelled against their own ruler on 31st August and took possession of the fort. (138) They consisted of a majority of Makrani, Vilayati and Pathan Muslims. (44-173; 141-316; 68-492) By October, their strength had grown to such an extent that they began opposing the British. Plundering and looting became commonplace. However, Anandrao was a British-loyalist. His mother, the Regent, appealed for British help. The latter captured and razed the fort on 31st October. (141-317; 44-173) Rebels then went away to Mundsore.

Bakhtawar Singh was ruler of Amjhera and his force had a large proportion of Arabs and Afghans. Sepoys such as these used to be regularly supplied from there. (44-173) Those sepoys rebelled on 3rd July and brought an end to British control. The Union Jack was taken off and burned. However, the revolt was put down completely by the British in the same month. The Raja tendered an explanation that he had nothing to do with the rebellion but that his courtiers had engineered it. (86-142)

Bhopal was a Muslim State which was ruled on behalf of a minor princess by Sikandar Begum. While she was loyal to the British, most of the prominent nobles, army commanders and kinsmen were anti-British. They had advised the Begum and indeed even been insistent that she ought to fight the British. (145) She had intimated the British about the rebellious mood of her armed forces and kept them abreast of conspiracies. Preparation for a rebellion and general public discussion about it was going on in Bhopal. She had even advised the British to leave Bhopal and go elsewhere for their own security. The rebel leaders here were the same people who hatched the conspiracy in Indore. (126, 145)

Sehore, 32 kilometers from Bhopal, had a British cantonment. It had to be abandoned because sepoys had rebelled on 9th July. Rebels ruled over the palace till the end of November. The British had handed over the cantonment to the Begum, but sepoys obeyed none of her orders. (86-153; 132-96)

Rebellions also occurred at Sipri, Agar, Mandaleshwar, Manpur and some other places in Malwa. All these were essentially of a similar nature.

Prince's Rule at Mundsore

Finally, we must review the significant Uprising at Mundsore in the Gwalior State. It had links to the Indore State and cantonments in Rajputana.

The 20–22-year old Firoz Shah, who hailed from the Mughal dynasty, came here in August 1857 with thousands of his followers and defeated the British to establish an Islamic state. (5-146; 141-310) He had gathered a fighting force exceeding 20,000. (72-175; 86-143) The number had increased in later times to between 1.3 and 1.5 lacs.[13] This force began attacking neighbouring principalities and regions with Mundsore as its base. Nahargadh was attacked, captured and plundered. Sitamau was also taken. In September, the prince captured Mahidpur and appointed his Subedar. (86-147) Mundsore became a center for revolution. An emergent situation developed in the region. Contacts were established with rebels at places like Dhar and Amjhera. (143, 4)

---

13. 1.3 lacs (3-463; 72-182); 1.5 lacs (4-656; 7-379; 87-62).

Besides all of this, the prince dispatched a force in October to attack Neemuch. By mid October, they had captured the fortified town of Jiran, 16 kilometers from Neemuch. A British force that had been detailed to drive them away, was defeated on 23rd October. (87-59) Captains Tucker and Reed were killed in the battle while five others were wounded.

Then, on 8th November, his force of 5,000 fell upon Neemuch. The British troops retreated into the fort. Rebels laid a siege for 15 days and rained cannon fire. Ladders were also put up against the walls to gain entry within.

But precisely at this time, news was received that British troops were advancing towards Mundsore. The prince's detachment of 2,000 had, on the same day as Neemuch was invested (i.e. 8th Nov.), also encircled and captured Mahidpur. Security of Mundsore being the top priority, the Neemuch siege was lifted and the troops, along with those that had taken Mahidpur, were called back. A battle ensued on 24th November in which the prince suffered a defeat and Mundsore went back under British control. (87-61; 44-176)

Bundelkhand — Jhansi

We now turn to Bundelkhand — Jhansi.

This was part of the kingdom ruled by Raja Chhatrasal Bundela. He had to engage in incessant struggle for independence against Muhammad Khan Bangash, Nawab of Farukhabad. Bangash enjoyed support of the Mughal Emperor while Chhatrasal was supported by the Peshwa from Poona. At a particularly critical juncture (1729 C.E.), when Bangash had made a concerted attack, Chhatrasal had sent a missive to Peshwa Bajirao I stating: "A united Muslim force is attacking me with the intention of destroying the Hindu religion. I am fighting for the cause of protecting the religion. So, send me help." (48-15) The Peshwa had dispatched a force of 70,000. In gratitude, Chhatrasal divided his territory into three parts and bestowed one on Bajirao. The latter, in turn subdivided it into three more portions and allotted the first (Banda and Kalpi) to his illegitimate son Samsher Bahadur, the second (Sagar) to Govindpant Kher and the third (Jhansi) to Raghunath Nevalkar.

While each of these parts saw rebellion in varying degrees in 1857, the uprising in Jhansi proved significant and historic. The last inheritor of the political title to Jhansi, Gangadharrao, died (November 1853) without natural heir and his widow, Laxmibai (age 18 years), began administration as Queen. The British disallowed adoption of a male heir and annexed the state in March 1854. While she was assured a monthly privy purse of Rs. 5,000, the responsibility of repaying debts owed by her husband was heaped upon her. Moreover, she was made to relinquish her late husband's prestigious residence in the fort, and shift to a mansion in the town. While all this had made her unhappy, she had neither turned hostile nor swerved from her loyalty to the British.

Sepoys' Threat to the Rani

The British had stationed a total of 881 native sepoys and 11 English officers in Jhansi divided into one infantry, one cavalry and one artillery regiment. Some sepoys suddenly torched a few officers' bungalows on 1st June 1857. Even then, the British Captain had not lost trust in native sepoys. In the meantime, sepoys in Jhansi had received written communication from their counterparts in Delhi asking the former to rebel. Infantry and artillery sepoys rebelled on 5th June, setting fire to the cantonment office and officers' houses, setting prisoners free and looting the cantonment. They then invested the fort, which had the treasury, ammunition store and some British officers. The cavalry joined the mutiny on the following day (6th June). Five officers and the Captain were put to death. (82-73; 110-70) Realizing they were not likely to be safe even in the fort, the British sent for the Rani's help. But three of them who were on their way to see the Rani, were identified by sepoys and killed. (141-269) On the other hand, sepoys threatened her that if she assisted the British she would be killed and the palace burnt down. (82-74) Despite this threat, the Rani secretly supplied food to the besieged British for two days and detailed 100 musketeers to guard over them. (36-80; 39-67; 48-69)

On 8th June, sepoys assured the English of the safety of their lives and asked them to leave. However, when they emerged trusting the assurance given, they were caught, taken to nearby Jokhanbagh and slaughtered.[14] The dead were buried in a common grave three days later.

The rebel leaders then went to the Rani and made demands for money and artillery pieces threatening to destroy the palace if she declined. After much haggling and most reluctantly, she gave them Rs. 3 lacs and 2 field guns. Sepoys raised slogans in praise of the Rani and some of them left for Delhi on 11th June.[15] The Rani was thus compelled under threat to assume the throne of Jhansi.

She did not tarry in explaining to British authorities that she was forced to help rebels because of the threat they had issued. An official inquiry established that the Rani's defence was true and that she had no hand either in the rebellion or the massacre of Englishmen. (141-277) On the contrary, she was given authority to conduct administration of the Jhansi province on their behalf. (110-76; 36-88) She accepted that responsibility and sought additional military assistance from the British for the purpose of maintaining law and order. (126-353)

She was now faced with new challenges. Sadashivrao, a claimant to the Jhansi title, amassed a rebel force, captured the fort of Karera, 48 kilometers from Jhansi, and declared himself King of Jhansi. However, the Rani sent a force against him, defeated him in battle and put him in prison. (110-77; 141-278)

Then, in August, a force of 40,000 under Natthe Khan, the Diwan and General from the neighbouring State of Orchha, attacked Jhansi and laid siege for a month and a half. The

---

14. Sources vary in respect of the number killed. For example, 60 (132-69); 61 (81-216); 66 (110-72); 60, 70, 76 or 114 (39-65); 60 or 76 (36-78); 67, 76 or 107 (36-68); 110 (1-240); 76 (131-96).

15. 82-76; 110-73; 81-216; 131-97; 141-274; 39-69; 48-70.

Rani repelled this attack, too. (111-525; 141-278) She had made adequate provisions, anticipating just such an attack.

So, while she was engaged thus in fighting her own compatriots during that period, she had maintained amicable relations with the British and had been faced with no reason to fight them till March 1858. We will go into details of her later conflict with the British subsequently.

A detachment of the infantry and cavalry units stationed at Jhansi was detailed at Nowgong, 360 kilometers away. Sepoys in that detachment rebelled on 9th June when they received news of the revolt in Jhansi. Several officers were killed. Survivors fled from the place with women and children. But most of them were later pursued and killed. (132-72; 82-76)

Similar mutinies occurred at other places in Bundelkhand like Lalitpur, Sagar, Jabalpur, Jalon, Hoshangabad and Rahatgadh. In effect, British rule had ended in whole of Bundelkhand by August 1857. (126-282; 82-i)

Bihar

The region in North India remaining to be discussed is Bihar.

Patna, the headquarters of the Waliullahi movement, was the centre of the mutiny in Bihar. Besides, Kunwar Singh of Shahabad in the same region had figured prominently as a rebel leader in the 1857 uprising.

A total of 3,000 sepoys in three native infantry regiments and a detachment of an artillery unit were stationed at Danapur, 20 kilometers from Patna. In addition to this, there was also a Regiment of British soldiers and artillery. Uprisings at Meerut (10th May 1857) and Benares (4th June) had caused much unrest among sepoys. Superiors did not give approval to Commissioner Taylor's decision of disarming regiments. One sepoy was hanged on 12th June on charges of treason. A comprehensive strategy to overthrow British rule was taking shape in Patna and its leaders were engaged in spreading rebellion among sepoys in cantonments. Taylor summoned three such leaders on 19th June to his residence and had them arrested. Martial law was imposed from Patna to Gorakhpur, and public movement after 9 p.m. was prohibited.

Despite such precautionary measures, rebels took out a march through the city on 3rd July, brandishing their flags and beating drums. One officer was put to death. Additional security forces were called out and the street revolt was crushed. One of the rebels was killed and several wounded. Their chief leader, Pir Ali, was arrested. Forty-three persons were tried and 19 of them, including Pir Ali, were sentenced to death by hanging, five were awarded life imprisonment and 16 were given various other punishments. These sentences were executed immediately. (141-247) A decision was then taken to disarm native regiments at Danapur. However, because the officer detailed to perform this duty did so (25th July) in an incorrect manner and without taking assistance of the British regiments, most of the rebel sepoys managed to escape towards Arah. British troops went in pursuit on the following day but failed to apprehend them. (130-147; 141-251)

Kunwar Singh of Jagdishpur

Arah was at a distance of 40 kilometers from Danapur, and headquarters of the Shahabad district. The octogenarian Kunwar Singh of Shahabad was a major landholder and wielded great influence over the region. His managers and employees, taking advantage of his illiteracy, had defrauded him in financial matters and the old man found himself in deep debt (Rs.13 lacs). (141-252) He had become bankrupt. (81-167; 153-18) He was a British-loyalist and had assisted them in 1853 to crush a rebellion in the Arah prison. (67-166) He enjoyed special trust of the Commissioner of Bihar, Taylor. (141-254; 153-21, 2) He had been making incessant appeals and entreaties to the British administration to help him in redeeming his debt. But, as the administration had done nothing to alleviate his situation, he was also upset with it. Kunwar Singh was courageous and valiant, and enjoyed immense popularity. Nearby Jagdishpur was his place of residence.

The situation in Arah deteriorated when more than 2,000 of the Danapur rebels arrived there on 27th July. The British treasury was plundered and 400 prisoners were set free. (153-28) Some Englishmen, who were at Arah, and 50 Sikh policemen took refuge in a Railway Engineer's house and defended it like a small fort against the siege laid by rebels.

After reaching Arah, sepoys demanded Kunwar Singh's men to fetch him from Jagdishpur, threatening to loot that town if they did not comply. In response to the threat, Kunwar Singh went to Arah. (144-255; 67-168; 153-20) He was forced to assume leadership of the rebels. (67-170) The siege continued under his leadership.

Capt. Dunbar, with 415 troops and 15 officers, was on his way to Arah on 29th July to force rebels to lift the siege. But they were ambushed and routed by Kunwar Singh's men one night, the Captain, his officers and 184 soldiers being killed. Many more were killed while they were attempting to flee. Only 3 officers and 50 men escaped with their lives. This was a shocking defeat for the British but a heartening triumph for the rebels.

Vincent Eyre, a British artillery officer, was on his way to Allahabad when he received news of this defeat. He had just 220 men and 3 field guns. Yet, he decided to head for Arah with barely half the number of soldiers that had been decimated.

Fall of Jagdishpur

Kunwar Singh tried to block Eyre's force at a number of places and several fierce skirmishes were fought. But the rebels were frustrated by Eyre's cannons every time. Ultimately, the British force put the rebels to a rout on 2nd August, defeating an enemy 9 or 10 times as numerous as themselves, and took Arah. Englishmen and Sikhs, who had courageously defended an ordinary house against besiegers 50 times as numerous as themselves, were at long last freed the next day.

3,000 of Kunwar Singh's troops fled towards Jagdishpur and were pursued by the British. This town, which was Kunwar

Singh's headquarters, was captured on 12th August. Three hundred of his soldiers were killed. The town was plundered and atrocities heaped on the population. Kunwar abandoned his native region to shift westwards in North India, joining up with local rebel groups there and continuing his conflict with the British.

It will thus be seen that Uprisings had taken place in most parts of North India while Delhi was still in rebel control, i.e. till August-September 1857. Rebel administrations had been established in some areas, which were still in place. Rebels were dominant in Delhi, Agra, Ayodhya Province, Rohilkhand, Gorakhpur and the Doab region. The British had put down rebellions in some places and reestablished their rule in areas like Punjab, Bihar, Kanpur, Benares and Allahabad. Remnants of rebel activity were still noticeable in Malwa and Bundelkhand. Let us now review how the British, beginning with Delhi, finally neutralized rebel rule, dominance and activity.

- 2 -

How the Mutiny was Quelled

The Emperor's rule had begun in Delhi on 11th May 1857. He was the 'object of inspiration' of the entire Uprising and resided in the city. Rebel sepoys from various parts had converged on Delhi amid roars of 'Chalo Delhi!' after the mutiny; 60,000 of them had assembled by 3rd August. (121-179) Moreover, Delhi was difficult to capture. The 11 – 12 kilometer circumference of the city was protected by a 24-foot high and 7-foot wide rampart on three sides with the natural barrier of the Yamuna River on the fourth. The wall was impregnable to cannon fire. A hundred and fourteen guns were mounted on the ramparts. Seven gates facilitated entry into the city but were adequately guarded. A large force was required to reduce such a formidable objective.

Battle of Hindan

The British, however, were making attempts from the end of May to establish a base at some vantage point with whatever troops then deployable. By that time, the Uprising in Punjab had been put down and their forces there were relatively free to be employed in the Delhi campaign. A division from Ambala was called in, and it was decided to move towards Delhi with a total force of 3,000 which included this contingent and another from Meerut. The Meerut contingent of 700, under command of Brig. Wilson, left first but was sought to be stopped in its march on 30th May by 3,000 rebel troops under Prince Mirza Abu Bakr at Ghaziuddinnagar on the banks of the Hindan River, 24 kilometers from Delhi. (132-56; 67-72) However, the Prince suffered a comprehensive defeat, with heavy casualties. Another encounter on the following day resulted in a second rout of Delhi forces similar to the first. This is known as the Battle of Hindan.

British Occupation of the Ridge

The Meerut and Ambala units combined on 7th June and halted at Badli-ki-Sarai, seven kilometers from Delhi. A fierce battle was fought the next day between the British and rebel forces under Prince Mirza Khizr Sultan who lost 350 to 400 men and 26 field guns. The British then occupied the strategically advantageous ridge around Delhi, at an elevation of 80 to 100 feet more than the city. Not only was the location excellent from the aspect of defence, it was also ideally suited as a base for launching an assault on the city. Moreover, it was adjacent to a portion of the city wall. The British had, within the space of a month since the rebellion, established a base in proximity of Delhi.

Many attacks were subsequently launched to dislodge them from their vantage point. Groups of fresh sepoy rebels arriving in Delhi from time to time, launched a succession of attacks. But they were all in vain. A total of 32 battles were fought within a span of 96 days from 10th June to 14th September but in none of them did Delhi sepoys succeed. 3,000 British troops were tenaciously holding their position against more than 40,000 sepoys who, incidentally, had been given military training by the British themselves. (130-187; 44-38)

Battle of Najafgarh

The British needed more troops to gain control of Delhi. A large force was dispatched in phases from Punjab under Nicolson's command. They were assisted on the way by British-loyalist Sikh rulers of Patiala, Nabha and Jind. The first unit reached Najafgarh, 32 kilometers from Delhi, on 25th August and halted there. It consisted of 2,050 soldiers and 16 cannons. A battle against Commander-in-Chief Bakht Khan and his 6,000 sepoys ensued. The Khan was put to a rout, losing 800 men. The British appropriated 13 cannons. (130-193; 69-111)

The last unit arrived from Punjab on 4th September. Now the British had a force of 11,000. Of them 3,317 were British and the remaining, Sikhs and other native soldiers. (126-291) A military strategy to gain victory over Delhi was then drawn up.

British Victory over Delhi

The assaulting force was divided into four units, each under independent command. One more unit was kept as a reserve. The force entered Delhi on 14th September from different directions. The Kashmere Gate was breached to facilitate British entry. After overcoming stiff resistance from the defenders, the British gained complete control over the city on 20th September. Many pages of history are filled with accounts of this struggle. A final fierce battle was fought in the Jama Masjid. The Red Fort and the Imperial Palace was occupied on the same day and a victory celebration was performed there. Wilson, the Chief of Staff, set up his headquarters in the Red Fort. The British had become masters of Delhi after 134 days.

Commander-in-Chief Bakht Khan found an opportunity on the same day to desert Delhi and escape towards Lucknow. Bahadur Shah left the Palace and moved to the nearby Humayun Tomb. He was asked to surrender after assuring him that his life would be spared. He went into British custody the following day. He was put on trial later on but was not sentenced to death, on account of the assurance of amnesty, but transported for life in September 1858 to Rangoon, where he died in 1862. All 24 princes of his household were executed either by firing squad or hanging. (141-106; 43-70)

The British had lost 3,000 soldiers in the struggle for Delhi that waged from 30th May to 20th September. (111-504) Nicolson, along with 1,042 soldiers, was killed during the last six days, while 2,795 were wounded. (126-308; 70-133; 141-104) Of them 2,151 were British and 1,686 were native soldiers. At least 3,000 persons were sentenced to death. (70-127) 27 to 30 thousand people lost their lives in a variety of ways. (17-147; 69-ix) Delhi had become virtually depopulated as people had fled in large numbers. (141-109) Soldiers were given permission to plunder the city to their heart's content. Delhi of that time is referred to as 'The City of the Dead'. (141-109; 126-307) [An entire chapter is entitled 'The City of the Dead' in Nigam's and Dalrymple's books. (69-148; 154-393)]

The victory over Delhi was a harbinger of the suppression of rebellion in other places. The very source of inspiration for rebellion — Bahadur Shah — was no longer the Emperor. British officers forthwith commenced the work of breaking up rebellions at other places. Their morale was on the rise and that of rebels, on the decline.

Battle for Agra

A flying squad of 2,790 soldiers was dispatched on 24th September to Agra under command of Edward Greathed. On 28th September, on the way to Agra, the force captured Bulandshahar, an important rebel base. It had been under the rule of Walidad Khan, Nawab of Malgadh, since 22nd May. Malgadh, too, was captured and the fort demolished. (130-209; 132-132) The Nawab fled to Bareilly.

Then the British army took Aligarh on 5th October. Rebel sepoys, who had been there since 22nd May, vacated the town and fled when they saw the approaching British army. They were pursued and 250 [400, according to another source (7-869)] of them were hunted down and killed. (130-209; 132-134)

The situation of the British in Agra, who had taken refuge in the fort, had become pitiable at the time. Rebel rule had commenced from 5th July. Moreover, rebel sepoys from Mhow and Indore under leadership of Prince Firoz Shah had camped 22 kilometers away with the intention of completing the conquest of Agra. As soon as this information was received, the British force moved quickly to reach Agra on 10th October. Almost at the same time, some rebel troops, too, had reached Agra in advance of the main party. A battle ensued between the two on the same day and the rebels suffered a defeat. Two thousand of them lay dead on the battlefield. (132-135) All of their war material fell into British hands. This is known as the Battle of Agra.

British administration was immediately set up in Agra and environs. The victorious British troops indulged for a few days in plundering and destroying the region. The rebel administration there, which had been in place since 22nd May, thus came to an end.

Lucknow: Battle for Relief of the Residency

Several British personnel had been besieged in the Lucknow Residency since 1st July. Forcing an end to the impasse had become imperative. Although some reinforcements had reached within the precincts, the siege still continued. Greathed had been replaced by Hope Grant, who received a desperate missive on 21st October from James Outram, the commander within the Residency, to rush to their rescue as supplies of essential commodities were almost exhausted. Hope Grant thus reached Kanpur on 26th October.

Then, Hope Grant from Kanpur and Commander-in-Chief Sir Colin Campbell from Calcutta joined forces on 9th November at Alambagh, six kilometers from Lucknow and under British control since 23rd September. The strength of the British force had now reached about 5,000. (132-143) As against this, the rebel Nawab commanded a force of 55,050 [1 lac, according to another source (141-219)]. (106-181)

An assault commenced on 13th November after drawing up a comprehensive strategy. Jalalabad, on the way to

Lucknow, was attacked on the same day and the Ayodhya defenders, with a loss of 212 dead, were put to flight. The British demolished the local fortress.

Then, on 16th November, the British troops entered Lucknow from two directions of less resistance. A fierce battle was fought that day at Sikandarbagh. 3,000 rebels offered stiff resistance but were helpless against British artillery and were defeated. More than 2,000 of them lay dead after the event. (141-225; 106-193) [Dr. Chaudhary states this figure as 3,000. (81-47)]

The British forces then attacked Shah Najaf, a place constructed by the first Nawab of Ayodhya, Ghazi-ud-Din Haider where he and his Begum had been buried. A large rebel force was concentrated there. The British prevailed after a hard, three-hour battle, fought till the last of the defenders had fallen. The British lost 122 men while 414 suffered wounds. (106-194)

Another encounter at Begum Kothi on 17th November left 672 rebel sepoys dead. (196) Likewise, Moti Mahal was demolished. Gaining one success after another, the Commander-in-Chief entered the Residency on 17th November. In this two-day campaign, the British casualties were 550 dead and wounded. (46-201)

The only objective of the campaign was to launch a surprise attack on the Residency and free personnel who were inside. This was successfully achieved and all of them were sent to Allahabad via Kanpur on 27th November, with Sir Colin Campbell personally accompanying them. The Residency was evacuated and forces withdrawn from Lucknow. However, Outram remained camped at nearby Alambagh with 4,000 troops. The 142-day long siege of the Residency was ended in this manner, but Lucknow continued to be ruled by Begum Hazrat Mahal. (132-146; 130-225)

Over One Lac Sepoys in Lucknow

Sepoys in Lucknow regarded the British exit as their triumph. They hoisted their flag over the now vacant Residency to replace that of the English. 101 guns were fired in token of victory.[16] Hazrat Mahal convened a war council and it was decided to oust the enemy from the entire Ayodhya province. It was also resolved to reinstate Bahadur Shah on the throne at Delhi after defeating the British with liaison and cooperation of other States. (106-200)

With British withdrawal from Lucknow began a flow of sepoys from everywhere. By the end of December 1857, almost one hundred thousand sepoys from places like Delhi, Kanpur and Farrukhabad poured into the town. (206) Assembled in Lucknow on 1st December were 85,000 trained sepoys and 45,000 volunteers who were untrained but wielded muskets.[17] (210) Besides this number, the local population had 2 lacs that wielded arms. They possessed lethal weapons like swords, spears and muskets. No other town in India had such militant inhabitants. (40)

Capturing Lucknow was as important to the British as gaining control over Delhi. However, on account of the circumstances discussed above, they felt they would need about 30,000 troops to achieve the conquest. (141-234; 46-224) By terms of a treaty with the Maharaja of Nepal, the British were awaiting the arrival in March 1858 of a force of 10,000 from that State. (141-236) The campaign for Lucknow was thus postponed for the time being.

In the meantime, Outram's camp at Alambagh came frequently under rebel attack under orders of M. Ahmad Shah. Indeed, as many as 30,000 sepoys marched upon them on 12th January 1858. (130-240) But the attack was repulsed. In a like manner, the British force remained determinedly entrenched bracing and repelling all such attacks.

---

16. Roshan Taqvi has this comment: "By the departure of Firangis from Lucknow, the first battle of Lucknow had been won by Indian patriotic forces." (106-205)

17. According to Malleson, they had 1,20,000 sepoys. 33,650 were trained while 20,000 were from various talukdars. The rest were armed volunteers. (130-241) Saul David also states the figure of 1,20,000. (126-336)

Victory over Lucknow

Sir Colin Campbell prepared to launch an attack on Lucknow in March 1858 after making thorough preparation. Including the Nepal contingent, he had a force of 30,000.[18] (141-237) Sepoys had secured three approaches to Lucknow reasonably well. However, the fourth on the north was somewhat neglected. Once Campbell had received this intelligence, he decided to force an entry into Lucknow from that direction.

The campaign began on 2nd March and lasted till the 21st. Skirmishes, big and small, occurred daily. M. Ahmad Shah led the rebels. It was from 13th March that confrontation began in all seriousness. A fierce battle at Begum Kothi left 860 rebels dead. (106-261) All important places in the city were under British control by 18th March.

Many soldiers along with Ahmad Shah were lying in wait in Musabaug. He remained there till 18th March. Campbell's attack on the place was bitterly resisted, but 400–500 rebels were killed. (46-229) Twenty thousand sepoys, including M. Ahmad Shah, managed to escape from there along the Faizabad road. (130-246; 141-237) However, they soon regrouped under the Maulvi's leadership and returned to the city, concealing themselves in a certain place. They were ultimately driven out on 21st March. They offered stiff resistance even at that time. The British casualties in the entire Lucknow campaign were just 127 dead and 597 wounded. (126-343)

The British had won a decisive victory over Lucknow. Begum Hazrat Mahal, Prince Firoz Shah and others had deserted the palace and slipped away. The city was plundered.

Thereafter, by the end of 1858, the entire Ayodhya province was brought under British control in phases. The

18. However, Roshan Taqvi states that the British strength (including the Nepal contingent) at the time was 69,517 — 59,840 infantry and 11,677 cavalry along with 132 field guns.

Begum's regime, which had come into existence on 5th July 1857, was completely uprooted from Lucknow in March and from the whole of Ayodhya in December 1858.[19]

Tatya's Victory over Kanpur

At about the same time as efforts were in progress to relieve Englishmen at the Residency in Lucknow, a large force of sepoys was gathering under Tatya Tope's command at the new headquarters of the Peshwa at Kalpi in Bundelkhand and was becoming a reason for anxiety for Kanpur, 65 kilometers away. Gwalior sepoys had rebelled as early as 14th June 1857, but the Maharaja had succeeded in his strategy to prevent them from leaving the town and going elsewhere. Tatya had visited Gwalior in September to try and win those sepoys over to his side. His efforts were fruitful and 5,000 sepoys with 40 cannons arrived in Kalpi. (111-477; 108-160) At the same time, Kunwar Singh of Jagdishpur, having suffered defeat at the hands of the British, came to Kalpi after first visiting Banda. A force of 25,000 had assembled under Tatya's command.[20] (130-228; 132-151)

---

19. The following statistics of the number of people killed and weapons recovered is sufficient to give an idea of how formidable the conquest of Ayodhya province must have been. A total of about 1.5 lac people fell to British arms during the entire period of the uprising in Ayodhya. 35,000 of these were soldiers and the rest were civilians. (44-130; 16-43) 1,400 fortifications in the province were demolished. 900 cannons were acquired from rebel forces. Besides this, 3,07,372 firearms, 14,21,223 swords, 6,64,015 spears and 12,15,275 daggers or similar lethal short bladed weapons were confiscated. These figures exclude the 14,00,000 weapons that continued to remain in possession of the people. (44-310) 75,000 Indians lost their lives to British army only in the single event of the conquest of Lucknow. This number includes those executed after the conquest. (111-567)

20. According to Misra's book, Tatya had 15,000 troops and 140 cannons. (111-482) This variation is on account of exclusion of untrained fighters from the number. (132-149)

The security of Kanpur at that time was entrusted to Windham. He initially had 500 soldiers under his command, but later reinforcements had increased his strength to 2,400. (111-479) Tatya crossed the Yamuna River to march towards Kanpur on the day after Campbell left in force for Lucknow in November. British attempts on 26th November to block Tatya's march near the Pandu River, 11 kilometers from Kanpur, ended in defeat. Both sides suffered heavily. This is known as the Second Battle of Kanpur. The British took refuge inside the fort on the following day. Tatya then proceeded to Kanpur and took control of the town on 29th November. (108-161; 141-230)

Kanpur Recaptured by the British

Campbell learnt of the fall of Kanpur when he was marching back after the Lucknow campaign. Tatya had left the bridge across the river intact. The British force crossed the Ganga River on 30th November and encamped in the vicinity of Kanpur. After completing the task of dispatching women and children rescued from the Lucknow Residency to Allahabad, Campbell concentrated on drawing up a strategy to retake Kanpur. He had 5,600 soldiers and 35 cannons. Tatya's army was suddenly and forcefully attacked on 6th December when his sepoys were preparing to eat. They ran helter-skelter in sheer panic. Tatya was defeated in the ensuing battle. (130-228; 111-482) They fled along the road to Kalpi and were chased to a distance of 22 kilometers. Tatya and some of his soldiers, who were fleeing towards Bithoor, were chased right up to their destination. Then that town was destroyed, Nanasahib's palace was plundered of its great wealth and burned down. A large cache of valuables that had been thrown into a well when Nanasahib had fled from the town was recovered. (108-165) This is known as the Third Battle of Kanpur. British control was once again established. Tatya's one-week regime came to an end.

March on Jhansi

The campaign for retrieving Bundelkhand was progressing in tandem with the one for taking Lucknow. Jhansi in this region was the prime objective. Although it had been established that Rani Laxmibai had no hand in the June Uprising and she was conducting administration on behalf of the British under the aegis of the Union Jack flying over the fort even after the revolt, higher British authorities had, on the one hand, resolved to capture Jhansi and her detractors, on the other, had prevented her letters and explanations from reaching them. (36-95) When armed conflict with the British became inevitable, she donned the mantle of a warrior and her subsequent heroism adorns the annals of history in letters of gold.

Three divisions of the army were readied for the conquest of Bundelkhand. They were to execute the campaign in co-operation with one another. One of the divisions was led by Hugh Rose. He was a brave soldier, skilled strategist and experienced commander. His accomplishments were acknowledged by his appointment on the Jhansi campaign.

He began moving from the direction of Sagar on 6th January 1858. The fort of Rahatgarh, which was on the way and had been in rebel control since July 1857, was taken on 26th January after a four-day struggle. (39-83; 82-107) Chief Mardan Singh of Banpur had arrived there with assistance for the rebels. Afterwards, rebel sepoys and Mardan Singh sought refuge in Barodia, 24 kilometers away. Rose went in pursuit and again routed them there. (100-108; 141-283)

Rose, with a force of 2,000, reached Sagar on 3rd February. He made short shrift of rebels there and freed British personnel in the fort. The formidable fort at Gadkot, 40 kilometers away, was wrested from rebels. (36-113; 110-108) Dealing with rebels in this manner, Rose arrived at a distance of 22 kilometers from Jhansi on 20th March.

The Siege of Jhansi

The fort was very strong. A protective wall, 30 foot high and 16–20 foot wide, encircled the town and fort. The rampart had many high towers embedded along its length and housed 51 cannons. A moat surrounded the walls. The garrison was 11,000 strong. (48-125; 130-260) The Rani had made necessary provisions for repelling attacks from the neighbouring Orchha and Datia states. That same preparedness was now going to be useful in fighting the British aggression.

Rose began a barrage of cannon balls on the walls on the following day. The defenders responded by firing the cannons from the ramparts. This exchange of cannon fire and the consequent loss of life continued till 31st March. The Rani sent an appeal for help to Raosahib Peshwa at Kalpi. Tatya Tope had just returned after his victory over Charkhari. He immediately set off with 22,000 soldiers and 28 cannons to the Rani's relief. (5-585; 110-119)

Rose became apprehensive at the approaching Tatya and his huge force. Lifting the siege would have sent signals of defeat; not lifting it or lifting it to direct it against Tatya would have exposed their rear to the Jhansi forces. Nevertheless, summoning a great deal of courage, he detailed 1,500 soldiers with some cannons to block Tatya's march. (131-133; 130-261) The strengths of the contending forces were heavily disparate. A battle was joined on 1st April in the vicinity of the Betwa River. The British opened fire with their cannons on both flanks of Tatya's army which created havoc in its rank and file, resulting in sepoys fleeing from the battlefield out of sheer fright.[21] British troops chased them to a distance of 25 kilometers. Tatya lost 1,500 men. The British casualties were just 15 dead and 66 wounded. (110-125; 36-135) This was a victory won within a few hours against a force 15 times as numerous. A large quantity of Tatya's war material fell into British hands and the detachment returned to Jhansi.

A remarkable aspect was that neither were cannons fired upon British soldiers from within the fort nor did soldiers emerge to attack them during this engagement. (39-95; 131-134) The siege was kept going by 500 British soldiers.

---

21. Savarkar writes about this: "Alas! A most shameful poltroonish cowardice was exhibited by the Revolutionary troops.... The English charged straight on the enemy. The cowards did not even offer to fight.... So, the army and its commander (Tatya Tope) were routed and ran away... mad men and fools!....." (1-468)

The Rani's Valour

Rose began his offensive against the fort. Ladders were put up against the ramparts on 3rd April to facilitate attackers to climb over the fortification and gain entry. British troops tenaciously persisted in ascending the ladders despite the fact that those who had gone up were being killed by the defenders. Alarms of the emergent precarious situation were passed around inside the fort. Many of the Rani's men had fallen. Tatya's rout had made the Rani aware of certain impending defeat. (39-97) Nevertheless, she continued raining cannon fire upon the British without losing hope.

The next day (4th April) the Rani personally took the sword in hand and led 1,500 soldiers to one of the gates to give battle. However, being advised by elders that it was improper to risk her life, she went back inside the fort. Two of her skilled and brave cannoneers were killed on the same day which snatched away a great source of her strength. She even considered suicide, but was dissuaded from doing so by elders.

Ultimately, she decided to escape and go to the Peshwa. She escaped on horseback from the fort in the darkness of night with her adopted son. Learning that she had slipped away, British troops went in hot pursuit for 40 kilometers but could not apprehend her. She reached Kalpi at midnight on 5th April after an arduous ride of 165 kilometers in 24 hours. (39-104; 126-360)

British Victory over Jhansi

The British took control of the fort after battling against determined and tenacious defenders for 13 days, losing 343 men in the process. (36-163) Soldier and civilian alike were treated with utmost cruelty in reprisal. The plunder of the town went on for seven days. Flames were seen everywhere. Corpses were strewn around in heaps. At least 5,000 civilians had been killed. (110-139; 132-187; 130-262) As Godse Bhatji wrote, "every street had become a cemetery". (123-101)

The Rani's valour during the defence of Jhansi and thereafter justly earned her an unassailable place in history as the veritable 'Goddess of War'!

Peshwa's Defeat at Kunch

Kalpi had become the Peshwa's headquarters and a rendezvous of rebel leaders after the British capture of Kanpur. Kunwar Singh of Jagdishpur, Nawab of Farrukhabad and Chief of Banpur had gone there. The Nawab of Banda, whose force of 6,000 had suffered defeat at the hands of Whitlock on 19th April, had arrived with 4,000 troops in Kalpi. (82-149; 126-362) Now the Rani of Jhansi had also reached.

Rose decided to capture Kalpi and left Jhansi on 25th April. Reinforcements had arrived and his army had gained in strength. The summer heat was taking its toll on British soldiers. Nanasahib's nephew, Raosahib Peshwa, left Kalpi with 10,000 sepoys and 12 cannons in order to stop Rose's advance, and halted at Kunch, 37 kilometers away. The Rani and Tatya accompanied him. But this force was defeated in a battle fought on 7th May, with a loss of 600 soldiers and six cannons. (126-362) The British forces occupied Kunch town and the nearby Lohari fort.

Defeat in Kalpi, too

The Peshwa and his army returned to Kalpi after the Kunch defeat, followed by Rose. A battle was joined on 22nd May at a distance of 10 kilometers from Kalpi. The Rani was in virtual command of the army. Its strength was 20,000. (131-152; 36-173) The battle continued for three or four days and Raosahib, seeing defeat facing them, contemplated retreat. But the Rani opposed such a move and displayed immense valour in falling suddenly upon the enemy with a detachment of her force. The surprise move succeeded in scattering the enemy for some time. It is said that the swiftness of her movements in battle and personal skill were akin to lightning. She held the reins of her steed between her teeth so that she could wield a sword in each hand. (39-119; 48-161) By such peerless courage and indescribable enterprise, she became known as 'Ranachandika', or incarnation of Goddess Kali. Indeed, the British went so far as to call her 'the only notable man in the enemy camp', 'the bravest and best military leader of the rebels'. (36-14;

50-162) Despite all this, she had to surrender to the British. Kalpi was taken by them on 24th May. (39-121) The entire quantity of the Peshwa's war material fell into their hands. The union Jack was Unfurled over Kalpi after 11 months.

It is believed that Tatya had gone to Gwalior after the Kunch defeat to assess the situation of the rebel forces there. All the leaders at Kalpi decided to move to Gwalior and reached Gopalpur, 75 kilometers from Gwalior, along with their troops on 26th May. Tatya met them there. All of them were sure of assistance and cooperation of the Gwalior sepoys. Some had already arrived. But the rest had been held back by the Maharaja.

The Peshwa Takes Gwalior

The Peshwa's force under Tatya's command reached Gwalior and halted near the Murar cantonment on 30th May. The total force was 20,000. (82-152; 131-161) The Maharaja came out the following day with 9,100 soldiers and 8 cannons to confront the rebel force. An order to attack was issued but his army, instead of obeying the order, rebelled and joined up with the Peshwa's forces amid loud sloganeering. (110-179; 82-153) Gwalior was occupied without any significant resistance. The Maharaja fled to take refuge with the British in Agra. After a victorious entry into the town, Raosahib established his throne in the palace, and the fort was taken without much ado. Great quantities of war supplies were appropriated from there and the old palace was looted. The British residency was demolished. (39-132)

Raosahib's Enthronement

Raosahib was installed as the official Peshwa in great style on 3rd June, witnessed by hundreds of invitees. Prolific gifts and largesse were distributed. Thousands of Brahmins were sumptuously fed and culinary skills reached their acme. Brahmins were given donations in gold. The Peshwa distributed these alms attired in a light yellow silk dhoti (*peetambar*) and, with jewellery of pearls and diamonds, he certainly must have made a most enrapturing picture. The air was reechoing with Vedic chants, expressions of delight and sounds of percussion musical instruments. (36-209; 110-180) Rupees 20 lacs were distributed among sepoys. Astrologers became busy preparing horoscopes and casting predictions. The Rani, however, was unhappy with these celebrations and stayed away. (139-134; 126-365) Raosahib then made appointment of his officials and commenced his rule.

Rani's Death and the Fall of Gwalior

Rose was not idle while all this was taking place. He planned an assault from all sides on Gwalior. The cantonment at Murar was occupied on 16th June. The main confrontation was sparked off on the following day (17th June). The Rani and Tatya were exerting their utmost to ensure victory, with the Rani having personally taken the field. In fact, according to her biography, this battle was fought under her leadership. (39-140) The British were compelled to retreat initially against the Rani who was fighting with unparalleled speed and dauntlessness. But British forces finally prevailed and the Peshwa's prominent commanders as well as troops bolted from the battlefield. The Rani, however, continued to battle well into the following day (18th June). Her person had become so dusty that none could recognize her. Her contingent was encircled by the enemy, but she managed to find a gap and shoot out at great speed. A chase by the enemy ensued during which she was severely wounded and brought down from her horse by an enemy bullet. Even at that trying moment she remained firm and unshaken, giving a final bitter battle to her attackers before succumbing to her wounds. (39-143; 36-226; 48-182) She was just about 22–23 years of age at the time.

As stated by a noted scholar, Narhar Kurundkar, "Her life was embellished by her martyrdom... Martyrs' antecedents are not to be examined. Only the glorious period that imparted piety to their lives is worth reviewing." (150-118)

The Peshwa's forces were defeated and Gwalior re-occupied by the British. They had suffered just 87 dead and wounded. (110-204) The Peshwa's regime, established a mere

16 days previously in great pomp and pageantry, had come to an end. Gwalior was handed back to the Maharaja on 20th June.

Fatehgarh Reduced

Rebels now had only one stronghold remaining — Rohilkhand. It became necessary to take Fatehgarh, which lay on the Kanpur-Agra route and was a link between Rohilkhand and the Doab region. If one approached after crossing the Ganga River, Fatehgarh was the only place which facilitated entry to Rohilkhand. Control over that town meant a severe breakdown of rebel communication between Rohilkhand and Ayodhya provinces. Demolition work on a bridge across the Kali River had been initiated by rebels in order to hamper British movement. Campbell immediately detailed some troops there and a confrontation that occurred on 2nd January 1858 near the river resulted in the rebel force fleeing to Rohilkhand instead of Fatehgarh. The British took control of the town and the local fort. A large cache of military equipment was recovered. The fort was demolished. The Nawab of nearby Farrukhabad had been ruling over the town since 18th June 1857 which came to an end after seven months. That Nawab, along with Prince Firoz Shah who was then in the area, left for Rohilkhand to assist Nawab Khan Bahadur Khan.

The British then went on a spree of hangings in the surrounding region. Trees were used as gallows. A stage was reached when there was left no room even on those trees to hang the next victim. An extant record says as many as 130 persons were seen hanging from a single tree. (111-590; 44-219) A gallows was erected in the center of the town for hanging the Nawab's kin, this event drew spectators in droves. In this manner, Fatehgarh and Farrukhabad districts were brought under British control.

Rohilkhand Campaign

A difference of opinion arose among British officers over the next objective after Fatehgarh — Rohilkhand or Lucknow. It was decided to take Lucknow first, which had been accomplished in March 1858. Plans for the Rohilkhand campaign were drawn up in April. (141-354)

The force was divided into four and it was decided to make assaults from different directions. The final destination of all divisions was convergence at Bareilly, the principal town. A fifth division was kept stationed at Fatehgarh. The campaign was set into motion.

Walpole, commander of one division, carelessly attacked a fortress, held by local rebel leader Narpat Singh, at Ruia in the course of his march on 15th April because he did not expect resistance. But, contrary to his belief, the assault was met with such bitter retaliation that it left 112 British soldiers dead or wounded. Moreover, the Chief managed to slip away. Walpole was forced to retreat. Thereafter, conducting his part of the campaign according to plan, he met with Campbell on 3rd May.

Jones, another Commander, crossed the Ganga at Haridwar and encountered much opposition on the way. His march was once blocked at a small rivulet by Multani horsemen but they were soon dispersed. The Nawab of Najibabad was ensconced within the Khot fortress with 500 troops. Jones took that fort and arrested the Nawab. He then had to fight a bitter battle on 21st April at Nagina with 12,000 rebels who had arrived there with six cannons. It was only after vanquishing them that British power could be established over Bijnor district. (132-190)

The force under Jones' command reached Moradabad on 26th April. Prince Firoz Shah was at the place from 22nd April. Having driven away the Rampur Nawab's officials, he had assumed power as Chief. Now, hearing of Jones' advance, he scampered away and hid himself in the town. The British force came to know where he was hiding and raided the place. Twenty-one rebel leaders were killed in the skirmish but Firoz Shah slipped away. Administration of the Moradabad district was entrusted to the loyalist Nawab of Rampur. Then Jones proceeded according to plan and met with Campbell at Bareilly.

Cambell had encamped near Bareilly from 3rd May. He received intelligence that M. Ahmad Shah had arrived in nearby Shahjahanpur after his defeat at Lucknow. The British force turned to go there but by that time the Maulvi had made his escape towards Mohammadi, 30 kilometers away. (44-242; 132-193) Campbell stationed a detachment in Shahjahanpur and returned to Bareilly.

All the British divisions had united. The objective now was the principal center and capital of Rohilkhand — Bareilly. Nawab Khan Bahadur Khan had a force of 36,000 and 40 cannons under his command. Prince Firoz Shah, too, was there. The number of *ghazis* was large. The British attack of 5th May, the fierce battle that was joined and valour displayed by *ghazis* and sepoys has been narrated by many writers. But the British forces prevailed and their power was established over Bareilly. The battle left huge loss of life.

Seeing that the British force was engaged in Bareilly, M. Ahmad Shah left Mohammadi with 8,000 men and arrived in Shahjahanpur on 3rd May. He had planned to launch a surprise attack and take the town. The British force stationed there took refuge in a certain place. The Maulvi took control of the town and from 3rd to 11th May unleashed incessant cannon fire on the British position. Accompanying the Maulvi at the time were Begum Hazrat Mahal of Lucknow and Prince Firoz Shah. (44-244; 141-356) The Bareilly affair was over by that time and Jones went to Shahjahanpur on 11th may for relief of the garrison by which time some reinforcements had reached the Maulvi. Thus, Jones was forced to go on the defensive. (132-194) A concerted assault was launched on British positions on 15th May and were given a thorough mauling. This continued for a further three days. However, the British could not be ousted from their place. Campbell arrived in Shahjahanpur with a large force on 18th May after which the Maulvi retreated to Mohammadi along with Begum Hazrat Mahal and Prince Firoz Shah. He captured the Fort there and established an Islamic State. (77-191) The British took Mohammadi after a hard struggle on 24th May. (132-196; 72-186)

Thereafter, the Maulvi trustingly went to Jagannath Singh of Powain who put him to death on 15th June, sent his severed head to British authorities and claimed the reward of Rs. 50,000 announced by the administration for the wanted man. Thus ended the career of the 'crown jewel' of the 1857 Uprising. The greatest leader and mainstay of the revolutionaries was extinguished.

Campbell then sent detachments to various places and soon brought the whole of Rohilkhand province under British control. Khan Bahadur Khan's rule, which lasted for eleven and a half months from 31st May 1857, came to an end.

About 80,000 British troops had now assembled under Campbell's command. (44-250) The back of the rebels had been broken. Their citadels had been destroyed, and the states and administrations they had founded in the aftermath of the rebellion had been vanquished. Almost all mutinies in North India had been put down by April 1858. The Queen of England issued a declaration on 1st November 1858 by which the British Indian Empire was transferred from the East India Company to the Crown. The Company's administration thus came to an end and the Queen of England became the *de jure* ruler of India. With the exclusion of those charged with killing Englishmen, an amnesty was declared in respect of all rebels if they surrendered before 1st January 1859. Many submitted to this concession and secured pardon. Others tried very hard to obtain it but could not succeed. The government was able to put down all remaining elements of mutiny by April 1859.

- 3 -

Struggles of Some Leaders in the Final Phases

Although the main Uprising had been suppressed, some rebel leaders continued in their struggle even when there remained absolutely no hope of victory. We will briefly review what some of them did in those final phases. The chief among them were Kunwar Singh, Rana Beni Madhav Singh, Prince Firoz Shah, Begum Hazrat Mahal, Tatya Tope and Nanasahib Peshwa.

Kunwar Singh

After the fall of Jagdishpur in August 1857, Kunwar Singh joined forces with other rebel leaders in North India. He went to the Nawab of Banda with 2,000 men on 29th September. From there, on 18th October, he went to Kalpi. He took part in the battle at Kanpur in November. He then went to the Begum in Lucknow after Tatya's defeat at Kanpur, was accorded a grand welcome by the Begum and permitted to rule over Azamgarh. He did not take part in any struggle thereafter till February 1858.

However, in February, he decided to take advantage of the situation when only a skeleton force had been kept in Azamgarh after the main contingent of British troops had left for the Lucknow campaign.[22] Access to his native Jagdishpur was going to open up with control over Azamgarh. Accordingly, on 17th March, he gathered a fighting force and attacked and took Atrauli, a place 32 kilometers from Azamgarh, driving away the British soldiers stationed there. Then on 26th March, he took Azamgarh after a bitter struggle. The British force took refuge in the fortification which was invested. A fresh force was immediately dispatched from Lucknow when the Commander-in-Chief heard of the incidents. That force retook Azamgarh on 13th April. Kunwar Singh left that place and went away. The British went in pursuit.

Kunwar Singh suffered a severe bullet wound in his right arm before he could cross the Ganga River on 21st April. Without so much as a second thought, he cut it off himself and consigned it to the Ganga waters as he crossed over. (153-82; 132-190) Jagdishpur was captured with assistance of his 2,000 brave soldiers on the third day after a battle in which the British suffered a humiliating defeat, losing 100 men. This final triumph over his birthplace must have made him very content. However, he succumbed to the fatal wound in his arm and died on 26th April 1858. (153-93) His brother, Amar

22. Savarkar writes about this: "In the meanwhile, news reached him that troops, Nepalese and English, were being sent from Azamgarh into Oudh to destroy Lucknow. As soon as with his keen scent he scented the prey, the lion of Jagadishpur took one leap out of the forest." (1-419)

Singh, continued the struggle for some time more even when there remained no hope of success.

Rana Beni Madhav Singh

It was Rana Beni Madhav Singh who continued the fight in the Ayodhya province against the British after the fall of Lucknow. He was a major talukdar and zamindar of Shankarpur in the Rae Bareli district. Of 223 villages that he held, he had to lose 119 as a result of British policy. (72-219) He was thus understandably disgruntled with the administration. He was Collector of Shankarpur during Nawab Wajid Ali Shah's time. His loyalty to the royal house of Ayodhya had earned him the distinction and title of 'Bahadur Diler Jung' conferred by the Begum. (87-36; 72-219) He was a very brave man and had provided 40,000 sepoys to the British Bengal Army. His own force was 20,000 strong. (87-37) Of course, it was meant exclusively for the Nawab's service.

The British began feeling his presence after the fall of Lucknow and end of the Begum's rule. Campbell detailed a large force to take Shankarpur in November 1858. When his fortress was invaded, he had 6,000 soldiers and 40 cannons with him. (72-228; 87-38) He was offered several concessions and asked to surrender. Declining all such overtures, he replied "I have pride for the Nawab...my person is devoted to him. It will either fall in his cause or be destroyed in the wilderness of ravines and hills." (44-251; 87-38) Three days later (15th November) he collected all his people, cannons, weapons and treasure and escaped from the fort in the darkness of night. The fleeing party was chased and in the battle that ensued, Beni Madhav suffered heavily.

He then went towards Ayodhya and wandered the territory in the cause of the Begum and her children, finally moving into the Terai region of Nepal. Nothing is known with certainty about when and where he died. (87-39; 72-235)

Prince Firoz Shah

This man slipped away towards Ayodhya when Nawab Khan's defeat became a certainty in the Bareilly battle and commenced anti-British propaganda there. (87-62) Beni Madhav Singh had become his right hand man. He took Rasoolabad in July and made it his base to raid surrounding areas. He had seven or eight thousand troops with him at the time. (63) A British force set out in December 1858 to curb his activities. As soon as he heard of the advancing force, he crossed the Ganga River and entered the Doab region. With the British in hot pursuit, he crossed the Yamuna River and went towards Central India and joined with Tatya's forces on 9th January 1859. (87-63; 72-189; 5-664) The combined rebel force lost 300 men in a battle on 16th January. Another defeat faced them on 21st January. Thereafter the two leaders went different ways. (87-64; 152-67)

Shahzada Firoz Shah kept wandering along with his companions. His initiative to forge a truce with the British fell through because of a disagreement about its terms. Finally in 1860, he left for several Muslim countries via Kandahar and died in Mecca in 1877 at the age of 45.

General Tatya Tope

Tatya Tope and Raosahib Peshwa left Gwalior after their defeat in a battle on 20th June 1858. Thereafter, till April 1859 Tatya's struggle against the British is a long series of conflicts fought with recourse to guerilla tactics. The British had formed a special group to apprehend him in addition to the general alert put out in all regular cantonments as well as military stations and outposts. For more than nine months, Tatya attacked and mauled British troops wherever he could to vanish from the scene before retaliatory action could be taken.[23] He continued in this manner till the end despite the impossibility of ultimate success. He forced the British to scamper and run from pillar to post.

His activity in this final phase was briefly as follows. He went from Gwalior to Jawaraalipur, 50 kilometers away. The British caught up with him there. Tatya lost 300–400 men and

---

23. It is said that he traversed an area of 16,17,000 sq.miles (41,00,000 sq. kms.) in that period. (152-77)

25 cannons in the engagement. (44-265; 132-202) He then crossed the Chambal River and went to Tonk in Rajputana. The Nawab of Tonk shut himself into the fort but his soldiers defected to Tatya *en masse*. (141-374) The principality was taken over by Tatya on 9th July. On 20th July, he reached the Bundi State. (72-148) However, he got no help there. Then, he was able to obtain 30 cannons and Rs. 5 lacs from the Jhalawar-Patan principality. The British attacked Tatya's force on 14th November at Rajgarh when the rebels abandoned their cannons and fled. He contemplated crossing the Narmada River and entering Maharashtra but his hope of getting help from the locals was futile. He then crossed the Narmada River again to enter the Maratha state of Baroda. Several British task forces were prowling around to catch Tatya. But he escaped into the forest before any confrontation could occur. (44-268) The British encircled the forest. Prince Firoz Shah joined Tatya in January 1859 but they parted ways after their combined defeat on 21st of that month. Tatya also left Raosahib who was accompanying him.

Now left all by himself, Tatya took asylum with a local zamindar whom he thought was trustworthy. But the latter betrayed him and handed him over to the British on 7th April 1859. He was tried and hanged on 18th April 1859 at the age of 45.

Nanasahib Peshwa

Once Nanasahib went underground after the defeat at Kanpur in July 1857, he was never seen again in any subsequent event. His existence was perceived by none. Instead, Raosahib is recognised everywhere as Peshwa. Nanasahib made a representation on 20th April 1859 to the British administration seeking pardon in accordance with the Queen's declaration. Of course, it was not granted. He took refuge in Nepal in 1859. None knows with certainty what happened to him then or when and where he breathed his last.

Hazrat Mahal, the Begum of Ayodhya, too, took refuge in Nepal. She remained there till her death in 1874.

Khan Bahadur Khan of Bareilly also took asylum in Nepal. But he was extradited in cooperation with the King of Nepal, brought to Bareilly and hanged on 24th March 1860.

The various insignificant revolts in southern India are discussed in Chapter 8, in the course of viewing the nature of the Uprising.

With this overall picture of the course of events during the Uprising in our minds, we will delve further to ascertain who its promoters, leaders and beneficiaries were and what their inspiration was. We may never understand the true and factual nature of the Uprising without doing so. The information contained in the Chapter just concluded, is sufficient for that purpose.

* * *

Chapter 5

Promoters, Leaders and Beneficiaries of the Uprising — I

(The Jihadi Core of the Uprising)

Bringing an end to the British power in India was only one part of the Uprising that was intended for political revolution. Who succeeded the British after they had been driven out, was a vital aspect. That 'Indians' were going to be freed from slavery to the British, is a vague statement. Aurangzeb was an Indian, yet Shivaji had to wage war against him. Who was slated to be Emperor of India and who were to become her kings, princes, subedars, nobles and administrators after a successful conclusion of the revolt? Who were its promoters and leaders? Let us examine the Uprising from the aspect of its promoters, instigators, leaders and beneficiaries.

- 1 -

Mangal Pandey's Instigator : Nakki Khan

Amaresh Misra's biography[1] of this 'first freedom fighter'

---

1. *Mangal Pandey: The True Story of an Indian Revolutionary*

(Contd.)

provides much information about what was Pandey's inspiration to rebel and who provided it!

Shah Waliullah and Sayyid Ahmad Barelvi had enthralled northern India with their thoughts on political revolution, while their all-pervasive network of secret activists had planted seeds of treason among native soldiers of the British army in India. Nakki Khan, a leader associated with the Patna centre of the movement and actively furthering its cause, had instigated Mangal Pandey to rebel.

They were good friends, of about the same age and residents of the Faizabad district of the Ayodhya province. Nakki would take Mangal to Muslim festivals and durgahs, as also rendered all kind of help to him. Other Muslims, too, were frequent visitors to the Pandey household. (29-19) Nakki was an activist of the Waliullahi movement in Patna and would function in conjunction with another leader, Pir Ali.[2] (67) Being

---

was published in 2005 and dedicated to 'the 1857 Hindu-Muslim solidarity'. This book is written in honour of Mangal Pandey by research and the use, for the first time, of indigenous (archival) material from an Indian perspective. He was honoured as the first hero of the first war of Indian Independence.' (29-xii,xiii, back cover). The comment, 'The legacy of Mangal Pandey must live to keep India's composite culture alive,' appears on the cover.

2. Pir Ali was hanged for treason during 1857 but Nakki Khan was both shrewd and alert, and functioned in extreme secrecy. Savarkar wrote about him: "A very prominent leader of this secret organization was a book-seller !" (1-88) "Peer Ali was originally a resident of Lucknow but had lately established himself as a bookseller in Patna. He had imbibed the ideas of independence... the conditions of dependence and slavery became unbearable to him. He placed himself in communication with Revolutionaries at Delhi and Lucknow... (H)e had great influence in the Revolutionaries councils of Patna. He collected together large number of armed men with the help of the wealthy members of the secret society and they were all sworn to rise against the British power at a given signal... He was by nature stern, spirited and brave... (Before being hanged) the martyr dying for his people said, 'you might hang me but you cannot hang our ideal. If I die, thousands of heroes will rise out of my blood and will destroy your kingdom."' (320)

a follower of the Waliullahi school, Nakki Khan was working for the expulsion of the British and was a firm believer in the prophesy that British power in India would come to an end after a hundred years of the Battle of Plassey. (49) Meanwhile, he became a great religious scholar like his father.

Nakki was in touch with Mangal while the latter was at Barrackpur, and began attempts to influence the latter's mind to rebel against the British. But Pandey was reluctant to entertain thoughts of disloyalty towards his employers. "The British were his masters and he had eaten their salt." (49) Mangal would not budge despite the innumerable tales Nakki spun against the British. However, at long last, Nakki's efforts were successful and Mangal veered around to the view that the Mughal Emperor ought to be reinstated. (52) Soon, his resolve was made so firm that he was believed to have dreamt two days before he rose in revolt that soldiers liveried in red, brandishing green flags, were marching along with Bahadur Shah through Faizabad; they reached Lucknow where the Nawab of Avadh was embracing the Emperor; wounded British officers lying around were trying to shoot at the Emperor and he (Mangal) was firing at them. (95)

'Mujhe Age Karke...'

Although he had expected that other troopers would follow him after he had actually acted on the 29th of March, none did. Inflamed with rage at their complete inaction, he cried out, "*Chale aao behanchod*! – *humko aage kar ke khud peeche rah rahe ho? Dharm ki khatir uth khade ho*!" (Come on sister fuckers, you instigated me to do this and put me in the front, and are now remaining in the background. Stand up in the name of religion and act!)" (79-68; 29-96; 126-72) It is well known that he was under the influence of *bhang* (an intoxicant made from the opium plant) when he had acted. (79-70; 57-29) It was quite possible that others did not follow him because he had perhaps acted arbitrarily in his intoxicated condition without consulting them, and with no preparation. Nonetheless, it is clear from his ramblings that someone had provided immediate incitement to him.

After Pandey had been hanged and cremated, Nakki accompanied by Pir Ali took the ashes to his hometown and delivered them to his mother; both had broken down with grief. (29-104)

In short, Pandey had been provoked into rebellion by persons wedded to the Waliullahi philosophy. Instigating Hindus to rebel was part of their conspiracy: they had realized their uprising could only succeed with Hindu participation. On several occasions, in fact, they had even put up a wholly Hindu façade while keeping themselves in the background, only to test the depth and sincerity of Hindu sympathy.

In the Barrackpur Cantonment, too

Pandey was not the only trooper to be incited by Nakki Khan. The latter was a regular visitor to the (Hindu) Sanatan Dharmasabha and had even become a member of that body. He used to be accorded a special place at its meetings. (62) He had also accompanied Pandey to Calcutta for holy dips in the Ganga. (52) This was how he had infiltrated the Hindu camp, and the Hindu psyche, to administer oaths for the Uprising. Several Hindus, too, had been inducted as members of the Waliullahi movement.[3] (50)

As opium addiction was widespread among sepoys, Nakki Khan had become an agent for an English firm dealing in the intoxicant in order to gain entry to cantonments and engage in the activity of preaching revolution. (50) His task was considerably simplified because Dadu Mian and leader of another similar movement, Titu Mir (see Chap. 2, footnote 39), had already succeeded in creating a Jihadi atmosphere. (50)

---

3. Actually, in principle, the Waliullahi movement was strictly a pristine Islam activity, with its slogan, 'Return to the Quran'. It sought to correct the influence that association with Hindus had had on Muslim lifestyles. An idea of the compromises, Muslims were prepared to make to obtain Hindu support may be gleaned from this. Of course, they had not abandoned their pristine philosophy in any way, and were indeed seeking political power in order to implement it. Being ignorant of that doctrine, it was characteristic of the typical Hindu to extend his cooperation to them.

Who Masterminded the 'Chapatis'?

The system of conveying messages to sepoys with the 'chapati' as a medium, had been prepared by Waliullahi activists. Nakki Khan had a significant role to play in this. (29-83) In Malleson's opinion, M. Ahmad Shah was the mastermind. (130-12) Needless to state, he subscribed to Waliullahi philosophy, too. The chapati was a Muslim symbol denoting the earth and how Hindustani Muslims ought to take their destiny in their own hands. (29-82) It was a powerful means of combining all classes of Mahomedans in the general cause.[4] (3-391; 106-44)

The work of spreading news about the new, fat-smeared cartridges, even before they had been issued to sepoys, had been undertaken by these Waliullahi activists. The Muslim tutors attached to other regiments were plotting an uprising. Already, they had sent letters to every other British cantonment urging them not to touch the hated cartridges. (60-29) Two of Nakki's trusted activists, Bacchan and Machhi, had been actively involved in this work. (29-85) It had been done so effectively that no explanation tendered by the administration was good enough to placate sepoys.

Nakki had formed a secret group of three sepoys of the 34th Platoon at Barrackpur. (85) News about the contentious cartridges had first been spread among this platoon; sepoys had informed their captain as early as 6th February that they were not prepared to accept the ammunition and warned him of their insubordination. (29-85; 132-35) Nakki Khan thereafter had gone to Bahrampur and conveyed a message to the 19th Platoon there, through Bacchan, to rebel. (29-88) He also held a secret meeting with leaders of the platoon. (88) Accordingly,

---

4. Savarkar, in poetic flair, addresses those chapatis and writes: "Dash on, Messenger (of Revolution to all ten directions.... The Mother (India) goes forth to the war (*Jihad*) ! March on ! March on !! Save her !!!...." (1-98) (Brackets added by us on the basis of Savarkar's Marathi original book (P.75). It should be noted that the word 'Jihad' is wrongly translated as simply 'war' by the translator.)

the sepoys refused to accept the cartridges and rebelled on 26th February. (88) Both the 19th and 34th Platoons were disbanded as rebellious, after the Mangal Pandey incident. Briefly, the 'cartridge' and 'Barrackpur-Bahrampur' affairs were well-planned conspiracies hatched by Nakki Khan, which generated an atmosphere conducive for garnering support of Hindu sepoys.

Seditious Propaganda at Meerut

In the foot steps of the Barrackpur-Bahrampur incident, but as one that involved actual armed rebellion, the next phase was reached on 10th May 1857 at Meerut. The work of inciting sepoys to rebel on the cartridge and other issues was continuing. A group of Waliullahi activists had settled down at Faridnagar near Meerut. (115-58) Among them were several associates of Sayyid Ahmad Barelvi, many of whom had travelled thence to Peshawar for *Jihad* in his time.

A European (Christian) ex-serviceman from the cantonment had converted to Islam and assumed the name Abdullah Baig. (121-60) He was particularly effective in conducting seditious propaganda. (154-153) Having paid visits from Meerut to cantonments at places like Ambala, Ludhiana and Firozpur, he had made his home in the vicinity of the Meerut cantonment. He would meet sepoys daily and incite them to rebel by telling them how pig and cow fat had been used in the new issue of cartridges. (121-39) Many envoys were making the rounds of various cantonments in April 1857 carrying the message of rebellion. One such, a fakir, had stopped along with his disciples near the Meerut cantonment for a few days. (3-397) He was later driven away.[5] "The minds of the native soldiery were kept in an agitated and inflamed state, by false and malicious reports busily circulated." (7-13)

---

5. About this Savarkar writes: "The authorities at Meerut were at last compelled to ask a Fakir, who was lodging near the Meerut military cantonment, to move away." (1-83) In the original Marathi book, it is said that 'he was engaged in preaching political *Jihad*.' (P.66) However, this part does not appear in the English version.

"The great interest of the Bahrampur episode is that its pattern closely resembles the pattern at Meerut some ten weeks later." (57-27) Not remaining restricted to mere refusal to accept the cartridges, the matter resulted in armed rebellion that snowballed into a public uprising. Sufficient preparation for it had been made.

Rebellion of Muslim Cavalry

Two troopers of the rank of 'naik' in the 3rd cavalry platoon, Pir Ali and Kudrat Ali, had obtained an assurance on solemn oath from sepoys that they would refuse to accept the cartridges. (131) They were members of the secret group. At a test of loyalty held on 24th April, 85 out of 90 sepoys on parade refused the cartridges. Forty-eight of them were Muslim.[6] (126-81) Pir Ali and Kudrat Ali were among the first to refuse. (57-63) They were sentenced to punishment for this insubordination on 9th May. "The walls were frosted with placards with a Mahomedan proclamation calling upon all true Musalmans to rise and slaughter the English." (57-70; 78-39; 79-81) Residents of the Sadar Bazar raised slogans of 'Deen, Deen'[7] in support of their brethren. (7-11) Witnessing the punishment meted out to them, their comrade sepoys rose up in the historic revolt on 10th May. With cries of 'Allah-I-Allah! Maro Firangi Ko'[8], they began putting the British to death. (60-35; 126-88) Sepoys and especially civilians then commenced a spree of loot and arson. While doing so, they raised cries of 'Ali, Ali!'.[9] (7-14) The

---

6. The names of all 85 are printed in the history of the 'Freedom Struggle in U.P.' published by the Government of U. P.. (7-6)

7. 'Deen' means Islam. The slogan was an expression of the desire that Islam should prevail. This slogan was raised at hundreds of places during the 1857 rebellion. (60-35)

8. It means 'to kill the Christians/English for and with the help of Allah'.

9. The then Maj.Williams commented upon these events thus: "....loud yells and cries of 'Ali Ali,' (for the Mahomedans soon took the lead, raising above all other sounds this watchword of their religion) bungalows blazing in all directions ..." (7-14) Ali was the Prophet's son-in-law and the fourth 'rightly guided Khalifa'.

infantry platoon, which had been brought around to its side by the cavalry, soon joined the mêlée.[10]

- 2 -

Delhi: Reinstatement of the Mughal Emperor

The rebels left for Delhi the same night.[11] Assembling before Bahadur Shah's residence, they told him: "You are the King of both the worlds — terrestrial and spiritual.[12] The whole of India is under your sway. The English have been ruling on your behalf. They want to convert everyone of us into Christians... We have also circulated the letters in our regiments of the Infantry and Cavalry to the effect that 'the entire army should break out on one and the same date all over India... (After the) revolt first at Meerut...we started towards Delhi and reached this place... Your Majesty should extend your...hand for we have done all this in the cause of religion."[13] (3-407; 7-990; 126-101)

---

10. The *Delhi Urdu Akhbar*, a paper published at the time, reported the Meerut revolt thus: "Meerut : The Risala of the victorious Turksawars (cavalry) and Paltan were already agitated. First, they marched to the jail and set the *Mussalmans* free." (7-974) These were also called as 'the renowned *ghazis*.' (975) Muslim writers particularly, refer clearly to the 3rd cavalry as 'Muslim cavalry'. (e.g. 112-327) In fact, Muslims formed the majority in each cavalry, which is why the cavalry was often also called 'Turkswar'. Free use of the term 'Turkswar' appears in Hakim Ahsanullah Khan's memoirs (Ref.# 85)

11. All of these troopers were Muslim. (85-1,2; 43-63) This notwithstanding, Savarkar writes that they had paid obeisance to the Yamuna river with the words, 'Jai Jamnaji'. (1-118) In fact, bowing before a river is un-Islamic. Savarkar at that time was not aware of the fact and has written thus in a flight of poetic fancy.

12. The word 'spiritual' is significant. It is an Islamic concept according to which the Khalifa or Muslim Ruler is both political and religious head. It may be gleaned who they were from the fact that they also regarded Bahadur Shah as their spiritual head.

13. Moinul Haq writes: "This is very clear indication of the object ot the revolution. The leaders of the Movement had prepared the sepoy and the common man for a holy war to safeguard their faith. This is why their war cry was *Deen*." (85-32n)

Bahadur Shah replied, "I did not call for you; you have acted very wickedly." They said, "unless you, the king, join us, we are all dead men." (126-104; 79-269; 107-65) When he said he had no money to pay for their services, they told him they would bring it to him as loot, for all they wanted were his blessings. (126-121; 85-2) Bahadur Shah, against his own wishes, but under pressure from courtiers, acceded to the sepoys' demands and consented to assume the leadership.[14] Included among those courtiers were his sons, too. Proclamations were issued in his name as Emperor. The Mughal Empire had been restored in Delhi and the green flag began flying proudly over the Red Fort again.

Bahadur Shah got his Imperial seal fashioned. Imperial decrees began carrying the following: "The Father of Victory! The Candle of Religion ! Muhammad Bahadur Shah, King, Defender of the Faith !" (107-58) Another seal, with 'Padshahi Ghazi' (Emperor of Holy Warriors) inscribed thereon, was also made. (36)

The Emperor immediately constituted an advisory council in which six Muslims were included. (59-63) He also made appointments of ministers and senior bureaucrats. Only one among them was Hindu, Mukundlal, a Kayastha (a caste), appointed to the office of writer, for he was renowned for his penmanship. He would be summoned when some document was to be prepared but not allowed to remain there during

---

14. However, according to Savarkar: "But this restoration of the old Moghal was a restoration, neither to the old power nor to the old prestige, nor to the old traditions. The Mughal dynasty of old was not chosen by the people of the Land. Bahadur Shah was raised by the free voice of the people, both Hindus and Muhammedans, civil and military, to be their Emperor." (1-283 to 5) "These (first) five days proclaimed by beat of drum the end for the time being at any rate of the continuous fight between the Hindus and Muhammedans, dating from the invasion of Mahmud Ghazni. It was proclaimed first that the Hindus and Muhammedans are not rivals, not conquerors and the conquered, but brethren. Be those grand days remain ever memorable in the history of Hindustan !" (1-126)

important discussions. (107-249, 51) The Chief Justice, Commander-in-Chief, prime minister, chancellor of the Exchequer, other commanders and officers were all Muslim. Prince Mirza Mughal who had never seen military action, was made Commander-in-Chief at the insistence of sepoys. Other princes of the Imperial household were appointed to various subordinate military commands. (79-270; 69-57) Shamshadullah, a grandson of Ahmad Shah Abdali, was made mukhtar. (85-14, 34) So, Muslims overwhelmingly became the beneficiaries.

Nominal Emperor

In reality, the Emperor was just a nominal figurehead. Real power was held by courtiers. He was forced to bend to the will of the sepoys who used to force their decisions on him. His constant refrain was that he had been made a prisoner. (107-344) He was powerless to stop the slaughter of Christians in Delhi. He complained that he was helpless. (126-119; 121-49) Unlike his courtiers, he had no prior knowledge of the Uprising. (126-99,100; 107-182; 121-120)

Bahadur Shah was not ambitious, but his sons and other Muslim leaders desired a reestablishment of the Mughal Empire. They only looked upon him as a leader generally acceptable to the populace and possessed of the ability to attract and unite them, which is why they wanted him as Emperor. (69-45) They had reduced him to a virtual puppet in their hands. (126-122; 141-xxvii; 121-87) They would have him sanction letters and affix his seal thereon; the administration was being run in the Emperor's name by these people. (107-345, 406). All that had remained with him was the semblance of moral authority. His son's (Mirza Mughal's) "desire was to ascend the throne even by dethroning his own father; for that purpose he had in a way assumed the post of C in C." (69-92) Even a threat to that effect had been given to the Emperor. (107-344) Indeed, apparently, so pathetic was his situation, that common soldiers showed no respect for him and often would speak their minds to him with epithets like "Are Badshah ! Are Buddha !" (79-271; 67-119; 121-87) He was required to issue orders and make appointments according to the wishes of persons like M. Fazal Haq and M. Sarfaraz Ali. (14-69,70) They would advise him on occasion to personally take to the battlefield. (14-74) He often complained that, "Those Maulvis rendered me powerless." (85-29) Obviously, seeking the opinion of Hindus was out of the question!

Jihad Begins in Delhi

Sepoys in Delhi welcomed their comrades from Meerut on their arrival in the city. Savarkar says: "This army of the heroes of liberty entered the town of Delhi (by Kashmere gate) with cries of 'Deen! Deen!' The second part of the Meerut Army was also trying to enter Delhi by the Calcutta gate. The watchman at gate joined the Sepoys with cries of 'Deen! Deen!'... (Then) wherever an English head was found, it was stuck at the ends of lances, and with such terror-striking flags did the army push forward at rapid pace (with cries of 'Deen ! Deen!')!" (1-119) This was an instance of Muslim soldiers greeting, welcoming and uniting with other Muslim soldiers.

Not just the sepoys in Delhi, but even civilian Muslims went over to side with the rebels. Forty percent of Delhi's population, or 66,120, was Muslim and fiercely anti-British. (69-37; 78-75) Many pages of history are full of the Jihadi colours shown by sepoys and civilians during the period of the Uprising.

Even before the rebels from Meerut had reached Delhi, the people there had begun saying, "Now swords will come into play and rivers of blood will flow through the city. Whatever is to happen will occur during this Ramzan." (47-265; 14-81) The agitated Muslim populace of Delhi joined the rebels with cries of 'Deen, Deen'. The throngs followed the sepoys through the town. "Everywhere it had been noised about from early morning that the King was on the side of the mutineers, and that to fight against the English was to fight for the King, to fight for the restoration of the Mughal throne, to fight for the religion of the Prophet (Muhammad)." (78-70) Here, the meaning of 'fighting' is 'waging Jihad'!

Their first act was to put the local British and Christians to death. Forty-nine of them, who had taken refuge inside the palace, were slaughtered on 16th May. (69-58) Not a single Englishman or Christian in the city was left alive. (130-57) They were so infuriated that, despite the palace-victims' readiness to convert to Islam and appeals on that ground for clemency made on their behalf by a moderate liberal like Zahiruddin Zahir,[15] none was spared the sword.[16] (14-82; 47-266) Moreover, they were not slaughtered by ordinary sepoys. "None of the sepoys took part in killing them. The privilege, so far it was considered, of murdering them was particularly reserved for the King's own servants, as it was believed by them, that the killing of an infidel would ensure them a place in paradise." (79-95)

Bahadur Shah had faith in the Islamic doctrine which declared Kafirs as impure and were the cause of pollution of the earth. In a letter dated 7th August 1857, sent to the ruler of Kachh-Bhuj, he wrote: "Muhammad Bakht Khan, Governor (and Military) general Bahadur affirmed that you, ever faithful one, having put the whole of the infidels to the sword, have thoroughly cleansed and purified your domains of their unclean presence. We have been extremely gratified to hear of such conduct on your part, and you are therefore honoured..." (107-157)

On hearing the ear-shattering report of the explosion in the ammunition dump, which the British had deliberately ignited on the very first day (11th May) of the outbreak of the rebellion, sepoys gave uproarious cries of 'Deen, Deen' and began moving in the streets brandishing their weapons. (79-105; 60-58) After this, two men mounted on camels and dressed in green with red turbans rode by at a trot, calling out, "Here, ye people, the drum of religion has sounded." The excited

15. Zahir was Bahadur Shah's hereditary nobleman and author of *Dastan-e-Gadar,* a book narrating events of the Uprising.

16. Nevertheless, many instances may be cited to show that British lives were spared under condition of conversion to Islam. Either option led to overall gain for the Muslim: sparing a life added to their population, killing guaranteed a place in heaven.

and livid crowds in the streets believed they were heavenly messengers. (121-48; 85-32n) Many observers or historians use the word 'Muslim' for 'rebel sepoys' in their descriptions of the Delhi Uprising.[17]

The editor of the *Delhi Urdu Akhbar*, M. Muhammad Bakar, was a loyal supporter of the Emperor. He believed that, "The rebellion had been sent by God to punish the *Kafirs*." (154-18) Using flowery language, he wrote in the issue dated 17th May 1857: "One venerable man had a dream that our Prophet Muhammad said to Jesus that your followers have become an enemy of my name and wish to efface my religion. To this Lord Jesus replied that the British are not my followers, they have joined ranks with Satan's followers.... Some people even swear that the day the troopers came here (from Meerut), there were camels ahead of them on which rode green-robed riders. These green riders instantly vanished from sight and only the troopers remained, killing whichever Englishman they found, cutting them up as if they were carrots or radishes." (18)

---

17. For example, the following reports from the *Delhi Gazette Press* may be cited: *30 May*: "Several Mahomedans (arrived from the North West) accompanied the force to fight for the religion." *31 May* : "Mutineers force have been totally defeated on the Hindun bridge, Mahomedans are quite disheartened." *8 June* : "Mahomedans are flocking in great numbers to the fields of battle in assistance of the rebels." *9 June* : "Fighting is the order of the day. Mahomedans continued to flock in great numbers to the fields of battles." *5 July*: "Mahomedans are assembling in great number from outstations to join the war against the British." *16 July* : "Mahomedans are gathering to join the war of religion." *3 August*: "The rebels (*Jihadis*) have fled away to their homes this day." *4 August*: "Swords, guns etc. are selling innumerably in the Jama Masjid." *3 Sept.* : "Some Mahomedans are also flying away with their families to the adjacent cities and villages through fear, when they were given to understand that British forces are at hand." *11 Sept.* : "A large portion of the Mahomedans assembled in Jama Masjid and prepared themselves to accompany with the force to attack the English." (85-40 to 57)

This editor consistently referred to the 1857 Uprising as a 'Jihad' for the cause of Islam. (159) In order to enthuse and excite his readers, he would also often quote from the Quran in his writings. (161)

In one issue of the Akhbar-ul Zafar, which used to be published from the Red Fort, it was written: "Though Christians may be found here and there, the Almighty Creator has removed their authority from the Mahomedan cities." (69-61) According to the view prevalent within the Red Fort, places like Delhi, Lucknow, Allahabad and Bareilly were regarded as Muslim cities. The comment was in context of the fact that those places had then passed under the control of rebels for some time.

Invitation to Persia for Invasion

What were the factors that gave the rebels confidence of success against the mighty British Empire? First, they evinced implicit faith in the prophesied demise of British rule in India after 100 years from the Battle of Plassey. (1757) Second, they were assured of an invasion by Persia and Afghanistan to free India from the British yoke. (107-xix) This confidence was a result of corroborative news reports and an atmosphere that had been created by them.

Bahadur Shah had personally sent an invitation to the Persian Emperor to launch an invasion of India.[18] Persia was under Shi'ah rule. To gain assistance from that state, Bahadur Shah had become an adherent of the Shi'ah sect. (107-407; 78-29) He had declared in a letter to the chief religious authority that those who had no love for the Prophet's relations (meaning Hazrat Ali and others) were not Muslim. He dispatched his nephew, Mirza Najaf, to Persia with an appeal for help. (107-

18. Issuing such invitations was an old habit with them. Shah Waliullah and Padshah Alamgir had invited Ahmad Shah Abdali (1761). Tipu Sultan had sent invitations to Turkey (1786), Afghanistan (1797) and Iran. Nawab Vazir Ali Khan of Ayodhya and Mughal Emperor Shah Alam, too, had invited Zaman Shah of Afghanistan (1798).

407; 54-276) It had been so arranged that news of the Mughal Emperor's conversion to the Shi'ah persuasion would become known to the Persian monarch through newspaper reports appearing in Persia before Najaf arrived there. (107-408) A few months later, at the insistence of a certain soothsayer Fakir Pirzada Hasan Askari, who wielded much influence over the Emperor (the latter's daughter had become the former's disciple), one Siddi Kambar was dispatched to Persia on the same errand. This fakir claimed to have dreamt that the Persian Empire extended over India, that Delhi had returned to her former glory and British rule in India had ended. (107-162; 70-129; 78-28) Muslims in Delhi had begun trusting this vision, while the happy prospect held citizenry as well as the Palace in its thrall. (78-31) Siddi Kambar had been sent with monetary gifts and a letter for Nasiruddin, the Persian Emperor, in the expectation of receiving military and financial aid from the latter. (107-408); 126-99)

A proclamation, issued by the Persian Emperor in March 1857, was displayed at the Jama Masjid in Delhi and began to be read all over the town. It contained an appeal to Muslims to participate in the *Jihad* against the British. It also stated that the Persian Emperor was intending to assume the Indian throne and make the people of India happy and contented. (107-315) It further stated that his armies had set out for India, that 900 of their troopers had already entered the territory, while 500 of them were in Delhi in disguise. (315)

Report after report about the approaching Persian host had been appearing from March in the *Sadiq-al Akhbar* ('Authentic News') of Delhi. It was reported in the 16th March 1857 issue that Persian courtiers had advised their Emperor to declare *Jihad* against the British and conquer India. Nasiruddin was so pleased with such solicitation that he announced the appointment of those advisors to governorships of Bombay, Calcutta, Poona and other places. (313) The same news report went on to state that Persia had declared war against the British because she desired to fulfil a desire to conquer India, which had eluded her for five generations,[19] that the present Emperor, Nasiruddin, too, had cherished the desire for many years, and that all things were now falling into place. (314)

Muslims in Delhi as well as in the rest of India were thus in a state of mental excitement and evinced keen interest in every news report connected with the imminent arrival of Persian forces. Animated expression about the expected Persian host, and even vociferous boasting about what they would do when they arrived, began making the rounds. (78-31; 107-208) Princes of the Imperial household attached great significance to such reports.[20] Prayers began to be said to hasten

---

19. The first of these five generations, it might be surmised, was that of Nadir Shah.

20. Savarkar writes: "(I)t was in the Diwan-i-Khas of Delhi, more than in any other Durbar, the seeds of Revolution began to take root. Zeenat Mahal, the beloved, clever, and determined Begum of the Emperor, had already decided that this last opportunity of regaining the last glory should not be allowed to go by. Seeing that simultaneous rising in India would be a help, the Shah of Persia, began to open diplomatic correspondence with the Emperor of Delhi. In the Declaration of the Emperor of Delhi, it had been made quite clear that a confidential agent had been sent to Persia from the Delhi Durbar. While this intrigue was going on at the Durbar of Shah, right in the city of Delhi agitation was started to stir public feeling to its very depths. For this work, even public Proclamations were sometimes posted on the walls of the town. In the beginning of 1857, a Proclamation couched in the following terms appeared boldly: 'The army of Persia is going to free India from the hands of Firangis. So, all Hindustanee brothers should leap forth into the field to free themselves from the *Kafirs*'. Indian newspapers used to publish these Proclamations. The various *Shahzadas* and their retainers in the Palaces of Delhi openly and secretly spread disaffection, and were engaged in weaving a network of conspiracies." (1-79)

One cannot wonder how the same Savarkar who, after 1923, unleashed a spate of criticism of Gandhi for his posture of welcome to the Amir of Afghanistan had the latter invaded India to liberate it from the British, should himself be here (in 1908) ushering the Shah of Iran!

that force. (78-28), Charles Metcalfe refers a writer who "believes the Mutiny to have been the result of fanaticism, created by a Royal Proclamation, emanating from the Court of Persia, copies of which had undoubtedly been circulated throughout India." (121-6)

The Commander-in-Chief of Waliullahi Thought

After rebelling in Rohilkhand, the Brigadier General Bakht Khan, reached Delhi in early July 1857 with 3,000 troopers[21] and Rs. 300,000 cash. (69-92) He had been specially summoned by the Emperor to disperse *kafir* Christians, entrenched in the hillocks around the city. Bakht Khan hailed from Rohilla stock and was a grandson of a brother of Najeeb Khan, the man who had instigated the Battle of Panipat in 1761. He held the rank of Subedar in the British Indian Army. His mentor, M. Sarfaraz Ali, had commanded him to rebel in May 1857. (127-15; 77-164; 154-285) He was at the forefront of the 31st may uprising at Bareilly, after which he became 'Brigadier-General' of the rebels. The Emperor appointed him Commander-in-Chief in place of his son, Prince Mirza Mughal, on 5th July 1857.

Why had the Emperor displaced his son in favour of this Bakht Khan? It was because influential Maulvis like M. Sarfaraz Ali, M. Imad Ali and Munshi Khairat Ali had told him to do so. "The Munshi gave a paper in which was written that Muhammad (Bakht) Khan was appointed Governor General and Commander-in-Chief of all the forces. The King signed it." (85-18; 14-62; 127-16)

Why had Maulvis chosen Bakht Khan? It was because all of them subscribed to Waliullahi thought, while Bakht Khan's mentor, M. Sarfaraz Ali, was a disciple of Sayyid Ahmad Barelvi and a principal leader of the movement. Bakht Khan

---

21. According to Zahiruddin, however, this number was 14,000. (14-85; 47-268) According to the contemporaneous *Delhi Urdu Akhbar*, : "A large number of *Jihadis* have come with him." (7-1003) William Dalrymple gives the figure as '4,000 Jihadis'. (154-285)

himself was a disciple of Barelvi and an ideologue of Waliullahi thought.[22] (70-104; 76-20; 112-326; 107-441; 154-285) The Jihadis accompanying him, too, were all followers of the same ideology of Sayyid Ahmad Barelvi. (127-18)

Organization of the Jihadi Force

Bakht Khan convened a meeting of Maulvis and leaders of his persuasion as soon as he had assumed powers as Commander-in-Chief. Those present included, among other leaders of the Barelvi persuasion, Ghaus Muhammad Khan, Imam Khan, Abdul Ghaffar Khan and Sarfaraz Ali. The last was elected by the assembly as Chief of the Jihadi force (Amir-ul-Mujahideen) and a separate force of Jihadis was raised and detailed to his command. (77-164; 85-20) In this manner, the teacher helped his pupil and the pupil his teacher to lead two independent armies.[23] Thereafter, all Muslims in Delhi were asked to report for service to Sarfaraz Ali. (85-20; 14-65)

---

22. About this Prof. Qeyamuddin Ahmad comments: "The Wahabis with their compact organization, covering the whole of Northern India, their secret cells in the Indian Army Units provided a solid organizational base. It also enabled the Wahabis themselves, at some places, to capture the leadership of the other movement for instance, Bakht Khan's supersession of Mirza Mughal in the control of the Delhi forces." (116-218)

The book *We Fought Together for Freedom: Chapters from the Indian National Movement*, edited on behalf of the Indian Council for Historical Research, which gives details of some selected agitations during the Uprising, Bakht Khan has been separately dealt with as a freedom fighter. (127-14 to 26)

23. Prof. Faruqi writes: "The 'Wahabis' sentiment had permeated the heart and mind of rugged soldiers like Bakht Khan who was the dominating figure of the revolt and the leader of the central government at Delhi (in 1857). He arrived at Delhi with a band of Wahabi organizers and appointed his spiritual guide Maulvi Sarfaraz Ali as the 'Imam' of the contingent of 'religious warriors' (*Mujahids*) numbering several thousands." (76-20)

At this juncture, troopers who had rebelled at various places, as well as volunteers[24] of the Waliullahi school, began converging on Delhi. (107-442; 81-69; 112-328) The Tonk state was home to a very large number of Barelvi's followers, "which had a history of welcoming extreme 'Wahabi' preachers, and which had long been regarded by British intelligence officers as a hotbed of fanaticism and an underground centre of the Mujahideen movement." (154-264) In fact, the Chief of the state had himself been a disciple in Sayyid's time. A contingent of 600 Jihadis from there arrived in Delhi on 21st July. They met the Emperor and informed him that 2,000 more had left Tonk. (121-160) At last count, 4,000 of them had arrived in Delhi from Tonk. (154-264) On 3rd August, someone went through the town proclaiming that Akand, Chief of Swat, was on his way to Delhi with 1,400 Jihadis in order to submit himself to the service of the Emperor. (121-179) Innumerable instances may be observed of rebelling troopers at various places raising cries of 'Chalo Delhi' (March to Delhi) and then proceeding to that city. There was a deviation from this general trend only in the case of Kanpur rebels; also, rebels at Gwalior had been detained there by the Maharaja's stratagem and had then proceeded to Agra. Even then, a contingent of suicidal *ghazis* had indeed reached Delhi from Gwalior. (154-338) Barring these exceptions, all rebels from all places had Delhi as their destination. (69-108) And, an overwhelmingly large number of those that had made their way to Delhi, were Muslim.[25] Delhi being the capital of the Mughal Empire where

---

24. How those *ghazis* were and how they fought may be surmised from a report: "Fully five thousand men from various quarters poured into Delhi as *Ghazis* dressed in blue tunics and green turbans. All *Ghazis* received two annas a day from the King. They usually joined in the attacks on the British lines: some Europeans were killed by them and (they) beheaded some of the dead Europeans, and after fixing the heads on poles, took them into the city, followed by enormous crowds. The bearer of every head brought to the King received five rupees." (79-279)

25. The few Hindus that had not grasped the true intent of the Uprising, those that had been beguiled by anti-British Muslim

(Contd.)

the Emperor lived, it was the attraction that had driven all of them to that city. As a result, 60,000 troopers had assembled there by 3rd August 1857. Half of them were *ghazis* (Jihadis). (154-338) On arrival, they would be welcomed and greeted with chants of 'Deen-Deen'. (121-63) This was the fruit of efforts made by Shah Waliullah, Shah Abdul Aziz and Sayyid Ahmad Barelvi. That a warrior inspired by their philosophy should become the Commander-in-Chief of the 1857 Uprising was their crowning triumph.

Proclamation of Jihad in Delhi

A religious decree (*fatwa*) against the British was then issued, to which many well known Maulvis were signatories.[26] (77-165) It had been invoked by the Commander-in-Chief, and imparted the status and complexion of *Jihad* to the overall political uprising against British rule. (142) Whatever it had meant to Hindus, to the Muslims it was nothing but *Jihad.*

---

propaganda, those that had participated for personal gain or those that had been merely carried upon the crest of the Jihadi wave had also arrived in Delhi along with the Jihadis. A mention of Raja Narhar Singh of Vallabhgarh, who was at the forefront of the Uprising, would be pertinent in this context. Sashi Bhushan Chaudhary, who eulogizes the rebellion as a war of independence, writes: "Narhar Singh was so very devoted to the cause of Islam that he seems to have embraced the faith." (81-68) M. Ahmad Ali had presented a token of fealty to the Emperor on his behalf. (7-983) A reason for 'Hindu-Muslim Unity' that had apparently manifested itself during the Uprising was of this nature.

26. Names of 15 of these Maulvis appear in two references. (77-165; 28-210) The first to sign was the renowned M. Fazal Haq Khairabadi. (15-82) Each one of the Maulvis who was party to the proclamation subscribed to Waliullahi thought. M. Nazir Hussain was disciple and successor of a trusted lieutenant of Barelvi, Shah Muhammad Ismail. Mufti Sadruddin was a disciple of Shah Abdul Aziz. Three others were disciples of Barelvi's senior associate, Shah Muhammad Ishaq. (25-210) M. Sarfaraz Ali was a disciple of Sayyid Ahmad Barelvi. (77-164)

Participating in it was a religious obligation for the latter. The proclamation itself had stated that it was the sacred religious and unavoidable duty of every Muslim to participate in the *Jihad*. It was also made clear that families — including children — of those who did not, would be liquidated. (107-442) This proclamation produced much enthusiasm and vitality among Muslims.[27] (77-142)

Thereafter, Maulvis and Ulemas embarked upon a campaign of preaching and put in untiring efforts to ensure a successful outcome of the *Jihad*. (127-18) A mechanism was set up to reach their philosophy to areas beyond the precincts of Delhi. Maulvis commenced travelling all over India preaching *Jihad* and the whole political milieu became charged with the doctrine.[28]

Declaration of Jihad against Hindus

Despite a formal declaration made at this time, *Jihad* had actually commenced in Delhi from 11th May. By the 16th, all Englishmen or Christians had been put to the sword. Forty percent of the population of the city, where large numbers of sepoys and *ghazis* had assembled, was already Muslim. So, against whom was this *Jihad* going to be waged now? *Jihad*, according to Islamic tenets, is to be waged against *kafirs* (or non-Muslims). Who, it might be asked, were slated to be targets of swords that had then been drawn for *Jihad*?

Many Maulvis and thousands of Muslims assembled at the Jama Masjid on 19th May, issued a declaration of *Jihad* against Hindus, and green flags were unfurled there and at other places in town. (121-69; 107-279; 85-38) M. Muhammad

---

27. Dr. Mahmood Ghazi writes in this context: "It was not just the *fatwa* but the entire *Jihad* movement of 1857 that was conceived and given full intellectual backing by the scholars of Shah Wali Ullah's school. Moreover, the followers of the WaliUllahi tradition actively participated in the War of Independence." (25-210)

28. Savarkar writes: "Influential and noble Maulvis were appointed to preach the political *Jihad* and they were rewarded with thousands of Rupees...." (1-82)

Sayyid had been in the forefront of this affair. The declaration had also stated that the *Jihad* was being conducted to re-establish Muslim paramountcy in India. (69-61) On 14th June 1857, Maj. General Reed who had been stationed there, wrote in his report to the Chief Commissioner: "They are displaying the green flags in the city and bullying Hindus who are praying for our Government — so says our secret intelligence." (67-230)

The Emperor, apprehensive that it might provoke Hindus to act against him, was upset by this development. (121-98) An order was issued to remove the Jihadi flags. (107-279) Aggrieved by the order, a delegation of Maulvis called on the Emperor on 20th May to represent their case. On enquiry by the Emperor, the Maulvis replied that the standard of Holy War had been erected for the purpose of inflaming the minds of Mahomedans against Hindus. The Emperor answered that such a *Jihad* was quite impossible and such an idea is an act of extreme folly. Moreover, such an act would create internecine strife/consequences, and that would be irredeemable. (121-98; 107-280) "He further said that the greater part of Nationalist forces fighting against the British were Hindus who were well armed and if the Muslims raised *Jihad* against them, the Hindu forces would finish off the *Jihadis* easily." (107-280; 69-62) The Maulvis pointed out to the King that the Hindus were leaning towards an alliance with the English and had no sympathy with Mahomedans, and were already holding themselves apart. (121-98) Certainly some of the *Jihadis* were convinced that the entire Hindu population was with the British. (154-268)

Bahadur Shah, of course, was well aware of this, but it was in his interest to abstain from waging *Jihad* against Hindus in order to win their sympathy through a conciliatory approach and extract as much support against the British as possible. It was impossible to conduct a *Jihad* against two powerful opponents simultaneously.[29] Editorials, imploring Hindus not

---

29. See this footnote on p.253

to despair, began appearing in the newspaper run by Imperial loyalist and supporter, Muhammad Bakar. (268)

A delegation of Hindus called on the Emperor to complain about declaration of *Jihad* against them. The Emperor clarified, "The Holy War is against the English; I have forbidden it against the Hindus."[30] (121-98)

British Victory — Hindus Elated

As discussion over the anti-Hindu *Jihad* was progressing, news was received that British troops were advancing on Delhi. Muslim forces set out to deal with them. A battle was fought on 30th and 31st May between the two at Hindan in which the Muslims faced a rout. (107-234) Many were killed and the wounded were brought back to Delhi. The subedar reported to the Emperor that "a great many Mahomedans had fallen in yesterday's engagement, claiming that they had fallen in *Jihad*." (121-109) Muslims in Delhi were grief-stricken. But, "The Delhi Hindus, who had suffered much at the hands of the mutineers since their arrival in the city, expressed their joy that these wicked men, like decapitated fowls, with bloody wounds, had now themselves been tossed hither and thither, and had lost all their manhood and bravery."[31] (121-108)

---

30. Savarkar writes: "(W)hen once some fanatic Muhammedans wanted to insult the Hindus by declaring *Jihad* against them, the old Emperor, seated on an elephant and with all his Imperial officers, went in a procession through all the city declaring that the *Jihad* was against the Firangis alone !" (1-287) The matter remaining unexplained is the need for the 82-year old Emperor to roam the streets of Delhi with his retinue to make such appeals if only a handful of demented fanatical Muslims had declared *Jihad* against Hindus. Several historians cite this incident of his appeals to illustrate how Bahadur Shah was a proponent of Hindu-Muslim unity. In actual fact, it is this very need to make appeals in this manner that speaks volumes for anti-Hindu sentiments harboured by Muslims.

31. Dr. Chaudhary, who calls the Uprising a war of independence, writes: "(I)t was not unlikely therefore that the disaster of the sepoy force at the Hindan bridge was welcomed, specially by the Hindus." (81-74)

Debate about *Jihad* against Hindus now receded into the background because Muslims had found a new adversary in the British.

This was the first battle sepoys in Delhi had fought against the British. The next encounter was on 8th June at Badli-ki-Sarai where they faced another rout. While 400 Muslim sepoys were killed in the battle, not a single Hindu lost his life. (117) British troops then occupied strategic positions on the Ridge near the city. Hindus within the city heaved a sigh of relief with two successive Muslim defeats and the firm encampment of British troops in close proximity. The prospect of respite from the fear of *Jihad* was going to continue as long as the British remained victorious.

It was but natural for Hindus to see that the British were not defeated. Hindus who had decided to cooperate with Muslims during the Uprising were now experiencing disillusionment. "The Hindu sepoys especially upbraided the Mahomedans; they also reproached the Mahomedans for having deceived them on pretences of their religion, and seemed to doubt greatly whether the English Government has really had any intention of interfering with their caste." (107-234) They awoke to the realization that they had been used by Muslims for political gain. "Great numbers of the Hindu sepoys at this time declared that if they could be sure their lives would be spared, they would gladly go back to the service of the Government." (107-234, 401)

Muslim Women to the Fore

This Uprising against the British was referred to in contemporary Muslim parlance as nothing but a '*Jihad.*' Here are a few examples.

Bahadur Shah had been informed on 2nd September about the 24th August battle at Aligarh in the following words: "It is reported also that several thousand *Jihadis,* under Maulvi Jalaluddin, had ventured to fight in the open, with the result that the Maulvi and several hundred of his followers had been killed, that English had taken possession of Aligarh." (121-217)

A British officer who was present in the battle at the Jama Masjid towards the end of the Uprising, described it thus: "The *Ghazis* made some desperate charges upon us. They came galloping down the street, their linen clothes flying in the wind, their *tulwars* waving round their heads, shouting '*Deen, Deen, Allah Deen*!', straight on the points of the bayonets. None ever went back, they came to die, and die they did, but every time they came, some one of us was killed or wounded." (91-163; 154-272)

Killings of the English had invariably been followed by Muslims giving victorious chants that their religion had prevailed. (107-263) The war cry *Deen-Deen* meant the same thing.

Being a struggle for Allah's cause, even Muslim women actively participated in the Uprising and would ride out for the *Jihad* just like their men folk. A British officer recorded his encounter with one such woman, 'who fought against us like a fiend.' (79-296) About two other women, he wrote: "They went far in advance with naked swords bitterly taunting the sepoys when they held back, calling them cowards and shouting to them to see how women went in front where they dared not to follow. The sepoys would excuse themselves, saying, 'We go to fetch ammunition.' But the women would reply, 'you stop and fight and we will get your ammunition for you.'" (296) These were women who took part for their faith without the slightest motive of individual worldly gain or power.[32]

---

32. Savarkar writes: "The women of Kanpur had left their Zenanas and jumped into the battlefield. But all these young soldiers and heroic women were put to shame by the dancing girl, Azizan: she had now put on a heroic grab. With her rosy cheeks and smiling lips, she was there on horseback, fully armed. And the artillery sepoys would forget all their fatigue at the sight of her.... 'Armed Azizan is flashing everywhere like lightning....' " (1-227)

Ban on Cow Slaughter — Only on the Day of Id and in Delhi

Bakrid fell on 1st August 1857. Anticipating the possibility of a Hindu-Muslim conflict, especially since such clash would have proved deleterious during the Uprising, the Emperor instructed (27th July 1857) the Commander-in-Chief to issue orders banning cow slaughter in the city on the day of Id, under pain of severe punishment to offenders. (69-62; 107-170) However, Muslims were loath to comply. (107-418) Even the Emperor's advisor, Hakim Ahsanullah Khan, took exception and proposed a consultation with Maulvis on the issue. The Emperor became furious after hearing this and retired in a huff to an inner chamber. Ultimately, however, the Commander-in-Chief did issue orders for a ban in the city on the day of Id.[33] (121-170) "The King has forbidden the killing of cows; but there is bad feeling between the Mahomedans and Hindus." (79-290)

The Emperor wrote Urdu poetry. On the auspicious occasion of Id, he sent the following couplet for the Commander-in-Chief:

"May all the enemies of the Faith be killed today;

The Firang his be destroyed, root and branch!

Celebrate the festival of Id Kurban by great slaughter;

Put our enemies to the edge of the sword – spare not!" (121-177; 79-277)

To Appease Hindus

The Muslim refrain was that Hindus were not cooperating in the fight against the British but, on the contrary, had joined hands with them and were supplying them with food. Many Hindus were arrested for this reason on 13th June 1857. (85-43) Hindus had given asylum to the English and Christians in several instances. One Christian recorded how Hindus had

---

33. Savarkar wrote that "A general order was issued prohibiting the slaughter of kine throughout the country." (1-287) This is incorrect. The ban was only for that day, that year and limited to the city of Delhi.

saved 14 Christian lives on 20th June 1857. (64-92) Likewise, records reveal cases where Hindus had extended a hand of friendship to Christians. (94)

At the time of the last conflict in September 1857, Bahadur Shah decided to personally lead his troops into battle in a bid to gain Hindu support and also quell Muslim wrath. (121-231) It was an attempt to end the dispute between the two communities. Announcers went around the city to inform citizens of the Emperor's intention of personally leading them against the enemy that night, calling upon all Hindus and Muslims to consider themselves obliged to assemble at the Kashmere Gate of the Palace. (121-229) Since the Emperor was going in person, more than 70,000[34] *ghazis* responded by assembling at the appointed place. (79-314) However, no record shows even a single Hindu having gone there. Ultimately, however, Bahadur Shah, on Hakim's advice and for reasons of security, abandoned the plan of going into battle in person. (79-314; 154-367)

After a decisive British victory over Delhi, "the Muslims began taking refuge with Hindus who they had upbraided for not cooperating with them, while others spent that entire day heaping abuses on them, menacingly recounting how they should have slaughtered all of them along with their women and children had they triumphed" [.] (121-231) Hindus, who were well aware of this, kept hoping that Muslims would not emerge victorious.

The Emperor's 'Generous Offer' of Relinquishing Power!

Full preparations to launch an assault on Delhi had been made by the British. Nicolson had defeated Muslim forces on 25th August at Najafgarh. Law and order in the city had collapsed completely. The Emperor could see his defeat vividly, and the question before him now was whether to prosecute the war or declare surrender. (1-335) Fully realizing that the

---

34. Other sources place this figure at 'upwards of 10,000' only. (121-229)

political revolution had failed, he wrote letters on 4th September to the Maharajas of Jaipur, Jodhpur, Bikaner and Alwar to inform them of his progressive powerlessness and to appeal to them to assume the mantle of leadership of the revolt. The letters also stated his willingness to step down as Emperor in their favour should any of them step forward to accept the responsibility. (121-219) Some authors use this document to establish that Bahadur Shah was free from a lure for power and was liberal, democratic, secular, nationalistic, and so on.[35]

However, such claims are meaningless. If any generosity had at all been shown, it was merely one of making over a failing revolution and a doomed throne to someone sufficiently gullible and unthinking to assume it! Such declaration might have made some sense had it been made on the first day, that is 11th May. This notwithstanding, whether on 11th May 1857 or later, in September of that year, had Bahadur Shah the right or authority of transferring power to a Hindu? He was no more than a puppet in the hands of Jihadi rebels. Moreover, would Muslims have supported someone like Nanasahib of Bithoor, the Shinde of Gwalior or Laxmibai of Jhansi even if one of them had been proposed to ascend the throne at the commencement of the Uprising? Would the same apparent solidarity with Hindus have characterized those events? Would history have been witness to scenes of seeming Hindu-Muslim unity?

---

35. For example, Savarkar writes: "This is the letter written by the leader of Indian Muhammedans, the Emperor of Delhi, to the Hindu kings in India ! This unique and typical letter shows how the noble words – Swatantrya, Swaraj, Swadesh and Swadharma – were thoroughly understood in Hindusthan." (1-334) "(The) noble and patriotic Emperor, fearing that, perhaps, the Revolution was being destroyed on account of his fault and that capable men were leaving his side on account of his being at the head, announced publicly that he was ready to give up all his power and abdicate." (333)

British Capture Delhi: Hindus Celebrate

When the British ultimately captured Delhi (20th September 1857), there is no saying how relieved Hindus must have felt! The unsettled milieu during the retribution unleashed by the victorious British might have prevented Hindus from open expression of their jubilation in Delhi, but those in Agra seem to have done so on behalf of their Delhi brethren. When news of the capitulation of Delhi reached Agra, the houses of the native inhabitants were richly illuminated. The Agra native community anxious to testify their loyalty towards the English Government, resolved to illuminate the city and indulge in other festivities in honour of the fall of Delhi. The mild Hindu was there in his Sunday best and evidently enjoyed the scene. Many followers of the Prophet likewise attended, but it was very evident by their sullen demeanour, etc., that the illuminations were not to their desire." (64-93) A British officer commented upon this scene that, "Had the Agra European population suffered the fate of their poor countrymen at Kanpur, we should have had every Mussalman in the city illuminating his house...." (93)

Well aware that the promoters, leaders and beneficiaries of the revolt were all Muslim, the axe of retribution fell primarily and selectively on that community. Bahadur Shah was dispatched to Rangoon, while the very dynastic seed, root and branch of the Mughal royalty was extinguished, not a single descendant was kept alive. Muslims were singled out for the severest punishment. (69-159) Innumerable pages of history are filled with descriptions of punishments thus meted out.

Sikhs Take Revenge

Sikhs made a significant contribution in suppressing the Uprising. The British could not have done without their co-operation.[36] British writers themselves gratefully acknowledged

---

36. Chief Commissioner Lawrence reported after the capture of Delhi: "Had the Sikhs joined against us, nothing, humanly speaking, could have saved us." (1-145q) (See also foot note 40 (infra)). Savarkar calls this act of the Sikhs helping the British as 'treachery.' (1-158)

the contribution of the Sikhs, saying "The Sikhs, whose thousands had perished in battle a dozen years before, were our friends in the Mutiny." (63-119) Why had the Sikhs co-operated with the British despite fresh recollections of how English cannons and muskets had conquered their kingdom not too long ago?

"It was because the Sikhs remembered the ferocious tortures with which their ancestors had been executed by the Mughal Empire 150 years ago. The Sikhs against Delhi were our (English) most savage and joyous auxiliaries." (63-47) "...as such, Sikhs had developed deep antagonism towards Muslims. Sikhs regarded Muslims as their staunch enemies" (158-33) "Sikhs unsheathed their swords with fervour against rebels who were attempting to rekindle Muslim power." (217) "The hatred felt for centuries by the Sikhs against the Mughal Emperor and their subjects. How could he (Sikh) forget the persecutions by the Mughal Emperors? To preach a holy war in favour of the restoration of the throne of Delhi, would have been an outrage on the memory of their martyrs, a disavowal of the prophecies of Guru Tegh Bahadur." (70-51) "The ill-will harbored by the Sikhs towards the Company's government disappeared before the ancient hatred and bloody reminiscences of the Mughal Emperor's oppression. The Sikhs were about to avenge their martyrs and the murder of their saint, Guru Tegh Bahadur." (70-62) They had desired to behead Bahadur Shah as an act of retribution. (44-86) Sikh soldiers satiated their wrath through mass slaughter and pillage.[37] Let us see what Khushwant Singh has to say about the intensity

37. A description of how they took revenge : "(After the fall of Delhi) the Sikhs dismounted to strip and plunder the dead Muslim fanatics whom they detested for they had a far longer and fiercer tradition of hostility to Muslim rule than they had to the British. They rolled the bodies over on to their back and slashed at their faces as they shouted, 'Take this for the Prophet, and this, and this, and this, and this for the four Imams (i.e. Gurus)." (79-326)

of Sikh sentiment, before we leave Delhi and turn to the Punjab of the Sikhs.

Khushwant Singh writes with reference to an event after the capture of Delhi: "(The) role of the Sikhs in suppressing the uprising was the most significant. Since the Meerut and Delhi mutineers had proclaimed the restoration of Mughal rule, Sikhs who had been brought up on tales of Mughal atrocities against their forefathers reacted sharply to Bahadur Shah's proclamation. (On the fall of Delhi) Hodson with his Sikh horsemen first captured Bahadur Shah, Begum Zeenat Mahal and their son Jawan Bakht. A day later they arrested two other sons and a grandson of the Emperor. In the security provided by the Sikhs, Hodson ignored the presence of an armed mob of several thousand, stripped the three princes naked and shot them with his carbine. Sikhs took the corpses of the princes to Chandni Chowk and laid them out for display in front of Gurdwara Sis Ganj, where 182 years ago, Guru Teg Bahadur had been executed by the orders of Emperor Aurangzeb."[38] (19-111)

The Sikhs thus expressed their exhilaration by taking revenge for atrocities committed on their ancestors and, by rendering help to the British in suppressing the Jihadi rebellion, they also removed the possibility of throning another Aurangzeb to torment their descendants.

- 3 -

Jihad in the Punjab Province

Punjab was under the overriding influence of the Sikhs. The Sikh populace, soldiers as well as chiefs of states that had not been annexed, had lent active support to the British during the revolt. Fresh in their minds were memories not only of atrocities under Mughal rule of a mere century and a half ago,

---

38. Two to three thousand armed Muslims were present at the time, guarded by just a hundred Sikhs. (79-315) The incident was remarkably stirring.

but also of the *Jihad* begun by Sayyid Ahmad Barelvi and his disciples in 1826, thereafter continued by the Ali Brothers till the British conquest of their kingdom (1849). They had firmly stood behind the British to prevent the resuscitation of the Mughal Empire or advent of another similar Islamic state.[39]

M. Inayat Ali had kept the anti-British *Jihad* going even after the British had annexed the Punjab. Sixteen British expeditions between the years 1850 and 1857, involving mobilization of 33,000 troops, were required to suppress that transborder *Jihad*. Infusion of treason among native soldiers of the British army was an important part of the *Jihad* agenda, which had been successful in causing the 4th Infantry Platoon in the Rawalpindi Cantonment to rebel in 1852. (42-14) As soon as indications of a possible rebellion became evident, Punjab had been secured by disarming or disbanding various platoons at 11 places in May 1857. Barring a single exception (of Hissar and Hansi), none of the rebelling forces had proclaimed independent administrations even for a short time. A majority of the sepoys, after rebellion or disbanding, had left for Delhi to serve the Emperor. It was this contingent of sepoys from the Punjab that had been mainly responsible for creation of an explosive situation in Delhi. (154-154) Even the British admit that it would not have been possible for them to put down the various rebellions without help from the Sikhs.[40] (111-632)

---

39. About this E. de Valbezen observes : "The Mussulmeen of the country, the towns and the frontier who were better disposed towards their coreligionists of Delhi, were separated from the Sikhs by the bloody barriers of the past. That hereditary hatred divided the children of the soil." (70-53) "The sympathies of the Hindus...were given...to the Government." (52)

40. Mohiuddin Ahmad writes: "The Punjab remained fairly calm in 1857 owing, chiefly, to the religious antipathy between the Sikhs and the Muslims, a legacy of the Sikh rule, and saved the Indian empire for the English." (112-330) (Here Sikhs have been held responsible for the estrangement.) See also footnote 36 (supra).

Conspiracy to Foster Rebellion in Platoons

Events occurring during the Uprising in the province have been recounted in the preceding chapter. Let us review from available sources, details of the essential nature of the Uprising.

Peshawar had the largest military base in the region, and it was there that the British suffered effects of the Uprising most. Places like Nawshera, Swat, Sitana, Panjatar, Mangalthana and Hotimardan were the very citadels of the Jihadi movement. M. Inayat Ali was leader of this movement during 1857. Their inability to secure victory against both Sikhs and the British had not prevented Jihadi sentiment and the cherished dream of founding an Islamic state from inspiring the entire region. Ali had concentrated the entire energy of the movement against the British during the 1857 Uprising.

The organization had succeeded in instilling rebellion among soldiery of the native platoons stationed in the region. One finds frequent mention of four platoons that had turned wholly rebellious. They were the 51st, 55th and 64th Infantry, and the 10th cavalry.

These four platoons had passed completely under the influence of Inayat Ali's Waliullahi teachings. (116-171; 112-331,2) Sepoys of these platoons were in secret correspondence among themselves as well as with those in other platoons. (112-331) The Indian headquarters of the movement was in Patna.

An administrative report dated 21st May 1857 would serve as an illustration of how rebellion was infused in sepoys. "The most rancorous and seditious letters had been intercepted from the Mahomedan bigots in Patna and Thaneswar and other soldiers of 64th Native Infantry and sending them messages from their own mothers that they should emulate these deeds, and, if they fell in the attempt, they would at least go to heaven, and their deaths, in such a case, should be pleasant news at home." It further reported that these letters alluded to a long series of correspondence that had been going on, through these men of the 64th Native Infantry, with the

Hindustani fanatics (*Mujahidin*) in Swat and Sitana." (3-353; 112-331)

Correspondence like this would be conducted through the naib (deputy commandant) of the platoon, Karimullah. (3-353) His father was an activist of the movement at Patna. He often travelled to Sitana, and from there to other places to meet chosen naibs and others in platoons. (116-170)

Preachers, disguised as fakirs, would be deputed to various cantonments to initiate sepoys into the rebellion. Fakirs enjoyed access to cantonments for religious purposes, or simply as mendicants. One such fakir was apprehended on suspicion on 19th May in the vicinity of the 24th Platoon. A letter in Persian containing a message for rebellion was found in his possession.[41] Such letters had been sent everywhere, and a few of them had accidentally fallen into British hands.

The following information, contained in a section entitled 'The War of Independence, 1857-59' in the book *Freedom Struggle in U.P.* published by the Pakistan Government, is noteworthy: " In Peshawar also in the beginning of June, emissaries from Delhi were preaching *Jihad*, and a number of *ghazis*, catching of cry, swarmed out of their fastnesses with a Maulvi at their head, and planted their standard in a strong mountain village called Nowrunjee, just outside the Peshawar frontier. The revolutionaries were, however, overpowered and village was destroyed. In August, a *faqir* was found preaching in the Lines of the 51st. The officer commanding took preemptory steps against the sepoys who had risen : they were defeated and slain in large numbers. The same

41. It reads : "My beloved Mullah ! Salam,....that instantly on receiving this, on the second day of the festival of the Id, you must – yes, must – come here, and if it be easy, bring a few pounds of fruits with you. Now is the time; admit no fear into your heart; such an opportunity will not again occur. Set out, I enjoin you." – Fakir Mullah. (3-355) Id was six days away (25th May). It was in cryptic language; 'fruits' meant 'weapons'. It was a message calling for revolt on the day following Id.

faqir suddenly reappeared in September with fresh followers, mainly Mahomedans...." (34-295)

Work of Waliullahi Maulvis

Mohiuddin devoted nine pages of his book to present information how M. Inayat Ali struggled against the British from May 1857 till his death in March 1858. (112-330 to 8) A separate seventeen-page section entitled 'The Wahabis and Movement of 1857–59' appears in Prof. Qeyamuddin Ahmad's book. (116-215 to 31) Nevertheless, the above information suffices to reveal who the promoters, inspirers and leaders of the Uprising really were. So explosive a situation had been created by the Waliullahi movement at the time, that Commissioner Lawrence had felt obliged to propose to his superiors that Peshawar ought to be ceded to Afghanistan. (34-393; 78-459)

Abdul Qadar, a Maulvi of the Waliullahi persuasion, was at the forefront of the movement in Ludhiana. Educated at the famous 'Madarsa-i Rahimmiya' established by Shah Waliullah, he had been associated with Barelvi and had plunged into the 1857 Uprising along with his four sons.[42] (25-216) He wielded much influence in the royal court in Afghanistan, and one of his sons, M. Saif Rahman, had settled in Kabul in later times and was a signatory to the Delhi *Jihad* Declaration. (216)

The rebellion at Ludhiana involved not just sepoys, but also the civilian populace. Dr. Chaudhary, who lauds the

42. Without stating this Maulvi's name, Savarkar writes: "In the (Ludhiana) city, there was a certain Maulvi who always used to preach to the people to break away from English slavery and establish Swaraj. On account of the Maulvi's lectures, this town had become a powerful centre of the Revolutionary party in Punjab. When the sign came that the time had come to deal the last blows at the chains of slavery, the whole town rose (with cries of 'Deen ! Deen !')." (1-155) "But it was desirable for the Revolutionaries to go to Delhi.... And they proceeded towards Delhi crying that they would now decide, at the walls of Delhi itself, the question of slavery or Swaraj." (156)

Uprising as a war of independence, writes: "The population of Ludhiana was of a mixed character consisting of many turbulent elements, the Kabulis and the Kashmiris, and the Mahomedan Gujars in particular, who were excited to a high state of fanaticism by a Maulvi. All of them were now foremost in plundering the government stores, in destroying printing presses and in other outrages." (81-236) "In Ludhiana, military preparations on the part of the city populace were going on in such a scale that the city had to be disarmed and eleven cart-loads of arms were seized." (236)

Rebellion by Muslim Population

Inhabitants of all villages around Sialkot rose in rebellion, encouraged by reports that British rule had ended and power had been restored to the Mughal Emperor. (235) This was entirely civilian in nature and independent of the separate revolt by sepoys stationed there. Their comrades in Delhi had invited these sepoys to hasten to that city. (132-96) Many had accordingly left and several had been apprehended and killed *en route*.

Sepoys stationed at Jalandhar and Philaur were in communication with those at Ludhiana. They shared the same philosophy and had together left for Delhi.

The 21st platoon at Karachi had planned to rebel on the 13th September, take support of the 14th platoon and Muslim residents of the town, kill all whites and proceed to Delhi. (44-283) But the platoon was disbanded as soon as this plan became known. (284)

Ahmad Khan and Sarfaraz Khan, who were prominent in the Uprising in the Multan province, had in fact initiated the revolt there, breaking into the Gogaria prison on 26th July. Ahmad Khan, who belonged to the Ravi tribe, was killed on 17th September, but the struggle was carried on by his successors, Walidad and Mir Fatwanah. (81-236; 67-65; 68-554)

Establishment of a State

The 14th cavalry at Hissar and Hansi rebelled on 29th May, put the Magistrate and twenty-one other Englishmen to death, and did other usual things like torching their bungalows and freeing prisoners. (81-237) Rebel leader Muhammad Azeem Shahzada became the head of the administration. (81-237; 67-65) The Uprising here had assumed the same nature as that in Rohilkhand. (67-65; 68-554) Four hundred Jihadis had gone from the area to Delhi "who believed it was their duty to free what they regarded as *Dar-ul-Islam* from the rule of the hated *kafirs.*" (154-264)

A detachment of the cavalry platoon was stationed at Sirsa. After rebelling, the sepoys looted the treasury, killed the tehsildar and other officials, while the terrified Hindu population fled abandoning their homes and belongings. Local Muslims then looted the town and surrounding villages, and burned official documents. (81-237; 67-65) The rebellion had developed into a communal, anti-Hindu pogrom. (67-65; 68-554)

Dr. Chaudhary writes about prevailing conditions when the revolt at the above three places was put down by the British: "Many villages were carried by storm and burnt and altogether 133 persons were hanged. The Mussalmans, in general, took an active part but Jats, Sikhs and deswalis maintained a defensive attitude." (81-237)

Three hundred sepoys from Delhi went on 11th May 1857 to neighbouring Gurgaon, where hundreds of locals declared their support, while Nawab Ahmad Mirza and Nawab Dulajan joined hands with the rebels. Ford, the local Collector fled. (38-48) The rebel leader in the district, Hakim Abdul Haq, was hanged on 2nd November 1857. (81-239)

Unrest erupted in Rohtak as soon as the Emperor had been reinstated in Delhi. When Tafzal Hussain arrived with a force from Delhi on 23rd May, the situation had gone out of control. The collector and other officials had fled. (7-984; 81-238) This was followed by customary looting and arson. All rebels rallied under a green flag hoisted in the town. (81-238) Like Delhi, Rohtak also remained under rebel control till mid-September. (239)

Two zamindar leaders, Darya Khan and Dil Murad, were making efforts to provoke sepoys in Sindh to rebel by infusing anti-British sentiment among them. The proximity to Iran had facilitated Iranian busybodies to spread a similar sentiment among Baluchis. (44-284, 6) The British, of course, dealt firmly with these insurgencies.

Promoters and Leaders

Stating it briefly, all promoters, instigators and leaders there, were Muslim. Even according to Dr. Chaudhary, at the forefront of every incident (except one) in the Punjab all were invariably Muslim. The lone exception was that of Narhar Singh, the Hindu Raja of Vallabhgarh, who had voluntarily submitted himself to the cause of Islam despite his religion. (see footnote 25 (supra)

As a consequence of the predominantly Jihadi nature of the Uprising in this province, the British were under constant fear that, if the then Amir (of Afghanistan) were to raise the green standard and to call upon the chiefs and people of Afghanistan, in the name of the great Prophet, to pour down upon the Firangis, all the great chiefs and leading tribes would have gathered around him and a great flood of Muhammadanism would have poured down upon us." (78-337) They had succeeded, through the diplomacy of a political treaty, in forcing the Amir of Afghanistan into inaction.

Help from Sikh States

Unannexed states of Patiala, Nabha, Jind and Kapurthala in the Punjab had backed the British with their entire strength. The passage of many a rebel sepoys from the Punjab towards Delhi had been blocked by them.[43]

---

43. Savarkar writes about the first three of these states: "These States had it in their hand either to establish the Revolution firmly or kill it. These States lay between Ambala and Delhi and without their support the English rear was quite defenseless. Even if these States had remained passive like the others, the Revolution had a great chance of success. But when (they)....began to deal blows at the Revolution even more cruel than those of the English, the chain between Delhi and Punjab was suddenly snapped." (1-132)

This invaluable Sikh cooperation finds mention in a book authored by a Secretary to the then Punjab Government: "During the disturbances of 1857–8, no prince in India showed greater loyalty or rendered more conspicuous service to the British Government than Narinder Singh, the Maharaja of Patiala. He was the acknowledged head of the Sikhs, and his hesitation or disloyalty would have been attended with the most disastrous results, but he unhesitatingly placed his whole power, resources and influence at the absolute command of the English, and during the darkest days of the Mutiny he never for a moment wavered in his loyalty." (35-234) The Maharaja personally led his army against rebels. Going further, he constantly expressed his earnest wish to lead a contingent to Delhi, but he was dissuaded from this by the British authorities. (235) He had supplied 156 commanders, 5,002 soldiers, 8 guns and a sum of Rs. 5 lacs to this effort. (236)

Similarly, when the mutiny broke out in May 1857, Raja Sarup Singh (of Jind) was not behind the Maharaja of Patiala in active loyalty. (390) Raja Bharpur Singh (of Nabha) was anxious himself to march to Delhi at the head of his troops, as the Raja of Jind had done. This was not allowed. (465) Raja Randhir Singh (of Kapurthala) took the earliest opportunity of evincing his loyalty towards the British Government. (The) Raja marched into Jalandhar with every available soldier, and remained there throughout the hot season at the head of his troops. (576) He had with him 1,700 troopers and five field guns.

In view of the nature of the 1857 Uprising, the following comment cannot be ignored just because it was made by the British: "If there be any feeling of nationality in India whatever, it may be most fairly looked for among the Sikhs." (35-vi)

- 4 -

Agra Province

Rebellion had erupted in all the six districts of the Agra province during May–June 1857, and every one of these had been spearheaded by Maulvis and Ulemas. (77-166) Besides fiercely opposing their rule and participating actively in the Uprising, these clerics were also engaged in a theological battle against the British. They had succeeded in propagating the superiority of Islam over Christianity. (166) (Dr.) Wazir Khan and Maulvi Rahmatullah were foremost among those who fought with their deep knowledge and tremendous courage both on the academic front and in the battlefield (in 1857). (166) M. Rahmatullah was a great scholar of Islam in the Waliullahi tradition. (25-206)

Aligarh under Muslim Rule

A Brahmin zamindar at Aligarh was hanged on charges of treason, and the leading bad characters in the 9th (N.I.) being ripe for mutiny, took advantage of this execution and broke out. (655) Stripping off their uniforms, sepoys rose up with cries of 'Yeh Khuda ka Hukm Hai' ('This is Khuda's Command')[44] (655) All British officials fled to Agra. After completing customary post-Uprising business, many sepoys left for Delhi amid roars of 'Deen-Deen'. (7-657; 5-172) Aligarh passed into rebel hands but they could not establish a state till the end of June.

On 30th June, Muslims in the town raised green flags, gave slogans of 'Deen-Deen' and loudly proclaimed the re-establishment of the Islamic state. They went out with the resolve to kill all Englishmen and began giving cries that their severed heads would be hung at the city gates. (7-659; 81-79; 43-64) M. Abdul Jaleel,[45] an adherent of the Waliullahi doctrine,

---

44. That Brahmin had no connection with the rebellion – he was neither instigator nor leader. Perhaps, like Mangal Pandey, he too had been used to obtain Hindu support. It is indeed astounding that the sepoys themselves had exposed the Brahmin's (seditious) conspiracy. (44-104) Would anybody betray the complicity of one's comrade? It would almost seem that the sepoys sent the Brahmin to the gallows and used the incident to their own advantage as an excuse to rebel. Hindu presence was not perceived in any subsequent event.

45. A disciple of Sayyid Ahmad Barelvi and Shah Muhammad Ishaq. He is buried in the Jama Masjid at Aligarh. (25-211)

had issued a declaration of *Jihad* on the same day. (25-211) The Nawab of Malgadh in the neighbouring Bulandshahar district, Walidad Khan, then commenced his rule. The Emperor sent him a charter appointing him as Subedar. Actual administration was delegated to the naib (deputy) subedar, Ghaus Muhammad Khan. (7-67, 667) He commenced his rule with the 6,000 sepoys under his command and appointed Muslims to all executive offices.[46] (81-79; 7-669)

Valour of the Ghazis

A fierce encounter with the British ensued on 24th August. M. Abdul Jaleel was performing the task of provoking the citizenry to perform *Jihad*. Proclamations of *Jihad* began to be heard from Aligarh's mosques. *Ghazis* attacked with great speed and agility, and managed to initially scatter the enemy. Seeing that they were gaining an upper hand, the British opened a barrage of the artillery in which many *ghazis* were killed. The Maulvi lay down his life in a duel with a captain. (44-106, 7) History records several engaging accounts of this man's heroism and the fierce battle given by the *ghazis.*[47] Although the defeated rebels quit the city, the British were unable to establish their administration. (7-670) The rebels began their rule again.

What had been the role of Hindus in this affair? They were helping the British. Thakur Govind Singh and Raja Tekum Singh, who were with the British commander Mr. Cocks, had been given charge of the place after the Aligarh victory. (670) However, despite this authority, Muslim rebels

46. For example, Naib and chief of the city: M. Naseemullah Khan; tehsildar: Mahboob Khan; kotwal: Hassan Khan. (81-79; 7-669) Naseemullah was a nephew of Abdul Jaleel and, like him, a Waliullahi. (25-211) After assuming charge of the city's administration, he had declared: "Khulk Khuda Ka, Mulk Badshah Ka, aur Hukum M. Naseemullah Ka." (212)

47. Dr. Chaudhary writes, "He (Jaleel) was most active in stirring up the religious bigotry of the Mahomedans." (81-80)

continued to hold sway over the area. It was only after the capture of Delhi that British forces finally wrested Aligarh from them on 5th October 1857. Local Muslims had offered bitter resistance during this final battle in which M. Naseemullah Khan and 400 others were killed. (7-869; 25-212)

Hathras, a town 20 miles from Agra, was threatened by Ghaus Khan in August 1857. But the local Hindu leaders assisted the British and preserved law and order. (7-669)

In like manner, Muslims of nearby Atrauli broke into open revolt on 25th September. (81-80; 7-865, 8)

Hindus Appointed to Administer on Behalf of the British

Local talukdar Tej Singh had declared independence after a rebellion at Mainpuri and after the rebels had left for Delhi. He harboured a grievance against the British for making laws that had forced him to cede 149 of the 200 villages he had held. (81-80) He wielded great influence in the district. Naturally, how were Muslims going to tolerate this situation? They had not engaged in the Uprising to suffer a Hindu ruler at the end of it all. So, Tafzal Hussain of neighbouring Farrukhabad launched an immediate military attack upon him. However, as both were opposed to the British albeit for distinct reasons, a superficial truce was hammered out between them. Yet, efforts to cause defections from mutual parties continued. (44-106) Tej Singh's cousin, Rao Bhavani Singh, was a British loyalist and was used by them to maintain British supremacy over Mainpuri. Indeed, after their complete victory over Mainpuri in October 1857, the British had entrusted the administration to Rao Bhavani Singh. (141-365) Ultimately, Tej Singh surrendered. It was only on account of these cousins that a Muslim state could not be established in Mainpuri.

Shahzada's and Walidad Khan's Troops in Etawah

Six Pathan horsemen of the 3rd Cavalry, who had arrived at Etawah with the objective of passing a message to sepoys in the district, after the Uprising in Meerut, were identified by sentries on guard duty. Five of them were killed in the ensuing skirmish, with some losses to the British. (7-632) The population of Etawah was all Muslim and all 2,000 of them were bitterly anti-British. (630) They possessed six cannons and a variety of other weapons. (774)

Many Hindu zamindars in the district were chieftains in their respective territories and a certain Kunwar Singh among them was pro-British. The Nawab of Farrukhabad dispatched 5,000 soldiers with 12 cannons to uproot the zamindar's rule. (87-85; 7-777) After the rout, Mewati Muslims looted the environs to their heart's content. (7-777) Soon thereafter, Prince Firoz Shah with 1,400 cavalry and Walidad Khan of Malgarh with his army arrived in the district, which intensified the already charged atmosphere. A fierce battle was also fought at Haracharapura against the British. (81-86) In short, the uprising in the district had taken on a completely Islamic hue.

Muslims versus Hindus and British in Etah

Events at Kasganj in Etah district are particularly significant. Sepoys who had rebelled in Aligarh and Mainpuri arrived in Etah on 23rd May, and all local officials fled. (7-673) A rebellion occurred on 24th May at Kasganj, the most important place in the district. Seeing that no Englishmen were present, a certain Dambar Singh proclaimed his independent rule over the Etah region. Durjan Singh, a brother of Tej Singh of neighbouring Mainpuri, came to Dambar's assistance. (7-679; 44-107) How could Muslims tolerate this?

So the Nawab of Farrukhabad sent his forces and assumed control of the region in July. Muslim officials were appointed: Hussain Mirza as tehsildar and Azamullah Khan as police chief of Kasganj. (7-680) They also enjoyed support of the Nawab of Malgarh. (44-107) The British won back the region in November 1857 and appointed Ghanshyam Das as nazim (collector) on their behalf. (7-680, 1)

All Pathans in the Etah region assembled at Bithaura, launched an attack on Kasganj on 2nd December, killed Ghanshyam Das and suspended his decapitated head from a *peepul* tree near the tehsil office. (682) Hindu households were ransacked. The town remained under their control for thirteen days, till 14th December. Many of these miscreants were deserters from service of the Nawab of Rohilkhand. (682)

The following entreaty, made by one Muhammad Ali Chaudhary on 26th June 1857 to the Nawab of Malgadh, is illustrative of the penchant for power and overlordship afflicting Muslim gentry after the Uprising. After the eight opening lines eulogizing the Nawab to the status of Emperor, the representation stated: "(In) these glorious days when the light of religion of Islam has dispelled the gloom hanging over the realm of India by the glad tidings of the coronation of the Heaven's favoured king of Delhi as Emperor of Hindustan and by grant of a *firman* to Your Excellency in which His Imperial Majesty has been pleased to confer on you a very high dignity, but the wicked Rajputs are bent upon causing anarchy and by their disaffection the crimes of murder, plunder and arson, have become common these days. The ancestors of your petitioner under the auspices of your illustrious forefathers, held high offices under the former Emperors of Delhi. Your poor petitioner is anxious that he may be appointed a *Nazim* (which rank was formerly held by his ancestors) over the district of Etah...." (684)

Was it not a pipedream to contemplate a Hindu for any office at all in such conditions?

Green Flag over Mathura

Sepoys from two platoons at Mathura rebelled in May and set off towards Delhi. Two *sethiyas* (traders/money-lenders), Radha Kishan and Govind Das, spent from their own wealth to raise a security force to give protection to British officers, and to maintain law and order. (686) The British officers, themselves, recorded that they would not have been able to continue staying there without the help of these *sethiyas.* (68-526) But soon thereafter, British officers left Mathura. Their absence prompted Devi Singh from a nearby village to proclaim his rule. (7-696; 44-110) But the British attacked and arrested him. He had acted rashly when he had no support. This was his undoing and he was later hanged. (44-110)

In July 1857, locals and some horsemen unfurled the Muhammadi flag over kotwali (police station). They began helping the rebels led by Saduddin. (7-892) Commencement of rule from Delhi was proclaimed and the Emperor appointed Karamat Ali as Subedar of Mathura. (81-82) It was only after the British capture of Delhi that this Muslim state was dissolved. Neither the Emperor nor Muslim population nor anybody else, however, supported Devi Singh's adventure, which clearly indicates the essential nature of the uprising there. It is significant that the green flag should be flying over Mathura, a sacred place of Hindu pilgrimage.

Nawab's Rule at Farrukhabad

No sooner the rebellion had broken out in the Farrukhabad district of the Agra province the than local Nawab Tafzal Hussain Khan, proclaimed his rule. The Fatehgarh fort was situated in his district. The usual slogan of 'Khulk Khuda ka, Mulk Badshah ka, Hukm Nawab Bahadur ka' was made and rule of Delhi promulgated. (7-731, 52) Muslims were appointed to all advisory and executive offices in the Darbar. (7-769; 81-87) Barring a singular exception, all administrative positions were filled by Muslims. Only Thakur Pandey was appointed as nazim at Fatehgarh (where the fort was located). (7-763)

This Nawab retained his own district and also sent help to rebels in the nearby districts to usher in Muslim administrations. He ruled for a period of seven months, being finally sentenced to death by hanging. However, the punishment was not implemented and he was later permitted to go to Mecca. (111-591)

Farrukhabad had become an important center for the *Jihad* of 1857. Principal leaders of the movement had paid visits to the place, including the Commander-in-Chief at Delhi, Bakht Khan, Nawab of Malgarh Walidad Khan and Shahzada Firoz Shah. This was not all. Even Tej Singh of Mainpuri had gone there. (7-927) The first thing the victorious British general did after the capture of the town in January 1858, was an order for the arrest of all Muslim leaders. (928)

Agra: Hindus Cooperate with British

When rebellion erupted on 31st May at Agra, British officers disbanded platoons and took refuge in the fort. The Muslim troopers who had arrived from Neemuch and Malwa had left for Delhi on 5th July as 'the victors of Agra', defeating the British at Shahganj. Next morning, the Mussalmans of the city on a rumour that they (British) had almost all been killed were debating whether (to proceed or not to the enemy camp). (723) The British took refuge within the fort.

The local Magistrate trusted Muslims implicitly and, as a result, many were employed in the revenue and police departments. But no sooner the revolt had occurred than all of them abandoned their posts and joined up with the rebels. (724) An intelligence report says: "The religious and Mahomedan element at this time was dominant in the mutineer movement. The whole Police Officers and men (almost all Moslems) quitted their post. The fierce anti-Moslem feeling pervaded in most civilians and almost all the military leaders. (724) This misplaced trust cost the magistrate his job.

The British could only trust Hindus. A government report says : "The lieutenant governor determined on the judicious plan of working mainly through Hindus, whom alone we can, at this juncture, as a body, depend upon. This policy, however, ran so counter to (Magistrate) Mr. Drummond's previous system and agency, that the government was obliged to supersede him (i.e. the latter), and appoint another officer to his post." (724) Consequently, Hindu help was taken to maintain law and order in Agra.

Wazir Khan's Rule

However, the force of the Muslim revolt was great. Rebel forces from all over were converging on Agra. As a result of the Uprising in Gwalior, the Maharaja too was unable to send sufficient military aid to Agra and, in this situation, the town passed under rebel control. The Emperor's rule was proclaimed and Dr. Wazir Ali Khan[48] became Subedar. (77-166; 17-144) He was a surgeon, having been educated in London and had engaged in a deep study of Islam and Christianity. (77-166) He was in the company of M. Rahimatullah,[49] a great theologian of the Waliullahi tradition.

Declaration of Jihad

Proclamation of *Jihad* was made from mosques immediately after promulgation of the state. The town reverberated with slogans of *Jihad.* (44-114) A huge *Jihad* procession was taken out under the leadership of the kotwal, Murad Ali, in which Muslims joined in big numbers. (68-527; 154-326) Thereafter, all remaining Christians without distinction of age, sex, colour or condition were put to death. (44-114) Fortunately, for the Hindus in Agra, the *Jihad* being only against the Christians, they did not challenge the Hindus. (114)

Had the forces that had arrived with Prince Firoz Shah not been defeated at Agra (October 1857), an Islamic state under his aegis would have been established.[50]

The following incident shows how the milieu was surcharged with Jihadi sentiment. Some British soldiers were conducting several civilian Englishmen from Agra to Aligarh when they were accosted and attacked by Jihadis *en route.*

---

48. After the fall of Agra, this man went to Lucknow to participate, along with M. Ahmad Shah, in the *Jihad* there. After Lucknow had been lost to the British, he went to Prince Firoz Shah to assist in the latter's *Jihad.* (25-217)

49. M. Rahimatullah (d. 1891) had accomplished much in the Uprising. He had popularized *Jihad* in Delhi. (25-211) He had authored several books to demonstrate the supremacy of Islam. (207) Among them, the four-volume *Izhar-ul Haq* was written at the behest of the Turkish *Khalifa* a Abdul Aziz (d. 1876) and has been translated into several languages including English. (207n)

50. A glance at the proclamation (Chapt. 9, Infra) issued by him will suffice to indicate what the nature of such Islamic state could have been.

The then British Magistrate describes the incident thus: "When the *Ghazis* charged, an old Mullah or priest, sat by the bank chanting the Quran to encourage the warriors; as the combat thickened, his voice rose louder; at length he worked himself up into an ecstasy of fanaticism. He closed his volume, seized a sword, and exclaiming, 'I too will be a martyr!' he rushed on our soldiers...." (79-162) Of course, all *ghazis*, along with him, perished.

Happy Hindus

As we have seen earlier, Hindus of Agra celebrated the fall of Delhi to the British with loud cries of jubilation and illuminating their homes. (64-93)

In brief, there ought to remain no doubt in our understanding of who the promoters, instigators, leaders and beneficiaries were in the Agra region, or how its essential nature was Jihadi to the core.

- 5 -

Meerut Province

We now turn to events in the Meerut province.

Rule of Walidad Khan

The Bulandshahar district had passed under rebel control with the rebellion on 22nd May. Walidad Khan, the Nawab of Malgarh in the district, declared his independent rule. Subsequently, the Emperor issued an order (26th May) appointing him as Subedar of the district. (7-51) Muslims were appointed to all important offices in the administration. Walidad was an important leader of the Uprising. Not limiting himself to administration of his own holdings, he had paid attention to neighbouring territories as well. Aligarh was fully under his control, while rebels in Etah were receiving assistance from him. Being a kin of Bahadur Shah, he also wielded considerable influence in the Imperial court at Delhi. (56)

Main Offensive Against Hindus

The overall balance of power in the district had Jats and Gujars siding with the British and Muslims on the side of the rebels. About 70 to 80 Gujars had been killed in conflicts. (41) About an incident Govt. Report says : "The Gujars now grew resolved in all eagerness to loot the town. Meanwhile the weavers and *Guddes,* and Hassan Buksh and Karim Buksh *Risaldars,* and Ali Raza *Daffadar* with other Mussalmans, came out to oppose them and a fight ensued." (41) On 31st May, twenty thousand Rajputs and Gujars came together, attacked the weavers' quarter, torched houses and wounded or killed several of them. A sack followed. (42) The Nawab reported in a letter to the Emperor that Gujars and other natives had killed all inhabitants of Sikandarabad (near Malgarh). (66) Although Rajputs and Gujars were creating anarchy and indulging in loot, they were neither sympathetic to the Uprising nor were they supporters of the Nawab's rule. As a result, Walidad had to engage in a dual *Jihad* — one against the British and another against Rajputs and Gujars. All Muslim talukdars and zamindars in the district were supporters of the Nawab's regime. (81-78) Till the fall of Delhi, Muslims had oppressive dominance over the city. (44-107)

Nawab's Jihadi Letters to the Emperor

The Jihadi essence of the Uprising in the district becomes clear after an overview of Hindu-Muslim relations and even the Nawab's correspondence with the Emperor.

In a letter dated 11th June, he wrote: Today I with a few soldiers attacked the *Kafirs*....and waged a fierce battle. The *Ghazis,* irrespective of the consideration of their small numbers and greater of the enemy, showered such a heavy fire from matchlocks that the opponents took to flight. The *Ghazis* pursued them. Many *Kafirs* escaped to Meerut. I am much worried as the *Kafirs* are many and (we are a few).... This country has come into our hands after great battle and much bloodshed; but would be lost upon us for nothing due to non-arrival of the help. The faithful *Ghazis* of Your Majesty would thus be greatly lowered in esteem. (If early help is reached) I may squeeze out the brains of the *Kafirs*. May the sun of glory and fortune ever shine (upon you)." (7-56)

In another dated 19th June, he wrote : "I have driven out the vainglorious *Firangis* but the innumerable Jats, who in this region with (the) three Englishmen have created disturbances, are harassing your subjects. Although General Mohd. Ismail Khan and the *Ghazis* have been appointed for extirpating these shameless people, still because of paucity of troops their total annihilation as desired by me is not possible." (58) He also requested military aid in the letter.

Jihad against Jats, Too

In a letter dispatched on the following day, he wrote: "Today in the morning the Englishmen accompanied by 2000 Jats, Foot soldiers, marched for a battle towards Malagarh. My relation General Mohd. Ismail Khan with 300 *Ghazis* and one piece of artillery reached over the heads of these wicked *Kafirs* and a serious skirmish ensued. At last, the indomitable *Ghazis* exhibited bravery and manliness....(so that) victory fell to the lot of followers of Islam. About 60 (*Kafirs*) were sent to hell and 12 (of us) were martyred in the battle, and one Jat village was put to fire. Although a handful of *Ghazis* are bent upon sacrificing their lives and winning over the crown of martyrdom yet our enemies become bold because of their (*Ghazis*) small strength." (59)

It is significant that Jats, like the British, have also been called 'kafirs' in the letter. Muslims, during the Uprising, regarded not just the British but even Hindus who opposed them as kafirs and were prepared to wage *Jihad* against both, wherever essential and possible.

On 22nd June, he wrote: "The Jats have given shelter to the *Firangis* and are devastating Your Majesty's country. I shall quell the power of miscreants after the arrival of (your) army, and massacring the *Firangis* and the Jats shall begin the realization of revenue... ." (60)

Included in the same book (*Freedom Struggle in U. P.*) are six other similar letters in which Jats and Gujars are categorized as *kafirs* along with the British, and a resolve to exterminate them mentioned. The real nature of the Uprising can be appreciated not by reviewing appeals Muslim leaders had made to Hindus, but by studying what sentiments and expression they used in private correspondence[51] among themselves.

Walidad Khan remained the Nawab and the same situation continued till British forces captured Bulandshahar soon after the fall of Delhi.

Muzaffarnagar : Jihadi attacks on Hindus

After revolt, district Muzaffarnagar, like Meerut, went under the control of rebels. Local Sayyid zamindars began raising militia from the population to attack British officials and Hindu bankers. (77) The latter along with Hindu mahajans became their special target. A twenty thousand strong force was raised and slogans of 'Ya Ali! Ya Ali!' used to be given during assaults. (90) Their first target was destruction of deeds and documents relating to lands mortgaged to Hindu mahajans and usurers. (91) They would go armed with muskets and other weapons and abduct or otherwise take such mahajans into custody, conduct them to the attackers' homes and threaten them with death while beef was forced into their mouths. (92) Rebels had resolved to kill all British officials and, on 21st June, raise the green flag over the town. At eight in the evening on that day, the 4th platoon issued a declaration ordering all true Muslims to rally around them and hand over all *kafirs*. (85) However, they could not kill all of them.

An incident of 14th May 1857 illustrates the view taken by the community whenever a Muslim official refused to rebel but continued in British service. Imad Hussain, a tehsildar, was performing the duty of protecting the treasury at that time. The Muslim subedar of the rebel sepoys "sent an abusive message to the *Tehsildar* saying that he had believed him a Mahomedan but that he had proved himself a *Kafir*...." (77) This clearly shows who was considered a *kafir*. Every Muslim was expected to rise against the British. Nonparticipation in the Uprising was considered '*kufr*' (disbelief').

---

51. In letters or applications to the Emperor, Muslim subedars and other officials referred to him as: "The representative of God, the sovereign of the world, may he ever reign." (7-62)

Muzaffarnagar was the birthplace of Shah Muhammad Ismail, a close associate of Sayyid Barelvi. The latter had even visited the town on his preaching tours. The entire district was under influence of his teachings. It was due to events during the Shamli and Thana Bhavan rebellions that this district became a subject of wide discussion. It provides a representative picture of the Uprising in this region.

Thana Bhavan: Declaration of Jihad

The Muhammadi flag was hoisted as soon as rebellion broke out in Thana Bhavan. (7-127) Proclamation of *Jihad* was made according to the *Shariat.* Holy warriors began converging at the town from all parts of the district. Orders were issued to kill *kafir* Firangis wherever found. Appeals were made to Muslims asking them to consider themselves subjects of the Delhi Emperor. (128)

This revolt was organized by Qazi Inayat Ali, assisted by the cavalry commander, Ghulam Mohiuddin. (147)

Rebels from Thana Bhavan went to nearby Shamli, the main center of the Uprising where renowned Maulvis had assembled, and an Islamic state was promulgated. M. Haji Imadullah (1817–99) was made Khalifa, M. Muhammad Qasim Nanautavi (1832–80) the Commander-in-Chief and M. Rashid Ahmad Gangohi (1828–1905), the Qazi (Chief Justice). (17-143; 24-214; 76-21) M. Rahimatullah was in actual command of the Jihadis. (77-167) All of these Maulvis were faithful adherents of the Waliullahi doctrine. (25-214; 43-65; 77-163) Khalifa Imadullah had twice visited Delhi and seen conditions there. (17-143) He was closely associated with the *Jihad* in that city. A military commander from the town, Khairat Khan, had also gone to seek help from the Delhi administration. (7-129)

Detailed descriptions are available of the *Jihad* waged against the British by rebels in Shamli. (17-143) For example, a report by a magistrate, Edwards, states: "The ferocity of the Mahomedans against government servants was shown at Shamali by their slaughtering all who fled into the *Masjid* which had always hitherto been deemed a sanctuary. They were brutally murdered. The main walls of the *Masjid* and *Shewallah,*....are crimsoned with blood." (7-141; 125-13)

The Khalifa appointed a 'Majlis-i-Shura' (legislative/ decision-making council), which included many Maulvis as members, when the decision to declare *Jihad* was taken with overwhelming majority. (25-213) Some members, however, expressed doubts about success in the absence of adequate military strength.[52] M. Muhammad Qasim replied that at the Battle of Badr (624 C.E.), the Prophet had few soldiers yet was able to vanquish a numerically superior *kafir* host, and wanted to know whether they were not as strong as the army of believers at Badr! The example of this precedent forthwith quelled all doubts and the decision for *Jihad* was taken. (125-11)

Haji Imadullah slipped away to Mecca in order to escape arrest and trial after the rebellion was crushed by the British. Nevertheless, his disciples M. Muhammad Qasim and M. Rashid Ahmad secured pardon and continued their work in India in various other ways.[53] (125-16)

---

52. Two of the Maulvis expressed a different opinion. According to them, *Jihad* was lawful only if the hope and possibility of success existed. They opined that *Jihad* was unlawful in that situation because there was no hope of success against the British. (15-82; 25-214; 125-10)

53. In later times (1867), M. Qasim founded the historic 'Dar-ul-Ulum' school of religious study at Deoband. M. Rashid assumed responsibility of the institute after Qasim's death (1880). Prof. Faruqi writes about this academy: "Shamli and Deoband are, as a matter of fact, the two sides of one and the same picture. The difference lies only in weapons. Now the sword and spear were replaced by the pen and the tongue. There, at Shamli, in order to secure political independence and freedom of religion and culture, resort was made to violence; here at Deoband, a start was made to achieve the same goal through peaceful means. There, for the cause of religio-political freedom, individuals were used; here, for that purpose individuals were to be produced. The roads, though diverging from each other, led towards the same destination." (76-23; 125-19q)

M. Haji Imdadullah

The following comment by a well-known Deobandi of the 20th century, M. Ubaidullah Sindhi, about Imdadullah's *Jihad* work is noteworthy in the context of 1857: "There had been a continuous *Jihad* movement in India going back to the time of Shah Abdul Aziz. This had reached its peak in the *Jihad* of Sayyid Ahmad Shaheed (d.1831) but continued in an organized form after his death, first under the leadership of Shah Muhammad Ishaq, a great grandson of Shah Waliullah and, after (him) under Haji Imdadullah (in 1851) (till the 1857 Uprising)." (17-143q.)

The situation in the third district of the Meerut province, Saharanpur, had worsened from 23rd May 1857. The Magistrate's report for that day read: "At this time the Mahomedan feeling in the city was not satisfactory. Hindu bankers and baniyas had completely lost heart. They have shut up their shops, buried their valuables and business was all but suspended. The close of *Roza* was approaching. I anticipate serious disturbances." (7-96) Even the Assistant Commissioner wrote: "It was considered not improbable that the Mahommedans might take advantage of the Id, which occurred on the 26th (May), to create disturbances." (99) This is an indication of how apprehensive were authorities about a Muslim uprising.

Like Muzaffarnagar, zamindars here too had begun attacks on Hindu moneylenders. (94) The Nawab of Najibabad in neighbouring Rohilkhand had created a situation of insecurity in the region, in which his nephew had been killed. (156) In short, the struggle in this region was nothing but a saga of looting moneylenders and the Nawab's assaults upon them.

Meerut Province is commonly known as 'the Doab'. The British Magistrate wrote about it: "The *Zamindars* there were chiefly Mussalmeen, and with scarcely an exception, they joined their brethren, with the object of exterminating the English, and upsetting the Government." (68-497q.)

Let us move from the Uprising in Meerut Province to another Province adjacent to it.

- 6 -

Allahabad Province

Situated at the confluence of the Ganga and Yamuna rivers, Allahabad is part of the 'Doab'. What one gets to see as a picture of the Uprising in the district is fiercer Muslim fanaticism than in other parts of the Doab. According to the 'Red Pamphlet' published at the time, "The population of Allahabad are bigoted Mahomedans." (6-539) Muslims were very powerful there. (78-192) All the troopers participating in the rebellion were Muslim. (90-68) The decision to revolt had been taken on 5th June at a meeting of Muslim sepoys held at the residence of their leader, Saif Khan. (6-459) Two Muslims in the city had arrived in the cantonment a few days before the rebellion to provoke the sepoys. (49-8) Accordingly, rebellion broke out the following day. The local Muslim population soon joined the fray under leadership of M. Liaqat Ali whose rule was established on 7th June. (6-549) They declared that they were representing the Emperor. (90-75) Soon thereafter, the Emperor sent a letter appointing M. Liaqat Ali as subedar of Allahabad district. (85-25; 25-215) This Maulvi is regarded as one of the important leaders of the 1857 Uprising. He was instigator and leader of the revolt there.[54]

---

54. Savarkar praises this Maulvi: "An ardent lover of liberty, called Leakat Ali, soon became the leader of the Revolution. He was a religious preacher among weavers. Before the Rising, he had worked as a teacher in a school. He was adored by all people for the holy purity of his life. When the province of Allahabad became free, he was proclaimed in great ceremony as the representative of Emperor of Delhi." (1-200) "Also, among the vast Mussalman population of the town, the Mullahs were very busy. Thousands of Mussalmans were only awaiting the signal with a firm determination to offer their blood in the cause of country and religion. The English seem to have (been) firmly convinced that all Mussalmans were their mortal enemies. They were most prominent in the management of the machinery of the secret society." (193)

Maulana Liaqat Ali's Rule

He had arrived in Allahabad many days before the actual revolt and a secret organization of Muslim rebels was already functional. (77-176; 90-68) Having served in the British army, he was familiar with the warfare. (90-74) He was a vehement subscriber of Waliullahi thought and a disciple of Barelvi. (25-215) He had become leader by unanimous choice of Muslims in 40 nearby villages,[55] besides Allahabad. (60-238) All local Muslim zamindars as well as commoners had supported him. (6-549, 556; 126-235) The entire district soon passed under his domination. (6-649; 109-73) Armed Pathan bodyguards kept a constant vigil around the Maulvi. (3-478)

The flag of Islam was hoisted over the police headquarters and main square of the town immediately after the rebellion.[56] (126-236; 6-648) " It proclaimed the restoration of supremacy of Islam." (90-74; 78-194; 34-324) Several Maulvis and Muslim talukdars were present along with Liaqat Ali.[57] (6-648; 90-75) Directions to kill 'Firangis' wherever found, were issued and the Maulvi cited the Quran and its precepts many times.[58] (90-75) His rule commenced. (6-648) A programme of awarding capital punishment to anyone not submitting to the oath of loyalty to the Emperor, was begun. (44-59) Bengali Hindus, who inhabited the region in large number, had to suffer punishment on the charge of being British sympathizers and collaborators. (59)

---

55. A list of all 40 villages may be found in some books. (6-550; 90-184)

56. Savarkar says about the unfurling: "Then, in the afternoon, a great Revolutionary (i.e. green) flag was taken in procession and hoisted on the police station and all the sepoys and the citizens saluted it." (1-197)

57. Dr. Choudhary lists influential local leaders who assisted this Maulvi. All 14 of them are Muslim. Maulvis, talukdars and other leaders are included with them. (81-90n)

58. Quotations from the 9th and 61st surah of the Quran were invoked for the purpose, which contain directives to "*Slay the polytheists wherever you find them.*" (*9:5*) Also, "*Allah loves those who battle in His way in ranks as if they were a compact wall.*" (*61:4*) (90-84n)

The Maulvi had set up his headquarters for administration and *Jihad* at Khusrubrgh. Needless to state, all officials he appointed were Muslim. (76) He had always propagated the prophesied end of British rule and reinstatement of the Emperor to incite people to rebel. (44-60; 90-183) He now declared that, "The real paradise lay beneath the strokes of the swords."[59] (90-76) He also published a detailed Proclamation of *Jihad*. With the exception of the fort, which was under British control, he ruled all over the Allahabad district till 16th June when the British recaptured it. (6-558) The Jama Masjid, which had been the center for the conspiracy, was demolished after the recapture. The Maulvi and 3,000 followers left towards Kanpur. (86-643; 90-115; 109-73) Although he ruled for just nine or ten days, he left a deep imprint on the region.

In a report, the local British Magistrate wrote: "Pergunnah Chail was the worst of all; the Maulvi was a resident of one of its villages, and every Mussalman there joined his standard. The Doab population, led by their Mohamedan Zamindars, has risen with enthusiasm to take part in a religious war, and had marked their rising with the usual accompaniments of Mahomedan fanaticism." (68-498; 90-98)

Conversions by Sword

The Maulvi was particularly zealous about augmentation of the Muslim population. He had permitted Christians the gift of their lives if they agreed to convert to Islam. Dr. Sen makes an insightful observation (in a Government Publication) about the Maulvi's piousness: "It stands to his credit that many Indian Christians were permitted to purchase their lives at the price of their religion." (141-151; 68-562q.)

Besides, the Maulvi had also commenced work of converting Hindus to Islam. Walker, the Deputy Collector, reported: "The Maulvi at Allahabad was said to be making converts of Hindus by the sword." (6-55)

---

59. This saying appears in the Prophet's *Hadis* (Sahih Bukhari : 2818; Sahih Muslim: 4314). (128-613)

During the hearing in a case filed later, this Maulvi told the Court with pride that the Allahabad rebellion had been engineered by him and that he was the leader of the rebels. (643) He was so popular in the region that Muslims had turned out in large number in his support at the hearings. (644) He had also been present at the Satichaura Ghat massacre in Kanpur. (644) Such was his sway over Muslims that some Christians at that Ghat incident had been spared of their lives when they had merely invoked his name, crying out 'Maulavi Saheb!'. (644) A defense presented during the trial on behalf of the Maulvi in order to mitigate his offence, was that he had spared the life of an eighteen-year old unmarried Christian girl, Miss Bennett, even though she had refused to convert to Islam. She was delivered to the custody of the sepoy who had captured her and with whom she lived for a subsequent period of ten months. (645) Such 'generosity' had helped him being sentenced to life imprisonment instead of death.

Muslim Conspiracy at Fatehpur

Soon after events in Allahabad, an uprising occurred at the district place of Fatehpur (9th June). The Deputy Collector Hikmatullah, had defected to the rebels. He approached his superior with a huge mob of rebel sepoys and Pathans. (562) They were armed with swords, muskets and other weapons. This man now had assumed leadership of the rebels.[60] Breaking open the prison houses, performing massacres, looting and arson commenced. The magistrate was put to death. (563) Two Hindus who said the Magistrate was a just and virtuous man, were also put to death. (78-276) "(The) Muslim conspiracy was hatched in the very heart of the city." (78-275; 90-80) The rebels ruled for just 32 days, till the British overthrew their

60. Sir John Kaye writes: "At the head of the Muhammedan conspiracy was a well-known native functionary — Deputy magistrate by office. It was believed that Mussalman treachery and ingratitude had culminated in the crowning crime of this man's life. When poor Tucker was shot by his orders, he himself was reading out the Quran whilst the guns were fired." (78-276)

regime. (12th July) Excepting acknowledgment of the authority of Nanasahib of Kanpur, who had recently declared independence, the nature of the short-lived rebel rule was entirely Muslim.[61]

Nawabi Rule at Banda

Muslim sepoys took the lead at Banda and rebelled on 14th June, declaring the Nawab, Ali Bahadur, as their ruler. The usual slogan ' Khulk Khuda ka, Mulk Badshah ka, Hukum Nawab Ali Bahadur ka' was given out. (92-47; 82-86) The Nawab began his rule over the Banda district on behalf of the Emperor, appointing Muslims to all senior administrative positions.[62] (90-91; 82-87; 92-47; 6-658) Muhammad Sardar Khan became the Collector of Banda. The Emperor appointed the Nawab as Subedar[63] of the district and a declaration of the end of British rule was issued.

Thereafter, Muslim rebels began roving the area giving slogans and singing songs of *Jihad.* (6-576; 92-43) Declarations

---

61. This essential nature of the rebellion may easily be gleaned from the orders issued to his subordinate Major General Neill who was on his way from Allahabad to Kanpur via Fatehpur: "Certain guilty villages were marked out for destruction, and all the men inhabiting them were to be slaughtered. The town of Fatehpur, which had revolted, was to be attacked, and the Pathan quarters destroyed with all their inhabitants. All heads of insurgents, particularly, at Fatehpur, to be hanged. If the deputy collector is taken, hang him, and have his head cut off and emplace it on one of the principal (Muhammedan) buildings of the town." (63-52; 90-119; 58-303)

62. He had appointed an advisory council, one member of which, however, was a Hindu *sethiya.* (81-209) The latter was an expert in financial dealings and was going to prove useful to the administration.

63. In a letter of gratitude, the Nawab wrote to the Emperor: "The obedience commanding *Firman,* being like revelation from the heaven having honoured me with its arrival here..." (92-121) "He called himself the Majesty's 'devotee' and as 'self-sacrificing' in the Royal cause." (121)

of *Jihad* were posted all over the town, all Muslims were called upon to come together to massacre Christians. (6-573, 7) Directions were also issued to that effect. A green flag was hoisted at the Tara fort. (81-209; 90-91)

Forcible Conversions

The Nawab began his rule according to Islamic law. A Mufti (qazi) was appointed for the district. (6-617) The *hijri* era was implemented by an edict. (90-92) A force of 12 – 17 thousand had assembled under his leadership. (111-582; 90-92) Many Christians were forcibly converted to Islam by the sepoys after the revolt. The head of the missionary school, Pappanah Paul, was forced to convert after the school had been sacked on 15th June. (6-567; 90-91)

The Hindu chief of Ajaygarh in the district, Raja Ranjor Dauwa, was an adversary of the Nawab and did not wish him to rule. Although this chief had defeated the Nawab in a fierce battle in August 1857, the Nawab had subsequently succeeded against him. The chief's fortress was razed. (90-93) Nanasahib backed the Nawab because the rebels supported him. Like his counterpart in neighbouring Fatehpur, the Nawab here too had maintained friendly relations with Nanasahib. Banda at that time had become a rendezvous for leaders of the Uprising. (82-87) Even Dr. Chaudhary writes about the rebellion in Banda : "The Mahomedans regarded the scene (of revolt) as a holy war to result in the extermination of the *Kafirs*."[64] (81-209)

---

64. The thought and feeling mutually evinced by Nawab who had declared independence during the 1857 Uprising may be judged from a letter that the secretary to the Nawab of Banda wrote to the Nawab of Farrukhabad. Therein, that Nawab had been referred to as, 'The Noble, the Shadow and *Khalifa* of God.' (6-619) The green flag of the state was called as 'the flag of your Kingdom raised on high.' (620) About himself he wrote, "being a true follower of the Prophet bears mortal enmity towards the English." (621) British officers and Hindu chieftains in Bundelkhand opposing the Nawab were called 'infidels' and 'enemies'. (621)

Ali Bakhsh – Ruler of Hamirpur

Sepoys in the fourth district, Hamirpur, rebelled on 14th June. It began like this: Rahimuddin, commander of a platoon, took the State cannons to his house, followed by the usual breaking into the prison, releasing prisoners and looting the treasury. (90-95) Thereafter, Ali Bakhsh, the subedar, declared his rule over the district as a representative of the Emperor. (96) Three days later, the local Magistrate and other officials were put to death. (126-391) Wahiduzaman began conducting the administration on behalf of Nanasahib from 1st July. (92-47; 90-96)

Contending Hindu Chief Defeated

The Chief of Charkhari, Ratan Singh, began opposing Ali Bakhsh. He frustrated the Subedar's attempts to carry the local treasury to Delhi as he too wanted a share in it. (90-96) But a Hindu was unlikely to become a beneficiary in an uprising by Muslims. He had command of an army, too, but when he realized he did not stand to benefit from the revolt, he became a British loyalist. [Tatya Tope had invaded this chief's territory for eleven days on account of his pro-British leanings. (97)]

Briefly stated, the overall picture in Hamirpur was no different from that in other districts of the province. The subedars in the three districts, discussed above, had accepted Nanasahib's leadership. But that need not mislead readers for we are yet to see what was Nana's position in his very own Kanpur.

We now turn to the remaining, and important, district of the Allahabad province — Kanpur. It was one of the two or three places where a Hindu assumed charge of post-Uprising administration.[65]

---

65. The second was Jhansi. Kunwar Singh's Jagdishpur may be regarded as the third.

Kanpur — Nana Enjoys Trust of the British

On receiving information about the Meerut and Delhi uprisings, Nana had publicly 'lamented the outbreak' and thought it 'most shameful.' (126–186) The irksome question is how Nana later assumed leadership of the rebels. It has been accepted by all historians that he had nothing to do with instigating the rebellion. British officials were not gullible to entrust the security of the treasury and armoury to Nanasahib on the eve of the Uprising. They trusted him implicitly. Arrangements for the stay of Collector Hillersdon's pregnant wife and two children were made within the Shaniwar Wada at Bithoor. (126-186) The amity and intimacy of relations between Nana and the British are worthy of note.

Nanasahib enjoyed the company of the English for whose stay and travel at Bithoor he had made special provisions like separate rooms and exclusive carriages. (108-6) Grand banquets were thrown in their honour; games with prizes used to be arranged for their entertainment. (72-13) He used to play billiards with them. (105-18) On one occasion a game had stretched over a full day and night. Minute details of banquets he gave may be read in narratives recorded by his English guests. (108-8) His doors were ever open for the British. (9); (also :159-245)

Perhaps he believed such cordial relations would ensure timely receipt of the political pension and facilitate other interactions with the administration. Historians are incredulous that someone of his disposition, who had adopted the path of bonhomie, should suddenly resort to armed rebellion. None is willing to credit him with the unscrupulousness, cruelty or treachery to betray British trust or waylay them in the manner that he is said to have done later. Suffice it to say, the trust Major Wheeler or Collector Hillersdon had put in Nanasahib was hardly misplaced.

Muslim Cavalry in the Lead

The Kanpur uprising was initiated by the 2nd cavalry platoon. Sepoys in that platoon (like other cavalry platoons) were predominantly Muslim.[66] (158-346) They had managed to win sympathy of the infantry platoons.[67] (8-61; 90-55; 141-131) One of the infantry platoons was commanded by Subedar Salamat Ali. (108-62). There were many Muhammadens in the corps, and Muhammaden feeling was then strong in the place. There had been great gatherings at the mosques, in which the Musalman Sipahis had taken a forward part, for the full discussion of the crisis. And it was thought, as had before been thought, in other places, that the festival of Id, on the 24th May, would prove the appointed day for a great Muhammadan demonstration.[68] (78-228) No actual outbreak of rebellion occurred that day, but preparations for one were being made everywhere. 4th June was fixed for Kanpur.

Azeemullah Khan was Nanasahib's advisor.[69] Azeemullah held complete sway over Nana. (159-245) Nana did not so much as lift his little finger without Azeemullah. (264) Although Nanasahib was in charge of security of the treasury and

---

66. Historian Sir John Kaye states: "The chief source of immediate danger at this time was the temper of the 2nd cavalry.... That the troopers were ripe for revolt was certain, for already they were quietly making arrangements to send away their families and their property, and soon they had nothing in their huts but their drinking-vessels." (78-228)

67. Tikka Singh was the commander of this cavalry. Savarkar writes: "The chief rendezvous of the secret societies of Kanpur was the house of Subedar Tikka Singh. Another place of meeting for the secret societies was the house of the Sepoy leader Shamsuddin Khan." (1-215)

68. Savarkar writes: "The 24th May was the great Id festival of the Mahomedans. The English in every town apprehended a rising on that day. But the leaders in 1857 were not such fools as to rise on such an easily marked day. Therefore even in Kanpur, on the day of the Id festival, there was not the slightest disorder." (1-217) (Who 'the heroes of 1857' were, becomes clear from this.)

69. Savarkar described him as the 'Mentor (Guru) of Nana' in the original Marathi book (p.165), but it was omitted in the English translation.

armoury, these had been commandeered by rebel sepoys. (104) All this had happened without his knowledge or consent.[70] It is interesting to see how sepoys had forced Nana to become their leader.

Leadership or Death

Rebel sepoys went to Nana and warned him that he would rule if he sided with them, but would be put to death if he declined or sided with the British. (109-57; 141-133; 108-72; 126-190) Realizing the gravity of the emerging situation, Nana reluctantly agreed to assume leadership.[71] Rebel leaders thus

---

70. Tatya Tope wrote about this: "Detachments of the Infantry and 2nd cavalry surrounded us (that is, Nana and himself) and kept us prisoner in the strong room of the treasury. The ammunition dump and treasury were looted completely and nothing was left remaining there. Sepoys handed over Rs.2,10,000 to Nana and placed their guard over it. Nana himself was placed under a guard of three sentries. Sepoys who were with us (Nana's contingent from Bithoor) also joined the rebels. The entire number of them then left from there, taking Nanasahib, myself and our retinue with them." (111-784)

71. Comments of some eminent historians and scholars on this:

i. Dr. S.N. Sen : "Tatya Tope deposed that Nana had been forced under duress vile (sic) to join the sepoys and assume their command. At first he refused to go to Delhi or to fight the British force at Kanpur but later yielded to force. Therefore, Tatya Tope's story might have a substratum of truth. At the last extremity Nana's men might have fraternized with the sepoys." (141-133)

ii. Sir George Forrest points out that Nana had 2 guns and 500 armed retainers with him and thus had no reason to bow to the rebels' will. Other historians debate this point by stating the fact that Nana had only two guns which were worse than useless and armed retainers numbered only 300 which were no match for three infantry and one cavalry regiments of the rebels. (141-233; 111-355)

iii. After citing Tatya Tope's deposition, Dr. P.C. Gupta remarks, "All these versions probably contain some elements of truth, and from them it is possible to get an idea of the general pattern of events." (108-72)

(Contd.)

coerced Nanasahib by giving him a choice between 'leadership and death'. The usual slogan, 'Khulk Khuda ka, Mulk Badshah ka, Hukum Nanasahib *aur Fauj Bahadur ka*' was raised.[72] (90-58; 109-62; 49-xii) The sepoys needed a leader like Nana because it was going to get them Hindu support. (108-72)

---

iv. Dr. S.B. Choudhary : "The recent researches go to the point of indicating that Nana Sahib was unaware of the mutiny of the sepoys until it actually broke out.... That there was absolutely no understanding between Nana Sahib and the disaffected sepoys in regard to plan of action.... It can be safely established that Nana had no hand in planning the mutiny of troops and it was not till they had actually broken out that he joined them." (81-96,8,9) The inquiry officer General Williams also found no evidence to support the theory that Nana Sahib organized the conspiracy." (81-99)

v. Dr. R.C. Mujumdar : "While there is no ground for the belief that Nana organized a conspiracy against the British, it is definitely opposed to his own conduct. In the first place, he was quite friendly to the British even after the outbreak of the mutiny at Meerut and Delhi.... When the sepoys mutinied at Kanpur and were proceeding towards Delhi to join rebels there, it was Nana himself who dissuaded them.... If there was any organized conspiracy to overthrow the English, the obvious thing for Nana would have been to march to Delhi with the troops." (67-191)

vi. Narhar Kurundkar : "It is a bitter fact of history that Nanasahib, in whose name the Peshwa Rule had been proclaimed, had been coerced to participate in the rebellion." (150-116)

vii. Richard Collier : "No valid evidence suggests that he was behind the Kanpur mutiny. Next morning rebels urged him, 'Come to Delhi, but the Nana was unwilling. Then, they said, 'Come with us to Kanpur and fight there.' Menaced by a strong guard of sepoys the Nana had no choice." (60-120)

72. The addition of 'Aur Fauj Bahadur ka' in this usual slogan shows that Nanasahib's authority was not exclusively his; it was equally shared by the brave sepoys.

Unfurling the Flag — Declaration of Jihad

Nana began his rule the following day. Administrative headquarters were established at the Duncan Hotel owned by a Muslim leader, Noor Muhammad. (126-197) Azeemullah Khan became Nana's Advisor and also Collector of Kanpur, Qazi Wasiuddin the Police Chief, Tikka Singh the Commander-in-Chief and Baba Bhatt the Chief Justice. (108-84; 126-191) A green flag was hoisted over the Old Residency to signify the end of British rule and commencement of self-rule. (111-358; 126-192) Another Mahomedan flag[73] was unfurled at the fort after it had been evacuated on 27th June. (90-59)

An inspiring, historic programme of flag hoisting as well as declaration of *Jihad* was held in the town two days later, on 9th June, in which M. Salamatullah and Qazi Wasiuddin took a lead. Nana's Advisor, Azeemullah Khan, who had originally conceived the programme, was also present with them. (6-600; 49-xi) Proclamations were made all over the town asking people to assemble in the main square. (49-xi) The green flag was unfurled at that place. (109-65; 108-81) *Jihad* was declared along with a warning that those staying away from it would be put to death. (49-xi; 109-65; 72-23) This event provided great inspiration to Muslims of Kanpur.

Sepoys by that time had already besieged the entrenchment, within which British officers, women and children had taken refuge. According to the original plan, an attack was to be launched upon the entrenchment immediately after the declaration of *Jihad*. In fact, Qazi Wasiuddin had even arrived mounted on his steed. However, the Maulvi present there said that the day was inauspicious according to Islam and that the attack ought to be deferred by a day. (108-81) All

---

73. After the words 'Mahomedan flag', Prof. Srivastava tenders his own explanation thereof as 'flag of freedom and religion' in parenthesis. (90-59)The impossibility of denying that such flag was indeed unfurled and the concurrent need for lauding the Uprising as a joint war of independence, has given rise to this typically 'Hindu' explanation.

decision making being in the hands of clergy, the proposed assault was made the next day. (6-600) Names of all twelve persons who took a lead in it, provided in the reference book, are Muslim except for one, who was Hindu and a government servant. (600)

Nanasahib's Equal Regard for All Religions

The attack was not made by a combined Hindu-Muslim force. Two flags had been planted — a green one for Muslims and the 'Mahavir Jhanda' for Hindus. (81-100) They were asked to assemble under their respective flag. "Some 2000 Musalmans repaired to the former; but only a few budmashs took service under the latter." (103-137) The former assembled in the cause of *Jihad* for religion and state with loot as an adjunct of holy war, while the latter had been animated only by the lure of pillage.

Apprehension loomed large that the Hindu complement might be dissuaded by the overall milieu of *Jihad.* Nana needed to take Hindus with him. He was firmly convinced that unity of action of the Hindus and the Muslims was indispensable for attaining victory; he therefore constantly emphasized his esteem for Islam just as for Hinduism and the complete equality of both religious communities. (109-64) He even began exhibiting this view through his actions. Two separate flags – one for Hindus and another for Muslims began to be unfurled at his headquarters.[74] He also began issuing his orders and appeals in Arabic script for Muslims and in Devnagari for Hindus. (64) Coins were minted in the Emperor's name, and all orders, too, were issued on his behalf. (141-xxvii)The Islamic *Hijri* calendar was implemented for all. (64) "However, these measures were obviously not enough. Nana Sahib and Azeemullah Khan established communications with Wasiuddin, the Qazi of Kanpur, and won his full support. A wonderful speaker and respected preacher, Wasiuddin became

---

74. About the two flags, Historian Malleson comments: "One (was) to propitiate the Hindus, the other to humour the Mahomedans." (130-110)

one of the most active and most consistent of the leaders of the rebels." (64) It is plain that Nana was not likely to receive and retain that support unless he behaved according to the dictates of Maulvis. An incident that occurred around 18th June may be cited as an illustration of this situation.

Nana's Appeal for Forgiveness: Complete Freedom to Slaughter Cows

Nanasahib's Chief Justice, Baba Bhatt, ordered the hands of two butchers to be cut off for the offence of slaughtering cows in the main market.[75] This resulted in angry outcries from the Muslim population including sepoys of the 2nd cavalry, who had enthroned Nana in the first place. They held a consultation among themselves and argued thus, "Who had made this Nana a ruler over us? Is he not a creature of our own hands; and can we not appoint any one else we like? If he has already commenced interfering with our creed, and preventing cows being killed, which is not only lawful, but is necessary to our very existence, how much more will he not meddle with our other religious callings when he is firmly established in authority and when our enemy, the English, shall have been completely exterminated ?" Thus arguing, they proceeded in a body to the Nana to call him to account for causing the butcher's hands to be cut off. In the meantime, the Nana was informed of what was going on and immediately ran out with barehead and barefoot in the sun to meet the troopers, and with clasped hands begged their pardon for what he had done, promising never again to interfere in this respect, and that the Mahomedans were perfectly at liberty to kill as many cows as they liked, only that they were to do it in a retired spot. The troopers used much abusive language on that occasion to the Nana, and threatened to displace him (as the ruler) if he did not do as they desired. From that day

75. Savarkar, writing about the incident, only says: "A Mahomedan butcher was given the same punishment (i.e. cutting off the right hand) for killing a cow" (1-228), without stating what happened afterwards.

the 2nd cavalry Mahomedans held the Nana's authority in contempt." (56-86; 126-204)

All of them began flouting Nana's word from that day, resulting in development of an air of suspicion between them. (126-204; 55-86) As stated by Shepherd, "They owned no master save the king of Delhi, who was their true and only Sovereign, being true believer and a Moslem." (56-8)

Nanasahib had no authority whatsoever. He was only Peshwa (Ruler) nominally with real power being controlled by rebel leaders in his name. As such, he was forced to do their bidding. All historians take note of Nana's unenviable condition.[76] It was an inevitable consequence of the situation

---

76. Comments by some scholars on this:

i. Sir John Kaye : "He was, after all, only a miserable tool in the hands of others. In his absence from Kanpur, his influence was declining. The Mahomedan party was waxing strong. It had hitherto overborne by the Hindu power, probably more than all else for want of an efficient leader (among the Mahomedans). But (now) there was a Muhammedan nobleman, known as the Nani Nawab. And, now there was some talk of setting up the Nawab as head of the new government. If this had been done, there would have been faction fights between Hindus and Mahomedans…". (78-264) "The authority of Nana Sahib had been nominally recognized, but in truth there was scarcely any semblance of Government." (277)

ii. Saul David : "Though Nana Sahib was the nominal head of the rebels at Kanpur, in reality he had to defer to rebel officers like Tikka Singh of the 2nd cavalry." (126-198) "….But the power still lay with the rebel troops at Kanpur…." (126-243)

iii. Anand Sarup Misra : "Nana and his Court had no control over rebel sepoys. Those sepoys used to act entirely according to their own will." (111-395)

iv. P.J.O. Taylor : "He may have been no more than a puppet in the hands of four regiments of Kanpur mutineers." (105-18)

v. Prof. P.C. Gupta : "Undoubtedly Nana Sahib was very much dominated by his advisors and had rarely the power to go against the wishes of his troops." (108-120)

(Contd.)

in which Nana had assumed leadership of the rebels. The incident cited above was but an instance of this subjection. The Satichaura massacre, or the one at Bibighar, was another glaring example of the same predicament in which Nana found himself.

Who was Responsible for the Kanpur Massacres?

Historians concur that Nanasahib had no hand in either of those massacres.[77] (90-61) Both had been perpetrated by rebel sepoys.[78] Nanasahib had no hold over them. (81-118; 111-395)

It is necessary to obtain a clear picture of 'who and how' of these events even for an understanding of the general nature of the 1857 Uprising.

A Christian survivor of the massacre at the Satichaura Ghat recorded that it was committed by Muslim sepoys of the cavalry. (56-82; 60-146,9; 108-117) According to a statement made later by the Kotwal of Kanpur, Qazi Wasiuddin was the man behind the deed. (49-cxvi; 141-146; 56-97; 72-78) He held authority over the cavalry. (49-cxvi) N.K.Behere establishes that Azeemullah Khan was responsible for the conspiracy. (158-354,5)

M. Liaqat Ali had arrived in Kanpur with 3,000 Jihadi followers just a few days before the incident. He recounted harrowing tales of British atrocities after the capture of

---

vi. N. R. Phatak writes: "There remains no doubt whatsoever that sepoys evinced only nominal feelings of solidarity with Nanasahib. They were more attracted by the Imperial rule (of Delhi). They had initially desired to take the Lord of Bithoor with them to Delhi, but later turned their backs to Delhi and returned to Kanpur not for the Peshwa's sake but in order to satiate their ambition to uproot the very seed of Whites." (44-48)

77. Also: 81-99; 108-117; 141-146; 56-85; 158-388.

78. John Lang writes: "The massacre was the act of those who wished to place forever between Nana Sahib and the British Government an impassable barrier." (108-117q; 111-449q)

Allahabad. (141-146; 90-61) He moved around the town with 20 or 25 horsemen in constant attendance. He had met Nanasahib several times. (49-cliii; 6-765) The task of further inciting local Muslims and sepoys of the cavalry had been accomplished by him.

Tale of Two Christian Girls

As the slaughter of the British at the Satichaura Ghat was in progress, troopers of the 2nd cavalry busied themselves with kidnapping beautiful girls from among their victims. A sepoy called Khan had abducted the pretty Margaret, 18 year old daughter of Maj. Wheeler, from one of the boats. (108-113; 56-87; 49-ciii; 79-195) She was later converted to Islam, kept as a concubine and was alive till 1880. (126-221; 111-381) Needless to state, she suffered the consequences of the 1857 *Jihad* all her life.

An equally tragic story of another 18-year old girl, Amy Horne, needs to be narrated. Richard Collier describes what happened on 27th June: She was kidnapped from the boat by a trooper of 2nd cavalry, Muhammad Ismail Khan. He took her to a Maulvi stationed three miles from the Sati-Chaura Ghat. There at one end of the tent, on a wooden dais, sat two Maulvis. Senior of them was Maulvi Liaqat Ali. She squatted on the carpet at their feet. A man with a drawn sword was standing on each Maulvi's side. A third man was behind her, his sword drawn, the razor- edge poised only a few feet above her dark tumbling hair. The favourite slogan of the senior Maulvi was, 'The true Paradise lies beneath the sword-stroke.' The Maulvi put two alternatives before her: Islam or death. The sword above her head was not an idle threat. She favoured Islam to save her life. The Maulvi gave her the oath of faith. Then a female attendant led her to an improvised bathing tank. After taking a bath she was absolved from all previous impurity. When she returned to the tent, she was for all the world a Moslem woman, dressed in Muslim fashion. Bareheaded, she stood to face Liaqat Ali, reciting: 'In the name of God, the Compassionate, the Merciful....' She was now irrevocably a bride of Islam, in duty bound to pray five times a day facing Mecca. (60-237 to 9) "She knelt to worship and worship again as the price of staying alive. 'Allahu Akbar ! Allhu Akbar !,' she cried that all might hear. What her heart said was, O God, please God, have mercy and let me die." (246)

Abduction of girls like Margaret and Amy was an integral part of practical *Jihad.*[79]

Why were the Women Kept at Bibighar?

One of the motives in attacking the British who were boarding or had boarded boats at the Satichaura Ghat was abduction of their womenfolk. A survivor, Shepherd, later wrote that, "Oh ! But it was torture to my breaking heart when they commenced to brag and boast about their conduct to the ladies. They (i.e. troopers) said, 'We have saved as many *bebee logues* as possible for ourselves; they are very handsome and fair and will easily be persuaded to become Mahomedans; they will be distributed to the most deserving of us in a few days; they are for the present kept in the Savada Kothee (*Bibighar*)." (56-85) Why, then, had it become necessary to first move them to the Bibighar and then divide them among sepoys instead of carrying them off directly from the site of abduction? They continued talking among themselves : "Some of our fellows actually ran away with their selections from the river side; a row took place between two troopers about a handsome lady, and was the cause of an order being issued to return all *Firangee* ladies to the *Savada Kothee.*" (85) In short, the cavalry troopers had attacked boats in the river out of their lust for the Christian women, who had then been transported to the Bibighar to facilitate easy and leisurely distribution.

The distribution never happened. British forces fell upon Kanpur before it could be done. Sepoys engaged in the ensuing

---

79. Such instances may be observed to have occurred from very early times. Khalid bin Walid, a renowned military commander during the rule of the first two Khalifas, was well known for such practice.

fighting, were defeated and all the women and children inside the Bibighar were mercilessly slaughtered. Historians conclude that Nanasahib had nothing to do with this affair. Hussaini Khanum, the Begum in charge of the Bibighar, had taken a lead in prosecuting the deed. (111-454; 126-253; 44-56) It is also believed that her paramour, Sarwar Khan, was also involved. (126-253; 72-28; 56-117) N.K. Behere shows how Azeemullah Khan, this Begum and Sarwar Khan were behind the affair.[80] (158-387 to 91) Sarwar Khan was later hanged. (126-373)

For a Place in Heaven

Even the manner in which these women and children were put to death indicates the nature of the Uprising. Shepherd narrated: "On every occasion, when a request was made by anyone, either to spare a child or man no sooner did they make their wishes known than the Mahomedans would get round and repeat a Persian verse as follows: That is to say 'to extinguish the fire and leave the spark, to kill a snake and preserve its young, is not the wisdom to men of sense.' Besides this, whenever a Mahomedan found the lifeless body of a European or Christian lying anywhere, he immediately drew out his sword, 'with a *bismillah,*' and made a gash upon the corpse. This act is considered by them to be equivalent to killing an infidel, and adds to their claim for entering Paradise after death." (56-93)

The following incident of around the same time (10th July) merits mention since it is further illustrative of the nature of

---

80. He also writes: "Not a single Hindu sepoy was willing to perform this unmanly act; it was done by Muslim butchers whose sensitivities had been dulled by their wonted practice of daily slaughtering poor, innocent mulching kine" (158-387, 489) Prabodhankar Thakare writes: "It was Azeemullah who caused women and children kept in the Bibighar to be butchered, thereby bringing infamy to Nanasahib's character, influence and public image." (159-264)

the Uprising. Rebel sepoys took three British officers, who had arrived in Kanpur from Fatehpur, into custody. They were accompanied by one Christian and one Hindu servant. The former was given the chance of saving himself by converting to Islam and was promptly hacked to pieces when he refused. The Hindu was asked to give up service of Christians and join their side. He declined to betray his master and was immediately shot in the head. Thereafter, the three officers were also killed. "The bodies were allowed to lie exposed for a couple of days for the troopers and other Mahomedans to try their swords upon. On such occasions these men were in the habit of bringing their own children — young lads – and instructing them how to make a cut; at the same time giving them to understand that a cut upon even the dead body of a Christian *Kafir* was of infinite value, entitling a true believer (Moslem) to place in Paradise." (113)

23rd June was the centenary of the Battle of Plassey, when the prophesied end of British rule was expected. Four thousand troopers charged upon the entrenchment, brandishing cutlasses high over their heads and giving cries of 'Deen-Deen'. (126-205) Many of them were killed. (111-363)

Jihadis throng to Kanpur

When it became known that a government of rebel forces had been established in Kanpur and the British had been scattered, "Mahomedans, calling themselves the descendants of the Prophet, wearing garments of the most extraordinary devices, and many covered over from head to foot with armour, laden with five or six different kinds of weapons — poured in from Oudh, and other parts of the country by hundreds. As for bragging and boasting, nothing could equal them." (56-114)

Nanasahib Appointed as Subedar

Nanasahib ordered a salute of 21 guns for himself and 101 for the Emperor after he had been enthroned on 1st July. (111-390; 90-62) The Emperor sent him a letter of recognition of his authority of Kanpur district on 12th July.[81] A great celebration was made of the event. (109-69) His rule lasted just four days after that. The Union Jack once again replaced the green flag on 17th July.

He left Kanpur and Bithoor to go towards Ayodhya. None of the sepoys went with him. On the contrary, they only had abusive language for him. (111-410) Perhaps it was best for him that British forces had arrived to rescue him from the stranglehold of sepoys and rebels, for it need not be presumed that the latter would have allowed him to continue ruling for too long.

'Nana is an Alien, We want Nanhe Nawab!'

While Nana was engrossed in the euphoria of his enthronement at Bithoor, which event had continued a good four or five days, news was received that Havelock was on his way to Kanpur with his force. Sepoys in Kanpur panicked and began levelling accusations against Nana. Demands were made to depose and replace him by Nanhe Nawab. (49-cccxxxi) Talk became rife that Nana was an alien to Kanpur and was therefore uncaring about its security. They also began saying, "He is a Maratha. He is a stranger here. Only a Muslim can rouse the people and guarantee the security of the citizens." (109-84) They declared their resolve of replacing Nana by Nanhe Nawab if the former did not show up at Kanpur that

---

81. Although Nanasahib's constitutional status and factual position might have been that of Subedar of the province, his authority at that time was limited only to Kanpur, which was not a province but a district. Hence his status was merely that of a collector nazim of a district. (Appointment and dismissal of subedars was the Emperor's prerogative). The first education minister of India, M. Azad, writes: "And he did not for a moment hesitate to declare himself a subedar or governor of the Mughal Court. The real ruler, he proclaimed, was the Emperor of Delhi. The coins struck were in the name of the Emperor and all orders were issued in his name." (141-xxvii)

very day.[82] (49-cccxxxi; 126-243) It was decided to bring Nana forcibly from Bithoor as the enemy was very close to Kanpur. (ibid) Commander-in-Chief Tikka Singh went on the double to Bithoor, apprized Nana of the situation and returned to Kanpur along with him. (109-84)

Nanhe Nawab (Muhammad Ali Khan) hailed from the ruling family and was both respected and popular among Muslims. (111-393; 108-758; 78-264) Nana had been made leader by rebels in order to obtain Hindu support, while Nanhe Nawab had ambitions of becoming subedar. It was at this juncture that he came forward to stake a claim. Muslims supported him unflinchingly. Realizing that he had intentions to rebel, Nana placed him under detention for some time. (78-264; 111-392) Sepoys, however, wanted him as chief of Kanpur. (108-98; 111-393) Conspiracies were hatched to achieve that end. As a result, Nana ceded to the demand and gave an assurance of making Nanhe the subedar after they had dealt with the immediate threat of the approaching British force. (111-393; 108-79; 49-cxlii; 78-264) However, the assurance never reached fruition because Nana's forces were defeated and Kanpur was lost to the British. Otherwise, had they been victorious, Nanhe[82] would have become subedar and Nana would have been destined to spend a retired life at Brahmavarta.

---

82. N. K. Behere writes: "Creation of Nawabs was proceeding on such industrial scale (during the Uprising), that in Kanpur, too, a worthless person called Nanhe Nawab was put up against Nanasahib." (158-280) "Sepoys contemplated, even during their short-lived rule, dismissing Nanasahib and making a vagabond called Nanhe Nawab the Nawab of Kanpur." (517) "History notes that Nanasahib was forced to make over chief control of Kanpur to Nanhe Nawab only to appease Muslims whose stranglehold over the city had increased." (388)

However, it is said that Nana had become wise to a plot by Nanhe and the sepoys to assassinate him and gain control of the subedari, for which reason he had dispatched them to obstruct British troops at Fatehpur. (49-cxlviii) History is silent on the outcome because of the ensuing defeat.

Nana went to the Begum of Avadh after his defeat without a single sepoy accompanying him. She conceded his entreaty and permitted him to enter Ayodhya. His arrival in the city on 1st August was greeted by eleven gun-salute. Thereafter, a special reception ceremony was arranged in his honour. Nana, however, complained to the Begum that only 11 guns were fired when he enjoyed the status and honour of 21. She replied through Mir Wajid Ali that the higher salute could not be given to him because he was no King. Finally, even the reception was cancelled. (4-116)

After that, Nanasahib went completely behind the scene, never again to be seen on the stage of the Uprising. Except for some obscure reports claiming to have seen him at one or another place, history never again felt his existence. (67-135; 108-165) It was his nephew, Raosahib, who is seen to be acting as Peshwa after his disappearance. All later orders were issued in the latter's name.

Nanasahib's Final, Realistic and Candid Statement

Nanasahib's *raison d'être,* status and authority as 'Peshwa' may be estimated from the representation (*Istiharnamah*) he sent to the British administration on 20th August 1859 with the intention of obtaining exemption from punishment. It exudes an honest but conflicting admixture of valour and pathos, as if he had resigned to the inevitability of his sentence — nay, almost as if he were inviting its pronouncement despite full knowledge that a price of Rs. 50,000 had been put on his head.

He had stated therein: "It is surprising that I who have joined the rebels from helplessness have not been forgiven. I have committed no murder. When your army mutinied and proceeded to take possession of the treasury, my soldiers joined them. Upon this I reflected that if I went into the entrenchments my soldiers would kill my family, and that the British would punish me for the rebellion of my soldiers. My ryots were urgent and I was obliged to join the soldiers. For two or three years I petitioned the *Sarkar* but no attention was paid to it. At Kanpur the soldiers disobeyed my orders and began killing the English women and the ryots.

"Now I have prepared to fight and up to this time I have been fighting with you, and, while I live, will fight. You are well aware that I am not a murderer, nor am I guilty. You have no enemy besides me, so, as long as I live I will fight. That my troops do not obey me and I have no possession of my country. You have forgiven the crimes of all—and I alone am left—We will meet, and then I will shed your blood and it will flow knee deep. I am prepared to die. If I alone am worthy of being an enemy to so powerful a nation as the British it is a great honour to me; death will come to me one day. What then have I to fear? You are wise, but have erred in your wisdom. A wise enemy is better than an unwise friend". [83](111-717; 6-773)

It becomes clear from this statement that Nanasahib was neither an instigator nor a leader of the rebellion, but had agreed reluctantly to assume leadership because he had been coerced into it by sepoys. Even after becoming leader, his orders were being flouted. He calls the British an 'unwise friend.' He used expressions of valour because he was certain in his mind that he would never be pardoned and, in that sense, the communication was more in the nature of a statement of fact than an entreaty for acquittal. Otherwise, there was nothing preventing him from utilizing the opportunity to acquire historic fame and martyrdom by claiming to have been the real, chief promoter, inspiration, leader and executor of the rebellion — something that might have been more consistent with the valorous outpourings

83. Nanasahib was prepared to surrender, but had insisted on the condition that the letter accepting his surrender ought to be issued not by someone like Maj. Richardson, but by the Queen's government under its seal. (111-718) The Kanpur massacres were becoming a hurdle in obtaining a pardon for him. Apparently Nanasahib was held responsible for those morally and legally, if not in actual fact.

contained in the document! Tatya Tope's deposition[84] before he was sentenced to be hanged, too, is concordant with Nanasahib's statement.

True history would be served and due justice done to the memory of Nanasahib and Tatya Tope by upholding the same truth that both fearlessly embraced in shunning the temptation of misusing that opportunity to falsely claim inspiration and leadership of the mutiny even after realizing that, whatever their defence, they would never be pardoned, and death was staring them fully in the face!

* * *

---

84. Tatya Tope wrote about this: "Detachments of the Infantry and 2nd Cavalry surrounded us (that is, Nana and himself) and kept us prisoner in the strong room of the treasury. The ammunition dump and treasury were looted completely and nothing was left remaining there. Sepoys handed over Rs.2,10,000 to Nana and placed their guard over it. Nana himself was placed under a guard of three sentries. Sepoys who were with us (Nana's contingent from Bithoor) also joined the rebels. The entire number of them then left from there, taking Nanasahib, myself and our retinue with them." (111-784)

29. While Bahadur Shah himself had not openly said so, his son and heir, Jawan Bukht, had at the time clearly enunciated the principle of 'one enemy at a time'. Despite being the youngest of the siblings, Jawan Bukht was Bahadur Shah's favourite son and it was the keen desire of the Emperor and his queen Zeenat Mahal that he succeed as heir to the throne. He was minister at the time. He said that, in a short time he would have all the infidel English under his feet, and after that he would kill the Hindus." (107-26; 78-25n; 67-194) He had simultaneously threatened such Christians as were present there that the Persian army was expected to imminently arrive for their succour. (ibid) He might have merely repeated what was being said in the Palace.

Chapter 6

Promoters, Leaders and Beneficiaries — II

(The Jihadi Core of the Uprising)

- 1 -

The Ayodhya State

Ayodhya was second in importance only to Delhi during the Uprising. The Nawab's rule in Ayodhya had also ended like the Emperor's in Delhi. As the nobility and people of Ayodhya were keen on restoration of the deposed regime, it is obvious that Muslims were slated to be promoters, instigators, leaders and beneficiaries of the Uprising. Nevertheless, we will take a closer look at some of the more important aspects of the revolt here in order to understand the picture with more clarity.

Wajid Ali Shah, the deposed Nawab, was under British detention at Calcutta, along with his prime minister, Ali Nakki Khan. Anti-British conspiracies had begun as soon as he was deported from Lucknow. Begum Hazrat Mahal had prepared a scheme to free the Nawab that involved engineering a blast in the ammunition dump at Calcutta. Ali Nakki Khan was the brain behind this plot.[1] However, it failed. (106-21; 67-200) It is said that, in addition to this, he was largely responsible for provoking rebellion among sepoys. (106-40)

Envoys to Persia for Assistance

The ruling family of Ayodhya was Shi'ah and, in an attempt to overthrow British rule, some of its members were making efforts to seek help from Persia, which subscribed to the same religious denomination. Assistance from the Emperor was also secured. The Emperor had even switched affiliation to become Shi'ah in an attempt to secure Persian aid. His nephew, Mirza Haider, who also became Shi'ah and had set up residence in Lucknow, had succeeded in influencing him to adopt the Shi'ah sect. (78-29; 107-407) A grandson, Mirza Bahadur Bakht, had travelled from Delhi to Lucknow, where he took an oath to fight the British. (106-53) The Ayodhya nobility had largely taken part in inviting a Persian invasion of India. An envoy was also sent to the Amir of Afghanistan for help.[2]

Commencement of Rebellion

The 19th and 34th Platoons that had rebelled at Barrackpur were originally from Ayodhya and had only temporarily been posted at the former place. (121-37) They were in Ayodhya during the annexation of the state and had thus become fiercely

---

1. Not to be confused with his Waliullahi namesake who had inspired Mangal Pandey. They were different persons.

2. A letter (August 1856) of the following import had been sent by the secret council at Ayodhya to the Amir at Kabul: "The Mahomedans of Lucknow had written to Dost Muhammad, informing him that Oudh had been taken by the British, and that as they supposed that Hyderabad would follow, *there would soon be no stronghold of Islam left in Hindustan, and unless some efforts were made the cause of true believers would be lost.* In the event of the Mahomedans of Lucknow entering on any plan, they wished to know what aid they might expect from Dost." (73-373; 1-147). It clarifies who were the promoters as also whose help was sought and for what fundamental purpose.

anti-British. (121-37; 81-15) They had, at that time, declared their willingness to serve the Nawab. (126-57) Which is why the instigators had been successful without much effort and within a short time to provoke them to rebel.[3]

Anti-British sentiment was becoming apparent from as early as February 1857. M. Ahmad Shah was leader of the Uprising. (106-41) As stated by John Pemble, "The Mutiny of 1857 began in February and March in Lucknow, the trouble had spread to Meerut and other parts of Oudh by the last week of April." (45q.) The 19th February issue of the *Central Star* reported that Ruqn-ud-Daulah, brother of the first Nawab of Ayodhya Ghazi-ud-Din Haider, was raising an army to drive the British out of Ayodhya and that it was undergoing training in the far west of city. (43) It was also around this time that chapatis — "a more powerful means of combining all classes of Mahomedan in the general cause" — had begun making the rounds in Ayodhya. (44)

Muslims were agitated that the British had commandeered a religious place called 'Qadam Rasool' in April and converted it into an ammunition dump. A stone, believed to have on it the imprint of the Prophet's foot, had been housed there. "They were ready and much excited and had been waiting for a direction but there was no leader." (106-53)

---

3. Savarkar writes: "The Nawab of Lucknow and his Vazir were now residing near Calcutta. Vazir Nakki Khan was much absorbed in his dangerous conspiracy near Calcutta. One cannot help feeling wonderstruck at the schemes — secret, extensive, and daring — which he was weaving to seduce the sepoys in Bengal and to prepare them to join him at the right moment already fixed upon. Confidential agents were sent by him, in the garbs of Fakirs or Sanyasis, to preach sedition to the sepoys." (1-80) "He had set on foot the Revolutionary secret organization among the Sepoys all over Bengal, and had woven terrible net in order to reestablish his master on the throne of Oudh. When he was imprisoned in Calcutta fort, the Revolution lost, as it were, its head." (1-270)

Call for Jihad

During the Friday prayers on 1st May, M. Syed Muhammad delivered a provocative speech calling upon people to fight against the British and be prepared to make sacrifices for the purpose. (57) Agha Mirza, inspired by the speech, led thousands of people in a demonstration on the third day. The Muhammadi flag was held aloft and Agha, sword in hand, was at the head of the procession which came to be known as the 'Nishan-e-Muhammadi'. (59) British authorities obstructed the throng when several persons including Agha were wounded in a skirmish. Many were arrested. Agha was hanged in his wounded condition outside the Machchi Bhavan the very next day. (59) Troopers of the cavalry rebelled the same day (3rd May). Because of these events, it is held that the 1857 Uprising was first sparked off on 3rd May in Lucknow.[4]

A large number of youths assembled and hoisted the Mahomedan flag for *Jihad* at Ayeshbagh on 9th May. (61) An appeal to fight against *kafirs* was issued in a meeting held at Ruqn-ud-Daulah's house. (64) The traditional day of mourning the death of Hazrat Ali during Muharram fell on 15th May that year. All Muslims were enraged at the British and were in every mood to kill them.[5] All they lacked was a leader. (65)

The British were monitoring Muslim activities minutely. Any case of rebellion or treason in the cantonment was severely dealt with. Henry Cotton wrote in his diary for the 15th May: "In the evening a Sikh sepoy came to me. After *cornish* he told me the condition of those Indian soldiers who were imprisoned last night. He also wanted me to go with him to see those bastards. You would like to see how we treated these Indians. I proceeded fast towards the camp, where I

---

4. Included in the list of those who share this view are: Michael Edward, John Pemble, P.J.O. Taylor, Harprasad Chattopadhyaya and Roshan Taqvi, among some others.

5. A British officer noted: "The Mussalmeen had determined on killing every Christian in Oudh before the end of the feast of *Ramazan*." (4-8)

saw those bloody Musalmans who were tight roped and laid on floors on their stomach. Their bodies were burnt by heated brass rods. I could not see their pains and cries and shoot them to their relax." (65) Who the instigators were, or who the British believed they were, needs no elaboration.

A Jihadi poster in Persian was posted in the cantonment and the town on 18th May, "calling on the Muslims to rise and fall upon us." (4-5) It had been distributed by some "high Muslim authority" of Lucknow. (4-5) Another poster in Hindi, "in which all Hindus and Mahomedans were called upon to join in murdering the Firangis", was distributed on the 20th. (4-5; 106-67) *Payame Azadi*, an Urdu newspaper edited by Mirza Bakht, published editorials to the same effect. (106-66) Similar posters in provocative language were being displayed all over town till 29th May. (4-7; 106-71) British officers recorded that all those posters had been distributed by Muslims. (4-8)

Jihad Procession

Plans for *Jihad* were drawn up at a meeting held on 28th May under the leadership of Fakir Muhammad Khan Goya at Malihabad, 22 kms from Lucknow. (106-71) Taking the law into their own hands, fierce rioting was begun by Muslims immediately thereafter, in which zamindars of Afridi descent had taken the lead. (46-161) British officers used the words 'insolent Mahomedan population' to describe the miscreants. (4-9)

Lucknow was reverberating with Jihadi slogans by the end of May. Every masjid was preaching and advocating *Jihad*.[6] A grand procession was taken out in the town on 30th May, in which effigies of 'Firangis' were carried up to Kaiserbagh and then 'beheaded' with swords. This scene was shown at several places in the city. (106-73) Sepoys there rebelled on the same day.

---

6. Savarkar wrote : "In Lucknow, Maulvis delivered in Masjid open lectures for preaching *Jihad*." (However, this statement, which appears in the original Marathi book (p.66) cannot be found in the English version).

"The Mutiny at Lucknow was followed by city riots on 31st May when green flags, the standard of the Prophet Muhammad, were raised." (126-171) Six thousand Muslims had gathered around that flag. (67-58; 81-128) A White clerk was done to death. Although the outbreak was brought under control, it revealed a deep and widespread conspiracy within the cantonment and the town. (126-171; 4-12)

The Ringleaders

It was discovered that members of the nobility had masterminded this outbreak — Sharf-ud-Daulah who was an influential personage in Wajid Ali Shah's court and had served as prime minister to two predecessor Nawabs, two princes from Bahadur Shah's family (Mirza Muhammad Humayun and Mirza Haider), Wajid Ali Shah's brother Mirza Muhammad Mustafa Ali, Nawab Ruqn-ud-Daulah, Nawab Muhammad Hasan Khan of Tulsipur and some others. (106-103; 126-171; 4-13) Rukn-ud Daulah had amassed a force of 7,000. The administration arrested these persons by 21st June. (106-90) Also arrested, on 20th June, was a wandering bard, Amir Hasan, and eleven of his companions who were using effigies of 'firangis' to demonstrate the method of putting them to death. (89)

These events are sufficient to illustrate whence the winds of rebellion began blowing and what was the true nature of the revolt. Very seldom, if at all, does the name of a Hindu figure in either the conspiracy or its conduct. In fact, no Hindu may be found to have performed any significant role.

Hindu Talukdars Sympathetic to British

There was a large number of zamindars and talukdars in the fertile Ayodhya region, who were predominantly Hindu and even maintained military or paramilitary forces. The point to be noted is that they had chosen to side not with rebels, but the British. John Pemble, who researched this aspect, writes: "During the first few weeks of the Mutiny, the great majority of the taluqdars made no move to support the rebels. Gubbins reported at the end of June that 'the taluqdars (were) hesitating about joining the mutineers'; and Wingfield wrote that in his Division 'none of the taluqdars has yet shown any indication of revolt'. The few large landholders who found themselves in a position to assist the British did not hesitate to do so." (46-183) He states further that during the Uprising, 15 or 16 talukdars had provided asylum to British refugees, for which reason ten of these had later become exposed to rebel ire. (183) Their names and how they helped the British is listed in Pemble's and Gubbins' writings. That all of them were Hindus, is of special significance.[7] (46-184,5; 89-137 to 42)

Names of just two Hindu talukdars figure in the list of important zamindars / talukdars who sided with the rebels, and of one Muslim who sided with the British. They were Raja Jaylal Singh (a talukdar in the Faizabad district) and Talukdar Beni Madhav Singh of Shankarpur, while the third was Yasin Khan (zamindar of Sultanpur). Raja Jaylal and Beni Madhav were sworn loyalists of the ruling family of Lucknow and had devoted themselves unremittingly to their service. Yasin Khan had given asylum to two British officers but had later turned them out of their shelter treacherously and then shot them to death. (89-140) Of all these various talukdars, Raja Man Singh, a British loyalist, was the most powerful. He had a standing force of 6,000. (4-219)

A Leader Found: M. Ahmad Shah

An able leader was soon found for the Ayodhya revolt on 8th June, when sepoys in Faizabad rebelled and set free a Maulvi from the prison house. It was this forty year old Maulvi — Ahmad Shah — who became the real leader of the Ayodhya uprising. He is universally eulogized as the 'crown jewel' and brain behind the 1857 Uprising and was the fiercest opponent

---

7. Their names: Man Singh (Shahganj), Lal Madhav Singh (Amethi), Rustum Shah (Dera), Hanumant Singh (Kalakankar), Digvijay Singh (Balrampur), Loni Singh (Mithauli), the Rani of Dhaurahar, Digvijay Singh (Maurmau), Ram Sahai (Harora), Hardeo Baksh (Katiyari).

of the British. It was also under his leadership that the British suffered a comprehensive defeat at Chinhat on 30th June. Moreover, he was the only leader of the revolt without any earthly ambition. (87-14) He was the greatest hero of the Uprising and gave up his life solely to promote Allah's Cause and fight for Islam.[8]

Malleson, a British officer of the time and contemporary chronicler, wrote about him: "Who all the active conspirators were may probably never be known. One of them, there can be no question, was he who, during the progress of the Mutiny, was known as the Maulvi. The Maulvi was a very remarkable man. His name was Ahmadullah. In person he was tall, lean and muscular, with large deep-set eyes, beetle brows, a high aquiline nose, and lantern jaws. (He was) a man of great abilities, of undaunted courage, of stern determination, and by far the best soldier among the rebels. Such was the man selected by the discontented in Oudh to sow throughout India the seeds which, on a given signal, should spring to active growth.... That very soon after the annexation of Oudh he travelled over North-West Provinces on a mission which was a mystery to the European authorities.... (H)e circulated seditious papers throughout Oudh.... That this man was the brain and the hand of the

8. Savarkar uses every possible adjective of praise he could in eulogizing this man: 'True patriot' (1-456); 'The great and saintly Ahmad Shah had woven finely and cleverly the webs of *Jihad*—the war of independence.' (1-88); 'Let everyone bow down his head to do honour to this hero of heroes' (410); 'careless of his life, mad with devotion to his country'(410); 'His voice was law in the royal family of Oudh' (251); 'the national hero' (403); 'extraordinary man, moving with lightning-like activity'(403); 'extraordinary brilliant hero' (508); 'whose very soul is on fire with a burning patriotism and who is dancing on the battlefield with shouts of 'Blood! Blood!' in order to quench that fire, knows no death....' (508); 'Venerable Maulvi' (509); 'after his death, his spirit, his ghost, began to fight with the English on the field in its terrible unhuman form.' (509) And so on.

conspiracy. During his travels (in U.P.) he devised the scheme known as the chapati scheme."[9] (130-12)

We need to find out more about this single most prominent Maulvi in order to understand the true nature of the Uprising. Whence had he arrived in Lucknow? Why was he imprisoned at Faizabad till 8th June? What was his inspiration and objective?

The Hanumangarhi Imbroglio in Ayodhya

The Maulvi was originally from Tipu's Mysore region and was clandestinely touring India to preach *Jihad*. He had arrived in Faizabad in November 1856 in connection with the Hanumangarhi affair. Let us trace this contentious issue to obtain an introduction not only to the Maulvi but also the Nawab's rule in Ayodhya, Hindu-Muslim relations in the region and one of the causes of annexation of the state.

A dispute had arisen between the two communities over a Hanuman temple at Faizabad, about five kilometers from Ayodhya. The temple had been razed during Aurangzeb's reign and the ruins had been used to construct an enclosure for Muslim worship. Hindu recluses ('bairagis') were in occupation of rooms (known as 'akhadas') within the enclosure. The temple was reconstructed in later times and, when Raja Darshan Singh was the Collector, a wall was also built around the entire enclosure. Use of the place as a mosque ceased. (47-150; 95-117) The place was known as the 'Hanumangarhi'.[10]

Muslims claimed in 1855 that a mosque was at the site and, under the leadership of Ghulam Husain and his disciple

---

9. Nigam writes: "Maulvi Ahmad Shah of Faizabad toured the same territory (Northern India) extensively; and visited Delhi, Agra, Lucknow, Meerut, Patna and even Culcutta. He adopted the queer but effective method of distributing chapatis which passed from village to village. These chapatis probably carried messages hidden inside them." (69-34)

10. It was probably in proximity of the Ram Temple.

M. Muhammad Shah, began agitating with the resolve of entering the enclosure and offering *namaz*. As soon as this plan reached the ears of Nawab Wajid Ali Shah, he appointed a committee of two Muslims to inquire into the matter and decide on the veracity of the claim. A request to suspend the agitation till the committee had decided, was dismissed and it was declared that *namaz* would be offered at the site on 28th July 1855. This led to development of an explosive situation as Hindu recluses, too, rose up with the support of Hindu zamindars. (95-118; 47-150)

Capt. Orr immediately rushed to the site and detained 150 soldiers as well as a field gun at the spot, simultaneously appealing to contending parties to maintain peace for a few days till the decision was reached. Hindus agreed, but Muslims refused to be patient. (95-118; 47-151) Threats were issued to the effect that bairagis would be attacked after the midday *namaz*. Riots broke out in the town. Hindus fell upon Muslims who had made their way into the disputed site, killing 70 of them and wounding many. The Muslim leader, Shah Ghulam Husain, ran away along with some of his companions by jumping over the wall. Thereafter, Hindus attacked and looted Muslims in the town.[11] (95-119; 47-152)

The incident provoked Muslims in Faizabad and their leaders began preparations to lead a large mob in an attack on Hanumangarhi. The British Resident cautioned the Nawab to arrest and detain Shah Ghulam Husain and M. Muhammad Shah. The Nawab agreed to the suggestion but did not act upon it as he feared it might provide further provocation to Muslims. (95-120)

---

11. According to a contemporaneous narrative of Mainuddin Khan, Hindus went to the disputed site, snatched the Quran from the Maulvi's hand and burned it. (121-34) Some soldiers in the Nawab's employ had also taken part in assaulting the Hindus. (34) According to another Urdu source, 269 Muslims had died there, the Quran had been torn into pieces, trampled and then burned. (34-135q.)

The Resident then suggested that a committee of three be appointed and their decision be made binding on all parties. Accordingly, the Nawab constituted a fact-finding committee consisting of a Hindu, a Muslim and a Christian (the Captain) to inquire into the issue. Four battalions of troopers and 20 cannons were detailed at the site to ensure adequate security. (120)

Jihad Against Hindus

Meanwhile the Muslim agitation escalated all over the kingdom. Maulvis declared *Jihad* against Hindus, leading to boisterous Jihadi shouts and slogans from mosques and in the streets. The green flag of Islam was hoisted in Amethi and appeals were made for people to assemble under it. Thousands of Muslims came together to proceed to Faizabad. (95-121; 47-153) Sloganeering like 'Islam khatre mein hai' ('Islam is in danger') was done to inflame Muslim sentiments in the state. (121-35)

This worried even the Nawab. He formed another committee of four, consisting entirely of qazis and Maulvis, to produce a decision favourable to the Muslim stand. Besides concluding that there was a mosque at the site, the committee also accused Hindus of insulting the Quran, persecuting Muslims, throwing the remains of a butchered pig near a mosque and destroying *dargahs* of two *pirs* (holy men of Islam). (95-122) These findings strengthened the cause of agitating Muslims and thousands of them gathered to rebuild the mosque, while threats were being issued of avenging those 'martyred' by Hindus. (126)

Within a few days, however, the three member committee appointed on the Resident's suggestion, concluded the unanimous decision that no mosque had existed at the disputed site. (127) Copious evidence had also been furnished to substantiate the finding. The Resident advised the Nawab to honour the verdict.

However, the verdict only served to further flare up Muslim sentiment. The matter was then taken up by the 'Firangi Mahal' in Lucknow and an action committee consisting of several Maulvis was set up with M. Amir Ali as the leader.

Jihad was declared. (128) Calls for laying down lives in the cause of religion, rent the air. Two hundred armed Jihadis set out on 2nd September 1855 from Lucknow under Amir Khan's command and set up camp on the way where hundreds of holy warriors from various areas joined them. A large contingent arrived from neighbouring Rohilkhand. (25-209) Preparations to obstruct the Jihadis, on behalf of the Nawab, had begun. Talks to seek a compromise were also begun, as it was difficult to stop such a large throng of Jihadis, and they were told that since the Nawab was prepared to rethink the committee's decision, the *Jihad* should be stayed till the conclusion of Muharram. (95-131) An agreement was reached and the *Jihad* was put off till 6th October.

The Nawab then proposed to the Hindus that a mosque be allowed to be built at the disputed site, that a wall erected to separate it from the remaining portion of Hanumangarhi and that, in return for this, a separate piece of land granted to them.[12] Rejecting the proposal, Hindus threatened to abandon all temples in protest and leave the region *en masse* if a mosque was built at Hanumangarhi! (131)

The Nawab, in an attempt to appease Muslims by another stratagem, proposed a third commission of inquiry. But the governor general dismissed the proposal. (132)

Then the Nawab called upon the highest Shi'ah authority to decide whether *Jihad* was lawful under Islamic jurisprudence in such circumstances. (54-247) The Shi'ah cleric opined that none but the head of state could declare *Jihad* but, the sovereign had the right to build the masjid and the Hindu Ryots ought not to disobey." (54-247; 95-133) This opinion was publicised and the Nawab urged Muslims not to pursue their agenda of *Jihad*.

---

12. In an attempt to pacify the Maulvi, the Nawab invited him to an audience during which he assured him that a mosque would be built. He expressed the desire to honour the Maulvi and also offered to send Rs.15,000 to Mecca on his behalf. But the Maluvi retorted haughtily that he was not a revenue collector to accept a robe of honour. (54-246)

The month of Muharram was drawing to an end. A large number of Muslims had rallied under the green flag during this period. At this juncture, M. Amir Ali proclaimed *Jihad* even before the month was over and attacked a temple in Suhali near the cantonment. The idols were thrown into a lake and the Brahmins driven out of town. Nearby places like Zaidpur and Nawabganj also saw incidents of temple destruction. Cows were forcibly taken from locals and slaughtered. (95-134; 47-160) *Jihad* was begun at other places, too. Two thousand Muslims of Khairi interrupted their Tazia procession to attack Hindus. A cow was slaughtered by the use of swords and a Hindu was beaten to death. (54-248; 95-234) Many followers of Sayyid Ahmad took part in this *Jihad*.[13] (25-209)

Seeing the explosive situation all over, the Nawab called upon the British Captain to provide more security to Hanumangarhi and the Hindu population. Additional troops were assigned to control the *Jihad*. Only Hindu troopers had been assigned to this duty because it was unwise to rely upon their Muslim counterparts. (121-36; 34-135; 54-246, 8) Receiving reports of atrocities being committed against their co-religionists, Hindus had made sufficient preparations and appeals had been sent to Hindu chiefs and zamindars in the state to rush to the aid of the Hindu population. While many of these sent money, Man Singh openly took the field with his forces. (4-222) The Maulvi, referring to the force that was being mobilized against him, asked the prime minister whether the latter had any pride at all for his religion. (47-161; 95-135) The Begum of Bhopal sent an elephant and some equipment as assistance to the Maulvi. (47-161)

The Nawab Sides with Muslims

In their heart of hearts, the Nawab and his courtiers were in favour of a mosque. The prime minister proposed to the Resident that another fact-finding committee be appointed

---

13. Dr. Cole in this context states that this proclamation of *Jihad* was but an echo of the one made by Sayyid Ahmad Barelvi thirty years ago. (54-246)

under the Nawab's chairmanship. In support of the need for such an exercise, he stated that a 1707 book had been found in the Nawab's library that confirmed the previous existence of a mosque. (95-137) Rejecting the proposal, the Resident wished to know from the prime minister what might happen if, on the same principle, Hindus insisted on demolishing mosques at Benares and every other place just because there happened to be proof of temples having existed there. "But the Chief (Prime) Minister expressed surprise that the Resident considered the two cases as analogous. To him they were altogether different, *as the Hindus had always been subject to the Muslims*; 'What matters if a dozen of their shrines were destroyed and their pollutions adorned with mosques? But the destruction of a mosque was an offence of the deepest hue; from all times it had been punished by mutilation, nay by death." (95-137; 47-162)

625 Holy Warriors Killed

Ultimately, conflict became inevitable. The Maulvi and his Jihadis gave a valiant fight on 7th November without caring for their lives against cannon-aided Hindus under British command. It is said that Ayodhya had never before witnessed such a fierce conflict. (95-138) Historians call this a 'civil war'. (54-244) The battle waged for two hours and 625 Jihadis, along with 100 Hindus, perished. Many were wounded. (95-139n; 34-136; 47-163)

A Reason for Annexation

The Resident had cautioned the Nawab as early as in October that the latter would be held personally responsible if Muslims persisted in their attempt to build a mosque or if Hindus were attacked. The governor general had issued a warning that the Nawab's failure to suppress the *Jihad* agitation would attract annexation of the state. (54-247) But, the affair flared up, and hundreds of lives were lost. The British now made up their mind to annex Oudh. (34-136)

The Court of Directors (of the East India Company) gave their consent to Lord Dalhousie's recommendation of annexation of Ayodhya on 21st November 1855, fourteen days after this battle. (95-142) After completion of due formalities, the state was annexed in February 1856. Dalhousie had long desired to take this step; the Hanumangarhi imbroglio enabled him to give a fresh instance of maladministration to his superiors in England and obtain their consent. The affair became a reason for annexation of Ayodhya!

The fracas threw up an overall picture of 'Hindu versus Muslim' in the Ayodhya province. The clarion call for *Jihad* had reverberated throughout the state for five months, from July to November. The powerful zamindar, Man Singh, was already backing the Hindu cause. "Since his championship of the Hindu party in the affray and Hanumangarhi in 1856 he had been regarded as the leader of the Hindu cause in Faizabad." (46-189) He had supported it from the very beginning. (121-34) Besides, he had been a member of the Inquiry Commission appointed at the Resident's suggestion. Contemporary British officer Gubbins wrote : "The Rajputs and Hindus of all the country round were flocking to defend their sanctuary. At this time Man Singh took the lead and placed himself at their head, becoming the acknowledged leader of the Hindu party. He raised a large body of men, with whom he took post at the deeply-shaded dells and ravines of Ayodhya. Fortunately, the British Resident's interposition prevented an encounter between hostile parties. The king's troops attacked and dispersed the Mussalmans, and the party which was headed by Man Singh remained victorious."[14] (89-292; 4-222) He further states: "It was commonly believed that Man Singh had then declared that but for the support which the king would be sure to receive

---

14. Without even so much as a passing reference to the Hanumangarhi affair, Savarkar writes: "Raja Man Singh was the great leader of all the Hindus in the province of Oudh. His sword was always drawn to protect the Hindu religion under the (reign of) Nawabs." (1-250) In fact, it was only during the Nawab's rule that Hinduism suffered humiliation. Man Singh had not risen up in arms to mitigate Hindu plight under British rule. Even Savarkar does not make such a claim.

from the British, he would have marched to Lucknow, destroyed the Mahomedan dynasty, and established a Hindu government in its place. The introduction of British authority into Oudh found Man Singh deeply embarrassed." (89-293; 4-202q.) (ibid)

Man Singh's Hindu Mindset

Hindus were never really happy with imperial, Nawabi or any other form of Muslim rule. Lack of unity among themselves had forced them to reluctantly suffer it in resigned silence. Nevertheless, their innermost thoughts would occasionally find visible expression. They were aware of — and dissatisfied about — the fact that Muslims would continue receiving the ultimate and real benefits of the anti-British agitation. (46-185) A letter written by Man Singh to Hindu talukdars is an indication of that Hindu awareness.

He wrote: "It is also surprising that people should aid and put into power those very Muslims who, on invading India, destroyed all our Hindu temples, forcibly converted the natives to Mahomedanism, massacred whole cities, coerced Hindu women and made them their concubines, burnt their religious books and levied taxes (*Jaziya*) upon every Hindu." (185)

Though not strictly part of the 1857 Uprising, the Hanumangarhi affair clearly mirrors its intrinsic nature especially in Ayodhya. It was just a few months later that the Uprising occurred. We can infer from all of the foregoing that:

One, Hindu-Muslim relations had hit their worst pass on the eve of the Uprising; a *Jihad* against Hindus had been declared; intervention by the British Resident and officers to uphold the just cause of Hindus had prevented a disastrous conflict and casualty. Which one of the two overlords might Hindus have perceived as their friend and helper on the eve of the Uprising? *Two*, when Muslims had issued hundreds of *fatwas* against the British in 1857, what might have prevented them from doing the same in respect of Hindus, too? The *fatwa* issued in the Hanumangarhi matter was hardly any different from others issued during the Uprising. Who had been more threatened as a result of any such *fatwa*, British or Hindus? *Three*, how had it been possible to totally resolve a grievous dispute of just four months ago and suddenly unify the two warring communities? Could Hindus have ever perceived that once the British had been driven out and the Nawab's rule restored, their Hanuman temple would become secure, the neighbouring Ram Temple liberated and Muslim insistence on mosque construction rescinded? *Four*, it was not just an odd Maulvi or two but the entire Muslim community that had demanded a mosque and had become surcharged with the spirit of *Jihad*. Moreover, the Nawab himself, along with his coterie, had become one with Muslim sentiment and was making one new proposal after another in a bid to build the mosque. But for British intervention, the mosque would most certainly have been built.[15] Had Hindus not realized in 1857 that there was none in the Nawab's regime to take up their cause? *Five*, what were the views held by the Nawab, his prime minister Nakki Khan[16] and the Maulvis about the Hindu religion, temples, idols and people? Their official and doctrinal outlook was that the mosque was superior to the temple; the temple was unclean and profane while the mosque, sacred and exalted; demolishing temples was their right, demolishing mosques was a capital offence; Hindus were subservient

15. Gubbins writes: "The Mahomedan aggression was secretly favoured by the bigoted and imbecile Court at Lucknow." (4-22; 89-292)

16. We have already seen Savarkar's glorification of Wajid Ali Shah and his prime minister, Nakki Khan. [footnote #3 (supra)] He also writes that, while inducing people towards work of the revolution, "Nawab of Ayodhya promised the Hindus to treat them generously." This part appears in the Savarkar's original Marathi book (p.70), but not in the English version. Even so, a question arises as to how a sudden change came about in the Nawab's views of a mere few months ago about profanity of temples and subjection of Hindus? Perhaps it was expedient political generosity after and because of his expulsion from power in Ayodhya!"

tributary while Muslims, their kings and masters. Is it plausible that Hindus could have supported the *Jihad* in the fond hope that Muslims would give up all such views after the British had left and treat them in an equitable manner? What does Man Singh's letter, quoted above, indicate?

Nawabi Regime's Outlook vis-à-vis Hindus

Dr. J. R. I. Cole, who made an in-depth study of the regime and religion in Ayodhya, wrote a peerless book on the subject. The royal court was under the firm and unremitting influence of Shi'ah clerics and the Nawab was obliged to act according to their directions. This was why the Nawab sought opinion of the clergy about legality of the *Jihad*. The clergy was reluctant to accord the status of 'zimmi' (protected peoples) to Hindu subjects because they were idol worshippers.[17] (54-246) "Their demand for the social exclusion of Hindus as ritually impure received scant response from the Shi'ah-ruled state, which depended on the Hindu elites to help the rule." [18] (250)

---

17. Islam only allows 'zimmi' (non-Muslim, protected subjects of an Islamic state) status to Jews and Christians who are regarded as the 'people of the Book'. In the absence of this status, conversion to Islam and death are the only choices available.

18. Some more thoughts: "As the Shi'ah ulemas began to influence state policy in the 1840s, however, their attitudes towards Hindus became important. They wished to bring Hindus into Shi'ah fold, to offer them conversion or death." (54-224) "He (the Shi'ah Maulvi) complained that the irreligious Sunni Mughal rulers of India neither made war against the Hindus nor forced them to accept Islam." (226) "The Ulema did not allow Shi'ahs to give food to Hindus. A Shi'ah, citing the *Quranic* statement that a full believer should help a hungry neighbour, inquired (of the Chief *Mujtahid*)...whether only Muslim neighbours were meant. He replied that apparently the verse meant only Muslims." (227)

"The King Amjad Ali Shah (1842-7) enacted anti-Hindu policies, founding Shi'ah shops to drive Hindu merchants out of business, and rewarding Hindu officials who adopted Imami Shi'ahism. The provision of government welfare monies to only the Shi'ah poor encouraged thousands of Hindus to convert to Shi'ahism in

(Contd.)

Although they were incapable of legally doing so, they still regarded Hindus as 'unclean', which was why views like those stated above about Hindus and their temples were voiced through the Nawab.

It was not only during the reign of the last Nawab Wajid Ali Shah (1847–57) that Hindu-Muslim tension prevailed, but had a tradition going back in time. Hindu subjects had been living under gross injustice for several decades.[19] Such a state of affairs is a useful guide to judge whether – as also why – Hindus could have supported the Uprising.

1840s." (54-229) "Always fiercely *Usuli* Government (at Lucknow) showed little understanding to their Hindu subjects, allowing communal resentment to fester, a policy that culminated in a major battle over a religious edifice in Faizabad." (229)

"Amjad Ali Shah, a blatant communalist, cut off stipends to many Sunnis and Hindus, employing Shi'ahs as the heads of every government office. Because he thought Sunnis and Hindus ritually impure, he forbade them to write name of God (i.e. Allah), the Prophet on official letters, and hired Shi'ah secretaries to write the holy names. The heir-apparent, Wajid Ali (1847–56), at one point forced several reluctant Sunni secretaries (munshis) to embrace Shi'ahism." (54-243)

19. Some instances of pre-1857 conflicts:

I. "(Those of) Nasiruddin Haider (1827–37) and Amjad Ali Shah (1842–47) being the most anti-Hindu. In 1829 the king forced a Brahman boy to undergo circumcision. He told the outraged Resident that he had a divine right to dispose of his subjects as he wished. The Resident Ricketts angrily retorted that the British government recognized no such right. When, three months later, Hindus provoked violence by defiling a mosque in Rikabganj, the king vindictively sent troops into the area, who plundered, ripped nose-rings off the faces of Hindu women, and destroyed all 47 Hindu temples in that quarter, putting to flight its entire population of three thousand." (54-228)

II. "When, in November 1840, some Hindus defiled a *Zamindar*'s mosque with pig's blood, his sons rounded up a crowd of angry Muslims to exact revenge. On 4 December two hundred Muslims killed cows, profaned temples, and damaged shops… ." (228)

A notable incident needs mention here. An inciteful handout called '*Risala Jihad*' was distributed in 1855 in Ayodhya as well as Delhi. It was issued by a leader of the Waliullahi school and had as its chief slogan: "Throughout Hindustan, let there be no sound (heard), but Allah." (3-302; 119-191)

M. Ahmad Shah's Jihad Against Hindus

It was on the backdrop of the Hanumangarhi affair that M. Ahmad Shah arrived on the scene in Lucknow in November 1856. People went in droves to meet him in Moti Masjid. The then Commissioner wrote that the locals had found a good leader. (106-37) Then, in February 1857, he entered Faizabad along with many followers. (106-41; 87-15) He had gone there from Lucknow to pray at the tombs of martyrs of the *Jihad* for the mosque and to avenge the death of M. Amir Ali. (87-15; 46-212) No sooner he reached the place, than *Jihad* was announced against Hindus. (87-15; 4-147) British officers feared that there was an evident intention on the part of the Faqir to raise a riot and dissension among the people." (59-264; 3-381) People queued up in order to meet the man. Fearing a breach of peace, the police chief went to see him accompanied by eight constables. The Maulvi was seated inside a mosque at that time with ten armed guards flanking him on either side. The police chief asked him to come out of the mosque, which he refused to do. He was ordered to surrender his weapons. Declining to do that as well, he told the police that those weapons had been given to him by his Pir (Muslim saint). Moreover, he also refused to quit the town. (3-382)

Then, on 17th February, a larger force was brought in. The Maulvi and his followers charged upon them with drawn swords, but was wounded in the ensuing skirmish while three of his men were killed. (3-383; 87-15; 59-264) He was arrested,[20] tried, sentenced to be hanged and incarcerated in the Faizabad

20. From him, "a number of letters from the Muslims alone showing their complicity in this affair were recovered. But there was none from a Hindu." (3-388)

prison pending execution.[21] In the meantime, on 8th June, sepoys at Faizabad rebelled and freed him from prison after which he assumed leadership of the revolt. (59-264; 118-426) He was even accorded a 'gun salute' by sepoys. (89-137)

Of the Waliullahi School

This Maulvi hailed from South India, and Tipu Sultan was his inspiration. (77-170) In the opinion of some, he belonged to Tipu's family. 25-217; 87-15) He had been engaged in preaching *Jihad* in the south but had moved north because Madras was not a particularly suitable region for the purpose. (68-499) Educated in Hyderabad, he had visited Arabia, Iran and England. (59-263; 77-170) He had also toured the whole of India to preach *Jihad*. He was in contact with Maulvis at Tonk, Gwalior, Delhi, Agra, Meerut, Patna and other places. (77-170; 130-12; 25-217) He possessed a maultifaceted personality and was an excellent orator and preacher. He would be accompanied by thousands of followers when he moved through the streets. Drums would be beaten at the head of such processions, which had earned him names like 'Dunka Shah' and 'Nagara Shah'. (87-15; 59-264) His followers swallowed burning charcoals before the crowds in the belief that the act would save them from the fires of hell. (59-264; 87-15) He believed he had been inspired by Allah Himself.[22] (4-144; 59-267)

---

21. Savarkar writes about his incarceration: "With the burning torch of Revolutionary War in his hand, he had been setting the whole country aflame, when the English authorities at Lucknow captured and ordered him to be hanged. But, before being executed, he was taken to the prison at Faizabad and there the storm of 1857 raised him from his cell in the alien's prison to the leadership of the Revolution." (1-403) (Probably, Savarkar was ignorant of the fact that the Maulvi had come to Faizabad to wage *Jihad* against Hindus). He glorifies the gaol as the prison which had been sanctified by the feet of the popular hero. (252)

22. In a book providing information about this man, a separate chapter is titled 'A God-sent Leader'. (87-14)

When a situation almost foreboding the end of British rule arose, Ahmad Shah declared he was going to march upon London and beat drums in the streets there. (4-144; 87-16) He even entertained thoughts of making Empress Victoria his 'Rani'. (60-245) His followers had implicit faith in him and used to regard him as a divine incarnation. (87-16) Interestingly enough, the Maulvi and his followers sincerely believed that a whip he was accustomed to carry around with him, and his kerchief, possessed divine power. (59-267)

All of this notwithstanding, his greatest attribute was that he belonged to the Waliullahi tradition, was infused by the Jihadi teaching of Sayyid Barelvi and was now conducting the agitation with the cooperation of others with the same inspiration. (76-20; 46-212; 22-94; 25-217) He was a proponent of pristine Islam for which reason apparently he had forbidden looting and killing women and children during the entire period of the Uprising. (87-14)

For his activism during the 1857 Uprising, this Maulvi commands a unique place among all revolutionaries. The British feared him the most; they faced a defeat at Chinhat because of him. As rebel leader of Lucknow, he had offered the greatest resistance to them till he left to participate in the Rohilkhand *Jihad* after British control had been reestablished over that town. An Islamic state had been founded by him at Mohammadi though it was short-lived. However, when he had gone to Powain to secure the local Hindu Raja's support, the latter had killed him. It was for that purpose, in fact, that Raja Loni Singh of Mithauli had advised Ahmad Shah to go to Powain. (87-19)

Historians name this Maulvi as the greatest and most influential leader of the 1857 Uprising.[23] The 'Fateh Islam' *Jihad*

---

23. Comments of some historians about him :

I. Dr. Chaudhary: "The Maulvi was the leader of the north-western front of rebels and *was acting as a focus of* Mahomedan *hostility*. His death on 5 June (1858) led to the collapse of the movement in north-western part of Oudh." (81-139)

(Contd.)

proclamation that he issued makes his Wahabi thinking and the true nature of the Uprising crystal clear.

II. The then Magistrate's report: "Due to his death, one of the most determined and influential of the rebel leaders has been got rid of. "(7-539) Their only leader of energy and ability." (545)

III. S. N. Chanda: "But during this short period he had left an indelible mark in the pages of history as a tactician and a 'spiritual guide' for the people of Oudh." (87-17)

IV. *A History of the Freedom Movement* published by the Pakistan Government: *The greatest of the heroes (in 1857).* (34-332)

V. John Pemble : "That he was a *Ghazi* or Islamic crusader, whose mission was the promotion of a holy war (*Jihad*).... *His mission to Faizabad appears to have been anti-Hindu rather than anti-British,* for he came to visit the tombs of the Muslims who had been killed in the religious riots of 1856 and to avenge the death of one of their leaders, a *Maulvi* called Amir Ali. As a Muslim extremist he was naturally suspect to the Hindu sepoys. Yet he is historic, for he was almost the only individual to leave his imprint on the Indian Mutiny. He was, in fact, the only character approximating to a popular leader (in the struggle). His rise to power changed the character of the revolt in Lucknow. The Maulvi gave a different colour to the Revolt. He appealed to popular religious susceptibilities and popular fears, and under his leadership the rising briefly assumed the character of a mass movement. 'The war is now fully believed to be a religious crusade." (46-212 to 4)

VI. Mujeeb Ashraf : "Ahmadullah Shah deserves special attention as he was easily the most prominent leader of the resistance movement in Oudh. In fact, in the final phase of Uprising, he became one of the all-India leaders of the movement. He was one of the ablest men to be thrown up by the struggle and excelled all other leaders in independence of spirit. He had hardly any rival as a tactician. This is acknowledged even by the British. He was from South India, a descendant of the Qutb Shahi family of the Deccan.' The remarkable courage shown by Tipu Sultan in his anti-British struggle was still in his memory. It served as an unfailing source of inspiration for him. He organized the Muslims there,

(Contd.)

Ten Year Old Qadar Enthroned

The proclamation, "Khulk Khuda ka, Mulk Badshah ka, Hukum Birjis Qadar[24] ka" was made after that 10-year old was enthroned as Nawab on 5th July. (4-89) A 21-gun salute was also given on the occasion. Fazal Haq Khairabadi, a renowned Waliullahi Maulvi, was appointed as his (i.e. his mother's) advisor. (77-167) This Maulvi had been in the forefront when the Delhi *Jihad* declaration had been issued. After the fall of Delhi on 20th September 1857, courtiers at Lucknow proclaimed Birjis Qadar as Emperor of India and gave him a 101-gun salute due to an Emperor. (54-277) His regent minted a coin with the couplet: "The Emperor (Badshah) of everybody, every eye, Birjis Qadar struck coins in gold and silver, like sun and moon." (277) All of this implied that the seat of imperial power had shifted from Delhi to Lucknow! Hindus, however, were to be given no role loftier or more glorious than that of porters with the burden of the imperial palanquin on their shoulders!

Officers of the administration were then appointed. The Prime Minister, Commander-in-Chief, Chief Justice, Chief of Police, Chief of Intelligence and eleven other key officials were all Muslim. (4-104) Real power lay with the Begum and Mammu Khan. (117) Only two other offices came to the lot of Hindus. The hereditary loyalist of the Nawabs, Zamindar Raja Jaylal

---

trained them and told them of the merit of participation in a *Jihad*." (77-170)

VII. T.R.Holmes: "The Maulvi, who, though not the equal of Haider or Shivaji, was probably the most determined of the men who fought against us in the Indian Mutiny." (77-172q.)

24. Other Begums were opposed to Birjis Qadar as Nawab because he was offspring of Hazrat Mahal who had been a concubine before becoming 'Begum'. They feared denigration of the royal house. But her paramour, Mammu Khan, had exerted every possible effort and influence he could, and had succeeded in enthroning the child. (4-140; 79-371) Obviously, only another Muslim could be considered as an alternative; even contemplating a mature, experienced and meritorious Hindu as king was a pipedream.

Singh, who had rendered valuable assistance to Mammu Khan in the accession of Birjis Qadar, was given an unimportant post of 'Collector of Army' whose duty was 'to command the forces sent to collect revenue from the rebellious people.' (113) The revenue department was offered to another Hindu, Balkrishnan, who declined the offer, being opposed to Nawabi rule. But he consented after being coerced through a threat that his house would be sacked. (4-106; 54-277) The two appointments had only been made to win Hindu sympathy.

Numerous Hindu zamindars were opposed to Nawabi rule and had sided with the British. Better known among them was Raja Loni Singh of Mithauli. He had extended asylum to several British personnel within his fortress. (4-128) Despite the Nawab's directive to give custody of the Englishmen, as well as a warning that he would be regarded as an enemy and stern action would be initiated against him, he had managed to stall compliance for four months. As a result, the Nawab had to march against him and take custody of the British refugees. (129)

Jihad Slogans

The revolt in Lucknow was primarily a conflict between Muslims and the British with a profusion of green flags and Jihadi sloganeering. Those flags were flying over government buildings. A British officer stationed there recorded that war cries of 'Ali! Ali!' were so frequent and deafening, that they could not sleep at night. (89-72)

One gets the impression from historians' descriptions of the conflict as well as eyewitness accounts that one is reading narratives of a *Jihad*.[25] The approach of Muharram would send signals of impending unrest to British officials. Special Jihadi

---

25. For instance, Savarkar writes about the battle of Sikandar Bagh: "More than two thousand rebel corpses lay heaped round (the Sikandar Bagh). Oh, you two thousand martyrs that died fighting for independence let this grateful history be dedicated to your memory ! The blood of two thousand patriots! This history is dedicated to that blood. Let your blood and bravery purify and adorn the Past and incite and inspire the Future." (1-373) In short, those fighting and dying were all Muslim '*ghazis*'.

names were assigned by rebels to campaigns intended to engage in armed combat. For example, one such expedition in August – September 1857 was named 'Operation Muharram', while holy warriors engaging in it were shouting 'Ali, Ali, Ya Ali!'. (6-142,5)

Entire Ayodhya Province Under Nawab

The Nawab's rule was not limited to the city of Lucknow but extended over the entire Ayodhya province. Rebels established administrations at various places in the region after respective local revolts, while the Collectors of such districts acted on behalf of the Nawab.

At Faizabad, rebellious sepoys installed M. Ahmad Shah as their leader. Mehndi Hasan began his administration at Sultanpur, and commanded a standing force in excess of 18,000. (81-123; 87-42) By February 1858, his sway extended over the southern part of the Ayodhya province. He recruited a force of 25,000 to counter the British. This man attacked the citadel of the pro-British Man Singh of Shahganj in Faizabad district with a force of 4,000 and invaded the fortress. The defenders appealed for British help but assistance was not quick in coming as they were themselves facing difficulties. Man Singh was thus confined to the fortress until help arrived. (87-45; 6-340, 4) Mehndi Hasan held sway over the entire Faizabad district and attempted several times to establish his rule over adjacent Azamgarh and Jaunpur by reducing British presence at those places. (6-174) The Begum confiscated all property owned by the pro-British Hindu Chief of Dera, Rustam Shah. (87-45; 4-480)

The Begum's rule was also established at Sitapur after a rebellion there. (81-126)

Beni Madhav Singh's Sacrifice for the Begum

Beni Madhav, who was a talukdar chieftain of Shankarpur, pitched himself stoutly behind the Begum. He dedicated himself completely to the ruling family of Ayodhya. He had no political ambition or expectation but was sore with the British on account of the 119 villages he had to forego as a result of their policies. Having mustered all his resources for the Begum's cause, he was awarded the title of 'Bahadur Diler Jung' by her. She had also appointed him nazim (collector) of Azamgarh for some time. As such, he can neither be regarded as a motivator, leader nor true beneficiary of the 1857 Uprising.

While many Hindu zamindars and talukdars in the region were intrinsically opposed to the Nawab's rule, they had to engage in armed conflict with Nawabi forces because they sided with the British. Their situation would have become unenviable had British power collapsed. Hence, during a short period when it had seemed British power might succumb or when it was felt that they (i.e. zamindars / talukdars) could not hold out against the Nawab's forces or threats, these landlords adopted a policy of conciliation. Their actions began to be dictated by who of the two, British or the Nawab, was more likely to emerge the ultimate victor. This does not imply that they supported the Nawab's rule; it only means they lacked the power to oppose it. Many such petty Hindu zamindars had inclined towards the Nawab for this reason and also because they hoped their land holdings would be secure. Thus, even those historians who call the 1857 uprising a 'sepoy mutiny', label the Ayodhya unrest as a 'national rising/war.' (95-153; 141-413) Be that as it may, it does not alter the essentially Islamic / Jihadi nature of the uprising in Ayodhya.

- 2 -

Muslim Uprising in Benares

Hindus were not just in majority in Benares, but it was also a district in which one of their holiest places of pilgrimage was located. The king here was Hindu. Signs of rebellion became apparent towards the end of May 1857. The agents of the king of Delhi were found to be busy amongst the Mahomedan sepoys;[26] the Hindus went openly to their

---

26. About this Savarkar wrote : "When the month of May came, there was quite a number of Mahomedan preachers in the Sepoy camp." (1-181)

temples, and prayed for the time to arrive when they might murder us; placards were posted up calling on the people to rise, and every thing indicated the approach of a crisis." (6-9) But was it a joint Hindu-Muslim effort?

Rebellion broke out on the same day as in Kanpur and Azamgarh (4th June). Muslim sepoys had risen in both places. However, Sikh sepoys took part in the Benares rebellion only as a result of misunderstanding, when the 37th Platoon was being disarmed, but reverted to their loyalist position once it had been dispelled. The local Hindu king, the prominent and influential leader Pandit Gokulchand, other leaders like Rao Deo Narayan Singh, and the Sikh leader Surat Singh gave valuable support to the British in putting down the rebellion. 6-12, 19,45; 34-324; 44-123) A British officer gratefully recorded that they preserved the great city of Benares for the British. (130-122; 78-174; 44-123) In respect of Deo Narayan Singh, Kaye wrote : "No words could exaggerate the importance of his services." (78-174) The British administration had recognized these services by titles and rewards. (130-122n) Not a single drop of Christian blood was shed because the local Hindu population responded positively to their leaders' appeals. (78-175) Coopland, an Englishwoman present in Benares at the time, recorded: "As this is completely a Mahomedan rising, there is not much to be feared from the Hindus of Benares." (55-86q) Since sepoys after rebelling left for Ayodhya to serve the Begum, it is clear under whose influence they acted.

The Green Flag Heads for the Temple

A green flag was hoisted in the city after the revolt. (81-157; 70-155; 78-175; 44-123) Soon, 'Mussalmans had determined to raise the Green Flag in the temple of Vishveshwar, the most holy of the many holy places.' (60-20; 55-87) Receiving news of this, Hindus mobilized and assisted British troops in preventing Muslims from prosecuting their design. It was thus that rebels of 1857 were precluded from actually hoisting the green flag of Islam at one of the holiest of Hindu shrines. (ibid) Even Dr. Chaudhary states: "At Benares Hindu-Muslim dissension also raised its head, the green flag was hoisted...". (81-157) Benares thereafter remained under British control and thereby the hazard posed to Hindus and their sacred temple was averted.[27] Whoever had prayed before the uprising for its success must have probably gone to the Vishveshwar Temple another time, after this incident, to express remorse!

A Green Flag at Azamgarh

Muzaffar Jahan, the zamindar chief of Azamgarh, Irzat Jahan and Fazat Jahan were in the forefront of the rebellion there. (6-101) A rebel administration was set up and, overnight, a green flag began flying over the fortress.[28] The Begum of Ayodhya appointed the Collector there.[29] Muzaffar Jahan

---

27. Savarkar writes: "At this time a Pundit, called Gokul Chand, had also joined the side of the English. Even the Raja of Benares placed all his influence, his wealth, and his power, his everything at the feet of his lord, not Kashi Visheshawara, but, the English !" (1-185)

28. Savarkar's description is more evidential for understanding the true nature of the revolt at this place: "The twilight of the 3rd of June was slowly changing to the darkness of night at Azamgarh. 'The sepoys have arisen !' Just then followed a thundering noise of drums and clarinets! (English) officers, women and children despaired of life. Sepoys ordered them to leave Azamgarh at once. The whole caravan, including all the flags and all the signs of English rule, started forth for Benares! Remaining all fell into the hands of the Sepoys. *And who was foremost in all this work*? When the sun rose the next day, it gazed in admiration at the marvellous transformation that had taken place during its short absence (of night), and shone delightfully of the revolutionary (*green*) flag flying at Azamgarh. The Sepoys, in the flush of victory, drew up a great military procession; and to the strains of martial music and (*green*) banners unfurled marched away to Faizabad." (1-183) (Here we have placed the word 'green' in brackets because in the original Marathi edition of the book, Savarkar had mentioned this flag / banners as 'green.' However in the English version this term is omitted.)

assumed chiefship of Mhow. (81-156) The other two Jahans were later hanged by the British. (6-102; 81-150) Plainly, Muslims alone had been the motivators, leaders and beneficiaries. Kunwar Singh had, at a later stage, acquired control over Azamgarh but it was short-lived.

The Begum of Ayodhya appointed a Collector and other officials after the Uprising at Jaunpur, the third district place of prominence in the province.[29] A well known Waliullahi Maulvi Karamat Ali played a leading role in inspiring locals to rebel.[30] (81-153)

British attempts to regain control over Azamgarh and Jaunpur were successful and their power was established in these districts. Mehndi Hasan of Sultanpur, however, continued efforts to oust them, under authority granted by the Begum of Ayodhya. It was decided that Mehndi Hasan would become ruler after a prospective victory. (6-174)

Muhammad Hasan at Gorakhpur

Rebel leader Muhammad Hasan set up his administration after an uprising at the fourth district of the Ayodhya province, Gorakhpur. The Emperor accorded him recognition as subedar. (6-224) The Hindu Raja of Bansi and the dowager Rani of Basti denied him the authority. (81-145; 6-158) A force of 4,000 was sent by the Subedar against Bansi, forcing the Raja to abandon everything and flee into the forests. (6-338) Both chiefs often assisted the British during their conflicts with the subedar. (303)

Likewise, Hindu chiefs of Tumkhoi, Mujovali and Gopalpur had also turned against the subedar and become pro-British. (156, 8, 60) The Chief of Gopalpur had, in fact,

---

29. The Nazim (Collector) and his deputies here and at Jaunpur kept changing. Names like Irzat Jahan, Beni Madhav, Mehndi Hasan appear in the context.

30. Savarkar writes: "(After sepoys' revolt) the city of Jaunpur marched out with slogans of 'Deen! Deen!'" (This statement containing 'Deen! Deen!' appears in the original Marathi book (p.147), but does not appear in its English version.) (1-183)

even formed a confederacy of British-loyalist zamindars like himself. (160)

On commencement of the subedar's rule, all senior offices in the administration, of course, went to Muslims. The naib (deputy) subedar, Musharraf Khan, was the most influential official, "who perhaps enjoyed more and real power than Muhammad Hasan himself." (157) He also held additional charge as Chief Justice and Collector. (157)

The subedar's force numbered 12 – 15 thousand and became a grave threat to the Azamgarh District. (172) British officials lived in constant fear of this man and Mehndi Hasan of Sultanpur.

News was received towards the end of September 1857 that local Hindu zamindars were planning to rise against him. (294) Muhammad Hasan had added the suffix, "High above the stars stands the name of Muhammad Hasan !", to his name. (296) He also attempted to entice the pro-British Hindu king of neighbouring Nepal through subtle incitement to his religious sentiments by expressing astonishment at the latter's sympathy for 'firangis', who "expresses surprise that 'His Excellency' should take part with those who 'tolerate the destruction of Brahmans and Cows.'"[31] (6-302)

The job of generating an atmosphere of unrest in Gorakhpur was being performed by a Waliullahi Maulvi Sarfaraz Ali who was party to the *Jihad* declaration of Delhi. His disciple Dumman Khan was also equally active in preaching the doctrine. (347)

---

31. However, he did not ban cow slaughter within his own Gorakhpur. The journal that published this report, 'The Friend of India', comments that "Muhammad Hasan is a Mahomedan as indeed his name imports, he therefore does not object to the slaughter of cows. The letter affords an insight to the way in which Hindus and Mussalmans have been united." (6-302) A description of this affair appears under the heading 'Hindu-Muslim Unity' in the Publication of the Government of Uttar Pradesh.

An army had been sent against the pro-British Chief of Shahganj, Man Singh. The Begum of Ayodhya also assisted in this expedition. Man Singh had appealed for British help. (6-355; 4-425) Gorakhpur had remained under Muhammad Hasan's control till January 1858 when the British reoccupied it. An alliance had been formed for some time between Hasan and Balarao Peshwa, which had ended when a dispute arose between them. (6-360, 3) Muhammad Hasan made an overture of surrender in October 1859. This statement is useful for an understanding of his thoughts and aims.

- 3 -

We now turn our attention to the Uprising in areas of the predominantly Hindu Rajputana and Malwa.

Rajputana: Uprising by Muslim Sepoys

The Hindu States in Rajputana "in general remained 'a rock of strength' to the British power during" the rebellion. (81-235) All the revolts that occurred here were initiated by Muslim sepoys in the cantonments of Ajmer, Nasirabad and Neemuch. Tonk was a Muslim State and the late Nawab, Amir Khan, had become a disciple of Sayyid Badshah. Muslim sepoys in Tonk rebelled and went away as Mujahiddin to serve the Emperor in Delhi. (43-65)

Muslim sepoys took the lead in rebellions at all three places and most of them had left for Delhi. (72-178) They had appointed their own 'brigadiers'. For example, subedar Shaikh Riyadat Ali had been made their brigadier by the Neemuch sepoys; he issued directives in the Emperor's name. (126-391) This Neemuch faction later offered stiff resistance to the British in Delhi. The sepoys from Nasirabad were referred to as 'Jihadis'. (121-179)

Rajputana remained peaceful because rebel sepoys had all left and Hindu potentates were pro-British.

Gwalior: The Maharaja versus Sepoys

While the Maharaja of Gwalior – the most important State in Malwa–was entirely pro-British, the forces assigned to him by the British became rebellious and took part in the revolt.

The Maharaja had already enlisted a special, independent force of trusted Maratha soldiers because he had no faith in the regulars. (64-74) These Maratha troopers had no sympathy for the latter and the Maharaja preferred to trust their own men. (64-74; 82-90;5-177) Id was on 25th May, and sepoys in the cantonment were itching to rebel; their wrath had reached fever pitch. (5-173) Around the same time, sepoys insulted the Maharaja's Divan in the cantonment. Cavalrymen were contemplating departure for Delhi on 29th May. (129) Of course, the cavalry was mostly Muslim.[32]

The Leaders: Amanut Ali, Jahangir Khan

The government report says : "On the 1st of June, of Maharajah's chosen Mahomedan guard at the residency, an officer and six men deserted to Delhi, and thenceforth parties of his men from our provinces followed them daily." (5-178; 82-91)

Sepoys rebelled on 14th June under leadership of Amanut Ali, who then became their Subedar General. (5-189; 126-392) As soon as the revolt broke out, Resident Macpherson along with some officers and his family left for the Maharaja's Palace for security. They were surrounded on the way by six musket-wielding *ghazis* led by Jahangir Khan, a favourite captain of the Maharaja before the revolt. They said they were going to kill them all. But the captain of the forty Maratha soldiers in the Resident's security escort threatened, in turn, to kill all the *ghazis* if they tried to do so. That ensured them safe passage to the Palace. (5-184)

However, when the Maharaja realized he would not be able to guarantee safety of the British refugees much longer, he decided to send them to Agra under escort. Accordingly, thirty refugees including the Resident were sent to Agra under a special security force of trusted troopers assigned to conduct them in safety upto the Chambal River, after which a force detailed by the Hindu Raja of Dholpur was to escort them to

---

32. Muslims, in the Maharaja's regular force, constituted 50% of the infantry, 67% of the cavalry and 75% of the artillery. (86-87)

Agra. The Gwalior contingent reached their charge to the Chambal where, unknown to the Gwalior party, the same Jahangir Khan with 200 armed *ghazis* in green attire was lying in ambush to kill them. This notwithstanding, the Thakur escort from Dholpur was successful in foiling the attempt and reaching the party to Agra. (5-185; 36-192) The Resident expressed gratitude to the Raja of Dholpur and, as a token of appreciation for saving their lives from the *ghazis*, made the grant of a village to the Thakur soldiers. (5-185)

Maharaja Receives Threat

Muslim rebels approached the Maharaja, asked him to lead them and threatened to imprison him if he declined.[33] (82-91) But the Maharaja shrewdly managed to hold them at bay for two months.

In the meantime, the Maharaja called upon Hindu chieftains in his dominion to assist him and enlisted 6-11 thousand additional soldiers in his army. (5-188) Resident Macpherson noted: "From the Marathas and the Gwalior Hindus alone could he hope for obedience." (188)

Rebel sepoys from Indore and Mhow had in the meantime arrived in Gwalior on 1st August with the aim of gathering local sepoys and proceeding to Agra. "It excited the contingent afresh like oil thrown on fire." (5-191) They were led by the rebel commander from Indore, Sadat Khan, and consisted of 1000 *ghazis*, 1300 sepoys and had 7 field guns. (86-105; 5-191; 50-140) Prince Firoz Shah of Delhi, too, had arrived in Gwalior during the same month with 1000 men. (111-475) The Gwalior sepoys went to the Maharaja and asked him to arrange for their conveyance to Agra. Again, he managed somehow in persuading them to wait for a month. The British were insistent that the Gwalior rebels should not be allowed to reach Agra.

33. Nanasahib had likewise been threatened by his Kanpur sepoys. But, unlike the Gwalior Maharaja, Nana lacked the necessary military strength and had to give in to the threat. The Maharaja's case was different.

By a clever move, the Maharaja proposed that the Indore and Mhow contingents should be the first to move out, followed later by those from Gwalior. As a result, 1000 Muslim horsemen, 700 'vilayatee' Muslim sepoys and a large body of fanatic fighters prepared to move out. (5-192) But the Maharaja had all the ferries across the Chambal removed overnight as soon as the Indore and Mhow contingents had crossed over, making it impossible for the Gwalior faction to move for want of transport across the river. (192)

The sepoys realized they had been tricked. A delegation of 300 met the Maharaja and told him : "We want to finish off the whites by attacking Agra. You also kindly help us in this task." He said they would now need to wait till the end of the rainy season. (39-128; 5-192)

They then returned to the cantonment and hoisted a green flag, while Hindus among them unfurled a white flag. (5-192; 50-150) An invitation was sent to the Nawab of Banda to assist them in crushing the Maharaja. (5-192) They made preparations to bombard the Palace, but the Maharaja had made adequate preparations by readying a force of 5,000 Marathas and 11,000 Thakurs. (5-193, 204) The rebels had planted their Batteries against the town and the Palace, but were bettered by the Maharaja in both power and stratagem so that nothing untoward occurred and the rebels were forced to wait patiently for the rains to cease. In the interregnum, however, Delhi fell to the British on 20th September and the British gained the upper hand.

The Resident's report of the overall Uprising at Gwalior states: "With great limitations and exceptions, the Mahomedans cooperated with the revolt; the Hindus wished it well, but having no religious grievance, while their civil grievances were inadequate to move them to arms they did not rise, and protected the lives of defenceless Europeans." (5-202) About the Maharaja it states : "Scindhia discredited the religious pretext for the revolt, believed that we must triumph, and unhesitatingly took part with us." (203)

The Maharaja had "most confidently" told the British that because seats of Hindu religious authority like "Benares or Gaya, and other centers of Hindu opinion, to whom all (Hindus) looked for (guidance), had abstained from sanctioning any religious pretext alleged for" the Uprising, the revolt would be arrested once Delhi was recaptured. (175)

It might be pertinent to see at this juncture how, at later dates, Kanpur (November 1857) and Gwalior (May 1858) fell to Tatya Tope's forces. Although Kalpi after Kanpur had become the headquarters of Raosahib Peshwa, the administration was actually conducted since June by the rebel, Muhammad Ishaq. (87) He used to issue orders in Nanasahib's name and appeal to Hindus and Muslims to kill enemies of religion. (211) Kalpi became a rendezvous for rebels.

What Army was Tatya Commanding?

In September, or around the time the Maharaja of Gwalior had succeeded in staying the Gwalior sepoys' advance to Agra, Tatya Tope went to that town and managed to bring 5,000 sepoys as well as 40 cannons to Kalpi. "But he could not get the Maharaja's Darbari (Maratha) Army." (111-477) Tatya took Kanpur with the help of this force. In effect, the Gwalior contingent which was eager to capture Agra had to be satiated with the capture of Kanpur!

Tatya invested Charkhari, principality of the pro-British Ratan Singh, in January 1858. Tatya wrote to Raosahib Peshwa asking for assistance: "The Rajah does not wish to side with us, the sepoys boast very much now but in time of difficulty they will desert us. In the battle fought day before yesterday, our troops fled before the enemy. I hope, therefore, that you will be pleased to send Vilayatee men (i.e. Mahomedans) to our assistance." (5-229) The import of the communication should leave no room for doubt who was fighting spiritedly and which force was responsible for victories gained even by the Peshwa and Tatya Tope.

Who Took Gwalior

The victory over Gwalior was something quite similar. Tatya had gone to Gwalior incognito after his defeat at Kunch to assess the situation there. The aim was to ascertain whether rebels there would assist him. It was only when conditions appeared favourable that a decision was taken to make an attempt to seize Gwalior. When the Peshwa's forces reached Gwalior, the local sepoys rebelled and joined with the former amid chants of 'Deen, Deen!' The Peshwa's forces also responded to their coreligionists with the same Islamic chants.[34] This was a significant event and most historians take due note of it. Those soldiers embraced one another. (50-152) Rahim Ali Khan arrived from Bareilly in Rohilkhand with 800 troopers to assist the Peshwa in taking Gwalior. (448)

The British recaptured Gwalior sixteen days later. But the Maharaja could not force an entry into the fort because of the *ghazis* within, who were determined to make a stand till the last man. Finally, all of them were killed. (5-465; 44-208) All these events clearly reveal the Jihadi core of the Gwalior uprising.

Indore Leader: Sadat Khan

The Uprising in Indore — the second most important state in Malwa — was similar in nature to that at Gwalior. The Holkar Maharaja was loyal to the British but his army had turned rebellious. Sepoys in the cantonments of Indore, Mhow and Mahidpur rebelled, put many of the British to death and reached the Maharajas's Palace. Their leader Sadat Khan was the cavalry commander in the Holkar's army. He went to the Maharaja immediately after the killings, his clothes all drenched in their blood, and demanded more troops. (86-126; 141-313) He recounted with great pride how he had killed his victims.[35] (141-313) The Maharaja wished to arrest him but

---

34. See: 126-365; 141-290; 82-153; 5-454; 110-179; 44-200; 48-170; 5-152.

35. Savarkar writes: "The Revolutionary spirit that exhibited itself among the masses and the Sepoys at Gwalior had also burst forth in a terrible manner at Indore. On 1st July, Sadat Khan, a Mahomedan nobleman at the Indore court, ordered the army to fall upon the English at the Residency. He declared (falsely) that the Maharaja Holkar had given him the order." (1-266)

allowed him to leave in prudent consideration of his powerful support. (141-381; 86-126) To avert the possibility of misunderstanding or misconstruction, the Maharaja forthwith dispatched a written explanation to the British administration:

"No one in the world regrets more than I do the most heart-rending catastrophe which befell at Indore and at Mhow. The mischief done was great; many lives were lost, the rascals then plundered the whole Residency. The next morning the Mhow troops arrived here; the whole town was in a panic. A greater part of my troops were in open mutiny, and what remained could not be trusted. The Mahomedans raised a standard of 'Deen', and the disorder was complete. I had no alternative left but to offer them my own person. The tale is a painful one, and will be described to you in detail by Rao Ramchandar and...who are bearers of this (letter) to you. I have not, even in a dream, ever deviated from the path of friendship and allegiance to the British Government. I know, their (i.e. of British) sense of justice and honour will make them pause before they suspect, even for a moment, a friendly chief, who is so sensible of the obligations he owes to them, and is ready to do anything for them." (5-143; 141-315; 50-64)

In the above statement, reference to "the Mahomedans raised a standard of 'Deen', and the disorder was complete," is significant and illustrative of the nature of the Uprising there.

The British were convinced, the Maharaja's explanation being both correct and true, and thereafter conducted themselves with full trust in him. (5-143)

The scheme of the entire revolt in Indore was well thought out. Sepoys at places like Neemuch, Mhow, Indore, Bhopal and Gwalior were in close communication with one another. Some detachments of the Bhopal army had been moved by the British around this time to Indore. Rebellion was rampant in the Bhopal army. Of their prominent leaders, Waris Muhammad Khan and Adil Muhammad Khan came to Indore along with those detachments. (86-126) They colluded with the local rebels. Although they had been brought to Indore to quell rumblings of rebellion, they went and joined the rebels instead of countering them. (86-124, 6; 44-137)

Maulvis had already inspired sepoys for *Jihad*. One, found lurking around the Mhow cantonment disguised as a fakir, was apprehended and arrested on 24th June. It was discovered that he was spreading the message of revolution. Many similar 'fakirs' were spotted in the Indore cantonment on 27th June.[36] (86-123)

Rebel rule lasted for three days after the revolt, during which time Sadat Khan became 'Nawab' Sadat Khan and began his rule. His troops moved about the town receiving ceremonious salutations. (181) The same contingent of troops had later gone to Gwalior and thence to Agra.

Dhar and Amjhera: Jihad Against Hindu Chiefs

Two other Hindu principalities in Malwa were Dhar and Amjhera. British-loyalist chiefs of both states had recruited Muslim troopers in large numbers in their armed forces who rebelled and brought the states to an end. They left for Mundsore after the rebellion was crushed. So, the first *Jihad* was, in fact, actually aimed at Hindus, not the British.

Located between these two principalities was another called Jhabua. What happened here is noteworthy. Some British officers, fleeing with their families from Indore, took asylum with this Chief for a few days on 5th July. He was a boy of sixteen and his grandmother bore charge of the administration on his behalf. A large number of Arabs and other Muslims, who had been recruited to the armed forces, demanded custody of the refugees as they desired to kill them. As luck would have it, the dowager also had some Rajputs in her employ to whom she had entrusted the British. "Not a Mussalman sepoy was allowed to approach" them during their five days stay in the Palace. (50-66; 141-316) Such incidents

36. Dr. S.B. Chaudhary, who views the Uprising as a war of independence, writes in this context: "The religious mendicants made their appearance among the troops on 27 June in Indore, and the Mutiny occurred on 1 July." (81-231) This clearly indicates the cause-effect nature of the two.

were a reason why the British viewed the revolt as a Muslim uprising!

Writing about the Malwa province generally, Surendra Nath Sen says: "In Malwa the foreign mercenaries (i.e. Arabs, Afghans, Vilayatees, Makranis, Armenians, Pathans etc.) took the principal part in the Mutiny." (141-316)

Begum Bhopal: Jihadi Atmosphere

The Begum of the Muslim state of Bhopal was loyal to the British, but her relations, courtiers and armed forces had turned rebellious. While those rebels were unable to do anything in Bhopal, they were active in the Indore revolt. Chief among them were Waris Muhammad Khan, Adil Muhammad Khan, Sarfaraz Khan and Fazal Muhammad Khan. (86-145; 77-179) Names of several other leaders also figure in sources. (86-41) Sepoys and local Muslim populace were sympathetic to the Emperor. (41) The Begum found herself in a pitiable situation as Maulvis, preaching *Jihad* all over the place and also to her own people, were threatening her for assistance in the fight against the British. (42) Muslim leaders were conversing on *Jihad*: "This is time to do whatever is to be done for the cause of religion and worldly interests will never come again." Adil Muhammad Khan wrote to her that, "Having waged religious war we have turned out the infidel Christians from Rahatgarh and we have embraced the cause of religion." (77-179) One sepoy stationed there wrote to his uncle in Hyderabad, "Listen all you Mahomedans: It is forbidden that you should eat your food with the accursed Christians. You will never get such an opportunity again. Send them all to hell." (179)

Thus, the whole atmosphere in Bhopal was charged with Jihadi sentiment but an explosion had been averted only because the Begum, even under such situation, had remained firm in her loyalty to the British.

The Shahzada's Islamic State at Mundsore

The remaining area of importance in Malwa was Mundsore district in the Gwalior state. We have seen how the Emperor's nephew, Firoz Shah, set up an Islamic state there in August and how he brought nearby places like Neemuch and Mahidpur under his control. Even this reveals the nature of the local uprising. As this prince may be numbered among selected, important and principal leaders of the 1857 Uprising, it would be in order to look at him in some detail.

When the rebellion broke out in Meerut and Delhi, this young prince in his early twenties was in Mecca. Having completed the Hajj pilgrimage, he returned to India during the Uprising and since it was felt unsafe to go to Delhi at the time, he chose to go to the Gwalior state. (72-173; 87-58) He set up habitation in the guise of a fakir from July at Kachrodi near Mundsore and gathered many followers. Rebellions had then already broken out at places like Neemuch, Indore, Mhow and Gwalior in the region but rebels had failed to establish their rule. The Maharaja of Gwalior had somehow restrained the Gwalior sepoys from going to Agra. All such rebel sepoys now found a new leader in the prince and, especially after his imperial antecedents became known, began flocking to his side in large numbers. No sooner he had acquired a following of a couple of thousand than he made declaration of *Jihad*. (87-58; 72-173) Capturing Mundsore on 20th August with the help of this Muslim force, he proclaimed the establishment of an Islamic State there and hoisted the green flag. (5-146; 72-175)

He assumed the title 'Humayun Shah'. (72-174; 87-59) His edicts carried the title: "Lord of the World and mankind, the son of the holy precept of the Universe and the inmates, Mirza Mahomed Firoz Shah Bahadur." (72-193; 87-64) He also used to write himself in letters, 'Firoz Shah Bahadur Ghazi'. (5-152) The following announcement was issued after enthronement: "I, Shahzada Humayun Shah, have been placed on the *Musnud* at Mundsore and the standard of the Prophet has been planted." (5-151; 72-175) As to why he chose Mundsore to establish his Islamic rule, he said, "That this Shahzada has selected his point Mundsore judiciously enough, for the neighbourhood abounds with turbulent Mewatees (i.e. Muslims)." (5-156)

Both the British as well as the Maharaja of Gwalior developed feelings of apprehension with the arrival of the prince. The Shahzada's appearance before Mundsore was the signal for a general rise of Mahomedan and Vilaytee (Muslim) mercenary troops of the Subah. With the appearance of Shahzada they found a leader under whom to rally round. 'Turbulent characters in all parts of central India girded their swords and hastened to join the Shahzada. (87-59) The Minister of Maharaja of Indore wrote to the British government: "His appearance is likely to lead to extensive disasters in Malwa if not crushed at once. The rebels will no doubt flock to the standard of revolt, and Mussalmans and others from all parts of the country, will readily gather round this nucleus of disorder and devastation." (5-149)

As soon as he took Mundsore, he commenced his *Jihad* work by arresting the Brahmin kotwal appointed by the Gwalior state and converting him to Islam. (87-59) Rebels from all directions began pouring into Mundsore. An official government report of 28th September 1857 states: "A party of 300 Afghans, after committing very offensive atrocities and carrying away four Hindu women, had joined the Mundsore insurgents." (5-154) Such activities of rebels was a routine affair.

The prince marched upon Neemuch from Mundsore. Defeating a British force at Jiran on the way, "Firoz Shah's men went back with the severed head of Captain Tucker as their trophy which was later on displayed over the gates of Mundsore. (87-60) On reaching Neemuch, the fort was invaded, won and soon a green flag began flying over it. (60)

Mirza as Subedar of Mahidpur

Sepoys in the Mahidpur cantonment rebelled and joined the prince. "That when British forces under Major Timins faced the men of Firoz Shah, the 'Mussalmans of the contingent refused to obey their officers and joined the enemy." The Subedar Major opened his jacket, took out a green flag and hoisted it. (61) With that act, all sepoys went and joined up with their new king. The prince appointed a certain Mirza as his subedar at the place. (72-177)

The Army — 1,50,000 Strong

Soon, the force under the prince swelled up to 1,50,000. It was made up of Arabs, Afghans, Rohilas, Mewatis, Vilayatees, Makranis, Pathans and other Muslims of various ethnicities hailing from different areas. (5-146, 8, 96; 72-177) Some sources provide details of these various divisions. (5-154; 72-180) It may be that some Hindus were carried away on the tide with such a large flow of Muslims.

A Well-Wisher of Muslims

The prince sent out royal decrees to neighbouring Muslim chiefs and his own officers. The following, addressed to the Chief of Jawra is a fair indication of the nature of instruments sent to Muslim chiefs: "You have been since long putting off your attendance here, but now I must tell you in plain terms that if you are willing to come to me you must make haste, you will be the most deserving of my favour of consideration. I am the well-wisher of the people in general and of the Mahomedans in particular. If you are a well-wisher of Islam and of the house of the Sultan you will do as desired." (5-153; 72-176; 86-216)

In orders issued to army commanders[37] (9th September 1857), it was stated: "The proverb 'Make the enemy to deal with a serpent,' should be the principle of your action, for should the serpent bite the enemy or the enemy kill the serpent in both cases we are to gain our object. We will destroy one of the two enemies[38]. It is proper to kill the enemy when it is in your power to do so." (5-152)

---

37. Names of cavalry commanders, of whom five were Mewati and three Makrani Muslims, appeared first. Then it was addressed to all the Makrani, Vilayatee, Sardars and Officers of the force. (5-151)

38. It is not clearly stated who were these two enemies. Clearly, one of them was the British. The second was probably one who was helping the British and refusing to side with rebels. It is noteworthy that the communication was only sent to Muslim commanders.

It was observed that the standards that appeared in numbers at the Battle of Mundsore (in Nov. 1857) had nearly all been green, i.e. Muslim. (132-147) After suffering a defeat, the prince's force got scattered when one faction attacked Pratapgarh, the principality of a Hindu chieftain of the area. The Chief of Pratapgarh collected Thakurs to humble and drive away the same Arabs and Pathans who had terrorized the local population barely a couple of months previously, after they had been defeated by the British. (44-176) Eighty rebels were killed by that chief. The severed heads of two of the prince's commanders, killed in the battle of Mundsore, were hung by the British at the same city gate where rebels had hung Capt. Tucker's head three months ago. (44-176)

The prince continued his *Jihad* against the British in alliance with other rebel leaders. He went to the Nawab of Farukhabad and, after the fall of that principality to the British, he went to the Rani of Jhansi. He was in Jhansi in February 1858 and it was from there (17th February) that he published his historic proclamation that explicitly mirrored his thoughts and objectives. Then, he went to the Begum of Ayodhya. He continued wandering thus after the fall of Lucknow. Ultimately, he visited several Muslim countries like Afghanistan, Persia, Turkey and Arabia to seek assistance from them. (5-661, 2; 72-194) He died in Mecca.

It is correct that, "The Shahzada of Mundsore dreamt of reviving the glory of House of Timur to which he traced his ancestry." (86-216) It is said that had he been in command at Delhi in the place of other vacillating and ineffective Shahzadas, Delhi would have survived longer than it did. [39] (72-198)

It is necessary to mention in passing some significant rebellions that occurred at adjoining places in the same province.

---

39. Savarkar describes him as: 'the brave prince of Delhi' (1-450), 'the illustrious hero' (534), 'a worthy son of Delhi dynasty.' (535)

Nawab of Rahatgadh

Rahatgarh, 39 kilometers from Sagar, was a veritable citadel of rebel Afghans and Pathans. The strong fortress was held by Nawab Fazal Khan who was kin of the Begum of Bhopal. (131-126; 36-112) Hugh Rose won the fortress in January 1858. Prince Firoz Shah, who was at Rahatgarh at the time, escaped to Jhansi. (132-164; 82-107) The Nawab was caught and hanged at the gate of the fortress along with 200 of his men. (82-108; 132-165)

At Hoshangabad, the local police rebelled and hoisted their green Islamic flag. (81-227) Of course, the uprising was later crushed.

- 4 -

Jhansi — A Royal Family of British Loyalists

We shall now see how events unfolded in Jhansi, principality of one of the brightest characters recorded in the annals of India's Freedom Movement — Rani Lakshmibai who transcended the natural limitations of her feminity to display unmatched valour and military prowess.

The Rani was loyal to the British before the Uprising and had persisted in her untiring petitions and entreaties to the British administration, ever since the Raja's demise (November 1853), for recognition of her adopted son as heir to the throne. Included in her petitions was proof of how the ruling family had been consistent in its loyalty to the British.

In an application made within a fortnight (3rd December 1853) of the Raja's death, she wrote: "The services rendered by Sheo Rao Bhau, the father of my late husband, to the British government are recorded and have been amply rewarded by the unceasing flow of benefits which his family have derived from the acknowledged favour and protection of such a mighty power. The concluding article of the Treaty with my late husband in 1842 guarantees to the Jhansi Government the continued existence of all the benefits (under former Treaty)." (31-253) Also clarified in the application was the fact that the late Raja had adopted Anandrao, in the presence of local British Officer, according to established religious prescriptions. (254)

Another letter sent on 16th February 1854 stated : "It was the good fortune of the father of my husband to be the first of the chiefs in this part of the country who tendered their allegiance to the British Government. (255) And thereafter also, Jhansi State was always foremost in the field when opportunity occurred for displaying its loyalty to the Paramount Power." (257) That letter also stated that Rao Ramchandra, a predecessor of the late Raja, had assisted the British in crushing a rebellion for which act of loyalty the governor general conferred upon him the title 'King of Kings' (Faithful to the Emperor of England) and ordered him to have it engraved on his seal, with permission to adopt the British flag.[40] (257) Narrating the history of loyalty of the royal family, this letter appeals the Government to sanction the adoption-deed. (258)

Jhansi and Ayodhya: Essential Difference

However, the adoption was not recognized and the state was declared to have lapsed in March 1854. The difference in public reaction when Ayodhya and Jhansi were annexed is very telling. Public outcry was widespread in Ayodhya; the subjects were infuriated; the deposed Nawab had to be imprisoned in Calcutta because of involvement in conspiracies; annexation became one of the chief causes for the 1857 Uprising. But did anything of the sort happen when Jhansi was annexed? It simply remained calm (131-72). The reason of this essential difference was: those who lost political power in Ayodhya were Muslim and sought restoration of their rule. Subjects of Jhansi entertained no such sentiment and the issue was limited to the Rani individually.

---

40. Parasnis writes: "Rao Ramchandra sought permission to fly the Union Jack over the fort, which was gladly conceded by the British. This establishes the royalty's deep sense of loyalty for the British." (36-10) This was not all. That same Union Jack was flying over the fort when mutiny broke out there and was still flying during the entire period of the battle with the British in March 1858. (123)

She preferred an appeal through her lawyer against the decision of annexation to the 'Court of Directors' of the East India Company in England. Even that appeal, and at such pass, displayed her feelings of loyalty and reminders of past acts of her family to that end. Some of those statements are particularly noteworthy : "The helpless petitioner chooses to submit the causes of appeal. She would respectfully beg the consideration of the facts to follow, taking into account her sheer helplessness like that Great God Himself who answers the wailing prayers of His creatures and does not withdraw subsistence from the sinners even. (3-492) "All claims concerning the territory, forts, taxes, property, disbanding of the troops were immediately surrendered on the order of confiscation issued by the illuminated Presence was received." The Queen of England was referred as, "the Refuge of the World (May All Dominions Remain With Her)." (493)

The appeal was dismissed in August 1854. The State armed forces were disbanded and replaced by fresh recruitment of sepoys. (36-63) The Rani was often humiliated. A certain sum was deposited in the name of her minor adopted son, with her as guardian. She was even denied withdrawal from this fund for the purpose of his thread ceremony. (66) Likewise, permission needed for going to Prayag (Allahabad) for ritual tonsuring was refused by Company officials in London. (123-61) Despite all such indignities, the Rani had not wavered in her loyalty. Thereafter, she resigned herself to a variety of religious observances that occupied her eight or nine hours every day. (36-65) It seemed she had no political ambition left. The 1857 Uprising broke out at a time when Rani Laxmibaisahib had thus renounced everything including hope of regaining her right to rule and, regarding the remaining days of her earthly existence as an inevitable misfortune, completely devoted herself to God's service. (66)

Rebellion of Muslim Sepoys

How, then, had the Rani become a leader of the rebellion? Sources suggest that she was coerced by her Muslim sepoys. The rebellion was primarily a Muslim affair and those sepoys demanded that she assume leadership, make over a sum of Rs. 3 lacs and arm them with field guns. They were led by Chief of Prisons, Bakhshish Ali, Cavalry Chief Kale Khan and Tahsildar Muhammad Hussain.[41] (39-65; 82-74; 110-72) Sepoys of the 12th Infantry Platoon rebelled on 5th June with war cries of 'Deen, Deen!' (50-vi; 5-113) They broke into the prison and released all internees with the same chant under leadership of Bakhshish Ali. (5-44; 50-4; 92-51) Then, the fort was invested. On the following day, the Muslim dominated cavalry led by Kale Khan, joined the revolt.[42] Five prominent British officers were put to death. (82-74; 141-269)

Three British officers in Muslim disguise[43], who were making their way to the fort to seek assistance from the Rani, were identified, brought before the Cavalry Chief and summarily killed. (5-44; 141-269; 48-66) British personnel inside the fort, assured of the safety of their lives by oath on the Holy Quran, were induced to emerge from within by the well-known Dr. Saleh Muhammad[44] and Bakhshish Ali, and later mercilessly massacred at the Jokhanbagh amid chants of 'Deen,

---

41. Messengers had arrived from Delhi with letters inspiring them to rebel. (48-61; 82-72) S. Thornton, the Deputy Collector of Jhansi, described the conspirators in Delhi as "most of them Skinners bigoted Mussalmans of Delhi," and "the ring leaders." (5-12)

42. P.G. Scot, an English official at Jhansi, states his reason for the infantry rebelling before the cavalry: "At Nowgong and Jhansi, they let the infantry begin the mutiny. I believe the reason was solely that they wished to conceal the character of movement, viz., its being a Muhammedan one. They were the most bloodthirsty when the mutiny did break out." (50-i)

43. Scott managed to escape from Jhansi disguised as a Muslim fakir. (5-11) One finds incidence of many instances like this at various places during the 1857 Uprising.

44. Savarkar called him a 'representative of the victorious rebels' in his original Marathi book (p.193). However, this was incorrectly translated in the English version as 'a prominent citizen of Jhansi." (1-240) Savarkar, too, states that the Jokhanbagh incident had occurred under the directive of cavalry chief Kale Khan. (240) He

(Contd.)

Deen!' and 'Maro *Kafir* Ko!'. (110-62; 39-65; 36-78; 48-67) Bakhshish Ali and Kale Khan took a lead in this affair. Bakhshish Ali would recount with great pride how he killed Capt. Skene with a single stroke of his sword. (5-18; 50-xi; 92-31) Of particular note is how Bengali Babus, who were British loyalists, were singled out for vengeance, hunted down and detained. (92-31; 141-271; 5-45; 50-6)

All historians and commentators accept that the Rani had no hand either in the rebellion or the Jokhanbagh massacre.[45] On the contrary, she had secretly provided them with security and food.

---

also adds: 'The able author (Parasnis, in his Marathi book on the life of the Queen of Jhansi) has established by an incontestable array of proofs that there was not the least incitement to this massacre from the young Queen." (1-241n)

45. Some comments on this:

I. Parasnis: "It is evident that the Ranisahib was not in favour of the rebels at the time of this horrible incident. On the contrary it is seen that she gave good assistance to the English during the rebellion. There is not an iota of doubt that she rendered no assistance to the rebels. She had no military strength at that time and the rebels had become very powerful." (36-79, 81)

II. Historian Sir John Kaye: "I know it with strong evidence that at the time of this *hatya-kand* (murder of the group) not a single servant of the Maharani was present there." (36-82q; 39-68q.)

III. Dr. Rana: "Whatever the case, our heroine Maharani Laxmibai had nothing to do with it. Not only this, the Maharani did not want to participate in this battle. The scholars have accepted Shri Parasnis' book 'Jhansi Ki Rani Laxmibai' as authentic in this respect. According to him also this opinion is correct." (39-66) Savarkar had also considered Parasnis' book as 'authoritative'. (1-241n)

IV. Martin, an Englishman present in Jhansi at the time, had later stated in a letter addressed to the Rani's adopted son: "A very cruel and unjust treatment has been meted out to your mother. The real story that I know about it, none else knows. The poor lady had no connection whatsoever with the murders of the Europeans in the month of June, 1857. Not only this, when Englishmen went

(Contd.)

The fact that the Rani was innocent of the massacre is important not just for proving that she was not cruel or merciless but also for appreciating that she had no power over her sepoys and was actually quite helpless.

Threat to Bombard the Palace

The sepoys then set up their artillery and directed all sepoys to join their ranks, warning them that those who failed to comply would be killed. (141-274) Then, proceeding to the Palace armed with muskets, they informed the Rani that they intended to proceed to Delhi, demanded money and field guns and asked her to come over to their side. They even threatened to shell the Palace with the field guns they had if she declined to meet their demands.[46] The Rani told them that she had no money to give them as all control was with the English; that it was improper to blackmail a lady. The sepoys, nevertheless, reiterated the threat and warned her that a kin and claimant to the throne, Sadashivrao Narayan, would be installed as Raja of Jhansi in her place.[47] Having no recourse

---

fort for safety, she supplied food to them for two days. She called a hundred armed soldiers from Karera and sent them to the fort for our assistance. After that Maharani advised them to run away from there and go to the Rajah of Datia for shelter. But they did not act upon it at that time. In the end our own army (the rebels) killed them." (39-68; 48-69)

V. Sir John Smith: "The matter of the killing of all the prisoners was taken out of her hands. It does not seem to be quite in character for the Rani to have *ordered* the massacre herself, though she may have known of it and been powerless to prevent it.... Had she tried to oppose it she would have been a dead duck." (110-73)

VI. Deo Narayan Varma: "Rani had not any remote connection with the revolt or massacre at Jhansi. On the other hand she had helped the Britishers in every possible way." (147-64)

46. See: 36-88; 39-69, 48-70, 1; 82-76; 92-32; 110-75; 131-97; 141-271 to 6; 67-155.

47. Sepoys had, on the previous day, brought this Sadashivrao to their camp. (110-71) A majority of them were opposed to the Queen

(Contd.)

whatsoever, the Rani made over a sum of Rs. 1 lac and two cannons after which sepoys made the proclamation 'Khulk Khuda ka, Mulk Badshah ka, Hukum Rani Laxmibai ka' and left for Delhi.[48]

This is how the Rani was threatened into assisting rebels, entirely against her will and because she had no alternative, assume the leadership for the time being and helplessly listen to the proclamation 'Khulk Khuda ka... ., Except for a few personal bodyguards, the Rani had no significant force under her command and wielded no power over those that had rebelled. If one understands and appreciates the desperate situation in which she found herself at that juncture, it is easy to see why she had to become leader of the rebels for some time, and an unwilling victim of the 1857 Uprising.[49]

The Rani only freed herself from the clutches of the rebels once they had issued the customary proclamation and left for Delhi on 11th June. She sent two successive letters on 12th and 14th June to the Commissioner explaining her situation in order

---

anyway because of her pro-British policy. Hence, the claimant had been kept in the wings in readiness for such contingency. (70) However, Laxmibai was eventually enthroned.

48. However, some sources state that, "The Rani was threatened with instant assassination, if she refused to side with the rebels." (5-45; 50-6; 92-46)

According to some books, the Rani had been issued a threat on the previous day that she would be put to death if she assisted the English. (82-74) Corroboration may be found in a book by Godse, the Brahmin priest. The Rani had informed British officers who approached her at the time for protection: "How can we guarantee your protection now? The native (Black) platoons will loot and decimate us". (123-61; 44-167q.)

49. Savarkar, after narrating how Muslim sepoys engineered the June uprising in Jhansi, writes: "After the uprising at Jhansi the Revolutionaries annexed the Kingdom of Jhansi to the Rani's crown as the guardian of her son. They declared, 'The Universe belongs to God, the country to the Emperor, and the authority to Rani Laximi Bai !" (1-241) Clearly, Savarkar admits the sepoys' role

(Contd.)

to avert the possibility of misunderstanding about her unwilling and forced actions and to dispel it if one had occurred.

Her Letters to the British

She wrote in the first letter: "The Govt. forces, stationed at Jhansi, through their faithlessness, cruelty and violence, killed all the European civil and military officers, the clerks and all their families and the Rani not being able to assist them for want of guns, and soldiers as she had only 100 or 50 people engaged in guarding her house she could render them no aid, which she very much regrets. That they, the mutineers, afterwards behaved with much violence against herself and servants, and extorted a great deal of money from her, and said that as the Rani was entitled to succeed the Riyasat, she should undertake the management since sepoys were proceeding to Delhi to the King." (110-74) Narrating how she had tried her best to maintain law and order, it further stated that the sepoys knowing her to be quite helpless sent her message to the effect that if she, at all hesitated to comply with their requests, they would blow up her palace with guns. Taking into consideration her position she was obliged to consent to all the requests made and put up with a great deal of annoyance, and had to pay large sums in property, as well as in cash to save her life and honour. She is in continual dread of her own life and that of the inhabitants." (110-75; 48-85; 141-275) It was also explained that the letter could not be sent earlier because of the presence of the rebels in Jhansi till the previous day. (110-75; 48-85, 131-99; 141-275)

Describing the situation of anarchy in Jhansi, she wrote in the second letter that it was beyond her capacity to provide security to the district because of financial constraints and requested that she might be favoured with orders which she would see carried out." (ibid)

---

as king-makers. But, because it was inconvenient for the thrust of his book, he avoids mentioning the fact that the Rani had been coerced into participation.

The entire course of events of the Uprising at Jhansi was narrated by the then local British Officer in which it is stated that, "Rani with the utmost difficulty managed to save her life, but her money and property were plundered. She was not able to report this before the Commissioner or Agent since the disaffected (rebels) had stopped all *Dawk* communication and had guarded all the roads round Jhansi which prevented anyone from going out." (131-100; 5-68)

The Rani Rules on behalf of the British

Convinced by her explanation, the Commissioner wrote on 2nd July to the Home Department that "It seems clear from the Rani's statement that she has not assisted rebels in any way. On the contrary, she was robbed through threats by them... information received by us through independent sources is fully consistent with her statement." (48-86; 131-101)

On the same day, he wrote to the Rani, "I beg, you will manage the district (of Jhansi), for the British Government collecting the Revenue, raising such police as may be necessary and making other proper arrangements... ." (5-69; 48-86; 131-101) The following gazette, according authority to rule over the Rani on behalf of the British, was published also on the same day: "Be it known to all people belonging to, or residing in the Government of District of Jhansi, that owing to the bad conduct of the soldiers some valuable lives have been lost and property destroyed. Until officers and troops reach Jhansi, the Rani will rule in the name of the British Government and I hereby call on all, great and small, to obey the Rani, and pay the Government Revenue to her...." (131-202; 111-541; 5-70)

These documents establish that the Rani had remained firm in her loyalty; she had nothing to do with the revolt and that, even after the Uprising, she continued to command the same trust that she had earlier. Otherwise it was impossible that the British could have entrusted the state administration to her after the rebellion.

She ruled on behalf of the British for a period of about ten months thereafter, a fact that is fully consistent with the above conclusion.[50]

Neighbouring Natthe Khan's Machinations

The Rani now had to engage in conflict not with the British, but a minister of the neighbouring Orchha State, Natthe Khan. She had to raise a force to contend with aggression from this quarter, a matter exceeding the authority delegated to her by the British. Enmity that developed between the two neighbours prompted Natthe Khan to create apprehension and misunderstanding in the minds of the British about the Rani. He succeeded in misrepresenting to the British that her war preparations for resisting Orchha

---

50. Conclusions of some authorities:

i. Dr. Sinha: "It is, therefore, quite evident that the Rani kept herself aloof from the insurgents and that it was only when she was faced with the alternative of the destruction of her property and perhaps even the loss of her life that she yielded to their demands and that too very reluctantly and that she had no concern with the massacre of Europeans." (82-137)

ii. P.J.O.Taylor: "She was forced, in my view, into rebellion.... The British, not she, had declared implacable enmity." (105-28)

iii. Pratibha Ranade: "The Rani was firm in her loyalty to the Company (even after the Uprising)." (131-99)

iv. Dr. Mujumdar: "This clearly shows that at first the sepoys did not recognize the Rani as the ruler, and completely disproves the idea that the mutiny was the result of a conspiracy organized by the Rani. If the sepoys were really goaded into the mutiny by her, she would immediately have been hailed as the ruler. If the Rani of Jhansi had been even then thought of rebelling against the British, it would undoubtedly have been to her interest to keep the sepoys at Jhansi, so that they might help her against the British in the forthcoming struggle. The more we think of the whole affair, the more does it appear that the mutiny of the sepoys at Jhansi early in June 1857, was purely an act of sepoys and the Rani had no hand in it, and she was only used as milch cow by the mutinous sepoys." (67-146)

(Contd.)

were really meant to be utilized against them. This man even actually pilfered letters, sent by the Rani to the British to dispel misunderstanding about her actions. The cause for an

---

v. N.R.Phatak: "There is no evidence to believe that the Rani secretly harboured any intention of armed conflict with the English. The rebel sepoys had a strong urge to go to Delhi. They deserted the Rani in Jhansi and headed for Delhi. P.V. Kelkar has said: 'Laxmibai had not rebelled. She had no intention of ousting the British from power…The treatment meted out to her by the Government at the end (in March 1858) drove her to desperation and she leapt into the Uprising'."(44-355 to 8)

vi. Surendra Nath Sen: "The Rani frankly admits that she had to subscribe to the rebel military chest but she did so under a threat of violence, that she took up the responsibility of administration and she invited the (British) Government to send troops for the maintenance of law and order. Had she been in league with the sepoys the best course for her would have been to persuade the sepoys to stay with her, for their departure left her helpless not only against British vengeance but (also) against the aggression of her neighbours and the machinations of her relatives (e.g. Sadashivrao). Erskine (the Commissioner) did not suspect her sincerity." (141–276)

vii. Narahar Kurundkar: "In 1854…the state was annexed. She evacuated the fort in perfect docility and preferred to live in the town. She is believed to have exclaimed, 'Meri Jhansi main kabhi nahin doongi' ('I shall never yield my Jhansi'). However, her own subsequent actions prove that the exclamation was quite in vain. She became embroiled, in the most peaceable manner, in a series of applications, requests and complaints till 1857. She first declined to accept the pension, but later helplessly relented after the Uprising (in June), she conducted the administration of Jhansi as a representative of the British under the Commissioner's orders. Her stance of amity with the British had not altered till February 1858." (150-117)

viii. Godse Bhatji: "Sepoys of the British platoons created an unrest and rebelled in June." (123-61)

ix. Dr. Tapti Roy: "Soldiers mutinied in Jhansi without the prior knowledge of the Rani. Soon after rising, however, they went to

advance of a British force against Jhansi is to be found in this misapprehension.[51]

It is seen that she continued in her attempts to convince the British of her fair intentions and loyalty even till their forces actually launched an attack on Jhansi. (67-155) She was again and again requesting the British for help. (131-115) She wrote on 1st January 1858 to the British representative in Jhansi, Sir Robert Hamilton: "My life has been saved by your arrival in India. I had written to (five different names are here listed) British officials when the regular British army rebelled and looted my belongings under threat, and when the Chiefs of Orchha and Datia intimidated me but some of the carriers of my letters just disappeared while others returned to Jhansi because they were attacked. I had again written on the 20th September and 19th October appealing for help because my supplies were dwindling." (131-116)

Referring to anarchy in Jhansi and aggression by Orchha and Datia, she wrote further: "Under these circumstances I can never expect to get rid of these enemies, and clear myself of the heavy debts without the assistance of the British

---

Laxmibai's palace 'with loaded guns and demanded assistance and supplies'". (92-103)

51. Comments by some authorities in this context:

i. Parasnis: "The Rani tried to tender an explanation about the affairs of the revolt by writing letters to the British. But Natthe Khan had agents to ambush and liquidate camel-mounted messengers, thus preventing any communication to reach its destination. Not only this, he even convinced the British that the Rani was colluding with rebels, a reason why he (Natthe Khan) had opened an armed offensive against her." (36-95)

ii. Pratibha Ranade: "Natthe Khan used to waylay the Rani's messengers dispatched to various British authorities and seize the letters they carried." (131-117)

iii. Dr. Sen: "But she feared that some of these letters might not have reached their destination." (141-277)

iv. Dr. Rana:

Government. So you will give me support in the best way you can and thus save myself and the people." (67-151; 131-117)

She did not omit to mention in conclusion that those short-sighted individuals (the rebels) seemed unmindful of the British supremacy and did their best to ruin her and the whole country. So she earnestly appealed for help in order to 'cope with the enemy.' (126-353; 131-117; 92-123)

When this letter was forwarded to the Secretary to the British administration, Hamilton was asked to see what he could gather about the Rani's possible involvement in the June uprising. Dr. Mujumdar writes: "This letter shows that even in March 1858, when the British army was advancing against Jhansi, the Government of India did not possess any definite evidence against the Rani." (67-151) Hamilton conducted an inquiry through evidence of depositions and witnesses and sent his report on 24th April to the administration. Dr. Mujumdar writes about the conclusions of the report that the confidential correspondence between the Government of India and Hamilton therefore fully supported the view that there was no reasonable ground for the belief that the Rani of Jhansi either instigated the mutiny

---

'A Dirty Plan of Natthe Khan'

"....He (Khan) was a highly cunning person of base temperament. So, when he lost to the Maharani in the battle, he thought of harming her in some other way. That when the Maharani dispatched to the Political Agent of Bundelkhand an account of her success in battle against him, his people intercepted and killed the messenger. On reading the account seized from the messenger, he chalked out a dirty plan. He thought that Maharani be made culpable for the massacre of Englishmen in Jhansi. So, in order to take revenge of his insult indirectly, he wrote a letter to Hamilton to the effect that Maharani Laxmibai had turned rebellious against the Britishers, and that he (Natthe Khan) was fighting to crush her. The Englishmen were massacred on the Maharani's instigation. This heinous plan of Natthe Khan worked. The Britishers took the Maharani as their enemy, and its consequence appeared before all in the form of an inevitable battle." (39-76)

of sepoys in June 1857, or ever took any part in their subsequent proceedings." (152)[52]

The Rani Opposed to Armed Confrontation

Reports of the British advance upon Jhansi had begun to reach her in January 1858. Actually, Hugh Rose's campaign was launched on 6th January 1858. The anti-British Chief of nearby Banpur, Mardan Singh, had joined the rebellion but regarded Laxmibai as his sister. He had helped her in forcing Orchha to lift a siege of Jhansi. He desired the Rani to join him in the revolt and was in Jhansi on 6th January 1858 to pursue his attempts to convince the Rani to defect to his side. But she did not flinch and he left disappointed. (126-353; 5-219; 92-123) As Dr. Sinha concludes "Even so the Rani continued her efforts to maintain friendly relations with the British Government." (82-139)

Most of the rebel sepoys had left for Delhi but some were still in Jhansi, including one of their leaders, Bakhshish Ali. He had fifty troopers under his command. (5-217) They were enough of a threat and the Rani was deterred from taking any action against him. On 8th January, two days after the Chief of Banpur left Jhansi, "Bakhshish Ali, *Daroga* of Jhansi Jail, asking Rani whether she would fight or not with the English forces, was informed by the Rani that she would not; but will return all the districts under her to the British Officers when they come to Jhansi. On getting this information , the *Daroga* did not take service with Rani." (5-218; 82-139; 141-281) He joined the Chief of Banpur. [53]

---

52. Stating that a hundred years had passed since the unfolding of those memorable events and that it was high time evidence regarding the Rani's involvement was studied without prejudice and in a detached manner, Dr. Mujumdar analyzes it in ten pages of his book before arriving at this conclusion. It is not possible to discuss that analysis here.

53. Also: 82-139; 126-354; 141-281; 131-118; 92-122, 3; 111-525, 6.

Intelligence reports state that the Rani had sent an envoy to the Commissioner on 26th January. Her intention was : "That should this Vakil be treated kindly, the Rani will in no way oppose the British force. She will pay obedience to our Government and return all the districts now in her possession. While on the contrary should the British officers show displeasure, she will fight to the last." (82-139; 141-281)[53] Another report dated 4th February mentions that "The Rani is said to have no intention of fighting with the English." (131-118; 141-281)

Hugh Rose was advancing upon Jhansi. The Rani called a meeting of courtiers to discuss whether or not to offer resistance. There were two opinions. One faction that advised against it included the seasoned and knowledgeable Nana Bhopatkar and Lalubhau Bakhshi. (48-111; 36-109) Nana said, "As I have served the Ruler of Jhansi for a considerable time, I beseech you to pay heed to my advice and dispatch an envoy to the British administration (in order to state facts and dispel misunderstanding). " (36-109) "The advice of the old and experienced Bhopatkar was appropriate and timely." (39-82) "On hearing what a seasoned and wise veteran like Nana advised, the Rani ordered her minister to send an envoy." (36-109) Lalubhau Bakhshi later deposed in the trial that, "It was not proper for him to think of anything else than loyalty (towards the *Sarkar*). But Rani's father and Gangadhar Bahia said that because no reply was received, they had no option but to fight and die." (82-140) The army was in favour of giving battle, and threatened to abandon her service and recover their dues if she did not agree to fight the British. They were led by Cavalry Chief Hasan Ali. He said they had continued in her service in the expectation that she would fight the British. (126-355; 48-111, 3) This tipped the scales in favour of giving battle. (126-355; 39-86)

The intelligence bureau reported that, "The Rani is prepared for both compromise and battle. She fears the sepoys. It is out of this fear that she is in favour of giving battle. However, she is willing to a truce on the advice of some of her advisors." (48-112)

Firoz Shah in Jhansi

An important event was the arrival of Prince Firoz Shah and Nawab Adil Khan of Bhopal in Jhansi in February 1858. (4-656; 72-182) The prince was visiting various principalities at the time to enlist military assistance. (3-462) It was from Jhansi that he had issued his historic proclamation on 17th February and had remained in that place till the end of the month. (4-656) The Rani's proclamation was published just three days before (14th February) the prince's. Both were unquestionably Jihadi in essence.

How is it that the Rani's proclamation was published at all when she had not then taken a decision to fight the British? This points to a possibility that the prince had utilized his sojourn in Jhansi to influence her to issue that proclamation, publishing his own after she had done so. It is also possible that he had inspired the sepoys at Jhansi to fight with the British. Is it not astonishing that this prince, who had been fighting the British for well over eight or nine months in places like Agra, Lucknow and Rohilkhand, and had even established Islamic rule in Mundsore for a while, issued from Jhansi the proclamation he had not felt like publishing during all those months? It must be remembered that he had been an important factor in Jhansi's decision to confront the British. A copy of the Rani's proclamation fell into Hamilton's hands, which he forwarded to the governor general. (48-112) This reinforced the misunderstanding planted by Natthe Khan and the British began truly suspecting the Rani.

Why did the Battle Occur?

In this manner, in the final stages, "The Rani's loyalty went unheeded by the British who marched upon Jhansi under the false notion that the Rani was opposed to them and that the town was a hub of rebels." She was forced to engage in battle. (36-108, 19) "Without surrendering timidly, she embraced the *Kshatriya* (warrior) spirit and took the sword in her hand; sad but infuriated that every overture and demonstration of loyalty had gone unrewarded, she finally resolved to wreak vengeance."[54] (118)

She made another attempt to dispel the brewing mistrust and avoid armed conflict even when Rose had halted close to Jhansi (21st March). He sent her a message, before investing the fort, to personally see him with her ministers within two days in order to decide upon the future action. (39-86; 123-81) She replied immediately, "We fail to understand why the British Government is insulting its old, well-wishing friends ! In such a situation how can we believe that there will not be a breach of trust with us in your camp? But we assure you that we do not want any dispute with you; nor have we done in the past. Therefore, if you want we are ready to send our Dewan Saheb so that he may decide with you the appropriate conditions of the treaty. (Being a woman I cannot come)." (39-87) Moreover, she informed him that "Our subjects do not entertain even the thought of war against the administration, whatever you have been given to understand notwithstanding." (123-81)

---

54. On this point some authoritative comments:

i. Deo Narayan Varma: "The British failed to appreciate the Rani's aspirations and ultimately viewed her as their enemy. Had they but even slightly utilized their intellectual faculty, the factual position would have revealed itself and no misunderstanding might have arisen. The Rani would never have needed to fight against them. However, the Rani had been destined by fate for immortal glory! Had she (even at the final hour) sided with the British by abandoning her countrymen, none today would have invoked her name with respect." (147-64)

ii. Dr. Sinha: "This in spite of her best endeavours to sustain friendly relations with the British Government, the Rani failed to get satisfactory response. In short, the Rani was convinced that she would not get justice at the hands of the British Government. Thus, the Rani was left with no other alternative but that of opposing the restoration of British rule in Jhansi." (82-140)

iii. Parasnis: (The Rani had adopted a policy of loyalty in the hope that) "she would be equitably compensated by the British government (by being restored to rulership of Jhansi)". (36-105)

(Contd.)

Surrender or battle were the only alternatives before her at the juncture. If she surrendered, there was always the possibility of her being charged for the massacre, it being entirely unpredictable what false evidence might be cooked up to implicate and punish her. She seems to have decided, instead, to be martyred. Her subsequent valorous exploits – and biography itself now adorn pages of history in letters of gold.

Her Mainstay — Afghani Soldiers

Not only was the uprising in Jhansi the handiwork of Muslim sepoys, they were also at her side once she had decided to fight. Her special bodyguard of thirty was a Vilayati (Afghan) Muslim. (5-333; 111-685) Several Muslim fakirs[55] were operating an artillery battery under the flag of Islam and encouraging others to give an honourable account

---

iv. Dr. Mujumdar: "The Rani made repeated attempts to disabuse their (British's) minds, but failed. No heed was paid either to her protestations of innocence or to her unequivocal declaration of loyalty to the British. When she was at last convinced that the British were determined to bring her to trial for the massacre of the Europeans – but not till then – she decided to defend her honour by armed resistance to the British. She was faced by two alternatives, namely death by hangman's rope or a heroic death in the battlefield. She chose a more honourable course." (68-489; 67-155)

v. Dr. Sen: "Sir Hugh Rose was already on his way to Jhansi and his intention did not appear friendly. To submit was to court dishonour, to fight was to save honour though everything else might be lost." (141-281)

vi. From the *Marathi Vishwakosh* (Encyclopaedia): "She remained loyal and ruled over Jhansi admirably during the Uprising. Rebels demanded Rs. 3 lacs from the Rani…finally threatened to demolish the fort and palace in the alternative… . After she had conceded their demands, they proclaimed her as ruler of Jhansi. But (even thereafter) she remained loyal to the British." (Vol.6, p.695)

55. Reporting these incidents, 'The Friend of India' used the words 'fakirs and fanatics.' It is observed that the English often used 'fanatic' to describe 'Jihadis/*ghazis*.'

of themselves. (5-337; 81-219; 82-143) Several references indicate that the Rani had "10,000 Bundelas and Vilayatees (Afghans) and 1500 sepoys" in the fort. (126-356; 111-527) No mention can be found of the precise number of Afghans among them. However, it may be surmised from the efficacy and valour displayed during the entire action that the number must have been large. Most historians mention an incident when on a certain day the Rani, accompanied by 1,500 trusted Afghans, fought bravely near one of the gates of the fort.[56] This is regarded as the most daring and thrilling incident of the entire period of the siege. It is amazing that not even a single Hindu soldier had accompanied the Rani when she emerged from the fort to give this battle.

The enemy was under greatest danger from the heavy cannons mounted on the ramparts. Two expert cannoneers, Ghaus Khan and Khuda Bakhsh find universal mention. (131-129) They were a source of immense strength to the Rani. But both were killed not too much later: "At this afflicting intelligence, Laxmibai's remaining fortitude collapsed in despair. She was distressed, she saw nothing but darkness all around. She contemplated suicide. She wept ... the two were expert marksmen with cannons. They were virtually her right and left arms. Both having been killed, she realized it was now impossible to hold out much longer... both were buried in the courtyard before the palace under her personal supervision. Two small cenotaphs may still be seen there." (131-135; 39-101; 48-134) Their graves within the fort precincts "have become a place of pilgrimage for the Nation." (48-134)

Realizing that she could not hold the fort much longer, the Rani took some trusted troops and made a daring escape on horseback. Even at that time, she had 400 Afghans and Pathans flanking her on both sides.[57] (81-220) Godse Bhatji, an

---

56. See : 39-100; 131-138; 44-183; 111-528; 141-286; 48-132; 82-145; 36-145; 123-90; 126-358.

57. The number varies from source to source: For example, 300 Vilayati (Afghan) and 25 horsemen. (5-334; 110-135; 111-530; 131-140); 200 (36-150)

eyewitness, wrote: "Baisahib (i.e. the Rani) took 1,500 Vilayati (Afghan) with her and emerged from the fort. A stiff battle ensued for a short time in which 400 – 500 Vilayatis[58] and 700 – 800 English were killed. The Rani escaped with the remaining 1,000/1,100 Vilayatis." (123-95) Dr. Sen calls the troopers who escaped as her 'faithful Afghans'. (141-286) Dr. Sinha calls them 'devoted 1500 Afghans.' (82-145)

She was attired as a Pathan, with a green turban tied around her head. Most historians take special note of this.[59] Pratibha Ranade, in fact, goes to write that even when the Rani was still defending the fort, she used to don 'male Pathan attire'. (131-114) However, none offers any explanation for this. It is possible that she did so to please the trusted Arabs, Afghans, Vilayatis and Pathans who were even prepared to sacrifice their lives for her.

Even when she reached Kalpi after her flight from Jhansi, the force with her was Afghan. (152) "The Rani's Afghan soldiers were blamed for not having shown their usual courage" for the defeat at Kunch. (82-148; 131-152) Sources state that the Rani held command of Muslim forces at Gwalior. (39-139) Even there, she had donned the Pathan headgear. (82-154) The Peshwa's force at Kunch, too, had a large number of Muslims. Which is why Parasnis had to write: "The Peshwa's Pathani troops fought bravely. The English were helpless against the Peshwa's Pathani force!" (36-173) Sepoys brought from Gwalior by Tatya Tope, Rohilas from Rohilkhand and those in service of the Nawab of Banda had swelled their proportion in the Peshwa's army, which is why they had entered Gwalior amid war cries of 'Deen, Deen!'

When an enemy soldier struck a blow on the Rani's head with his saber in the final encounter, Ghulam Muhammad, a

58. Some sources say 200 Afghans were killed. It is written about their bravery: "The Rebels, who were chiefly Vilayatees and Pathans, generally sold their lives as dearly as they could, fighting to the last with their usual dexterity and firmness." (5-335; 110-141)

59. See: 82-154; 5-423; 44-186; 111-530 (male attire).

loyal Pathan officer who was close at hand, fell upon the assailant and hacked him to pieces. (122-76)

It was thus that the noose of a rebellion engineered by Muslim sepoys ultimately fell around the Rani's neck, while her subsequent bravery and martyrdom imparted to her, along with Jhansi and its uprising, an immortal place in history, casting a veil of emotion on the past.

***

Chapter 7

Promoters, Leaders and Beneficiaries — III

(The Jihadi Core of the Uprising)

- 1 -

Rohilkhand

It was Rohilkhand that offered the longest and most determined opposition to British rule. This was the same province that had produced Afghan Rohilas who had invited the Amir of Afghanistan to invade India, and it was also here that any conflict with the British invariably assumed the nature of a *Jihad*. The locals suffered none but a Rohila to rule over them.[1] A massive agitation against house tax levied by the

1. It is said in a contemporaneous administrative report: "Rohilkhand is inhabited by a race of Mahomedan warriors, the descendants of the victorious Afghans who settled in that country nearly a century and half ago. They were brave, treacherous, revengeful, very idle, careless of any occupation save that of a soldier. Hence this race supplied many recruits to our Irregular Cavalry." (7-177)

British administration had occurred in 1816. This tax equally affected Hindus and agitating Muslim leaders had secured their support, too. Nevertheless, the principal leader, Mufti Muhammad Iwaz, declared that India was no longer a 'Dar-ul-Islam' but had become a *'Dar-ul-Harb'*. Green flags were immediately hoisted and *Jihad* declared against the British. (13-30) So, even if the grievance was economic and Hindu support was needed, the struggle invariably ended up as a *Jihad*.

'1857' was plainly a political struggle for which *Jihad* was a religious duty. We have already seen the course of events in Chapter 5. We now take a look at inner workings.

Jihad Propaganda by M. Kifayat Ali Kafi

Although the leader of the *Jihad* was Khan Bahadur Khan[2] (1790-1860), Waliullahi Maulvis were in the forefront to provide Jihadi inspiration to him and his people. The real leader and inspiration for the *Jihad* was Khan Bahadur Khan's right hand man, M. Kifayat Ali Kafi. (25-213) A disciple of Shah Abdul Aziz, Kafi had lectured on *Jihad* extensively and copies of his religious decree for *Jihad* had been sent to all places. He was hanged for treason in April 1858. (213)

In the third week of May, a retired local munsiff, Niyamatullah Khan, attempted to induce sepoys to defect. He told sepoys, "I have been appointed as representative of the Emperor who has been enthroned in Delhi. Other representatives like me are active in various places. if you agree to my bidding, the Emperor will be pleased to enhance your status; on the other hand, should you not follow my

---

2. In respect of him, Govt. Report says: "This man, in fact, received a double pension, one as the heir of Hafiz Rahmat, (Rohilla Chief), and other in his capacity of retired Principal *Sudder Ameen* (i.e. Judge)...that he himself was the soul of the conspiracy, that the entire district, and the infantry regiments, were ready to rise at a signal from him, and that he was busily engaged in seducing the Irregulars by means of Mahomed Shafi, a *Resaldar*." (7-179)

directives, you will, willingly or otherwise, be compelled to do so by the Imperial army that is expected in two days. And when that happens, your reward will be the gallows. " (158-262) However, he did not succeed in his attempts.

The Waliullahi ideologue and Chief of Artillery, 'Brigadier' Bakht Khan, who had led the uprising at Bareilly in this region, was a disciple of M. Sarfaraz Ali and had in fact later become commander-in-chief of the imperial army at Delhi.

'Islam ka Bolbala...'

The Khan began his rule after the rebellion. A well-known writer of the time, Sayeeda Anees Fatima, wrote in her memoirs: "People used to say that God (i.e. Allah) has liberated us from *kafir* rule... large crowds of people would frequent shops selling weapons. Swords were got made. Swarms of Mujahids (Muslim holy warriors) would make the rounds on horseback, and heaven and earth would reverberate with their chants of 'Islam ka bolbala, Firangi ka muh kala!' (Islam is ascendant, the Firangis are disgraced)" (14-101q.) This saying[3] had become quite a part of common parlance. (44-374) That amply indicates for whom and for what objective the uprising there truly was.

British officers in Rohilkhand had become vigilant after the Meerut and Delhi rebellions. Anticipating declaration of *Jihad*, they had persuaded one Maulvi to express a view against it. Accordingly, on 22nd May during the sermon at the Friday *namaz* in Bareilly's principal mosque, M. Muhammad Ahsan from the Government College said it was against Islam to

---

3. N. R. Phatak writes: "The saying 'Islam ka bolbala' was most discomfiting for Hindus, and the unilateral ascendancy of Islam hardly squared with the overall nationalistic concept of freedom. It was not just in the Bareilly region that domineering Islam was experienced; it may be shown how it suffered in innumerable other places, too. Hindu society was free for two generations from the unbridled 'bolbala' of Islam (because of the British)." (44-374) (Is it possible, under such circumstances that Hindus might have earnestly participated in an uprising to drive away the British?)

wage *Jihad* against the British. This produced sharp adverse public outcry among local Muslims. Indeed, so fierce was the sentiment that British officers were obliged to move the Maulvi out of the district to a safer place for his security. (7-170; 81-111)

25th May happened to be Id and a sermon by M. Rahimatullah was arranged in the same mosque on behalf of the rebels, in which this Maulvi was going to tell the congregation how *Jihad* against the British was fully consistent with Islamic principles. Several army commanders and sepoys were present along with Bakht Khan. When the thrust of the sermon became apparent, the British kotwal intervened and prevented the Maulvi from continuing the harangue. (7-171; 81-111) But the damage had been done — the audience had received the intended message.

M. Sayyid Qutb — Author of Many a Proclamation

Another important leader who preached *Jihad* was M. Sayyid Qutb, a teacher of Persian at the Bareilly college. He did the work of getting *Jihad* edicts and other material of mass communication printed at the Government Bahaduri press and distributing it. The *Jihad* Proclamation issued in the name and with consent of Khan Bahadur Khan had been prepared by this man.[4] (7-373; 81-111) Moreover, he had even appointed agents to bring *ghazis* together. (7-373)

When artillery and infantry sepoys in Bareilly rebelled on 31st May the British commander "ordered the cavalry regiment to march on the Revolutionaries. Mahoomd Shafi (the head of the regiment) galloped towards the Revolutionaries and ordered the horsemen to follow him. They followed him shouting, 'Die for religion, the green flag is calling you !'" (1-171)

---

4. Not just this one, but it can be seen that several other declarations in Rohilkhand were printed at the Bahaduri press and published by this man. Included in these were declarations by Nanasahib, Rani Laxmibai, Firoz Shah and others.

Not just sepoys but even the lay public was fully prepared to wage *Jihad*. (7-280) The leading Mahomedans of the city were fully aware of the intention of the troops, and had prepared the people to join in the rebellion against the British Government.[5] (193) Accordingly, they joined the *Jihad* also, which signaled the end of British control over Bareilly district.

Khan Bahadur Khan's Islamic Rule Begins

A grand procession along with all the trappings of sovereignty was taken out through the town, and the end of British rule and reinstatement of the Emperor was proclaimed. (279) A green flag was unfurled at the kotwali. (194) A makeshift throne was erected there "and Madar Ali Khan speaking in the name of the Pathans of Rohilkhand, called upon Khan Bahadur to seat himself upon it, and declare himself ruler, under the King of Delhi." (194) He commenced his rule as Nawab and Imperial Subedar. A declaration calling for death to every Englishman was also issued. (194)

The Nawab constituted his council of ministers. With the single exception of Shobha Ram[6], all department heads were Muslim. (281, 5) Shobha Ram wielded much influence and was needed for obtaining sympathy of Hindus. (283) He was an able administrator and loyal to the Khan. He was put in charge of finance and was as such responsible for the unpopular task

---

5. An invitation to rebel and come to Delhi was received by Rohilkhand sepoys: "Brothers, there is a fight with English at Delhi Innumerable Swadeshi heroes are coming to Delhi. At such a time, if you are dining there, come here to wash your hands. The Padshah of Shahs and the Home Splendour, our Emperor of Delhi, will give you a great welcome and fitly reward your services. Our ears are anxious for the sound of your cannon and our eyes are thirsting to see you. Come ! Come at once !" (1-169)

6. Setumadhavrao Pagdi writes: "Bahadur Khan's executive council had ten Muslims and two Hindus. Jaimal Singh was one of them." (14-101) With Jaimal as (a minister or) a member, the number of Hindus in the council becomes two. However, of significance is the fact that no vital office was allotted to a Hindu.

of fixing and recovering taxes. Draconian measures were employed. Lower echelon Muslim officials would place bones of cows before Hindus during the process of such recovery. Defaulters were made to sit on heated iron strips. (287) It was advantageous for the Nawab to have a Hindu at the head of such a department. Jaimal Singh, a Hindu, was a subordinate of Shobha Ram in the same department.

Later, the Nawab also minted his coin and introduced it in circulation. (287)

The Khan then organized his army. He had a total strength of 30,000 of which 25,000 were infantry and 5,000 cavalry. (289) The figure varies from one source to another: 30–40 thousand (43–65), 40 thousand (68-535), 50 thousand (14-100), 100 thousand (7-446). (Quite possibly, these varying figures pertain to different times as the strength progressively increased.) Importantly, a majority of the force was Pathan. (43-65) The 88 cavalry platoons had an average of 55 horsemen in each. Names of all commanders (*risaldars*) of those platoons are available. Only one of them was Hindu. (7-290 to 4). The infantry had 57 platoons with an average of 415 troopers in each. 52 of their commanders (subedars) were Muslim. (294) In effect, only six out of a total of 145 platoon commanders were Hindu. There was no possibility whatsoever of a Hindu being appointed to any of the higher commands.

Emperor's Orders: Implement Shariat

The Emperor's order sanctioning the Nawab's rule was received on 9th July. The Khan had been guided thereby to... "Among other necessary things, you should also care to see that on all occasions and in all cases nothing should be done contrary to the *Shariat* or the Mahomedan Law and everyone of the subjects and the soldiery should also strive in achieving this object."[7] (284)

---

7. A question remaining unanswered is whether Hindus, too, were expected to 'strive in achieving this object.' If they were so expected, it necessarily follows that they had to accept the *Shariat*. On the other hand, if they were not so expected, they could not

(Contd.)

Thus, the law of the *Shariat* was slated to be implemented in 'independent' India after a successful conclusion of the Uprising. There remains no doubt that the Emperor was going to implement in his Empire what he was asking his subedar to do in Rohilkhand.

Hindus Support British

The Khan's rule soon became characterized by the adage 'might is right'. (158-269) The state became a curse for Hindus. Rohilkhand became an open field for growing Hindu-Muslim friction, and it is necessary to discuss this conflict separately. (Chapter 10). However, it will suffice to state at this juncture that, "Rohilkhand had been the traditional home of warlike *Rajput Thakurs* who disliked Mahomedan suzerainty and proved to be a constant source of trouble to the Rohila Chiefs in the past. He could not fully win over confidence of the *Thakurs*... ." (87-52) "Rohilkhand contained a significant number of pro-British Hindus who were anxious to be released form Muslim rule, particularly that of Khan Bahadur Khan." (126-347) "The Hindus, oppressed by the Muslims, were depressed at the success of the mutiny, and daily offered prayers to God for the return of the English." (67-177; 68-520)

Preconditions for Cow-slaughter Ban

Khan Bahadur Khan made attempts to obtain Hindu sympathy. Efforts began to ensure that Hindus do not join the British. (158-274) Nanasahib was in Bareilly at that time. An administrative report says: "Nana arrived at Bareilly on 25 March and remained there till the end of April (1858). He found that the rebellion had assumed an entirely Mahomedan character; he made some attempts to put a stop to cow-killing

---

qualify as subjects/citizens of the state. By a less stringent interpretation of the *Shariat*, Hindus qualified as zimmis (protected peoples) and were required to remit *jaziya* to the Islamic state in token of subservience. This was implicit in the Emperor's directive of doing nothing that went against the *Shariat*. But because Muslims could not do without Hindu sympathy and cooperation during the Uprising, it is obvious that the Emperor had avoided clear mention of it in his decree.

in the city and also to induce the Hindus to join the Mahomedans in opposing the English,[8] but without success." (68-556n) This notwithstanding, the Khan appealed to Hindus, as part of a joint effort, by issuing a directive regarding cow slaughter in Rohilkhand. It was stated therein: "If the Hindus and Mahomedans join together, the extermination of Europeans will appear very easy. The Mahomedans are already engaged on their part in attaining this end but the Hindus are careless of this important point. The reason for this appears to be none other than the prevalence of the practice of cow killing among Mahomedans, which is opposed to the tenets of the Hindu faith. It is resolved that if the Hindus shall exert themselves in the extermination of these infidels and expel them from this country, they shall be rewarded for their patriotism with the extinction of the practice of slaughter of kine throughout my dominions. For the present no cows shall be killed in any Mohallas of this town in which the Hindus may be residing, but the entire prohibition of this practice is made conditional with the complete extermination of the infidels from India. If any Hindu shall shrink from joining in the cause, the evils of revival of this practice shall rest upon him."[9] (87-53; 7-349)

---

8. The task of pacifying Rajput Thakurs and persuading Hindus to back the Khan had fallen to Nana's lot. It was on his advice that the Khan had issued the directive. (7-400, 34; 72-37; 90-169) (Is it not amazing that when he was ruling in Kanpur he had permitted any number of cows to be slaughtered, but was now advising the Khan to ban it? How was it going to be possible for the Khan to do something that was impossible for Nana? Of course, the Khan had included such conditions in the directive that might deceive gullible Hindus, but no Muslim was going to complain.)

9. Savarkar quotes the directive but uses 'gomata' (or, 'cow mother') for 'cow' and 'gomatecha vadh' (killing of the cow) for 'slaughter of kine'. In later times (1930), he regarded the cow not as 'mother' but a 'beast', but at the time of writing his book (1908) he was forcing (through incorrect translation) Muslims to regard the cow with filial veneration.

This directive had been issued 10 months after establishing the state. It was a conditional sop offered in time of difficulty when Hindu support was desperately needed. So severe and unrealistic were the conditions of 'complete extermination of the infidels from India' and 'all Hindus joining the cause', that the eventuality of ever acting upon the promise might never have arisen![10] Thus, the possibility of honouring the assurance after the British had been successfully driven out was beyond the realm even of imagination.

Scintillating Jihad by Ghazis

Most sources refer to those who fought the British in Rohilkhand as '*ghazis*'. All historians make special mention[11] of the dazzling resistance they offered to the British in the last stand (May 1858) at Bareilly. Here are two examples.

"About a hundred *Ghazis* (Muslim fanatics) issued from the broken walls, and came hounding forward like panthers, shouting 'Bismillah Deen' (for God and the Faith), covering their heads with a leather shield, and brandishing their formidable 'tulwars'. They were grey-bearded men; all wore turbans and waistcloths of green, the colour dear to the Prophet; and on the little finger was a silver ring with a stone, on which was engraven a long text from the Quran." "A hundred and thirty-three corpses were counted after the action." (70-324)

This is Savarkar's eulogy: "The sword belonged to the martyr-spirits, who, in spite of the hopelessness of success, nay, in virtue of the hopelessness of success, instead of leaving the battlefield, preferred to embrace death with a smile on their lips. To die while fighting in a good cause is the key to the gates of Heaven, that was their belief. So they unsheathed

10. N. K. Behere writes that the last condition in the directive was: "If any Hindu joins the British instead of supporting our cause will be imprisoned for six months and cow slaughter will be resumed with renewed vigour" (158-274)

11. See: 61-146; 44-243; 141-356; 81-113n; 72-185; 14-102; 7-457, 8, 63.

their swords and dashed like thunderbolt on the British forces. With green turbans on their head, with a *Kumerbund* girded round their loins, and a silver ring inscribed with chosen sentences of the Quran in their finger, these terrible-looking *Ghazis* rushed up from the right, holding their head behind their shields, with their swords shining aloft in the sun, and shouting wildly their war-cry of 'Deen, Deen !' They closed with the British troops with a tremendous shock, and, at this desperate attack, though they were few, the British soldiers were startled and confused and swept away; but the death-dealing *Ghazis* still advanced. Not one of them returned back — all of them fell while fighting and mowed down by the British soldiery like sheaves before the scythe ! They fell; they fell like lions. Of the few instances of the immortal bravery of martyrdom in the history of the world, none can be greater than this !" (1-451)

Bahadur Khan was later put on trial (1860) and sentenced to death by hanging.

M. Sarfaraz Ali at Shahjahanpur

While the revolt in Shahjahanpur occurred on 31st May , preparations were underway for a month before that date. M. Sarfaraz Ali[12] had arrived from Gorakhpur and was busy provoking people for the *Jihad*. He had many followers in the town. (7-297; 44-102; 34-300) As in Gorakhpur, it was this Maulvi who was the inspiration for the rebellion here. (81-116) Green flags were used to inspire people. (117)

Several sources cite a provocative speech given by the Maulvi at a meeting convened on 1st May at Mazhar Kareem's house. Among the many Muslims present were some Hindus, too. Guards had been positioned at the entrance during the meeting. The Maulvi said: "The question for debate is : Shall they continue to be our masters any longer? By the last Prophet,

12. This man is lauded as the 'One of the most prominent leaders of the movement.' (34-300) A proponent of Waliullahi philosophy, he was greatly influenced by Barelvi's Jihadi thought. He was a signatory to the Delhi *Jihad* Declaration. Moreover, commander-in-chief Bakht Khan was his disciple.

they shall not defile our native soil any longer. I am here to devise ways and means to accomplish that object. Consider what instruments they used to acquire from this country? It is the *sipahi* army which conquered India for them, and by the sword of Ali! That very instrument shall be employed to destroy them." (81-25)

Referring to the humiliation perpetrated by the British, he stated further: "But ai bhaio ! our religion is now in danger. Having lost the sovereignty of the land, having bowed in subjection to the impure *Kafir*, shall we surrender the inalienable privileges which we have received from the Prophet ?" (25)

Turning to the Hindus present, he said: "O brothers of the Hindu race ! the purity of your caste is threatened, and the religious distinctions so much prized by you invaded by the proselytizing and annexing *Firangi* ! Rise in arms ! Just a hundred years ago the rule of the infidel began, and I declare to you that it must now end. The centenary approaches, my friends, and have I your unanimous vote to declare that the *Kafir* blood shall be stamped out on that date ?" (26)

Overwhelmed with emotion and forgetting for the time being that their blood, like that of 'firangis', was no different from that of *kafirs* of yesterday and tomorrow, Hindus present on the occasion assented uproariously to the Maulvi's call. "The Hindus cried out *Jai Ram Laxmanji Ki,* while the Mahomedans yelled *Ek nara Haidari, ya Husain."* (26). The local subedar, Ghanshyam Singh, was so overcome with emotion that he fell at the Maulvi's feet, drew his sword, touched his sacred thread (janew) and roared, "By the sacred cord which I wear as *Chatri of Chatries,* this blade shall lick up the blood of him who dares to bring the greased cartridge to my mouth." (26)

The incident is a fine example of the manner in which Hindus were induced to join.[13] There was no possibility that

13. Dr. Chaudhary, who regards the Uprising as a war of independence, comments thus on this incident: "The over excited political sentiment as reflected in the above speech was typical of the attitude of the general body of the rebels." (81-26)

Hindus of that time and place could have had even an inkling of 'the inalienable privileges' bestowed upon Muslims by their Prophet.

Muslim Rule Begins

Two Nawabs, Qadir Ali Khan and Ghulam Hussain Khan, commenced their rule over the district. Nizam Ali became the kotwal. On 1st June, a procession proclaiming the overthrow of the British rule was led by Hamid Hasan Khan and Nizamali Khan. (44-102; 7-296; 81-116) A fortnight later, with the assent of the Nawab of Bareilly, Ghulam Qadir was made nazim (collector) to replace the former two. He appointed Muslims to all senior positions in the district (including talukas/tehsils). Only the charge of finance was given to Sital Singh. (7-299) Names of the more important officials in the civil hierarchy are listed in sources, and it may be observed that of 114 such officials, 97 are Muslim and 17 Hindu. (301 to 11) All names of army commanders — nine cavalry and 4 infantry — that are available, were Muslim. (300)

Hindu Challenge to Rebels

A Muslim state was unacceptable to Hindus. The main problem in the district was to suppress the recalcitrant Hindu Zamindars. They could not be suppressed by local authorities, who requested to Khan Bahadur Khan to send help. In response to this appeal Mardan Ali Khan arrived with a large force and overpowered the Rajputs, many of them were killed in the action. (34-301)

Upon cessation of British rule in the district, the state sponsored *Jihad* was directed at Hindus. Various descriptions are available. Rajputs gained an upper hand at one stage in the conflict between Hindus and Muslims in this district but Khan Bahadur of Bareilly sent his troops and neutralized their resistance. Many Rajputs were beheaded, and their severed heads displayed in procession, while the entire community was thoroughly looted." (44-102)

Emperor's Directive: Extermination of 'Kufr' and 'Shirk'

Pleased at the manner in which Khan Bahadur Khan was ruling over the Shahjahanpur district in keeping with imperial directives, the Emperor dispatched the following order: *"By God's grace Kufr and Shirk (the rule of the heathens)*[14] *have been purged from Hindustan* and the Islam[15] has been established. As you have carried on administration of Bareilly and Shahjahanpur nicely that part of country has been given to you. You should now carry on the administration according to the tenets of the religion and pray wholeheartedly for the stability of the King's rule." (7-320)

Hindus were praying fervently for such a draconian regime to come to an end. And that time had arrived. "Muslim rule in this district came to an end in April 1858. Elation of Rajputs knew no bounds when their chief tormentor, Ahmad Yar Khan, was hanged by the British." (44-102)

---

14. 'Kufr', according to Islamic principles, means 'denying faith in Islam', while 'shirk' means 'worshipping gods other than or along with Allah (polytheism)'. 'Shirk' is the most grievous and unpardonable crime and injustice imaginable. (128-308,15,38,563) Likewise, regarding any human power as sovereign in place of Allah is also tantamount to polytheism. (300n) This is a reason why maulvis of the Waliullahi school were making frenzied attempts to establish an Islamic state in India. The meaning of 'shirk' given here in parentheses as 'the rule of heathens' is not an accurate rendering of the concept. The correct meaning is 'existence / prevalence of polytheism'. It ought to be sufficiently clear that, like one ruled by the British, a state governed by Hindus, too, qualifies as 'kufr' and 'shirk'.

15. Government editors supply a footnote about the word 'Islam': "Islam in these documents is broadly used in the sense of peace." This is clearly an attempt to mislead the Hindu reader. A little further down, the word 'religion' 'according to the tenets of the religion' implies 'Islam'. In the previous directive issued by the Emperor there is a clear instruction to abide by the '*Shariat* or Muhammedan law'. Such deliberate misdirection has helped the emergence of an incorrect picture of the 1857 Uprising, especially the regimes of the Emperors and the Nawabs.

Muslim Rule at Badaun

Let us turn to the Badaun district of Rohilkhand that was adjacent to the two we have just seen. There was a revolt here on 1st June but the collector had received information on 25th May that the Mahomedans of the town assembled for prayers on the occasion of the Id festival, were to rise on noon. (7-216; 34-299) The next day in Badaun the mass of the population rose in a body, and the entire district became a scene of anarchy and confusion. (7-217) After this they set the bungalows of (officers) on fire. The residents of Sarai Jalandari, Sarai Nai, Ibrahimpur and others looted all they found without the fear of God and the Day of Judgement. (211) The entire police force had thrown away its badges and joined them. (219) The situation became uncontrollable and, on the same day, British power in the district came to an end with the proclamation of Khan Bahadur Khan's rule. (7-219; 81-115) The Khan appointed his nephew, Abdur Rahman, as collector while Ahmad Yar Khan became his deputy. (7-213; 34-299; 81-115)

Abdur Rahman then made appointments of senior administrative officials. Of the fourteen so appointed, only one was Hindu — Lakshman Singh, — as tehsildar of a taluka. (7-314) Rehman also immediately organized a 2,000 strong army. (312)

Hindu - Muslim Strife

The conflict that waged in the district till the British re-established control over Rohilkhand, was between the Khan's forces and Hindu zamindars and Thakur chieftains. The latter were unwilling to recognize the Nawab's rule or the local collector's authority. In effect, the Uprising in the Badaun district is a tale of an armed struggle between the Nawab's Muslim state and the local Hindu population. This being an important feature, we have included details in Chapter 10. However, reference to one incident would suffice for the present.

The local collector (*Nazim*) used to dispatch armed detachments to suppress acts of rebellion against his authority.

A report of one of those reads: "The *Nazim* with his army went to the spot and, besides these ruffians, put 307 persons to sword and brunt their villages." (312) Concluding the news item, the newspaper that reported the incident (25th June 1857) offered prayer for the success of the *Nazim* and of the religion of the Prophet. (312)

This should provide an idea of the inner reality of the Badaun uprising.

Same at Pilibhit

It was Muslims once again who had rebelled in the fourth district of Rohilkhand, Pilibhit. The large mob assembled between the Tehsil and Kotwali was Muslim. (229) The Muslim population of this small town enthusiastically took up the cause of the Revolution; they accepted the authority of Khan Bahadur Khan. In the vicinity of Pilibhit a few Hindu Zamindars, particularly the Thakurs of Nawabganj, refused to submit to the officers of the new government; they were, however, soon punished for creating trouble. (34-299) The Nawab appointed Fazal Haq as collector, and Muslim rule commenced. (7-327)

Moradabad: Majju Khan's Rule

A Waliullahi Maulvi, Kifayat Ali, had done the groundwork of inspiring Muslims in the Moradabad district to rebel. He was in the forefront of preaching activity there. (34-302; 25-213) Preparations for the 1st June rebellion[16] had

---

16. Savarkar describes it as: "(The Sepoy told the English authorities) : 'The rule of the Company is at an end ! Therefore, you should leave this country immediately and go away, or else you will be massacred. We will allow you two hours to prepare for departure. But you must vacate Moradabad as soon as the two hours are over.' The Moradabad police also announced that thenceforth they would not obey the orders of the English, and the citizens supported them. The Englishmen who were found in Moradabad after the time limit had expired, were killed. Commissioner Powell and others became Mahomedans and thus saved their lives. And before sunset the green flag began to fly on Moradabad. (1-175)

commenced well in advance. The tehsil and police station at taluka Amroha, 33 kilometers from Moradabad, were burned down under leadership of a certain Sayyid Gulzar Ali on 27th May, the station officer killed and treasury looted. (7-239) Ali declared himself as ruler after 3rd June. (68-522) M. Mannu Khan was leader of the revolt. On the following day, a contingent of 200 *ghazis* from neighbouring Rampur arrived in Moradabad in response to Mannu's invitation and the green flag was hoisted. (34-302; 7-240) In the meantime, Mannu was killed in an encounter with the British, and Nawab Mujahiddin Khan (Majju Khan) took over as leader of the *Jihad.*

Local Muslims had been exchanging the following cryptic verse in Urdu among themselves on the previous day: "The fowler this day announced to the captive birds, 'ye all shall obtain freedom next day.'" (7-241) The British were under the constant apprehension of Muslim attack. (242) Throughout the district the Mussalmans as a body had shown in the clearest manner their antipathy to the British Government. In Moradabad, as in other districts of Rohilkhand, there was a general revolt on the part of Mussalman community, inflamed by fanaticism to an active hatred of everything English." (34-303)

The revolt broke out in the town as well as the district, and those who assumed leadership or participated in it were Muslim.[17] (7-242 to 5)

Majju Khan was then appointed Collector of Moradabad by the Nawab of Bareilly and the usual proclamation, "Khulk Khuda ka, Mulk Badshah ka, Aur Hukum Majju Khan ka" was made. (329)

The Shahzada's Regime: Tax on All Hindus

Nawab Muhammad Yusuf Ali Khan of neighbouring Rampur was loyal to the British. Prince Firoz Shah haa launched a surprise attack on Moradabad with 1,000 *ghazis* in

17. Besides this information contained in the Government Publication, Dr. Chaudhary provides in his own book names of 14 prominent maulvis, nawabs and sundry leaders who took part. All were Muslim. (81-110)

April 1858, defeated the Nawab and retained control of the district for some time. (7-409, 41; 68-558n) His rule lasted just two days, but even in that negligible interval he had imposed a tax on all Hindu residents.[18] (68-556n) Then, with the help of the British, the Nawab of Rampur regained control once again in which local Hindus helped him. (7-420)

Since the Nawab of Rampur in Rohilkhand was a British loyalist, no rebellion had occurred in that town. Nevertheless, even the British were certain that "not a single Rampur Pathan subject, except the Nawab and perhaps three or four of his confidants, could be trusted." (360) Hindu residents of Rampur had, in fact, always been referred to by the British as 'loyalists' (419, 20) The Nawab gained control over Moradabad which was ceded to him by the British after they had won the final victory. A notable event was that the Prince had attacked Rampur with a large force from Bareilly in May 1858, and after defeating the Nawab took possession of his territory in the name of Prophet. (446). Of course, that occupation, too, had not lasted too long.

Mahmud Khan at Bijnor

What remains to be seen now is the last district, Bijnor. Sir Sayyed Ahmad was district judge here during the Uprising and amassed detailed information of events unfolding around him, to collate them in a book form. As a consequence of those efforts, as much detailed information as is available about events in Bijnor is not available in respect of the Uprising not just in other districts of Rohilkhand but also other places in the rest of India.

Sensing the gathering storm of an Uprising, British officers stationed there invited influential and loyalist Hindu Chaudharies (Randhir Singh of Haldaur and Pratap Singh of

---

18. It is not stated clearly in any source whether this tax was '*jaziya*'; but it is quite plain that it was imposed on Hindus as something in the nature of punishment for their pro-British (and pro-Nawab of Rampur) leanings.

Tajpur), requesting them to assume charge of administration after their departure. (260) The two declined the request for the simple reason that Muslims in the district were never going to suffer the authority of anyone other than the Muslim Nawab, Mahmud Khan.[19] (260) This nawab lived at Najibabad, a prominent town in the district. He was great grandson of the well known Najib Khan Rohila who had played a key role in the Battle of Panipat in 1761. (14-94) Ultimately, the officials decided to entrust administration to this nawab. (7-260) Sir Sayyed Ahmad, at this juncture, had taken him aside and told him, "Mubarak ho (be glad) you have received the country of your ancestors." (99-17)

After the British went away, the Nawab had the usual proclamation made: "Khulk.... Hukum Nawab Mahmud Khan ka". (7-331; 81-109) A messenger was dispatched to obtain traditional symbols and tokens of sovereignty from Delhi. New weights and measures were introduced. (7-332) Sanction was received from the Emperor in due course. The nawab was described therein as: "our special servant, worthy of kindness and protection, the object of our favours...." (337) Senior administrative officials were then appointed. Of course, none of them was Hindu. (338)

Return of British rule: Hindus Happy

However, local Chaudharies refused to recognize the nawab's rule. (45-39) The revolt here was a relentless saga of Hindu-Muslim armed conflict till the British finally retook the district. Since it forms an important part of the Uprising, we have included details in Chapter 10. Suffice it to say, "The British district officials returned to Bijnor for a triumphant entry (after the fall of Rohilkhand) with the Hindu chiefs who had continued their struggle against the Pathan rebels." (45-

---

19. The population of the district at the time was 6,20,552—4,15,570 was Hindu and 2,04,982, Muslim. Although (or since) the latter formed 30 percent of the population it had become a dominant section of society. (45-xix) They were not likely to permit anyone else to rule over them.

xix) (Their) re-entry into this district, has given confidence to the loyal Hindus. (7-420) The British Army marched into Najibabad. The city was sacked and then burnt. The Nawab had left his blazing palace and gone to Bareilly with fifty followers.... The Hindus....from all sides were delighted with the progress of our force and the Mussalmans were neither to be seen or found. (401)

These conditions prevailed not just in Bijnor but the entire Rohilkhand region. Lord Canning, the Governor-General, clarified before sending in an army to take control of Rohilkhand, that most of the Hindus in Rohilkhand were still quite kindly disposed towards British and looked to them for release from the tyranny of Khan. (79-369) Dr. Mujumdar observed, "The Hindus, disaffected by the communal policy of the (Nawab) Government, welcomed the return of the British forces." (68-535)

Let us take leave of the district by taking note of what Dr. Sashi Bhushan Chaudhary writes about Rohilkhand: "The Mahomedan population in this area was strong both in number and in influence. The revolt in Rohilkhand was mostly confined to the Muslim community who were inflamed by fanaticism to an intense hatred of the English. They raised the green flag,[20] shouted for the revival of the Islamic State and despoiled the Hindu bankers and merchants."[21] (81-108)

- 2 -

---

20. Savarkar writes: "In this manner, the whole province of Rohilkhand rose in a day ! British flags were torn down, and green flags began to fly in the courthouses and police stations and offices." (1-176)

21. Despite this, he writes in the same breath, as it were, that: "But these features did not warp the popular character of the rising." (81-108) Quoting this entire comment, Dr. Mujumdar says insightfully: "It seems to be the view of Dr. Chaudhari that the hatred of the English is the only factor that counts in a popular national movement. The popular character, it seems, is not lost even though the Hindus fight against Muslims...." (68-534)

Bihar: Centre of the Waliullahi Movement

Patna in the Bihar province, was the headquarters of the Waliullahi Movement in India.[22] It was the source for money, war material, manpower and inspiration for the transborder *Jihad.* British officers had knowledge of the all India secret conspiracy of these Waliullahi leaders. Many letters of treasonable nature dispatched towards the Peshawar region had been intercepted. (3-353) Patna had been the centre of the movement for *Jihad.* The Maulvis were now endeavouring to induce the Muslim troops to desert the Company's service and join the holy war. (32-33) The work of sowing seeds of treason among sepoys was being performed by this organization in a well-planned and clandestine manner through special agents appointed for the purpose. (116-158) This was going on incessantly since 1854. (160) A majority of the three hundred thousand population of the town was Muslim. (132-90; 81-161) Hence it had become a source of much apprehension for local officials before the actual Uprising. (81-161) As the government report indicated, that for months past conspiracies had been systematically and extensively carried on and subscriptions raised to finance the projected plot and communications and contacts established with many disaffected centres for the restoration of Mahomedan sovereignty." (161)

22. Hunter writes about the movement in Patna: "The missionary zeal of the Patna Caliphs, and the immense pecuniary resources at their command, once more raised the sacred banner from the dust. They covered India with their emissaries, and brought about one of the greatest religious revivals that has never taken place. The two Caliphs themselves went through Bengal and Southern India. The minor missionaries were innumerable, and a skilful organization. In this way, almost every one of the fanatic Districts had its permanent preacher...." (42-42) "Besides their seditious literature, and the central propaganda at Patna, the Wahabis have a permanent machinery throughout the rural districts for spreading their faith." (63)

Maulvis Arrested

Before the actual rebellion had broken out, the Commissioner, Taylor, had summoned three prominent ring leaders to his residence and had them arrested. They were M. Shah Muhammad Hussain, M. Ahmadullah and Waziul Haq. They were renowned Islamic scholars and wielded great influence over the local Muslim population. (141-244) All three were disciples of Sayyid Barelvi. (34-368)

Although these men were arrested, the movement had no dearth of leaders and M. Ali Karim[23] and Pir Ali stepped forward to fill the vacancy. (34-326; 77-181) Of the two, the former was the kingpin. (81-162) An attempt was made to arrest him as well, but he managed to escape. (34-326)

Pir Ali was primarily a bookseller, but had been so enthralled by Waliullahi thought that he had become one of the most active workers and leaders of the movement. He was 'a brutal but brave fanatic.' (3-359) "The letters found in Peer Ali's house disclosed an organized Mussalman conspiracy to reestablish Mahomedans supremacy and to overthrow the British Government." "A plot has been in existence for some months, and that men were regularly paid and money distributed to incite the people to fight for religion and the Padshah of Delhi." (359) He functioned under an

23. Qeyamuddin Ahmad has written an essay on the subject 'Contribution of M. Ali Karim in the 1857 Uprising.' Ali Karim hailed from a family of respected zamindars and was son of a renowned advocate. The essay sheds light on his relations with Pir Ali as well as general activism behind the Bihar uprising. He slipped away to Gorakhpur in apprehension of being arrested after the administration laid its hands on his correspondence. In later times, he had established contact with Kunwar Singh's brother, Amar Singh. He finally went to the Begum of Bhopal who used her influence to manage a pardon for him after the Uprising had been finally suppressed. (146-44) Savarkar also lauds him: "The seeds of the *Jihad* had taken such a root in Patna that the whole city was a regular haunt of the Revolutionary party. A very prominent leader of this secret organization was a bookseller." (1-88) (See Savarkar's view about Pir Ali, Chap. 6, footnote 2).

understanding with the Kotwal of Patna, Mehndi Ali. (116-220) He was skilled in spreading the message of treason among native sepoys of the British Army. Not only was he in regular correspondence with the Lucknow leader Majih-uz Zaman, being himself originally from that town, but he had also established relations with Kunwar Singh in Bihar. (29-66; 3-359) He had spread tentacles of the movement in the latter's territory of Arah and Jagdishpur.[24] (29-66) Mangal Pandey's motivator, Nakki Khan, and Pir Ali used to function in conjunction with one another. (66)

The Patna rebellion of 3rd July had been organized by the same man. On that day, a large crowd of his followers marched through the streets armed with swords and muskets, brandishing green flags, beating drums and shouting slogans of 'Ali, Ali!'. (132-90; 141-246; 3-359) The mob attacked the Catholic Church[25] and destroyed part of it. One officer was put to death, while one Jihadi was killed. (81-161; 34-326) Pir Ali and many of his followers were arrested, put on trial and sentenced to various punishments. Nineteen of them were hanged along with him. All three platoons at Danapur rebelled after hearing of the hangings[26] (25th July) (1-258)

The same Waliullahi revolutionaries had succeeded in inducing sepoys at Danapur near Patna to rebel. Thus, when

---

24. Every historian takes note of Pir Ali. (132-18) He even finds mention in a section entitled 'Pir Ali Hanged' in the *Hindu Panch: Balidan Ank,* a Hindi Publication giving information about just five selected personalities of the 1857 uprising. The concluding sentence says: "The lesson bequeathed to Indians by the valorous Pir Ali will remain written in letters of gold! He is immortal even in death!" (146-113)

25. Savarkar writes: "On the 3rd of July, Mussalmans began to crowd towards the house of a leader, Peer Ali by name. They entered his house and settled their plans. In a short time, they came out one by one, with green flags and shouts of 'Deen, Bolo ! Deen !' About two hundred *Jihadis* came out in procession and attacked the Church. Peer Ali shot him (i.e. Lyall) dead, and his infuriated followers hacked his body to pieces beyond recognition !" (1-319)

26. See Ch. 6 footnote 2 for Savarkar's assessment of Pir Ali.

an attempt was made on 25th July to disarm them, 2,000 troopers managed to escape to Arah. A majority of them were Waliullahi adherents and had risen in the name of the Emperor. (32-78)

On arrival in Arah, they threatened Kunwar Singh's troopers into fetching their master from Jagdishpur. Thenceforth, the Bihar rebellion was conducted under Kunwar Singh's leadership. This man had no independent political identity and had assumed leadership because the Danapur rebels had presented him with an opportunity of leading them and also winning back his lost zamindari holdings, but had thereafter fought the British with zeal, courage and determination. In later times, he went with his force to the Begum of Ayodhya, Prince Firoz Shah, the Nawab of Banda and Tatya Tope. After allying himself with various principals and offering stiff resistance to the British at various places, he finally returned to his native Jagdishpur, over which he had gained temporary control. But on the third day after his homecoming, he succumbed to the wounds he had sustained. Ten days later, on 10th May 1858, the British took Jagdishpur. (132-194)

All the glorious descriptions of Kunwar Singh's valour and bitter struggle against the British do not alter the nature of the 1857 Uprising. Even assuming for the sake of argument that the Uprising had been successful, his status and position was never likely to exceed that of a zamindar or, perhaps, Imperial Subedar; indeed, he seems to have aspired for nothing more than obstinate loyalty to the Begum of Ayodhya or the Emperor.

The Uprising in Bihar, thus, was inspired by leaders subscribing to Waliullah's ideology. It was, plain and simple, an agitation for *Jihad*.[27]

---

27. Savarkar's view about the Bihar revolt: "The historical town of Patna was the centre of the powerful Wahabi sect of Muslim religion. The town of Patna which thoroughly hated the English

(Contd.)

- 3 -

Nature of the Uprising in Southern India

No Uprising in the South

Every historian concedes that the Uprising of 1857 was mainly confined to North India, which is why serious note has not been taken of those minor and rare or local incidents of rebellion that occurred in the south as faint echoes of events in the north. The British themselves viewed the rebellion as one limited to North India, a reason why armed forces had been detailed from the south to suppress revolts in the north. Had there been a significant rebellion in the south, troops would scarcely have been moved out of the region. Thus, it is obvious that the British felt no anxiety about developments in the south. A complaint that South India had not yet woken up and risen, was made in a proclamation to rulers in that region purportedly addressed by Nanasahib in as late as June 1858. It stated that those southern states and their people would be called 'effeminate and foolish' if they did not rebel. Would such remarks have ever been made if a rebellion of any significance had occurred in the south?

Nevertheless, because the Uprising is currently sought to be presented as the 'War of Independence', a search with a

---

yoke had started a secret society with the object of overthrowing the English power as far back as 1852. This secret society had amongst its members influential and rich merchants, bankers and zamindars, a fact which gave the society immense funds for its work. The prominent Maulvis accepted leading positions in the society, the work soon assumed a grave turn. They had correspondence and communication with the secret society at Lucknow as well as with the Sepoys at Danapur." (1-315) "They had no lack of funds and even sent some money to the distant frontier districts in the west to organise a Revolution against the English. Since the police had also joined, the nightly secret meetings went on without a hitch. Soon communication was established with the Sepoys stationed for the protection of the province. The Sepoys in the camp at Danapur began to hold secret meetings and form plans at nights, under cover of the trees !" (316)

microscope, so to say, is underway to show how 'our' region, too, had participated with gusto and 'we' were not lagging behind in any manner whatsoever. A painstakingly authored book, *South India in 1857: War of Independence* by V. D. Divekar, is an example of this quest.[28] Those who might not have studied the north Indian rebellion or those without adequate information about it, are more than likely to come away with an impression of mistaken awe for events in the south after reading such works. With so many revolutionaries arrested, hanged or transported for life to the Andamans, they are led to believe that the entire South India, too, had been engulfed in flames of revolution! It is no different from someone who has yet to see the magnitude of the ocean, to look at a largish lake and exclaim, 'Oh! How vast is this ocean!' On the other hand, someone who knows what had happened in the north cannot but wonder what there was in southern incidents that might qualify them for description as 'uprisings'. In terms of both number and intensity, the southern rebellion appears negligible in comparison with its northern counterpart. Divekar mentions about 55 incidents that occurred in the whole of South India. But such events had occurred almost in every street and town in Uttar Pradesh. A majority of incidents in the south had been quelled even before they had broken out. The remainder had been suppressed within a very short time of their eruption, and even those had not needed much military force. Only a few stray sparks of the northern conflagration had fallen in the south and historians view them as mere echoes — faint ones at that — of what had come to pass in North India, just as they were regarded by the British themselves.

---

28. Thirty-eight scholars read their research papers on the subject "Contribution of Our Province in the Freedom Struggle of 1857," at the annual convention of the 'Akhil Bhartiya Itihas Sankalan Yojana' at Kurukshetra in November 2006. Included therein were papers on events in regions like Andhra Pradesh and Tamil Nadu. ('Vivek' Weekly dated 24th December 2006)

1857 was a political revolution. The proclamation, 'Khulk Khuda ka, Mulk Badshah ka,...' in the name of Bahadur Shah as the new ruler, had reverberated all over North India after British rule had ceased. Three distinct categories may be identified in the south from this aspect. The first comprised, as in the north, loyalists of the Emperor; the second, those desiring restoration of the Peshwa's rule under Nanasahib; the third, those wishing to exploit the reigning anarchy and enrich themselves through pillage. It is generally said that 31st May was the appointed date for the Uprising in the north. Of course, this date did not apply to the south simply because no date was fixed for the region. What seems to have actually happened, is individual uprisings were initiated after gauging the northern situation and local convenience. On the whole, every northern rebellion had occurred by mid-June 1857 and the British had begun suppressing them by September. In the south, however, revolts took place even after July 1857 and continued to occur till May 1858. Bhimrao Desai of Mundargi in Karnataka had fixed 27th May 1858 for a rebellion in his territory. (155-273) By that time, the back of almost every revolt in the north had been broken. It is amazing that Bhimrao Desai had remained a peaceable citizen when the enemy was in dire straits in the north but had now decided to rise, when the latter had become free from the peril, almost with a death wish and aspiration to be comprehensively mauled by him!

Let us review some of the so-called southern rebellions being projected as the war of independence to understand their real nature.

Statement by Madras Administration : Muslim Revolt

The nature of the Madras revolt has been clearly enunciated in a statement issued on 3rd September 1857. It reads, "Hyderabad is always inflammable and was sure to be deeply excited. Our Provinces of Kurnool, Cuddapah and Malabar contain a large Mussalman population which would participate in these feelings, and at Madras itself and the towns of Arcot, Vellore and Tiruchirappalli animosity was felt in consequence of extinction of the Nawabship of Karnatak."

On 28th July 1857, a conspiracy was discovered, the ramifications of which extended (from Belgaum) to Mysore, Kurnool and Madras generally. In the middle of June 1857, bands of armed Rohillas (who proclaimed that they were the servants of Nanasahib Peshwa) crossed from the Nizam's country, into the Kurnool and Cuddapah districts with a deeper object. They were apparently connected with the party who attacked the Hyderabad Residency on 17th July. In Mysore, about the middle of July, it was found necessary to dispatch some European Infantry and guns to overawe the Mahomedans near Srirangapatnam and Mysore.

"In Machilipatnam, a green flag and a proclamation, urging the slaughter of the English were seized on 10th July and it was reported on 15th August that prayers for success of King of Delhi were offered in the mosques.

"In Madras itself, the state of feelings in Triplicane became so suspicious that on 29th June, military posts were established in different parts of the town and other precautions taken. Among other signs of disaffection, proclamations and seditious letters were seized urging the Nizam and his minister to begin a holy war in which they were ready to join. Both in Madras and in the surrounding provinces much seditious language and correspondence was going on. The approaching downfall of our power was openly talked of.

"There was the presence of seditious foreign (i.e. of neighbouring states) emissaries and Bengal Sepoys in various parts of the Madras Presidency. They entered the provinces in large numbers and there was no room to doubt their mischievous designs of trying to tamper with our sepoys." (155-xi)

It is plain from this statement that the rebellions in Belgaum (Karnataka), Hyderabad State, Mysore and Madras had assumed Muslim overtones and was emotionally connected with its pervasive counterpart in the north.

Hyderabad : Jihad against Christians

While the Nizam had shrewdly and tactfully remained loyal to the British, his Muslim subjects were sympathetic to the rebellion. Waliullahi (Wahabi) thoughts held tremendous sway in the state.[29] The 1839 'Hyderabad Conspiracy' had been hatched by these very people. No sooner the holy warriors in Hyderabad began preaching rebellion than they received news of revolts in Meerut and Delhi. (77-180; 64-66) Provocative posters were put up at the Mecca Masjid and Charminar,[30] in which appeals were made to wage *Jihad* against Christians.[31] (70-273; 155-112) People thronged at the Mecca Masjid in huge

---

29. Divekar comments on the Wahabi influence during 1857 as: "Wahabi movement was one of the preludes to the Uprising of 1857. It was started by a puritanical sect of Muslims led by Abdul Wahab in Saudi Arabia. It soon spread to many countries. In India at Patna, under the leadership of Syed Ahmad Barelvi, it became a strong anti-British movement. After Syed Ahmad's death in 1831, his followers kept up the anti-British agitation. In Hyderabad (1839), Nawab Mubarizudduallah played a leading role as part of the Wahabi movement, in anti-British activities. He was the younger brother of Nizam... and, therefore, held high rank in the royal family... Due to the Wahabi movement, there already prevailed anti-British feelings in the Hyderabad state." (155-21)

30. Some of the statements in those numerous posters were as follows: "A new subedar shall be appointed by Delhi (if the Nizam is unwilling to wage religious war)." "This proclamation is being made for the sake of Islam and waging war against *kafirs.*" (14-161) "Oh, Allah! Multiply the Islamic faith!" "Help comes to Muslims from Allah… assemble under the banner of Islam and begin your work." (162)

31. Savarkar describes the Hyderabad revolt in the following words: "So, on 12th June 1857, Hyderabad assumed a more terrible form. On that day, proclamations signed by important Maulvis began to adorn the walls; revolutionary handbills were seen everywhere in heaps; there were crowded meetings of Muslims in the mosque and violent revolutionary lecturers bound the people by oaths to drive the *Kafir* Britishers out of the land. Therefore, towards the evening of the 17th of July, the city of Hyderabad actually rose and ran with shouts of 'Deen, Deen !' to release their imprisoned leaders and, following the (green) flag signifying independence, rushed at the British Residency." (1-504)

numbers in June and a programme of rebellion from 17th July under the leadership of M. Allah-ud-Din was drawn up. Accordingly, 500 Rohillas and innumerable other Muslims[32] attacked the Residency under direction of this Maulvi and the subedar Turrebaz Khan. The Nizam's forces did not stop them. (77-55) Both leaders were then arrested and awarded life sentences. The subedar was later killed when he made an attempt to break out of prison, and his dead body was hung in chains for a few days in a busy square for the public to view. (14-171)

The Nizam, although sympathetic towards his subjects, had overtly supported the British and assisted them in suppressing the revolt in his state. The British gratefully record that had the Nizam not sided with them but declared *Jihad* instead, it might not have taken Hyderabad too long to become another Lucknow, and South India to be engulfed in the flames of rebellion. (64-64, 66, 9, 71q.)

Aurangabad : Revolt of Muslim Cavalry

It is said that "the honour for pioneering the Hyderabad uprising goes to Aurangabad." (14-133) The 3rd cavalry was on its way north from Ambajogai via Aurangabad. While they took a halt in Aurangabad on 12th June, news was received that the British were on the retreat in Delhi. The cavalry, thereupon, refused to ride to Delhi in conflict with their religion and the Emperor, and raised the flag of rebellion. Their slogan was 'Nizam ki sarhad ke bahar nahi jayenge aur Deen ke upar kamar nahi bandhenge [or, 'we shall neither go outside the Nizam's territories nor act against religion (i.e. Islam)].' (136) The two other cavalry platoons in the town also assumed the same stand and all of them entered the city shouting slogans of war against the British. The local population also lent its support. (155-105) The flag of religion (of course 'Green') was hoisted. (155-105; 14-134) Troopers of the cavalry, under command of Chhedi Khan, tied strips of green cloth on their arms and rebelled on the night of 13th June. (155-105)

---

32. A British Officer described this mob as : "an ocean of human faces, exhibiting ferocity in its worst forms." (155-114q.)

This revolt, engineered by Muslim cavalry troopers, was suppressed on 23rd June by other troopers brought in from outside. Ringleaders were Amir Khan, Mir Fida Ali, Muhammad Hashim, Chhedi Khan, Waheed Khan and some others. Amir Khan escaped. Mir Fida Ali was sentenced to death by being blasted by cannon. Many were arrested and put on trial. Divekar provides names of many horsemen who took part.[33] (109)

The cavalry unit at Buldhana rebelled under leadership of Chheda Khan on 24th. This 'revolt' involved nothing more serious than the risaldar and fifteen horsemen deserting from the camp. (107)

Andhra Pradesh : Muslim Revolt

Wall posters in Telugu containing matter with the following import were displayed in the second week of August in Vishakhapatnam in Andhra Pradesh: "Under the orders of the Emperor of Delhi, the people of Mahomed (i.e. the Prophet), do, on this 21st July 1857, hereby openly notify to the rich inhabitants of Vizagapatnam attached to the (E.I.) Company, that the said Company, who were always obedient to the Emperor of Delhi have, with the ambition of subduing all the country, done many injustices. There is not the least doubt of their quitting this country. With the assistance which we expect from the Emperor, we the people of Mahomed remaining in the Company's Territories will destroy several towns." (155-42)

Rohilas began forays into Cuddapah and Kurnool districts as soon as the June rebellion broke out. In one such attack, 400 of them looted the village of Rudravaram on 15th June and

---

33. Divekar begins a separate section giving details of the Aurangabad rebellion by discussing the Wahabi movement. Stating that, "For a long time before 1857, there prevailed anti-British feelings and like activities in different areas in the Nizam's Territory. The Wahabis had planned a widespread uprising in 1839." (155-103) He further refers to the context of the Wahabi agitation. (155-103) In a nutshell, this rebellion stemmed from Wahabi teachings.

escaped Hyderabad territory. (83) They belonged to the same group of Rohilas who later attacked the Residency in Hyderabad on 17th July. (84) Several other villages also received their attention. (84)

The rich town of Cuddapah was "an important Muslim centre, and insurgent leaders there looked to Hyderabad for their signal and instructions. (155-84) The British were aware that a revolt was likely to occur. Shaikh Pir Shah was the rebel leader there, and had garnered support of local Maulvis. Mufti Sadramin and M. Syed Abdul Aziz Hussain were among them. He used to say that British power would soon cease and a repentant Nizam would join their cause, and tried to win support of Hindu sepoys. He was later arrested.

Eleven persons were arrested on charges of treasonable offences at Rajahmundry in Andhra Pradesh on 21st August 1857. All of them were Muslim. (120) A local British official, in his report to superiors, wrote: "I am now endeavouring to obtain further evidence against the accused, but have small hopes of success, as all those who know anything of the plot, are, of course, Mahomedans and they will not give evidence against their coreligionists." (155-121) The conspiracy extended to Machilipatnam and Guntur.[34]

As Muslims in Machilipatnam were in close contact with their fellows in Hyderabad, signs of revolt began to be apparent as soon as the revolt occurred in Hyderabad. (124) A week earlier, that is on 10th July, a green flag[35] was hoisted at the parade ground. Fastened to the flag was a poster containing an appeal to kill all Englishmen. (124)

Mysore

Tipu Sultan had died in 1799, but still commanded immense fascination among Muslims in Mysore. Their urge for independence had not withered. (31) The 1806 rebellion at

---

34. Divekar writes that "the 'plot' was of general nature involving a large number of men, especially Muslims." (155-121)

35. Divekar glorifies it as 'a green flag of Independence'. (155-124)

Vellore had been engineered by these same people, in which 800 rebels had been killed. (90) Mussalmans had not forgotten the glorious days of Tipu. (155-31) As we have seen, due note of the Muslim conspiracy of 1857 in Mysore was taken in the statement issued by the Madras government. A leader, Zain-ul-Abideen, had been moving around in the Mysore, Kurnool and Madras regions with plans for rebellion. He wrote letters of very treasonable nature.[36] (33) Fierce rebellion took place during the 1857 Uprising at various places in the Mysore state as well as in the city. (34) The Hindu Maharaja assisted the British in every possible way to suppress those revolts and, on one occasion, even provided 2,000 troopers. The British repeatedly expressed their gratitude for Maharaja Krishnaraj's loyalty and help. (34, 5)

Muslim Conspiracy at Belgaum

Muhammad Hussain was the key leader in the Belgaum uprising. He was a disciple of the chief of Wahabis in Poona, Nur-ul-Huda who had dispatched envoys to the southern regions including Belgaum, Zain-ul-Abideen being one such. These people were engaged in inciting platoons in their respective areas to rebel. About these letters, Divekar writes: "They showed how widespread was the organization and how large in number the sepoys in south India in every army station were ready to join the war of Independence." (80) Muhammad

---

36. In narrating the Mysore uprising, Divekar quotes the following noting from an administrative report: "Letters of the most treasonable and seditious character were intercepted from Aurangabad, Bhopal, Ahmedabad, Belgaum, Kurnool and Mysore." (155-33) It is clear that the Mysore incident was part of a larger conspiracy masterminded by Muslims in all parts of South India. However, he also cites a report by Maj. Jacobs, according to which Nanasahib had apparently sent envoys to Chimasahib at Kolhapur, one of whom had visited other areas in the south and finally returned after paying a call at Mysore to report that support of 40 platoons was secured. (33) We have seen elsewhere how such things were being routinely done by others in Nanasahib's name.

Hussain, who had engaged in extensive conspiratorial correspondence with numerous parties, was executed on 14th August 1857 by cannon shot. (80)

The 8th cavalry at Bangalore revolted by refusing to go to Kurnool. The administration prosecuted six subedars, five of them were Muslim. (138)

Madras

We have already reviewed the official government statement about the rebellion-prone situation in Madras. Proclamations had been published in January 1857 calling upon all true believers to rise against the English infidels. It was told that the English were bent upon appropriating the possessions of the Muhammedans, and hence there was but one way of resisting their encroachments – a holy war.[37] (68-499) Divekar writes: "From the early days of the war of Independence in 1857, Madras became an important centre in South India where anti-British activities, both in the army and among the civilians, were organized. Many activists from Madras also instigated those in other areas to join the freedom struggle. Thus Sultan Bukhsh went from Madras to Chingleput, in July 1857, to help the Uprising. (155-46) This Sultan Bukhsh hailed from the Emperor's family. (131) Workers from Madras had been present at the 12th June meeting at the Mecca Masjid

---

37. Savarkar writes: "In Madras, in the beginning of the year 1857, the following Proclamation began to appear from the walls of the city : 'Countrymen and faithful adherents of your religion, rise, rise ye, one and all, to drive out the Firangi *Kafirs* ! There is only one remedy now, to free India from the insufferable tyranny of the *Kafir* Firangis, and that remedy is to wage a bloody war. This is *Jihad* for independence. Those who fall in such battles will be their country's *shaheeds.* Opened wide are the doors of Heaven for the *shaheeds.* But Hell is burning fierce to engulf (cowards). Countrymen, of these, which would ye have ? Choose now, even now !'" (1-89)

Dr. Mujumdar says, "This was a handiwork" of M. Ahmad Shah (who later came to Lucknow and began to be regarded as the 'crown jewel' of the Uprising). "Madras did not prove a fruitful soil for his propaganda. So he turned his attention to North India."(68-499)

in Hyderabad and had interrupted proceedings to demand a decision to fight the British. They had managed to escape from the clutches of the police. (forty-six) Sepoys of the Madras Cavalry were moving freely in Hyderabad on 17th June without permission from their superiors. (46) Madras had revolutionary links also with other centers in the south, like Belgaum, Kolhapur etc. (155-47)

Extremely treasonable posters were put up in Madras.[37] Leaders of the rebellion, Amir Khan, Ghulam Gaus and Shaikh Mannu, were in the forefront. The first could not be apprehended, but the other two were arrested and awarded life sentence. (49) In Madras, the rebel troops raised the shouts of "Long Live the Padshah of Delhi." (32-100)

Of course, the British had prepared in advance against an eventuality of rebellion and did not allow one to break out. As to why a large scale rebellion did not happen, Valbezen writes: "The Mahomedan sepoys (here) no doubt entertained a secret sympathy for the cause of the Mutineers; but living at a greater distance than their Bengal comrades from the centre of the traditions of the Mughal Empire, they did not share their impatient longing to throw off the yoke of the European conquerors." (70-175)

In short, while no rebellion like the north took place in South India, it can be seen that where tremors were felt, conspiracies discovered or a few actually occurred, they were generally of the nature of a Muslim uprising. The statement issued by the Madras government provides a guideline in this context.

Wahabi (Waliullahi) Center in Poona

The fountainhead for the uprising in Maharashtra was Poona. In Divekar's words, "In 1857, the Wahabis in Western India had an active centre in Pune, whose chief was Maulvi Nurul Huda, who then lived in Sadar Bazar in Pune. Wahabis were then organizing a strong anti-British movement in India. Nurul Huda, the chief, sent his disciples from Pune as emissaries to different British army stations like Kolhapur, Belgaum etc., to organize revolts there. He had his many disciples also in the 27th N.I. Regiment at Kolhapur. One of his emissaries, a Munshi (Muhammad Hussain)[38] sent from Pune, was later apprehended in Belgaum and executed there by the British on 14th August 1857. Later, Nurul Huda, the Wahabi leader in Pune, himself for his 'treasonable' activities and his correspondence with the men at Belgaum, Kolhapur, etc., was arrested and imprisoned in jail at Thane."[39] (155-65)

It does not require much time to unravel identities of the real instigators of the Uprising in Western India once it is appreciated that Nur ul Huda was the 'Wahabi chief of Western India', and the overall preeminence of Wahabis in the 1857 Uprising is considered.

Huda was in correspondence, in connection with organizing a revolt, with people in the Maratha country as well as with Muslim leaders in Hyderabad. (77-180)

Poona became restive once news of the Meerut revolt was received. "On Friday, of 22nd May 1857, for example, Jaffer Mulla, Mahomed Hayat, Hussain Arab, Imam Pattewala and Jamaluddin offered prayers in the Jama Masjid in Pune for the success of the freedom fighters at Delhi. The whole party besought the help of the Prophet on behalf of the Mutineers." (155-62) Prayers were offered on behalf of the rebels for help from the Prophet. (62)

---

38. Without stating his name, Savarkar writes: "The above-named munshi was a government servant and incriminating letters from him were found on the Sepoys at Poona and Kolhapur. So, on the evidence of these, he was blown from the mouth of a canon." (1-501)

39. Without mentioning the name of this Maulvi, Savarkar wrote, "In the inquiry held in respect of Uprising at Kolhapur it was revealed that the Wahabi Maulvi residing at Pune had sent secret emissaries and conspired with the rebel leaders at Kolhapur and other parts of Maharashtra." [However, this statement which appears in his original Marathi book (p.390) does not appear in its English version.]

Kolhapur Uprising

The 27th Infantry Regiment at Kolhapur rebelled on 31st July 1857. "The sepoys of the Regiment had established links with revolutionaries in other parts of the country. Consultations for planning the revolt were held with the men of the Belgaum Regiment." (155-163) They were led by Ramji Shirsat. (163) He deserted along with 200 sepoys on that day, looting the treasury on the way, attacking bungalows of some Englishmen and shouting slogans like 'Maro firangi ko'. (156-258; 155-164) Protection was afforded to British officers by forces belonging to the local British-loyalist Raja. (156-258) The rebels took control of the town on the following day. Thereafter, British troops were brought in to suppress the revolt. Many rebel sepoys were arrested and punished. (155-166)

Despite the fact that a Hindu had led the revolt here, its connection with Wahabis cannot be overlooked. Work had been going on for many days on their behalf to induce rebellious tendencies among sepoys. Their main center was at Poona with a branch at Belgaum. Nur-ul Huda's disciple at Belgaum, Muhammad Hussain, had done the work of spreading the disaffection among Kolhapur sepoys with co-operation from Abdul Rahman, a subedar in the platoon. Correspondence was going on between the two. (175) Letters calling for rebellion were also sent to civilians. (177)

Here is a sample of what those letters were: "Fakir Sahib[40] has been prohibited from visiting the camp owing to some information supplied by a traitor. The regiments are all ready. They will suddenly make a night attack on the fort and seize it. You do the same there (at Kolhapur) also. Here they are all disturbed and agitated and are looking out for cry of 'Deen'. Let there be no delay. We are all ready here. This is the opportunity for us. There is again no European regiment and Christian themselves are few in number here. The

---

40. This man was probably a Wahabi Maulvi who frequented cantonments to spread rebellion among sepoys.

Maulvisahib[41] has written a letter to Raja Balwantrao. I have sent its answer by the same man together with an account of affairs here. I also sent to you letters which had been received from Madras. This is no time for delay. Now you know everything. The Raja of Shorapur is also ready with his army...." (156-267) Two subedars of the platoon, Imam Khan and Daud Baig, told sepoys that they would be issued fat-smeared cartridges on 10th August 1857. (155-168) Hawaldars Shaikh and Chand Khan, in fact, even said that the consignment of cartridges had reached Kolhapur.[42] (176, 7) Subedar Daud Baig, too, was in correspondence with Satara and Belgaum. (168) It was this Daud Baig who had conveyed news about the cartridges to sepoys in Belgaum. (168) These people had also weaned Hindu civilians of Kolhapur to their side.

The second rebellion in Kolhapur occurred in December 1857 when, at dawn on the 6th, sepoys under command of Godaji Naik and Bhausaheb Ghatge, suddenly attacked and took control of the city. They issued a threat of opening cannon fire and destroying the palace if the British loyalist Raja did not surrender. But British forces regained control the following day. Many rebels were arrested and severely punished. (155-182; 156-259) Chimasahib, younger brother of the Raja, was arrested four months later on 31st March 1858 on suspicion of complicity and sent to Karachi on 12th May.

This was perhaps the only revolt in the south that might be said to have achieved some success. Editors of the Maharashtra Government Publication state: "Kolhapur is the only place in Western India where the sepoys had rebelled

---

41. The Maulvi was from Kolhapur. It is evident that he took efforts to wean the Raja to his side. It is to be noted that Muhammad Hussain had sent the reply on behalf of the Raja. It throws light upon their relation and the nature of the revolt there.

42. In fact, nothing of the sort had occurred. Issue of cartridges was suspended after the Meerut incident. These were mere rumours intended to incite sepoys.

as a part of the plan made by the leaders of 1857 Rebellion." (156-258) A notable aspect was the large participation of Hindus. An interesting feature was rumours put abroad during the period. Cartridges, of course, was one of those rumours but several others about Nanasahib were rife: his imminent arrival with a huge army; Chimasahib's assurance to Nana's envoys that the native British army in south Maharashtra and north Karnataka was under their control; Nana's gift of a sword to Chima, and the like. (155-182, 4; 156-259) All of this was propagated just for creating 'atmosphere'.

However, nothing of this kind was ever likely to happen. At this time in the north, Nanasahib was himself neck deep in trouble, having gone underground since 16th July and fled to the Begum of Lucknow for refuge. There was absolutely no possibility that he could have gone to South India. And, having himself laid down his sword in despair, it was a far cry for him to send one for Chimasahib.[43] It is clear that such tales were being fed to Hindus to induce them to rebel. Keeping in mind that others were issuing even declarations in Nana's name, it is easy to imagine who might have been behind such propaganda. [44]

---

43. The description of that 'sacred' Bhawani sword: "a silver-handled sword, with the blade of waving or serrated edge, covered with Shia religious inscriptions in gold....(sent) from the Lucknow Durbar." (155-184) Is it not amazing that Nanasahib, who respected the hallowed tradition of Shivaji's Bhawani sword, should present such a sword to Chimasahib?

44. Dr. S. B. Chaudhary, too, writes, "The Mahomedan population of Belgaum formed a conspiracy which had its ramifications at Kolhapur, Hyderabad and at Poona. Kolhapur was 65 miles distant from Belgaum. Malleson says that the regiments in these stations and also the one at Dharwar were showing symptoms of mutiny and were in communication for a simultaneous action. They were secretly supported by the discontented chiefs and openly by the Mahomedans. Accordingly, the 27th (regiment) at Kolhapur rose in arms on 31 July (1857)." (81-230)

Proclamation in Nana's Name

The following episode is an apt illustration of how it was attempted to incite people in those parts by making statements as Nanasahib's. It is said that a certain Rangrao Pagay of Narkhed (Hyderabad) had visited Kanpur in 1857–58 and obtained from Nanasahib several edicts, almost identical in nature and calling for a rebellion, addressed to various persons. Those stated: "To Jagirdars, Deshmukhs, Deshpandes, Patils, Kulkarnis, etc., and the soldiers, officers and to the general public, residing in the districts of Sholapur, Ahmednagar (etc.) in the Deccan. Be it known to you that Hindus and Muslims in North India, out of regard for their faith (*Deen*), have revolted against the British Government, and in order to make them quit this country, have killed Englishmen everywhere in their military camps. Such a revolt has not taken place in your districts. It is hereby ordered, therefore, that Shri Rangrao Ratnakar Pagay of Narkhed and Sonaji Pant of Hyderabad have been charged with the responsibility of organizing effective resistance in those parts. You are, therefore, enjoined to act in the name of your faith (*Deen*) and destroy the Englishmen wherever they may be found...." (155-23; 14-144) (Words in brackets have been reproduced exactly as they appear in the original Marathi book.)

It is dated 18th April 1858. (155-22) Some supplementary information in this regard is as follows: A certain Sonaji Pant was a record officer to Raje Rai Rayan, a jagirdar of the Hyderabad state. He wrote to Nanasahib for organizing a rebellion, his letter being carried by this Rangrao to Kanpur in February 1857. Meeting Nana at Barvathoda, 40 miles west of Lucknow, he returned to Hyderababd after February 1859 along with those edicts addressed to various people. Sonaji Pant had died in the meanwhile. With those edicts in his possession, Rangrao then met the various addressees as an envoy of Nanasahib. He was rendered valuable assistance in this task by Safdar-ud-Dowllah and Shaikh Madar. Safdar-ud-Dowllah was himself one of the recipients of the edicts. Shaikh Madar did the work of carrying messages to and from Deshmukhs, Deshpandes and others. Safdar-ud-Dowllah had readied 25,000 rockets for use on the battlefield. The British confiscated some letters from Rangrao and he was awarded a life sentence along with Safdar-ud-Dowllah. (155-22 to 4; 14-143 to 51)

It does not seem possible for the following reasons that Nanasahib could have issued and entrusted those edicts to Rangrao:

1. Not much is known about who this Sonaji Pant was, or what was his importance and status. (14-51) It, therefore, seems unlikely that Nanasahib would have issued edicts only on the strength of a single letter from him.
2. When the plan for the Uprising was not yet disclosed even in North India in February 1857, it is most unlikely that Sonaji Pant could have anticipated or thought about it sitting in Hyderabad, and advised Nanasahib accordingly.
3. Rangrao left Hyderabad in February 1857, met Nana in April 1858 (since the letters are dated April 1858) and returned to Hyderabad after February 1859. This period of two years is suspect.
4. According to Rangrao's claim, he met Nana at Barvathoda. In Pagdi's opinion, this might have been 'Brahmavarta'. (148) (It could be an incorrect English rendering of 'Bithoor'). It is interesting to note that Nana was neither at Bithoor nor Kanpur during that period. He had left these places permanently on 16th July 1857 and had gone underground. Hence it is improbable that he could ever have met Rangrao, and that too at Bithoor.
5. The northern uprising was on the decline on the date of the edicts, it being almost certain that the British would prevail, and by the time Rangrao returned to Hyderabad, everything was over. It was futile issuing such edicts at such a juncture. Moreover, false information about having killed all Englishmen in northern cantonments was suicidal. People in the south were certain to be misled by it.

6. Obviously nobody had given any serious heed to Rangarao, and Nana's edicts were totally ignored by all and rendered ineffectual.
7. How had Nana, sitting in Kanpur, been able to think up names of all the recipients of the numerous edicts in the south? It is obvious that those names were added subsequently.
8. Reference to 'Deen' appearing in them is most significant.

To sum up, all those edicts were prepared by someone else in Nanasahib's name in order to incite Hindus in the south to rebel.

Naik of Shorapur Misled by Muslims

The example of Raja Venkatappa Naik of Shorapur in Gulbarga district would suffice to illustrate how chiefs in South India had been incited to rebel. This Naik rose against the British with a large force.

Events unfolded thus: "He was told that the English had lost everything and were flying to England, that the Arabs and Rohillas of Hyderabad and all the Mussalmans had declared a crusade against the English, and the Brahmans from Pune promised by their incantations to make him Raja of the whole country from Shorapur to Rameshwar. Hopes were also held out for a general rising of the Marathas. The Raja collected a force, about 5000–7000 strong, consisting of Arabs, Rohillas and Bedars, and attacked the British camp at night on Feb. 7, 1858. As soon as British reinforcement arrived, he surrendered." (67-64) He spoke out his mind after arrest: "One of the Arabs and Rohilas who assembled around me told me on oath on the Quran that Muslims in India had declared a religious war against the English. Even the native troops stationed at Madras were not going to support the British and were going to join up with me as soon as I had risen." (14-176)

The Naik rebelled by trusting all of this. He was sentenced to death by hanging. Possibly because the Government felt the man had been tricked, the sentence was commuted first to life imprisonment and then to four years. But later, out of a feeling of remorse and humiliation, he chose to end his life. The leader of the Arabs and Rohilas, Tasdiq Hussain, who had put the Naik in the forefront, was hanged at a public square in Shorapur. (177)

Satara

Rango Bapuji is regarded as the kingpin of the rebellion in Satara. The claim that he had, for this purpose, kept in close contact with Nanasahib does not seem true. This is because Rango Bapuji's work for rebellion had been between December 1856 and June 1857, whereas Nanasahib had conceded, albeit under pressure from rebel sepoys, to join the revolt at Kanpur only after 6th June 1857. Rango Bapuji was, on his own, preparing for a revolt in Satara but that could not have been related to Nanasahib in any way.

Rango Bapuji had plans of rising in December 1856 by bringing in 40,000 Rohilas (and not Maratha Mavalas!). (155-7) The kingdom was Maratha, but its freedom fighters were going to be Rohilas! The government got wind of this plan on 11th June and immediately arrested him along with many belonging to the group. The uprising did not happen. Rango Bapuji escaped from prison but was never heard of again. (155-191,3; 156-8, 11)

Thus, the rebellion in Maharashtra, too, was similar to others in South India. While actual rebellions were few, the conspiracies that came to light were identical in inspiration to those in North India. Their aim was reestablishment of the Mughal Emperor of Delhi. The kingpin of the uprising in Poona, the erstwhile capital of the Maratha Empire and the Peshwas, was a Waliullahi Wahabi while the fate of Satara, where resided the Chhatrapati, was entrusted to Rohilas. Even if all this seems astounding, it was in complete consonance with the general nature of the 1857 uprising!

* * *

Chapter 8

Jihadi Proclamations During the Uprising

After the fire-worshippers and Christians shall have held sway over the whole of Hindustan for a hundred years, and when injustice and oppression shall prevail in their Government, an Arab prince shall be born, who will ride forth triumphantly to slay them.

(– a prophesy current during the Uprising, according to which British power was to end after a century of the Battle of Plassey of 1757.) (72-28n)

Major Source of Causes and Nature of the Uprising

"After the outbreak of violence in 1857, proclamations were issued by many of the Indian leaders calling upon the people to support them against the British. These proclamations constitute a major source of evidence for the causes of the Uprisings, and are among the few documents we have from the Indian, in contrast to the British, point of view."[1] - (Ainslie T. Embree) (55-1)

---

1. Savarkar writes: "These Proclamations were not issued by

(Contd.)

The proclamations are a useful source for answers to questions like, what kind of appeals had been made to the public; what was the motive for the revolt; what was the nature of Uprising? They had all been published with the intention of inciting and inspiring civilians and sepoys alike. One of the motives of a majority of those publications was to bring Hindus and Muslims together for a common cause. Muslim and Hindu leaders of the period of the revolt, or rulers, administrators and Maulvis had published their proclamations independently. Some of them had issued more than one, with minor changes that were deemed expedient. Likewise, some of them were appeals to other Rajas and chiefs while others were in the nature of directives to their own subordinates and officials.

Original proclamations were mainly in Persian. Others might have been issued in Urdu. We have, however, referred to translations in English. Because of religious terminology and metaphor used by their authors, translations are sometimes incapable of reflecting originally intended meanings. For instance, the word 'God' appearing in renderings in English must have been 'Khuda' or 'Allah' in the original. Such translation, therefore, is incorrect. However, some translations do retain the words 'Khuda' or 'Allah' as they must have appeared in originals, which is more logical and meaningful from the point of view of understanding the core import of the text. Also, the correct translation of 'Deen' is not merely 'any religion', but 'Islam'. We have retained the original rendering.

Some proclamations are undated, but their probable period can be estimated from internal evidence. It is likely they had been deliberately left undated to be used at any time and still appear as if they had just been issued. Of course, the absence of dates does not hamper one's understanding of the nature thereof.

---

nonentities; but they were orders issued from adorable and powerful thrones. They were burning expressions of the agitated feelings of the time. In these the real heart of the Nation had spoken out, when at the time of war, there was no occasion to conceal real sentiments through pressure or fear." (1-9)

Some of the more significant proclamations and declarations issued during the period were as follows.

Proclamation by the Shah of Persia, as distributed in Delhi

As early as in March 1857, this Proclamation issued by Shah Nasiruddin of Persia had been posted at various places in Delhi. It reads:

"Let it be known that the English Government first planted their victorious standard in India, and step by step subjugated all the powerful princes of the Eastern provinces. Some short time ago they conquered Afghanistan, but relinquished it in consequence of what they suffered from the restless turbulence of the Afghans. After this they took possession of the cities of Lahore and Peshawar, and of other free and independent countries.... Shah Nasiruddin, King of Persia, therefore, has the greatest pleasure in making the following *Proclamation*.

"Let all the troops assemble at the different places on the frontiers of Persia to resist these enemies professing an antagonistic faith. It behoves the Arab tribes to act up to the precepts of the Prophet. It is now necessary that old and young, high and low, wise and foolish, peasant and soldier, should all without hesitation rise to the assistance of their coreligionists, assume arms, raise the Mahomedan standard declare in the name of God — a religious war of extermination.

"I have sent an army of 1.1 lac soldiers under four Nobles. These forces have been thus distributed, that they may conquer the provinces of Afghanistan and then move onwards. They (names of four Commanders) have been appointed to join in the conquest of India. It is fully to be expected, from God's blessing, that they will be victorious.

"Accordingly, now it is the time for all the tribes of Afghanistan, and the inhabitants of India, who believe in the Quran, and walk in the precepts of God's Prophet, to join openly in the religious war of extermination, to stand by their faith, and to hold out the hand of support to their brother Mahomedans, for by doing so they will reap advantages both temporal and eternal. It is incumbent on all Mussalmans to assist with zeal and energy in this matter. Moreover, let it be known that it is no intention of the King of Persia to conquer and annex Afghanistan (or India) as a dependency; but that, on the contrary, his real desire is that India should be subject to the house of Taimur.

"It is incumbent on the (Afghanistan's) Amir Dost Muhammad Khan personally that he should assist the Mahomedans, acting up to the traditional precept of the Prophet that he who will assist a member of his faith will receive a good reward for doing so.

"Hitherto, previous to the publication of this notice, Amir Dost Muhammad Khan always used to say, that if the armies of Persia should go against a people of a different religion, he would join them with armies and money. It is manifest that now the time he used to speak of, has arrived, that is, that I have declared war against the English solely in defence of the faith. Let the Amir Dost Khan now remember his promise and join me against the enemies of the Mussalmans. If he is killed he will be exalted to the dignity of a martyr, and if he lives he will be called a defender of the faith. In every point of view a religious war of extermination is the most meritorious undertaking.

"But (God forbid it should be so !) if the Amir acts in a different way, first, he will have denied his religion; second, he will be disgraced in the estimation of the world; third, he will be called a coward; and fourth, the wrath of God is certain to visit him.

"The Amir evinced much respect for this letter, and resolved on coming in this direction himself accompanied by the Chief of Swat. The King of Persia has entered Herat, and the troops at Kandahar have totally cut up the English, who had gone forward in advance." (107-318 to 26)

Whether it was actually written and sent by the Persian monarch or had been prepared in India, it may easily be imagined how much excitement and provocation it must have instilled in the Muslim sentiment in the country in general and Delhi in particular.[2] It throws much light upon the nature of 1857 uprising.

The Emperor's Proclamations

Many declarations had been published in Bahadur Shah's name in the period between his enthronement on 11th May and defeat on 20th September 1857. Although many of these had been issued on his behalf by his courtiers or leaders of rebel sepoys, they are vital for a clear understanding of the motives and nature of the Uprising.

1. The following *firman* (Imperial decree) was issued under his seal at the *durbar* (court) held on the day following his enthronement:

"To all the Hindus and Mussalmans of India:

"Taking my duty by the people into consideration at this hour, I have decided to stand by my people.... It is the imperative duty of Hindus and Mussalmans to join the revolt against the English....(But) before doing so, they should get themselves armed and declare war on the English." (69-56)

Historians conclude in the context of this decree that, "The *Firman* must....have been issued by the Nationalists (rebels) who would have encountered not much difficulty in getting it signed by the King." (56)

2. A second declaration, addressed to rulers and citizens, was then issued:

---

2. News of the imminent arrival of Persian forces had been doing the rounds even as late as 23rd August 1857. There spread the spurious rumours that the Persian Army was coming to save the rebels, that it had fought its way through Afghanistan and into India via Peshawar, and was crossing the Indus at Attock. Another seaborne assault of Iranian troops was said to be on its way via Bombay. (154-322) The *Delhi Urdu Akhbar*, a pro-Emperor paper, commented at the end of this news "It is not an impossibility." (322)

"All you Rajas are protectors of your own faith and the faith of others. God has given you bodily existence to defend your faith.[3] It is, therefore, incumbent that you should destroy those who harm your religion.[3]

"The English have been overthrowing religions through various means. They have adopted systematic policy to destroy the religions and cultures of India by introducing remarriage of widows, stopping of the *Sati* system, propagating Christianity, by introducing the law that only legitimate son of the ruler would be recognized as heir-apparent, forcing the prisoners to eat bread cooked in a common kitchen, supplying atta (wheat flour) in the market mixed with crushed bones and supplying sugar whitened with bones. They have now introduced new orders of biting the grease cartridges. It is my conviction now that if the English continue their rule in India, they would kill all of us and destroy our religion.

"You *Hindus are solemnly adjured by your faith in Ganges, Tulsi and Saligram and all you Mussalmans by your belief in God and* Quran, that it is your bounden duty to kill the English and thus protect your religion and yourself..." (60)

The conclusion of historians is that, "Mirza Mughal was almost certainly behind (this) circular sent out in Zafar's name." (154-220)

It is sufficiently clear from the contents of this declaration that the Uprising had occurred mainly for Islamic concerns.

---

3. It is stated in the Quran: *"I have created....men merely so that they should worship Me (i.e. Allah)." (51:56)* (Of course, worship of Allah is the same as 'following the religion of Islam'.) *"Strive hard in the cause of Allah with all the striving that is due to Him; it is He who has elected you for that cause". (22:78) " And fight them until there is no more persecution and there prevails religion for Allah." (2:193, 270) '...persecution is worse than slaughter.' (2:191)* (Here, the essential meaning of persecution is '*Kufr*'. (128-420))

The negligible effect of reasons pertaining to Hindu concerns mentioned in it, had been added only to gain Hindu support; it has been discussed in Chapter 4. In actual fact, conversion activities of Christians posed no threat to Muslims either. It was only with the aim of recovering political power that recourse to spreading the apprehension, 'Islam is in danger', had been taken. From their point of view, this document was nothing but a *Jihad* declaration in the sense of a struggle for religion.

Presented in the above quotation, are two significant issues that are not clearly discernible from a superficial perusal, but become obvious after a deep study.

Purpose of Human Birth

First, the belief that God brings man into existence for the sake of religion, which he is then expected to protect by killing rivals, is an Islamic concept. Doctrinal support for this may be found in the Quran and *Hadis.* On the other hand, such a concept is absent in Hindu thought, according to which religious conduct becomes a necessary adjunct of life because man is born. It is not for religion that the Hindu takes birth, nor indeed does God grant him human existence for that purpose. Therefore, an appeal to Hindus on the basis of this concept was, from the aspect of their religious world view, both unacceptable and inapplicable.

'Religious war' that Hindu thought envisages, too, is essentially different from *Jihad.* Indeed, Hindus are commanded by their religion to fight injustice and persecution, but not by viewing someone as guilty of those crimes just because he is not of their religion. Polytheism ('*shirk*'), according to Islam, is the greatest crime and injustice. (31:13; 4:48, 116) *'Those who disbelieve in the revelations of Allah they are wrongdoers / liars / ingrate." (2:154; 21:77; 29:47; 31:32; 40:4)* Contrastingly, the Hindu religion sanctions all religions, besides doctrines of monotheism, polytheism and deems that all these lead to God. It accepts the right of someone not to be a Hindu, and does not prescribe holy war against him for that reason alone. Likewise, there is no doctrine among Hindus commanding the killing of others because their religious propagation or movement might be detrimental to their own. Had all these things been so, would Hindus not have declared and waged a holy war during the entire period of erstwhile Muslim rule? Even Shivaji, who fought Muslim regimes to free Hindudom from the threat of extinction, had neither declared 'holy war' nor ever issued orders to kill those who were a perceived source of detriment to his religion. On the contrary, he had assumed a stand that contemplated equal regard for all religions, with his opposition to Muslim rule being strictly on a political level. Thus, the mindset that prescribed killing the English or Christians was Jihadi in essence and alien to Hindus. During the 1857 Uprising, it had been foisted upon them by Muslim leaders.

Dissimilar Manner of Taking Oaths

The second significant issue was that Hindus were called upon to take oaths with 'Ganga, Tulsi and Shaligram' as sacrosanct objects, while Muslims by 'Khuda and the *Quran*'. Deep thinking on Islamic principles had obviously been done before prescribing these diverse methods of taking oaths. God is One and Only Allah and His Book, the One and Only Quran. Thus, to prescribe that Hindus would take oaths in the name of their God and the *Vedas* or the *Gita* as their scripture, was tantamount to conceding equal reverence for gods other than Allah and sacred writings other than the Quran. This was nothing less than the cardinal offence of '*shirk*'.[4] So, the presumed exclusive uniqueness and superiority of Islam had been expressed even in the Emperor's appeals for solidarity of Hindus.

For Religion Alone

3. The following declaration was issued on behalf of rebel sepoys in Delhi:

"To all Hindus and Mussalmans, citizens and servants of Hindustan, the Officers of the Army now at Delhi and

---

4. The same prescription is followed not just in this proclamation but in many others issued during the period, providing more than an inkling of who might have been their real authors.

Meerut send greeting : It is well known that in these days all the English have entertained the evil designs: first, to destroy the religion of the whole Hindustani Army, and then to make the people Christians by compulsion. Therefore we, solely on account of our religion, have combined with the people, and have not spared alive one infidel, and have reestablished the Delhi dynasty. Hundreds of guns and a large amount of the treasure have fallen into our hands; therefore, it is fitting that whoever of the soldiers and people dislike turning Christians should unite with one heart, and, acting courageously, not leave the seed of these infidels remaining." (68-513)

Here, too, 'religion' appears as the reason and uprooting and destroying the very seed of the *kafirs*, as the remedy. Hinduism does not regard any non-Hindu as a *Kafir*. Also, it is unlikely that having become accustomed to being referred as '*kafirs*' for several centuries, Hindus might have used the very same expletive for Christians. (They regarded the British as 'mlenchhas', which only means 'aliens'. '*Kafir*' is an altogether distinct concept.)

Here it is clearly stated that the Mughal dynasty had been reestablished after the Uprising at Delhi.

4. Besides this proclamation, sepoys of Delhi had issued two more. The first was addressed to native sepoys in Punjab and contained the following:

"To our brothers, Hindu and Mussalman, who are employed at Lahore and other places in Punjab,

"Salam ale kum and Ram Ram !

"It is a matter of great regret that although for the sake of our religion we revolted against the English and have killed all the European soldiers, the enemies of our faith, and through the kindness of God have been victorious, you, who are our relatives and...are our brothers in arms are sitting idly there. Such conduct is unbecoming. In whatever way you can, destroy the enemies of our religion and come to Delhi. All the revolting troops from Calcutta to Peshawar are collecting at Delhi. Thousands of Hindus and Mussalmans have joined us. Those who die in this battle will attain Ghazidom, if Mussalman and Baikunth (Heaven), if Hindus." (69-84)

This was nothing else than a *Jihadnama* identifying Christians as enemies of the religion. It is interesting to note that it appealed to Hindus and Muslims to fight on the same terrestrial battlefield despite the fact that they were believed to be destined for separate paradises in the event of their death in battle.

Kill Enemies of the Religion

5. Another declaration reads :

"To all the inhabitants, Hindus and Mussalmans.... Be it known : There are too many tyrannies (by the English) to be detailed here. Gradually, matters have come to such a pass that the Government aims at subverting our religion. Therefore, the whole army of Hindustan, both Hindu and Mussalman, from Calcutta to Peshawar, has risen up in arms. After all man dies but once. To die denying one's religion is disgraceful in both the worlds. Destruction of oppressors and enemies of faith is laudable in every creed. It is surely the right path to attain paradise.

"Therefore, all Hindus and Mussalmans, siding with the army, have assembled at Delhi and other places with the view of fighting for their religion. It has been decided by all that we should kill the enemies of our faith wherever found. For this contest is simply for the defence of religion. If our faith is preserved we have everything. Otherwise death any day is preferable.

"The force of the English consists of only four to five thousand Europeans of whom some are sick. Whoever plunders the enemy of our faith, however, will not be called to account, but will win a good name." (69-88)

The directive to 'kill the enemies of our faith wherever found' is most significant and requires no elucidation.

The Standard of Muhammed

6. All these declarations pertain to the early period of the Uprising (May-June 1857) when rebels were in complete control of Delhi. Later, on 25th August 1857, sepoys at Azamgarh published a proclamation in the Emperor's name. Known as the 'Azamgarh Declaration', it is long enough to fill 5 or 6 pages and spelled out British injustice done to various classes of people, calling upon them to join in the rebellion. It addressed five categories: zamindars, traders, government servants and soldiers, artisans and fakirs, pundits and intelligentsia. The several benefits that would accrue to all of them under self-rule after departure of the British were listed therein. For instance, that landholdings of zamindars would be restored to them had been enumerated as a benefit. It was stated, in the earlier part of the declaration, that:

> "It is well known to all, that in this age people of Hindoostan, both Hindus and Mahomedans, are being ruined under the tyranny and oppression of the infidel and treacherous English. It is, therefore, the bounden duty of all the wealthy people of India, especially of those who have any sort of connection with any of the Mahomedan royal families, and are considered the pastors and masters of their people, to stake their life and property for the well-being of the public. With the view of effecting this general good, several princes belonging to the royal family of Delhi, have dispersed themselves in the different parts of India, Iran, Turan and Afghanistan. That one of the aforesaid princes has, at the head of an army of Afghanistan, etc., made his appearance in India; and I, King of India... have, by the aid of the Mujahideens or religious fanatics, erected the standard of Muhammad, and persuaded the orthodox Hindus, who had been subject to my ancestors, and have been and are still accessories in the destruction of the English, to raise the standard of Maḥavir.
>
> "Several of the Hindu and Mussalman chiefs, have presented themselves to me, and taken part in the reigning

Indian crusade, and it is more than probable that I shall very shortly receive succours from the West (i.e. from the Muslim countries). That all (astrologers etc.) agree in asserting that the English will no longer have any footing in India or elsewhere. Therefore, it is incumbent on all to give up the hope of the continuation of the British sway, side with me, and deserve the consideration of the Badshahi....

"Lastly, be it known to all, that if any of you still cling to the British Government, all his estates shall be confiscated and his property plundered, and he himself, with his whole family shall be imprisoned, and ultimately put to death." (3-453 to 8; 55-3)

Notable aspects of the proclamation were references to relations with ruling Muslim families, help from Muslim countries and holy war against *kafirs*. It should also be noted that Hindus had been called 'accessories' in the *Jihad*.

A Special Official for Recruitment of Ghazis

7. It was stated in a proclamation issued on 11th August 1857 that:

"To – All Hindus and Mahomedans who wish the Advancement of Religion.

"Be it known to you! That Falakuddin Shah, being one of those who have pledged themselves to fight for the Mahomedan faith, the religious war against the infidels, and being director of Finance and the Army, is sent to collect *Ghazis* as well as money for the expenses of the armies bestowed by God, which have come here from all directions for the destruction of Christians; and which have already sent thousands of them to hell... You will, moreover, give the above named Falakuddin Shah such aid...for the slaughter of Christians, as he may demand. Those who will join in the cause of the faith and of religion, will receive distinctions; and those who will confederate with the Christians, will be utterly despoiled of life and property." (107-159)

Hindus, too, had been thereby called upon to assist in the *Jihad* to be waged for the sake of Muhammad's religion and, it would seem, that they were to go to Delhi as '*ghazis*'.

Islamic State: The Law of Shariat

The following two *firmans* (decrees) may be cited to illustrate the nature of directives that the Emperor had issued to his newly appointed Subedars:

1. He wrote to the Chief of Kachchh-Bhuj on 7th August:

"Muhammad Bakht Khan, Governor General Bahadur....affirmed that you, ever faithful one, having put the whole of the infidels to the sword, have thoroughly cleansed and purified your domains of their unclean presence. We have been extremely gratified to hear of such conduct on your part. Be assured of our kindness." (158)

2. The Nawab of Rohilkhand was sent an order on 9th July:

"Among other necessary things, you should also care to see that on all occasions and in all cases nothing should be done contrary to the *Shariat* or Mahomedan Law and everyone of the subjects and the soldiery should also strive in achieving this object." [5] (7-284) "By God's grace *Kufr* and *Shirk* have been purged from Hindustan and Islam has been established."[5] (320)

Nanasahib Peshwa's Proclamations

1. Nanasahib issued a proclamation on 1st July after his enthronement at Kanpur :

"As, by the bounty of the glorious Almighty God,[6] and the enemy-destroying fortune of the Emperor, the yellow-faced and narrow-minded people have been sent to hell, and Kanpur has been conquered, it is necessary that all the subjects and landholders should be as obedient

---

5. For comments see footnotes 7, 14 and 15 in Chap. 8.

6. Tnis is a typically *Quranic* manner of addressing Allah. However, Dr. Dhamdhere provides an equally typical 'Hindu' translation as, 'By the Grace of Ishvar'. (111-392)

to the present Government as they have been to the former one.... That it is the incumbent duty of all the ryots to rejoice in the thought that Christians have been sent to hell, and both the Hindu and Mahomedan religions have been confirmed... ." (6-602; 111-692)

It is clear that the proclamation was written in Islamic metaphor. 'Sending Christians to hell,' did not square with Nanasahib's religion. The belief that followers of certain religions were destined for hell was unacceptable to his faith. Why had Nanasahib, then, included it in his proclamation?

The answer is plain. Although it was Nanasahib who had been enthroned, his mentor and advisor, Azeemullah Khan, had held all real power along with rebel Muslim sepoys. Azeemullah could do anything he pleased because of the absolute power he enjoyed. (158-374) The proclamation had been issued from the headquarters located inside Noor Muhammad's hotel in Kanpur. Nana's policy to please Muslim sepoys, and eulogies to the Emperor was thus inevitable. It had been issued after the Satichaura massacre, with which affair Nanasahib had no connection whatsoever but, as is obvious from the contents, Azeemullah and Muslim sepoys had shifted its responsibility to him. The following proclamation will further clarify who were the actual authors of Nanasahib's proclamations.

2. It had been stated in a proclamation of 6th July, written in Persian and using the Hijri Era, that:

"A traveller just arrived at Kanpur from Calcutta states that before cartridges were distributed a council was held for the purpose of taking away the religion and rites of the people of Hindustan. The members of the council came to the conclusion that as the matter was one of affecting religion, seven or eight thousand Europeans would be required and it would cost the lives of 50,000 Hindustanis but that at this cost all the natives of Hindustan would become Christians. To this Queen Victoria gave her consent.[7]

---

7. A reference of similar import, but historically completely false, had also appeared in a proclamation by M. Ahmad Shah.

"A second council was then held. It was resolved there to ask for the assistance of a body of English troops equal in number to the native Army. When the dispatch containing this application was read in England, 35,000 Europeans were very rapidly embarked upon ships and started for Hindustan, and intelligence of their dispatch reached Calcutta. The English in Calcutta then issued the order for the distribution of the cartridges. The whole object of which was to make the native army Christians as it was thought that if the army were made Christians there would be no great delay in converting the people generally.

"Meanwhile, while they were occupied in carrying out the plan, the Ambassador (Vakil) of the Sultan of Turkey in London sent word to his Sovereign that 35,000 Europeans had been dispatched to Hindustan to christianize the natives. The Sultan of Turkey (May Allah perpetuate his kingdom)[8] issued a *firman* to the Pasha of Egypt...as follows: 'You are conspiring (for friendship) with Queen Victoria. This is not the time for peace, for I learn that 35,000 European soldiers have been dispatched to Hindustan for the purpose of forcibly converting the army and the people.

---

8. This is typical usage in the nature of greeting utilized in addressing the Khalifa. At that time, the Sultan of Turkey was, in principle, both the religious and political head of all Muslims throughout the world as Khalifa (Allah's representative on Earth). This greeting for him, which only Muslims would have used, has been ascribed to Nana.

Authors translate the original Persian greeting as: "May God give honour to his Kingdom"; (6-604) "May God perpetuate his sovereignty;" (70-493; 78-499; 67-134) "May Allah perpetuate his kingdom." (3-452) As the word 'Allah' appears for 'God' in one of these renderings, it is clear that it must have been used universally in the original. In another translation, the content in parentheses has been omitted as insignificant because the import of the greeting appearing in a Hindu Nana's proclamation was perhaps completely lost on the translator. (56-41)

If we neglect this matter what face shall we show to God[9] (*Khuda*) and this day will come upon us too one day, for if they succeed in christianizing natives of Hindustan, they will attack our country as well.'

"When this *firman* of the Sultan of Turkey reached the Pasha of Egypt, the Lord of Egypt assembled his army in the city of Alexandria (which was on the road to India) before the Europeans arrived. As soon as the European troops arrived, the troops of the Pasha of Egypt began to fire into them with guns on all sides and destroyed and sunk all the ships so that not even a single European escaped… .

"Thus the *Almighty* ('Haq Ta'ala' – a Mahomedan Title)[10] by the exercise of his power made an end of them at the very outset. When intelligence of the destruction of the Army from London arrived, the Governor General (at Calcutta) was much grieved and distressed and beat his head.

"Printed by order of Peshwa Bahadur, 13th Zilkad, 1273."[11]

In a meaningful comment, a newspaper of the time *The Friend of India,* quoting the entire text of the proclamation, wrote: "It is very remarkable for the Mahomedan tone and language used although issued by the Nana — a Hindu." (3-453)

It is obvious that the above proclamation had been issued in Nana's name by Muslims with only a formal consent from him. It must have been the handiwork of his advisor, Azeemullah, who knew Persian, had toured Turkey and other

---

9. In one English translation, the word 'Khuda' is mentioned in parentheses after the word 'God.' (3-452) It implies that the word used in the original document had been 'Khuda' or 'Allah'.

10. This explanation given in parentheses by the translator is very important. Here 'the Almighty' is the translation of original Persian word 'Haq Ta'ala.' So it is beyond doubt that this proclamation was drafted by someone well versed in Islam.

11. See: 3-453; 6-605; 56-41; 67-134; 70-494; 78-500.

lands and was known for his familiarity with international affairs. There was no need whatsoever for Nana's proclamation to contain references to an undue affinity for Muslim Empires like Turkey or Egypt on the one hand, and expressions of an equally unwarranted desire that the Turkish Khalifa's Empire may become strong, glorious or eternal, on the other. Apparent from this proclamation is an anxiety not just for Islam in India, but all over the world. It would almost seem that Nana's own apprehensions about the religious conversion of Hindu India were of no significance compared with what the Khalifa of Turkey or the Shah of Egypt, as portrayed in the proclamation, apparently perceived and felt as the real and greater threat to international Islam. The overall emerging picture is of a proclamation issued by Nanasahib expressing anxiety for international Islam. Virtually saying that the successful remedies were already being devised by the Khalifa, the Shah, and perhaps Allah Himself, it is amazing Nana omits to state what his own role was going to be in the entire matter. Evidently, giving his formal consent to proclamations authored in his name by Muslims was the only work left for him.

Who Perpetrated Those 'International' Falsehoods?

A second remarkable matter was the false nature of claims, like the army that had set out from London, the Turkish Khalifa's edict to the Egyptian Shah or the drowning of British forces in the sea. Nothing even remotely like this had happened. Fictions had been deliberately fabricated to incite Indian Muslims, which people trusted and the aim was achieved. Other rumours such as "Nanasahib has sought assistance from Russia for which people have urgently gone there, that Nanasahib will drive away all Englishmen to Calcutta and then establish his unhindered rule over India (158-362) were also floated in those days, which the sepoys believed. These rumours were spread by Azeemullah, (162) who was adept at such 'international' rumour mongering.

In a lengthy speech made by Azeemullah at a time when Nana was ruling, he had claimed that British rule over India was all but over; that he had visited England and knew more about its natives than anybody else, and had gone on to say:

"It (England) is a very small piece of an island, and very scantily populated; no more troops can be spared to send out to India. If it were not so, why would not more soldiers have been sent long ago? I have been to all their little villages and know it for a fact. What fools, then, we natives have made of ourselves, so quietly to surrender our country to a handful of tyrannical foreigners, who are trying in many ways to deprive us of our religion and our privileges ! It behoves us, therefore — and I call upon you all to join heart and hand – to extirpate our enemies, root and branch, from the face of all India. Let not a soul escape, let not the name of a Christian be ever named in Hindustan...

"When I was in England, I made friendship with all the plenipotentiaries of France, Russia,[12] and other States; these are all my friends, and are willing and ready to do anything for me." (56-42)

A contemporaneous comment about this by a British officer, Shepherd, reads: "After a long harangue of this nature, the audience ended. Many of the natives, who did not know better, were inclined to believe what they heard, especially as they all well knew that Azeemullah had actually been to England and had remained there two years. Apprehension and doubt arose in their minds for the fate of the English in India; they calculated on the immense body of the mutinous troops, all well-trained soldiers, with vast resources at their

---

12. Dr. Mujumdar writes: "That he was at least partly responsible for the canard, then widely prevalent in India, that Russia, as a military power, was far superior to the British, and was ready to help India in case of any fight against the latter. This propaganda had some share in instigating the mutiny of the sepoys and in sustaining or stiffening their resistance. (67-165)

N.K. Behere states that he had seen the valiant Russians fighting (against the British) in the Crimean War and had not fully recovered from effects of that euphoria. (158-362)

command. Thus many wavered in their allegiance to the British Government, and joined the rebel cause. (56-42)

Azeemullah used to do the work of conducting such subtle propaganda. The contents of the speech, on the one hand, were effective for strengthening the views of those who believed the British had no army. On the other hand, Nana's proclamation, conveying information that the army was destroyed *en route*, was useful in the case of those who believed otherwise. All of this was his brainchild. In short, this was a proclamation issued by the mentor on behalf of the disciple!

Against English Kafirs

3. A well-known proclamation, apparently issued by Nanasahib after the British had prevailed over the Uprising not just in Kanpur but practically all over India, addressed to potentates in the South, stated:

"From Dhondo Pant Nana Peshwa, Pant Pradhan to all the Saranjamdars, Jagirdars, Desmukhs, Despandeys and other Zamindars, Patels, Kulkarnis, Naikwads, Seth-Sahukars and the whole of the population of the Deccan and the Karnatak, it is ordered to be proclaimed that –

"The English, who are '*Kafirs*' came to this country under pretence of carrying trade. Afterwards instigating sedition among our Saranjamdars and practising treachery they seized all the Hindu and Mahomedan Kingdoms.

"The *Kafirs* upon the strength of their acquisition of the Empire have turned arrogant. They have been endeavouring to delude and convert the population of the country by inducing them to abandon their own religion and caste.

"Tyranny, wickedness and injustice having been much practised by the '*Kafir*' English on the faithful and sin-fearing, I have been commissioned by God to punish the '*Kafirs*' by annihilating them and to reestablish the Hindu and Mahomedan Kingdoms as formerly and to protect our country and I have conquered the country north of the Narmada river.

"To submit to and live under such wicked '*Kafirs*' is very disgraceful. So immediately on the perusal of this Proclamation you are bravely to take up your swords and without mercy destroy the '*Kafirs*'...

"Ye heroes ! This is the best time for you to avenge the wrongs and wickedness perpetrated by the '*Kafir*' English on your grandfathers and on your Kings. By allowing such an opportunity to escape do not suffer the stain of being effeminate and foolish to attach to the people of the South.

"At the present time the English having disagreements among themselves about their religion are quarrelling and fighting and killing each other. The French and the Russians who entertained from a long time a hatred against the English and a design to turn them out of Hindustan have thought this a proper time to carry it out and with this intention they have been sending armies by sea these three months past.

"The Chinese also have declared war against the '*Kafirs*', and the latter having no army to send against the Chinese are much alarmed. The Persians, Afghans and Baluchis moreover are ready with their armies collected to help us. In short, this is the golden time to root out completely the English from this country.

"The '*Kafir*' English, in order to discourage the population , fabricate false information of their having retaken Delhi and other places and having defeated us and make it known among the public; but such ought not to be believed. If you allow this time to escape all of you will be liable to punishment from us and for that guilt whatever jagirs, lands and other subsistence you may possess will be brought under attachment.

"This Proclamation is published by order of 'Ullee Shah' 'Bundeegan' 'Ullee Hozoor' the Emperor of Delhi by Rao Pant Pradhan Peshwa."[13]

---

13. See: 156-254; 111-715; 109-136; 6-590; 90-166; 131-88; 68-221; 108-166; 155-330.

In the opinion of some, the proclamation was issued in September 1858. (111-714, 917; 109-253) Others say it was issued in June 1858 from the fact that it was found among documents pertaining to that month seized from some nobles. (156-253) Even assuming the earlier date of June 1858, many questions still emerge about the contents. But, before considering them, let us review the situation of the rebellion in India at that time.

The Situation of the Uprising at that Time

It is evident from the proclamation that no noteworthy rebellion had occurred in the South till June 1858, for it was because people there had remained passive that their particular attention has been directed to expletives like 'effeminate and foolish'. The British had been victorious in the entire North. The provinces of Delhi, Punjab and Bihar, and divisions like Agra, Allahabad and Meerut, as well as Ayodhya (province), Rohilkhand, Jhansi and Malwa had all of them, without exception, passed under British control. Not a single rebel State remained. Lord Canning's offer of amnesty dated 15th March 1858 had also been proclaimed.

The Delhi Emperor was in British imprisonment for the past nine months. He had been put on trial for treason in January 1858, convicted in March, and it was being debated at this time where he ought to be sent — Andaman or Rangoon. M. Ahmad Shah, Rani Laxmi Bai, Kunwar Singh of Bihar were dead. Nawab Khan Bahadur Khan of Rohilkhand and the Begum of Ayodhya had taken refuge in Nepal. Tatya Tope, Raosahib Peshwa and Prince Firoz Shah were the only prominent leaders still remaining, chased by British forces with whom they were fighting a guerilla war while fleeing from pillar to post without any hope of victory. It was in this period of a rapidly waning revolt all over North India that this proclamation was issued.

It cannot be stated with certainty where Nanasahib was at the time. He had been with the Begum of Lucknow till the end of May but thereafter there was no place to which he could turn for safety. In a way, since his departure from

Kanpur on 16th July 1857, he had gone underground. Later, when the Peshwa's forces took Gwalior, Raosahib was enthroned there on 3rd June 1858 as Peshwa and had begun officially issuing proclamations in that capacity. In that sense, Nanasahib had not remained the 'authorized' Peshwa in June 1858. When Gwalior was retaken by the British during the same month, Raosahib, having no fixed headquarters, had been wandering, along with Tatya Tope from place to place offering the British resistance while on the move.

Why the Proclamation at such Juncture?

Some issues emerge on the backdrop of this scenario. Why had Nanasahib issued the proclamation calling for a rebellion in the South at a time when the Uprising in the principal (or, sole) Northern theatre had all but ended? Why had it not been issued while he was ruling at Kanpur (or within a reasonably short time thereafter)? Why did he wait all of about eleven months for the Northern Uprising to be completely suppressed? If it had been issued at that earlier date, and if it had been met with the expected response and support, the British would have been prevented from mobilizing their southern platoons to supress the northern revolt. Troops from the Bombay province had been sent to Jhansi and Malwa, while those from Madras had gone to Allahabad and Benares. Had an Uprising broken out at that time in the south, the British would have been caught in a serious predicament.

Why had Nanasahib chosen to issue his proclamation from some unknown place in the north instead of personally coming to south and mould public opinion in favour of a revolt? Why was the proclamation silent about the fact that the Emperor, whose 'Bandeegan' (obedient servant) Nana claimed to be, was in prison? Why had the proclamation lied about conquest of the region north of the Narmada? On the other hand, in an equally untenable bid, why did it ask people to disbelieve British claims that Delhi and other places had been won by them, and that the revolutionaries had been defeated? Why had other falsifications been included about the arrival of help from international quarters like France, Russia, Iran,

Afghanistan and Baluchistan, or that China had risen up in war? Why had the final death rattle of northern revolutionaries been distorted as a 'golden opportunity'? Had the south believed in all these statements and risen up in rebellion, would it not have courted unimaginable vendetta and slaughter, success being the least of possibilities?

Answers to such questions can be obtained only when it is appreciated that others had been issuing proclamations in Nana's name. Azeemullah had previously propagated the rumour that France, Russia and some Muslim countries were going to send help. "From 16th July (1857) onwards Nana is heard of here and there but not Azeemullah." (72-83) It is clear that not Azeemullah perhaps, but someone else like him had been behind issuing this proclamation.

Unacceptable to Nana's Religion

It is remarkable that the word '*Kafir*' appears nine times in this comparatively short proclamation.

Moreover, appointment of someone by God with the specific duty of annihilating *Kafirs*, was something unfamiliar to Nana's religion, according to the beliefs of which God Himself incarnates to reestablish religious order. There is no evidence to affirm Nana believed *he* was *that* incarnation. Moreover, 'establishment of religion' is not 'destruction of followers of other religions' just because of their beliefs, but the uprooting of injustice, where injustice does not imply 'belief in another religion' but 'injustice' in its sense conforming to universally accepted norms.

So, it should not need too much effort to unravel who might have issued the proclamation in Nana's name.

Who Wrote to the Maulana?

4. It is also believed that Nanasahib wrote a letter to rebel leader of Allahabad M. Liaqat Ali, after the Meerut revolt but during the month of May, as follows:

   "May 31st was fixed as the date for a nationwide uprising for regaining freedom. This programme was finalized by main leaders of the revolution. England and other European countries are at war with our neighbour, China. Eighty percent of the British forces (in India) have been dispatched to China by sea on 7th May. As such, security of the East India Company's Indian territorial possessions is entirely dependent on its native forces. With the European contingent having thus gone to the east now (an insignificant number has remained in India). Hindu and Muslim sepoys are duty bound to assist establishment of independence with all their heart. You can therefore appreciate that 31st May is a golden opportunity to win back our all.

"Impatience on the part of the Meerut sepoys has done our cause a great harm; we, however, will act as per the predetermined plan. We shall fire the first cannon on 31st May; Lucknow, Faizabad, Benares and Allahabad will (thereafter) rise." (111-609; 37-17)

It is unlikely that Nana wrote this letter for the following reasons:

- It is an established fact of history that Nanasahib had no hand in the 4th June Kanpur revolt, but had been threatened thereafter by rebel sepoys to assume leadership. It is thus unlikely that he might have written such a letter in May.
- What was the need of informing M. Liaqat Ali of the date fixed for the rebellion when this Maulana was one of the main leaders of the revolution?
- If the Meerut sepoys had shown impatience, they were obviously aware of the date, and it naturally follows that it must have also been communicated to all leaders of sepoys who desired to rebel. In that case, how could the date be unknown to the Maulvi before he received this letter?
- What was the need to tell the Maulvi that Allahabad would rise immediately after Kanpur, when the Maulvi himself was the leader of the Allahabad revolt?
- Why had Kanpur not actually rebelled on the 31st despite the insistence in the letter that it was going to be the

first to do so on that date? On the contrary, rebellions had already taken place at Aligarh, Etawah, Mathura, Bulandshahar, Lucknow, Bareilly, Shahjahanpur, Bijnor and other places on or before that date. Moradabad, Badaun and Pilibhit districts had risen on 1st June. Still, there had been no revolt in Kanpur. Had Nanasahib really been a principal leader of the rebellion, why had he incited others to rebel and himself stayed put?

Thus, it is likely that the letter was sent in Nana's name or forged by leaders of rebel sepoys at a later date to secure Nana's indictment as a principal leader of the revolt. Rebels are known to have made such attempts at that time to ensure that Nana did not distance himself from the Uprising. (See Chap. 6, footnote 78.)

Proclamation by Nanasahib's Subedar, Muhammad Ishaq

5. While Nanasahib had gone underground after the fall of Kanpur, Kalpi had become the headquarters of Raosahib Peshwa. Muhammad Ishaq was running the administration on his behalf as his subedar. He issued, on his own, a letter addressed to chiefs in Bundelkhand on 2nd January 1858. It read:

"My master, Shrimant Maharajah Peshwa Bahadur, has for the purpose of defending the religion both of the Hindus and Mahomedans, prepared himself to slaughter the followers of Christ as they are enemies of the faith of the Mussalmans and Hindus. The said Maharajah has, by engaging a war with the Christians, put several of them to the sword, and he resolved not to refrain from killing them as long as he breathes and to annihilate at once the people of this race now in India. The object which the Maharajah has in view to expel all the Christians from Hindustan, is not to take possession of the territories and property of the Rajahs and Chiefs of India, or to assume the supreme command of the country, but on the other hand, it is his sole desire that after a victory all the chiefs may in peace enjoy the possession of territories which they at present hold. Those provinces which are now exclusively in the British possession, shall be distributed to such Chiefs for their services in slaughtering the followers of Christ.

"If all the Chiefs for the purpose of defending their religion and faith, join together and be of one mind, it will not be difficult to annihilate through the divine favour, all the remaining Christians." (3-459; 5-512; 92-59)

It was nothing but a *Jihadnama,* for the destruction of *kafir* Christians, written by the subedar expressing the desire of his master.

The Same Letter in Tatya's Name

Tatya was in Kalpi at that time. A letter, containing the same text of 43 lines and issued on the same day, was sent to the same chiefs in Tatya's name. Only the following two lines were added at the end: "Pandit Baba Devi Gir will wait upon you with this letter and verbally communicate to you all other particulars." (5-214)

Neither letter contained Muhammad Ishaq's or Tatya's names. It is clear that some third person prepared a single draft and issued the two letters in the names of the two persons. The contents are a sufficient clue to the possible identity of that third person.

Raosahib Peshwa's 'National Religion'!

6. Declarations issued by Raosahib Peshwa are of a similar nature.

a) He wrote in an order issued on 17th April 1858: "It is the wish of the Sarkar that such steps as may regulate its affairs and lead to the extermination of the infidels, should be taken. Those who will perform meritorious services will be rewarded with suitable jagirs, titles." (5-359)

b) He had declared in a proclamation dated 7th November 1858 which said: "Let it be known to all people that the army bearing the standard of victory has marched in this direction, only for the destruction of the infidel Christians" (3-464; 5-522)

c) And, in another declaration issued on 26th February 1858 in connection with the Hindu chief of Charkhari, it was written:

"The chief of Charkhari district did not come to terms with this government, neither did he embrace the course of religion; the army on several occasions wrote to him to embrace the course of religion. Yet that infidel having no regard for religion is prepared to fight with us. I am desirous to extirpate infidel Christians and preserve the national religion. It is hereby proclaimed that all officers, subedars, sardars and sepoys should consider the chief of Charkhari as an Englishman and send him to hell." (3-464; 92-63)

It is not clarified what was the 'national religion' to which he referred. Also notable is the classification of a Hindu chief as an 'infidel'.

7. Two subedars (Moha Singh and Shamsher Khan) of the army under the Peshwa also wrote a letter on 2nd January 1858 to the chief of Charkhari : "It is therefore incumbent on you to hold yourself steady in the cause of 'Deen'. If you send troops and money, we shall know that you are for the 'Deen'. All chiefs upto Delhi are ready in the cause of 'Deen'". (92-61)

Proclamations of the Nawab of Ayodhya

For Hindus and Muslims

1. In a declaration dated 17th August 1858, issued by Nawab Birjis Qadar of Ayodhya it was stated: "I have, therefore, decided to exterminate the cruel, ill-behaved *kafir* Firangis from my hereditary dominions, both old and new. Consequently I have nominated the brave Raja Beni Madhav Singh for the administration of the *ilaqa* of Jaunpur and Azamgarh, and order that you should capture, put to the sword and annihilate the entire group of these perverted nonbelievers." (4-121; 72-221)

2. Addressed to zamindars and subjects of Ayodhya, another proclamation stated:

   "All the Hindus and Mahomedans are aware that four things are dear to every man; 1st • Religion, 2nd • Honour,

3rd • Life, 4th • Property. All these four things are safe under a native government. No one under that Government interferes with religion. The English are enemies of four things mentioned above.

"They wish to deprive the Hindus and Mahomedans of their religion, and wish them to become Christians. Under their government, thousands of people have embraced Christianity and are continuing to do so. Therefore, the Hindus and Mahomedans are hereby warned that whosoever among you wishes to protect his faith, honour, life and property, may come forward to fight against the English in conjunction with the forces of this *Sarkar*." (3-451; 4-123)

Three other matters besides religion had been broached in the proclamation. While a special attempt may be seen in this to obtain support of the large population of aggrieved zamindars in the Ayodhya province, whose land holdings had become jeopardized by British legislation, the primacy emphasis was on religion.

Only for Muslims

3. Both those proclamations were intended for Hindus as well as Muslims. However, specifically addressing Muslims in Rohilkhand, he wrote:

"In the Holy Quran, the great and glorious God has said *'O ye, believers*[14] *! don't make friendship with the Jews and Christians. He who befriends them is surely one of them, that is to say, the friend of a Jew is a Jew, and the friend of a Christian is a Christian…'*

---

14. One source translates this as 'O ye believers!' with precision. (3-448) Here, the Quran is addressing 'believers' (or Muslims) alone. However, in another book the phrase is incorrectly translated as, 'O ye, the people who follow the religion!' (4-123) 'To believe' means to believe in Islam. This incorrect rendering fails to particularize 'religion' as 'Islam', and creates the erroneous impression that all followers of all religions in the world had been addressed. It is the style used in the Quran to address Muslims. (For ex. *Ayat* 5:51,7)

"This sacred text plainly shows that the forming of friendship with the Christians is an act of infidelity and that consequently he who is on friendly terms with them is not at all a Mussalman. These considerations render it a bounden duty of all the Mussalmans who are the brethren of each other, to become with heart and soul the implacable enemies of the Christians and in no respect be their friends at any time. The nonexecution of this duty by them will lead to the loss of their faith and they will in consequence become apostates.

"Those who are not staunch in their religion and whose views are directed to temporal affairs, say that if they be at enmity with the Christians, misfortune will befall them when the authority of that nation will have been reestablished. In regard to these people, God has enjoined thus in the text (i.e. the Quran) next to the foregoing one : "Did you mark those men whose minds are afflicted with the malady of faithlessness?' They are very hastily in contracting friendship with Christians. They say they are afraid lest they might meet with some mishap. In order to remove their whim, God had said, 'Be confident, God will give a speedy victory[15] to Mussalmans or give such a turn to the events that they will repent of their folly in having entertained groundless doubts." (5:52)....

"If all the Mussalmans unite together and remain firm in their faith, they will undoubtedly gain victory over the English inasmuch as God has said in the Holy Quran : 'It is for me to give success to the Mussalmans.'[15] If the Mussalmans will show cowardice, and will not persevere, nor unite, the English will surely triumph, and then they will disarm, and hang, shoot, and blow up the Mussalmans, seize their wives and children, dishonour their females, force them to embrace Christianity, burn the Quran, or throw them among filth and sweepings, knock down the mosques, and will not keep a single vestige of Islam. Therefore if the Mussalmans have any shame or desire to uphold their cause let them unite and resolve to kill the English.

15. Quran – *3:123,7; 5:56; 9:25; 33:71; 37:173.*

"To die in battle with the English for the sake of religion is glorious, and he who falls thus is sure to become martyr. Every Mussalman eagerly wishes for such a death, therefore no one ought to shrink from dying thus. Remember that man is mortal; therefore why should you fear to die? Men and women should think it their duty to extirpate the English. The fatwa of the religious men of both the sects (Shi'ah and Sunnis) is herewith annexed. To all of you God will assist and furnish us with resources of every kind." (3-449; 4-125)

Because Jihad Was Only Against Christians

The appeal for *Jihad* had been more openly made in this proclamation because it was addressed specifically to Muslims. While the *Quranic* directive, "Don't make friendship with Jews and Christians" was included in the proclamation, no mention was made about polytheists and idolaters because this 1857 *Jihad* had been declared against Christians.

4. In a representation made to the British administration, the Begum of Ayodhya, commenting on the English Queen's proclamation of amnesty, wrote:

"In the Proclamation it is written that the Christian religion is true, but that no other creed will suffer oppression, and that the laws will be observed towards all. What has the administration of justice to do with the truth or falsehood of a religion? That religion is true which acknowledges one God, and knows no other.[16] Where there are three gods in a religion (like Christianity), neither Mussalmans nor Hindus — nay, not even Jews–can believe it true...

"The rebellion began with religion, and, for it, millions of men have been killed. Let no subject be deceived by the Proclamation (of the Queen)." (3-467; 4-531)

---

16. Although 'Islam' was not specified here, the Quran states in innumerable places that it is the one and only true divine religion. (e.g. 2:132; 3:19; 12:40; 30:30; 98:1)

It was unambiguously stated in her representation that Christianity was not a true faith. However, whether Hinduism was a 'true' religion was a matter left unaddressed because the conflict at that time was against the British Christian.

Appeal by Muhammad Hasan, Subedar of Gorakhpur

Jihad: A Noble Cause

We quote below a significant portion of a lengthy representation for surrender to the British made in October 1859 by Muhammad Hasan, the leader of the rebellion at Gorakhpur, who then became subedar:

"Subsequently (i.e. after the revolt), I, with God's help, restored Gorakhpur (district) to the Kingdom of Oudh, to which it had been in former times attached. The Almighty, whose name is 'strong' and the 'Protector' is omnipotent, if an enemy is mighty, He is more mighty; He, if He chooses, makes the strong weak, and the weak strong; whom He wills, He exalts, and whom He wills He debases[17] Save with God's permission no one can slay or burn....

"If I am killed while fighting for my religion and my earthly sovereign, I then attain the prosperity of the two worlds. I also consider it ennobling and sure to benefit me now and hereafter to fight and die in the tenets of my creed and in the cause of my illustrious sovereign.

"My business is with the King of Oudh. This rebellion arose solely out of the annexation of Oudh. Had that not taken place, there would have been no bloodshed. If Her Majesty even now acts justly and gives back his Kingdom, to the King of Oudh, all this disturbance will be brought to an end, the justice and mercy of the queen will be blazoned forth and extolled in the seven regions of the world....

"That we servants and dependants of the King of Oudh consider it essential to our prosperity in both worlds, to display devotion in protecting the Kingdom.... If we fail in doing so, we are traitors, and will have our faces blackened in both worlds." (6-391)

---

17. Quran : *3:26.*

In a letter he wrote about a month and a half later, he stated:

"And if I valued my life and worldly wealth more than my religion, I would certainly come to you, but I am here companion of my King and my faith, and what you have written about Bala Rao's coming, the following is the case that I am not a servant of Bala Rao's or Nana Rao's nor did I come into his camp at Kanpur. I am hereditary servant of the Kings..." (394)

The reason for the Uprising and its nature, as well as his view of his relationship with Nanasahib and the kind of sentiments he held for him, need no elaboration. Their religion and political supremacy of their religionists was the chief inspiration for the rebellion.

Proclamation of Prince Firoz Shah

Only for Religion/For Purifying the Land from Kufr

Shahazada (Prince) Firoz Shah had stated in a proclamation he had issued on 17th February 1858[18] while he was at Jhansi. The proclamatin read: "To all Hindus and Mahomedans of Hindustan who are faithful to their religion know that sovereignty is one of God's chief boons, one which a deceitful tyrant is never allowed to retain.

"For several years the English have been committing all kinds of excesses and tyrannies being desirous of converting all men to Christianity by force. When God saw this fact, He so altered the hearts of the inhabitants of Hindustan, that they have been doing best to get rid of the English themselves; now the *Firangis* have been (mostly) destroyed. Soon they (those remaining) will have been, by the grace of God, so utterly exterminated, that no traces of them will remain.

"When the army mutinied to preserve their faith, and in various places sent the *Kafirs* to Hell".

---

18. The date was 18th February according to some authorities (7-376; 132-171) and 17th according to others. (4-656; 72-182)

(Information about 15 articles constituting the British plan for religious conversion is then given. These included burning of scriptures, forbidding worship, prohibiting construction of masjids and temples, disallowing marriages and other ceremonies according to religious prescription, implementing the law of the Bible, banning religious discourses by Maulvis and Pundits, and disarming the native population, among others.)

"Oh Hindustani Brethren ! You must now wash your hands, and becoming their enemies exert themselves in exterminating them for the sake of your religion and of your lives. Through God's grace we shall be victorious.

"Before the commencement of these calamities of the English, I went on a pilgrimage to Mecca; on my return (to India), I travelled from Bombay to Gwalior and (persuaded the people on the road to make *Jihad*), made all chiefs and armies promise to exterminate the (Nazarenes) Christians. I took a small army with me from Gwaliar, intending first to arrange and consolidate affairs and then to fight. However, the soldiers were so excited by religious zeal, that they hastened on impetuously, and made an attack on Agra. Notwithstanding their own small numbers they behaved with becoming valour and courage, and although apparently defeated, yet in reality they gained a signal success, having slain 1000 *Kafirs.* After that battle, my property and comrades were scattered, hither and thither. From that time until now I have been busy in my endevours to collect an army, and have been for four months meeting kings[19] and armies to rise and slaughter the infidels.

"Through the aid of God, from various quarters, 1,50,000 men,[20] old and new soldiers, have been induced to swear to

19. He was at that time in Jhansi, and it is clear he had incited the Rani and her troops to fight the British. It seems he had induced her to also issue a proclamation.

20. Some sources give this figure as 1,50,000 (7-379; 87-62; 4-656) while others put it at 1,30,000 (3-462; 72-182; 132-172).

join me, and I will soon, collecting all of these, purify the land from these Nazarenes. All sorts of material and treasure have been collected, there is only a little delay in the commencement of the movement.

"Let it be known that the only inducement to enter into these plots, is the call of our ancient religion. After the receipt of this Proclamation, it is expected that all will join the *Jihad.*

"When you determine on joining the rank of the *Jihadis,* you must consider the following points:

"1st •The Chiefs subject to the King of Oudh and Nawab of Bareilly must not join me without first obtaining the permission of their sovereigns, because they are doing all they can to destroy the *Kafirs...*

"2nd •Let zeal for religion alone be the motive which prompts those who determine to join me (in this religious war), not by worldly aspiration...

"3rd •The reason of the delay there has been in burying the English, that the commands of God have been disregarded in as much as the soldiers have wickedly put women and children to death and the common people have been much oppressed. When you have rectified these faults, you will succeed...

"4th •Great and small will all be on an equality in this army because all brethren are equal...

"Placing my trust in God; devoting myself solely to God's service; observing the precepts of religion; strengthening my determination; having wrapped round my head the cerements of the grave (*Kaffan*) and having armed myself with the sword of '*Jihad*' I rise repeating the holy '*Bismillah*' and relying on the blessing of God, I am sure of obtaining victory.

"Therefore again I urge you, and urge you one and all, join me, prompted solely by the desire of doing God's work.

"O Hafiz, do you decide which is better of the two courses.

"Printed at the Bahaduri Press in Bareilly, by the order of the Nawab, the Ruler of Kathair (i.e. Rohilkhand), under the superintendence of Maulvi Sayyid Qutb Shah...dated 18 Feb. 1858." (3-463; 7-380; 72-183; 132-173; 87-115)

Although appeals to Hindus were included in the document, its Jihadi nature comes through clearly enough. Religion was the only reason given for the Uprising. The concept that sovereignty of the country was a boon granted by 'God' was a significant feature of the proclamation. For, only the representative of Khuda, or the Khalifa, had the right to this boon, and being a 'believer' was an unbreakable precondition to become the Khalifa. The prince evidently sought to purify the land from *Kufr* by exterminating all Christian *kafirs.*

Well-wisher of Muslims

The Prince had established an Islamic state at Mundsore and assumed the title of Khalifa. At the time, he had issued an edict to the Muslim Chief of Jawra to join him. He had stated therein: "Should you take the advice of one like myself who is the well-wisher of the people in general and of the Mahomedan in particular, it would be better for you. If you are a well-wisher of Islam and of the house of the Sultan you will do as desired." (72-176)

The religious message and expression of well intentioned goodwill contained in the document are amply clear.

Proclamation by the Nawab of Rohilkhand

1. An important proclamation issued by Nawab Khan Bahadur Khan of Rohilkhand reads as follows:

 "Proclamation for the religious and faithful, promulgated by authority (of Nawab):

 "Let it be known...that it is the duty of every wise and vigorous Mussalman youth to take part in the crusade (against Christians) both according to religious books and the opinion of all orthodox *Ulemas.* And, that whoever at this juncture playing the coward will not answer our Call and (not) assist the faithful....shall certainly bring upon himself the wrath of the Almighty and prove himself a useless creature both in this world and the other.

 "You Mussalmans consider when, according to the words of the Prophet 'Those who die for their honour and property are martyrs' you get martyrdom simply by dying in defence of your honour and property, is it not worth the dignity of a thousand martyrs to die in such a noble cause? God forbid, if Christians overcome the faithful, thousands of His creatures shall be indiscriminately slaughtered, hundreds of thousands obliged to leave their houses and property, innumerable respectable women Sayyidins dishonoured, innocent children murdered, the religion of Islam totally destroyed, and every surviving individual forced to adopt Christianity.

"Fye! What Mahomedanism is that to which infidelity is so much superior? Is it not forbidden for one Mussalman to flee before the infidels ? Now here in this town you are a hundred to one Christian and still display cowardice.

"For God's sake attend to this, wash your bodies, put on fine cloths, apply perfume, take whatever arms and weapons you can get and on Sunday the 14th of the month proceed to Aysh Bagh (Public garden) for the support of Islam and the welfare of God's creatures; and being certain that every step you put in this way shall be of more real benefit to you than all the niceties of this world[21] and your adoration in the whole of your life grace the Army of Islam by your presence and please yourselves by the following promise (by God) 'Verily I shall favour my followers.'[22]

"Be sure if you put your trust entirely in God and act according to His commands, obey God, your Prophet and your Ruler, you shall be victorious as He Himself says 'Verily I give victory to the faithful.'[23] If you die in the cause of God you shall be freed from the pangs of death, miseries of the grave and fears of the day of justice and adopted in His service and favoured with a place near Him.

---

21. This has support in the *Hadis* – 'Sahih Bukhari' : 2792, 3250, 6415; 'Sahih Muslim' : 4639 – 43; 'Sunnah Ibn-i Majah' : 2755 to 7. (128-612)

22. Quran – 3:152; 33:43.

23. Directive in the Quran: see footnote 15 (supra).

"O followers of God, bring to your mind all the stories related in the Quran and you shall find that whenever it pleases God to let His vengeance fall on any nation, He especially provides for the safety of His followers;[24] hence one might hope that if all the faithful rise in the cause of God, without having in view any worldly advantage, they might be the objects of His particular favour. The Will of God must ultimately prevail.

"By God I have undertaken the task of proclaiming God's orders for God's sake only and not from any selfish motives...." (7-351)

No Prevalence of Kufr

This was a coherent *Jihadnama*, embellished with thoughts and citations from the Quran, specifically issued only for Muslims by their leader-ruler. The desire that 'infidelity' may not prevail over Islam is a significant aspect of the document. Rebellious Muslims were opposed to the British because the latter were Christians by persuasion; that they were also unjust and oppressive was an inevitable consequence of their disbelief.[25] Hindus had neither been mentioned in the proclamation, nor an appeal made to them. This very proclamation can be used, without making any change, for Hindus instead of Christians.

A *Jihadnama* for Hindus and Muslims

2. In an attempt to obtain support of Hindus in Rohilkhand, who had been reluctant to help Muslims in the rebellion, the Nawab had issued the following declaration:

---

24. This has reference to how 'Khuda' had destroyed disbelieving peoples by inflicting natural calamities, but saved believers in those respective regions, after He had sent His message during the period of prophets from Adam to Muhammad. (128-362,6,402,4)

25. 'Belief', according to Islam is the source of all righteousness, justice and virtues; 'disbelief', that of all evil, injustice and vice. (128-542 to 7)

" 'Victory of Religion'

"O Rajahs !... God has provided you with bodies for the performance of His sacred rites[26].... God has created you, Oh Rajahs, for the destruction of the destroyers of your creed; for the same purpose, He has given you (State) power. The *Shastra* declares that it is best to follow one's own religion, and not to adopt another's, and God Himself has so declared;[27] but it is evident to all men that these English are perverters of all men's religion. From time immemorial have they endeavoured to contaminate the Hindu and Mahomedan religions[28] by the production and circulation of religious books through the medium of missionaries.

"(We) have heard from creditable sources the various endeavours they have made to contaminate our creed.

"1st. The forcible remarriage of Hindu widows.

2nd. The abolition of the ancient rite of *Sati*.

---

26. For some details about this Islamic concept: see under 'Emperor's Proclamations.'

27. Two essentially dissimilar kinds of doctrinal substantiation had been proffered for the belief that martyrdom was preferable to acceptance of another faith. Of these, 'the Shastra declares' implied that it was written in Hindu scriptures, while 'God himself has so declared' implied that 'the one and only Allah' of the Muslims had also said so. What actuated these distinct validations was the belief that Hindu *Shastras* were not of divine origin and that Allah was the one and only Supreme Being. Had it not been so, a single rationale — either of God or the Scripture — would have been presented to both Hindus and Muslims because what Allah or God had said is anyway included in the (scripture) Quran.

28. Allah, according to Islamic thought, had given the Scripture to every group of human beings but every such Book and the teachings contained therein became corrupted in later times. The Bible of the Christians is one such scripture that had not retained its original purity. This is why Allah sent the original pure scripture, intended for the whole human race, through the Final Prophet Muhammad. (128-534 to 41)

3rd . The exaltation of those who may embrace the Christian faith, so also succession to the thrones of Hindu princes is only permitted to the legitimate sons, the adopted sons are prohibited from succession. Finding that these measures still proved to be ineffectual, they powdered bones and mixed them with flour, sugar etc. and exposed it for sale; in every way they tried their best to destroy our creeds. That consequently they ordered the Brahmins and others attached to the army to bite greased cartridges. The Mahomedans refused to use them although they were sensible that the use of these cartridges would affect only the religion of Hindus. The Europeans have determined to destroy the religion of both....

"I conjure the Hindus in the name of Ganga, Tulsi and Saligram, and the Mahomedans by the name of God and the Quran[29] and entreat them to join us, in destroying the English, for their mutual welfare.

"The killing of cows being esteemed one of the greatest of sins amongst the Hindus, the Mahomedan chiefs have agreed to abolish that custom from the day the Hindus come forward to kill the Europeans.... Perhaps Europeans for their own ends may stipulate with the Hindus not to kill cows if they will join them; I assure the Hindus that no man of sense will be deceived by this pretence, as they have notoriously violated their promises.

"Let not this opportunity pass away. Know Oh people ! You will never have such another.

"This letter calling for the joint alliance of Hindu and Mahomedan is published by Maulvi Sayyid Kutb Shah at the Bahaduri Press in the city of Bareilly." (5-227; 3-444; 7-348; 107-289)

Embellished with Islamic Concepts

This proclamation is significant for several reasons. A large part of Bahadur Shah's proclamation appeared verbatim in it,

---

29. An explanation for the different methods of obligating Hindus and Muslims: see under 'Emperor's Proclamations.'

especially such references as the purpose for which Khuda bestowed human birth, the concept of killing those who undermined religion. British plans for religious conversion and separate methods of obligating Hindus and Muslims, among others. This was probably so because both proclamations had been drafted by the same expert. It is important to note in this context that M. Sayyid Qutb Shah's name appears distinctly in this and other proclamations.[30]

The belief, appearing in the proclamation, that Khuda had bestowed a superior status[31] on Man, and a kingdom to rule over, is Islamic. Needless to state, 'man' here implies 'a believer' (a Muslim). Believers, according to the Quran, are made heirs to the kingdom of earth.[31] Muslim rulers and administrators during the Uprising had obviously not forgotten this concept; nay, the Uprising was for the realization of this concept.

Nanasahib, at the time this proclamation was issued, was with the Khan in Bareilly. Perhaps because of Nana's presence, an assurance of banning cow slaughter, conditional though it was, had found its way into the document to favourably influence Hindus.

While dispatching the proclamation to his superiors, the local British Commissioner observed that it threw some light upon the manner in which the followers of Islam had inveigled the Hindus to join them in the Mutiny. (7-343)

One More Proclamation: Stringent Conditions for Cow Slaughter Ban

Perhaps because the Nawab's people thought that the conditions imposed in this proclamation were inadequate, a second one was issued a few days later, which stipulated such rigorous conditions that the need for imposing a ban could

---

30. Dr. Chaudhary cites a portion of this proclamation that deals with the ban on cow slaughter and the different methods for obligating Hindus and Muslims as an excerpt from a letter issued by Maulvi Kutb Shah. (81-281n)

31. E.g. *5:20; 6:165; 10:14; 17:70; 21:105; 24:55; 35:39.*

never have arisen at all. We have reproduced that proclamation and discussed this aspect in Chap. 8 under the subhead 'Pre-conditions for Cow Slaughter Ban.'

Rani of Jhansi's Proclamation

Just a Copy of the Nawab's Declaration

This proclamation was issued under the title 'Victory of Religion' on 14th February 1858, i.e. before the Rani had taken her final decision to fight the British. (5-226 to 8; 48-95 to 9) We have already seen how Prince Firoz Shah, who was in Jhansi at that time, may have had a hand in inducing the Rani to issue the proclamation. His own proclamation was issued three days after the Rani's.

The Rani's proclamation is nothing but a word-by-word copy of the second one issued by Nawab Khan Bahadur Khan of Rohilkhand.[32] (We have cited this proclamation under the subhead, 'A *Jihadnama* for Hindus and Muslims', in the section dealing with the Nawab, above.) Both proclamations had been titled 'Victory of Islam'. Both contained the reference: "This letter calling for the joint alliance of Hindu and Mahomedan is published by Maulvi Sayyid Kutb Shah at the Bahaduri Press in the city of Bareilly."[33] Except in the title (perhaps assigned by researchers/editors), the name or reference of either the Nawab or the Rani does not appear anywhere in the body of the respective proclamations. Both are unsigned. This notwithstanding, researchers' conclusion that these particular proclamations were indeed issued by them, is correct. There is no doubt that the same proclamation was separately

---

32. The original proclamations are in Persian. While numerous translations have been done of the more important portions of these proclamations, we have before us four English and one Hindi translations of the whole document running into about three pages. The only difference observable in these is a natural consequence of style and ability of the various translators.

33. When this proclamation was issued, Prince Firoz Shah was at Jhansi. It is likely that he has some hand in issuing it.

circulated in the name of both. So, it is beyond reasonable doubt that these identical proclamations issued by both had been drafted by some third person who could only have been M. Sayyid Qutb Shah. (Besides, some portions of these proclamations appeared verbatim in the one issued by Bahadur Shah, too. (390)

Considering the Jihadi essence of her proclamation, assuming of course that it was issued by her, one is left wondering whether she had at least been permitted to read it! Ideas like, God granting human life for the sake of religion, liquidating opponents of the religion or the original pure scripture having undergone corruption, were all not just alien but also unacceptable to her faith.

Why Conditions for Ban on Cow-slaughter?

Indeed, the Rani's conditional assurance on behalf of Muslim chiefs of banning cow slaughter is shocking. What was the need for her to thus reassure Hindus on behalf of Muslims? Similar attempts by the Nawab of Rohilkhand to win favour with his reluctant Hindu subjects with such sops, could be understood, but why was the Rani also indulging in such measures? As she was ruling over Jhansi at the time, she could easily have issued a royal decree to enforce the ban that was so dear and significant for her and her religion. Her proclamation mentions the possibility of the British also offering a similar assurance, implying that although she was ruling on their behalf, she had no apprehensions about the British opposing such ban. Why had she, then, told Hindus about a conditional Muslim assurance of a ban instead of ordering one on her own? One inference that may be drawn from this is that she had indirectly all but conceded the right of Muslims to unhindered cow slaughter under prospective self-rule had they succeeded in the rebellion without the expected measure of Hindu support. In short, the same proclamation that M. Sayyid Qutb Shah had drafted for the Nawab of Bareilly,[34] and which conveyed many Jihadi thoughts

34. Government editors explain the identical nature of the two proclamations in a footnote: "Khan Bahadur reutilized the

(Contd.)

contained in the earlier proclamation issued by Bahadur Shah, had been used for the Rani.

Inapplicable Reasons

Of the three reasons stated in the proclamation, the first two do not apply in the Rani's case. If the British had indeed enforced widow remarriage, why did the law not apply to the 21-22 year old Rani, herself a widow? On the other hand, the British had tacitly honoured her, in a manner of speaking, by entrusting her with administration of the state for about 10 months on their behalf. Also, how had the ban on committing *sati* affected her? While it might have been impossible under the new dispensation for her to undertake the ordeal with due solemnity and religious ceremonial observances, it was certainly not so in the form of suicide. The new law must obviously have appealed favourably to her. Also, Hindu society had not ostracized her for not committing *sati*, nor had their respect or love for her diminished in any way. In a way, therefore, the ban had obviously only made a positive impact on collective Hindu consciousness. Thus, these two reasons had hardly, if at all, seemed to Hindus serious enough to warrant bloody rebellion. So why had they found their way into her proclamation?

The simple answer is that rebellious Muslims had proffered these reasons in the name of Rani only to incite Hindus!

Thus, her proclamation was allied to her name, but not her ideals, thoughts or motives.[35]

Proclamation of Rani of Jhansi in March 1858." (7-389n) However, for the reasons discussed above, the situation was exactly the reverse. The editors rely on dates of issue to venture their conjecture. But it appears that proclamations that had been drafted and kept ready, had been published in a sequence decided by expediency. What matters here is who purportedly issued them and what their contents convey!

35. It may be seen in the following example how ignorance of Islamic terminology results in misleading interpretations to be drawn from proclamations. To begin with, a certain specific word in the

(Contd.)

M. Liaqat Ali's Proclamation

The following is an important excerpt from a declaration made by the rebel leader and postuprising administrator of Allahabad, M. Liaqat Ali, who Savarkar glorifies as 'an ardent lover of liberty' and 'the leader of the Revolution.' (1-200):

"In the name of the beneficent God, the absolver of sinners.

"All praise to the Great and Merciful God. May the Merciful God and Preserver shine upon the Great Prophet, his descendants and his companions. May the mercy of God also alight upon the Votaries of the Great Religion of Islam !!!

"After praising God.... I, Liaqat Ali, of Allahabad beg to publish some of my observations, based upon precepts from the sacred Quran and the Holy Book (i.e. *Hadis*) of our Prophet, and trust that the faithful Mussalmans will attend to my appeal, as I am only discharging a great religious duty viz. inculcating the doctrines of our sacred scriptures, (so) that I may not be held responsible on the day of salvation for being backward in doing my duty.[36]

"The tyranny, oppression and cruelty practised by the fraudulent Christian infidels on the Mussalmans of the whole

---

original proclamation must have been used for what appears as 'God' or 'Khuda' in translations. Vivek Mohan, while translating proclamation for his informative book in Hindi, uses the following variety of nouns for that word appearing in the original: Ishwar, Paramatma, Brahma, Bhagwan and Allah. (48-96 to 8) A significant statement in the proclamation is translated by him as: "Brahma has created you for you should destroy those who harm your religion" (96) This rendering fails to convey what M. Qutb Shah actually wished to say. The word 'dharma' (religion) cannot be taken in its Hindu sense, but as 'Allah's religion'. It needs to be kept in mind that since 'Allah' is unique, His religion, too, cannot be more than one.

36. It is the religious duty of every Muslim to recount and alert people to Khuda's ordinances about His grace and punishment; failure to do so entails answering for it before Khuda on the Day of Judgement.

India...by plundering, burning, murdering, demolishing, fighting and killing the learned men...and burning the Quran and other religious books, are as clear as the sun. It is therefore necessary and incumbent on all the Mussalmans to prepare themselves for a *Jihad* and follow the words of Muhammad who says that, 'there has been particular work appointed for every *Nabi* and fight in *Jihad* is fixed for me'....

"You all should act according to the following precept quoted from the Quran, 'The real paradise lies beneath the strokes of swords.' You will then obtain salvation and the honour of martyrdom, which is eternal life. You will then obtain the blessings of Paradise, and get Elysian nymphs for your wives. You should never entertain in your minds any kind of fear or doubt...

"You should comply the following precept quoted from the Quran, 'Consider *Jihad* as your duty and engage in it under a leader whether he be good or bad.' Our Holy Quran is full of the promises of blessings attainable by undertaking *Jihad*, and they are also mentioned in several places in the chapter designated 'Surah-Tobah' (no.9)....

"In a *Jihad* it is specially necessary to place confidence in God and ask His assistance, which the Almighty has already bestowed on the Mussalmans on this occasion.

"Mussalmans of India being destitute of resources, and having no ammunition, guns, or army, have been all along in a helpless condition, but the Gracious God Who has strengthened the religion of Islam internally...furnished us with the resources formerly enjoyed by the useless and misconducting Christian Infidels (Kuffar, Nabukar, Nisara, Bud Utwar) and made them over to the Mussalmans of India with much ease and facility. Our being backed by a large Army of Infantry, Cavalry and Artillery, our having obtained an immense treasure, the arrival of the letter from the King of Delhi, the bonafide ruler of Hindustan who is the shadow and representative of God (May his dominions ever extend !), the assistance given to us by the Army of Birjis kadar, Ruler of Lucknow (May God always bless him with prosperity !)...are clear proofs that the people are determined to extirpate these rebel Christians now.

"O my Mussalman brethren ! As soon as you hear the above glad tidings, prepare yourselves for *Jihad,* come to Allahabad, subdue and put to sword the besieged Christians there, and try to expel the remnant of their bodies from this country, and then rule the country according to Laws and Institutions of Muhammad (after reestablishing the Mahomedan rule)....

"I quote for your perusal some lines from the Quran :

"....That he who believes in God, leaves his house (*Hijrat*), fights and devotes his life and property in His cause, obtains great glory and gains his final wishes."..... 'O you faithful believers ! Don't side with your fathers and brothers if they attach themselves to heresy (i.e. *Kufr*), and if you befriend them you will certainly be great sinners.' 'Say, do you prefer to God, to His Prophet, and to fighting in His cause, your fathers, sons, brothers, females, tribe, the money which you have earned, your trade....and your houses ?' 'If you do so, God will let fall his wrath upon you.' .... 'O you believers! How is it that when you march to fight in the cause of God, you all look pulled down, and your spirits are drooping, and that you do act upon this world in preference to your eternal life?' 'The worldly gains are nothing in comparison to eternal life.' 'If you will not go out of your house to fight, God will let fall his vengeance upon you, and substitute in your room other people'.... 'O you low and great! Come forward, fight in the cause of God, and devote both your life and property....' .... 'God loves those, who fight in His cause in battle, array like a wall stuffed with lead.' .... 'May God forgive your sins and admit you into His Elysian Gardens abounding in fountains, and into His Holy mansions.' .... 'God will assist you and give you a speedy victory.'

"Report this good news to the Believers." (3-448; 6-615; 90-197)

Like the first proclamation issued by the Nawab of Rohilkhand, this document too was a cogent *Jihadnama* and contained neither reference nor appeal to Hindus. Other *Jihad* declarations had contained assurances to Hindus for obtaining their support, with appeals for joining in the *Jihad* and for unity. Although the *Jihad* was primarily against *kafir* Christians, the fact that Hindus were also equally guilty of '*Kufr*' had thus created a contradiction in those declarations of *Jihad,* which inconsistency had been removed in these proclamations by the Nawab and the Maulvi. It is interesting to note that in the event of rule or domination by any *kafir* other than the British, the latter proclamations could have been utilized equally well by merely substituting the words 'British' or 'Christian' appearing therein.

Needless to reiterate, this declaration of *Jihad* mirrors the nature of the 1857 Uprising in an unadulterated, undisguised, pure and clear form!

M. Ahmad Shah's Proclamation

In his 12-page (about 5,500 words) historic proclamation entitled 'Fateh Islam', M. Ahmad Shah, the veritable 'crowning glory' and the most influential leader of the 1857 Uprising, in eulogizing whom Savarkar leaves no appellation of praise unused,[37] stated:

"Fateh Islam"

"Praise be to God who gives victory to the followers of the Mahomedan faith.

"Praise be to His Prophet Muhammad whose religion is glorious; and also to all the believers of the Mahomedan Faith, and to the *Ghazis* who are exalted.

"O Brethern ! At this present time, the execrable Christians are openly committing oppression and tyranny; they are killing innocent men, plundering their property, setting fire to their houses. It has been very difficult for the *Hafizes,* the learned and the pious, to live in their houses. The said Christians felt no hesitation whatever in hanging great chiefs. The accursed

37. For these appellations see Chap. 7, footnote 8. He also wrote: "Wherever this political saint went, there was seen an extraordinary awakening among the people. His voice was law in the royal family of Oudh. He was beloved by the masses of Oudh. With his body, his mind, his speech and his intelligence, he worked incessantly in preaching freedom and weaving a perfect net of secret societies. He then took up the pen also. In one hand the sword and in the other the pen!" (1-251)

Christians are so ungodly and inhuman that they forcibly press many poor people into their service, tie the hands of one with those of another...by pricking them with bayonets, force them to go in front to the field of battle, using them as shields for their own defence. Such has been the state of anarchy, that the whole country has been insecure.

"In fact, these outrageous acts are prelude to the downfall of these accursed people. As their past conduct in attempting to deprive the troops of their religion by applying impure substances to the cartridges...led to their destruction like dogs...; so their present proceedings have converted their subjects also into enemies.

"These accursed people have considered themselves as equal to the great Pharaoh, but they will all, please God, be butchered in the same manner as Pharaoh.[38] If they succeed in reestablishing their authority, great misfortunes will befall all the Hindus and Mahomedans, the people, the sepoys, the Kings and the Vazirs. A circumstance which renders the waging of a religious war at once with the execrable Christians is one of our bounden duties, enjoined by the Prophet. God be praised that the necessary material for the execution of that duty has, through His assistance, been now put in our possession i.e. the guns etc., which are required for a religious war. These are, through divine favour, now in the possession of the Mahomedan Kings of Delhi and Lucknow. May God save the Kings of the Mahomedans and make them victorious. A few troops of the English are still alive but they are paralyzed. Whoever will not take advantage of this opportunity to make a religious war, will repent in future as such chance will never again offer....

"The sepoys should now proceed to every country (i.e. province) and city and put the Christians to death. It is said

---

38. Pharaoh was the oppressive ruler of Egypt, whom Khuda had punished by drowning him in the sea because he had persecuted a past prophet of Islam, Moses. (128-382) This narrative in the Quran is a source of great inspiration to Muslims.

that they are about to practice enchantment on you, but…it cannot avail them, as it becomes defeated by the repetition of the invocation 'Allah-O-Akbar'.

"It is you sepoys who have kindled the flames and these cannot be extinguished but by you. You should therefore fight and pray (God for help). Do not put off till tomorrow that which can be done today and whatever it is possible to do today, let it be done forthwith. It is incumbent on the sepoys to consider the protection of Delhi and Lucknow as their first care, inasmuch as these two places are the asylums of the sepoys and the people high and low, and the enemies have fixed their teeth on them. A sufficient number of sepoys should be stationed in these two cities to protect them. The remaining sepoys, after receiving orders from the King, should proceed to the East being accompanied by the fanatics (*Ghazis*) who desire to make a religious war. They should kill and pursue the unbelieving (infidel) people as far as Calcutta. By doing so Delhi and Lucknow will be well protected. It is above all things a duty to collect the people desirous of waging a religious war…. If the Troops do not proceed to the East, the result will not be good. The advantages which will result need not be described, as they are manifest.

"Arise quickly in the name of God, and go forth to slay the infidels. May the Almighty give you strength, courage and victory. Cause it to be proclaimed by beat of drum that the sepoys are prohibited from plundering…the people of the places which they may conquer. It is however lawful to plunder the property of the enemy; such plundered property is designated 'Prize.' The Chief (Commander) will explain to you how that prize is to be divided among you.

"That you have recently succeeded in killing the English of high dignity and thousands of Europeans;[39] but, you are now flying before a small body of Europeans, whom even the shoemakers and spirit-sellers can put to death. It is the part of

39. This is a reference to the Battle of Chinhat in which this same Maulvi's forces had inflicted a crushing defeat on the British.

the sepoys, and religious fanatics, to destroy the infidels in the field of battle. The people also should at present, offer thanks to the Almighty, and fight valorously.

"In the time of the Prophet (Muhammad) 1000 Mahomedans, living on the leaves of trees, fought with 80,000 infidels. It is stated in the Quran, that 100 pious Mahomedans can, by the power of God, overcome 200 infidels and in like manner 1000 Mahomedans can overcome 2000 infidels. This blessing can be obtained if a holy leader be first appointed and then a religious war be undertaken. Now unite together, invoking God, and become of one mind. (Your leader should be from the Quraysh). If you do not find a Quraysh at this time when the infidels are paramount in power it is no consequence. Appoint a Mahomedan who is a Chief and in power, to be the leader of the Mahomedans and solemnly declare yourselves as his followers. It is incumbent on 1000 *Ghazis* to be steadfast in opposing 2000 infidels[40] but it is unlawful for them to take flight. The more obstinately they will fight, the greater spiritual benefit will accrue to them. Hence, the *Ghazis,* through 1000 in number, will please God, never flee even before 10,000 Europeans.

"History of the term Quraysh: Quraysh...was one of the ancestors of the last Prophet... His descendants are designated Quraysh... The Arabs are the bravest of all the nations in the whole world and the Quraysh are the most courageous amongst the Arabs. Hence God made the last Prophet a descendant of the Quraysh family of Arabia and caused the Quraysh and all other Arabs, to be his descendants and the followers of his faith, in order that when the Arabians and the Quraysh should be zealous for their religion, such religion might be propagated throughout the world. Certain sages have therefore pronounced it unlawful to appoint Commanders except of the Quraysh family.[41] But if at the time when infidels

40. Quran : 8:66. But this proportion (1:2) was when Muslims were weak. However, *Ayat* 8:65 mentions it as 1:10.

41. Leader of Muslims is the same as 'Khalifa' or 'Commander of Believers'. The Prophet is quoted in the *Hadis* to have said: "The Caliphate will remain among the Quraysh even if two persons are

(Contd.)

become paramount in power, a Quraysh be not found, any Mahomedan Chief endowed even with a few of the qualities of a leader and observing the tenets of the Mahomedan Law can, as a matter of necessity, be selected as Chief. This leader will be called 'Imam Akbar'. In short, it is held unlawful, even by the religious books, that the orders of a Mahomedan Chief, of whatever description he may be, should be obeyed. Commonsense and a regard of faith point out that servitude under the Mahomedan Chiefs and such Rajahs as are dependants of the Mahomedan Kings is infinitely better than that, under the infidel Victoria and the English, the enemies of our faith[42]....

"The Hindus should join the Chief (so selected) with a view to defend their religion, and should solemnly pledge themselves to be faithful; the Hindus and the Mahomedans, as brethren to each other, should also butcher the English inasmuch as formerly the Mahomedan Kings protected... the lives and property of the Hindus with their children in the same manner as protected those of the Mahomedans, and all the Hindus with heart and soul were obedient and loyal to the Mahomedan kings[43]....

"Our object in repeatedly requiring you to appoint Chiefs, is to gain for you the spiritual benefit and speedy mercy of God, from the execution of the injunctions of Mahomedan

---

left (on the earth)." ('Sahih Muslim' : 4476; 'Sahih Bukhari' : 7139). "People are subservient to the Quraysh." ('Sahih Muslim' : 4473) "People are the followers of Quraysh in good as well as evil." ('Sahih Muslim' : 4475)

42. Government editors print this part in italics, probably wishing to emphatically demonstrate how anti-British and freedom-loving the Maulvi was. (However, even in that prospective self-rule, Hindus were only destined for subservience.)

43. This entire paragraph has been printed in italics by government editors perhaps to show how the Maulvi's thinking was replete in sentiment of Hindu-Muslim unity and fraternity. (But it is plain that this unity and fraternity was to become manifest only after Hindus had accepted a Muslim king and taken a subservient position in the polity.)

Law. The fact is that the English have a Chief over them, but not God in their favour; whereas He sides with us. He had provided us, the Mahomedans, with a King to arrange our affairs. It is therefore incumbent on us to appoint a leader or chief forthwith and to obey his commands for the purpose of destroying English.

"The adoption of the following measures will lead to their destruction, viz: the *Ghazis*, among the people, as well as those among the troops...who are very brave and experienced in War, should with one accord slay the Christians in the field of battle, invoking at the same time '*Allah-O-Akbar*.' The people should seek opportunities to harass the enemy and render every service to the sepoys. That if the English sit down, they (sepoys) should lie down; if the English divide their Army into three or more parts, our sepoys should make as many divisions of troops or more than those divisions, and two or three divisions of our army should proceed to kill one division of theirs. They are to surround the English by stratagem and kill them. Several guns are to be fired at once. The Artillery men are to take the usual rest, but the fire is to be kept up. If they have to fight for three hours, they should keep with them a sufficient quantity of ammunition to last them for 24 hours. The time has now come for the appointment of a leader to wage a religious war. After that a report of the commencement of a religious war will be spread. The *Ghazis* will come from every direction, and your troops will be as innumerable as locust.

"It is a fact, that the solemn promise of a sepoy to his commander on the occasion of a religious war, is as binding as that of a person to his Spiritual Guide, at the time of the expiration of his sins. When a man makes such solemn declaration to his Spiritual Guide, he feels that he will derive spiritual benefit from him; he entertains strong feelings of attachment and devotion towards him; he looks upon all his acts as correct and good and he considers it easy under his orders to sacrifice his life, property and honour in the path to God. In like manner the sepoys in obeying the orders of their commander (who is regarded as a Spiritual Guide) will, with readiness, devote their lives to the service of the Almighty.

"When there is already a chief in power in any city, it is unnecessary to seek for another Chief to make him leader, for Almighty has already provided that place with a Chief and it is unlawful to appoint two leaders at one and the same place. It is incumbent on the people to appoint that Chief as their commander and act up to his orders and to consider him as their Spiritual Guide and also with one accord, under his command, to butcher all the Europeans. A good General obtains victory by a skilful disposition of his forces.

"We give as a specimen the following rules of warfare. In the first place count the number of fighting men and prepare their muster rolls; appoint intelligent and faithful men as your spies...since spies are the hands and legs of the person who employs them. The accursed English have been saved from destruction only by the help of spies. When they hear of the attack of an enemy, they should hold consultation with all the troops. After the consultation has been held, they should select 500 to 1000 of the strongest youths...fit for making an attack unawares. Some of them should cut the ropes of the tents, others should sever the heel ropes and hind stalls of the horses. Some should seize upon the arms and guns, others should fire volleys on the enemy, and put down them to the sword. Some should hide themselves in the jungles, ravines, and valleys and cut off the supplies of the enemy. They should make satisfactory arrangements regarding the rivers.

"All the Hindus and Mahomedans will afterwards invoke God and commence fighting. It is lawful to attack unawares and deceive the enemy but mutual promises should not be broken. All should be unanimous and vigilant in the field of the battle.

"The commanders and chiefs should encourage the troops, and incite them by shouts, exclaiming thus, '"Oh Warriors brave'; 'Oh Warriors, you have fought desperately'. 'Oh Warriors, you have overcome the enemy'; 'A hundred thanks are due to your mothers, whose milk has proved so invigorating'. 'Oh, Warriors, now the victory is gained'... 'Advance Heroes, we have now gained the victory'. 'Behold the enemy are turning their backs'. 'Oh my tigers, pounce upon the Jackals'. 'Oh brethren, you have saved my nose today';.... 'Oh *Ghazis,* you have upheld my honour'. 'Oh *Ghazis,* be careful, lest you incur shame, if I lose my beard'. 'Oh Brethren, kill the enemy. 'Oh *Ghazis,* I have sacrificed my parents to you.'

"Sometimes they should taunt the enemy in the manner : 'Why? Oh ye noxious ones, Whither are you flying now?' '....you are now fighting with Tigers?' 'Are you not under the influence of liquor?' 'Oh cowards, have you now forgotten manoeuvres? Why are you running away? Are the swords now brandished?' and so on.

"This proclamation is to be circulated to the Hindus and Mahomedans of Hindustan (Upper India); they may deeply reflect upon its contents and that they may be ready to destroy the English for the purpose of defending their respective religions.

"Before quarrel regarding the cartridges took place, these accursed English had written to the Impure Victoria thus: 'If Your Majesty will permit us to kill 15 Maulvis out of every 100 in India, and the same number out of every 100 Pandits, as well as five lac Hindus and Mahomedan sepoys and *ryots,* we will in a short time make all the people of India Christians." Then that ill-starred, polluted bitch gave her consent to the spilling of this innocent blood. The accursed men, on receipt of her permission, commenced committing general slaughter on the pretext of the cartridges. As no one was in a condition to oppose them, they would in a short time have killed every one who refused to become a Christian, had it not been that, by God's blessings, the bold sepoys butchered the English and put an end to all their power.

"It has become the bounden duty of all the people, whether women or men, slave girls or slave men, to come forward and put the English to death. The adoption of the following measures will lead to their destruction, viz. the Kings, Wazirs, Rajahs and Nawabs ought to slay them in the field of battle, the people should not leave their city...but on the contrary should shut up their doors and all the people, ought to put these accursed English to death by firing guns, carbines and pistols, from the terraces shooting arrows and pelting them with stones, bricks, earthen vessels, ladles, old shoes and all other things which may come to their hands. They should stone to death the English in the same manner, as the swallows stoned the Chief of the elephants.[44] The sepoys, the nobles, the shopkeepers, the oilmen, etc. and all other people of the city, being one accord should make a simultaneous attack upon them, some of them should kill them by firing guns, pistols, and carbines and with swords, arrows, daggers, poignards, etc. some lift them up on spears, some dexterously snatch their arms and destroy the enemy, some should cling to their necks, some to their waists, some should wrestle, some should strike them with cudgels, some slap them, some throw dust in their eyes, some should beat them with shoes, some attack them with their fists, some scratch them, some drag them along, some tear out their ears, some break their noses. In short, no one should spare any efforts, to destroy the enemy and reduce them to the greatest extremities. They will all be put to death.

"It is necessary to make the Proclamation generally known." (4-150 to 62)

'Dangerous and Inflammable Document'

We have reproduced above only about half of the Maulvi's proclamation, but it is sufficient to gauge how fanatical, extreme, inciting and provocative the entire piece must have been. It is not without justification that M. Ahmad Shah is regarded by historians as the most significant leader and veritable crown jewel of the 1857 Uprising! And it is not

---

44. An army consisting of elephants had been dispatched against the *Kaba* by the Christian ruler of Yemen in 570 CE (the year of the Prophet's birth). Khuda had sent a force comprising birds which pelted countless stones, held in their beaks, upon that Yemen army and destroyed it. (128-82) The reference here is to that historic event, which could only have made sense to Muslims.

without like reason that the British called this proclamation as "a highly dangerous and inflammable document." (59-270q.) This Maulvi was not just an Islamic scholar but also a skilled preacher, gifted organizer and proficient soldier. This 'Fateh Islam' proclamation was issued when the Maulvi was at the zenith of his achievements (July 1857) after vanquishing the British at Chinhat. (72-29; 132-1)

An Important Document

P.J.O. Taylor rightly observed that this historic proclamation is "a significant statement of the cause and nature of the struggle against the British." (132-1) As Dr. Bhargava says : "*Fateh-Islam*...gives true insight into the struggle." (72-79) According to the editors of the Government Publication, "(It) is an important document revealing the character of the Freedom Struggle in Awadh and pointing to its having been planned meticulously." (4-150n)

Who Should be the Leader?

There is no need to elaborate upon the proclamation. Or, no amount of elaboration can be excessive! Undoubtedly, this was a *Jihad* declaration for victory of Islam drafted by a Maulvi who was a follower of the Waliullahi philosophy. It is remarkable indeed that a stipulation had been clearly expressed therein, in conformity to Islamic doctrine, that the post Uprising head of state ought to be a Muslim belonging to the Quraysh tribe of the Arabs. Also stated was the reluctant readiness, only as a temporary compromise, to make do with some Muslim from a different ethnic stock if a Quraysh could not readily be found in India at that juncture. That leader or commander was also going to assume spiritual leadership, and be bound by the implicit requirement of spreading Islam all over the world. Obviously, therefore, no Hindu despite all his merit for leadership was ever going to get the right of becoming such leader. The proclamation thus shackled Hindus to remain loyal, obedient and subservient (or tributaries) to Muslim rulers under the envisaged self-rule, just as they had been under previous Muslim regimes. All that had come to the share of Hindus was to help the Muslims in slaughtering the *kafir* British. And, Hindus and Muslims are called 'brethren of each other' only as a ruse to encourage the former to give their unstinted support in this undertaking.

It would be sufficient, in the context of this proclamation, to quote a comment made by Gautam Bhadra in his essay included in an anthology edited by historian Ranjit Guha: "What was there in the Maulvi's ideas to account for 'the wonderful influence possessed by him over his followers?' For an answer we may turn to the pamphlet, *Fateh-i-Islam,* published after the battle of Chinhat, (when) Ahmadullah Shah's influence was at its highest. Written as a proclamation, it served as a vehicle of the ethical and political ideas of the rebellion. 'The proclamation,' said a loyalist Indian of Awadh at that time, 'is a highly dangerous and inflammable document for its contents are explicitly believed by the common people who are consequently much exasperated against the English.' The idiom in which the proclamation was written was religious. It represented the loss of religion as the loss of life, property, home and finally, honour. The direct condemnation of the Queen of England in the most abusive terms sets the *Fateh-i-Islam* apart from the contemporary statements of this genre.... (In it) the recommendation (of choosing a leader) is clearly sectarian as well as theological. It has been sacralized by *Quranic* precepts and *Shariat* Laws." (59-270 to 2)

Mirrors of the Nature of the Uprising

In conclusion, it becomes amply clear that all proclamations and declarations issued during the period of the 1857 Uprising were, in reality, declarations of *Jihad* founded on the Quran and the *Hadis,* based upon Islamic principles, and representing Muslim thought. Even proclamations issued in the names of Hindu rulers were not free of this bias or nature. Veritably, all those documents are mirrors reflecting the fundamental cause and true spirit of the 1857 Uprising!

* * *

Chapter 9

Hindu-Muslim Struggle During the Uprising

Hindus and Muslims have coexisted in India for several centuries. This long coexistence is marked by occasions of understanding and unity as well as opposition and strife. This notwithstanding, it is particularly and emphatically said that during the 1857 Uprising — not just with respect to that period, but even present times — this coexistence had reached an acme of unprecedented and exemplary amity between the two communities. It is often referred to as inspirational, and a remarkable incidence of Hindu–Muslim unity[1]. The entire

1. Savarkar's comment on this: "These first five days proclaimed by beat of drum the end for the time being at any rate of the continuous fight between the Hindus and Mahomedans, dating from the invasion of Mahmood Ghazni. It proclaimed first that the Hindus and Mahomedans are not rivals, not conquerors or conquered, but brethren. They unanimously raised the flag of national freedom at Delhi." (1-126) "Besides, the sight of Hindu and Mahomedan fighting side by side for Hindusthan realizing their true interests and natural comradeship, was truly magnificent and inspiring." (1-199)

advent of the Uprising is often sought to be viewed in terms of the stimulation it provided in this respect for future generations. If indeed such was the case, it might have delighted one and all. However, history does not permit idealism or wishful thinking, only for their sake, to be accepted as reality. It is founded on evidence and fact, not goodwill or sentiment!

It thus becomes essential from the historical perspective to determine the nature of this unity during the Uprising. A review of the history of the period reveals that the same inter-community relations usually found to prevail at other times, were also in play during the Uprising. Thus, the idealistic picture that is conjured up is not true.[2]

A great deal had been said and written by historians about this much vaunted unity. Without repeating it, we will merely see details of the more serious Hindu-Muslim conflicts so as to obtain a comprehensive picture of the nature of the Uprising.

The Conflict in Rohilkhand

It is generally observed that resistance to the British was more intense in regions that were under Muslim domination; it was also these areas that saw greater incidence of Hindu-Muslim friction. Clashes between Hindus and Muslims were more pronounced in areas that remained longer under rebel Muslim administrators or comparatively free from British campaigns to suppress the rebellion, and which had enjoyed freedom for slightly greater periods than others. Foremost among such provinces was Rohilkhand, which was under Muslim domination (not by demographic majority) and had been ruled by Khan Bahadur Khan for eleven and a half months

---

2. For example, Minister for Education Maulana Azad writes in the Preface of a book on '1857' published by the Union Government: "We do not, however, find during the whole period (of the Mutiny) a single instance when there was a clash or conflict on communal basis. All Indians — whether Muslim or Hindu — looked at things from the same point of view and judged events by the same standards." (141-xxv, vi)

before the British had turned to deal with rebellion in this region. "Rohilkhand was the only region in Northern India where the British were routed during the Revolt." (45-xviii) As a majority of incidents of communal conflict occurred there, we will take a look first at Rohilkhand.

Bijnor District

Detailed information about the happenings in Bijnor, 64 kilometers from Meerut, are recorded by Sayyed Ahmad Khan (knighted in later years), who was appointed by the British at the place as judge and administrative officer. He wrote a 121-page book *History of Bijnor Rebellion,* of which 80 pages are devoted to information about this conflict. The nature of that clash was briefly as follows.

Of the 6,20,000 population of the district 33 percent was Muslim and the remaining, Hindu. Mahmud Khan, Nawab of Najibabad, was ruling since the rebellion. His nephew, Ahmadullah Khan, was the *de facto* ruler and used all the powers of sovereignty on his behalf. The nawab lived at Najibabad while the district headquarter was at Bijnor. Muslims were dominant in urban areas and Hindus, in the villages. Thakur Chaudharies were landholders in rural areas, possessed fortified citadels and were powerful[3]. But they were opposed to the nawab's rule — a reason for friction between them. This burgeoned into armed Hindu-Muslim conflict. These Chaudharies assisted one another.

Nawab's Attack on Sherkot

The Nawab began extorting money from these Choudharies upon assuming power.[4] A sum of Rs. 1 lac was

---

3. The following names of the Chaudharies appear frequently: Ram Dayal Singh of Nagina, Umrao Singh of Sherkot, Pratap Singh of Tajpur, Randhir Singh and Budh Singh of Haldaur, Nain Singh and Jodh Singh of Bijnor.

4. Dr. Mujumadar writes: "After setting himself firmly in his authority, the Nawab began to oppress the Hindu chiefs. These, however, combined and drove him from Bijnor. Then followed a bitter and prolonged fight between the Hindus and the Muslims in which ultimate victory vested with the latter. This was celebrated by a wanton massacre of unoffending Hindus." (67-60; 68-521)

demanded from Umrao Singh of Sherkot and, even as negotiations were in progress, Ahmadullah Khan attacked the town on 23rd July. The fortress was invested, the Chaudhary's uncle was put to death, other zamindars' properties plundered and several Hindu men and women were killed. Their houses were torched. (45-47) Many were taken into custody. Umrao Singh escaped and went to Pratap Singh of Tajpur for refuge. Sherkot and its fort fell into the Khan's hands and the large quantity of material within the citadel was appropriated. Orders were issued to demolish the fortification. (49)

The local temple was also destroyed. (48)

This affair caused all Chaudharies in the district to unite. A meeting between them was held on 31st July and appeals were sent out in the district through criers for all Hindus to prepare themselves for struggle. Some of the nawab's officers and kin were taken into custody at Dhampur. Two soldiers in the Nawab's employ were killed. Then began a programme of putting everyone of the Nawab's men to death wherever found. (49) "However, in this fighting, the growth of hatred between Hindus and Muslims became more and more pronounced. On the one side there was the group of Hindu leaders, while there was the group of Muslim leaders on the other side. To Hindus new support was exclusively Hindu. The same happened for the Nawab; the support which he brought together was all Muslim." (50) Muslims demolished temples in Sherkot, while Hindus did the same to masjids in Chittawar and Sawahari. "This hatred grew so intense that it proved impossible to rescue Hindus whenever the Muslims had upper hand, or to rescue Muslims whenever the Hindus had upper hand." (50)

Hindus Attack Bijnor

Another battle was fought on 5th August. Chaudharies went for the relief of Sherkot and encircled Ahmadullah Khan who was still there. Many Muslim men and some women were killed. The Khan was defeated and fled to Najibabad. Hindus got their fortress back. (53)

But Hindus were not content with this. They suddenly attacked Bijnor on the following day with 4,000 men. Nawab Mahmud Khan lost his nerve. (55) Nevertheless, he mustered all his courage and went out to resist them with a force of 400, but was defeated and forced to flee to Najibabad.

Hindus took control of Bijnor and proclaimed a state in their name. (57) Several Muslims from villages in the vicinity were killed, and many mosques plundered and demolished. A similar conflict began in Bijnor. But for mediation of a Chaudhary leader, Nain Singh, every Muslim might have been slaughtered. (58) The British had previously asked the Nawab to take over administration of the area. Now they asked the Chaudharies to do so. (67) A proclamation was made on their behalf, 'Mulk Maharani Victoria ka, Hukum Company Bahadur ka!' (Here, 'Mulk Badshah ka' is absent).

Incidents of violence like this were occurring frequently. "The tree of Hindu-Muslim aversion for each other, which had been planted in the fighting at Sherkot, became very tall and too firmly rooted to dig out." (58)

The upper hand gained at Bijnor by Hindus was temporary. It had only been the result of their surprise attack. They lacked trained, professional soldiers. The nawab was better placed in that respect. (59)

News spread everywhere that the nawab was advancing upon Bijnor with a force of 4,000. Chaudharies, on their own, were unwilling to continue administration because they knew well that in truth, it was impossible that the people of the district would accept anyone other than Nawab Mahumad Khan as their ruler."[5] (30) They were aware that the Nawab and people of the district would not allow them to rule. They desired, instead, that the British should take over administration. (65)

---

5. Despite the fact that Muslims formed just 33 percent of the population, they were united in the demand for self rule and were solidly behind the Nawab; Hindus were neither united nor desirous of self rule — a reason for reluctance of the Chaudharies.

In the meantime, the Nawab began harassing the Hindu populations. Their houses were plundered and villages torched. Many Jat villages like Musapur, Hasanpur, Mohanpur, Shafiabad, Narayanpur, Patijatan and Kardili were reduced to ashes. (72)

Battles at Nagina

The Nawab also attacked Chaudhary Ram Dayal Singh's Nagina. A fierce battle was fought on 21st August in which both sides suffered much casualties. The Nawab was defeated. (86) A part of the town where Shaikh Muslims lived was torched. Thereafter, all Muslims in Nagina came together and another skirmish ensued. Both sides suffered casualties. (86) Ram Dayal Singh then made a compromise with Muslims, but the truce was not approved by Hindus, leading to another encounter. Fifty to sixty Muslims were killed, while 200 to 500 Hindus died in the Muslim counterattack. Muslims occupied the fortress and Ram Dayal Singh was forced to flee. (87)

In the meantime, reports of Muslim killings in Nagina reached Najibabad. Nawab Mahmud Khan told his people, "Look what the Hindus have done to the Muslims! All the Muslims ought to come together to kill the Hindus!" (88) Immediately, the Muhammadi flag was hoisted (22nd August 1857) and war declared against Hindus. A large force came together, since many Muslims were ready to fight a religious war to kill the Hindus. (88)

Ram Dayal Singh, who had been defeated in Nagina, went to Bijnor and met all the principal Chaudharies. Taking cannons with them, thousands of people left for Nagina to avenge atrocities on Hindus. Muslim men and women left the town when the attack was launched. They were looted and wounded by the attackers on the way. Hindu Chaudharies gained control over Nagina. (88)

The force of 3,000 that had assembled under the Muhammadi flag in Najibabad had left for Nagina at this time. It torched the village of Sawahari *en route*. (89) After reaching Nagina, this army looted the town completely and put 52 Hindus to death. (91)

The Nawab's Attack on Haldaur

After taking vengeance on Hindus in Nagina, the Nawab's army fell upon the second stronghold of the Chaudharies, Haldaur. (92) Chaudhary leaders came out to resist the attackers, a battle was engaged in the vicinity of a river in which the Hindus were defeated and they took refuge within their heavily fortified citadel in the town, which had been encircled by a moat for protection against the Nawab. The Hindus opened musket fire on the attackers but the Nawab's force proved stronger. It breached the wall and entered the town. The ensuing attack left 50 – 60 Hindus dead. (92) Their houses were set on fire and, within a short time, all structures except one were reduced to ashes. About a dozen Hindus died in the conflagration. Muslim residents of the town had lit the fires from within. The fire was so intense that the Khan's army was forced to wait outside the fortification. Indeed, the attackers left for Bijnor without attempting an entry into the town, burning the Hindu Pheriyapur village on the way. They faced no resistance at Bijnor because Chaudhary leaders had left in fear. The Nawab took control of that town. (93)

Khan then decided to reduce Tajpur. However, when his intention became known, Pratap Singh of Tajpur and all Hindu inhabitants evacuated the town completely. (93) So the Khan did not venture there at all.

Choudharies Retake Haldaur

Hindus from surrounding areas got together as soon as the Khan left the burning town and 3,000 of them, under leadership of Chaudharies, went to Haldaur (28th August 1857). While all houses belonging to Hindus had been burnt down, Muslims who had lit the fires yet inhabited the place. Closing all exit routes from the town, Hindus ensured that not a single Muslim was alive by evening. The womenfolk were taken into custody — some were killed. (94) Their houses were torched. Having mutually destroyed every house by fire, just one fortified mansion, belonging to Randhir Singh, remained in the town. Indeed not a single bit of straw remained in Haldaur.

A bird in search of some straw for its nest at that time could not have borrowed even a tiny bit in Haldaur." (94)

While the Chaudharies were busy restoring and strengthening their mansion after taking control of Haldaur, the Khan attacked them another time. All Hindus who had come together in the town fled as soon as the attackers arrived. The mansion was surrounded and subjected to heavy musket fire. Some of the Nawab's men were killed in retaliatory fire. (97) The Khan ultimately gave up and went back to Bijnor. On the way (1st September 1857), he killed several people in the Hindu village of Nangal, looting and destroying it by fire. (98)

A Chaudhary Defeated at Najibabad

Although the Khan had gained an upper hand in the district militarily, the Choudharies were yet unwilling to submit. They attacked Najibabad in force but were defeated. (101)

Realizing that they were making no headway, some Chaudharies sued for a compromise. Pratap Singh met the Nawab on 26th September and even made a gift of a few gold coins as a token of fealty. (102)

However, the Nawab's people were unwilling to make a truce. On the very same day two of the Nawab's commanders went to Sherkot with the intention of killing Hindus. They killed 32 people in a most cruel manner, subjecting 29 others to a less painful death. Many had already fled. The mere mention of the Nawab's army would send chills of dread up Hindu spines. In the words of Sir Sayyed Ahmad Khan, "From this time on, the fear of (the Commander of Nawab) became overpowering especially for the Hindus, whose hearts were so repressed they began to tremble and shiver wherever his army appeared." (103)

Randhir Singh Captured

The Nawab's army attacked Haldaur a third time and were successful in capturing Randhir Singh on 3rd November 1857.

Six or seven of his close relatives were killed. He was taken to Najibabad in chains, his wealth looted and the mansion burnt down. Haldaur had now become 'an absolute waste.' (103)

The Nawab felt secure once the Hindu threat had been neutralized in this manner. The Hindu-Muslim conflict in the Bijnor district had waged for over three months at a time when the British were fighting revolutionaries in Delhi and other places[6]. This nawab ruled until the British finally conquered the district in April 1858. The Nawab freed Chaudhary Randhir Singh only when it became amply clear that the British would triumph. (121) No doubt, both the Chaudhary and the local Hindu population must have been overjoyed when the British reestablished control![7] Thereafter, Randhir Singh continued to fight on the side of the British and against the *Jihad*. It should astonish none that the Rajputs and other Hindus had throughout (the period of the Mutiny) stood firm in their allegiance (to the British). (99-23)

---

6. N. R. Phatak writes: "The Nawab slaughtered Hindus in September. However, Hindu-Muslim strife continued till the military strength of the British increased." (44-97)

Dr. Chaudhary, who calls the 1857 Uprising a war of independence, writes: "But he could not restore law and order; far less stop the bloody wars between the Hindus and the Mahomedans." (81-109) (In fact, the Nawab was himself the chief party to these wars. Thus, expecting him to have done anything at all to stop the 'bloody wars,' which he had himself initiated, is absurd.)

7. The then British Commissioner reported about this district: "The Hindus we hear from all sides delighted with the progress of our force and Mussalmans are neither to be seen nor found." (7-401)

N. K. Behere writes: "Nawab Mahmud Khan of Bijnor torched many villages in the region and slaughtered Hindus. As a result of heinous atrocities, the local Hindus sincerely helped the British and uprooted the rebels." (158-281)

Sir Sayyed Ahmad clarifies that the British had no hand in provoking Hindus against Muslims during the conflict.[8] (45-61, 97)

The Conflict in Badaun District

The situation in the Badaun district was no different.

Abdur Rahman Khan had begun administration as collector (*nazim*) on behalf of Nawab Khan Bahadur Khan. Thereafter, all the clashes that occurred were between this Khan's administration and local Hindu Thakurs. The main problem in the district (facing the Nawab) was to suppress the recalcitrant Hindu Zamindars. (34-301)

His first act after assuming power was to lead an army against opposing Thakurs, put 307 of them to death and burn their villages. (7-312)

Hindu resistance to the Nawab's rule became manifest far and wide. Nehal Singh, a Thakur leader of a northern part of the district, Bisauli, defied authority of Azeez Khan, the local representative of the Nawab, and drove him away. However, this Khan brought in troops from Bareilly and reestablished his sway. Hindus from surrounding areas came together and intended to attack Bisauli, but returned without doing so.

---

8. However, it was this same Sir Sayyed Ahmad who had, in post-Uprising times, solicited just such a rift to the British by suggesting: "Government certainly did put the two antagonistic races into the same regiment, but constant intercourse had done its work and the two races in the regiment had almost become one. If separate regiments of Hindus and separate regiments of Mahomedans had been raised, this feeling of brotherhood could not have arisen." (45-171) In this respect, he had indicated Nadir Shah as an ideal for emulation: "When Nadir Shah conquered Khurasan and became master of two kingdoms of Persia and Afghanistan, he invariably kept two armies at equal strength. The one was composed of Persians, and the other of Afghans. When the Persian Army attempted to rise, the Afghan army was at hand to quell the rebellion and vice versa. The English did not follow this precedent in India (and hence the Mutiny)." (171)

(313) Thereafter, the Khan sent soldiers to the Thakurs and began extorting money. Villages of Khanak and Rafiyabad, belonging to opposing Thakurs, were torched. The Thakurs attacked Badaun but were defeated. (314) The Thakurs in the Hatauli area, too, denied the Nawab's authority and marched upon Badaun. But they were defeated as well. (315)

Hindu Challenge to Nawab from Bisauli and Bharauti

A detachment under Fasahatullah was sent to chastise Hindus in Bisauli because the latter were refusing to submit to the Nawab's authority. Hindus came together with a force of 2,000 and defeated this detachment at Wazirganj. The Nawab then dispatched a force of 4,000 and 5 cannons, which put the Hindus to flight, committed innumerable atrocities on them and amassed immense war booty. (321)

A Muslim zamindar looted affluent Hindus in the wealthy town of Ganj Gunbara. Thakurs, Jats, Ahirs and other classes of Hindus united to attack that zamindar and wreak vengeance by plundering his belongings thoroughly. (676)

A force of 10,000 volunteers and 10 cannons under command of Chhiddu Singh had been kept ready by Ahir Hindus of Bharauti in order to disown the Nawab's rule and engage in armed conflict if necessary. (322) This force engaged in a protracted combat with the Nawab's general, Niyaz Ali Khan.

Frustration of Defeat turned against Hindus

The Nawab's forces decided to attack a detachment of British soldiers near the Surajpur pass. "The General made an announcement in the town that all Mussalmans who are prepared for *Jihad* should accompany him.[9] (323) 2,000 Jihadis responded to the call. (324) When soldiers began clamouring for wages, the commander demanded an immediate sum of Rs.3 lacs from Hindu moneylenders. One of them, Mohanlal, was subjected to corporal torture. (324)

---

9. This illustrates how commanders during the Uprising used to lure Muslims alone, and that too by invoking 'Jihad', while fighting against the British.

However, this Jihadi army was mauled by the British in the ensuing battle, leaving hundreds of them dead. Many drowned in the Ganga River. This frustration found an outlet against Hindus. The commander invited five prominent Thakur leaders for talks, had them arrested and severely beaten up for having allegedly given asylum to Christians. Two of them were half-dead after the beating, one was paraded through the town mounted on a mule and then executed by cannon and the remaining two were threatened with a similar death unless they paid ransom of Rs. 40,000. They were kept in prison for two months and then sent to Bareilly. (325) Likewise, 50 Hindus were arrested for defaulting in payment of taxes. (325)

Nawab's Atrocities on Hindus

The same communal bitterness showed at Moradabad, too. The result was the disaffection of the Hindus who welcomed the return of the British forces. (67-60; 68-535) When Shahzada Firoz Shah was in Moradabad, he had issued a directive to impose a tax on every Hindu. Not too much later, British forces established control over the region and Hindus were liberated from this new *jaziya*.

The Nawab of Bareilly began his rule over Pilibhit district after the Uprising. The same communal conflict began between the Muslim administration and Hindu zamindars. Thakur Hindus of Nawabganj refused to submit to the Nawab and, as usual, an army was sent to neutralize them and establish authority. (34-299)

The Bareilly Nawab's rule was also established over the Shahjahanpur district and Hindu zamindars presented a challenge to it here as well. The army sent from Bareilly killed many Hindus. (68-522) Severed heads of Rajput Hindus were paraded in the streets. A Hindu goldsmith, who had advanced money against mortgage of jewellery, was put to death by the local *nazim* when he refused to return them without settlement of loans. (7-298) Hindus were praying fervently for deliverance from the Nawab's draconian rule.

The situation in Bareilly, capital town of Rohilkhand, was similar to other districts. Rather than narrate incidents of very much the same essence, we would prefer to present some comments of historians about conditions there.

Rise of the Communal Demon

Dr. Mujumadar writes: "The demon of communalism also raised its head. The Muslims spat over the Hindus and openly defiled their houses by sprinkling them with cows' blood and placing cows' bones within the compounds. Concrete instances are given where Hindu sepoys came into clash with the Muslim hooligans engaged in defiling Hindu houses, and a communal riot ensued. The Hindus, oppressed by the Muslims, were depressed at the success of the Mutiny, and daily offered prayers to God for the return of the English." (67-177; 68-520)

N. R. Phatak describes the situation as follows: "Bareilly had a class of fanatic Muslims who held the view that Hindus should have nothing to do with governance in Khan Bahadur's regime. The show of harmony and understanding[10] put up by Khan Bahadur faded and open conflict between Hindus and Muslims commenced. Disgruntlement between the two communities continued till the British finally captured Bareilly. Khan Bahadur had given the assurance[11] of imposing a ban on cow slaughter 'if Hindus assisted Muslims in the fight against the British'. That 'assistance' was a pre-condition for the ban may easily be noted... (Thereafter) atrocities (on Hindus) crossed all limits. Looting and forcible invasion upon women's chastity became rampant... spitting on Hindus... the blood and bones of cows...all this led to Hindu-Muslim conflicts."

---

10. One part of this show was the cooption of the one Hindu, Shobha Ram, in his council of ministers. The second part was his assurance of a conditional ban on cow slaughter. (See supra. p.401).

11. Not just superficial assurances like this one, but, "efforts of all kinds are still being made to raise the Hindu population against us, extending even to threats of forcibly converting to Mahomedanism, those who show any sympathy with the British Government." (7-344)

(44-367) "A popular slogan of the time was 'Islam ka bolbala, Firangi ka muh kala.' 'Islam ka bolbala' (or fame of Islam) was immensely disquieting to the Hindu heart. The British were capable of suppressing both, which was why the Hindu society had remained free from the independent 'bolbala' of Islam for two generations (previously)." (374)

Such communal conflict had flared up generally everywhere in Rohilkhand. The state had taken up the cause of Muslims. Dr Mujumadar writes: "The communal hatred led to ugly communal riots in many parts of U.P. Green Flags were hoisted and bloody wars were fought between the Hindus and Muslims in Bareilly, Bijnor, Moradabad and other places where the Muslims shouted for the revival of the Muslim Kingdom." (67-231; 55-87) Usha Sanyal writes: "The disappearance of British authority in Rohilkhand in the first phase of the revolt led to a struggle for control by Rohilkhand's old rivals, the Rajputs and Pathans." (13-31) Even Dr. Chaudhary is obliged to concede: "In Rohilkhand the movement took the form of a Mahomedan rising and was marked by communal distemper." (81-290)

Hindus Welcome English Troops

Hindus in Rohilkhand were loath to accept political domination of Khan Bahadur Khan. They were agitating continuously against it. Confidence that "The Hindu population of Rohilkhand is sick of Muslim rule, and eagerly awaits the return of British power" (44-237) felt by Lord Canning was not misplaced. The British were certain that Hindus would join them in any campaign they undertook in Rohilkhand. (7-369,466) Indeed, Hindus were delighted to welcome the return of British rule.

We have discussed the Rohilkhand uprising in some greater detail because those events are eulogized as 'popular' or 'national uprisings'. (81-108, 290) It may be viewed as representative of the overall success of the various rebellions that occurred in North India.

Let us now review happenings in other important places.

In Meerut Province

Nawab Walidad Khan commenced his rule immediately after the revolt at Bulandshahar in the Meerut province. All conflicts thereafter were between Hindus and Muslims. How local Hindu Jats and Gujars struggled against the Nawab's rule, and how the latter's armies fought battles and committed atrocities has already been seen in Chapter 6. The Nawab had declared a *Jihad* against Hindu Jats, naming them as *kafirs*, along with the British.

The situation in the Muzaffarnagar district was no different. Post-Uprising incidents was a saga of Hindu-Muslim conflict. Hindu moneylenders here, too, were attacked like in Rohilkhand. Beef would be stuffed into their mouths. These incidents have already been narrated in Chapter 5. An Islamic State had been established according to the *Shariat* at Thanabhavan in the district.

Saharanpur, another district place, saw similar incidents. Local Hindu moneylenders and *mahajans* had given up all hope. This, too, has been reviewed earlier in Chapter 5.

The Kasganj Struggle

A power struggle commenced in the Etah district of the Agra province as soon as the revolt occurred and the English had withdrawn. Dambar Singh first established his rule which was wrested from him militarily by the Nawab of Farukhabad.

Rebellion and atrocities on Hindus had begun from the month of May. Hurmat Khan was leader of the Muslims. He entered the prominent town of Kasganj (23rd May) and seriously wounded a certain Zunnilal, a moneylender, who had initiated civil proceedings against the Khan. His son's shop was plundered. Three temples were looted on the following day and their idols were broken. On the third day, the market was looted.

Then began a conflict between Pathans from Bisauna and Hindus from Etah. A nephew of the Hindu Raja of Etah was killed in the ensuing battle. Unable to suffer this injustice and persecution any longer, Hindus united to launch an attack on Bisauna and destroy it. (7-681)

The British captured this region in November and appointed the Hindu Ghanashyam Das as collector. Muslims in the vicinity of Bisauna came together and attacked Kasganj under leadership of Matin Khan. Ghanashyam Das was put to death and his severed head was hung on a tree outside the tehsil office. But 'the Tehsildar, Shaikh Faizuddin, being a Mussalman was of course spared.' (7-681) Hindus were looted in the aftermath. All this enjoyed active support from the Nawab of Farukhabad. Hindus were tied to muzzles of loaded cannons and threatened to be blown apart in order to extort money. (682) The British recaptured the area after two weeks and Hindus were spared further persecution.

Hindus in Agra had publicly celebrated the British recapture of Delhi, which indicates how intensely they must have been opposed to the Muslim rule that had been established after the Uprising.

Struggle in Allahabad Province

Subedar M. Liyaqat Ali had ruled over Allahabad for just nine or ten days. He was particularly attentive to religious conversions and used to forcibly proselytize Hindus. He was a leader who believed in the saying: "True heaven lies beneath the strokes of the sword." Although his proclamation (see Chapt. 6) was *prima facie* against English *kafirs*, it could as well be used verbatim against Hindus. However, his regime was short-lived and provided little scope for internal squabbles to manifest themselves.

Nanasahib was made leader at Kanpur, but sepoys had later put up Nanhe Nawab in opposition to him. Schemes to depose Nanasahib were being hatched. Even assassination was being contemplated. After the incident in which a butcher had been chastised, thousands of Muslims had marched upon his residence and Nanasahib had profusely apologized to them, granting permission to slaughter as many cows as they wished. Hindu-Muslim discord had reared its head here. (44-50) The rebel regime had lasted for 15 days, leaving no opportunity for the conflict to surface.

Banda came under Nawab Ali Bahadur's rule after the revolt. The Hindu Raja of Ajaygarh, Ranjor Dauwa, was opposed to the Nawab and stood up firmly against the new regime. Armed conflict between them ensued. In a battle fought in August, Dauwa emerged victorious and took control of Bhurgarh. The Nawab dispatched a large force in November, comprehensively defeated Dauwa and arrested him. His Nimnipur fort was razed. (90-93) Dr. Chaudhary writes about the revolt in Banda, "The Mahomedans regarded the scene (of revolt) as a holy war to result in the extermination of the *kafirs*. The (Hindu) mahajans were made to contribute to the royal treasury by forced and unacknowledged loans." (81-209)

In Hamirpur, it was AliBakhsh who began ruling after the revolt. Ratan Singh, Chief of Charkhari, who was powerful and nonsubmissive, had prevented Ali Bakhsh from transporting the local treasury to Delhi. Armed conflict began between them. This Chief was loyal to the British for which reason Tatya Tope had invaded his territory.

Benares Division

Immediately after the rebellion in Benares, sepoys had advanced upon the famous Vishveshshwar temple with the intention of unfurling the green flag there. However, their attempt was frustrated and undesirable consequences averted because Hindus united and assisted the British. Even Dr. Chaudhary admits that, "Hindu-Muslim dissension also raised its head (at Benares), the green flag was hoisted." (81-157) The Hindu Raja and population stood firmly behind the British. The rebellion was soon quelled and no major manifestation of communal strife was seen.

Muhammad Hasan began ruling in Gorakhpur after the rebellion. Hindus in Bansi and Basti were opposed to the regime, resulting in the Raja and Rani respectively of those places disowning it. Muhammad Hasan sent 4,000 troopers against Bansi and defeated the Chief who fled into the woods. The army took possession of the town and the palace. Hindu Chiefs of Gopalpur and two other principalities, too, were against the Nawab. All of them sincerely helped the British. The British, in turn, had supplied some troops and field guns in the aforementioned battle. (6-338)

In Ayodhya Province, Too

A conflict between Hindus and Muslims had been initiated in Ayodhya on the eve of the Uprising over the Hanumangarhi affair. The Nawab was entirely sympathetic to the Muslim cause. He subscribed brazenly to the belief that the mosque was superior to the temple and that there was nothing wrong in demolishing the latter to build the former. It was only because of British intervention that Hanumangarhi was secured to the Hindus. (See Chap. 6). This contentious issue had become one of the topical reasons at the time for annexation of the state.

Most of the talukdars and zamindars in the province had stood behind the British in opposition to the Nawab's rule. Indeed, Man Singh of Shahganj had stood firmly behind the Hindu cause from the time of the Hanumangarhi entanglement. He used to recount history of Muslim regimes to the Hindus in an effort to appeal to them to unite for the cause of religion and the honour of their womenfolk. (See Chap. 6). The Muslim leader, M. Ahmad Shah, had declared *Jihad* against Hindus before the Uprising. Man Singh openly sided with the British in later times for which precise reason Mehdi Hasan of Sultanpur and Muhammad Hasan of Gorakhpur had invaded his territories.

Fate of Hindu Sepoys in Punjab

The British had thwarted any possibility of internecine communal conflict by crushing the rebellion in Punjab province as soon as it broke out. However, an incident may be cited as a representation of the outlook of Muslims towards Hindus. Many deserted after the 55th N.I. as Hotimardan rebelled.

Historian Kaye writes about the fate of Hindu sepoys as they fled through Muslim areas: "(They), disappointed and destitute, were turning their faces towards the country of Rajah of Kashmir, sick of Mussalman fanaticism, and hoping to excite sympathy and obtain service under a Rajput Government. These poor deluded Hindus, who had abandoned pay, pension, peace, everything of that was dear to them, under a blind besetting belief in the bigotry of their Christian masters, now found themselves breast high in the bitter waters of Mahomedan persecution. They had escaped the chimera of greased cartridges to be despoiled of their sacred threads and circumcised. (78-371) Such were events that unfolded *en route*: "Many a sleek Brahman was made a compulsory Mahomedan, doomed to servile officers in their masjids; others were sold for slaves." (371n)

The Conflict in Delhi

Delhi remained the main centre of the 1857 Uprising. We have already seen in Chapter 5 the nature of Hindu-Muslim relations in Delhi during the Uprising. Maulvis had declared a *Jihad* against Hindus after all Christians in Delhi had been liquidated. They insisted that such a *Jihad* declaration should also be officially issued by an Imperial decree. But the Emperor had declined to do so. A son of the Emperor and Prime Minister (Vazir), Jawan Bakht, had stated that they would first finish Christian *kafirs,* and then kill Hindus. Hindus in Delhi were terrified during the Uprising, living in constant fear and praying for a British victory. They were also rendering what assistance they could to the British and expressing joy when the latter won one victory or another. Sikhs had expressed their extreme anti-Muslim feelings by openly siding with the British. All these happenings are not indications of Hindu-Muslim unity, but of its contradiction.

Let us see what some experts have to write in this context. William Dalrymple, who believes the 1857 Uprising was a united struggle by Hindus and Muslims, and that Bahadur Shah Zafar was like Akbar, 'an attractive symbol of Islamic civilization at its most tolerant and pluralistic', provides the following noteworthy information: On 20th May the Maulvi turned up at the Palace to remonstrate with Zafar, claiming that Hindus were all supporters of the English, and that a *Jihad* against them was therefore perfectly legitimate. Zafar declared that in his eyes Hindus and Muslims were equal and that 'such a *Jihad* is quite impossible, and such an idea is an act of extreme folly, for the majority of the *Purbia* soldiers were Hindus.[12] Such an act will create a civil war and the results would be deplorable. The Holy war is against the English. I have forbidden it against the Hindus.'" (154-229; also: 67-230)

He continues thereafter: "At this point of the Uprising, Zafar seems to have succeeded in silencing the Jihadis. But eight weeks later, when large numbers of 'Wahabi' Mujahidin had collected in the city from all over northern India, it would prove far more difficult." (154-229) About *Jihad,* he writes: "The one thing that the Jihadis did succeed in doing was alarming and potentially alienating Delhi's Hindus." (266) About the number of Jihadis, he writes: "As the numbers of the *Jihadis* in the city increased and the Uprising in Delhi assumed an increasingly Islamic flavour, so the dormant underlying tensions seem to have exacerbated, and many Hindus became increasingly anxious and disturbed." (268) "The arrival of groups of Muslim Jihadis eventually came to make up at least half of the rebel army in Delhi." (154-290, 338) According to what a certain commander had to say, in August: "Of the total estimated insurgent army remaining in Delhi of around 60,000 men as many as 25,000 were Jihadis." Dalrymple states further, "Lieutenant Coghill thought the Jihadis made up at least half the rebel numbers :

---

12. Hindus were not a majority among rebel sepoys who were in Delhi. No exact statistics on the Hindu-Muslim proportion at the time of the rebellion are available, but there is sufficient evidence to conclude that subsequently (August 1857) Jihadis were half the total number of rebel sepoys. Moreover, the other half who were strictly not 'Jihadis' must also have had Muslims among them. Thus, the Emperor's statement cannot justly be taken at face value exclusively in the context of Delhi, but the whole (at least northern) of India. This is because Delhi had a very small contingent of sepoys to begin with. Most of the rebels had gone there from other places. Dalrymple's premise about 'overwhelming Hindu sepoys' (154-264, 439) renders his conclusions misleading.

'The enemy had about 25 to 30,000 sepoys,' he wrote to his brother, 'and about 30,000 more *ghazis*, a race of devils and fanatics.'" (338)

Dalrymple tells his readers about the treatment meted out to Hindus by Jihadis: "The Jihadis went out of their way deliberately to offend Hindu feelings... 'The *Ghazis* who have come from Tonk are determined to kill a cow on the open space in front of the Jama Masjid on the day of Id, some three days hence. They say that if the Hindus offer any opposition to this, they will kill them, and after settling accounts with the Hindus they will then attack and destroy the *Firangis*. 'For,' they say, 'we are to be martyrs for the faith and the honours of martyrdom are to be obtained just as well by killing a Hindu as by killing a *firangi*.'" (295)

Muslims had opposed the Emperor's decision to ban cow slaughter in the city of Delhi during Id that year. To ensure complete implementation of his decree, the Emperor had instructed the kotwal to order every Muslim to deliver custody of cows in his possession at the kotwali. Dalrymple makes an insightful observation on this: "Zafar may have been unwilling or unable to lock up the Jihadis, but he could lock up the cows." (296)

Thus, such was the nature of the prevalent communal milieu in Delhi at the time. As a result, "Occasionally the tension between the overwhelmingly Hindu sepoys and the militantly Muslim *mujahidin* erupted in full-scale street fights." (264) As Darlymple observers, "Certainly some of the *Jihadis* were convinced 'that the entire Hindu population is with them (the British),' and that 'the moneychangers and Hindus were in alliance with the Christians.'" (154-268; also: 67-230)

Need for Proclamations Invoking Unity

To summarize, such was the overall picture of Hindu-Muslim relations or strife in 1857. Leaders of the rebellion therefore felt obliged to issue proclamations calling for unity between the two communities. Such proclamations are often proffered as a positive proof that Hindus and Muslims had really and truly united at the time. However, much to the contrary, such proclamations are actually indications that such unity was missing.

Dr. Mujumadar writes in this context: "But the communal spirit was too deep-rooted to be wiped out by mere pious wishes embodied in proclamations, even of the King himself. It raised its ugly head in the city of Delhi itself even when its siege by the British was imminent...." (67-230; 55-86) He also clarifies that, "Such communal feelings were not, of course, universal, but it is clearly proved by the proclamations and Hindu-Muslim riots that they largely prevailed in U.P., the only province in which the outbreak developed into a general revolt." (67-231) The conclusion drawn by him provides a guideline: "That the great difference between the Hindus and the Muslims loomed large in the territories where the revolt of civil population was most widely spread." (229)

N. K. Behere arrives at the following significant conclusion: "To Muslims, Hindus were as much of '*kafirs*' as Christians. However, because they could not have done without Hindu help at that time, they had momentarily overlooked their 'kafirhood' in self-interest. Nevertheless, Muslims in places like Bijnor and Nagina forgot even selfish benefit in the stupour of their bigotry and fanaticism." (158-281)

Nor can a comment by N. R. Phatak be ignored: "A hypothesis is zealously, emphatically and enthusiastically forwarded that in 1857 Hindus and Muslims conducted themselves in perfect amity with one another, but a rift between them was nurtured in later times by the British initiative of 'divide and rule'. We have briefly exposed the hollowness of the hypothesis earlier (in Phatak's book). Even those singing odes to unity among the people have been unable to hide the bloody conflicts that Muslims foisted upon Hindus. The historical record of the sepoy mutiny abounds in accounts of massacres inflicted on one another at many places. Hindus (in Delhi) made a celebration when (rebel) sepoys were defeated in the very first engagement at Hindan. Muslims were engaged in a game of crushing Hindus in the districts of Rohilkhand like Bijnor, Badaun and Shahjahanpur. Muslims in Aligarh plundered Hindus, killed them and often even forced them into Islam. Incidents of violent unrest cannot be ignored in interests of Hindu-Muslim unity just because those districts were dominated by Muslims. Benares district was populated predominantly by Hindus, chroniclers of those times have been unable to conceal the incident in which Muslims had unfurled the green flag to terrorize Hindus." (44-384) "Instances abound in which *Jihad* would first be declared by Muslims and an explanation, that it was directed against Christians, later provided as an afterthought only to quell Hindu anxiety." (374)

It is thus a parody of truth to claim that a golden age of Hindu-Muslim amity had dawned during the Uprising. Nevertheless, M. Abul Kalam Azad, in his capacity as Union Minister of Education, displays extraordinary confidence when he states, "We do not, however, find during the whole period a single instance when there was a clash or conflict on communal basis." (141-xxv). A greater travesty of history may rarely be found. Unity cannot be forged by distorting true history, nor can true happenings and events be brushed under the carpet for very long. Remedies for disunity and strife can and need to be found only by an understanding and appreciation of history, however harsh it may seem.

***

Epilogue

No other subject in Indian history has as many books written on it as the 1857 Uprising. The event has been viewed from many aspects. To some, it appeared as a sepoy mutiny; to others as Uprising by erstwhile rulers of Indian states; still others viewed it as the unrest of landed gentry, an economic agitation against capitalists, a war of independence, the first manifestation of Hindu-Muslim unity, a conspiracy by Muslim nobility, or a *Jihad*. Each view undoubtedly has some substance and justification. Needless to state, an eruption on such a large scale and spread over a vast geographical area inhabited by millions of people was bound to have many causes. Equally obviously, everyone participating in such a widespread revolt could not possibly have done so with the same objectives, inspirations or reasons, but was part of one or another of innumerable factions that formed the whole. There may also have been some who took advantage of prevailing anarchy to pillage and loot, while others saw the weakening administrative grip as an opportunity to settle old scores. Innumerable lands in Uttar Pradesh had been bought by moneylenders in auctions conducted by judicial orders under new zamindari laws. Dispossessed zamindars, utilizing the opportunity presented by the Uprising, raised paramilitary forces to drive out new buyers of their original holdings. Even under a democratic polity, a change of government brings with it new laws that adversely affect some interests and cause a degree of discontent. Ascertaining the precise nature of an armed uprising against the administration under such conditions is a difficult task and every observer or student perceives it according to his own abilities and viewpoint. This has also happened in the case of the 1857 Uprising.

Be that as it may, it is vital to identify what was the most central and crucial factor that caused the Uprising. It is only on the basis of such principal and decisive cause that a conclusion about the nature of the revolution is made, not by a summation of all the causes that could have brought about the event. What was that reason in the context of the 1857 Uprising? One qualifying test is to identify a motive whose absence might have rendered an uprising unlikely. Seen from this aspect, and from the contents of this book, it becomes clear that it was Muslim perception and discontent at having lost political hegemony to the British, combined with their cherished hope of restoring it, that had been the principal and decisive motivation for the 1857 Uprising; every other cause was only secondary or supplementary.

Muslim clerics and thinkers had become alarmed with the decline and disintegration of the Mughal Empire which had commenced after Aurangzeb's death. Shah Waliullah was one such great and influential cleric, without an appreciation of whose philosophy a comprehension of 1857 is impossible. Panipat (1761) had been brought about to destroy Maratha power. However, Abdali had not stayed back to rule over his gains and the Mughal throne became threatened first by the Marathas once again, and then by the British. Many players like the Mughal Emperor, the Nawabs of Ayodhya, Murshidabad and Dhaka, and Tipu Sultan of Mysore had hatched international conspiracies with Muslim states like Turkey, Persia and Afghanistan in an attempt to drive the British out of the country. However, the British proved to be adept at diplomacy and intrigue, and all those attempts had come to a naught; the Muslim empire could not be restored. These were events before 1800 C.E. In the nineteenth century, a *Jihad* programme was launched by declaring India a *Dar-ul-Harb*. The 1857 Uprising was the acme of this activism. Little doubt should remain in readers' minds about the essential nature of this Uprising after reading the two Chapters about 'A Century before the Jihad'.

There is general agreement that it was a 'holy war' or 'war for religion'. The point is whose holy war was it ? Hindus lack a tradition of waging such war against followers of other religions just because they are not Hindus. On the contrary, it is by assimilation of religious aliens into their culture and making compromises or adjustments in their own world view that the Hindu has historically sought to make his life under their rule as tolerable as possible. Had the concept of holy war indeed existed in their tradition, would Hindus not have risen against erstwhile Muslim regimes? Even Shivaji had not portrayed his struggle for *Swarajya* (self-determination) as a holy war. Thus, the term 'holy war' used in the context of the 1857 Uprising only applies to *Jihad*. Muslims have a long tradition of waging war for religion and State that is sanctioned by their doctrine. It was precisely this tradition that dominated the 1857 Uprising.

At every place of rebellion, the slogan given was 'Khulk Khuda ka, Mulk Badshah ka, *Amal* (of the respective Subedar)'. It was as clear as daylight that the Muslim Empire would be restored in India when the British had been successfully driven out. The Mughal Emperor had issued clear orders to the Nawab of Rohilkhand to implement the *Shariat* in the State and to uproot *kufr* (disbelief in Islam) and *shirk* (polytheism). The Hindus were going to fare no better under the restored Mughal regime than they had under the previous, deposed one. The head of the new state was also going to be the spiritual leader. Without reiterating the circumstances in which Nanasahib became a leader of the Uprising, it is beyond question that his status was going to be no higher than that of a Subedar of the Mughal Emperor. Dismissing subordinates like subedars was one of the Emperor's *ex-officio* privileges. Moreover, the crown jewel of the Uprising, M. Ahmad Shah, had declared that the king or head had to be a Muslim, preferably an Arab and ideally hailing from the Quraysh tribe, but was prepared to relent and make do with another Muslim not so qualified in case that ideal was unrealizable. Thus, there was absolutely no possibility that some Hindus might have ascended the throne in the near or even remote future; another 'war for independence' would have become necessary to bring that about. Gandhi's methods of truth, non-violence and *satyagraha* would have been utterly useless; it might have been necessary to expectantly await the advent of another Shivaji.

That Muslims, almost exclusively, were instigators, leaders and beneficiaries of the Uprising, is another clear and sufficient indicator of its essential nature. Hindus were entirely free of any ambition of replacing the British regime by their indigenous one. Besides, that would have entailed a conflict with both Muslim and British rulers. Muslims would never have supported a struggle to usher in a Hindu Emperor, and there would never have been the much-vaunted Hindu-Muslim unity. For, Muslims were not struggling to replace one *kafir* by another. Muslims consistently referred to the British as '*kafirs*' during the Uprising. Their cherished desire was *Dar-ul-Islam*, not a regime of *kafirs*. By their own reckoning, Muslim rebels viewed the Uprising essentially as a struggle against 'alien' Christian *kafirs*[1] who, by sheer coincidence, happened to be ruling over India at the time. But had they not fought, not too long before that, as tenaciously against Marathas and Sikhs — both 'natives' of India — for the very same purpose?

The question before Hindus was plain. Those from the 'nawabi' belt of Uttar Pradesh, where the Uprising was most pronounced, had been suffering political slavery under Muslim rule for centuries. It was almost as if every aspiration for freedom was extinguished from their heart and soul. As such,

1. The Uprising being against Christian *kafirs*, rebels had killed all native Christians in Delhi after the revolt but had spared those white foreigner Christians who offered to embrace Islam. As Smith George wrote: "Native Christians were simply identified by the rebels with the governing class, but were generally offered their lives at the price of denying their Lord..." (3-486n)

success of the Uprising only meant a change of masters to them, and it made no difference whether he was British or Muslim. It is quite natural that many of them felt more comfortable with their old Muslim feudal masters, who appeared to have conceded to them at least the semblance of their traditional values and mores, than they imagined they would under a new, unknown and modernistic ruler. However, those Hindus who had established their independent rule — albeit for short periods — by staking their lives against Muslim imperialism and who still retained collective memories of their independence, had scrupulously remained aloof from the Uprising. Foremost among them were Sikhs of the Punjab, Rajputs of Rajasthan and Marathas of Maharashtra. The Holkar of Indore and Shinde of Gwalior had sided with the British. Even Lakxmibai had remained loyal to the British for as long as 10 months after the Uprising in Jhansi. It is unfortunate that India in general and Shivaji's Maharashtra in particular should not realize even now that the pro-British stance adopted by Shindes, Holkars and Lakxmibai was not a betrayal of the Indian Nation but, on the contrary, an expression of patriotism.

We request such of our readers as might have been unable to read this book in its entirety to at least read the Chapter on 'Jihadi Proclamations and Declarations issued during the Uprising'. Proclamations issued by ten prominent leaders of the Uprising that are discussed therein, are mirrors reflecting the inspiration, causes and nature of the event. They will suffice to establish that the Uprising was actually a *Jihad*. It is not astonishing that even proclamations issued by Nanasahib or Lakxmibai should be replete in Jihadi sentiment; the documents had actually been drafted by quite somebody else. According formal consent for their publication was all that had been left in their power. The Nawab of Rohilkhand had issued two proclamations – one meant for both Hindus and Muslims and another, exclusively for Muslims. This feature — of soliciting Hindu support by telling them one thing, and then separately unfolding your inner mind to Muslims — was a startling differentiation employed in the production of those proclamations.

It will be clear from Chapter 9 how entirely false is the claim that a 'golden age' of Hindu-Muslim amity and unity had dawned during the Uprising.

It is observed that, during the period of the Uprising, the British generally referred to Muslims as 'rebels' and Hindus as 'loyal'. Even after suppressing the rebellion, they had singled out Muslims as objects of vendetta. Detailed descriptions of this retribution are available in literature and we do not feel the need to repeat them in the present book. To state it in the words of Mirza Ghalib, the Urdu poet who was in Delhi at the time, "The Chowk is a slaughter ground, and homes are prisons; Every grain of dust in Delhi, thirsts for Muslims' blood." (154-418) Let us consider a few incidents just by the by. Hindus who had left Delhi during the Uprising were permitted to return by November 1858, but Muslims were not allowed to do so till the end of December 1860, and then only after they had submitted to the condition of proving their loyalty. (461) Demolition of the Red Fort, a visible symbol of the Mughal Empire, had begun in right earnest but stopped later by mediation of a British officer, after a good eighty percent of it had been razed. (458) The Jama Masjid was in Sikh possession till 1862 and there were plans to demolish it, too. Fortunately, however, those plans were not executed. Nevertheless, innumerable other Muslim structures were destroyed, while many others were auctioned and bought by Hindu moneylenders. Among the latter, were the famous Fatehpuri Mosque, the Zeenat-ul-Masajid and the historic Madarsa-i-Rahimiyya that had been established by none other than Shah Waliullah himself. (462,3) Actually, 'the plan' had been 'to completely level Delhi as a punishment' for the revolt. "The plan had many powerful supporters, both in India and London, one of whom, Lord Palmerston (the Prime Minister), wrote (to Canning) that Delhi should be deleted from the map, and 'every civil building connected with the Mahomedan tradition should be levelled to the ground without regard to antiquarian veneration or artistic predilections.'" (154-454; 43-71) Lord Canning was also of the same view but it was John Lawrence who 'persuaded him not to order the levelling of the city.' (154-454) While such comprehensive acts of revenge were undoubtedly condemnable, they are sufficient to tell us who the British administration held responsible for the Uprising.

We are neither the first nor alone in regarding the Uprising as a *Jihad,* for several authorities reach the same conclusion. Foremost among them are Muslim scholars and writers. They take immense pride in asserting that 'we' rebelled against the British and that the Uprising was a *Jihad*. Even Sir Sayyed Ahmad Khan, who spared no effort in his attempts to prove that Muslims were loyal to the British, indirectly said the same thing. Moreover, he had also defined the logical, historical and political rationale for the Uprising. The British, too, called it a *Jihad.* In Appendix II that follows, we present conclusions drawn by 45 erudite and reputed authorities. We entertain no doubt, that after reflecting upon what they have to say, readers will not accuse us of stating the bizarre.

* * *

Appendix – I

List of Reference Books

1. Savarkar, VD: *Indian War of Independence,* Phonex Publications, Bombay, 1947
2. Ambedkar, BR: *Pakistan or The Partition of India,* Vol 8, Education Department, Government of Maharashtra, 1990
3. Rizvi, SAA: Bhargav ML (Ed), *Freedom Struggle in Uttar Pradesh,* Vol 1, Information Department, Govt, of U.P, 1957-61
4. —— Supra Vol 2.
5. —— Supra Vol 3.
6. —— Supra Vol 4.
7. —— Supra Vol 5.
8. —— Supra Vol 6.
9. Sardesai, GS: *British Riyasat* (British Rule), Vol I, Popular Prakashan, Mumbai, 1993
10. —— Supra Vol II
11. Ikram, SM: *Modern Muslim India and the Birth of Pakistan,* Renaissance Publishing House, New Delhi, 1991
12. Robinson, Francis: *Separatism Among Indian Muslims,* Oxford University Press, New Delhi, 1993.

13. Sanyal, Usha: *Devotional Islam and Politics in British India,* Oxford University Press, New Delhi, 1999
14. Pagadi, Setumadhavrao: *1857 Che Anakhi Kahi Pailu* [Some More Facets of 1857] Parchure Prakashan, Mumbai, 2000.
15. Metcalf, Barbara Daly: *Islamic Revival in British India, Deoband, 1860–1900,* Oxford University Press, New Delhi, 2002
16. Chandra, Bipin, et al: *Freedom Struggle,* National Book Trust, New Delhi, 1972.
17. Robinson, Francis: *Islam and Muslim History in South Asia,* Oxford University Press, New Delhi 2000.
18. Singh, Khushwant: *A History of the Sikhs,* Vol 1, Oxford University Press, 2001
19. ——— Supra Vol. 2, 2002
20. Heehs, Peter: *India's Freedom Struggle,* Oxford University Press, New Delhi, 2000
21. Ahmad, Aziz: *Studies in Islamic Culture in the Indian Environment,* Oxford University Press, New Delhi, 2002.
22. Bhat, Abdul Rashid: *Political Thought of Shah Waliullah,* Adam Publishers, New Delhi, 1996
23. Friedmann, Yohanan: *Shaykh Ahmad Sirhindi,* Oxford University Press, 2000.
24. Ansari, Asloob A (Ed): *Sir Syed Ahmad Khan, A Centenary Tribute,* Adam Publishers, New Delhi, 2001.
25. Ghazi Mahmood Ahmad: *Islamic Renaissance in South Asia (1707-1867): The Role of Shah Waliullah and his Successors,* Adam Publishers, New Delhi, 2004
26. Dehlvi, Muhaddis & Jalbani, GN: *Teachings of Hazrat Shah Waliullah,* Kitab Bhavan, New Delhi, 1997.
27. Jalbani, GN: *Life of Shah Waliullah,* Kitab Bhavan, New Delhi, 1997
28. Allana, G: *Eminent Muslim Freedom Fighters,* Low PP, New Delhi, 1993
29. Mishra, Amaresh: *Mangal Pandey: The True Story of an Indian Revolutionary,* Rupa & Co, New Delhi, 2005

66. *Dacoitee in Excelsis or The Spoilation of Oude by the East India Co.*, Pustak Kendra, Lucknow, 1971.

67. Mujumdar, RC: *The Sepoy Mutiny and the Revolt of 1857*, Published by Srimati S Choudhary, Calcutta, 1957.

68. — (ed), *British Paramountcy and Indian Renaissance*, Part I, Bhartiya Vidya Bhavan, Bombay, 1988

69. Nigam, NK: *Delhi in 1857*, S Chand & Co, New Delhi.

70. Valbezen, E de: *The English and India*, Translated by a Diplomat, Gian Publishing House, New Delhi, 1986.

71. Ghalib, Mirza: *Dastanbuy* (A Diary of the Indian Revolt of 1857), Translated and Published by KA Faruqi (1992)

72. Bhargava, M L: *Architects of Indian Freedom Struggle*, Deep & Deep Publishers, New Delhi, 1981.

73. Mathur, YB: *Muslims and Changing India*, Trimurti Pub. Pvt Ltd. New Delhi, 1972

74. Karandikar, MA: *Islam: India's Transition to Modernity*, Orient Longman Ltd. New Delhi, 1968.

75. Titus, Murray T: *Indian Islam*, Oxford University Press, New Delhi, 1930.

76. Faruqi, Ziya-ul-Hasan: *The Deoband School and the Demand for Pakistan*, Asia Publishing House, New Delhi, 1963.

77. Ashraf, Mujeeb: *Muslim Attitudes towards British Rule and Western Culture in India (in the First Half of the 19th century)*, Idara-e-Adbiyat, Delhi, 1982.

78. Kaye, John, *The History of Indian Mutiny*, Vol I, Oriental Publisher, Lahore, 1976.

79. Hibbert, Christopher: *The Great Mutiny: India 1857*, Penguin Books, New Delhi, 1980.

80. Chaudhary, SB: *Civil Disturbances during the British Rule in India: (1765–1857)*

81. Chaudhary, SB: *Civil Rebellion in the Indian Mutinies (1857–1859)*, The World Press Pvt. Ltd. Calcutta, 1957

48. Vivek Mohan: *Jhansi Ki Rani Laxmibai* [The Rani of Jhansi-Laxmibai], Raja Books, Delhi, 2001
49. Forest, GW (ed): *The Indian Mutiny : 1857–59*, Vol III, 2003
50. —— Supra Vol. IV Low PP, Delhi
51. Holt, PM (ed): *The Cambridge History of Islam*, Vol 2A, Cambridge University Press, Cambridge 1992.
52. Abbott, Freeland: *Islam and Pakistan*, Cornell University Press, New York, 1968.
53. Mahmood, Safdar & Zafar, Javaid: *Founders of Pakistan*, Uppal Publishing House, New Delhi, 1988
54. Cole J.R.I: *Roots of North Indian Shiaism in Iran and Iraq*, Oxford University Press, New Delhi, 1989
55. Embree, Ainslie T (ed): *Mutiny or War of Independence?*, DC Heath and Co. Lexington, 1968.
56. Shepherd, WJ: *A Personal narrative of the Outbreak and Massacre at Cawnpore*, Academic Books Corp, New Delhi, 1980.
57. Palmer, JAB: *The Mutiny Outbreak at Meerut in 1857*, Cambridge University Press, Cambridge, 1966
58. Khan, Syed Ahmad: *The Causes of the Indian Revolt*, Medical Hall Press, Benaras, 1873
59. Guha, Ranajit (ed), *Subaltern Studies IV*, Oxford University Press, New Delhi, 1994
60. Collier, Richard: *The Sound of Fury*, Collins, St James Place, London, 1963
61. Russel, William H: *My Indian Mutiny Diary*, Cassel & Co. London, 1957
62. Mishra, JP, *The Bundela Rebellion*: Sundeep Prakashan, Delhi, 1982
63. Thomson, Edward: *The Other Side of the Medal*, Leonard & Virginia Woolf, London, 1926
64. A Hindu: *The Mutinies and the People*, I C Bose & Co., Calcutta, 1859
65. Talib Abu (ed), *History of Asafu'd Daulah*, translated by W. Hoey, Pustak Kendra, Lucknow, 1971.

30. Rizvi, SAA: *Muslim Revivalist Movement in Northern India*, Munshi Ram Manohar Lal, New Delhi, 1965

31. Fisher, Michael H (ed): *The Politics of the British Annexation of India: 1757–1857*, Oxford University Press, New Delhi, 1999

32. Tara Chand: *History of Freedom Movement in India*, Vol II, Publications Division, Govt. of India, New Delhi, 1956

33. Govt. of Pakistan, *A History of the Freedom Movement*, Vol I, Renaissance Publishing House, Delhi, 1984.

34. —— Supra Vol.2

35. Griffin, LH: *The Rajas of Punjab*, LPP, Delhi, 2000

36. Parasnis, DB: *Jhashichi Rani* [The Rani of Jhansi], Varada Books, Pune, 1996.

37. Varhadpande, NR: *1857 Che Nindak* [Vilifiers of 1857] translated by Sakhdeo PM, Shri Babasahib Apte Samarak Samiti Prakashan, Nagpur, 1994.

38. Jogalekar, JD: *1857 Cha Prasphot* [Explosion of 1857], Manorama Prakashan, Mumbai, 2000.

39. Rana, Bhawan Singh, *Rani of Jhansi*, Diamond Books, New Delhi, 2004

40. Ahmed, Nur: *Forty Great Men and Women in Islam*, Adam Publishers, New Delhi 1999

41. Nadvi, Md. Ilyas: *Tipu Sultan (A Life Story)* Institute of Objective Studies, New Delhi, 2004

42. Hunter, WW: *The Indian Musalmans*, Rupa & Co. New Delhi, 2002

43. Hardy, P, *The Muslims of British India*, Cambridge University Press, Cambridge, 1972.

44. Phatak, NR: *1857 Chi Shipai Gardi* [The Sepoy Mutiny of 1857] Chitrashala Prakashan, Pune, 1958.

45. Malik, Hafeez (ed): *Political Profile of Sir Sayyed Ahmad Khan*, Adam Publishers, New Delhi, 1993.

46. Pemble, John, *The Raj, The Indian Mutiny and the Kingdom of Oudh, 1801–59*, The Harvester Press, Sussex, 1977

47. Pagdi, Setumadhavrao, *Bhartiya Musalman: Shod ani Bodh* [Indian Muslims: Inquiry and Lessons], Parchure Prakashan Mandir, Mumbai, 1992.

82. Sinha, Shyam Narain: *The Revolt of 1857 in Bundelkhand*, Anuj Publications; Lucknow, 1982.
83. Kaviraj, Narhari: *Wahabi and Farazi Rebels of Bengal*, People's Publishing House, New Delhi, 1982.
84. Domin, Dolores: *India in 1857–9 (A Study in the role of Sikhs in the People's Uprising*, Academic, Berlin, 1977.
85. Haq, S Moinul (ed): *Memoirs of Hakim Ahsanullah Khan*, Pakistan Historical Society, Karachi, 1958.
86. Srivastava K, *The Revolt of 1857 in Central India—Malwa*, Allied Publishers, Pvt.Ltd. New Delhi, 1966.
87. Chanda, SN: *1857: Some Untold Stories*, Sterling Publishers Pvt. Ltd., New Delhi, 1976.
88. Ray, Aniruddha: *The Rebel Nawab of Oudh*, K P Bagchi and Co. New Delhi, 1990.
89. Gubbins, MR: *The Mutinies in Oudh*, Janaki Prakashan, Patna, 1978.
90. Srivastava, MP: *The Indian Mutiny 1857*, Chugh Publishers, Allahabad, 1979.
91. Wilberforce, Reginald W: *An Unrecorded Chapter of the Indian Mutiny*, The Academic Press, Gurgaon, 1976.
92. Roy, Tapti: *The Politics of Popular Uprising: Bundelkhand in 1857*, Oxford University Press, 1994.
93. Hasan, Mohibbul: *History of Tipu Sultan*, The World Press Pvt. Ltd., Calcutta, 1971
94. Forrest, Denys: *Tiger of Mysore (The Life and Death of Tipu Sultan)*, Allied Publishers, New Delhi, 1970.
95. Bhatnagar GD, *Awadh under Wajid Ali Shah*, Bhartiya Vidya Prakashan, Varanasi, 1968.
96. Troll, Christian W, *Sayyid Ahmad Khan*, Vikas Publishing House Pvt. Ltd. New Delhi, 1970.
97. Mohammed, Shan (ed): *Writings and Speeches of Sir Syed Ahmad Khan*, Nachiketa Publishers, Bombay, 1972.
98. Nizami, KA: *Sayyid Ahmad Khan*, Publications Division, Government of India, New Delhi, 1980.

99. Graham, GFI: *The Life and Works of Sir Syed Ahmed Khan*, Oxford University Press, 1974.

100. Jog, BN: *Hindu-Musalman Aikya: Bhram ani Satya* [Hindu-Muslim Unity: Illusion and Reality], Unnati Prakashan, Bombay, 1990.

101. Nehru, Jawaharlal: *The Discovery of India*, Meridian Books Ltd. London, 1956.

102. —— *An Autobiography*, Allied Publishers Pvt. Ltd., New Delhi, 1962.

103. Mead, Henry: *The Sepoy Revolt*, Gian Publishing House, New Delhi, 1986.

104. Hodgson, Marshall G S: *The Venture of Islam*, Vol III, The University of Chicago Press, Chicago, 1974.

105. Taylor PJO, *Chronicles of the Mutiny and Other Historical Sketches*, Harper Collins, New Delhi, 1992.

106. Taqvi, Roshan: *Lucknow: 1857*, New Royal Book Co., Lucknow, 2001

107. Yadav, KC (ed): *Delhi 1857 (The Trial of Bahadur Shah,)* Vol I, The Academic Press, Gurgaon, 1980

108. Gupta, PC: *Nana Sahib and the Rising at Cawnpore*, Clarendon Press, Oxford, 1963.

109. Shastitko, Pyotr: *Nana Sahib*, Translated by Savitri Shahani, Shubhada Saraswati Publishers Pvt. Ltd. Pune, 1980.

110. Smith, John: *The Rebellious Rani*, Frederick Muller, Ltd., London. 1966.

111. Misra, Anand Swaroop: *Nanasaheb Peshwe ani Swatantryayudhha* [Nana Sahib Peshwa and the War of Independence] Translated by VR Dhamdhere, Maharashtra Rajya Sahitya va Sanskruti Mandal, Mumbai, 1973

112. Ahmad, Mohiuddin: *Saiyid Ahmed Shaheed: His Life and Mission*, Academy of Islamic Research and Publishers, Lucknow,1975.

113. Mahmood, Safdar: *Pakistan: Political Roots and Development*, Sterling Publishers Pvt. Ltd. New Delhi, 1990.

114. Cunningham, JD: *History of the Sikhs*, Low P.P., Delhi, 1996.

115. Balkhi, Fasihuddin: *Wahabi Movement*, Classical Publishing Co., New Delhi 1983.

116. Ahmad, Qeyamuddin: *The Wahabi Movement in India*, Firma K L Mukhopadhyay, Calcutta, 1966.

117. Datta: K K: *Anti-British Plots and Movements before 1857*, Meenakshi Prakashan, Meerut, 1970.

118. Mujeeb, M: *The Indian Muslims*, Munshiram Manoharlal Publisher Pvt. Ltd., New Delhi, 2003.

119. Akbar, MJ, *The Shade of Swords*, Rolli Books, New Delhi, 2002.

120. Nizami, Taufiq Ahmad: *Muslim Political Thought and Activity in India During the First Half of the 19th Century*, IM Publishers, Aligarh, 1969.

121. Anonymous, *Two Native Narratives of the Mutiny in Delhi* Translated by Charles Metcalfe, Seema Publications, Delhi, 1974.

122. Gupta, Sankar Sen (ed): *War of Independence: Centenary Souvenir*, Indian Publications, Calcutta, 1957.

123. Godse, Vishnubhat: *Maza Pravas (1857 Chya Bandachi in Hakikat)* [My Journey: A narrative of 1857 Revolt] ed. DV Potdar, Venus Prakashan, Pune, 1974.

124. Maitra, Jayanti: *Muslim Politics in Bengal 1855–1906: Collaboration and Confrontation*, K.P. Bagchi & Co, Calcutta, 1984.

125. Haq, MJ: *Muslim Politics in Modern India*, Meenakshi Prakashan, Meerut,1970.

126. David, Saul: *The Indian Mutiny 1857*, Penguin Books, New Delhi, 2002.

127. Dayal, Ravi (ed): *We Fought Together for Freedom*, Oxford University Press 1995.

128. More, Shehrao: *Muslim Manacha Shodh* [An Inquiry into Muslim Mind], Rajhans Prakashan, Pune, 2003.

129. —— *Preshitanantarche Pahile Char Adarsh Khalifa* [The Four Ideal Caliph Successors to the Prophet], Rajhans Prakashan, Pune, 2006.

130. Malleson, GB, *The Indian Mutiny of 1857*, Rupa & Co. New Delhi, 2005.

131. Ranade, Pratibha: *Jhashi chi Rani Laxmibai* [Laxmibai, Rani of Jhansi], Rajhans Prakashan, Pune 2006.

132. Taylor, PJO: *What Really Happened During the Mutiny: A Day-by-Day Account to the Major Events of 1857–1859 in India*, Oxford University Press, 1999.

133. Majumdar, RC et al: *An Advanced History of India*, Macmillan, Madras, 1991.

134. Mahajan VD, *India Since 1526*, S.Chand & Co, New Delhi, 2000.

135. Ram Gopal: *Bharateeya Musalmanancha Rajakeeya Itihas 1858–1947* [The Political History of Indian Muslims 1858–1947] (Translated by Kamal Padhye), Maharashtra Rajya Sahitya va Sanskruti Mandal, Mumbai, 1988.

136. —— *How the British Occupied Bengal*, Asia Publishers, New Delhi, 1963.

137. Baig, M.R: *Bharateeya Musalmananpuddheel Pech* [The Predicament before Indian Muslims] Translated by Achyut Khodave, Maharashtra Rajya Sahitya va Sanskruti Mandal, Mumbai, 1988.

138. Noorani, AG: *Islam and Jihad*, Leftword, New Delhi, 2002

139. Bakshi, SR & Sharma, SK: *Marathas in Panipat, 1761*, Deep and Deep Publishers, New Delhi 2002.

140. Nagarkar, Vasant: *Pakistanche Janmarahasya* [Enigma of the Birth of Pakistan] Translated by Madhav Limaye, Maharashtra Rajya Sahitya va Sanskruti Mandal, Mumbai, 1998.

141. Sen, SN: *Eighteen Fifty-Seven*, Publication Division, Government of India, New Delhi, 1995.

142. Dua, Shyam (ed), *The Luminous Life of Mangal Pandey*, Printline Books, New Delhi, 2004.

143. Azimabadi, Badr (Compiler), *Great Personalities of Islam*, Adam Publishers, New Delhi, 1998.

144. Dua, Shyam (ed): *The Luminous Life of Tipu Sultan*, Printline Books, New Delhi, 2004.

145. Ishwari Prasad & Subedar, SK: *Hindu-Muslim Problems*, Chugh Publication, Allahabad, 1974.

146. Sengupta, Kalyankumar: *Recent Writings On the Revolt of 1857: A Survey*, FCHR, New Delhi, 1975.

147. Pandeya, Kamaladatta (ed), *Hindu Panch Balidan Ank*, National Book Trust, New Delhi, 1996.

148. Bhivagde, Dyaneshwar, *Rani Laxmibai*, Lakhe Prakashan, Nagpur, 2001.

149. Walimbe, VS, *1857 Chi Sangramgatha* [An Epic of 1857 Conflict] National Book Trust, New Delhi, 1996.

150. *Parichay—Narahar Kurundkar* [Narahar Kurundkar–An Introduction] Indrayani Sahitya, Pune, 1987.

151. Agarwala, BR: *Trials of Independence*, National Book Trust, New Delhi, 1999.

152. Shevade, Indumati: *Tatya Tope*, Translator Sundarlal Shrivastava, National Book Trust, New Delhi, 1999.

153. Uday, Narayan Singh, *Veer Kumar Singh*, [The Gallant Kunwar Singh], Shabdapeeth, Allahabad, 1988.

154. Dalrymple, William: *The Last Mughal: The Fall of Dynasty, Delhi, 1857*, Penguin, New Delhi, 2006.

155. Divekar, VD: *South India in 1857, War of Independence*, Lokmanya Tilak Samarak Trust, Pune, 1993.

156. Source Material for a History of the Freedom Movement in India, Vol I (1818–85), Govt of Bombay, Bombay, 1957.

157. Norman, Henry W & Young, Keith: *Delhi 1857*, LP Publishers, Delhi 2001.

158. Behere, NK & Kulkarni, Mangesh Narayan: *San 1857 [The year 1857]* Mumbai, 1927.

159. Thakare, Prabodhankar: *Pratapsinh Chhatrapati ani Rango Bapuji*, Maharashtra Rajya Sahityava Sanskruti Mandal, Mumbai, 1998.

160. Bose, Subhash Chander: *The Indian Struggle (1920-42)*, Oxford University Press, 1997.

Appendix – II

The Nature of the Uprising: Conclusions of Reputed Authorities/Eminent Scholars

1. **Dr. Thomas R. Metcalfe:** "The first sparks of disaffection, it was generally agreed, were kindled among the Hindu sepoys but the Muslims then fanned the flames of discontent and placed themselves at the head of the movement, for they saw in these religious grievances the stepping stone to political power. In the British view, it was Muslim intrigue and Muslim leadership that converted a sepoy mutiny into a political conspiracy, aimed at the extinction of the British Raj." (112-327; 43-62)
2. **Smith George:** "That the grand proximate agency in exciting the rebellion was a treasonable Mahomedan influence brought skillfully to bear on a soil prepared for its action. Brahmanical and other influences had doubtless their share in it; but the preponderent central element has been of Mahomedan origin, directed to the realization of the long-cherished dynastic designs of Mahomedan ambition." (3-486)

3. **Barbara Metcalf:** "Muslims were disproportionately blamed for their part in the Mutiny, for many British believed that Muslims had fought from political grievances, Hindus from economic; and the former motive was understood to be more invidious and more dangerous." (15-85)
4. **Charles Raikes** (1812-85) (then Collector of Agra) who 'saw the Muslims as innately hostile to the British' wrote: "The green flag of Islam, too, had been unfurled. The mass of the followers of Prophet (Muhammad) rejoicing to believe that under the auspices of the Great Mughal at Delhi, their lost ascendancy was to be recovered, their deep hatred for the Christians got vent, and they rushed forth to kill and destroy. But the great agricultural communities, the Jat, the Brahmin, Rajput, looked on the English race with unfeigned compassion." (67-220; 43-63) "And so it was all over the North-Western Provinces, a Mahomedan was another word for a rebel." (67-228; 68-616)
5. **Roberts** (later Field Marshal) wrote that he would "show these rascally Musalmans that, with God's help, Englishmen will still be masters of India." (63-40; 67-228; 68-616; 55-86; 123-60; 158-281)
6. **Mrs. Coopland** (the wife of a British officer) wrote: "As this is completely a Mahomedan rising, there is not much to be feared from the Hindus of Benares." (67-228; 68-616; 55-86)
7. **Mr. Colvin,** lieutenant governor of the N.W.P. believed that "the mutiny was a Mahomedan movement." (130-73) Colonel **H. Fraser,** the chief commissioner of Agra, called it "the Mahomedan rebellion." (43-64)
8. Captain **P. G. Scot** remarks in his report on the Mutiny at Jhansi: "At Nowgong and Jhansi the Muslim Cavalry let the Infantry composed mostly of Hindu Sepoys begin the mutiny. I believe the reason was solely that they wished to conceal the character of the movement viz. its being a Mahomedan one." (67-228; 68-616; 55-86)
9. **Sir Alfred Lyall,** an Officer in the Agra Province "put the whole rebellion down to the Mahomedans." (68-617; 67-242)

10. British officers, writers and the English Press of that time regarded it 'as a Mahomedan rebellion.' (112-101,23; 103-95; 135-25; 7-3; 124-91; 67-242) The very title of a book written by **W.H. Carey** was 'The Mahomedan Rebellion' (1857). Mohiuddin Ahmad writes, "most of the British writers believed that the Mutiny was the result of Muslim conspiracy. It was then widely assumed in Britain that the British rule in India had been saved mainly because of anti-Muslim feeling of the Hindus." (112-101)
11. **R. Spankie,** the Magistrate, narrates in his report: "The common brotherhood of all Mahomedans is a very different matter, and I think it would be impossible to deny that they were in heart and soul against us. The Mahomedan population is ever against us." (3-474)
12. **M. H. Court,** the magistrate of Allahabad, narrates in his report, "One and very large party, the Mussalmans are, influenced by ambition and the hope of regaining supremacy, reviving their decaying religion, and destroying those professing the Christian faith." (3-477) "That the Pathans were the most prominent in the mutiny." (478) "Everybody knows that the Mahomedans regard us as usurpers and would gladly see us knocked on the head. That their religion and power will be restored and established everywhere and that all infidels will be destroyed, are matters believed in and hoped for by them." (43-88)
13. **E. I. Brokin** (historian) : "When the British returned (after victory), they usually looked upon the Hindu faction as loyal and the Muslims as rebels." (92-134)
14. **Sir William Muir** narrates in his intelligence report, "It is in the very nature of the Mahomedan faith to seize on such an incident as a religious principle, impelling the more devoted or fanatical to an attempt for reestablishing the ascendancy of Islam." (7-705) "The Mussalmans, while they thought their cause had a fair chance of final success have frequently compromised themselves by flagrantly traitorous acts. At Aligarh, for instance, the Mussalmans were for a considerable time dominant; they forcibly converted many Hindus; they defied our government in the most insolent manner; all the ancient feelings of warring for the Faith, reminding one of the days of the first four Caliphs, were resuscitated." (43-63)

15. **Alexander Duff** (1806–78), the first missionary in India, (wrote on 26-8-1857): "Every disclosure goes to demonstrate that the tremendous rebellion has been the result of a long concocted Mahomedan conspiracy against the British power, with a view to reestablish the old Mughal dynasty instead." (55-14; 90-135)
16. **W. H. Russel,** war correspondent, (wrote on 6-6-1958): "The fact is, that the Mahomedan element in India is that which causes us most trouble and provokes the largest share of our hostility. Above all, the recollection of the days when the Mahomedans were paramount is more recent and active in their minds. Our antagonism to the followers of Muhammad is far stronger than that between us and the worshippers of Shiva and Vishnu. They are unquestionably more dangerous to our rule." (61-179; 43-70; 124-92)
17. **Michael Edwardes** (historian): "The Mutiny was essentially a religious war, with all the flavour of those other religious wars, the Crusades...." (61-xviii)
18. The private secretary to Governor General Canning: "The rebellion is now pretty well understood to be a Mahomedan one and the cartridge question to have been only a pretext to unite the Hindus with them." (126-264)
19. **G. B. Malleson** (senior British officer): "The revolted soldiery throughout India were called upon to fight for the restoration of the Mughul. The 'cry' was not altogether a happy cry for the revolters. Though it might conciliate and bind together many Mahomedans, it could scarcely fail to alienate the Maratha princes who had contested umpire with the Mughal family. The result proved that the princes of Central India preferred the safe position they held under British suzerainty to aiding mutinied soldiers to restore a dynasty which they had been the first to trample under foot." (130-58)
20. **Henry Thomas** [of the Bengal Civil Service (1858)]: "(The Revolt) was the result of a Mahomedan conspiracy. The Hindus never would or could have compassed such an undertaking. They (the Mahomedans) have been uniformly the same from the time of the first (four) Caliphs to the present day, proud, intolerant, and cruel, ever aiming at Mahomedan supremacy by whatever means, and ever fostering a deep

hatred of Christians. They cannot be good subjects of any government which professes another religion; and the precepts of the Quran will not suffer it." (74-136; 140-25; 100-31)

21. **Lester Hutchinson** (historian): "The leaders of the rebellion planned to declare Bahadur Shah, the titular Mughul Emperor, as the head of the rebellion, of which the object was to restore the old Mahomedan Empire. This move at once antagonized many of the Hindu chiefs, and ensured that the Sikhs, who still remembered the persecutions of Aurangzeb, went over to the side of the British." (55-57)

22. **P. Hardy** (historian): "It was the British belief after 1857 that Muslims were by nature fanatical and irreconcilable." (43-60) "For most British observers in 1857 a Muslim meant a rebel." (62) "Events in the countryside pointed also to the Muslim character of the rising." (64) "Members of the Muslim religious classes were prominent in revolt. The case for a general Muslim conspiracy was strengthened by events hundreds of miles distant from the outraged sepoys of Bengal Army." (65) "After the capture of Delhi in Sept. 1857, a dire vengeance befell the Muslim there, catastrophe befell the Muslim intelligentsia in Delhi."(70)

23. **Sir Charles Wood,** "the first Secretary of State for India, during discussion over the Indian Penal Code on June 1861 told the House of Commons that they had to Legislate for India where there were different aspirants, 'ranging from the bigoted Mahomedan, who considered that we have usurped his legitimate position as the ruler of India, to the timid Hindu, who was bowed to every conqueror.'" (74-140)

24. **W. S. Blunt** (historian) acknowledged even in 1883 that "in England we were perpetually scared at the idea of a Mahomedan rising in India, and any word uttered by a Mahomedan was paid more attention than that of twenty Hindus." (112-124)

25. **Sir James Outram** (Chief Commissioner of Oudh) wrote (in January 1858): "What can be more ridiculous than the cry that the rebellion was caused by the annexation of Oudh, or that it was solely a military mutiny? Our soldiers have deserted their standards and fought against us, but rebellion

did not originate with the Sipahis. The rebellion was set on foot by Mahomedans long before we rescued Oudh from her oppressors. It has been ascertained that prior to that Mussalman fanatics traversed the land, reminding the faithful (i.e. Muslims) that it had been foretold prophecy that a foreign nation would rule in India a hundred years, after which the true believers (i.e. Muslims) would regain their ascendancy. When the century elapsed, the Mussalmans did their best to establish the truth of their Prophet's declaration, and induced the Hindu Sipahis, ever as you know, the most credulous of mankind, to raise the green standard, and forswear their allegiance, on the ground that we had determined to make the whole of India involuntary converts to Christianity." (78-27n)

26. **M. R. Gubbins** (the Financial Commissioner and an Intelligence Officer) observed: "The King of Delhi endeavoured to revive his fallen dynasty. That they (Musalmans) disliked us more than the Hindus is both natural and true. The latter had been long accustomed to subjection: the first could not forget that where we now rule they had long been masters." (89-51) "That the Mahomedans, who dislike our rule in India the most, viewed with satisfaction the disaffection of the Hindu soldiers, fanned the flame, joined in the movement, and endeavoured, with characterstic energy, to turn it to their own advantage." (52)

27. **Henry Mead** (historian): "The relatives and adherents of the Delhi family were spread all over the country, and had tampered, no doubt, with the major part of the Mussalman Sepoys, urging them to seize the first favourable opportunity to rise for the recovery of their ancient dominions. They would say that although the Padshah was too old to place himself at the head of such an enterprise, his son was willing to be declared their king and leader." (103-102) "The shout of the Mussalman troopers was 'Deen, Deen!' — a word of fear equally to Hindu and Christian under ordinary circumstances. It was the battle-cry of Mahmood of Ghazni and Nadir Shah of Persia, and had been heard over the din of falling pagodas and the death-shrieks of thousands of Hindu worshippers in many a dark cycle of Eastern history. To

suppose that the Mahomedan soldiers would raise it now, merely to excite the Hindu Sepoys to join them against the Firangis, is as reasonable as to believe that the officers of an English army would, if (Catholic) Ireland were invaded by a foreign power, seek to animate the loyalty of the Roman Catholic population, by marching through the villages with shouts of 'Down with the Pope and the priests!'" (103)

"The Mussalmans still continued to regard him (i.e. the Emperor) as being the fountain of honour, the rightful monarch of Hindustan. The Mughal is the only person to whom the Mahomedans can look up as their natural head. The founders of the royal houses of Deccan, Carnatic, and Oudh, of Holkar and Scindhia were the deputies and servants of his ancestors. His divine right to universal dominion still exists. Nothing was more natural than proclamation by Mussalmans of Delhi Raj (of the Mughal) when they fancied they saw a chance of throwing off the English yoke. They used the King of Oudh as they have used the credulous Hindus. The corps that commenced the revolt were Mussalmans almost to a man." (95)

28. **Sir William Hunter** (1857): "The Musalmans of India are, and have been for many years, a source of chronic danger to the British power in India. For one reason or the other they have held aloof from our system." (42-3) "The plain meaning of the Quran is, that the followers of Islam shall reduce the whole earth to obedience, giving to the conquered the choice of conversion, or of a submission almost amounting to slavery, or of death." (106) "During the mutinies of 1857, the first act of a Musalman rebel, when he proclaimed the Delhi rule in a city, was to call on some Mahomedan local saint for a *Fatwa* declaring Holy War against the English." (107) "The whole Quran is based upon the conception of the Musalmans as a conquering, and not as a conquered people." (133) "We may enforce submission, but we can no longer claim obedience (from Mahomedans). Any serious wrong done to the Mahomedan would render such a (non-Muslim) Government impossible. Even minor grievances attain in their case the gravity of political blunders, blunders of which the cumulative

effect, according to the law of Islam, would be to entirely change the relation of the Musalmans to the ruling power, to free them from their duty as subjects, and bind them over to treason and Holy War." (138)

The British Government commissioned Hunter after the Revolt to study the question: "Whether Indian Musalmans are bound by their religion to revolt against the Queen's Government?" Hunter concluded: "No (non-Muslim) Government can expect honest loyalty from Musalman subjects." (140-25)

29. **M. T. Titus** (historian): "Thus a discussion was started in the Muslim community which lasted for half a century (before 1857), as to whether India was *Dar-ul-Harb* or *Dar-ul-Islam*. That under the leadership of Sayyid Ahmad, (they) actually did declare a holy war, preached the necessity of emigration (*hijrat*) to lands under Muslim rule, and carried their agitation all over India. In fact, it is believed that the mutiny of 1857 was partly due, at least, to a recrudescence of this spirit, which sought to establish the Mughul power." (75-192) "Along with the processes of direct action which were aimed at the overthrow of alien domination and the reestablishment of Muslim power in all its ancient glory and influence with truly religious significance for the protection of Islam, there arose an effective conspiracy on the part of Muslims everywhere." (192)

30. During the trial of Bahadur Shah Zafar, Harriott, the advocate general submitted before the court: "That this possessor of mere nominal royalty has ever been looked upon by Mahomedan fanaticism as the head and culminating star of its faith. In him have still been centered the hopes and aspirations of millions." (107-349) He termed this revolt as 'the Mahomedan conspiracy' throughout his speech, repeating it 14 times, and his whole speech comprising 53 pages was devoted to prove this theory of conspiracy.

He concluded that the facts on record demonstrate that to Mussalman intrigue and conspiracy we may mainly attribute the dreadful calamities of the year 1857. They induced the Hindus to join them, by speciously exciting them on that most vulnerable point, the fear of being forcibly deprived of their caste. I again say, they induced the Hindus to join them, for such is the evidence before us, and this too on a pretext in which the Mahomedans could have had no possible sympathy with them. Nor indeed were the Hindus long in discovering this deception. After the first victory of British at Hindan, they had rejoiced. They also already spoke in terms of much regret of the turn that affairs had taken, reproached the Mahomedans for having deceived them on pretences of their religion. Great numbers of the Hindu Sepoys at this time declared that if they could be sure that their lives would be spared, they would gladly go back to the service of the Government.

"That we shall perceive how exclusively Mahomedan's are all the prominent points that attach to it. A Mahomedan priest with assumed miraculous powers; a Mahomedan King, his dupe and his accomplice; a Mahomedan clandestine embassy to the Mahomedan powers of Persia and Turkey resulting; Mahomedan prophecies as to the downfall of our power; Mahomedan rule as the successor of our own; the most cold blooded murders by Mahomedan assassins; a religious war for Mahomedan ascendancy; a Mahomedan press unscrupulously abetting; and the Mahomedan sepoys initiating the mutiny. Hinduism, I may say, is nowhere either reflected or represented; if it be brought forward at all, it is only in subservience to its ever aggressive neighbour." (401)

31. **Dr. R. C. Mujumdar** (historian) : "It is a significant fact that the contemporary Englishmen generally viewed upon the outbreak mainly as a handiwork of the Muslims". (67-227) "Not only the Europeans, but even the Muslims themselves, at least a section of them, believed that they were the senior partners in the great undertaking. This is quite clear from the many proclamations issued by the Muslim chiefs who had assumed independent authority in various localities. (For example, by Khan Bahadur Khan of Bareilly). Throughout his proclamations runs the assumption that while the Muslims are exerting themselves to their utmost, the Hindus are lukewarm in their efforts. He had declared a reward for the Hindus for their patriotism if they helped him in the Uprising." (67-228; 68-617; 55-86)

He also wrote: "The Sikhs hated the Mughuls, and joined the British in order to prevent the restoration of Mughal rule under Bahadur Shah. There can be hardly any doubt that the Sikhs were largely influenced by such considerations (of taking full revenge) in wholeheartedly offering their services to the British Government. There are good grounds to believe that the same spirit alienated the Rajputs and the Marathas, as they too, for historical reasons did not favour the restoration of the Muslim Rule. It is to be noted that none of the Rajputs and Maratha Chiefs responded to the invitation of Bahadur Shah, and all the propaganda in Maharashtra was carried on in the name of Nana." (68-618; 55-88)

32. **Pandit J. Nehru :** "After 1857 the heavy hand of the British fell more on the Muslims than on the Hindus. They considered the Muslims more aggressive and militant, possessing memories of recent rule in India, and therefore more dangerous." (102-460; 120-92; 43-70) "This Revolt also put an end finally to any dreams or fantasies of the revival of the Delhi Empire. The shadow emperor sat in the Delhi palace, still he was a symbol of a famous dynasty. The ending of the Revolt meant also the smashing of the symbol" (101-345)

33. **Dr. Ishwari Prasad** (historian): "The Revolt and its consequences that followed virtually wiped out the Muslim nobility." (145-4) "The English attitude towards the Muslims till 1870 was one of suspicion and repression. Till that year the doctrine laid down by Lord Ellenborough, the Governor General in 1848 held the field. He had written 'I cannot close my eyes to the belief that this race (Muslims) is fundamentally hostile to us and therefore our true policy is to conciliate the Hindus'. The mutual hostility of the British and the Muslims was increased in consequences of the Great Revolt and its cruel suppression. To the Muslims, Hindustan again became a *Dar-ul-Harb*, not fit for the abode of Islam." (5)

34. **Ashok Mehta** (socialist leader and thinker): "The Mahomedans had evinced a keener and more widespread sympathy for the Rebellion. Even in South India, where their number was negligible, many conspiracies among the Muslims were uncovered between 1857 and 1859. The

accounts of British refugees are replete with such statements as follows: 'As it was a Hindu village we were not afraid to venture to it.' 'The Hindus all expressed the most merciful feelings towards the Firangis, while the Mahomedans could not disguise their murderous feelings.' It was not a rebellion of one community. But the Mussalmans for historical and ideological reasons, were more violently anti-British than the Hindus. To many of them, inspired by the philosophy of Shah Waliullah, India under British rule was *Dar-ul-Harb* and a *Jihad* against the alien ruler was not only a national necessity but a religious duty. The British, therefore, feared the fiery and excitable Muslim more than the proverbially mild Hindu." (122-59) "The hand of repression fell heavily on the Muslims, they were as it were tattooed with terror. Muslim quarters were everywhere the target. Muslim property was widely confiscated. The wrath of the rulers was mainly directed against the Muslims. The sufferings of the Muslims were great; innocent and guilty alike perished in the flaming vengeance of the victors". (60)

35. **Jayanti Maitra** (scholar) : "Many Muslim scholars believe that the impact of Sayyid Ahmad Shaheed (Barelvi) and his followers resulted in a great revival of Muslim enthusiasm that proved to be 'the chief sustaining power' of the insurrection of 1857." (124-90) Among others he refers to K. M. Ashraf ('Muslim Revivalists and the Revolt of 1857') stating that "The Wahabis were the only people who came not only armed with a consistent anti-British ideology but also with the backing of a network of organized centres and a moral influence on the Muslim intelligentsia throughout the country, remarked Ashraf. An anti-British stand as the only true path a Muslim could follow, irrespective of the fact whether he was a Wahabi or not, was also the symbol of the Muslim spirit of 1857. It is no wonder, therefore, if the British authorities considered them a persistently belligerent class and 'a source of permanent danger to the Empire." (91) "For most British observers in 1857, 'it was Muslim intrigue and Muslim leadership that converted a sepoy mutiny into a political conspiracy, aimed at the extinction of the British Raj. The British saw the Muslims as a source of constant trouble. It convinced many of the Britishers that the real

danger to their rule came from the Muslims. The view held almost universally amongst the British that the 'mild Hindu' was suffering from some temporary aberration, but that the Muslim was our implacable foe."(91) "The establishment of British rule in India was looked upon by the followers of the Prophet fundamentally as the challenge of Christianity to Islam."(93) "With its (the Revolt's) suppression all hopes of recovering Muslim hegemony were dashed to the ground." (94)

36. **N. K. Behere:** "Muslims were involved to a far greater extent than Hindus in the northern rebellion...sepoys who rebelled at various places used to immediately take the road to Delhi because the Mughal Emperor had been reinstated there in the very first thrust by rebels; it became a kind of holy war for Muslims. Despite the primary political nature (and aim) of the Uprising, it turned into a *Jihad.* Muslim predominance in the rebellion ushered in the advent of new nawabs at different places, and it was these nawabs that promulgated all kinds of laws to commit untold atrocities." (158-280)
37. **Prof. Taufiq Ahmad Nizami** (Aligarh Muslim University): "By 1857 every part of India had organized enthusiastic camps of the Wahabis and these camps were waiting for a chance to rise against the British Raj. Hunter's analysis is absolutely correct that the Wahabis had created and nourished the anti-British feeling which was expressed in the upheaval of 1857." (120-91) "The 'Mutiny' was crushed by an iron hand by the British. The main sufferers were the Muslims who, on no account, were prepared to lose political power." (92) (Also see Chap. 2, footnote no. 31(vi)).
38. **M. J. Akbar** (journalist and scholar) : "(Sayyid Ahmad Barelvi's) martyrdom gave new life to this movement..... Disparate groups were scattered across India, fomenting discontent that displayed its part in the outburst that is called the Mutiny of 1857. The *Risala-Jihad,* a war song of one of the groups, extolled the rewards of martyrdom and left little doubt about intentions: 'Fill the uttermost ends of India with Islam, so that no sounds may be heard but Allah! Allah!'" (119-191)
39. **Aziz Ahmad** (professor at University of Toronto and Osmania): "The Indian Sepoy Mutiny 1857 or the 'War of

Independance' (as now portrayed) was an 'archaic' attempt of the Indian Muslims to recover their lost power in India." (21-55) (See also, Chap. 2, footnote no. 31(ii)).

40. **Mujeeb Ashraf** (professor at Jamia Millia University): "The Muslims began to consider themselves a class of superior human beings." (77-9) "Thus it is that the Muslims do not accept any truth, of whatever nature, unless it is Islamized. Secular interests may divide them only for a brief time, but they can never be a permanent barrier to their union. A Muslim, whoever he may be, submits to the strict discipline of Islam. He acts always in conformity with the higher interest of Islam. He would never willingly sacrifice even a fraction of the Muslim world to a non-Muslim Power." (11)

"The Muslim may bend to foreign authority when he is not strong enough to resist. He may even make terms with it and accept titles and favours. However, as soon as he feels himself in a position to revolt, he would immediately do so. It is his imperative duty. This is what happened during 1857 in India. The government, like others, is a religious institution to them. The Muslim may only be ruled by an Imam (Caliph) having right and authority (of so doing)." (13)

"Under British rule the change in the status of the Muslims automatically brought into play a new set of obligations on their part, and the first of these obligations was to expel the foreigners; for the Quran is based upon the conception of the Muslims as a conquering, and not a conquered people." (120)

"To the Muslims, the Uprising was the logical culmination of their vigorous resistance to alien rule. It was based on definite ideals and objectives which converged towards a single purpose viz. to reestablish Muslim rule in India." (159)

"As a matter of fact the movement was mainly organized by the Muslims. Of course some Hindu leaders and a large number of Hindu sepoys, notably Rani Laxmi Bai of Jhansi, Nanasahib, and Madho Beni joined them. In the struggle of the Hindus too the Muslims played an important role." (160)

"In fact all the sections of the Muslim community participated (in it) wholeheartedly except for a minuscule group of nobles and elite. Of the various sections of the Muslim community the Ulemas played a significant role in the Uprising. They provided a basis, a philosophy, for the struggle. They were more determined in their opposition to the British than even the sepoys. Besides issuing *fatwas* calling upon the Muslims to join the *Jihad,* they actively participated in the war. They carried the masses with them." (162)

"(Then) the *Jihad* idea became very popular. Hence, the *Jihad* became synonymous with national war against alien rule. The call for a *Jihad* issued by the Ulemas thus overcame all religious barriers during 1857. From the religious point of view it was not binding upon the Hindus to join the *Jihad* but they too responded to the call of *Jihad* whole-heartedly." (176)

"Religion played a great role in the Uprising of 1857. Whatever may be the general nature of the Uprising, for the Muslims, its suppression meant the tragic end of all their efforts to revive the Muslim power and restore Muslim prestige in India." (267).

41. **Dr. I. H. Qureshi** [historian and minister in the Pakistan Government (1957)] "That such was the desire for the recovery of lost power that the movement gathered great support among the Muslims. The British singled them out for revenge and the penalty which the Muslims paid was heavy. It seemed that the Muslims of North India had made one blind superhuman effort and had failed. A movement created by deep emotions which had been smouldering in Muslim hearts, without proper leadership or plan, had emerged unpremeditated with consuming energy and violence...." (33-43)

"The failure of the *Jihad* Movement led by Sayyid Ahmad Shaheed (d. 1831) resulted in great frustration among the Muslims. But, it could not be expected that the Muslims would easily reconcile themselves to defeat. A people which still cherished the memory of having so successfully sustained a brilliant and benevolent empire found it hard to believe that there was no avenue left of reviving it. There were men of spirit who had not lost all hope. The average Muslim never lost the hope that he might again witness the rule of his own people. The Muslim masses have been surprisingly empire-conscious in the subcontinent. When the war (1857) was over, the British instinctively blamed the Muslims, thinking that they were responsible, being implacable enemies of foreign rule; the part played by the Hindus was considered to have been merely 'a temporary aberration.'

"It is true that the Muslims were not entirely responsible for organizing the great Mutiny of the sepoys, but the rising was in greater accord with their sentiments, and they threw themselves into it with great enthusiasm. That the Muslim sentiment against the British was strong. The political humiliation of the Muslims would have been quite sufficient a cause for them to rebel." (232) (From 'A History of Freedom Movement,' published by the Government of Pakistan (1957).

42. **S. M. Haq,** the Pakistani historian, in his book, 'The Great Revolution of 1857' "has stressed the role of the Muslims during the Revolt. He sees in the uprising a Muslim effort to free India from the British yoke and emphasizes the role of Islamic inspiration in the revolt." (146-13)

43. **Sir Sayyed Ahmad Khan** was the district judge during the Mutiny. "To erase the conviction of the rulers that the Mutiny was a Muslim rebellion to regain their lost grandeur and establish that the Muslims were not disloyal, he wrote two books." (97-5) Even though advocating that Muslims were loyal during the Mutiny, he indirectly emphasizes their role in it :

"That the Mahomedans were, in every respect, more dissatisfied than the Hindus, there is little doubt. Hence, it was that in many districts the greater proportion of rebels were found in their ranks." (58-10) "There was no atrocity committed then of which the blame was not imputed to Mahomedans! In newspapers and articles I find the most bitter denunciations against the Mahomedans, who are freely represented as being everything that is vile, treacherous, and contemptible. There was no prickly thorn in those awful times, respecting which it was not said that it was planted by a Mahomedan; there was no fiery whirlwind that was not raised by a Mahomedan! I must deprecate that wholesole denunciation against the entire community of Mahomedans, in which the newspapers are wont to indulge, and which stains the pages of those who have written upon the events of 1857." (45-193 to 5)

Stating various causes of the revolt, he concludes: "All these causes rendered the Mahomedans more uneasy than the Hindus. The reason of this, I take to be that the Hindu faith consists rather in the practice of long established rites and forms, than in the study of doctrine. The Hindus recognize no canons and laws, or appeals to the heart and conscience. Their creed does not admit of such things. They insist upon nothing, excepting strict observance of their old rites, and of their modes of eating and drinking. It does not annoy or grieve them, to see such rites and observances, as they considered necessary, disregarded by other men. Mahomedans, on the contrary, looking upon the tenets of their creed as necessary to Salvation; and upon the neglect of them as damnation, are thoroughly well-grounded in them. They regard their religious precepts as the ordinances of God. Hence, it was that the Mahomedans were more uneasy than the Hindus, and that, as might have been expected, they formed the majority of the rebels." (58-23)

He states historical and political reasons for Muslim unrest: "For centuries the Mahomedan's position in India has been an honourable one. There is an element of shame in his disposition. He has no grasping desire for money, he esteems honour above all other things; that the Mahomedan is not easily brought to do that, which under the influence of temptation, other races in India will do (i.e. submit) without compunction. It may be that this is wrong but God having instilled it into him, his views and feelings cannot easily be changed. It may be unfortunate but, it is inculcated into them by their religion and is no fault of theirs." (44)

44. **M. Abul Kalam Azad**, Minister of Education, Government of India (1957), wrote in the Government Publication : "There was unanimous and spontaneous agreement (between Muslims and Hindus) that he (i.e. Bahadur Shah) alone had the right to become the Emperor of India. The story of the old conflict between Marathas and the Mughals was however forgotten and he (i.e. Nanasahib of Kanpur) did not for a

moment hesitate to declare himself a subedar or governor of the Mughal Court. The real ruler, he proclaimed, was the Emperor of India. The coins struck were in the name of the Emperor and all orders were issued in his name. He, i.e. Bahadur Shah' had neither army nor treasure. Nor had he any influence or power. The only thing in his favour was that he was a descendant of Akbar and Shah Jahan. The loyalty which the people of India offered to Bahadur Shah was not to him as a person but for the descendant of the Great Mughals ." (141 –xxvii)

45. For some more comments: see footnote 31 in Chap. 2; footnote 3 to 6, 9, 10 & 12, 13 in Chap. 3.

* * *

Appendix – III

The So-called 'Constitution' Drafted by Revolutionaries of 1857

An impression is sought to be created in recent times that, after their victory over Delhi (11th May 1857), revolutionaries had drafted, adopted and implemented a democratic constitution for India. A three-page document containing twelve articles is proffered as evidence of this belief. Numerous authors, historians and commentators including Savarkar cite this document. Some of them use it to emphasize how the then administration headed by Bahadur Shah was founded upon 'democratic' and 'secular' principles. The following two opinions are noteworthy in this context.

Prof. K. C. Yadav, reproducing that twelve articled document's in support of his contention, writes in the Preface to 'Delhi in 1857': "These unnamed leaders of the movement, at least in Delhi, were forward-looking persons, and believed in secularism, equality and justice. They were no restorers of the old, rotten monarchy of the past. In fact they stood for a democratic setup." (107-xxii)

Prof. Irfan Habib, also relying on the same document, writes in a subsection entitled 'Democratic Sentiments': "Of particular significance is the republican or democratic sentiments of the Bengal Army sepoys. When they formed representative bodies, they called them 'councils,' and elected their peers. In Delhi, they acknowledged the titular Emperor, Bahadur Shah Zafar, but actually constituted a 'Court of Administration' consisting of the representatives of different rebel contingents to administer Delhi." He writes further, "If the revolt had succeeded, then we might have had, instead of the Central Legislative Assembly, the Court of Administration of Delhi as the initial Parliament in India." ('Frontline', June 29, 2007)

Glorification of that document has also begun making the rounds in Shivaji's Maharashtra, and it is amusing to find a sudden advent of even eulogizers of Shivaji (along with those of Aurangzeb and Jinnah) telling us how democratic and secular was Bahadur Shah's rule (and, perhaps by implication, how utterly superfluous were Shivaji's efforts to found the indigenous 'Hindavi Swarajya'!). We therefore felt it necessary to review and discuss that 'constitution' with a view to dispel the false impression or misunderstanding that such attempts might create in the minds of some people.

Here is an English version of that document, along with the Editors' footnotes, as it appears in the book, *Freedom Struggle in U.P.*, published by the Government of Uttar Pradesh. (3-419):

"CIVIL ADMINISTRATION

DELHI

Court of Administration

In the name of God most merciful

Framing of a Constitution in order to dispel the confusion in Departments and to remove mismanagement from the Military and Civil Administration which is proper and indispensable for the working of the Constitution and the institution of a Court which is essential — the following being the important regulations for the same:

I. A Court shall be instituted which shall be named "Court of Administration" i.e. *'Jalsa-i-Intizam-i-Fauji Wa Mulki'*.

II. Ten members shall be appointed (elected) to this Court, as per details — six from Military and four from Civil: From amongst those of the Military two from Infantry, two from Cavalry and two from Artillery; four from Civil.

III. Out of the above ten, one shall be unanimously elected as a President and one as Vice President. The President shall have two votes, and Secretaries shall be appointed in every department as needed. Five of these shall form a quorum.[1]

IV. The following oath shall be administered to each at the time of their taking over, 'I shall discharge my duties with honesty and sincerity and shall not show any nepotism and shall work with great labour and profound deliberation and deep thought and will not miss even the minutest details of administration and shall not directly or indirectly resort to extortion, force or partiality but shall make efforts to carry on the administration in a manner, as to ensure the solidarity of the Government and the well-being and comfort of its subjects and will not disclose to anyone either directly or indirectly, the decisions arrived at by the Court, without the permission of the Court or that of Sahib-e-Alam'.[2]

V. The election of the Court shall take place thus: Two members from the Infantry, two from the Cavalry and two from the Artillery with majority of votes. They should be senior in service,[3] competent, experienced, suitable and wise. But if there is a person who is competent, wise, intelligent and capable of serving at the Court but is not senior in service, this alone cannot debar him from appointment (election) to the Court. The other four Civilian members shall also be likewise appointed (elected).

VI. If after the appointment of the above ten members, anyone of them would express any opinion, in the general meeting of the Court, prompted by insincerity, dishonesty and nepotism, he shall be expelled from membership with the unanimous decision of the Court and his substitute shall be appointed in accordance with Clause V.

---

1. This sentence is not clear in the manuscript and only a general sense has been given.

2. Apparently Mirza Mughal. (*This is incorrect. It was Bakht Khan –Author*)

3. The Constitution in question is available in the form of a draft. It is very interesting to note that though originally the basis of election was made communal i.e. of the two, one was to be Hindu and the other a Muslim, it was later on deleted from the draft and the seniority and capability were recognized as the criteria of election.

VII. All the administrative matters shall first be reported for decision to the Court. After the decision of the same by a majority of votes it shall be submitted for the concurrence of the Sahib-e-Alam Bahadur to whom the Court shall be subordinate. After the concurrence of Sahib-e-Alam Bahadur the decisions shall be submitted for information to His Majesty. No order regarding Military or Civil Administration shall be given to effect to without the *decision* of the Court, *concurrence* of Sahib-e-Alam and the *information* of His Majesty. If Sahib-e-Alam does not concur in any decision of the Court it will be referred back to the latter for reconsideration. If again there is a difference of opinion between the Sahib-e-Alam Bahadur and the decision of the Court, it shall be submitted to His Majesty whose orders shall be final.

VIII. No one else but the members of the Court, Sahib-e-Alam Bahadur and His Majesty shall be allowed to attend the meetings of the Court. If anyone among the members of the Court is absent from the meeting on strong valid grounds, the decision of the remaining members of the Court arrived at by majority of votes shall be considered as the decision of the full Court.

IX. If a member wants to move a resolution into the Court, he shall get it seconded by some other member and shall then submit it with the unanimous opinion of two members.

X. When a resolution is moved in the Court in accordance with Clause IX, the mover shall first of all deliver a speech and he shall not be interrupted by others, till he finishes. If any member of the Court raises any objections he shall be allowed to do so without being interrupted during his speech. If some third person makes a speech against the objector and moves an amendment or modification and the rest of the Court is silent, each member shall pen down his views separately and the decisions shall be arrived at with majority of votes. After the approval, the decisions shall be communicated to the Secretary of each Department.

XI. The members of the Court elected by the different departments of the army stipulated in Clause II shall act as the administrators of the department (of the army) concerned and a Committee of four persons shall be constituted under them, in accordance with Section IV. Secretaries shall also be appointed on this Committee as needed. The decision arrived by the majority of opinion in the Committee shall be placed before Court through the officers concerned and the

Court shall act according to Clause VII and the same procedure shall be followed in all Military and Civil Departments.

XII. The Court shall have the powers to amend the Constitution by majority of votes at anytime." (3-419)

The text is reproduced above in full. Hence we do not feel the need for quoting from it at length. The original is in Urdu and a facsimile may be found in Dr. Sen's work published by the Government of India. (141-80)

We wish to emphasize at the very outset that this document is nothing in the nature of a 'constitution', in the sense it is being construed, but merely a set of *rules of order* formulated for the conduct of a 'Court of Administration' that was established to deal with internecine squabbles among rival Muslim rebel leaders resulting from Avarice and mutual envy. This is already amply evident from the twelve articles themselves, but becomes all the more apparent after a close review of events that were unfolding at the time.

Mirza Mughal, the eldest son of Bahadur Ṣhah, was appointed Commander-in-Chief after the 11th May 1857 Uprising in Delhi when the latter was proclaimed Emperor of India. At the same time, his other sons were assigned to commands of various rebel regiments. (Included in such appointees were Mirza Khijr Sultan, Mirza Abu Bakr, Mirza Suhrab Hind, Mirza Bakhtkhar Shah, Mirza Abdullah, Mirza Qadar Sultan, Mirza Sidoo Baig.) (121-58) The entire rebel force in Delhi had thus been distributed among themselves by the various princes. The child Jawan Bakht, the favourite youngest son of the Emperor who had not yet reached his teens, was made Prime Minister of India. (85-6) Except for the scribe Mukundlal, not a single Hindu was included in either the Imperial Court or senior administrative hierarchy. One reason for taking special note of this fact is that everyone in any senior administrative position was exclusively Muslim. Similar was the case with the Court of Administration appointed in accordance with the 'constitution'. Another reason was that, the pillage and loot of the citizenry of Delhi (largely composed of Hindu traders, moneylenders and *mahajans*) was perpetrated by these very princes, who had seized complete control of the administration.

The Emperor expressed his despair at this state of affairs : "Thus, without my knowledge or orders, they (mutinous soldiers) plundered, not only many individuals, but several entire streets, plundering, robbing, killing and imprisoning all they chose; and forcibly extorting whatever sums of money they thought fit from the merchants and other respectable residents of the city, and appropriating such exactions to their own private purposes. All that has been done, was done by that rebellious army. I was in their power. They made me a prisoner. I was helpless. I did whatever they required, otherwise they would immediately have killed me. This is universally known. In this state of things, I resolved...to go first to...thence to Ajmer, and from Ajmer...to Mecca; but the Army would not allow me..." (107-345) It must be recalled that the Emperor had been coerced by rebel sepoys into appointing Mirza Mughal and other princes to their respective commands.

On 2nd July 1857, however, the Emperor removed Mirza Mughal from office and replaced him by 'Brigadier General' Bakht Khan who had arrived from Rohilkhand. This man was an adherent of the Wahabi school and his appointment had been a result of the pressure that Wahabi maulvis in Delhi had brought to bear on the Emperor. Mirza Mughal was appointed as deputy Commander-in-Chief. Immediately upon appointment, the titles 'Farzand' and 'Sahib-e-Alam' were bestowed on Bakht Khan. (121-86; 154-186) The meaning of the title, 'Sahib-e-Alam' is 'Lord of the World', and used to be conferred upon Commanders-in-Chief. The 'Sahib-e-Alam' referred to in the 'constitution' was this Bakht Khan. (121-167) He was also simultaneously given the responsibility as Governor General, the highest office in the civil hierarchy. Bakht Khan thus became both Commander-in-Chief and Governor General.

A correct appreciation of this development is necessary because it was as the fallout of this appointment that the rebel force was split into two contending factions within Muslim sepoys, and Bahadur Shah was obliged to constitute the Court of Administration in an attempt to find an amicable settlement of the rift.

One faction of the rebel force, loyal to Mirza Mughal, took strong exception to the removal of the Prince and his replacement by Bakht Khan. Shortly, a lengthy memoir was presented to the Emperor by some among them, which stated : "Bakht Khan was an officer of artillery. You have conferred on him the title of Governor General and proposed to place us all under his order. It is contrary to the rules of Government. He is not fit for such a trust. You have dismissed your sons and appointed him. This does not please us. What claims has he? If your Majesty wishes us to help you then allow us to select in concert with the princes, from the several regiments, such men as are fit to be general, and bring them up to you for confirmation of their appointment. Let the sepoys fight under their own officers so that there can be no new complaints that no help is sent out to them." (85-18)

On assuming his new office, Bakht Khan informed the Emperor, "I shall not hesitate to strike off the ears and nose of even a Prince, should he be apprehended in the act of looting or engaging in bloodshed." The Emperor replied, "You have been given the necessary authority. Do expressly everything that you may deem proper." (1-238; 121-135)

How sepoys, under patronage of the princes, had gone on a spree of looting and atrocity in Delhi is well documented. Innumerable complaints had reached the Emperor. The appointment of Bakht Khan, however, had a new effect. The princes now stood up against him and the rebel force became split into two factions, with the Bareilly Brigade in support of Bakht Khan and the Neemuch contingent behind Mirza Mughal. Sepoys loyal to Mirza Mughal began flouting Bakht Khan's orders, resulting in a series of defeats at the hands of the British. Every military setback became an occasion for making newer complaints against Bakht Khan to the Emperor on behalf of the princes. It even began to be alleged that Bakht Khan had secretly defected to the British.

Munshi Jiwanlal, who was present in Delhi at the time, notes that: "The officers of the Neemuch force accused Bakht Khan of negotiating with the English. The King was induced to issue an order that General Bakht Khan should not be admitted to the Palace. The officers of the Neemuch force then suggested that they should be allowed to disarm the Bareilly troops, which they offered to do with four regiments of infantry and one of cavalry. The King gave no answer to this proposal, but later in the day (i.e. on 23rd August 1857) he issued orders to all the officers to obey neither the orders of Mirza Mughal nor of any other General, inasmuch as His Majesty had appointed a Court of twelve members, six to be appointed by the King and six by the Army, for the future conduct of the siege (of Delhi). The Army was to obey all orders issued by the Court." (121-205)

Such were the circumstances under which the 'Court of Administration' was appointed and the much vaunted twelve articled 'constitution' formulated. Despite the mention of twelve members, it appears that the 'court' actually had only ten. Clearly, this Court was an expedient primarily for resolving the power struggle between Mirza Mughal and Bakht Khan.

The Emperor paid no heed to the numerous complaints he was receiving against Bakht Khan. The latter had declared by oath on the Quran that he had no connection with the British as was being alleged. Munshi Jiwanlal notes : "General Mahommad Bakht Khan, in the presence of all the principal officers of the Army, and of Mirza Mughal, swore upon the Quran that he had opened no negotiations with English." (121-205) Being pained by the charges, levelled at him, Bakht Khan requested the Emperor to relieve him of the office of Commander-in-Chief. As Munshi Jiwanlal noted : "He proposed in the future to concern himself only with the command of the Bareilly column. The King replied: 'No one has censured your conduct, and I am quite satisfied to leave the chief command in your hands.'" (121-212,167) Hence, the Emperor had continued to trust him and had retained him as Commander-in-Chief even after the constitution of the Court of Administration.

Mirza Mughal had demanded the establishment of such a Court in order to regulate Bakht Khan's authority. The following entry appears in a diary of the Emperor's advisor, Hakim Ahsanullah Khan: "Mirza Mughal sent a petition on the part of all the officers of the Regiments that the affairs of the army could not be administered until the Court was established; that the following individuals were eligible. Many names were given." (85-20) Thus, it is clear that the prince had made the demand in the expectation that his supporters would be co-opted on the Court, and had even sent a list of names of persons he considered fit for appointment.

Iqbal Hussain, a student of the rebel administration in Delhi, makes the following statement, which is very useful in this context:

"Not surprisingly, his (Bakht Khan's) sudden rise aroused the jealousy of the Princes, who were not willing to recognize his role. A letter, with the King's signature forged and censuring Bakht Khan, was dispatched; but Bahadur Shah immediately denied writing such a letter (11 July 1857). Bakht Khan's strong measures restoring law and order won him popular support in Delhi....

"Though on paper Bakht Khan was assigned absolute power in revenue affairs, intriguers continued to bypass his authority. On 9th July, with a strong force supported by the *Jihadis,* Bakht Khan attacked English positions and captured Tihari Hazari (Tis Hazari). Unfortunately, this success, the first important one since the rebels had captured Delhi, caused much jealousy among the sepoys who had come from Meerut and Neemuch. The attitude of the Princes was already unfriendly. Bakht Khan made some effort towards conciliating the sepoys... But Bakht Khan's efforts to reform the administration could do little to pacify the Princes and the conspirators. Mirza Mughal ignored his orders and tried to poison the ears of Bahadur Shah. At one stage he asked the King to relieve Bakht Khan of his supreme military position. But Bahadur Shah showed him increased favour by sending presents and publicly expressing his satisfaction with Bakht Khan's role.

"Of the available contingents, the Neemuch contingent has a reputation for bravery but its generals, Sidhari Singh and Ghaus Khan, held aloof and accused Bakht Khan of being complacent about the English. Mutual discord made it impossible to take joint action, and the delay proved to be a boon for the English. Differences between them came to a head on 5th August after their failure to capture the English position at Alipur Sidhari Singh was a supporter of Mirza Mughal, and it was alleged that Neemuch forces had given only a show of fighting and left Bakht Khan high and dry. Now Bakht Khan decided to fight alone to expel the enemy from their positions.

"Factionalism within the army and intrigues against Bakht Khan were adversely affecting the administration. Bakht Khan reported to the King that Mirza Khizr and other Princes were collecting funds from various bankers ostensibly to pay the troops; but the troops had not received anything. As a result of this complaint, Mirza Khizr was compelled to surrender all the money he had realized. Orders were issued to the bankers to negotiate directly with Bakht Khan.

"Intrigues against Bakht Khan continued to undermine his position. On 21st August a joint military campaign against the English did not materialize on account of mutual discords. Mirza Mughal blamed Bakht Khan for his failure and urged the King to prohibit his entry to the Palace and to disarm the Bareilly contingent. Such measures were fraught with danger for the personal safety of the King as Mirza Mughal was becoming increasingly powerful day-by- day with the support of Neemuch contingent.

"The King now issued orders to all officers forbidding them from obeying the commands of both Mirza Mughal and Bakht Khan. He appointed a Court of Administration, to consist of ten members, four to be appointed by the King and six by the army."

He further writes, "Evidently the formation of the 'Court of Administration' (the English words were used in the Urdu text) was the work of those with some background of service in the British Army and it seems very likely that Bakht Khan himself was the prime mover in this measure." (127-17 to 21)

Thus, although the Court of Administration had been constituted at the behest of Mirza Mughal, it had been populated according to the wishes of Bakht Khan, which is why sometimes the document is referred to as the 'constitution' framed by the latter. This is also the reason for Commander-in-Chief Bakht Khan's supreme position in the Court as 'Sahib-e-Alam' and the stipulation that decisions by the Court had to be accorded "concurrence" by him. In the event of a disagreement between the decision of the Court and Sahib-e-Alam, the matter was to be submitted for final disposal by the Emperor. In any case, the Emperor being completely in favour of Bakht Khan, it was plain that he was merely going to ratify Bakht Khan's decision. Thus, this 'Court of Administration' and its 'constitution' comprising twelve Articles had been farmed primarily to pacify Mirza Mughal while keeping Bakht Khan's supreme authority intact.

After reviewing the need and genesis of that 'Court', let us turn to the provisions of the *'dastur'*. (The 'constitution' has been referred to in that Urdu document as *'dastur'*).

1. The aims and objectives of the document have been spelled out in the preamble. It states that the constitution was being framed "in order to dispel the confusion in Departments and to remove mismanagement from the Military and Civil Administration". Indeed, a Council of Advisors of such nature exists even under autocratic or dictatorial regimes. The king or dictator, too, seeks opinion and advice of some. This is imperative for the sovereignty or dictatorship to function in a progressively efficient manner. As such, the mere existence of a 'council of advisors' is by no means proof of the existence of democracy. The members of such advisory council are the King's appointees and their decisions are not final or binding

on the King — it is entirely upto the latter to accept or reject them. This does not constitute a democratic system. The 'Court of Administration' in post-Uprising Delhi was no different.

2. Six out of ten members of this 'Court' were to be drawn from the army, two each from its three wings — infantry, cavalry and artillery. But to say that they were to be 'elected' (according to the currently accepted sense of the word) is patent falsification. The word 'elected, to appear in parentheses after the word 'appointed' in one English translation. Which of these alternatives was intended? If they were to be appointed, who was the nominating authority? If they were to be elected, who were the voters? Is one to suppose that all rebel soldiers, whose numbers in Delhi were constantly increasing by the day, were the constituents? How were the four members from the civil administration to be chosen? The answer is plain: no 'election' was envisaged. They were not to be 'elected' by voters, but 'selected' by their superiors. The Urdu word appearing in the original is *muntakhab* (chosen). Two nominees each from the infantry, cavalry and artillery were to be 'selected' by the respective commanding officers and nominated to the Court, while four members were to be 'selected' by the Emperor from the civil hierarchy. Besides, considerable ambiguity remains over whether seniority of service or merit was the criterion for 'selection'. Even assuming that either criterion was taken to apply to an 'election', it could only be a qualification for the candidate contesting the 'election' without in any manner making the process of 'election', *per se*, democratic. But this is not clearly spelled out in the document. Dalrymple's observation in this connection is pertinent: "According to its remarkable twelve-point constitution, there were ten members. Six of these were chosen (*muntakhab*) from the military; two each from the infantry, cavalry and artillery. The four remaining members were from the Palace." (154-293)

It is therefore clear that the 'Court' was certainly not constituted according to the will of either the rebel sepoys or the general public; the latter, in fact, had no connection with it. Thus, propagation of the idea that the 'Court' was a 'democratic institution', that it possessed the nature of the Central Legislative Assembly and that, had the Uprising been successful, it would have become 'India's First Parliament', is not mere misinterpretation of this 'constitution' but a grievous attempt to willfully mislead.

3. If viewed from the aspect of a constitution, the document lacks certain indispensable provisions. It was no more than establishment of an advisory council and a set of rules by which it was to function. It is quite obscure in details as nothing is clearly stated about which matters it was empowered to address and decide. The Court was authorized to amend its constitution by a majority vote, but it is clear that such amendment was going to need the Sahib-e-Alam's concurrence. If he declined, the matter would have to be referred to the Emperor. All of this means that the actual scope of the Court was no more than tendering advice and making proposals. If we assume that this Court enjoyed powers to amend its constitution, legislate, administer the state and give justice, would such arrangement be acceptable to a democratic system?

More remarkable is complete silence on rights of citizens, which are or ought to be of paramount importance in a democracy. How can a constitution that does not contemplate 'people' even in passing be construed as democratic? So, it was nothing of the sort, being no more than a set of rules and regulations for military administration. Even those rules were not entirely free from considerable ambiguity.

4. Some commentators laud this 'constitution' as secular because they find in it a commitment to secular principles. However, what were the rights guaranteed to Hindus, who formed 80 percent of the population, is a question that remains unanswered. There is no mention of 'religion' in the document. Is one to naïvely presume that this by itself constitutes evidence that it was secular? How many Hindus were inducted in the Court? No names are available, but history is witness that there was not a single Hindu in a position of senior responsibility in either the Imperial Court of Delhi or its administration. Plainly, all ten members of the Court, therefore, were Muslim. Thus, where there was no likelihood of a Hindu being inducted in this Court, it is difficult to contemplate that some Hindu could ever have been considered for becoming 'Sahib-e-Alam', much less the Emperor of India.

We need to take note of the fact that in the original Urdu document that is available, certain portions have been scored out and substituted by inscribing new matter over it and in the margin. The editors of the book published under the aegis of the Uttar Pradesh Government, in a footnote regarding one such substitution, mention: "The Constitution in question is available in the form of a draft. It is very interesting to note that though originally the basis of election was made communal i.e. of the two, one was to be Hindu and the other a Muslim, it was later on deleted from the draft and the seniority and capability were recognized as the criteria of election." (3-419)

Although the purpose of including this footnote is to lionize the then Delhi administration as noncommunal and duly committed to considerations of merit and ability alone, the scoring out of certain portions in the original had, in fact, been a consequence of the fact that the administration was wholly communal. Clear signs were being seen around 23rd August (the day when the 'Court' was constituted) that rebel forces were doomed to defeat at British hands, and the original portion might have been included only to appease Hindus whose cooperation was urgently needed at that critical juncture. However, some provisions were perhaps later scored out under pressure from other quarters. If the editors view the amended document as 'secular', it may never be known how much they might have eulogized the unmodified one.

5. Details in Article IV, pertaining to the manner of swearing in members, need special note. Eleven lines, out of a total of eighty-one in the document, are devoted to a procedural matter that cannot strictly form part of a 'constitution'. It charges members to avoid, among other matters, nepotism, dishonesty, extortion and partiality. It binds them to ensuring welfare of the people and maintaining complete secrecy about decisions of the Court. This only indicates that such ills and malpractices were rampant in the administration at the time. A reflection of this state of affairs can be seen in Article VI. "Insincerity, dishonesty and nepotism" were designated as reasons for expulsion of a member from the Court.

6. It is astonishing to note that such a brief 'constitution' contains not a charter of rights and duties of subjects, but entirely trifling rules of order like the procedure for presenting resolutions to the Court, and engaging in speeches, arguments, debates and discussion thereupon; refraining from obstructing the speech by a member; the method of recording dissent; how other members should keep notes; how secretaries should be appointed. Thus, the document, far from being a charter of the rights and duties of citizens (which any constitution necessarily needs to be), is no more than a compilation of rules and regulations to be followed for conduct of meetings. What was the propriety for a 'constitution' to contain rules of order?

7. The document was prepared on 23rd August 1857. The Emperor was in power in Delhi till 20th September 1857, or for just 27 days after the Court was constituted. Defeat loomed large over rebel forces during this entire period. The so-called constitution was not operative for even a month. It had nothing whatsoever to do with people's welfare or progress. It is thus most doubtful if this undated, unsigned document containing several hastily made corrections could ever have become really operative or useful. History is mute about who were its members or Chairman. It is also not known how the dispute between Mirza Mughal and Bakht Khan, for which express purpose the Court was brought into being, was resolved through the medium of the Court. What was the status of Mirza Mughal *vis-à-vis* the Court? Had he been made its chairman? The document provides no clear answers to all such questions.

Most researchers and commentators of the 1857 Uprising do not take cognizance of this document at all. However, the following observations made by those who do, might be useful.

Dr. Surendra Nath Sen writes: "A 'Court' or 'military and civil management committee' was appointed 'to do away with mismanagement and to remove disorder from the civil and military establishments.' It was not clear who were to elect the civilian members and how... The Court was under the Commander-in-Chief without whose approval its decisions could not be implemented... On paper, the Court was a democratic body...it should have served as an efficient curb on military licence. But in practice, it achieved nothing. When exactly the Court was appointed is not precisely known, for its constitution bears no date. It could not make its power felt either over the army or over the civil officers, and anarchy and disorder continued as before." (141-72)

William Dalrymple writes: "(The Court) never acted as a unified central command, and Bakht Khan always kept his distance from it: in the records that survive among the Military Papers, it appears to have been very much the organ of Mirza Mughal and his military allies." (154-293) What he means to say is, that Mirza Mughal was Chairman of the Court. He writes further about the final outcome of the institution : "Given this, the Court seems in fact to have achieved the direct opposite of what was intended for it. Rather than coordinating the different rebel regiments, it emphasized the existing divisions between them, polarizing them even more dramatically than before into competing factions acting under their own independent warlords." (154-294)

Savarkar writes : "The Emperor...was quite inexperienced in war and unequal to military leadership. There was wanted at least one capable head to command the sepoys...Even the old Emperor whom they had placed on the throne was...anxious to find a good leader for them. He gave all the power in the hands of Bakht Khan. He appointed three generals to manage the army. He then ordered that a committee of six – three (?) Delhi citizens and three (?) Sepoy leaders should together look after all the affairs of the army. And when this representative council also proved fruitless, the noble and patriotic Emperor...announced publicly that he was ready to give up all his power and abdicate." (1-333)

In fine, the only aim of the Court of Administration and its twelve-articled 'constitution' was to provide unified leadership for rebel sepoys. Perhaps, had a suitable and non-controversial commander-in-chief been found, the need for the Court might never have been felt. In a way, the 'constitution' was a compilation of rules for administration of the military. It was the conflict between predominance of Mughal princes and the influence of Wahabi Maulvis that gave birth to this ineffectual offspring. Neither democracy, nor indeed secular principles, had anything whatsoever to do with it. Moreover, the effort was a total failure. Even Mughal Emperors of yore had appointed councils of advisors. However, neither their Empires, for that reason, nor this 'constitution', for use therein of some stray Urdu synonyms indicative of Western democratic parlance, can ever be regarded 'democratic'. However, it is amazing indeed that the constitution should also be lauded as 'secular' when there was neither the presence, nor the least possibility of the presence, of even a single Hindu member in the Court.

xxx

Index

Abdul Hai, Maulana, 52, 53
Abdul Qadar, Maulvi, 208
Abdul Rehman, Subedar, 353
Abdullah Baig, 179
Abdur Rahim Khan, 426
Abdur Rahman, Collector, 331
Abu Bakr, Caliph, 32
Abul Hasan Ali Nadvi, 50
Adil Muhammad Khan, 290, 292
Administration, 27, 94, 106, 119, 120, 121, 125, 126, 131, 133, 134, 135, 137, 159, 168, 170, 178, 183, 205, 210, 214, 215, 230, 234, 235, 258, 276, 278, 282, 283, 330, 335, 402, 421
  Delhi, 225
  Muslim, 218
Adoption of Male Heir, 144
Afghan (s), 295, 315, 362, 363, 379
  Army, 28
  Rohillas, 318
  Soldiers, 314
Afghanistan, 20, 29, 37, 56, 58, 187, 208, 211, 296, 362, 370, 382
Agha Mirza, 256
Agra, 117, 118, 139, 140, 141, 153, 192, 202, 215, 219, 220, 221, 273, 286, 293, 312, 432
  European Population, 202
  Province, 116, 212, 218
Ahir Hindus of Bharauti, 427
Ahmad Khan, 209
Ahmad Shah Abdali, 27-29, 57, 80, 82, 187, 274, 441
  Invasion, 82

Ahmad Yar Khan, 331
Ahmudullah Khan, 419, 420
Ajaygarh, 233
Ajmer, Nasirabad and
Neemuch, 136
Akand, Chief of Swat, 192
Akbar, 22, 123
And Sirhindi, 17
Emperor, 17-19
Akhbar-ul-Zafar, (Newspaper),
187
Akor, 60, 62, 64
Al Azhar University Egypt, 45
Alambagh, 15, 155
Alauddin Khilji, 14, 15
Alexandria, 375
Ali Baksh, Ruler of Hamirpur,
234, 433
Ali Brothers, 71, 72, 75, 205
Ali Nakki Khan, 253, 254
Ali Raza, 222
Aligarh, 117, 119, 152, 216, 439
Mosques, 214
Under Muslim Rule, 213
All India Secret Conspiracy,
337
Allah's Law, 16
Allahabad, 54, 120, 122, 123,
126, 154, 158, 187
And Benares, 381
Division, 120
Province, 228, 234, 432
Rebellion, 231
Allah-i-Allah, Maro Firangi Ko,
180
Amanut Ali, 285, 286
Ambedkar, Dr. Baba Saheb
Bhim Rao, 7, 8, 11, 13-16, 43,
49
Amethi, 263
Amir Akbar, Shah of Swat, 76
Amir Dost Muhammad Khan,
363
Amir Khan, 57
Amir of Afghanistan, 89, 318
Amjhera, 142
Ammunition
Dump, 121, 131, 185, 254,
255
Store, 120
Amritsar, 42
Anandrao, 141, 298
Andamans, 342
Annexation of Ayodhya, 87
Anti-British
Agitation, 268
Conspiracies, 253
Muslims, 192
Propaganda, 171
Sentiments, 33, 211, 255
War, 105
Anti-Hindu
Jihad, 196
Program, 210
Anti-Islamic Forces, 35, 37
Anti-Sikh Jihad, 56
Arab, 147, 148
Prison, 147
Arabia, 296
Arabs, 295, 296
And Rohillas, 358, 359
Arah, 338, 340
Arcot, 343
Armed
Azizan, 198
Forces, 19
Rebellion, 102, 179
Revolt, 102
Struggle, 102, 103

Army
Camps, 112, 114
Camps, Meerut, 112
Atrocities on Hindus, 428
Attock, 21, 82
Aurangabad, 346
Aurangzeb, 14, 19, 21, 80, 101, 174, 261
Anti-Hindu Policies, 20
Bigotry, 19
Death in 1707, 20
Emperor, 204
Reign, 20
Religious Fanatism, 19
Autonomous Nawabs of-, 21
Ayodhya, 21
Bengal, 21
Hyderabad, 21
Rohilkhand, 21
Autonomous States, 21
Ayodhya, 1723, 21
Bengal, 1740, 21
Hyderabad, 1724, 21
Awadh, 416
Ayodhya, 88, 90, 97, 105, 133, 154, 157, 170, 248, 250, 254, 255, 258, 259, 261, 266, 267, 268, 270, 272, 278, 280, 386, 434, 441
A Muslim State, 89
As Garden of India, 88
Centre of Islamic Culture, 90
Defenders, 154
Province, 51, 53, 127-131, 155, 156, 165, 170, 175, 267, 278, 434
State, 253
State Army, 108
Aysh Bagh, 395
Azad, Abdul Kalam, 18, 439
Azamgarh, 125, 169, 280, 282, 386
Declaration, 370
Azeemullah Khan, 120, 216, 373, 375-376, 377, 378, 382
Nanasahib Adviser, 236, 239, 240, 243, 246
Azeez Khan, 426

Baba Bhatt, Chief Justice, 239, 241
Baba Devi Gir, 385
Badaun, 427
Badli-ki-Sarai, 150, 197
Bahadur Shah (1707-12), Aurangzeb's Son, 20
Bahadur Shah (Zafar), 9, 87, 112, 151, 152, 155, 176, 181-183, 185, 187, 195, 197, 200-203, 204, 221, 252, 364, 401, 402, 435-37
As Emperor of Free India, 9
Family, 258
Firman, 364
In British Custody 151
Mughal Emperor, 13, 76, 109
Proclamation, 204, 398, 402
Transportation to Rangoon, 152
Raja, 365
Trial, 101
Baharan Mulk, 89
Indian Representative of Shah of Iran, 89
Nawab of Ayodhya, 89
Bahraich, 130
Bahrampur, 178, 179
Bahrampur Episode, 180

Bahuri Press, Bareilly, 393, 398
Bakhshish Ali, 310
  Chief of Prisons, 300, 301
Bakht Khan, 218, 320, 321
  British Gen., 190
  Commander-in-Chief, 151
  Subedar, 133, 134
Bakhtawar Singh, Ruler of Amjhera, 141
Bala Rao, 391
Balakot, 33, 68, 69, 70, 75
Baluchis, 379
Baluchistan, 58, 211, 382
Ban on Cow Slaughter, 401
Banda, 157, 232, 433
Banpur, 310
Bareilly (Rohilkhand), 135, 152, 166, 167, 173, 187, 289, 321, 324, 334, 336, 393, 398, 399, 400, 428, 429, 430
Barelvi, 208, 229 *see also* Sayyid Ahmad Barelvi
Barely, Gen, 112
Baroda, 172
Barrackpore Cantonment, 177, 179
Barrackpore-Bahrampur Incident, 179
Barvathoda, 356
Battle
  at Aligarh, 197
  Jama Masjid, 198
  of Agra, 152
  of Badr, 226
  of Buxar, 30
  of Chinhat, 130, 408, 416
  of Hindon, 149
  of Kanpur, 169
  of Mundsore, 296
  of Najafgarh, 151
  of Panipat, 1761, 28, 29, 82, 109, 190, 335
  of Plassey, 1757, 8, 29, 30, 80, 176, 187, 247
  of Shahganj, 118
  of Sikandar Bagh, 277
Battles at
  Nagina, 422
  Unnao and Bashratganj, 132, 133
Begum
  Hazrat Mahal, 154-157, 168, 170, 253
  Regime, 157
  Kothi, 154, 156
  of Ayodhya, 281, 282, 284, 296, 340, 380
  of Bhopal, 265, 292, 297
  of Lucknow, 355, 380
  Zeenat Mahal, 204
Belgaum and Kolhapur, 350
Benares, 52, 53, 54, 125, 280, 281, 433
  Division, 124
  or Gaya, 288
  Rebellion, 280
Bengal, 21
  and Bihar, 106
  and Dacca, 41
  Army, 107, 108, 116
  Irregulars, 108
  Muslims, 47
  Population, 112
  Sepoys, 344
  Zamindars, 44
Bengali Hindus, 229

Beni Madhav Singh
  Nazim of Azamgarh by
    Begum, 279
  of Shankarpur, 168, 171, 259, 386
  Sacrifice, 278
  Title Bahadur Diler Jung by
    Begum, 279
Bhagat Singh, 11
Bharatpur and Kota, 135
Bhagalpur, 54
Bhopal, 37, 141, 142, 290-292
  Army, 290
  Sepoys, 140
Bibighar, 122, 127, 243, 245, 246
Bihar, 54, 146
  Province, 337
  Rebellion, 340
Bijnor, 334, 336, 421, 430, 438
Birjis Qadar, 131, 276, 277
Bithoor, 158, 235, 248, 249, 252
Bloody Revolution, 99
Bose, Subhash Chandra, 11
Brahmin Zamindars, 213
British
  Administration, 10, 87, 119, 140, 147, 153, 172, 250, 280, 297, 309, 311, 319, 446
  and Marathas, 42
  Army, 77, 106, 133, 152, 175, 205, 229, 309, 336, 339, 355
  Army at Hyderabad, 72
  Army in Bengal, 88
  Army Stations, 351, 352
    Belgaum, 351
    Kolhapur, 351
  Artillery, 139, 154
  Atrocity, 243
  Authority, 113
  Bengal Army, 170
  Camp, 37
  Campaign, 418
  Christians, 390
  Conquest of Delhi, 83
  Control, 118, 127, 141, 143, 156, 158, 165, 230, 274
  Defeat at Chinhat, 130
  Domination in India, 94
  Empire, 187
  Expeditions, 205
  Forces 141, 116, 154, 155, 164, 167, 171, 215, 224, 224, 327, 336, 383, 380, 428
  Government, 11
  Imprisonment, 381
  In Agra, 163
  India, 38, 106
  Indian Army, 77, 190
  Indian Empire, 168
  Intelligence Department, 92
  Intelligence Network, 42
  Intelligence Officers, 192
  Law Courts, 74
  Legislation, 103
  Loyalists Sikh Rulers of-, 151
    Jind, 151
    Nabha, 151
    Patialia, 151
  Military Base, 139
  New Policies, 97
  Official Reports, 9
  Perceptions, 10
  Plan for Religious
    Conversion, 392
  Policy, 170
  Policy of Annexing Native
    States, 88

Power, 40, 116, 136
Emergence, 29, 30
Foundations, 31
In India, 174
Proposal of Amnesty for Inayat Ali, 77
Reactions on Zaman Shah's Invasion of India, 43
Rebellion, 10
Refugees, 122, 259, 277, 285
Regime, 125
Residency, 163
Rule, 34, 41, 46, 48, 80, 83, 91, 92, 98, 99, 103, 104, 109, 146, 187, 188, 193, 232, 239, 247, 274, 318, 322, 329, 335, 376
Economic Consequences of-, 96
Rule India, 50
Rulers, 45, 443
Soldiers, 113, 124
Sovereignty, 85
Treasury, 148
Troopers, 115
Troops, 106, 113, 114, 118, 119, 129, 136, 137, 143, 153, 154, 160, 161, 169, 171, 196, 197, 280, 327
Women and Children, 138
Bulandshahar, 119
Revolt, 431
Bundelas, 315
Bundelkhand, 143, 149, 158, 159
Bundi State, 172
Buxar (Battle of-), 89

Caesar, 24
Calcutta, 374, 376, 408
Gate, 184
To Peshawar, 368, 369
Caliphs, 24
Campbell, Sir Colin, 153, 154, 156, 158, 165-168, 170
Cantonment (s), 179, 284, 289
Ajmer, 284
Ambala, 179
Ferozepore, 179
Indore, 291
Ludhiana, 179
Mahidpur, 294
Meerut, 179
Mhow, 291
Murar, 163, 164
Nasirabad, 284
Neemuch, 284
Rawalpindi, 205
Capitalists, 97
Capture of Delhi, 114
Cartridge greased with Cow and Pig Fat, 111, 178, 179, 354, 435
Cavalry and Artillery Sepoys, 124
Ceylon, 126
Chalo Delhi, 149, 192
Chapati Scheme, 261
Charminar, 345
Chaudhury Muhammad Ali, 217
Chema Sahib, 354, 355
Chhatrapati of Satara, 87
Chhedi Khan, Commander, 346
Chief of Swat, 363
China, 126, 382, 383
Chinese War, 379
Chinhat, 260, 274
Chittagong, 54
Chittawar and Sawahari, 420

Chosroes, 24
Christian
  Infidels, 403, 404
  Kafir, 435, 438, 443
  Mission School, Bithoor, 100
  Women, 245
Christianity, 98, 100
Citadal of Jihadi Movement, 206
  Hotimardan, 206
  Mangalthana, 206
  Nawshera, 206
  Panjatar, 206
  Sitana, 206
  Swat, 206
Cocks, British Commander, 214
Cole, Dr. JR, 270
Commission of Inquiry, 264
Communal
  Conflict, 419
  Policy, 336
Confluence of Ganga and Yamuna Rivers, 123
Conspiracies, 298
Conversions, 230, 233
  Hindus to Islam, 15, 101
Coronation at Bithoor, 122
Court
  Martial, 112
  of Directors (East India Company), 266
  of Persia, 190
Cow Slaughter, 401
  Ban, 18, 199, 324
Cows and Pigs Fat, 98
Cuddapah, 348

Dacca, 54, 441
Dadu Miyan, s/o Shariatullah, 46, 47, 177
Dalhousie, Governor General, 77
Dambar Singh, 216
Danapur (near Patna), 107, 339, 341
  Rebels, 340
Dar-ul-Harb, 8, 32, 33, 40, 55, 56, 319, 441
  HQ Peshawar, 56
Dar-ul-Islam, 31, 55, 56, 65, 210, 319, 443
Darya Khan, 210
Datia, 308
Daud Baig, 354
Dauwa, Raja Ranjor, 233
Day of Judgement, 331
Death or Islam, 15
Declaration of
  Early Period of Uprising, 370
  Jihad, 239, 320
  Jihad Against Hindus, 196
  The Emperor of Delhi, 189
Declaration on
  Behalf of Rebel Sepoys of Delhi, 367
Delhi, 114, 115, 117, 119, 155, 184, 187, 192, 202-204, 208-212, 218, 217, 224, 225, 273, 284, 285, 287, 319, 320, 346, 352, 364, 369, 370, 408, 425, 435, 445
  Dynasty, 368
  Jihad, 276
  Jihad Declaration, 208
  Mutineers, 204
  Palace, 86
  Political Circles, 27
  Politics, 21

Population, 184
Uprising, 186
Urdu Akhbar, 191, 192
Demolishing
Mosques at Benares, 266
Temples, 269
Devi Singh, 218
Dewas, 137
Dhampur, 420
Dhar, 137, 141, 142
Dhar and Amjhera, 291
Dholpur, 141
Dhondo Pant, 378
Dil Murad, 210
Din-e-Ilahi, Akbar's New Religion, 18
District
Azamgarh, 283
Badaun, 134, 331, 384, 426
Banda, 123
Bijnor, 134, 166, 419, 425
Bulandshahar, 214, 221
Charkhari, 386
Etah, 216, 431
Faizabad, 175
Farrukhabad, 118, 165
Fatehgarh, 165
Kanpur, 248
Mohammadi, 129
Moradabad, 332, 384
Administration, 166
Muzaffarnagar, 441
Pilibhit, 135, 384
Rohilkhand, 438
Shahjahanpur, 134, 428
Diwani Rights to Bengal-Orissa, 30, 44
Dost Muhammad, 254
Draconian Measures, 323
Dum Dum Musketry Depot, Calcutta, 111
Durjan Singh, 216

East India Company, 30, 84, 168, 299, 383
Economic
and Administrative Control, Removal From, 96
Injustice, 45
Policies and Reforms, 96
Education, 93
Arabic, 93
Egypt, 376
English
Education, 92
Education and Culture, Hatred Against-, 93
Education Boycott, 93
Language & Education, 91, 92
Queen's Proclamation, 389
Slavery, 208
Etawah, 117, 119, 215, 216
Exploitation of Muslim Peasants in Bengal, 44

Fact Finding Committee, 265
Fadak and Khaibar, 32
Faizabad, 129, 176, 259, 261-263, 267, 272, 273, 278
Prison, 130
Fakir Pirzada Hasan Askari, 188
Fakirs, 207
Falakuddin Shah, 371
Fanaticism, 190, 192, 221, 333, 336, 434
Farazi (s), 47, 48
Farazi Movement of Bengal, 44, 45, 83

Farrukhabad, 155, 165
Fateh-al-Mujahideens, (Tipu's Work), 39
Fatehgarh, 118, 165, 166
  Battle, 126, 127
Fatehpur, 54, 118, 127
Fatehpuri Masjid (Mosque), 27, 445
Fat-Smeared Cartridge, 111, 178, 354
Fatwa, 9
  (1803), 8
  against British, 268, 269
  India as Dar-ul-Harb, 31
Fazal Haq, Collector, 331
Fazal Muhammad Khan, 292
Fazat Jahan, 281
Firangi Mahal, Lucknow, 263
Firman
  of Sultan of Turkey, 375
  to Subedars, 372
Firoz Shah, 216, 286, 292, 293, 294, 400, 428
Firoz Shah, Prince, (Mughal Dynasty), 140, 142, 147, 153, 156, 165, 166, 168, 170, 172, 297, 312, 340, 380, 391
  Shahazada, 171
Firozepur, 114
Forcible Conversion of Hindus to Islam, 101
Foreign Islamic Power, 41
Fort,
  Ajaygarh, 233
  Fatehgarh, 118, 218
  Gadkot, 159
  Jhansi, 161
  Karera, 145
  Kotla, 77
  Lohari, 162
  Rahatgarh, 159
  Tara, 233
France (French), 377, 381

Gandhi's Methods of Truth, 443
Gangadhar Bhau, 311
Gangadharrao, 144
Ganges, 365
Ghatge, Bhausahib, 354
Ghaus Muhammad Khan, 214, 215
Ghazis, 167, 194, 198, 200, 207, 212, 214, 221, 223, 285, 286, 321, 327, 333, 371, 406, 409, 411, 436
Ghazi-ud-Din Haider, Nawab of Ayodhya, 154, 255
Ghaziuddinnagar, 150
Ghazis and Mujahids, 14
Ghazni, 58
Ghulam Hasan Khan, 53
Ghulam Hussain Shah, 261, 262
Ghulam Muhammad, 316, 317
Ghulam Qadar, Nawab of Bareilly, 329
Ghulam Mohiuddin, Cavalry Commander, 225
Global Muslim Community, 16, 33
God Plurality, 14
Godse Bhatji, 315
Gogaria Prison, 209
Gokulchand, 280
Gomti and Ganga, 88
Gonda, 130
Government Employment, 94
Goya, Fakir Muhammad Khan, 257

Grant, Hope, 153
Great Pharaoh, 407
Greathed, Edward,
    Commander, 152, 153
Green Flag at
    Azamgarh, 281
    Heads of Temples, 280
Green Islamic Flag, 297
Greased Cartridge, 111, 178,
    354, 435
Guerilla
    Tactics, 61
    Warfare, 62
Guidelines for 1857, 14
Gujars, 119, 222
Gulab Singh of Kashmir, 75
Gurdwara Sis Ganj, 204
Gurgaon, 210
Guru Tegh Bahadur, 203, 204
Gwalior, 57, 137-140, 163, 164,
    171, 192, 273, 286-290, 293,
    316, 381, 392
    Army at Hathras, 117
    Sepoys, 157, 163, 293
    State, 117
    Troops, 137

Hadis Literature, 32
Haider Ali, 34
Hajj Pilgrimage, 45, 46, 54, 71
Hakim Abdul Haq, 210
Hakim Ahsanullah Khan,
    Emperor's Adviser, 199
Haldaur, 423, 424
Hamid Hasan Khan, 329
Hamilton, Sir Robert, British
    Representative in Jhansi,
    208, 209, 312
Hamirpur, 123, 234, 433
Hamirpur Detachments, 123
Hanuman Temple, Faizabad,
    261, 269
Hanumangarhi, 261, 262, 264,
    265, 267, 269, 272, 434
Hari Singh, 64
Haridwar, 166
Hasan Ali, Cavalry Chief, 311
Hasan Nizami, Historian, 14
Hassan Bukhsh, Risaldar, 222
Hathras, 215
Havelock, Gen., 126, 127, 132,
    133, 248
Hazara
    Province, 75
    Region of Kashmir, 69, 74, 75
Hazrat Ali, 256
Hazrat Mahal, Begum of
    Ayodhya, 172
Hillersdon, Collector, 120, 235
Hindu
    and Muslims, 98, 200
    Attack on Bijnor, 420
    Chaudheries, 334, 335
    Chiefs, 282
        Gopalpur, 282
        Myovali, 282
        Tumhoi, 282
    Customs and Traditions, 23,
    46
    Ghanashyam Das, 432
    King of Kashmir, 115
    Kingdoms, 82
    Leaders, 420
    Martyrs, 103
    Muslim Relations, 222
    Muslim Unity, 7, 11
    Muslims, 13
    Muslims Soldiers, 11
    Participation in the
        Uprising, 102, 103
    Population, 98, 422

Principles and Traditional Practices, 23
Raja of
Bansi, 282
Dholpur, 285, 286
Etah, 431
Mithauli, 129
Sepoys in Punjab, 434
Shrines, 280
Soldiers, 101
Status, 15
Zamindars, 45, 216, 279, 331, 426, 428
Hinduism, 15, 240, 368, 390
Hindu-Muslim
Conflicts, 418, 419, 425, 429, 431
Relations, 268, 435, 437
Riots, 438
Struggle, 417
Unity, 417, 439, 440, 443
Hindupad Padshahi, 21, 29
Hindurao, 57
Hindus and Converts, 23
Hindustani
Army, 368
Fanatics in Swat and Sitana, 207
Muslims, 178
Hissar, Hansi, Sirsa, 115
Hodson, 204
Holkar, Tukojirao, 139
Holker Maharaja, 289
Holker of Indore, 444
Holy
Prophet Muhammad, 14, 15, 18, 23, 28, 32, 35, 47, 184, 186
War, 442
Warriors, 266, 278, 345
Horne, Amy, 244
Hoshangabad, 297
Hotimardan, 434
House of Timur, 296
Humayun Tomb, 151
Hume, Magistrate, 117
Hussain Mirza, 216
Hussaini Khanum, Incharge Bibighar, 246
Hyderabad, 73, 137, 343, 348, 351
Conspiracy (1839), 72, 73, 345
Residency, 349
State, 356
Uprising, 346

Ibrahimpur, 331
Ideal Muslim State, 39
Idol Worship, 14
Idolatry, 37
Idolatry and Polytheism of Hindus, 14
Iman Ali, 76
Imperial
Army, 320
Court of Delhi, 21
Inciting Sepoys to Rebel, 179
India
and Afghanistan, 78
as Dar-ul-Harb, 46, 47, 51, 92, 93
as Dar-ul-Islam, 7
India's
Freedom Movement, 50, 297
Political Independence, 7
Security, 42

Indian
  Army Units, 191
  Border, 37
  Music, 23
  Muslim Powers, 42
    Conspiracy by-, 41
  Muslims, 28, 49, 61, 78, 79, 81, 84, 90, 376
  National Congress, 117
  Nationalist, 18
  or Pakistan, 22
  Troops, 114
Indore, 137, 139-142, 153, 286, 287
Indore and Mhow, 290
Indus, 20, 58
Industry, 120
Infantry Platoons, 109
Infidelity, 14
Infidels, 14, 26, 28, 32
Inquiry Commission, 267
Instigators, 211, 443
Insurgencies, 211
Inter-Community Relations, 418
Intrigues of Succession, 21
Invasion of Hindustan, 14
Iran, 21, 187
Irzah Jahan, 281
Islamic State at Mundsore, 394
Islam, 14, 15, 17-19, 22, 23, 24, 33-36, 51, 53
  And Christianity, 220
  Conversion to, 15, 101
  Death or Islam, 15
  Protection and Propagation of-, 9
Islamic
  Administration, 13, 74
  Brotherhood, 34
  Civilization, 435
  Culture, 90, 105
  Doctrine, 185
  Hijri Calendar, 240
  Law, 15, 67, 74, 233
  Movement, 18
  Names to Towns and Places, 39
  Principles, 16, 17, 19, 24, 25, 60, 61, 321, 367
  Rule, 17, 100, 312
  State, 16, 17, 19, 39, 60, 61, 66, 68, 70, 73, 75, 90, 92, 206, 225, 274, 372, 431
    In India, 48, 56
    Dar-ul-Harb, 16, 46, 47, 51, 92, 93
    Dar-ul-Islam, 7, 16

Jagdishpur, 148, 340
Jaggannath Singh of Powain, 167
Jahandar Shah, 20
Jahangir, Akbar's Successor, 19
Jahangir Khan, 285, 286
Jaimal Singh, 323
Jalalabad, 153
Jalbani, Biographer of Shah Waliullah, 24
Jama Masjid, 76, 151, 188, 230, 437, 445
Jat Villages, 422
  Hasanpur, 422
  Kardili, 422
  Mohanpur, 422
  Musapur, 422
  Narayanpur, 422
  Patijatan, 422
  Shafiabad, 422

Jats and Gurjars, 221
Jaunpur, 125, 386
Javed Jafar, Historian, 22
Jawan Bakht, Begum Zeenat
  Mahal's Son, 204, 252, 435
  Prince, 87
Jayajirao Shinde, Maharaja, 117
Jaylal Singh, Zamindar Raja,
  276
Jaziya, 428
Jehadis, 220
Jehanabad, 54
Jesus, Lord, 186
Jhalawar Pattan, 172
Jhansi, 143, 144, 145, 146, 158,
  296, 297, 304, 308, 310-314,
  316, 317, 391, 400
  and Ayodhya, 298
  and Malwa, 381
  Campaign, 159
  Capture of-, 159
  Seige of-, 159
  State, 298
Jhelum, 115
Jihad, 7-11, 13, 16, 17, 24, 25,
  28, 33, 36, 38-40, 49, 51-55,
  57, 58, 60-62, 64, 66, 69, 70-
  72, 74, 76, 78, 79, 187, 188,
  193-197, 205-207, 214, 220,
  221, 225, 226, 230, 232, 233,
  239, 240, 244, 245, 256, 257,
  261, 263-270, 272, 273, 277,
  291, 292, 318, 319, 321, 322,
  327, 337, 340, 346, 366, 372,
  404-406, 425, 427, 431, 434-
  436, 440, 442, 444, 446
  A Sacred Religious
    Obligation, 9
  Against British, 42, 296
  Against Christians, 344, 345
  Against Hindus, 194, 195,
  263, 272
  Against Jats, 223
  Agenda, 205
  Aims, 56
  By Ghazis, 324
  Centre, 65
  Declaration, 283, 366, 405,
  415
  Edicts, 321
  Headquarters, Peshawar, 55,
  56
  in Delhi, 184, 193, 435
  in Punjab Province, 204
  Movement, 50
  of 1857, 218
  Only against Christians, 389
  Philosophy of-, 52
  Procession, 257
  Proclamation, 321
  Program, 55
  Propaganda, 319
  Re-establishing Islamic
    Empire, 43
Jihadi (s), 60, 64, 65, 68, 75-77,
  184, 191, 192, 197, 210, 21,
  225, 247, 264, 266, 339, 401,
  416, 427, 436, 437
  Army, 428
  Attack on Hindus, 224
  Flags, 195
  Force, 58, 67, 191
  Movement, 44
  Proclamation, 360
  Proclamations and
    Declarations, 444
  Rebels, 201, 204
Jihadnama, 400, 405

Jihadnama for Hindus/
 Muslims, 396-398
Jiziya, 17, 18, 61, 82
 Abolished on Hindus, 17
 Concession to Hindus, 15
 Poll Tax, 15
Jokhanbagh, 300
Jones, Commander, 166, 167
June Rebellion, 332
Jwala Prasad, 127

Kabul, 42, 58, 208
Kabulis and Kashmiris, 209
Kachchh-Bhuj, 372
Kachch-Bhuj Ruler, 185
Kafirs, 185
 British, 416
 Christians, 405
 English, 379
Kale Khan, Cavalry Chief, 300, 301
Kalpi in Bundelkhand, 157, 158, 160-163, 169, 288, 316, 384, 385
Kamran, Prince, 64
Kandhar, 42, 58, 171, 363
Kangra, 115
Kanpur, 54, 118, 120-127, 132, 133, 153-155, 157, 162, 172, 202, 234-236, 243, 245, 247,249, 251, 28C, 288, 356, 372, 373, 378, 381, 383, 384, 391, 432
 Massacre, 243
 Rebellion, 123
 Rebels, 192
 Recapture, 158
 Second Battle of-, 158
 Security of-, 158
Kanpur-Agra Route, 165
Kanpur-Delhi Route, 123
Karachi, 209
Karamat Ali, 282
 Subedar of Mathura, 218
Karera Fort, 145
Karim Khan, Shah of Iran, 38
Karimullah, Dy.Commandant, 207
Kasganj, 216, 431, 432
Kashmir, 434
Kashmiri Gate, 200
Khairabadi, Fazal Haq, 276
Khalifa, 19, 25, 33, 55, 56, 64, 60, 66, 68, 70, 226, 394
 of Islam, 37
 Sayyid, 66
 Vilayat Ali, 73, 75, 77
  Works, 77
Khan Bahadur Khan, 134, 319, 321, 322, 324, 327, 329-332, 418, 429
Khot Fortress, 166
Khulk Khuda Ka, Mulk
 Badshah ka aur
  Hukum Azeemullah ka, 214
  Hukum Nawab Bahadur Ka, 218
  Hukum Birjis Nawab ka, 276
  Hukum Rani Laxmibai ka, 303
  Hukum Nawab Ali Bahadur ka, 232
Khushwant Singh, 203, 204
Khusrubagh, 230
Kifayat Ali, 332
Koh-i-Noor Diamond, 20

Kolhapur Uprising, 353, 354
Kudrat Ali, 180
Kunch
Defeat, 163
Town, 162
Kunwar Singh of
Bihar, 380
Jagdishpur, 147-149, 157, 162, 168, 169, 216, 339, 340
Shahabad, 146
Kura, 54

Lahore, 42, 65, 362
Lahore Fort, 103
Lalubhau Bakhshi, 311
Land Grants, 97
Lashkar-e-Mujahideen, Tipu's Army Name, 39
Law and Order, 145, 200
Law of Shariat, 372
Lawrence, Chief Commissioner, 116, 208
Lawrence, Sir Henry, 127-130
Laxmibai of Jhansi, 144, 201, 310, 315, 444
Leaders of Rebellion, 351
Amir Khan, 351
Ghulam Gaus, 351
Shaikh Mannu, 351
Looting
and Arson, 210
Treasury, 117
Lord
Canning, Governor General, 106, , 336, 380, 430, 445
Dalhousie, Gov. Gen., 85, 266, 267
Harding, Gov. Gen., 85
Palmerston, 445
Lucknow, 128-133, 153, 154, 155, 158, 165, 166, 169, 170, 176, 187, 264, 268, 272, 274, 276, 277, 296, 312, 356, 408
British Withdrawal from-, 155
Campaign for-, 155, 156, 169
Residency, 153, 158
Security Arrangement at-, 130
Victory War-, 156
Ludhiana, 209

M Abdul Jaleel, 213
M Ahmad Shah, 130, 166, 167, 178, 259, 272, 278, 380, 442
Proclamation, 406, 414
M Ahmedullah, 338
M Ali Karim,, 338
M Allah-ud-Din, 346
M Amir Ali, 263-265, 272
M Fazal Haq, 184
M Inayat Ali, 243, 244
M Kifayat Ali Kafi, 319
M Liaqat Ali, 228, 229, 403
Rebel Leader of Allahabad, 382, 383
Rule, 229
M Mannu Khan, Leader of Revolt, 333
M Muhammad Ahsan, 320
M Muhammad Qasam, 225, 226
M Muhammad Shah, 262
M Naseemullah, 215
M Nurul Huda, Wahabi Chief, 351, 352, 353
M Rahimatullah, 220, 321
M Saif Rahman, 208
M Salamatullah, 239

M Sarfaraz Ali, 184, 190, 191, 320, 327
M Sayyid Abdul Aziz Hussain, 348
M Sayyid Qutb Shah, 399-401
  Persian Teacher, 321
M Shah Muhammad Hussain, 338
M Syed Muhammad, 256
M Ubaidullah Deobandi, 227
M. Ahmad Shah, 155, 156, 255
M. Haji Imadullah Khalifa, 223, 226, 227
M. Inayat Ali, 205, 206, 208
Macpherson, Resident, 137, 138
Madarsa-i-Rahimiya, 22, 208, 445
Madras, 350, 354, 381
  Administration, 343
  Nature, 343
  Army, 108
  Fusiliers, 125
  Presidency, 344
Mahar, 67
Maharaja of
  Gwalior, 284, 285, 286, 287, 288, 290, 293, 294
  Kashmir, 115
  Kota, 137
  Nepal, 155
Maharaja Ranjit Singh, 60, 62, 65, 67, 68, 79
Maharajas of-, 201
  Alwar, 201
  Bikaner, 201
  Jaipur, 201
  Jodhpur, 201
Mahavir Jhanda for Hindus, 240
Mahmood Ghazni, 14, 232
Mahmood Shafi, 321
Mahmud Hasan, Subedar of Gorakhpur, 390
Mahmud Khan, Nawab of Najibabad, 135, 334, 335, 419, 421, 422, 426
  Administration, 426
Mahomedan
  Bigots in Patna, and Thaneshwar, 206
  Gujars, 209
  Kings of Delhi, 407
  Law, 410
  Persecution, 435
Mainpuri, 117, 119, 215, 216
Majju Khan, 333
Makrantis, 295
Malgarh, 216
Malihabad, 128, 257
Malleson, British Officer, 260
Malwa, 118, 139, 149, 284, 289, 291, 292
  Malwa Province, 137
  Malwa-Bhil Force, 139
Man Singh of Shahganj, 434
Mangal Pandey *see* Pandey, Mangal
Maratha, 27-29, 31, 34, 35, 82
  Armies, 21
  Empire, 21
  Guards, 137
  Power, 28
Mardan Ali Khan, 322, 329
Mardan Singh of Banpur, 159, 310
Margaret, 244
Maritime and Naval Power, 36
Martial Law, 147

Massacre, 109, 233, 302, 314
- in Delhi, 89
- of Christians, 129
- of Englishmen, 145
- of Englishmen in Jhansi, 309

Mathura, 117, 217, 218
Matin Khan, 432
Maulana Ahmad Shah, 9
Maulvi, 167
- Jalaluddin, 197
- Rahmatullah, 213
- Vilayat Ali, 71, 75

Maulvi's
- Leadership, 156
- Proclamations, 414

Majih-uz-Zaman, 339
Mecca, 33, 45, 46, 54, 55, 76, 171, 218, 226, 245, 293, 393
Mecca Masjid, 345, 350
Meditátion, 57
Meerut, 128, 134, 136, 179, 180, 181, 184, 204, 224, 255, 320, 368, 419
- Army, 184
- Division, 119, 120
- Province, 133, 221, 227, 431
- Revolt, 113, 117, 352, 382
- Sepoys, 383
- Uprising, 113, 114

Mehndi Hasan, 278, 282, 283
Mewati Muslims, 216, 295
Mhow, 139, 140, 153, 290
Mhow Chief, 282
Mian Mir, 113
Mian Vilayat Ali, 74, 75, 76
- Death, 1852, 76

Military
- Services, 88
- Skills, 51

Militia, 224
Mir Wajid Ali, 250
Mirza Abu Bakr, Prince, 150
Mirza Bahadur Bakht, 254, 257
Mirza Ghalib, 90, 445
Mirza Haider, 254, 258
Mirza Khizr Khan, Prince, 150
Mirza Mahal, 113
Mirza Mahomed Firoz Shah Bahadur, 293
Mirza Mughal, 365
- Prince, 183, 190

Mirza Muhammad Mustafa Ali, 258
Mirza Najaf, 187, 188
Missionaries, 397
Missionary Activities, 98
Mohamedan Power, 441
Mohammad Beg, 35
Mohammad Islami Khan, Gen., 223
Moradabad, 333, 430
Moti Mahal, 154, 272
Mufti Muhammad Iwaz, 319
Mughal
- Army, 101
- Atrocities, 204
- Dynasty, 86
- Emperor, 21, 181, 182, 183, 203, 207, 209
    - as Enemy of British, 85
    - as Pensioner and Prisoners, 84
- Emperors, Candle of Religion, 182
- Emperors, Padshahi Ghazi, 182
- Emperors, Reinstatement at Delhi, 181
- Emperors, Seal, 182
- Empire, 82, 203, 351

Decline, 20
Royalty, 202
Rule, 97, 98, 204
Rule in Delhi, 113
Muhammad
Ali, 217
Azeem Shahzada, 210
Bakar, 196
Bakht Khan, 372
Bakht Khan, Governor Gen., 185, 191
Bin Qasim's Invasion, 13
Bin Tughluq, 95
Hasan (Gorakhpur), 125, 433
Hasan, Rebel Leader, 282, 283, 284
Hussain, 300, 349
Ishaq, 288, 384, 385
Islmail Khan, 244
Khan Bangarh, 143
Muhammadi Flag, 218
Mujahideen, 284, 370
Movement, 192
Mujahids, 320
Mulk Maharani Victoria Ka, Hukum Company Bahadur ka, 421
Multan, 21, 115
Multan Province, 209
Mundsore, 141-143, 292-294, 312, 394
Murshidabad, 54, 441
Muslim(s)
Administration, 418, 428
Aggressors, 13
Cavalry, 181
Rebellion, 180
Troopers, 347
Cities, 187
Clergy, 18
Community, 269, 336
Conspiracy, 338
Conspiracy (Fatehgarh), 231
Conspiracy at Belgaum, 349
Conspiracy of 1857 in Mysore, 349
Countries, 296
Fakirs, 314
Fanaticism, 228, 230
Feudal Masters, 444
Freedom Fighters, 18, 44
Imperialism, 444
Invasions, 14, 15
Invasions of India, 17
Jagirdars, 97
Killings in Nagina, 422
Laity, 9
Language and Culture, 91
Law, 16
Leaders, 26, 183, 420
Ahmad Shah, Amir of Afghanistan, 26
Najeeb-ud-Daula Khan, 26-28
Makrani, 141
Masters, 101
Monopoly in Muslim Trade, 96
Nawabs and Subedars, 26
of North India, 82
Paramountcy in India, 195
Pathan, 141
Political Power, 86, 91, 94
Population, 218, 331
Power, 21, 22, 23, 26, 30, 33, 86, 91, 94, 203
Maratha Challenge to-, 21
Power in India, 36
Religious Organizations, 22

Revolt, 219, 343
Revolt in Andhra Pradesh, 347
Rule, 16, 40, 43, 44, 99
Sepoys, 373, 383
Social System, 91
Society (ies), 22, 23, 32
South Asia, 31
States, 441
Afghanistan, 441
Persia, 441
Turkey, 441
Uprising, 351
Uprising in Benares, 279
Vilayati, 141
Women in Uprising, 198
Zamindars, 105
Mutineers, 351, 352
Mutinies at, 146
Bundelkhand, 146
Hoshangabad, 146
Jabalpur, 146
Jalon 146
Lalitpur, 146
Lucknow, 258
Rahatgary, 146
Sagar, 146
Mutiny, 1857, 72, 78, 99, 83, 190, 203, 212, 213, 255, 260, 324, 429
Mutiny of States, 88
Muzaffarnagar, 119, 224, 225, 227
Muzzaffer Jahan, Chief Azamgarh, 281
Mysore, 344, 348, 349

Nadir Shah, 89, 189
Amir of Persia, 20
Nadvi, Tipu's Biographer, 34
Nagina, 166, 423, 438
Nahargadh, 142
Naik, Godaji, 354
Najafgarh, 200
Najeeb Khan, as C-in-C of Mughal Army, 27, 29
Najibababd, 335, 420, 425
Nakki Khan, 9, 174-179, 269, 339
Nana
Bhopatkar, 311
Peshwa, 378
Rao, 391
Nanasahib (Nana, Nana Sahib) of Kanpur, 7, 158, 232, 233, 235-244, 246, 247, 249-252, 324, 341, 355, 357-359, 380, 381, 383, 384, 432, 442, 444
Force, 127
of Bithoor, 201
Peshwa's Proclamation, 372, 376, 378
Nanhe Nawab (Muhammad Ali Khan), 249
Narhar Singh, Hindu Raja of Vallabhgarh, 211
Narinder Singh, Maharaja of Patiala, 212
Narpat Singh, Rebel Leader, 166
Nasirabad, 284
Nasiruddin of Delhi, Maulvi, 70
Nasiruddin, Persian Emperor, 188
National
Movement, 105
Revolt, 41
Natthe Khan, 145, 306
Dirty Plan, 309

Naushera, 60, 65
Nawab
Adil Khan of Bhopal, 312
Ahmad Mirza, 210
Ali Bahadur, 232, 433
Amir Khan, 284
Birjis Qadar of Ayodhya, 386
Dulajan, 210
Fazal Khan, 297
Ghulam Hussain Khan, 329
Khan Bahadur Khan of Rohilkhand, 165, 167, 173, 380, 394, 399, 400
Mubari Zuddaulah, Nizam's Brother, 72, 73
Muhammad Hasan Khan of Tulsipur, 258
Muhammad Yusuf Ali Khan of Rampur, 135
Mujahideen Khan, 333
of Avadh, 176
of Ayodhya, 30, 44
of Ayodhya as King, 84
of Ayodhya, Ghazi-ud-Din Haider, 255
of Banda, 162, 169, 287, 316, 340
of Bareilly, 135, 401
of Bengal, 30
of Dacca, 42, 44
of Farrukhabad, 143, 162, 216, 218, 296, 431
of Karnataka, 34
of Kurnool and Bhopal, 72
of Malgadh, 120, 214, 217, 221
of Murshidabad, 41, 44
of Najibabad, 166, 227
of Rahatgadh, 297
of Rampur, 166, 334
of Rohilkhand, 217, 372, 401, 405, 442, 444
of Tonk, Amir Khan, 51, 172
Qadir Ali Khan, 329
Sadat Khan, 140
Tafzal Hussain Khan, 218
Wajid Ali Shah, 131, 170
Walidad Khan, 431
Nawab's Jihadi Letters, 222
Nawabganj, 265
Nawabi Rule in Banda, 232
Nazrana by British to Emperor, 84
Neemuch, 118, 137, 139, 143, 290, 293, 294
Sepoys, 284
Nehru, Jawaharlal, 93
Neil, Brigadier Commander, 126, 133
Nepal, 88, 170, 172, 173, 380
Nepal Singh, 426
Nicolson, 115, 200
Nicolson's Command, 151, 152
Nishan-e-Muhammad, 256
Niyamatullah Khan, 319
Niyaz Ali Khan, 427
Nizam, 34, 35
Forces, 346
Nizam Ali, 329
Non-Violence, 443
Noor Muhammad, Muslim Leader, 239
North India Uprising, 106
North West Provinces, 66
Nowrunjee Village, 207
Nur-ul-Buda, 349

Operation Muharram, 278
Orchha
    And Datia States, 160
    State, 145, 306, 310
Orissa, 21
Orr, Captain, 262
Oudh, 247, 254, 255, 260, 268, 390, 393
Outram, James, Commander, 132, 153, 154, 155

Pagay, Rangrao, 356, 357
Pakistan and Bangladesh, 11
Pandey, Mangal, 111, 174-177, 179, 254, 339
    First Freedom Fighter, 112
    Tried by Court Martial, 112
Panipat, 30
Panjatar, 65, 70
Paramountcy, 85
Pasha of Egypt, 374, 375
Pathan Tribes, 56, 62, 65, 68
Pathans, 295, 296
Patna, 39, 207, 273, 337
    Centre, 175
    Centre of Mutiny, 146, 147
    Rebellion, 339
Peacock Throne, 20
Peasants Workers Agitation, 45
Permanent Land Settlement Law, 97
Pershadipur, 130
Persia, 188, 296, 362, 363
Persia and Afghanistan, 187
Persian
    Army, 252
    Emperor, 188
    Forces, 189
    Language used in
        Administration and
            Education, 91
Persians, 379
Peshawar, 21, 57, 58, 179, 207, 208, 363
    Largest Military Base, 206
Peshwa, 242, 250
    Bajirao I, 21, 143
    Balarao, 284
    Nana Sahib, 100, 120-123, 127, 168, 172 *see also* Nanasahib Raosahib, 160, 163, 164, 288, 380, 381, 384
        Enthronement, 163
Peshwa's
    Defeat, 162
    Force at Kunch, 316
    Forces, 163, 164, 289
    Pathani Troops, 316
    Rule under Nanasahib, 343
    War Material, 163
Pig and Cow Fats, 111, 178, 179, 354, 435
Pilibhit, 331
Pir Ali, Chief Leader, 147, 150, 175, 177, 338, 339
Political
    Pensions, 235
    Revolution, 174, 175, 201
Polytheism, 14, 64, 366
Post-Uprising British Ire and Vendetta, 10
Pratap Singh of Tajpur, 420, 423
Pratapgarh, 296
Prayag, 299
Pro-British Hindus, 324
Proclamation
    against English Kafirs, 378
    by Shah of Persia, 362
    for Cow Slaughter Ban, 399, 400

in Nana's Name, 356, 382
Khulk Khuda Ka--, 343
of Firoz Shah, Prince, 391-394
of Jihad, 220, 230
of Nawab of Ayodhya, 386
of Nawab of Rohilkhand, 394-396
Proclamations, 361, 362, 437, 438
Propagation of Christianity, 365
Prophet Muhammad, 51, 258, 406, 409
Provinces, 343
Cuddapah, 343, 344
Kurnool, 344, 349
Malaba, 343
Provinces/divisions under British Control, 380
Agra, 380
Allahabad, 380
Ayodhya, 380
Bihar, 380
Delhi, 380
Jhansi, 380
Malwa, 380
Meerut, 380
Punjab, 113, 380
Rohilkhand, 380
Punjab, 21, 65, 76, 82, 106, 125, 151, 204, 205, 211, 380
and Bihar, Kanpur, Benares and Allahabad, 149
Province, 113, 380
Punjab-Peshawar Border, 107
Purlia Soldiers, 436
Purwa, 130
Qazi
Inayat Ali, 225
Wasiuddin, 239, 240, 243
Queen Victoria, 373, 374
Declaration, 172
Quetta, 58
Quran and Hadis, 16, 39, 366, 416
Quraysh, 25, 409,410, 415
Qutb-ud-Din, Nawab, 54
Qutubuddin Aibak, 14

Rahim Ali Khan, 289
Rahtgarh, 297
Rai Bareli, 51, 52, 54
Raja
Balwantrao, 354
Bharpur Singh of Nabha, 212
Chhatrasal Bundela, 14
Darshan Singh, 261
Jaylal Singh, 259
Loni Singh, 274, 277
Man Singh, 259, 267, 268, 270, 278, 284 *see under* Man Singh *also*
of Shorapur, 354
Randhir Singh of Kapurthala, 212
Sarup Singh of Jind, 212
Tekum Singh, 214
Venketappa, Naik of Sorepur, 358
Rajamundry in Andhra Pradesh, 348
Rajgarh, 172
Rajput Princes, 136
Rajputana, 284
And Malwa, 106
Province, 135

Rallying Point of Confederacy, 87
Ram Dayal Singh, 422
Ramayana Era, 88
Rameshwaram, 358
Rammohan Roy, Raja, 102
Rampur, 333
Rana Beni Madhav, 97 *see also under* Beni
Rango Bapuji, 359
Rangoon, 202
Rani Laxmibai, (Rani) 7, 159, 160, 161, 162, 164, 296, 297, 298, 299, 302-307, 309-311, 315, 316, 380, 402
  Rani and Tatya, 164
  As Ranachandika, 162
  Proclamation, 400
  Widowed, 103
Rao Bhavani Singh, 215
  Hindu Ruler, 117
Rao Dev Narayan Singh, 280
Rao Pant Pradhan Peshwa, 379
Rao Ramchandra, 298
Raosahib, 171, 172, 250 *see* also *under* Peshwa Raosahib
Rasoolabad, 171
Ratan Singh, 234
  Chief of Charkhari, 234
  Pro-British, 288
Ravi Tribe, 209
Rawalpindi, 115
Rebel
  Administration, 153, 281
  Afghan and Pathans, 297
  Arms, 149
  Christians, 404
  Communication, 165
  Dominant Areas, 149
  Forces, 118, 140, 163, 171
  Leaders, 145, 168, 296
  Rule, 153
Rebellion of 1857, 113-116, 120, 123, 125, 126, 128, 129, 130, 136, 140, 142, 144, 145, 152, 179, 186, 205-209, 210, 216, 212, 221, 235, 254, 256, 258, 278, 280, 290, 291, 298, 299, 301, 305, 310, 328, 331, 341, 345, 346, 355, 359, 390, 419
Rebellions at-, 129, 142, 384
  Amongst Sepoys, 254
  Agra, 142, 219
  Aligarh, 384
  Bareilly, 384
  Bijnor, 384
  Bulandshahar, 384
  by Muslim Population, 209
  Dariabad, 129
  Etawah, 384
  in Kolhapur, 354
  in South, 381
  Lucknow, 384
  Mainpuri, 215
  Malwa, 142
  Mandaleshwar, 142
  Manpur, 142
  Mathura, 384
  Meerut and Delhi, 293
  of Muslim Sepoys, 299
  Salini, 129
  Shahjahanpur, 384
  Shamli, 225
  Sipri, 142
  Sikrora, 129
  Sultanpur, 129
  Thana Bhavan, 225
Recruitment of Ghazis, 371
Red Fort, 84, 86, 151, 187
  Demolition, 445

Reed, Maj. Gen. 195
Reforms, 91
Regiment,
  British, 112, 117, 118, 127, 125, 147
  Fatehpur, 123
  Infantry, 112, 115
  Kanpur, 123
  Ludhiana, 124
  Native, 114, 116, 118
  Punjab, 116
  Sikh, 125
Reh, 353
Religious
  Leaders of Delhi, 92
  War, 311, 366
Remarriage of
  Widows, 365, 397
Renauld, Maj. 126
Revenue Collection, 97
Revolt
  in Meerut and Delhi, 345
  in Rohilkhand, 336
  of Kanpur, 359
Revolutionaries, 9, 207, 208, 321, 342, 353, 381
Revolutionary Party in Punjab, 208
Richardson, Major, 251
Right to Rule, 16
Rights of Kingship, 84
Ring Leaders, 347
  Amir Khan, 347
  Chhedi Khan, 347
  Mir Fida Ali, 347
  Muhammad Hashim, 347
  Waheed Khan, 347
Riots, 262
Risala Jihad, 272
River
  Betwa, 160
  Chambal, 137, 138, 172, 285, 287
  Ganga, 105, 120, 132, 133, 158, 165, 166, 169, 171, 177, 228, 428
  Hindon, 150
  Indus, 70, 77
  Jhelum, 42
  Kali, 165
  Narmada, 104, 139, 172, 378, 381
  Pandu, 158
  Yamuna, 76, 105, 149, 158, 171, 228
Rohilla Afghan Stock, 27
Rohillas, 295, 316
Rohilkhand, 21, 28, 105, 108, 129, 165, 190, 210, 227, 264, 312, 316, 318, 320, 322, 333, 334, 324, 326, 331, 332, 336, 387, 418, 419, 430, 431
  Campaign, 165
  Conflicts in-, 418
  Jihad, 274
  Province, 133, 135, 168
  Uprising, 430
Rohtak and Gurgaon, 115
Roman and Persian Empires, 24
Rose, Hugh, 159-161, 162, 164, 297, 310,311, 313
Roy, Raja Rammohun, 102
Ruqn-ud-Daula, 255, 256, 258
Russia (Russian), 377, 379, 381
Rustam Shah, Pro-British Hindu Chief of Dera, 278

Sadashivrao Narayan, 145, 302
Sadat Khan,
  Indore Leader, 289, 291

Safdar Mahmood, Prof.
Historian, 22
Safdar-ud-Dowllah, 356, 357
Sagar, 159, 297
Saharanpur, 119, 431
Saif Khan, 228
Salamat Ali, Subedar, 236
Saleh Muhammad, 300
Salim Khalifat of Turkey, 36
Saltanat-i- Khudadad, Tipu's
Kingdom, 39
Sanatan Dharma Sabha, 177
Sarai Jalandari, 331
Sarai Nai, 331
Sardar Budh Singh, 60, 62, 64
Sarfaraz Ali, 283
Sarfaraz Khan, 209, 292
Sarvar Khan, 246
Satara, 359
Sati, 103, 402
Abolition, 365, 397
Custom, 102
Prohibition, 102
Satichaura Ghat, 122, 243, 244,
245
Satichaura Ghat Massacre,
(Kanpur), 122, 231
Satyagraha, 443
Savarkar, 8, 9, 11, 105, 184, 189,
403, 406
Sayyid Ahmad, 7, 33, 57, 58, 61,
62-65, 66-71, 73, 77, 78, 84
Badshah, 71, 72
Migration to Pathan Tribal
Area, 69
Movement, 70
Sayyid Badshah, 60,62, 65
Sayyid Ahmad Khan, Sir, 10,
95, 334, 335, 419, 424, 426,
446
Sayyid Ahmad Barelvi
(Shaheed), 8, 49, 51-56, 175,
179, 191-193, 195, 205, 225,
274, 338
Greatest Reformer and
Mujahid, 49
India's First Freedom
Fighter, 49, 50
Sayyid Akbar Khan, 70
Sayyid Gulzar Ali, 333
Scot, PG, English Official in
Jhansi, 300
Secret Groups, 180
Sehore, 1421
Seizure of Lucknow Residency,
132
Sen, Keshav Chandra, 102
Sepoy
Anarchy of 1857, 110
Mutiny, 11
Sepoys at Jalandhar and
Philaur, 209
Shah Abdul Aziz, 8, 31, 33, 44,
46, 50, 51, 80, 193, 227, 319
Shah Alam
As Emperor of India, 29, 30
Mughal Emperor, 35, 42, 89,
187
Successor, 86
Shah Jahan, Emperor, 14, 19, 95
Shah Muhammad Ishaq, 33
Shah Muhammad Ismail, 225
Shah Najaf, 154
Shah Nasiruddin of Persia, 362
Shah of Iran, 37, 89
Shah Sulaiman, 63

Shah Wahabi Teachings, 50
Shah Waliullah (1703-62)
Clergy, 8, 22, 23, 24-31, 33, 39, 44, 45, 80, 175, 187, 193, 208, 227, 441, 445
Activism, 8
Islam, 23
Pilgrimage to Mecca, 23
Quran, 25
Second Great Reformer of Islam in India, 22
Skillful Preacher, 26
Teachings, 39
Shahzada Firoz Shah, 218 *see also under* Firoz Shah
Shahzada of Mundsore, 296
Shahjahanpur, 167, 327, 330
Shaikh Ghulam Ali, 53
Shaikh Pir Shah, 348
Shaikh Ruyadat Ali, 284
Shaikh Sirhindi, 49, 50
Teachings of-, 50
Shaikh Wali Muhammad, 70
Shamli, 225
Shamshudullah, Grandson of Ahmad Shah Abdali, 183
Shaniwar Wada at Bithoor, 235
Shankarpur, 278
Sharf-ud-Daulah, 258
Shariat, 25, 26, 32, 55, 68, 70, 78, 225, 323, 324
Shariat Laws, 66, 416
Shariatullah, Cleric, 44, 45, 46
Sheo Rao Bhau, 297
Shercot, 419, 420
Shiah, 89, 254, 264
Shiah Rule, 187
Shiah Sect, 187, 188
Shiah's Cleric, 270
Shinde of Gwalior, 137, 201, 444
Shinde, Jayajirao, 137
Shipbuilding, 96
Shivaji, 101, 174, 367, 442
Shobha Ram, 322, 323
Shorepur, 358
Shuja-ud-Daula, Nawab of Ayodhya, 28
Sialkot, 115, 209
Siddi Kambar, 188
Sikandar Begum, 141, 142
Sikandarabad, 154, 222
Sikh
Army, 61, 69
Kingdom, 82
Sepoys, 124
Soldiers, 203
States, 62, 116
Jind, 116
Kapurthala, 116
Nabha, 116
Patiala, 116
Sikhs and Gurkhas, 9
Sindh, 210
Sirhindi, Shaikh Sayyid, 18-20, 22, 23
As Indian Nationalist, 18
Muslim Theologian, 18
Renewer of Faith, 13
Teachings, 19, 51
Sirsa, 210
Sital Singh, 329
Sitana, 70, 76, 207
Sitapur, 129
Slavery, 174
Social
Customs, 98
Reform Laws, 101
Reform Movement, 102
Reformers, 98

Society,
  Hindu, 102, 104, 402
  Indian, 98
  Muslim, 44
Sonaji Pant, 356
Southern Rebellion, 342
Spiritual Guides, 411, 412
Stopping of Sati System, 365
Suicidal Ghazis, 192
Sultan
  Bukhsh, 350
  Firoz Shah, 14
  Muhammad Khan, 58, 67, 68
    Subedar of Peshawar, 68
  of Bukhara, 63
  of Ghazni, 63
  of Kabul, 63
  of Turkey, 374, 375
Sultanpur, 278
Surajgadh, 54
Surat Singh, Sikh Leader, 280
Swarajya, 208, 442, 443
Swat, 65, 76
Swat Valley, 65
Sylhet, 54

Tafzal Hussain, 210, 215
Taimur, 14, 363
Tajpur, 423
Talukdars, 97, 104
Tara Fort, 233
Tatya Tope, (Tatya), 7, 127, 158, 160, 161, 162, 163, 168, 172, 237, 252, 288, 316, 340, 380, 381, 385, 433
  Army, 158, 160
  Command, 157
  Defeat at Kanpur, 169
  Forces, 171
  General., 171, 172
Taylor, 328
  Commissioner of Bihar, 147
Tazia Procession, 265
Tej Singh, 216
  Local Talukdar, 215
  Fortress, 115
Thakur
  Chaudhuries, 419
  Govind Singh, 214
  Pandey, Nazim at Fatehgarh, 218
Thana Bhavan, 225
Third Battle of Kanpur, 158
Thornton, S, Collector of Jhansi, 300
Tikka Singh, 239, 249
Tipu Sultan (1740-1799), Son of Haider Ali, 34-39, 41, 42, 43, 81, 187, 273, 348, 349
  As Freedom Fighter, 40
  As Sword of Islam, 39
  Career, 40
  Death, 40
  Family, 55, 273
  of Mysore, 43, 261
  Shah Waliullah's Ideal Khalifa, 39
  Sons, 54
  Mysore, 43, 261
Titu Mir, 177
Tonk (Rajasthan), 51, 57, 172, 192, 273, 284, 437
Transborder Jihad, 205
Transfer of Power, 74
Treasury, 120, 121, 123, 124, 129, 137, 236, 237
Treaty of 1765, 44
Tribe (s), 211
  of Afghanistan, 362
  Quráysh, 442
  Ravi, 201

Tripartite Agreement, 30
Tucker, Capt., Hanged by Rebels, 296
and Reed, 143
uprising, 294
Tughlaqabad, 95
Turkey, 33, 296, 376
Turkish
Empire, 376
Khalifas, 376
Turks, Afghans, Mughals Infightings, 15
Turrebaz Khan, Subedar, 346

Umrao Singh of Sherkot, 420
Unannexed States of Punjab, 211
Jind, 211
Kapruthala, 211
Nabha, 211
Patiala, 211
Uprising 1857, 7-9, 10, 11, 34, 40, 44, 47, 49, 77, 81, 82, 83, 88, 90, 91, 95-100, 102-104, 107-110, 112, 116, 117, 119, 124, 127, 133, 141, 146, 149, 150, 159, 168, 173, 174, 177, 178, 183, 184, 187, 193, 197-199, 201, 202, 204, 206, 208-213, 215, 217-219, 221, 223, 224, 227, 233, 235, 243, 246, 247, 250, 253, 255, 256, 259-261, 268, 269, 271, 274, 275, 279, 284, 293, 297- 299, 303, 305, 309, 317, 324, 334, 335, 340-342, 349, 350, 359, 360-418, 428, 432, 435, 440, 441, 442-446
Aimed at wresting Political Powers form the British, 13
As a Sepoy Mutiny, 7, 88
As War of Independence, 209
Causes, 83
First War of Indpendence, 11, 12
Hindu Participation in -, 98
Jihadi Core, 253
Major Causes and Nature of-, 360
Meerut and Delhi, 235
Nature of-, 341
Political Dispossession, 100
Political Revolution, 343
Sepoy Mutiny, 10
The Great Northern Revolt, 105
War of Independence, 11, 40
Uprising at,
Benares, 146
Badaun, 331, 332
Bareilly, 190, 320
Bihar, 342
Delhi, 368
Gwaliot, 219, 287
Indore, 289
Jaunpur, 282
Jhansi, 305
Meerut, 146, 215
Mundsore, 142
Punjab, 150
Uprising, 150th Anniversary, 2008, 11
Urdu Poetry, 199
Uttar Pradesh, 90, 105

Vazir Ali Khan,
Nawab, 41, 42, 89
Of Ayodhya, Revolt by-, 83, 191

Vedas and Gita, 367
Vellore, 343, 349
Vidyasagar, Ishwar Chandra, 102
Vilayatis, 295, 316
Vishveshwar Temple, 280, 433

Wahabi, 45, 275
  Centre in Poona, 351
  Movement, 8, 50
    Anti-British, 50
  Mujahideen, 436
  Slogan of Jihad, 80
Wahabis, 93, 191, 208, 353
Wahabis in Poona, 349
Wahidu Zaman, 234
Wajid Ali Shah, 131, 170, 253, 258, 262
  Deposed Nawab, 253
  King of Avadh, 89
Walidad Khan, 214-216, 218, 224, 431
  and Mir Fatwanah, 209
  Nawab of Malgadh, 152
  Rule, 221, 222, 224
Waliullah, 178, 179, 229
  Activism, 178, 179
  Doctrine, 213, 225
  Ideology, 320, 340
  Maulvis, 208, 319
  Movement, 146, 175, 177, 208, 337
  Movement's Contribution, 78
  Philosophy, 177, 178, 415
  Revolutionaries, 339
  School, 176, 192, 272, 273
  Teachings, 206
  Thought, 190, 193
  Traditions, 213, 274
Walker, Dy Collector, 230
Walpole, Commander of Division, 166
War
  Council, 155
  for Religion, 442
  of Independence 1858, 80, 88
Waris Muhammad Khan, 290, 292
Warring Communities, 269
Wazir Ali Khan, Subedar, 220
Wazir Khan, 213, 219
Wazirganj, 427
Waziul Haq, 338
Weaving Mills, 96
Western
  Civilization, 96
  Education, 95
  Institutions Boycott, 92
Wheeler, Maj. Gen., 120, 121, 122, 244
Widow Remarriage, 102
Wilson,
  Brig., 150
  Chief of Staff, 151
Windham, 158

Yar Muhammad Khan, Sultan of Peshawar, 64, 65, 67
Yasin Khan, 259
Yusufi, Pathan Tribe, 58

Zahiruddin Zahir, 185
Zaidpur, 265
Zain-ul-Abedeen, 349

Zakat, 32, 68, 74
Zaman Shah of Afghanistan, 41, 42, 74, 75, 80, 187
  Amir of Afghanistan, 37
  Grandson of Ahmad Shah Abdali, 37
Zamindars, 97, 104
Zeenat Mahal, 87, 189, 252
  Empress, 76
Zeenatul Masjid, 445